D0771751

FEB   2010

The Tax Law of Unrelated Business
for
Nonprofit Organizations

The Tax Law of Unrelated Business for
for
Nonprofit Organizations

Bruce R. Hopkins

WILEY

John Wiley & Sons, Inc.

For general information on our other products and services, or technical support, please contact our Customer Care Department within the United States at 800-762-2974, outside the United States at 317-572-3993 or fax 317-572-4002.

Wiley also publishes its books in a variety of electronic formats. Some content that appears in print may not be available in electronic books.

For more information about Wiley products, visit our Web site at http://www.wiley.com.

Library of Congress Cataloging-in-Publication Data

Hopkins, Bruce R.

The tax law of unrelated business for nonprofit organizations / Bruce R. Hopkins.

   p. cm.

     Includes index.

     ISBN-13: 978-0-471-73836-7 (cloth)

     ISBN-10: 0-471-73836-0 (cloth)

   1. Nonprofit organizations--Taxation--Law and legislation--United States. 2. Tax exemption--Law and legislation--United States. 3. Unrelated business income tax--United States. I. Title.

KF6449.H67 2006

343.7305'266--dc22

                                        2005025151

Printed in the United States of America

10 9 8 7 6 5 4 3 2 1

About the Author

Bruce R. Hopkins is the country's leading authority on the law of tax-exempt organizations and is a lawyer with the firm Polsinelli Shalton Welte Suelthaus PC. He is also the author of nineteen books, including *Nonprofit Law Made Easy; 650 Essential Nonprofit Law Questions Answered; The Law of Tax-Exempt Organizations, Eighth Edition; Planning Guide for the Law of Tax-Exempt Organizations; The Law of Fundraising, Third Edition; Private Foundations: Tax Law and Compliance, Second Edition; The Tax Law of Charitable Giving, Third Edition, The Law of Intermediate Sanctions*, and *The Law of Tax-Exempt Healthcare Organizations, Second Edition*, all published by John Wiley & Sons. Mr. Hopkins also writes the monthly newsletter *Bruce R. Hopkins' Nonprofit Counsel*, also published by John Wiley & Sons.

Contents

Because of the rapidly changing nature of information in this field, this product will be updated
with annual supplements or with future editions. Please call 1-877-762-2974 or email us at
subscriber@wiley.com to receive any current update at no additional charge. We will send on approval any
future supplements or new editions when they become available. If you purchased this product directly
from John Wiley & Sons, Inc., we have already recorded your subscription for this update service.

Chapter Ten   **Unrelated Business and the Internet**   275

Appendices

Tables

Index   379

Preface

A significant component of the federal law of tax-exempt organizations is the body of tax law concerning the conduct and taxation of unrelated trade or business. This is one of the few areas of the law in which there is a significant statutory structure. Not surprisingly, this aspect of the law concerning the conduct of trades and businesses is substantially augmented by regulations, IRS rulings (public and private), and court opinions. It is indeed a rich feature of the exempt organizations law.

The purpose of this book, therefore, is to summarize this aspect of the federal tax law applicable to nonprofit organizations. The book introduces the unrelated business rules (including a history of and rationale for these rules), analyzes the meaning of the term *trade or business* and the factors taken into account in determining whether a business is related or unrelated, explores the many modifications and exceptions that enrich this part of exempt organizations law, and summarizes the unrelated debt-financed income rules and the doctrine of commerciality.

This book delves much deeper than I could in the *The Law of Tax-Exempt Organizations (Eight Edition)* , digging into topics such as the special rules for social clubs, the advertising rules, the corporate sponsorship rules, and the application of this aspect of the law to private foundations. It explores the unrelated business rules as they relate to the use of separate entities (such as partnerships and limited liability companies). Contemporary applications of these rules are addressed in some detail, such as those applicable to educational institutions, health care providers, museums, and associations, and attention is paid to application of these rules in other areas, such as the fundraising and travel opportunity contexts. A full chapter is devoted to the unrelated business rules in the context of use of the Internet.

In this book, I was able to do much more in the area of the reporting requirements. The annual information return (Form 990) is analyzed from the unrelated business perspective. Much of a chapter focuses on details pertaining to the unrelated business income tax return (Form 990-T) and its many schedules. Six appendices and six tables round out the analysis.

I hope, of course, that this book will be of interest and assistance to practitioners and others who need to cope with the complexities of the tax law of unrelated business applicable to tax-exempt nonprofit organizations.

This book is based, in part, on a spinoff of material previously published in various chapters of the *Exempt Organizations* book. It came about because of two diametrically competing considerations: my desire to provide much more detail about the federal tax law concerning related and unrelated businesses, and my ongoing efforts to reduce the size of the *Exempt Organizations* book. This book will, for the most part, substitute for the pages in *Exempt Organizations* concerning the unrelated business rules. When the ninth edition of the *Exempt Organizations* book is written, it will contain a chapter providing a relatively brief overview of the unrelated business law.

This is not the first time the *Exempt Organizations* book has been trimmed in this manner. In 1997, the same approach was taken with respect to the public charity and private foundation rules. The result is *Private Foundations: Tax Law and Compliance*, now in its second edition. *Exempt Organizations* also contains a chapter providing an overview of those rules.

My thanks are extended to Susan McDermott, who has been supportive from the outset of this project; and to Natasha Andrews for editing services. I have had marvelous experiences on many other occasions in working with editors at Wiley, and the support I have received in connection with this book is a continuation of this fine tradition.

BRUCE R. HOPKINS
July 2005

CHAPTER ONE

Tax Exemption and Unrelated Business: Introduction

The unrelated business rules constitute one of the most important components of the law of tax-exempt organizations. These rules influence nearly every operational decision made on behalf of an exempt organization, including the nature and scope of activities, financing and investments, use of a subsidiary, and involvement in joint ventures. Though some exempt organizations have an innate aversion to unrelated business activities, others aggressively embrace them as a way to generate needed revenue. Whether avoided or accommodated, the unrelated business rules—approaching 60 years of existence—are among the continually expanding bodies of tax law affecting the activities of nearly all nonprofit organizations.

§ 1.1 TAX EXEMPTION: A PERSPECTIVE

Nearly all tax-exempt organizations are subject to the unrelated business rules.[1] Thus, before it need concern itself with those rules, an organization must first qualify for tax-exempt status.[2] Once that is accomplished, the organization may

---

[1] See § 1.7.

[2] Hopkins, *The Law of Tax-Exempt Organizations, Eighth Edition* (John Wiley & Sons, 2003) (hereinafter *Tax-Exempt Organizations*), particularly chapter 23 (concerning the exemption recognition process). The basic tests for qualification for exemption are summarized in *id.* chapter 8, and the various categories of tax-exempt organizations are discussed in *id.* chapters 5–18.

have to contemplate the extent to which it can engage in unrelated business and retain its exemption.[3]

The term *tax-exempt organization* is an anomaly, inasmuch as few organizations are, as a matter of federal tax law, wholly exempt from tax. Aside from governmental entities, just about every nonprofit organization that enjoys general tax exemption is subject to one or more federal income or excise taxes (as well as state and/or local taxes). Levies that may be imposed on otherwise exempt organizations include taxes on charitable organizations that engage in excess expenditures to influence legislation[4] or for political activities,[5] a tax on the investment income of social clubs,[6] taxes on private foundations,[7] taxes on exempt organizations that are disqualified persons in excess benefit transactions,[8] a tax on membership organizations that engage in forms of advocacy,[9] and a tax on charitable organizations that pay premiums on personal benefit contracts.[10] Nonetheless, the federal tax that tax-exempt organizations in general are most likely to pay (or engage in planning to avoid) is the tax on unrelated business income.

§ 1.2   SOURCE OF TAX EXEMPTION

Section 61(a) of the Internal Revenue Code provides that "[e]xcept as otherwise provided in this subtitle [Subtitle A—income taxes], gross income means all income from whatever source derived," including items such as interest, dividends, compensation for services, and receipts derived from the conduct of business. The Code provides for a variety of deductions, exclusions, and exemptions in computing taxable income. Many of these are contained in IRC. Subtitle A, Subchapter B, entitled "Computation of taxable income." Pertinent in the tax-exempt organizations context, however, is the body of exemption provisions contained in Subtitle A, Subchapter F, captioned "Exempt organizations."

Exemption from federal income taxation is derived from a specific provision to that end in the Internal Revenue Code. *Derivation* of exemption is here used in the sense of *recognition* of exemption by the appropriate administrative agency (the Internal Revenue Service (IRS)) or as a matter of law, as opposed to exemption that is a byproduct (albeit a resolutely sought one) of some other tax status (such as a cooperative or a state instrumentality).

A federal tax exemption is a privilege (a matter of legislative grace), not an entitlement,[11] and—being an exception to the norm of taxation—is often strictly

---

[3] See § 1.10.

[4] Internal Revenue Code of 1986, as amended (IRC) § 4911 or § 4912. See *Tax-Exempt Organizations*, §§ 20.3(b), 20.6.

[5] IRC §§ 527(f) and/or 4955. See *Tax-Exempt Organizations*, §§ 21.2, 21.3.

[6] IRC § 512(a)(3)(A). See *Tax-Exempt Organizations*, § 14.3.

[7] IRC §§ 4941–4948. See *Tax-Exempt Organizations*, § 11.4; Hopkins & Blazek, *Private Foundations: Tax Law and Compliance, Second Edition* (John Wiley & Sons, 2003) (hereinafter *Private Foundations*), §§ 5.14(d), 6.6(c), 8.4, 9.9, 10.1.

[8] IRC § 4958(a)(1), (b). See *Tax-Exempt Organizations*, § 19.11(f); Hopkins, *The Law of Intermediate Sanctions: A Guide for Nonprofits* (John Wiley & Sons, 2003) (hereinafter *Intermediate Sanctions*), § 3.1.

[9] IRC § 6033(e)(2). See *Tax-Exempt Organizations*, § 20.8(b).

[10] IRC § 170(f)(10)(F). See Hopkins, *The Tax Law of Charitable Giving, Third Edition* (John Wiley & Sons, 2005) (hereinafter *Charitable Giving*), § 17.6(b).

[11] As discussed, however, the federal tax exemption for many nonprofit organizations (such as charitable ones) is a reflection of the heritage and societal structure of the United States (see *Tax-Exempt Organizations*, § 1.3).

construed.[12] (The same principle applies with respect to tax deductions[13] and tax exclusions.[14]) This type of exemption must be enacted by Congress and will not be granted by implication.[15] Two related tax precepts are (1) that a person requesting exemption must demonstrate compliance with the requirements set forth in the statute that grants the exemption,[16] and (2) that the party claiming the exemption bears the burden of proof of eligibility for the exemption.[17] Thus, a court wrote that the federal tax statutory law "generally consists of narrowly defined categories of exemption" and is "replete with rigid requirements which a putatively exempt organization must demonstrate it meets."[18] The IRS and the courts are alert for efforts to gain a tax exemption when the underlying motive is the purpose of "confounding tax collection."[19]

At the same time, provisions granting exemptions for charitable organizations are usually liberally construed. Thus, a court wrote that the "judiciary will liberally construe, and rightfully so, provisions giving exemptions for charitable, religious, and educational purposes."[20] Another court said that "in view of the fact that bequests for public purposes operate in aid of good government and perform by private means what ultimately would fall upon the public, exemption from taxation is not so much a matter of grace or favor as rather an act of justice."[21] Similarly, it has been held that the exemption of income devoted to charity, by means of the charitable contribution deductions, should not be narrowly construed.[22] These provisions respecting income destined for charity are accorded favorable construction, as they are "begotten

---

[12] *E.g.*, Knights of Columbus Bldg. Ass'n v. United States, 88-1 U.S.T.C. ¶ 9336 (D. Conn. 1988) ("A tax exemption is a benefit conferred by the legislature in its discretion. Because there is no entitlement to an exemption absent allowance by the legislature, the exemption provisions are strictly construed"); Mercantile Bank & Trust Co. v. United States, 441 F.2d 364, 366 (8th Cir. 1971) ("Special benefits to taxpayers, such as tax exemption status, do not turn upon general equitable considerations but are matters of legislative grace"). See *also* Conference of Major Religious Superiors of Women, Inc. v. Dist. of Columbia, 348 F.2d 783 (D.C. Cir. 1965); Am. Auto. Ass'n v. Comm'r, 19 T.C. 1146 (1953); Associated Indus. of Cleveland v. Comm'r, 7 T.C. 1449 (1946); Bingler v. Johnson, 394 U.S. 741 (1969) and authorities cited therein. In general, Murtagh, *The Role of the Courts in the Interpretation of the Internal Revenue Code*, 24 *Tax Law.* 523 (1971).

[13] Deputy v. DuPont, 308 U.S. 488 (1940); White v. United States, 305 U.S. 281 (1938). In Alfred I. duPont Testamentary Trust v. Comm'r, 514 F.2d 917, 922 (5th Cir. 1975), a case involving tax deductions claimed by a trust, the court wrote that the deductions "must fit into a statutory category of deductibility, else the trustees must carry out their fiduciary duty at the expense of the trust, rather than the public fisc."

[14] *E.g.*, Estate of Levine v. Comm'r, 526 F.2d 717, 717 (2d Cir. 1975), in which the court was prompted to observe that "[o]ne suspects that because the Internal Revenue Code . . . piles exceptions upon exclusions, it invites efforts to outwit the tax collector."

[15] *E.g.*, Mescalero Apache Tribe v. Jones, 411 U.S. 145 (1973).

[16] *E.g.*, Christian Echoes Nat'l Ministry v. United States, 470 F.2d 849 (10th Cir. 1972), *cert. denied*, 414 U.S. 864 (1973); Parker v. Comm'r, 365 F.2d 792 (8th Cir. 1966), *cert. denied*, 385 U.S. 1026 (1967).

[17] *E.g.*, United States v. Olympic Radio & Television, Inc., 349 U.S. 232 (1955); Bubbling Well Church of Universal Love v. Comm'r, 670 F.2d 104 (9th Cir. 1981); Senior Citizens Stores, Inc. v. United States, 602 F.2d 711 (5th Cir. 1979); Kenner v. Comm'r, 318 F.2d 632 (7th Cir. 1963).

[18] Knights of Columbus Bldg. Ass'n v. United States, 88-1 U.S.T.C. ¶ 9336 (D. Conn. 1988).

[19] Granzow v. Comm'r, 739 F.2d 265, 268–69 (7th Cir. 1984).

[20] Am. Inst. for Econ. Research v. United States, 302 F.2d 934, 937 (Ct. Cl. 1962), *cert. denied*, 372 U.S. 976 (1963), *reh'g denied*, 373 U.S. 954 (1963).

[21] Harrison v. Barker Annuity Fund, 90 F.2d 286, 288 (7th Cir. 1937). The court also said that "courts quite generally have extended liberal construction to statutes furthering the encouragement of bequests for purposes which tend toward the public good, without reference to personal or selfish motives" (*id.*).

[22] SICO Found. v. United States, 295 F.2d 924, 930, n.19 (Ct. Cl. 1962), and cases cited therein.

from motives of public policy,"[23] and any ambiguity therein has traditionally been resolved against taxation.[24]

The provision in the Internal Revenue Code that is the general source of the federal income tax exemption is IRC. § 501(a),[25] which states that an "organization described in subsection (c) or (d) or section 401(a) [the latter relating to employee benefit funds] shall be exempt from taxation under this subtitle [Subtitle A—income taxes] unless such exemption is denied under section 501 or 503." The U.S. Supreme Court characterized IRC. § 501(a) as the "linchpin of the statutory benefit [exemption] system."[26] The Court summarized the exemption provided by IRC. § 501(a) as according "advantageous treatment to several types of nonprofit corporations [and trusts, unincorporated associations, and certain limited liability companies], including exemption of their income from taxation and [for those that are also eligible charitable donees] deductibility by benefactors of the amounts of their donations."[27]

Thus, to be recognized as tax-exempt under IRC. § 501(a), an organization must conform to the appropriate descriptive provisions of IRC. §§ 501(c), 501(d), or 401(a). This exemption, however, does not extend to an organization's unrelated business taxable income.[28] An organization that seeks to obtain tax-exempt status, therefore, bears the burden of proving that it satisfies all the requirements of the exemption statute involved.[29]

§ 1.3 TAX-EXEMPT ORGANIZATIONS

In this book, the term *tax-exempt organization* refers to a nonprofit organization that is generally exempt from (excused from paying) the federal income tax. There are, of course, other federal taxes (such as excise and employment taxes), and there are categories of exemptions from them as well. At the state level, there are exemptions associated with income, sales, use, excise, and property taxes.

Nonetheless, the term *tax-exempt organization* is not literally accurate; there is no category of nonprofit organization (other than certain governmental entities) that is not subject to some form of federal tax. The income tax that is potentially applicable to nearly all tax-exempt organizations is the tax on unrelated business income. Exempt entities can be taxed for engaging in political activities;[30] public charities are subject to tax in the case of substantial efforts to influence legislation[31] or participation in political campaign activities;[32] and some exempt organizations, such as social clubs and political organizations, are taxable on their

---

[23] Helvering v. Bliss, 293 U.S. 144, 151 (1934).
[24] C.F. Mueller Co. v. Comm'r, 190 F.2d 210 (3d Cir. 1951).
[25] Also IRC §§ 521, 526–529.
[26] Simon v. E. Ky. Welfare Rights Org., 426 U.S. 26, 29, n. 1 (1976).
[27] *Id.* at 28.
[28] IRC § 501(b); Income Tax Regulations ("Reg"). § 1.501(a)-1(a)(1). See § 1.3.
[29] See, *e.g.*, Harding Hosp. v. United States, 505 F.2d 1068, 1071 (6th Cir. 1974); Haswell v. United States, 500 F.2d 1133, 1140 (Ct. Cl. 1974). See *Tax-Exempt Organization*, ch. 21.
[30] See *Tax-Exempt Organizations*, § 17.5.
[31] See *id.* § 20.5.
[32] See *id.* § 21.4.

investment income.[33] Associations and like organizations can be subject to a proxy tax when they engage in attempts to influence legislation or engage in political activities.[34] Private foundations can be caught up in a variety of excise taxes.[35]

No nonprofit organization has an entitlement to tax exemption; that is, there is no entity that has some inherent right to exempt status (other than certain governmental entities). From a pure-law standpoint, tax exemptions and the kinds of entities that may claim them exist essentially as whims of the legislature involved. No constitutional law principle mandates tax exemption.

An illustration of this point is the grant by Congress of tax-exempt status to certain mutual organizations—albeit with the stricture that, to qualify for the exemption, an organization must have been organized before September 1, 1957.[36] Before that date, exemption was available for all savings and loan associations. The purpose of the exemption was to afford savings institutions that did not have capital stock an opportunity to accumulate a surplus, so as to provide their depositors with greater security. This exemption was repealed because Congress determined that its purpose was no longer appropriate, because the savings and loan industry had developed to the point where the ratio of capital account to total deposits was comparable to that of nonexempt commercial banks. A challenge to this law by an otherwise qualified organization formed in 1962 failed, with the U.S. Supreme Court holding that Congress did not act in an arbitrary and unconstitutional manner in declining to extend the exemption beyond the particular year.[37]

There are other illustrations of this point. For years, organizations such as Blue Cross and Blue Shield entities were tax-exempt;[38] Congress, however, determined that these organizations had evolved into entities that were essentially no different from commercial health insurance providers, and thus generally legislated this exemption out of existence.[39] (Later, Congress realized that it had gone too far in this regard and restored exemption for some providers of insurance that function as charitable risk pools.[40]) Congress allowed the exempt status for group legal services organizations[41] to expire without ceremony in 1992; it also created a category of exemption for state-sponsored workers' compensation reinsurance organizations, with the stipulation that they must have been established before June 1, 1996.[42] Indeed, in 1982, Congress established exemption for a certain type of veterans' organization, with one of the criteria being that the entity be established before 1880.[43]

There is a main list of tax-exempt organizations,[44] to or from which Congress periodically adds or deletes categories of organizations. Occasionally, Congress

---

[33] See *id.* § 14.3, ch. 24.
[34] See *id.* §§ 20.7, 21.7.
[35] See *id.* § 11.3.
[36] IRC § 501(c)(14)(B).
[37] Md. Sav.-Share Ins. Corp. v. United States, 400 U.S. 4 (1970).
[38] By reason of IRC § 501(c)(4).
[39] See *Tax-Exempt Organizations,* § 22.1.
[40] See *id.* § 10.6.
[41] See *id.* § 16.6.
[42] See *id.* § 18.5.
[43] See *id.* § 18.10(b).
[44] IRC § 501(c).

extends the list of organizations that are exempt as charitable entities.[45] Otherwise, it may create a new provision describing the particular exemption criteria.[46]

§ 1.4 PHILOSOPHICAL PRINCIPLES OF EXEMPT ORGANIZATIONS LAW

The definition in the law of the term *nonprofit organization,* and the concept of the nonprofit sector as critical to the creation and functioning of a civil society, do not distinguish nonprofit organizations that are tax-exempt from those that are not. This is because the tax aspect of nonprofit organizations is not relevant to either subject. Indeed, rather than defining either the term *nonprofit organization* or such an organization's societal role, the federal tax law principles respecting tax exemption of these entities reflect and flow out of the essence of these subjects.

This is somewhat unusual, as nearly all of the provisions of the federal tax laws are based on some form of rationale inherent in tax policy. The fundamental reason for the law of tax-exempt organizations, however, has little to do with any underlying tax policy. Rather, this aspect of the tax law is grounded in a body of thought far distant from tax policy: political philosophy as to the proper construction of a democratic society.

This raises, then, the matter of the rationale for the eligibility of nonprofit organizations for tax-exempt status: the fundamental characteristic that enables a nonprofit organization to qualify as an exempt organization. In fact, there is no single qualifying feature; however, the most common one is the doctrine of private inurement.[47] This circumstance mirrors the fact that the present-day statutory exemption rules are not the product of a carefully formulated plan. Rather, they are a hodgepodge of statutory law that has evolved over more than 90 years, as various Congresses have deleted from (infrequently) and added to (frequently) the roster of exempt entities, causing it to grow substantially over the decades. One observer noted that the various categories of exempt organizations "are not the result of any planned legislative scheme," but were enacted over the decades "by a variety of legislators for a variety of reasons."[48]

Six basic rationales underlie qualification for tax-exempt status for nonprofit organizations. On a simplistic plane, a nonprofit entity is exempt because Congress wrote a provision in the Internal Revenue Code according exemption for it.

---

[45] IRC §§ 501(e), 501(f), 501(k), 501(m), 501(n).

[46] IRC §§ 521, 526–529. The staff of the Joint Committee on Taxation and the Department of the Treasury measure the economic value (ostensible revenue losses) of various tax preferences, such as tax deductions, credits, and exclusions (termed *tax expenditures*). Although the income tax charitable contribution deduction tends to be the fifth or sixth largest tax expenditure, the ones that are larger include the exclusions for pension plan contributions and earnings, the exclusion from gross income of employer contributions for health insurance premiums and health care, the deductibility of mortgage interest on personal residences, the reduced rates of tax on long-term capital gains, and the deduction for state and local governments' income and personal property taxes. The Joint Committee on Taxation staff estimated that, for the federal government's fiscal years 2005–2009, the tax expenditure for the income tax charitable deduction will be $228.5 billion. *Estimates of Federal Tax Expenditures for Fiscal Years 2005-2009* (JCS-1-05).

[47] See § 1.9; *Tax-Exempt Organizations,* ch. 19.

[48] McGovern, *The Exemption Provisions of Subchapter F,* 29 *Tax Law.* 523 (1976). Other overviews of the various tax exemption provisions are in Hansmann, *The Rationale for Exempting Nonprofit Organizations from Corporate Income Taxation,* 91 *Yale L.J.* 69 (1981); Bittker & Rahdert, *The Exemption of Nonprofit Organizations from Federal Income Taxation,* 85 *Yale L.J.* 299 (1976).

Thus, some organizations are exempt for no more engaging reason than that Congress said so. Certainly, there is no grand philosophical construct buttressing this type of exemption.

Some of the federal income tax exemptions were enacted in the spirit of being merely declaratory of, or furthering, then-existing laws. The House Committee on Ways and Means, in legislating a forerunner to the provision that exempts from federal income taxation certain voluntary employees' beneficiary associations,[49] commented that "these associations are common today [1928] and it appears desirable to provide specifically for their exemption from ordinary corporation tax."[50] The exemption for nonprofit cemetery companies[51] was enacted to parallel then-existing state and local property tax exemptions.[52] The exemption for farmers' cooperatives[53] has been characterized as an element of the federal government's policy of supporting agriculture.[54] The provision exempting certain U.S. corporate instrumentalities from tax[55] was deemed declaratory of the exemption simultaneously provided by the particular enabling statute.[56] The provision according exemption to multiparent title-holding corporations was derived from the IRS's refusal to recognize exempt status for title-holding corporations serving more than one unrelated parent entity.[57]

Tax exemption for categories of nonprofit organizations can arise as a byproduct of enactment of legislation. In these instances, exemption is granted to facilitate accomplishment of the purpose of another legislative end. Thus, exempt status was approved for funds underlying employee benefit programs.[58] Other examples include exemption for professional football leagues, which emanated from the merger of the National Football League and the American Football League;[59] and for state-sponsored providers of health care to the needy, which was required to accommodate the goals of Congress in creating health care delivery legislation.[60]

There is a pure tax rationale for the existence of a few tax-exempt organizations. The exemption for social clubs, homeowners' associations, and political organizations is reflective of this category.[61] Under general tax principles, an organization of this nature may not be considered as having any income, inasmuch as there has been no shift of benefit from the member to the organization; the organization merely facilitates a joint activity of its members. Under these circumstances, the individual is in substantially the same position as if he or she had

---

[49] See *Tax-Exempt Organizations*, § 16.3.

[50] H.R. Rep. No. 72, 78th Cong., 1st Sess. 17 (1928).

[51] See *Tax-Exempt Organizations*, § 18.6.

[52] Lapin, *The Golden Hills and Meadows of the Tax-Exempt Cemetery*, 44 *Taxes* 744 (1966).

[53] See *Tax-Exempt Organizations*, § 18.11.

[54] *Comment*, 27 *Iowa L. Rev.* 128, 151–55 (1941).

[55] See *Tax-Exempt Organizations*, § 18.1.

[56] H.R. Rep. No. 704, 73d Cong., 2d Sess. 21–25 (1934). This policy has changed, however (see *Tax-Exempt Organizations*, § 18.1, text accompanying note 1).

[57] See *Tax-Exempt Organizations*, § 18.2(b).

[58] See *id.* ch. 16.

[59] See *id.* § 13.5.

[60] See *id.* § 18.14.

[61] See *id.* § 1.5.

spent his or her income for purposes of pleasure, recreation, or similar benefits without the intervention of the separate organization.

The fourth rationale for tax-exempt status is a policy one—not tax policy, but policy with regard to less essential elements of the structure of a civil society. This is why, for example, exempt status has been granted to fraternal organizations,[62] title-holding companies,[63] and qualified tuition programs.[64]

The fifth rationale for tax-exempt status rests solidly on a philosophical principle. Nevertheless, there are degrees of scale here; some principles are less grandiose than others. Thus, there are nonprofit organizations that are exempt because their objectives are of direct importance to a significant segment of society and indirectly of consequence to all society. Within this frame lies the rationale for exemption of entities such as labor organizations,[65] trade and business associations,[66] and veterans' organizations.[67]

The sixth rationale for tax-exempt status for nonprofit organizations is predicated on the view that exemption is required to facilitate achievement of an end of significance to the entirety of society. Most organizations that are generally thought of as *charitable* in nature[68] are entities that are meaningful to the structure and functioning of society in the United States.[69] At least to some degree, this rationale embraces social welfare organizations.[70] This rationale may be termed the *political philosophy* rationale.[71]

Related to this rationale is the concept that promotion of certain activities may be viewed as desirable policy; tax exemption is accorded to encourage the activity. This may explain tax exemption for arrangements to provide employee benefits; arrangements for individuals to save for health, retirement, and education; and the exemption for small or rural commercial organizations that engage in activities such as farming, provision of financial services, insurance, electricity, or other public good.

§ 1.5   CATEGORIES OF TAX-EXEMPT ORGANIZATIONS

The categories of tax-exempt organizations are as follows:

- Instrumentalities of the United States[72]
- Single-parent title-holding companies[73]

---

[62] See *id.* § 18.4.
[63] See *id.* § 18.2.
[64] See *id.* § 18.6.
[65] See *id.* § 15.1.
[66] See *id.* ch. 13.
[67] See *id.* § 18.10.
[68] These are the charitable, educational, religious, scientific, and like organizations referenced in IRC § 501(c)(3).
[69] In general, Brody, *Charities in Tax Reform: Threats to Subsidies Overt and Covert*, 66 *Tenn. L. Rev.* 687 (no. 3, Spring 1999); Brody, *Of Sovereignty and Subsidy: Conceptualizing the Charity Tax Exemption*, 23 *J. Corp. L.* 585 (no. 4, Summer 1998); 22 *Exempt Orgs. Tax Rev.* 421 (no. 3, Dec. 1998).
[70] Tax exemption for social welfare organizations also originated in 1913; the promotion of social welfare is one of the definitions of the term *charitable* for federal tax purposes (see *Tax-Exempt Organizations,* § 6.7).
[71] *Id.* § 1.4.
[72] Organizations described in IRC § 501(c)(1) (see *Tax-Exempt Organizations*, § 18.1).
[73] Organizations described in IRC § 501(c)(2) (see *Tax-Exempt Organizations*, § 18.2(a)).

- Charitable organizations[74]
- Social welfare organizations[75]
- Labor and agricultural organizations[76]
- Business leagues[77]
- Social and recreational clubs[78]
- Fraternal beneficiary societies[79]
- Voluntary employees' beneficiary societies[80]
- Domestic fraternal beneficiary societies[81]
- Teachers' retirement funds[82]
- Benevolent life insurance associations[83]
- Cemetery companies[84]
- Credit unions[85]
- Mutual insurance companies[86]
- Crop operations finance corporations[87]
- Supplemental unemployment benefit trusts[88]
- Employee-funded pension trusts[89]
- War veterans' organizations[90]
- Black lung benefit trusts[91]
- A veterans' organization founded prior to 1880[92]
- Trusts described in section 4049 of the Employee Retirement Income Security Act[93]
- Title-holding companies for multiple beneficiaries[94]
- Organizations providing medical insurance for those difficult to insure[95]
- State-formed workers' compensation organizations[96]

---

[74] Organizations described in IRC § 501(c)(3) (see *Tax-Exempt Organizations*, pt. 2). The entities referenced *infra* in notes 98–100 are also charitable organizations.

[75] Organizations described in IRC § 501(c)(4) (see *Tax-Exempt Organizations*, ch. 12).

[76] Organizations described in IRC § 501(c)(5) (see *Tax-Exempt Organizations*, ch. 15).

[77] Organizations described in IRC § 501(c)(6) (see *Tax-Exempt Organizations*, ch. 13).

[78] Organizations described in IRC § 501(c)(7) (see *Tax-Exempt Organizations*, ch. 14).

[79] Organizations described in IRC § 501(c)(8) (see *Tax-Exempt Organizations*, § 18.4(a)).

[80] Organizations described in IRC § 501(c)(9) (see *Tax-Exempt Organizations*, § 16.3).

[81] Organizations described in IRC § 501(c)(10) (see *Tax-Exempt Organizations*, § 18.4(b)).

[82] Organizations described in IRC § 501(c)(11) (see *Tax-Exempt Organizations*, § 16.6).

[83] Organizations described in IRC § 501(c)(12) (see *Tax-Exempt Organizations*, § 18.5).

[84] Organizations described in IRC § 501(c)(13) (see *Tax-Exempt Organizations*, § 18.6).

[85] Organizations described in IRC § 501(c)(14) (see *Tax-Exempt Organizations*, § 18.7).

[86] Organizations described in IRC § 501(c)(15) (see *Tax-Exempt Organizations*, § 18.8).

[87] Organizations described in IRC § 501(c)(16) (see *Tax-Exempt Organizations*, § 18.9).

[88] Organizations described in IRC § 501(c)(17) (see *Tax-Exempt Organizations*, § 16.4).

[89] Organizations described in IRC § 501(c)(18) (see *Tax-Exempt Organizations*, § 16.6).

[90] Organizations described in IRC § 501(c)(19) (see *Tax-Exempt Organizations*, § 18.10(a)).

[91] Organizations described in IRC § 501(c)(21) (see *Tax-Exempt Organizations*, § 16.5).

[92] Organization described in IRC § 501(c)(23) (see *Tax-Exempt Organizations*, § 18.10(b)).

[93] Organizations described in IRC § 501(c)(24) (see *Tax-Exempt Organizations*, § 16.6).

[94] Organizations described in IRC § 501(c)(25) (see *Tax-Exempt Organizations*, § 18.2(b)).

[95] Organizations described in IRC § 501(c)(26) (see *Tax-Exempt Organizations*, § 18.14).

[96] Organizations described in IRC § 501(c)(27) (see *Tax-Exempt Organizations*, , § 18.15).

- The National Railroad Retirement Investment Trust[97]
- Religious and apostolic organizations[98]
- Cooperative hospital service organizations[99]
- Cooperative service organizations of educational institutions[100]
- Farmers' cooperatives[101]
- Political organizations[102]
- Homeowners' associations[103]

This enumeration of tax-exempt organizations does not include references to multiemployer pension trusts,[104] day care centers,[105] or shipowners' and indemnity organizations.[106] Because no data have yet been compiled as to them, there is no listing of charitable risk pools[107] or prepaid tuition plan trusts.[108]

The federal tax law recognizes 68 categories of tax-exempt organizations.[109]

§ 1.6   RATIONALE FOR UNRELATED BUSINESS RULES

Taxation of the unrelated business income of tax-exempt organizations—a feature of the federal tax law introduced in 1950—is predicated on the concept that this approach is a more effective and workable sanction for enforcement of this aspect of the law of exempt organizations than denial or revocation of exempt status because of unrelated business activity.[110] This aspect of the law rests on two concepts: (1) activities that are unrelated to an exempt organization's purposes are to be segregated from related business activities, and (2) the net income from unrelated business activities is taxed in essentially the same manner as net income earned by for-profit organizations. That is, the unrelated business income tax applies only to income generated by active business activities that are unrelated to an exempt organization's tax-exempt purposes.

---

[97] Organization described in IRC § 501(c)(28).

[98] Organizations described in IRC § 501(d) (see *Tax-Exempt Organizations*, § 8.7).

[99] Organizations described in IRC § 501(e) (see *Tax-Exempt Organizations*, § 10.4).

[100] Organizations described in IRC § 501(f) (see *Tax-Exempt Organizations*, § 10.5).

[101] Organizations described in IRC § 521 (see *Tax-Exempt Organizations*, § 18.11).

[102] Organizations described in IRC § 527 (see *Tax-Exempt Organizations*, ch. 17).

[103] Organizations described in IRC § 528 (see *Tax-Exempt Organizations*, § 18.13).

[104] Organizations described in IRC § 501(c)(22) (see *Tax-Exempt Organizations*, § 16.6).

[105] Organizations described in IRC § 501(k) (see *Tax-Exempt Organizations*, § 7.7).

[106] Organizations described in IRC § 526(d) (see *Tax-Exempt Organizations*, § 18.12).

[107] Organizations described in IRC § 501(n) (see *Tax-Exempt Organizations*, § 10.6).

[108] Organizations described in IRC § 529 (see *Tax-Exempt Organizations*, § 18.16).

[109] See *Tax-Exempt Organizations*, app. C. As the preceding footnotes indicate, the many categories of tax-exempt organizations are discussed in various chapters throughout *Tax-Exempt Organizations*. Nonetheless, as the following observation by the U.S. Tax Court affirms, "[t]rying to understand the various exempt organization provisions of the Internal Revenue Code is as difficult as capturing a drop of mercury under your thumb." Weingarden v. Comm'r, 86 T.C. 669, 675 (1986), *rev'd on other grounds*, 825 F.2d 1027 (6th Cir. 1987).

[110] Analyses of developments leading to enactment of the unrelated business rules include Stone, *Adhering to the Old Line: Uncovering the History and Political Function of the Unrelated Business Income Tax*, a University of Iowa Legal Studies Research Paper (No. 04-06), available at http://ssrn.com/abstract=634264 (hereinafter Stone Research Paper); Brody, *Of Sovereignty and Subsidy: Conceptualizing the Charity Tax Exemption*, 23 *J. Corp. L.* 585 (1998); Hansmann, *Unfair Competition and the Unrelated Business Income Tax*, 75 *Va. L. Rev.* 605 (1989); Myers, *Taxing the Colleges*, 38 *Cornell L.Q.* 388 (1953). An analysis of the state of the law prior to enactment of these rules appears in Blodgett, *Taxation of Businesses Conducted by Charitable Organizations*, 4 *N.Y.U. Fourth Ann. Inst. on Fed. Tax'n* 418 (1946).

The primary objective of the unrelated business rules is to eliminate a source of unfair competition with for-profit businesses. This is achieved by placing the unrelated business activities of tax-exempt organizations on the same tax basis as the nonexempt business endeavors with which they compete.[111] The House Ways and Means Committee report that accompanied the Revenue Act of 1950[112] contained the observation that the "problem at which the tax on unrelated business income is directed here is primarily that of unfair competition," in that exempt organizations can "use their profits tax-free to expand operations, while their competitors can expand only with the profits remaining after taxes."[113] The Senate Committee on Finance reaffirmed this position nearly three decades later when it noted that one "major purpose" of the unrelated business rules "is to make certain that an exempt organization does not commercially exploit its exempt status for the purpose of unfairly competing with taxpaying organizations."[114]

This rationale for the unrelated business rules has begun to be subjected to revisionist theories, specifically the view that other objectives are equally important. A federal appellate court observed that, "although Congress enacted the [unrelated business income rules] to eliminate a perceived form of unfair competition, that aim existed as a corollary to the larger goals of producing revenue and achieving equity in the tax system."[115] Another appellate court, electing more reticence, stated that "while the equalization of competition between taxable and tax-exempt entities was a major goal of the unrelated business income tax, it was by no means that statute's sole objective."[116] At a minimum, however, elimination of this type of competition clearly was Congress's principal aim; the tax regulations proclaim, as noted, that such was the federal legislature's "primary objective."[117]

Without doubt, the most interesting and innovative rationale for the unrelated business income rules is that their primary function is "political"; that is, that this body of law "deters charities from engaging in activities that do not comport with policymakers' perceptions of the type of activity subsidized by the charitable exemption."[118] This view asserts that Congress really was not concerned about unfair competition or revenue loss, but used the unrelated business rules concept as a "political expedient" for avoiding an analysis of the policies underlying the tax exemption for charitable organizations.[119] Proponents of this view argue that policymakers "simply acted to eliminate the cognitive dissonance" by giving charitable organizations a tax incentive to avoid active unrelated business and instead engage in passive investment (as well as related business activities).[120] Pursuant to this view, Congress and others were

---

[111] Income Tax Regulations (Reg.) § 1.513-1(b).
[112] 64 Stat. 906.
[113] H.R. Rep. No. 2319, 81st Cong., 2d Sess. 36–37 (1950). See *also* S. Rep. No. 2375, 81st Cong., 2d Sess. 28–29 (1950).
[114] S. Rep. No. 94-938, 94th Cong., 2d Sess. 601 (1976).
[115] La. Credit Union League v. United States, 693 F.2d 525, 540 (5th Cir. 1982).
[116] Am. Med. Ass'n v. United States, 887 F.2d 760, 772 (7th Cir. 1989).
[117] Reg. § 1.513-1(b).
[118] Stone Research Paper at 4.
[119] *Id.* at 4.
[120] *Id.* at 58.

concerned about a tax-exempt university's acquisition of a spaghetti company,[121] not unfair competition. This notion has it that the unrelated business income rules were "designed to channel charities away from problematic activities by setting up a tax gradient that favors income-generating activities compatible with perceptions of charitable activity" and to disfavor "highly visible activities that challenge perceptions of charitable activities—active business endeavors unrelated to any charitable purpose."[122] This approach sees the function of the unrelated business rules as forcing charities to stick with activities that are "more compatible with perceptions of charitable activity—traditional, passive investment and active business endeavors related to accomplishing a charitable objective"; hence, charitable organizations that were "willing to 'adhere to the old line' of good works and passive investment were rewarded."[123]

Generally, unrelated business activities must be confined to something less than a substantial portion of a tax-exempt organization's overall activities.[124] This is a manifestation of the *primary purpose test*.[125] According to traditional analysis, if a substantial portion of an exempt organization's income is from unrelated sources, the organization cannot qualify for tax exemption. Thus, for example, an organization failed to qualify as a tax-exempt social welfare organization because its primary activity became the operation of a commercial resort.[126] The IRS may deny or revoke the exempt status of an organization that regularly derives more than one-half of its annual revenue from unrelated activities.[127] In one instance, the agency ruled that an organization could not qualify as a tax-exempt social club,[128] in part because 75 percent of its gross income was derived from commercial rental activity that was held to be a business, regularly carried on, and conducted for profit.[129]

Although there generally are no specific percentage limitations in this area,[130] it is common to measure substantiality and insubstantiality in terms of percentages of expenditures or time.[131] Thus, generally, if a substantial portion of a tax-exempt organization's income is from unrelated sources, the organization cannot qualify for exemption. For example, a court barred an organization from achieving exempt status because the organization received about one-third of its revenue from an unrelated business.[132] Another court held that an organization

---

[121] "The fact is that, in 1947 and 1950, the Treasury, Congress and the press alike were obsessed with Mueller [the company], not unfair competition." *Id*. at 63. In general, Note, *The Macaroni Monopoly: The Developing Concept of Unrelated Business Income of Exempt Organizations*, 81 *Harv. L. Rev.* 1280 (1968).

[122] Stone Research Paper at 66.

[123] *Id*. Cf. § 7.5 (concerning the social enterprise movement).

[124] IRS Revenue Ruling (Rev. Rul.) 66-221, 1966-2 C.B. 220 (holding that a volunteer fire department was tax-exempt, notwithstanding an incidental amount of unrelated business activities).

[125] See *Tax-Exempt Organizations*, § 4.4.

[126] People's Educ. Camp Soc'y, Inc. v. Comm'r, 331 F.2d 923 (2d Cir.), *cert. denied*, 379 U.S. 839 (1964).

[127] See, *e.g.*, IRS General Counsel Memorandum (Gen. Couns. Mem.) 39108.

[128] See *Tax-Exempt Organizations*, ch. 14.

[129] Rev. Rul. 69-220, 1969-1 C.B. 154.

[130] See, however, § 1.11, text accompanied by notes 176–177.

[131] Similar definitional issues pertain with respect to the limits on allowable lobbying by public charities (see *Tax-Exempt Organizations*, § 20.3) and allowable political campaign activities by other types of exempt organizations (see *id.* §§ 21.4–21.4C).

[132] Orange County Agric. Soc'y, Inc. v. Comm'r, 893 F.2d 647 (2d Cir. 1990), *aff'g* 55 T.C.M. 1602 (1988).

could not retain its exempt status because about 50 percent of the time of its employees and nearly 60 percent of its income over a two-year period were attributable to unrelated business activities.[133] A 10-percent rule has been both relied on[134] and rejected[135]—by the same court.

Still, this approach is not always taken by either the IRS or the courts. As the IRS framed the matter, there is no "quantitative limitation" on the amount of unrelated business in which a tax-exempt organization may engage.[136] Likewise, a court wrote that "[w]hether an activity [of an exempt organization] is substantial is a facts-and-circumstances inquiry not always dependent upon time or expenditure percentages."[137] This is not a type of determination that is "based upon some economical and moral calculus."[138] In this context, there is no "percentage test which can be relied upon for future reference with respect to nonexempt activities of an organization," inasmuch as "[e]ach case must be decided upon its own unique facts and circumstances."[139]

Yet there are countervailing principles. The IRS, from time to time, applies the *commensurate test*, which compares the extent of a tax-exempt organization's resources to its program efforts.[140] Pursuant to this test, an organization may derive a substantial portion of its revenue in the form of unrelated business income, yet nonetheless be exempt because it also expends a significant amount of time on exempt functions. Thus, in one instance, although a charitable organization derived 98 percent of its income from an unrelated business, it remained exempt because 41 percent of the organization's activities, as measured in terms of expenditure of time, constituted exempt programs.[141] Using another approach, the IRS permitted an organization to remain exempt even though two-thirds of its operations were unrelated businesses, inasmuch as the reason for the conduct of these businesses was achievement of charitable purposes.[142] On that occasion, the IRS said that one way in which a business may further exempt purposes "is to raise money for the exempt purpose of the organization, notwithstanding that the actual trade or business activity may be taxable." The agency reiterated that the "proper focus is upon the purpose of [the organization's] activities and not upon the taxability of its activities."[143]

An organization may qualify as a tax-exempt entity, even though it operates a trade or business as a substantial part of its activities, when the operation of the business is in furtherance of the organization's exempt purposes. In determining the nature of a primary purpose, all the circumstances must be

---

[133] Ind. Retail Hardware Ass'n, Inc. v. United States, 366 F.2d 998 (Ct. Cl. 1966). The court dryly wrote that the fact that a "large percentage" of the organization's income was from unrelated activities was a "strong indication" that these activities were "more than merely incidental" (*id.* at 1002).

[134] World Family Corp. v. Comm'r, 81 T.C. 958 (1983).

[135] Manning Ass'n v. Comm'r, 93 T.C. 596 (1989).

[136] IRS Technical Advice Memorandum (Tech. Adv. Mem.) 200021056.

[137] Nationalist Movement v. Comm'r, 102 T.C. 558, 589 (1994), *aff'd*, 37 F.3d 216 (5th Cir. 1994).

[138] Christian Stewardship Assistance, Inc. v. Comm'r, 70 T.C. 1037, 1042 (1978).

[139] Church of God in Boston v. Comm'r, 71 T.C. 102 (1978).

[140] See *Tax-Exempt Organizations*, § 4.7.

[141] Tech. Adv. Mem. 9711003.

[142] Tech. Adv. Mem. 200021056.

[143] The fact that a business generates net income for exempt activities is, by itself, insufficient to cause the business to be regarded as a related one. See *infra* text accompanied by note 178.

considered, including the size and extent of the trade or business and of the activities that further one or more exempt purposes.[144] For example, an organization that purchased and sold at retail products manufactured by blind individuals was held by a court to qualify as an exempt charitable organization, because its activities resulted in employment for the blind, notwithstanding its receipt of net profits and its distribution of some of these profits to qualified workers.[145]

Funds received by a tax-exempt organization that is acting as an agent for another organization are not taxable income to the exempt organization, and thus are not unrelated business income.[146]

§ 1.7 ORGANIZATIONS SUBJECT TO UNRELATED BUSINESS RULES

The unrelated business rules apply to nearly all categories of tax-exempt organizations.[147] These entities include religious organizations (including churches), educational organizations (including universities, colleges, and schools), health care organizations (including hospitals), scientific organizations (including research institutions), public charities of various types, and similar organizations. Beyond the realm of charitable organizations, the rules apply to social welfare organizations (including advocacy groups), trade and professional associations, fraternal organizations, employee benefit funds, and veterans' organizations.[148] These rules also apply to charitable trusts.[149]

Special rules tax all income not related to exempt functions (including investment income) of social clubs, homeowners' associations, and political organizations.[150]

Some tax-exempt organizations are not generally involved with the unrelated business rules, simply because they are not allowed to engage in any active unrelated business endeavors. The best example of this is private foundations, whose operation of an active unrelated business (internally or externally) would trigger application of the excess business holdings rules.[151] These rules do not apply to governmental entities, however, other than colleges and universities that are agencies or instrumentalities of a governmental or political subdivision of a government, or that are owned or operated by a government or such political subdivision or by any agency or instrumentality of one or more governments or political subdivisions of them. The rules also apply to any corporation wholly owned by one or more of these colleges or universities.[152] These rules also do not

---

[144] Reg. § 1.501(c)(3)-1(e)(1).

[145] Industrial Aid for the Blind v. Comm'r, 73 T.C. 96 (1979).

[146] See, *e.g.*, IRS Private Letter Ruling (Priv. Ltr. Rul.) 7823048.

[147] IRC § 511(a)(2)(A).

[148] Oddly, the tax regulations, in the tax exemption context, expressly identify only some of the types of exempt organizations that are subject to the unrelated business rules: single-member title-holding companies (Reg. § 1.501(c)(2)-1(a)), charitable organizations (Reg. § 1.501(c)(3)-1(e)(2)), and business leagues (Reg. § 1.501(c)(6)-1).

[149] IRC § 511(b)(2).

[150] See § 6.1.

[151] See § 6.3.

[152] IRC § 511(a)(2)(B).

apply to instrumentalities of the federal government, certain religious and apostolic organizations, farmers' cooperatives, and shipowners' protection and indemnity associations.

§ 1.8   TAX EXEMPTION AND COMPETITION

The presence or absence of competition—fair or unfair—is not among the criteria, in a statute or regulation, applied in assessing whether an activity of a tax-exempt organization is an unrelated business. This is so notwithstanding the fact that concern about competition between exempt and for-profit organizations is the principal reason for and underpinning of the unrelated business rules.[153]

Thus, an activity of a tax-exempt organization may be wholly noncompetitive with an activity of a for-profit organization and nonetheless be an unrelated business. For example, in an opinion finding that the operation of a bingo game by an exempt organization was an unrelated business, a court wrote that the "tax on unrelated business income is not limited to income earned by a trade or business that operates in competition with taxpaying entities."[154] Yet, in a case concerning an exempt labor union that collected per capita taxes from unions affiliated with it, a court concluded that the imposition of these taxes (which enabled the union to perform its exempt functions) "simply is not conducting a trade or business," in part because the union was not providing any services in competition with taxable entities.[155]

§ 1.9   CONCISE HISTORY OF THE UNRELATED BUSINESS RULES[156]

Until the introduction of the unrelated business income tax in 1950, tax-exempt organizations enjoyed full exemption from federal income tax. If a charitable or other exempt organization met the organizational and operational tests,[157] there was no statutory limitation on the amount of business activity an exempt organization could conduct, as long as the earnings from the business were used for exempt purposes. Courts even extended this *destination of income test* to the exemption of charitable organizations that did not conduct any charitable programs, but rather operated commercial businesses for the benefit of a charitable organization, thus acting as *feeder organizations*.

In the years before 1950, charitable organizations also were acquiring real estate with borrowed funds. In a typical transaction, a tax-exempt organization would borrow money to acquire real property, lease the property to the seller under a long-term lease, and service the loan with tax-free rental income from

---

[153] See § 1.6, text accompanied by notes 111–114.

[154] Clarence LaBelle Post No. 217 v. United States, 580 F.2d 270, 272 (8th Cir. 1978).

[155] Laborers' Int'l Union v. Comm'r, 82 T.C.M. 158, 160 (2001). In general, Note, *Unfair Competition and the Unrelated Business Income Tax*, 75 *Va. L. Rev.* 605 (no. 3, 1989); Bennett, *Unfair Competition and the UBIT*, 41 *Tax Notes* 759 (no. 7A, 1988).

[156] This section is based on a portion of a report prepared by the staff of the Joint Committee on Taxation, titled *Historical Development and Present Law of Federal Tax Exemption for Charities and Other Tax-Exempt Organizations* (JCX-29-05) (Apr. 19, 2005). This report was prepared in connection with a hearing before the House Committee on Ways and Means, held on April 20, 2005, on an overview of the tax-exempt sector.

[157] See *Tax-Exempt Organizations*, §§ 4.3, 4.5.

the lease. Concern arose that exempt organizations were in effect leveraging their tax exemption through such transactions and thereby threatening the nation's tax base by acquiring, by means of debt, income-producing assets that, following the acquisition, no longer generated revenue for the federal government.

As a response to these practices, Congress in 1950 subjected charitable organizations (other than churches) and certain other exempt organizations to tax on their net unrelated business income. The tax was intended to prevent unfair competition. Excluded from this tax were passive investment income and certain gains and losses from the disposition of property. Excluded from the definition of an *unrelated trade or business* was a trade or business in which substantially all of the work in carrying on the business is performed without compensation; a trade or business carried on primarily for the convenience of the members and certain others; and a trade or business that sells merchandise, substantially all of which was received by the organization as contributions.

To address the matter of feeder organizations, the 1950 legislation provided that, in general, an organization that is operated primarily for the purpose of carrying on a trade or business for profit may not be recognized as tax-exempt merely because all of the organization's profits are payable to exempt organizations. To cope with the leveraging of exemption, the 1950 enactment, by expanding the unrelated debt-financed income rules, taxed certain rents received in connection with the leveraged sale and leaseback of real estate.

When writing the Tax Reform Act of 1969, Congress made significant changes to the unrelated business rules, including an extension of the unrelated business income tax to all tax-exempt organizations.[158] In addition, the 1969 act expanded the tax on debt-financed income to cover not only certain rents from debt-financed acquisitions of real estate, but also other debt-financed income. To prevent evasion of the unrelated business income tax through the use of controlled subsidiaries, the 1969 act also generally provided that payments to a tax-exempt organization of interest, annuities, royalties, or rent from a taxable or tax-exempt subsidiary of the organization may be subject to tax. These provisions were intended to prevent an exempt organization from "renting" assets to a subsidiary for use in an unrelated business, thereby permitting the subsidiary to escape income taxation by means of a large deduction for rent. Since 1969, although Congress has made a number of changes to the unrelated business rules, the structure of this aspect of the law of tax-exempt organizations has remained largely intact.

In general, tax-exempt organizations have greater discretion than taxable organizations in determining whether to report income as taxable, by asking whether income is from a regularly conducted trade or business, and whether the conduct of the trade or business is substantially related to exempt purposes. In addition, even if an exempt organization treats income as being unrelated and therefore subject to tax, an exempt organization might allocate expenses for an exempt activity to an unrelated activity, in order to minimize or eliminate the tax.

Issues often arise as to whether certain types of receipts constitute royalties, which generally are excluded in determining an exempt organization's

---

[158] That is, to entities described in IRC §§ 401(a) and 501(c).

unrelated business income. Two issues that have been the source of considerable debate in this area are (1) whether income from an affinity credit card program constitutes a royalty, and (2) whether income from a mailing list rental constitutes a royalty. Several court decisions have been issued on these points. Also, an exempt organization that provides more than a small amount of clerical services may risk having payments received in exchange for a license classified as payments for services rather than as excludable royalties.

§ 1.10 PRIVATE INUREMENT AND PRIVATE BENEFIT

To become, and to remain, tax-exempt, organizations are required to satisfy various tests.[159] One set of these requirements is adherence to the doctrine concerning avoidance of private inurement, which doctrine applies to most categories of exempt organizations. Private inurement transactions are distinguishable from unrelated business, yet there can also be some overlap of these two areas of the law of tax-exempt organizations.

The doctrine of *private inurement* is one of the most important sets of rules within the law of tax-exempt organizations—it is the fundamental defining principle distinguishing nonprofit organizations from for-profit organizations.[160] The private inurement doctrine is a statutory criterion for federal income tax exemption for nine types of exempt organizations:

1. Charitable organizations

2. Social welfare organizations

3. Associations and other business leagues

4. Social clubs

5. Voluntary employees' beneficiary associations

6. Teachers' retirement fund associations

7. Cemetery companies

8. Veterans' organizations

9. State-sponsored organizations providing health care to high-risk individuals

Thus, aside from being organized and operated primarily for a tax-exempt purpose and otherwise meeting the applicable statutory requirements for exemption, an organization subject to the doctrine must comport with the federal tax law prohibiting private inurement. Despite the fact that this law is applicable to several categories of tax-exempt organizations, nearly all of the law concerning private inurement has been developed involving transactions with charitable organizations.

The oddly phrased and utterly antiquated language of the private inurement doctrine requires that the tax-exempt organization be organized and operated so that "no part of . . . [its] net earnings . . . inures to the benefit of any

---

[159] See, *e.g.*, *Tax-Exempt Organizations*, chs. 19–21.
[160] See *id.* § 1.1.

private shareholder or individual."[161] This provision reads as though it were proscribing the payment of dividends. In fact, it is rare for a tax-exempt organization to have shareholders,[162] let alone to make payments to them. Moreover, the private inurement doctrine can be triggered by the involvement of persons other than individuals, such as corporations, partnerships, limited liability companies, estates, and trusts. The meaning of the statutory language today is barely reflected in its literal form and transcends the nearly century-old formulation: None of the income or assets of a tax-exempt organization subject to the private inurement doctrine may be permitted, directly or indirectly, to unduly benefit an individual or other person who has a close relationship to the organization, particularly those who are in a position to exercise a significant degree of control over the organization.

The *private benefit doctrine* is considerably different from the private inurement doctrine, although it subsumes the latter doctrine. As an extrapolation of the operational test,[163] the private benefit doctrine is applicable only to charitable organizations. The rules pertaining to *excess benefit transactions* are applicable to public charitable organizations[164] and social welfare organizations.[165]

§ 1.11 DETERMINING ALLOWABLE UNRELATED BUSINESS

To be tax-exempt, a nonprofit organization must be organized and operated primarily for exempt purposes.[166] The federal tax law thus allows an exempt organization to engage in a certain amount of income-producing activity that is unrelated to its exempt purposes. When the organization derives net income from one or more unrelated business activities, a tax is imposed on that income.[167] An organization's tax exemption will be denied or revoked if a certain portion of its activities is not promoting one or more of its exempt purposes.

A tax-exempt charitable organization may operate a trade or business as a substantial part of its activities, if the operation of the trade or business furthers the organization's exempt purpose or purposes and if the organization is not organized or operated for the primary purpose of carrying on an unrelated trade or business. In determining the existence or nonexistence of this primary purpose, all of the circumstances must be considered, including the size and extent of the trade or business and the size and extent of the activities that are in furtherance of one or more exempt purposes. An organization that is organized and operated for the primary purpose of carrying on a trade or business cannot be exempt even

---

[161] In a fine characterization, this phraseology was termed a "nondistribution constraint." Hansmann, *The Role of Nonprofit Enterprise*, 89 *Yale L.J.* 835, 838 (1980).

[162] The law in a few states permits a nonprofit corporation to issue stock. This type of stock, however, does not carry with it rights to dividends. Thus, these rare bodies of law are not in conflict with the private inurement doctrine.

[163] See *Tax-Exempt Organizations*, § 4.5.

[164] See *id.* §§ 11.1, 11.3.

[165] See *id.* ch. 12.

[166] See *id.* § 4.4.

[167] See § 11.1.

though it has religious purposes, its property is held in common, and its profits do not inure to the benefit of individual members of the organization.[168]

An organization cannot be a tax-exempt social welfare organization if its primary activity is carrying on a business with the general public in a manner similar to organizations that are operated for profit.[169] An exempt business league cannot have, as one of its purposes, engagement in a regular business of a kind that is ordinarily carried on for profit, if that engagement is more than insubstantial.[170] A club cannot be exempt as a social club if it engages in business, such as making its social and recreational facilities available to the general public or by selling real estate, timber, or other products.[171]

Business activities may preclude the initial qualification of an otherwise tax-exempt organization. If the organization is not being operated principally for exempt purposes, it will fail the operational test.[172] If an organization's articles of organization empower it to carry on substantial activities that are not in furtherance of its exempt purposes, it will not meet the organizational test.[173]

A nonprofit organization may still satisfy the operational test, even when it operates a business as a substantial part of its activities, as long as the business promotes the organization's exempt purpose. If the organization's primary purpose is carrying on a nonexempt business for profit, it is denied tax-exempt status, perhaps on the ground that it is a feeder organization.[174] Generally, there are no formal percentage-based quantifications in this context.[175] An exempt title-holding company usually cannot have income from an actively conducted unrelated trade or business;[176] an exception permits such income in an amount up to 10 percent of the company's gross income for the tax year, when the income is incidentally derived from the holding of real property.[177]

Occasionally, the IRS will assume a different stance toward the tax consequences of one or more unrelated businesses when the question is qualification for tax exemption. That is, the IRS may conclude that a business is unrelated to an organization's exempt purpose and thus is subject to the unrelated business income tax, but the IRS may also agree that the purpose of the unrelated business is such that the activity furthers the organization's exempt functions (by generating funds for exempt programs), even if the unrelated business activity is more than one-half of total operations.[178] In this circumstance, then, the exempt organization can be in the anomalous position of having a considerable amount of taxable business activity and still being tax-exempt.

---

[168] Reg. § 1.501(c)(3)-1(e)(1). *Cf. Tax-Exempt Organizations*, § 8.7 (concerning religious and apostolic organizations).

[169] Reg. § 1.501(c)(4)-1(a)(2)(ii).

[170] Reg. § 1.501(c)(6)-1.

[171] Reg. § 1.501(c)(7)-1(b).

[172] See *Tax-Exempt Organizations*, § 4.5.

[173] *Id.* § 4.6.

[174] *Id.* § 28.6.

[175] See § 1.6.

[176] Reg. § 1.501(c)(2)-1(a), which has not been amended to reflect the exception referenced in text accompanied by *infra* note 177.

[177] IRC § 501(c)(2), last sentence; IRC § 501(c)(25)(G).

[178] *E.g.*, Tech. Adv. Mem. 200021056.

CHAPTER TWO

Unrelated Business: The Basics

The federal tax law generally categorizes the activities of tax-exempt organizations as being one of two types: those that are substantially related to the performance of exempt functions and those that are not. The former are *related trades or businesses*; the latter are *unrelated trades or businesses*. The net revenue generated by an unrelated business—absent application of a modification[1] or an exception[2]—is subject to federal income tax. The judgments underlying the assignment of activities to these two categories are at the heart of some of the greatest tax law controversies facing exempt organizations.

The fundamental unrelated business rules entail a determination as to whether a particular activity amounts to a business, whether the activity is regularly carried on, whether the activity substantially furthers the purposes of the tax-exempt organization involved, and (if needed) whether an exception is available. The rest of the basics are essentially refinements of these four determinations.

---

[1] See ch. 3.
[2] See ch. 4.

Somewhat similar issues are brewing in relation to eligibility for tax-exempt status, by virtue of the *commerciality doctrine*.[3]

§ 2.1   THE ANALYTIC FRAMEWORK

An analysis of a factual situation surrounding a tax-exempt organization's potential unrelated trade or business may involve as many as nine steps:

1. Ascertainment of whether the exempt organization is subject to the unrelated business rules[4]

2. Ascertainment of whether the activity involved constitutes a *business*[5]

3. Determination of whether the business is *regularly carried on*[6]

4. Determination of whether the regularly carried on business is *related* to the purposes of the exempt organization[7]

5. Determination of whether the regularly carried on business is *substantially* related to the purposes of the exempt organization[8]

6. Determination of whether one or more modifications or exceptions for types of *income* may be available[9]

7. Determination of whether one or more modifications or exceptions for types of *activities* may be available[10]

8. Marshalling of available expenses that can be deducted in computing *unrelated business taxable income*[11]

9. Determination of whether the unrelated activity, or combination of unrelated activities, poses a threat to the organization's tax-exempt status[12]

§ 2.2   DEFINITION OF *TRADE OR BUSINESS*

As noted, some or all of the gross income of a tax-exempt organization may be includable in the computation of unrelated business income if that income is derived from a *trade or business*.

(a) General Rules

The statutory definition of the term *trade or business*, used for unrelated business law purposes, includes "any activity which is carried on for the production of

---

[3] See ch. 7.
[4] See § 1.3.
[5] See §§ 2.2–2.4. Although the technical term is *trade or business*, in practice, the law looks to whether the activity is a *business* rather than whether it amounts to a *trade*. Years ago, there was a court opinion in which the judge repeatedly made reference to "trader business," but that opinion was withdrawn and reissued with the accurate terminology.
[6] See § 2.5.
[7] See § 2.6.
[8] See § 2.7.
[9] See chs. 3 & 4.
[10] See chs. 3 & 4.
[11] See ch. 11.
[12] See § 1.11.

income from the sale of goods or the performance of services."[13] This sweeping definition encompasses nearly every activity that a tax-exempt organization may undertake. Indeed, the federal tax law views an exempt organization as a cluster of businesses, with each discrete activity susceptible to evaluation independently from the others.[14]

The definition of the term *trade or business*, however, also embraces an activity that otherwise possesses the characteristics of a business as that term is defined by the federal income tax law in the business expense deduction setting.[15] This definition, then, is even more expansive than the statutory one, being informed by the considerable body of law as to the meaning of the word *business* that has accreted in the federal tax law generally.

Consequently, in general, any activity of a tax-exempt organization (subject to the unrelated business rules) that is carried on for the production of income and that otherwise possesses the characteristics required to constitute a trade or business (within the meaning of the business expense deduction rules)—and that is not substantially related to the performance of exempt functions—presents sufficient likelihood of unfair competition[16] to be within the ambit of the unrelated business income tax. For purposes of the unrelated business rules, the term *trade or business* has the same meaning that it has in the context of the business expense deduction rules, and thus generally includes any activity carried on for the production of income from the sale of goods or the performance of services. The term *trade or business* is not, therefore, limited to the integrated aggregates of assets, activities, and goodwill that constitute *businesses* for other federal tax law purposes.[17]

A third element to consider in this regard stems from the view that, to constitute a business, an income-producing activity of a tax-exempt organization must have the general characteristics of a trade or business. Some federal courts of appeals have recognized that an exempt organization must carry out extensive business activities over a substantial period of time to be considered engaged in a trade or business.[18] In one case, a court held that the proceeds derived by an exempt organization from fundraising operations were not taxable as unrelated business income, inasmuch as the organization's functions in this regard were considered insufficiently "extensive" to warrant treatment as a business.[19] In another instance, the receipt of payments by an exempt association pursuant to involvement in insurance plans was ruled not to constitute a business, because the association's role was not extensive and did not possess the general characteristics of a trade or business.[20] This aspect of the analysis, however, is close to a

---

[13] IRC § 513(c).
[14] See the discussion of the fragmentation rule in § 2.3.
[15] Reg. § 1.513-1(b). The business expense deduction is the subject of IRC § 162.
[16] See § 1.8.
[17] Reg. § 1.513-1(b).
[18] In the tax-exempt organizations context, see, *e.g.*, Prof'l Ins. Agents v. Comm'r, 726 F.2d 1097 (6th Cir. 1984). In the business expense deduction context, see, *e.g.*, Zell v. Comm'r, 763 F.2d 1139 (10th Cir. 1985); McDowell v. Ribicoff, 292 F.2d 174 (3d Cir. 1961), *cert. denied*, 368 U.S. 919 (1961).
[19] Vigilant Hose Co. v. United States, 2001-2 U.S.T.C. ¶ 50,458 (D. Md. 2001).
[20] Am. Acad. of Family Physicians v. United States, 91 F.3d 1155 (8th Cir. 1996).

separate test altogether, which is whether the business activities are regularly carried on.[21]

When an activity carried on for profit constitutes an unrelated business, no part of the business may be excluded from classification as a business merely because it does not result in profit.[22]

Traditionally, the IRS has almost always prevailed on the argument that an activity of a tax-exempt organization constitutes a trade or business. In recent years, however, courts have been more willing to conclude that an exempt organization's financial undertaking does not rise to the level of a business.[23]

(b) Commerciality

When there is competition, a court may conclude that the activity of a tax-exempt organization is being conducted in a commercial manner[24] and thus is an unrelated business. For example, a television station run an exempt university was held to be an unrelated business because it was operated in a commercial manner; the station was an affiliate of a national television broadcasting company.[25]

Historically, the IRS (like the courts) has used the commerciality doctrine in assessing an organization's qualification for tax-exempt status; the doctrine was not used to ascertain the presence of an unrelated business. This appears to be changing, however, with the IRS employing the doctrine in rationalizing that a business is an unrelated one.[26]

(c) Charging of Fees

Many tax-exempt organizations charge fees for the services they provide. When the business generating this revenue is a related one, the receipts are characterized as *exempt function revenue*.[27] Universities, colleges, hospitals, museums, planetariums, orchestras, and similar exempt institutions all generate exempt function revenue, without adverse impact on their exempt status.[28] Exempt organizations such as medical clinics, homes for the aged, and blood banks impose charges for their services and are not subject to unrelated business income taxation (nor deprived of exemption) as a result.[29] Indeed, the IRS, in a ruling discussing the tax status of homes for the aged as charitable organizations, observed that the "operating funds [of these homes] are derived principally from fees charged for residence in the home."[30] Similarly, the agency ruled that a nonprofit theater may charge admission for its performances and nonetheless qualify as an exempt charitable organization.[31] Other fee-based exempt charitable

---

[21] See § 2.5.

[22] IRC § 513(c).

[23] *E.g.*, Laborer's Int'l Union v. Comm'r, 82 T.C.M. 158 (2001).

[24] See ch. 7.

[25] Iowa State Univ. of Sci. & Tech. v. United States, 500 F.2d 508 (Ct. Cl. 1974).

[26] *E.g.*, Tech. Adv. Mem. 200021056.

[27] *E.g.*, § 11.3(a).

[28] IRC § 170(b)(1)(A)(ii), (iii); Reg. § 1.170A-9(e)(1)(ii); Reg. § 1.501(c)(3)-1(d)(3)(ii), Example (4).

[29] *E.g.*, Rev. Rul. 72-124, 1972-1 C.B. 145; Rev. Rul. 78-145, 1978-1 C.B. 169, *modifying* Rev. Rul. 66-323, 1966-2 C.B. 216.

[30] Rev. Rul. 72-124, 1972-1 C.B. 145.

[31] Rev. Rul. 73-45, 1973-1 C.B. 220.

entities include hospices,[32] organizations providing specially designed housing for the elderly,[33] and organizations providing housing for the disabled.[34] Moreover, for some types of publicly supported charities, exempt function revenue is regarded as support enhancing public charity status.[35] Several categories of exempt organizations, such as business associations, unions, social clubs, fraternal groups, and veterans' organizations, are dues-based entities.

Consequently, as a general principle, gross income derived from charges for the performance of exempt functions does not constitute gross income from the conduct of an unrelated trade or business.[36] For example, suppose that a tax-exempt school trains children in the performing arts, such as acting, singing, and dancing. It presents performances by its students and derives gross income from admission charges for the performances. The students' participation in performances before audiences is an essential part of their education and training. Because the income realized from the performances derives from activities that contribute importantly to the accomplishment of the school's exempt purposes, it does not constitute gross income from an unrelated business.[37]

Another example is a tax-exempt union that, to improve the skills of its members, conducts refresher training courses and supplies handbooks and technical manuals. The union receives payments from its members for these services and materials. The development and improvement of members' skills is one of the exempt purposes of this union, and these activities contribute importantly to that purpose. Therefore, the income derived from these activities is not unrelated business gross income.[38]

In a third illustration, a tax-exempt industry trade association presents a trade show in which members of an industry join in an exhibition of industry products. The association derives income from charges to exhibitors for exhibit space and admission fees charged to patrons or viewers of the show. The show is not a sales facility for individual exhibitors;[39] its purpose is the promotion and stimulation of interest in and demand for the industry's products in general, and it is conducted in a manner reasonably calculated to achieve that purpose. The stimulation of demand for the industry's products in general is one of the purposes for which the association was granted tax exemption. Consequently, the activities that produce the association's gross income from the show—that is, the promotion, organization, and conduct of the exhibition—contribute importantly to the achievement of an exempt purpose, and thus that income does not constitute gross income from an unrelated business.[40]

Nevertheless, the receipt of fee-for-service revenue occasionally is regarded, in some quarters, as evidence of the conduct of an unrelated business. For example,

---

[32] Rev. Rul. 79-17, 1979-1 C.B. 193.

[33] Rev. Rul. 79-18, 1979-1 C.B. 194.

[34] Rev. Rul. 79-19, 1979-1 C.B. 195.

[35] IRC § 509(a)(2). See Hopkins, *The Law of Tax-Exempt Organizations, Eighth Edition* (John Wiley & Sons, 2003) [hereinafter *Tax-Exempt Organizations*] § 11.3(b)(iv).

[36] Reg. § 1.513-1(d)(4)(i).

[37] *Id.*, Example (1).

[38] *Id.*, Example (2).

[39] Cf. § 4.5.

[40] Reg. § 1.513-1(d)(4)(i), Example (3).

from time to time someone contends that an organization, to be charitable in nature, must provide its services and/or sell its goods without charge. In fact, the test for charitable and other exempt organizations is how the fees received are expended; the rendering of services without charge is *not* a prerequisite to tax-exempt status.

In one instance, the IRS opposed tax exemption for nonprofit consumer credit counseling agencies. The agencies asserted that their services, which were provided to individuals and families and included facilitating speeches and disseminating publications, were educational in nature as being forms of instruction of the public on subjects (such as budgeting) useful to the individual and beneficial to the community.[41] They also contended that their activities are charitable because they advance education and promote social welfare.[42] The IRS sought to deny these agencies exempt status on the ground that they charged a fee for certain services, even though the fee was nominal and waived in instances of economic hardship. This effort was rebuffed in court.[43] Thereafter, the IRS's office of chief counsel advised that if the "activity [of consumer credit counseling] may be deemed to benefit the community as a whole, the fact that fees are charged for the organization's services will not detract from the exempt nature of the activity" and that the "presence of a fee is relevant only if it inhibits accomplishment of the desired result."[44] (Earlier, the chief counsel's office wrote that the fact that a charitable organization charges a fee for a good or service "will be relevant in very few cases," that the "only inquiry" should be whether the charges "significantly detract from the organization's charitable purposes," and that the cost issue is pertinent only when the activities involved are commercial in nature.[45]) At about the same time, the IRS ruled that an organization that is operated to provide legal services to indigents may charge, for each hour of legal assistance provided, a "nominal hourly fee determined by reference to the client's own hourly income."[46]

There have been instances in which the IRS determined that an organization is charitable in nature, and thus tax-exempt, because it provides services that are free to recipients. This is, however, an independent basis for finding an activity to be charitable, usually invoked when the services, assistance, or benefits provided are not inherently charitable in nature. This distinction may be seen in IRS's treatment of cooperative service organizations established by tax-exempt colleges and universities. In one instance, a computer services sharing organization was ruled to be an exempt charitable organization because the IRS concluded that the services provided to the participating institutions of higher education were charitable as advancing education; no requirement was imposed that the services be provided without charge.[47] In another instance, a similar organization was found to be charitable even though the services it rendered to

---

[41] Reg. § 1.501(c)(3)-1(d)(3)(i)(B). See *Tax-Exempt Organizations,* § 7.4.

[42] Reg. § 1.501(c)(3)-1(d)(2). See *Tax-Exempt Organizations,* § 6.6.

[43] Consumer Credit Counseling Serv. of Ala., Inc. v. United States, 78-2 U.S.T.C. ¶ 9660 (D.D.C. 1978).

[44] IRS General Counsel Memorandum ("Gen. Couns. Mem.")

[45] Gen. Couns. Mem. 37257.

[46] Rev. Rul. 78-428, 1978-2 C.B. 177.

[47] Rev. Rul. 74-614, 1974-2 C.B. 164, amplified by Rev. Rul. 81-29, 1981-1 C.B. 329.

the participating education institutions were regarded as nonexempt functions (being "administrative"); the distinguishing feature was that the organization received less than 15 percent of its financial support from the colleges and universities that received the services.[48] Thus, the recipient entities were receiving the services for, at most, a nominal charge. Had this latter organization been providing only insubstantial administrative services and a substantial amount of exempt services, its exemption would have been predicated on the basis that it was engaging in inherently exempt activities. The 15-percent rule was employed only as an alternative rationale for exemption as a charitable entity.[49]

On occasion, the issue will be whether there is an unrelated business, not so much because fees are being charged but because the charges result in a *profit* (excess of revenue over expenses). Profit-making is not an automatic indicator of unrelated trade or business; indeed, a profit motive may be a requirement for a finding of business activity.[50] In its regulations concerning travel tours and similar opportunities,[51] the IRS stipulated that, in the case of both related and unrelated activities, the travel tours were priced to produce a profit for the exempt organization.[52]

Consequently, the law does not require, as a condition of tax exemption or avoidance of unrelated business income, that the organization provide services without charge.[53] Likewise, the fact that an exempt organization charges a fee for the provision of goods or services, though perhaps an indicator that the underlying activity is a business, should not lead to an automatic conclusion that the business is unrelated to exempt functions.

(d) Nonbusiness Activities

Not every activity of a tax-exempt organization that generates a financial return is a trade or business for purposes of the unrelated business rules. As the Supreme Court observed, the "narrow category of trade or business" is a "concept which falls far short of reaching every income or profit making activity."[54] Specifically in the exempt organizations context, an appellate court wrote that "there are instances where some activities by some exempt organizations to earn income in a noncommercial manner will not amount to the conduct of a trade or business."[55]

The most obvious of the types of nonbusiness activities is the management by a tax-exempt organization of its own investment properties. Under the general

---

[48] Rev. Rul. 71-529, 1971-2 C.B. 234.

[49] In general, see *Tax-Exempt Organizations,* § 10.5.

[50] See § 2.4.

[51] See § 9.7.

[52] Reg. § 1.513-7(b).

[53] The "position that the test of a charitable institution is the extent of free services rendered is difficult of application and unsound in theory." S. Methodist Hosp. & Sanatorium of Tucson v. Wilson, 77 P.2d 458, 462 (Ariz. 1943).

[54] Whipple v. Comm'r, 373 U.S. 193, 197, 201 (1963).

[55] Steamship Trade Ass'n of Baltimore, Inc. v. Comm'r, 757 F.2d 1494, 1497 (4th Cir. 1985). *See also* Adirondack League Club v. Comm'r, 458 F.2d 506 (2d Cir. 1972); Blake Constr. Co. v. United States, 572 F.2d 820 (Ct. Cl. 1978); Monfore v. United States, 77-2 U.S.T.C. ¶ 9528 (Ct. Cl. 1977); Okla. Cattlemen's Ass'n, Inc. v. United States, 310 F. Supp. 320 (W.D. Okla. 1969); McDowell v. Ribicoff, 292 F.2d 174 (3d Cir. 1961), *cert. denied,* 368 U.S. 919 (1961).

rules concerning the business expense deduction, which define *business activity*, the management of an investment portfolio composed wholly of the manager's own securities does not constitute the carrying on of a trade or business. The Supreme Court held that the mere derivation of income from securities and keeping of records is not the operation of a business.[56] On that occasion, the Court sustained the IRS's position that "mere personal investment activities never constitute carrying on a trade or business."[57] Subsequently, the Court stated that "investing is not a trade or business."[58] Likewise, a court of appeals observed that the "mere management of investments . . . is insufficient to constitute the carrying on of a trade or business."[59]

This principle of law is applicable in the tax-exempt organizations context. For example, the IRS ruled that the receipt of income, by an exempt employees' trust, from installment notes purchased from the employer-settlor was not income from the operation of a business. It noted that the trust "merely keeps the records and receives the periodic payments of principal and interest collected for it by the employer."[60] Likewise, the agency held that a reversion of funds from a qualified plan to a charitable organization did not "possess the characteristics" required for an activity to qualify as a business.[61] For a time, there was controversy over whether the practice, engaged in by some tax-exempt organizations, of lending securities to brokerage houses for compensation was an unrelated business; the IRS ultimately arrived at the view that securities lending is a form of "ordinary or routine investment activities" and thus is not a business.[62] A court held that certain investment activities conducted by a charitable organization were not businesses.[63]

Other similar activities do not rise to the level of a business. In one instance, a tax-exempt association of physicians was held not to be taxable on certain payments it received annually by reason of its sponsorship of group insurance plans that were available to its members and their employees. The court wrote that the payments "were neither brokerage fees nor other compensation for commercial services, but were the way the parties decided to acknowledge the . . . [association's] eventual claim to the excess reserves while . . . [the insurance company involved] was still holding and using the reserves."[64] In another case, an exempt dental society that sponsored a payment plan to finance dental care was held not

---

[56] Higgins v. Comm'r, 312 U.S. 212 (1941).

[57] *Id.* at 215.

[58] Whipple v. Comm'r, 373 U.S. 193, 202 (1963).

[59] Continental Trading, Inc. v. Comm'r, 265 F.2d 40, 43 (9th Cir. 1959), *cert. denied*, 361 U.S. 827 (1959). See also VanWart v. Comm'r, 295 U.S. 112 (1935); Deputy v. duPont, 308 U.S. 488 (1940) (concurring opinion); Moller v. United States, 721 F.2d 810 (Fed. Cir. 1983); Comm'r v. Burnett, 118 F.2d 659 (5th Cir. 1941); Rev. Rul. 56-511, 1956-2 C.B. 170.

[60] Rev. Rul. 69-574, 1969-2 C.B. 130, 131.

[61] Priv. Ltr. Rul. 200131034.

[62] Rev. Rul. 78-88, 1978-1 C.B. 163. This issue was subsequently further resolved by statute (see § 3.4).

[63] Marion Found. v. Comm'r, 19 T.C.M. 99 (1960).

[64] Am. Acad. of Family Physicians v. United States, 91 F.3d 1155, 1159 (8th Cir. 1996). Nonetheless, the IRS remains of the view that these types of oversight and like activities with respect to insurance programs constitute unrelated business. (*e.g.*, Tech. Adv. Mem. 9612003 (concerning a charitable organization, fostering competition in a sport (see § 10.2), that provided certain administrative services in connection with an insurance program covering its members for practices and other sports activities).

to be taxable on refunds for income taxes and interest on amounts paid as excess reserve funds from a bank and as collections on defaulted notes.[65] A comparable position was taken by a court in concluding that an exempt organization did not engage in an unrelated business by making health insurance available to its members, in that the organization did not control the financial result of the insurance activities.[66]

In still another case, a court held that the proceeds derived by a tax-exempt organization from fundraising operations were not taxable as unrelated business income, because the economic activity did not constitute a business.[67] The fundraising involved the use of "tip jars," with the exempt organization's role confined to applying for gambling permits and purchasing the tip-jar tickets; the significant and substantial portion of the activities was the sale of the tickets at participating taverns. The exempt organization's functions in this regard were considered insufficiently "extensive" to warrant treatment as a business.[68]

(e) Real Estate Activities

A tax-exempt organization may acquire real property under a variety of circumstances and for a variety of reasons. The acquisition may be by purchase or by contribution. Such acquisition activity is often undertaken to advance exempt purposes or to make an investment. When an exempt organization decides to dispose of the property, the activity may be, or may be seen as being, a dealing in property in the ordinary course of a business. When exempt functions are not involved, the dichotomy becomes whether the exempt organization is a passive investor or is a dealer in the property. The issue frequently arises when the property, or portions of it, is being sold; the exempt organization may be liquidating an investment in an attempt to maximize the value of the property, or may be selling property to customers in the ordinary course of business.

The IRS applies the following factors in determining whether property being or to be sold has been held primarily for investment or for sale to customers in the ordinary course of business (in the latter case, the resulting revenue is ordinary income rather than capital gain):

- The purpose for which the property was acquired
- The cost of the property
- The length of time the property was held
- The owner's activities in improving and disposing of the property
- The extent of improvements made to the property
- The proximity of the sale to the purchase

---

[65] San Antonio Dist. Dental Soc'y v. United States, 340 F. Supp. 11 (W.D. Tex. 1972).

[66] Carolinas Farm & Power Equip. Dealers Ass'n, Inc. v. United States, 541 F. Supp. 86 (E.D.N.C. 1982), *aff'd*, 699 F.2d 167 (4th Cir. 1983).

[67] Vigilant Hose Co. v. United States, 2001-2 U.S.T.C. ¶ 50,458 (D. Md. 2001).

[68] On occasion, as an alternative argument, the IRS will assert that the tax-exempt organization is involved in a joint venture with one or more for-profit entities, and attempt to tax net revenues received by the exempt organization on that basis (see § 8.16).

- The purpose for which the property was held
- Prevailing market conditions
- The frequency, continuity, and size of the sales[69]

The factors are derived from case law. In one of the principal cases on the point, the court held that the frequency of the sales and the level of development and selling activities are the most important criteria. This court wrote that "although a taxpayer may have acquired property without intending to enter the real estate business, what was once an investment or what may start out as a liquidation of an investment, may become something else"; thus, "where sales are continuous[,] the nature and purpose of a taxpayer's acquisition of property is significant only where sales activity results from unanticipated, externally introduced factors which make impossible the continued pre-existing use of the realty."[70]

Other court opinions provide similar lists of factors.[71] In one case, the court relied primarily on the frequency-of-sales factor.[72] A corporation that did not engage in any development or subdivision activity, and did not engage in any solicitation or marketing efforts, with respect to about 200 sales of lots over a 33-year period, was found to be a dealer because the sales activity was substantial and continuous.[73] A person who made 107 sales over a 10-year period was found to be a dealer,[74] whereas another person who sold 25 lots in 1 year was held not to be a dealer.[75] The only aspect of this matter that is clear is that there is no fixed formula or other rule of thumb for determining whether property sold by a person was held by that person primarily[76] for sale to customers in business or for investment.[77]

As examples of the IRS's decision-making in this context, the agency ruled that the gain from the sale by tax-exempt organizations of leased fee interests in condominium apartments to lessees was not taxable because of the exclusion for capital gain.[78] Likewise, the IRS ruled that the sale by a charitable organization of its entire interest in an apartment building, to be converted to a condominium, would generate excludable capital gain, with the agency emphasizing that the organization did not play any role in the subsequent marketing or sale of the

---

[69] *E.g.*, Priv. Ltr. Rul. 9619069.

[70] Houston Endowment v. United States, 606 F.2d 77, 82 (5th Cir. 1979) (internal quotations omitted). The court added (*id.*) that "[o]riginal investment intent is pertinent, for example, when a taxpayer is coerced to sell its property by acts of God, new and unfavorable zoning regulations or other uncontrollable forces."

[71] *E.g.*, Byram v. Comm'r, 705 F.2d 1418 (5th Cir. 1983); Winthrop v. Comm'r, 417 F.2d 905 (5th Cir. 1969); Heller Trust v. Comm'r, 382 F.2d 675 (9th Cir. 1967); Barrios Estate v. Comm'r, 265 F.2d 517 (5th Cir. 1959); Kaltreider v. Comm'r, 255 F.2d 833 (3d Cir. 1958), *aff'g* 28 T.C. 121 (1957); Brown v. Comm'r, 143 F.2d 468 (5th Cir. 1944); Buono v. Comm'r, 74 T.C. 187 (1980); Adam v. Comm'r, 60 T.C. 996 (1973); Also Rev. Rul. 59-91, 1959-1 C.B. 15.

[72] Biedenharn Realty Co. v. United States, 526 F.2d 409 (5th Cir.), *cert. denied*, 429 U.S. 819 (1976).

[73] Suburban Realty v. United States, 615 F.2d 171 (5th Cir.), *cert. denied*, 449 U.S. 920 (1980).

[74] Wineberg v. Comm'r, 326 F.2d 157 (9th Cir. 1963).

[75] Farley v. Comm'r, 7 T.C. 198 (1946).

[76] The word *primarily* in this setting means "of first importance" or "principally." Malat v. Riddell, 383 U.S. 569, 572 (1966). By this standard, the IRS ruled, ordinary income would not result unless a "sales purpose" is "dominant." Priv. Ltr. Rul. 9316032.

[77] Mauldin v. Comm'r, 195 F.2d 714 (10th Cir. 1952).

[78] Priv. Ltr. Rul. 9629030.

condominium units.[79] Further, a tax-exempt university was found to be engaged in a "passive" and "patient" property disposition; it followed a land use plan that envisioned sale of the property in up to nine tracts to different developers over a period of time so as to maximize the institution's return from the disposition. In this instance, the capital gain exclusion was ruled to be available.[80] Conversely, the improvement and frequent sale of land by an exempt organization were held by the agency to be an unrelated business.[81]

In a typical instance, the IRS reviewed a proposed sale of certain real estate interests held by a public charity. In that case, substantially all of the property had been received by bequest and held for a significant period of time. The decision to sell the property (liquidate the investment) was precipitated by the enactment of legislation adverse to the investment, so as to receive fair market value. Availability of the property for sale was not advertised to the public. Applying the primary purpose test, the IRS concluded that the proposed deals did not involve property held primarily for sale to customers in the ordinary course of business.[82]

In another instance, a tax-exempt charitable organization presented four alternatives to the IRS for development of its real property. The first alternative was to continue a leasing arrangement with annual rental income of approximately $100,000. The second choice was sale of the property as is for about $4 million. The third alternative was to complete some preliminary development work (such as obtaining various permits) and sell the property in large tracts to a few developers, resulting in about $6 million. The fourth alternative was further development of the property, including design and construction of streets, curbs, gutter, sidewalks, lighting, and utilities, with sales of individual lots to the general public. The agency ruled that the organization would escape unrelated business income taxation if it chose any of the first three alternatives, but would be subject to tax if it opted for the fourth alternative.[83]

By contrast, a tax-exempt charitable organization purchased real estate, divided it into lots, and improved the lots. The project evolved into the equivalent of a municipality. Lots were sold to the general public pursuant to a marketing plan involving real estate companies. The IRS concluded that the subdivision, development, and sale of the lots was a business that was regularly carried on, "in a manner that is similar to a for-profit residential land development company." The organization advanced the argument that the land development and sales were done in furtherance of exempt purposes, by attracting members who participated in its educational programs.[84] The IRS concluded, though, that the relationship between the sales of lots for single-family homes and the organization's goal of

---

[79] Priv. Ltr. Rul. 200246032.

[80] Priv. Ltr. Rul. 200510029.

[81] Priv. Ltr. Rul. 200119061.

[82] *Id.*

[83] Priv. Ltr. Rul. 8950072. Thus, obviously, an exempt organization in this position, in seeking to maximize value from the disposition of property (particularly real property) in adherence to principles of fiduciary responsibility, must balance the amount of projected revenue against the projected income tax consequences. An attempt at full maximization of value may cause the entity to be classified, for federal tax purposes, as a dealer in the property.

[84] An argument of this nature was accepted in Junaluska Assembly Hous., Inc. v. Comm'r, 86 T.C. 1114 (1986).

increasing program attendance was "somewhat tenuous." Therefore, the agency held that the resulting sales income was unrelated business income.[85]

An IRS private letter ruling illustrates how fine these distinctions can be.[86] A tax-exempt school owned land underlying a residential condominium project, which had been developed and marketed before the school received the property by devise. Sale of the land to the condominium association failed, in part because of enactment of a law that enabled the association to acquire the land through a condemnation proceeding. The school decided to offer the land directly to the owners of the condominium units, using a process that would span several months. The IRS took into account the "political climate" in which the school was operating, and emphasized the facts that the availability of the property was not advertised, the property had been obtained by gift, and the school had owned the land for a considerable length of time. These facts led the agency to observe that the proposed sales process was "completely contrary to the short turnaround period experienced by a typical buyer and seller of real property."

In another of these circumstances, a tax-exempt vocational school sold 8,500 acres of property over a 25-year period, yet was found by the IRS not to be selling property in the ordinary course of business.[87] The original reason for acquisition of the property was to support the school's mission, which was to prepare students for life in an agrarian society. When the school's farming operations eventually ceased, it desired to sell the farmland. Its position was that the land must be sold over a lengthy period of time in an attempt to realize the fair market value of the property. The IRS agreed, emphasizing that the school had held the property for more than 50 years, and writing that the property sales were a "liquidation of investment assets or a sale incident to the school's exempt property."[88]

The exception in the law for capital gain,[89] which interrelates with these rules, is not available when property is sold in circumstances in which the tax-exempt organization is a dealer in the property. When dealer status exists or is imposed, the property is considered to be property sold in the ordinary course of business, giving rise to ordinary income.

Even if the primary purpose underlying the acquisition and holding of real property is advancement of exempt purposes, the IRS may apply the *fragmentation rule*[90] in search of unrelated business. As the agency stated the matter in one ruling, a charitable organization "engaged in substantial regularly carried on unrelated trade [or] business as a component of its substantially related land purchase activity."[91] In this instance, the IRS looked to substantial and frequent sales of surplus

---

[85] Tech. Adv. Mem. 200047049.

[86] Priv. Ltr. Rul. 9505020.

[87] Priv. Ltr. Rul. 9619069.

[88] In another instance, the IRS allowed capital gain treatment for procurement of detailed site engineering plans and the proposed sale of real estate by a charitable organization, where the property had been held for some time, the sales revenue was needed to further exempt functions, and there will be no more than two sales of parcels annually over a 20 year period. Priv. Ltr. Rul. 200530029 In general, Nugent, *Possible Approaches for Avoiding UBIT on Real Estate Investment*, 37 *Exempt Org. Tax Rev.* 285 (no. 2, Aug. 2002).

[89] See § 3.10.

[90] See § 2.3.

[91] Priv. Ltr. Rul. 200119061.

land that was not intended for exempt use, and found that those sales were unrelated businesses. The same factors as are used in the general context (such as the sale of land shortly after purchase and the extent of improvements) were used to reach that conclusion.

(f) Efficiencies of Operation

On occasion, a court will focus on the fact that a tax-exempt organization is operating in a fashion that is considered "efficient," "effectively managed," "run like a business," and the like.[92] This can lead to a finding that the organization, or an activity of it, is—for that reason alone—a business undertaking.[93]

(g) Occasional Sales

Another illustration of a transaction involving a tax-exempt organization that is not a business undertaking is the occasional sale of an item of property. For example, the IRS held that a sale of property by an exempt entity was not made under circumstances in which the property was held primarily for sale to customers in the ordinary course of business.[94] By contrast, as noted, the subdivision, development, and sale of real estate parcels by an exempt organization was held by the IRS to be a business carried on in a manner similar to the activities of for-profit residential land development companies.[95]

The IRS reviewed a situation involving a group insurance trust, affiliated with a tax-exempt membership association, that experienced a substantial increase in its net worth and reserve balance because of the demutualization of an insurance company that provided insurance products to the association's members through the trust. The association decided to transfer all of the trust's assets to a related supporting organization. This transfer of assets was cast by the IRS as a one-time transfer, triggered by the unforeseen occurrence of demutualization; thus, it held that the transfer would not incur unrelated business income taxation.[96] This aspect of the law, however, is closely analogous to the *regularly carried on* test.[97]

§ 2.3 FRAGMENTATION RULE

The IRS has the authority to tax net income from an activity, as unrelated business taxable income, when the activity is an integral part of a cluster of activities that further a tax-exempt purpose. To ferret out unrelated business, the agency regards an exempt organization as a bundle of activities and evaluates each of the activities in isolation to determine if one or more of them constitutes a trade or business. This assessment process is known as *fragmentation*.

---

[92] See ch. 7.
[93] *E.g.*, Inc. Trustees of Gospel Worker Soc'y v. United States, 510 F. Supp. 374 (D.D.C.), *aff'd*, 672 F.2d 894 (D.C. Cir.), *cert. denied*, 456 U.S. 944 (1981); Presbyterian & Reformed Publ'g Co. v. Comm'r, 79 T.C. 1070 (1983).
[94] Priv. Ltr. Rul. 9316032.
[95] Tech. Adv. Mem. 200047049. See § 2.2(e).
[96] Priv. Ltr. Rul. 200328042.
[97] See § 2.5.

The *fragmentation rule* states that an "activity does not lose identity as trade or business merely because it is carried on within a larger aggregate of similar activities or within a larger complex of other endeavors which may, or may not, be related to the exempt purpose of the organization."[98] Thus, as noted, the IRS is empowered to fragment the operations of a tax-exempt organization, even when operated as an integrated whole, into component parts in search of one or more unrelated businesses. For example, the regular sale of pharmaceutical supplies to the general public by an exempt hospital pharmacy does not lose its identity as a trade or business merely because the pharmacy also furnishes supplies to the hospital and patients of the hospital in accordance with its exempt purposes or in compliance with the requirements of the convenience doctrine.[99] Similarly, activities of soliciting, selling, and publishing commercial advertising do not lose their identity as a trade or business even though the advertising is published in an exempt organization's periodical that contains editorial matter related to the exempt purposes of the organization.[100]

The fragmentation rule was fashioned to tax the net income derived by a tax-exempt organization from the soliciting, selling, and publishing of commercial advertising, even when the advertising is published in an exempt organization's publication that contains editorial matter related to the exempt purposes of the organization.[101] That is, the advertising functions constitute an unrelated business even though the overall set of publishing activities amounts to one or more related businesses and the advertising is an integral part of the larger publication activity.[102]

There are no stated limits as to the level of detail the IRS may pursue in application of the fragmentation rule. A tax-exempt university may find the agency's examiners probing its campus bookstore operations, evaluating goods for sale on nearly an item-by-item basis. An exempt association may watch as the IRS slices up its various services to members into numerous businesses. An exempt charitable organization may be surprised to see the IRS carve its fund-raising program into a range of business activities. The agency evaluated the status of one tax-exempt charitable organization and analyzed nine discrete businesses of the entity.[103]

A tax-exempt blood bank that sold blood plasma to commercial laboratories was found by the IRS not to be engaging in unrelated business when it sold byproduct plasma and salvage plasma, because these plasmas were produced in the conduct of related businesses. It was, however, ruled to be engaged in unrelated business when it sold plasmapheresis products and plasma purchased from other blood banks.[104] An exempt organization, the primary purpose of which was to retain and stimulate commerce in the downtown area of a city where parking

---

[98] IRC § 513(c); Reg. § 1.513-1(b).
[99] Reg. § 1.513-1(b). The convenience doctrine is the subject of § 4.1. In general, § 9.2(b).
[100] Reg. § 1.513-1(b).
[101] The caption of IRC § 513(c), which also contains the basic definition of the term *business* (§ 2.2), is "Advertising, etc." The rules by which advertising revenue is cast as unrelated business income are the subject of § 6.6.
[102] Reg. § 1.512(a)-1(f).
[103] Priv. Ltr. Rul. 200512025.
[104] Rev. Rul. 78-145, 1978-1 C.B. 169.

facilities were inadequate, was ruled to be engaged in related businesses by virtue of operating a fringe parking lot and shuttle service to the downtown shops; Its conduct of a park-and-shop plan was ruled to be an unrelated business.[105]

The use of a tax-exempt university's golf course by its students and employees was ruled not to be an unrelated business, whereas use of the course by alumni of the university and major donors was found to be unrelated business.[106] The fragmentation rule was applied to differentiate between related and unrelated travel tours conducted by an educational and religious organization.[107] An exempt charitable organization was held to be a dealer in certain parcels of real property, and thus engaged in unrelated business with respect to those properties, even though the principal impetus for the acquisition and sale of real property by the organization was achievement of exempt purposes.[108] An exempt monastery, the members of which made and sold caskets, was ruled to be engaged in a related business as long as the caskets were used in funeral services conducted by churches that were part of the religious denomination supporting the monastery; the monastery was held to be conducting an unrelated business when the caskets were used in services conducted by other churches.[109] An exempt organization was established to benefit deserving women, in part by enabling them to sell foodstuffs and handicrafts; its operation of a consignment shop was held to be a related business, but a retail gift shop and a small restaurant were found to be unrelated businesses.[110] If a fitness center[111] operates as part of a larger charitable organization, the IRS uses the fragmentation rule to determine whether the center is a related or unrelated business.[112]

When an activity carried on for the production of income constitutes an unrelated trade or business, no part of the trade or business may be excluded from classification as an unrelated trade or business merely because it does not result in profit.[113]

§ 2.4 PROFIT MOTIVE REQUIREMENT

The most important element in the federal tax law for determining whether an activity is a trade or business, for purposes of the business expense deduction (aside from the underlying statutory definition), is the presence of a *profit motive*. The courts have exported the profit objective standard into the unrelated business rules applicable to tax-exempt organizations.

The U.S. Supreme Court held that the principal test in this regard is that the "taxpayer's primary purpose for engaging in the activity must be for income or profit."[114] In the tax-exempt organizations context, the Court said that the inquiry

---

[105] Rev. Rul. 79-31, 1979-1 C.B. 206.
[106] Tech. Adv. Mem. 9645004.
[107] Tech. Adv. Mem. 9702004. See § 9.7.
[108] Priv. Ltr. Rul. 200119061.
[109] Priv. Ltr. Rul. 200033049.
[110] Tech. Adv. Mem. 200021056.
[111] See § 9.2(d).
[112] INFO 2005-0002.
[113] IRC § 513(c); Reg. § 1.513-1(b).
[114] Comm'r v. Groetzinger, 480 U.S. 23, 35 (1987).

should be whether the activity "was entered into with the dominant hope and intent of realizing a profit."[115] An appellate court stated that the "existence of a genuine profit motive is the most important criterion for . . . a trade or business."[116]

Various federal courts of appeal have applied the profit motive element to ascertain whether an activity of a tax-exempt organization is a business for purposes of the unrelated business rules. For example, an appellate court employed an *objective profit motivation test* to ascertain whether an exempt organization's activity is a business. This court wrote that "there is no better objective measure of an organization's motive for conducting an activity than the ends it achieves."[117] Subsequently, this court held that an activity of an exempt organization was a business because the organization "received considerable financial benefits" from performance of the activity; this was found to be "persuasive evidence" of a business endeavor.[118] On this latter occasion, the court defined as a *business* the situation in which a "non-profit entity performs comprehensive and essential business services in return for a fixed fee."[119] Thereafter, this appellate court wrote simply that for an activity of an exempt organization to be a business, the activity must be conducted with a "profit objective."[120] Another appellate court observed that an insurance company's payments to an exempt association were not taxable: "It does not matter whether the payments were brokerage fees, gratuities, to promote goodwill, or interest," because the association was not engaging in business activity for a profit.[121] Other courts of appeals have adopted this profit motive test.[122]

A court concluded, in the case of a tax-exempt labor union[123] that collected per capita taxes from unions affiliated with it, that, other than the services the union provides its members and affiliated unions in furtherance of its exempt purposes, the union "provide[d] no goods or services for a profit and therefore cannot be a trade or business."[124]

The IRS applies the profit motive test. In one example, a tax-exempt health care provider sold a building to another provider organization; the building was used as a skilled nursing and personal care home. The selling entity provided food service to the patients for about seven months, at a net loss. The agency characterized the food service operation as merely an "accommodation" to the purchasing entity.[125] Finding that the activity was not conducted in a manner

---

[115] United States v. Am. Bar Endowment, 477 U.S. 105, 110, n.1 (1986). The Court cited for this proposition the appellate court opinion styled Brannen v. Comm'r, 722 F.2d 695 (11th Cir. 1984).

[116] Prof'l Ins. Agents v. Comm'r, 726 F.2d 1097, 1102 (6th Cir. 1984).

[117] Carolinas Farm & Power Equip. Dealers Ass'n, Inc. v. United States, 699 F.2d 167, 170 (4th Cir. 1983).

[118] Steamship Trade Ass'n of Baltimore, Inc. v. Comm'r, 757 F.2d 1494, 1497 (4th Cir. 1985).

[119] *Id.* This latter statement, however, is a mischaracterization of the law. There is no requirement, for an activity to be a business, that the endeavor be comprehensive, nor is there a requirement that the activity be essential. Also, the mode of payment is irrelevant; whether the payment is by fixed fee, commission, or some other standard has no bearing on whether the income-producing activity is a business.

[120] W. Va. State Med. Ass'n v. Comm'r, 882 F.2d 123, 125 (4th Cir. 1989), *cert. denied*, 493 U.S. 1044 (1990).

[121] Am. Acad. of Family Physicians v. United States, 91 F.3d 1155, 1159–60 (8th Cir. 1996).

[122] *E.g.*, La. Credit Union League v. United States, 693 F.2d 525 (5th Cir. 1982); Prof'l Ins. Agents v. Comm'r, 726 F.2d 1097 (6th Cir. 1984).

[123] See *Tax-Exempt Organizations*, § 15.1.

[124] Laborer's Int'l Union v. Comm'r, 82 T.C.M. 158, 160 (2001).

[125] Tech. Adv. Mem. 9719002.

characteristic of a commercial enterprise—that is, as an operation motivated by profit—the IRS looked to these factors: There was no evidence, such as a business plan, that a food service business was being started; the organization did not take any steps to expand the food service to other unrelated organizations; the organization did not actively solicit additional clientele for a meal (or food catering) business; the organization did not take any steps to increase the per-meal charge, which was substantially below cost; and the service relationship between the organizations was not evidenced by a contract. On another occasion, the IRS concluded that, although the development of a housing project and sales of parcels of land were an unrelated business of an exempt planned community, the provision of water, sewer, and garbage services in conjunction with the project lacked a profit motive; thus, the income received for the services was not taxable as unrelated business income.[126]

A tax-exempt organization may have more than one activity that it considers a business. An activity of this nature may generate net income or it may generate a net loss. When calculating net taxable unrelated business income, an exempt organization may offset the loss from one business against the gain from another business in determining taxable income.[127] If, however, the loss activity consistently produces losses (year-in and year-out), the IRS may take the position that the activity is not a business, because of absence of a profit motive, and disallow the loss deduction. Occasional losses, however, do not lead to this result.

§ 2.5 DEFINITION OF *REGULARLY CARRIED ON*

As noted, gross income of a tax-exempt organization may be includable in the computation of unrelated business income when the trade or business that produced the income is regularly carried on by the organization.

(a) General Rules

In determining whether a trade or business from which an amount of gross income is derived by a tax-exempt organization is regularly carried on,[128] attention must be paid to the frequency and continuity with which the activities that produce the income are conducted and the manner in which the activities are pursued. This requirement is applied in light of the purpose of the unrelated business income rules, which is to place exempt organization business activities on the same tax basis as the nonexempt business endeavors with which they compete.[129] Thus, for example, specific business activities of an exempt organization will ordinarily be deemed to be regularly carried on if they manifest frequency and continuity, and are pursued in a manner generally similar to comparable commercial activities of nonexempt organizations.[130]

---

[126] Tech. Adv. Mem. 200047049.

[127] The IRS had occasion to observe that when a tax-exempt organization carries on two or more unrelated businesses, its "unrelated business net income" is its gross income from all of the businesses, less the allowed deductions. Rev. Rul. 68-536, 1968-2 C.B. 244.

[128] IRC § 512.

[129] See § 1.6. This is one of only two aspects of the unrelated business rules where the commerciality doctrine (see ch. 7) is expressly taken into account in the statute or tax regulations. The other aspect is the subject of § 7.3.

[130] Reg. § 1.513-1(c)(1).

An illustration of this body of law is the case of a tax-exempt organization that published a yearbook for its membership. The publication contained advertising; the organization contracted on an annual basis with a commercial firm for solicitation of advertising sales and printing, as well as collection of advertising charges. Although the editorial materials were prepared by the staff of the organization, the organization, because of its contract with the commercial firm, was ruled by the IRS to be "engaging in an extensive campaign of advertising solicitation" and thus to be "conducting competitive and promotional efforts typical of commercial endeavors."[131] Therefore, the income derived by this organization from the sale of advertising in its yearbook was deemed to be unrelated business income.

By contrast, a one-time sale of property (as opposed to an ongoing income-producing program) by a tax-exempt organization is not an activity that is regularly carried on, and thus does not give rise to unrelated business income.[132] For example, an exempt organization that was formed to deliver diagnostic and medical health care developed a series of computer programs concerning management and administrative matters, such as patient admissions and billings, payroll, purchases, inventory, and medical records. The organization sold some or all of the programs to another exempt organization comprised of three teaching hospitals affiliated with a university. The income derived from the sale was held to be from a "one-time only operation" and thus not taxable as unrelated business income.[133] Likewise, the transfer of investment assets from a public charity to its supporting organization[134] is exempt from unrelated business taxation under this rule,[135] as is the infrequent sale by an exempt organization of parcels of real estate.[136]

(b) Determining Regularity

When income-producing activities are of a kind normally conducted by nonexempt commercial organizations on a year-round basis, the conduct of the activities by a tax-exempt organization over a period of only a few weeks does not constitute the regular carrying on of a business.[137] For example, the operation of a sandwich stand by an exempt hospital auxiliary organization for two weeks at a state fair is not the regular conduct of a business.[138] The conduct of year-round business activities for one day each week, such as the operation of a commercial parking lot once a week, however, constitutes the regular carrying on of a business.[139]

If income-producing activities are of a kind normally undertaken by nonexempt commercial organizations only on a seasonal basis, the conduct of the

---

[131] Rev. Rul. 73-424, 1973-2 C.B. 190, 191.
[132] See § 2.2(e).
[133] Priv. Ltr. Rul. 7905129.
[134] See *Tax-Exempt Organizations*, § 11.3(c).
[135] See, *e.g.*, Priv. Ltr. Rul. 9425030.
[136] The gain from transactions of this nature may be protected from taxation by the exclusion for capital gain. See § 3.10.
[137] Reg. § 1.513-1(c)(2)(i).
[138] *Id.*
[139] S. Rep. No. 2375, 81st Cong., 2d Sess. 106–07 (1950).

activities by a tax-exempt organization during a significant portion of the season ordinarily constitutes the regular conduct of a business.[140] For example, the operation of a track for horse racing for several weeks in a year is the regular conduct of a business if it is usual to carry on the business only during a particular season.[141] Likewise, a distribution of greeting cards celebrating a holiday was deemed to be an unrelated business; the IRS measured regularity in terms of that holiday's season.[142]

In determining whether intermittently conducted activities are regularly carried on, the manner of conduct of the activities must, as noted, be compared with the manner in which commercial activities are normally pursued by nonexempt organizations.[143] In general, tax-exempt organization business activities that are engaged in only discontinuously or periodically will not be considered regularly carried on if they are conducted without the competitive and promotional efforts typical of commercial endeavors.[144] As an illustration, the publication of advertising in programs for sports events or music or drama performances will not ordinarily be deemed to be the regular carrying on of business.[145] Likewise, when an exempt organization sells certain types of goods or services to a particular class of individuals in pursuit of its exempt functions or primarily for the convenience of these individuals[146] (as when, for example, an exempt college bookstore sells books to students or a hospital pharmacy sells pharmaceutical supplies to patients of the hospital), casual sales in the context of this activity that do not qualify as related to the exempt function involved or are not sheltered by the convenience doctrine are not treated as regular.[147]

Conversely, when the nonqualifying sales are not merely casual, but are systematically and consistently promoted and carried on by an exempt organization, they meet the requirement of regularity.[148] Thus, a leasing arrangement that was "one-time, completely fortuitous" was held to constitute a business that was not regularly carried on;[149] a lease of extended duration can constitute a business that is regularly carried on.[150]

In determining whether a business is regularly carried on, the functions of a service provider with which a tax-exempt organization has contracted may be attributed to the exempt organization. This is likely to occur when the contract denominates the service provider as an agent of the exempt organization, inasmuch as the activities of an agent are attributed to and deemed to be the acts of the principal for legal analysis purposes. In such a circumstance, the time

---

[140] *Id.*
[141] Reg. § 1.513-1(c)(2)(i). Applying this rule, the IRS held that the conduct of horse racing by a county fair association was a business that was regularly carried on, even though the racing meet occupied only two weeks each year. Rev. Rul. 68-505, 1968-2 C.B. 248. This application of the law was changed by statute; § 4.5.
[142] Priv. Ltr. Rul. 8203134.
[143] Reg. § 1.513-1(c)(1), (2)(ii).
[144] Reg. § 1.513-1(c)(2)(ii).
[145] *Id.*.
[146] See § 4.1.
[147] Reg. § 1.513-1(c)(2)(ii).
[148] *Id.*
[149] Museum of Flight Found. v. United States, 63 F. Supp. 2d 1257, 1259 (W.D. Wash. 1999).
[150] Cooper Tire & Rubber Co. Employees' Ret. Fund v. Comm'r, 306 F.2d 20 (6th Cir. 1962).

expended by the service provider is attributed to the exempt organization for purposes of determining regularity.[151]

Noncompetition under a covenant not to compete, characterized as a "one-time agreement not to engage in certain activities," is not a taxable business, because the "activity" is not "continuous and regular."[152]

(c) Fundraising and Similar Activities

Fundraising activities by charitable and other tax-exempt organizations can constitute unrelated business activities.[153] Inasmuch as these activities rarely are inherently exempt functions, the rules as to regularity are often the only basis on which the income from these activities can escape taxation as unrelated business income.

Certain intermittent income-producing activities occur so infrequently that neither their recurrence nor the manner of their conduct causes them to be regarded as trades or businesses that are regularly carried on. For example, fundraising activities lasting only a short period of time are not ordinarily treated as being regularly carried on if they recur only occasionally or sporadically. Furthermore, activities will not be regarded as regularly carried on merely because they are conducted on an annual basis.[154] It is for this reason that many special-event fundraising activities, such as dances, auctions, tournaments, car washes, and bake sales, do not give rise to unrelated business income.[155] In one instance, a court concluded that a vaudeville show conducted one weekend per year was an intermittent fundraising activity and thus not regularly carried on.[156]

(d) Preparatory Time

A somewhat controversial issue is whether the time expended by a tax-exempt organization in preparing for a business undertaking should be taken into account in assessing whether the activity is regularly carried on. The IRS asserts that this preparatory time should be considered, even when the event itself occupies only one or two days each year.[157] This preparatory-time argument has, however, been rejected on the occasions it was considered by courts.[158] In the principal case, a federal court of appeals held that the preparatory-time argument is inconsistent with the tax regulations, which do not mention the concept. The court referenced the example concerning operation of the sandwich stand at a state fair,[159]

---

[151] NCAA v. Comm'r, 92 T.C. 456 (1989), aff'd, 914 F.2d 1417 (10th Cir. 1990).

[152] Ohio Farm Bureau Fed'n, Inc. v. Comm'r, 106 T.C. 222, 234 (1996). This opinion caused the IRS to issue Gen. Couns. Mem. 39891, revoking Gen. Couns. Mem. 39865 (which had held that refraining from competition in this context was a business activity).

[153] See § 9.6. In general, Hopkins, *The Law of Fundraising, Third Edition* (John Wiley & Sons, 2002) (hereinafter *Fundraising*), § 5.7.

[154] Reg. § 1.513-1(c)(2)(iii). "[I]ncome derived from the conduct of an annual dance or similar fund raising event for charity would not be income from trade or business regularly carried on." *Id.*

[155] *E.g.*, Orange County Builders Ass'n, Inc. v. United States, 65-2 U.S.T.C. ¶ 9679 (S.D. Cal. 1965); Priv. Ltr. Rul. 200128059.

[156] Suffolk County Patrolmen's Benevolent Ass'n, Inc. v. Comm'r, 77 T.C. 1314 (1981).

[157] *E.g.*, Tech. Adv. Mem. 9147007.

[158] NCAA v. Comm'r, 92 T.C. 456 (1989), aff'd, 914 F.2d 1417 (10th Cir. 1990); Suffolk County Patrolmen's Benevolent Ass'n, Inc. v. Comm'r, 77 T.C. 1314 (1981).

[159] See text accompanied by *supra* note 138.

denigrating the notion that preparatory time should be taken into account as follows: "The regulations do not mention time spent in planning the activity, building the stand, or purchasing the alfalfa sprouts for the sandwiches."[160]

Nonetheless, the IRS disagrees with these holdings,[161] and writes private letter rulings and technical advice memoranda that are openly contrary to these case decisions. One of these instances concerned a tax-exempt labor organization that sponsored a concert series, open to the public, that occurred on two weekends each year, one in the spring and one in the fall. The preparation and ticket-sale solicitation for each of the concerts usually took up to six months. Taking into account the preparatory time involved, the IRS concluded that the concerts were unrelated business activities that were regularly carried on.[162]

§ 2.6 DEFINITION OF *RELATED BUSINESS*

Gross income derives from an unrelated trade or business if the conduct of the trade or business that produces the income is not substantially related (other than through the production of funds) to the purposes for which exemption is granted. This fundamental rule of law necessitates an examination of the relationship between the business activities of a tax-exempt organization that generate the particular income in question—the activities, that is, of producing or distributing the goods or performing the services involved—and accomplishment of the organization's exempt purposes.[163]

A trade or business is *related* to the tax-exempt purposes of an exempt organization when the conduct of the business has a causal relationship to the achievement of one or more exempt purposes (other than through the production of income). Whether activities that produce gross income contribute to the accomplishment of an organization's exempt purpose depends in each case on the facts and circumstances involved.[164]

For example, a tax-exempt charitable organization had as its purpose enabling needy and worthy women to support themselves. To this end, it operated three businesses, each of equal size: a consignment shop, a retail gift shop, and a tearoom. The IRS concluded that the consignment shop was a business that was substantially related to achievement of the organization's exempt purpose.[165] The organization contended that the gift shop was a related business on the ground that the existence of the shop enhanced the likelihood of purchases of items in the consignment shop, because the gift shop attracted upscale consumers who were unlikely to patronize only the consignment shop. The IRS agreed that there was a causal relationship between the organization's exempt purposes and the operation of the gift shop, recognizing that the gift shop items were purchased by the organization "with the intent of imbuing the consignment items

---

[160] NCAA v. Comm'r, 914 F.2d 1417, 1423 (10th Cir. 1990).
[161] AOD No. 1991-015.
[162] Tech. Adv. Mem. 9712001. In AOD No. 1249 (1984), the IRS acquiesced in the *Suffolk County Patrolmen's Ass'n* case. That acquiescence had no bearing in this instance, the IRS said, inasmuch as the preparatory time in that case was "much shorter."
[163] Reg. § 1.513-1(d)(1).
[164] Reg. § 1.513-1(d)(2).
[165] See § 2.7.

with an aura of sophistication and tastefulness." The agency concluded, however, that this relationship was not substantial.[166]

§ 2.7 DEFINITION OF *SUBSTANTIALLY RELATED BUSINESS*

As noted, gross income of a tax-exempt organization may be includable in the computation of unrelated business income when it is income from a trade or business that is regularly carried on and that is not *substantially related* to the exempt purposes of the organization.[167] (The fact that the organization needs or uses the funds in advancement of an exempt purpose does not make the underlying activity a related business.[168]) Thus, it is necessary to examine the substantiality of the relationship between the business activity that generates the income in question—the activity, that is, of producing or distributing the goods or performing the services involved—and accomplishment of the organization's exempt purposes.[169]

To determine whether the conduct of an activity by a tax-exempt organization is substantially related to its exempt purposes, it is necessary to ascertain the organization's primary purpose or purposes, and then ascertain the organization's primary purpose in conducting the activity. When the primary purpose underlying conduct of the activity is to further an exempt purpose, the activity meets the substantially related test. According to the IRS, this exercise entails examination of the "nature, scope and motivation" for conducting the activity.[170] As an example, the agency concluded that the construction and operation of a regulation-size 18-hole golf course, replete with warm-up area, snack bar, and pro shop, was substantially related to the purposes of an exempt school operated to rehabilitate court-referred juveniles, inasmuch as the course was utilized primarily as part of the school's vocational education and career development department.[171]

(a) General Rules

A trade or business is *substantially related* only if the causal relationship is a substantial one. Thus, for the conduct of a business from which a particular amount of gross income is derived to be substantially related to exempt purposes, the production or distribution of the goods or the performance of the services from which the gross income is derived must contribute importantly to the accomplishment of these purposes. When the production or distribution of the goods or the performance of services does not contribute importantly to accomplishment of an organization's exempt purposes, the income from the sale of the goods or the performance of the services does not derive from the conduct of a related business.[172] A court wrote that resolution of the substantial relationship

---

[166] Tech. Adv. Mem. 200021056.
[167] IRC § 513(a); Reg. § 1.513-1(a).
[168] Cf. text accompanied by §1.11 note 178.
[169] Reg. § 1.513-1(d)(2).
[170] Priv. Ltr. Rul. 200151061.
[171] Id.
[172] Reg. § 1.513-1(d)(2).

test requires an examination of the "relationship between the business activities which generate the particular income in question . . . and the accomplishment of the organization's exempt purposes."[173]

Certainly, gross income derived from charges for the performance of a tax-exempt function does not constitute gross income from the conduct of an unrelated business.[174] Thus, as noted, income is not taxed when it is generated by functions such as performances by students enrolled in an exempt school for training children in the performing arts, the conduct of refresher courses to improve the trade skills of members of a union, or the presentation by a trade association of a trade show exhibiting industry products to stimulate demand for the products.[175] Also, dues paid by bona fide members of an exempt organization are forms of related income.[176]

Whether activities that produce gross income contribute importantly to accomplishment of an organization's exempt purpose depends in each case on the facts and circumstances involved.[177] A court observed that each of these instances requires a case-by-case identification of the exempt purpose involved and an analysis of how the activity contributed to the advancement of that purpose.[178] Court opinions and IRS rulings have provided many determinations over the years as to whether particular activities are substantially related businesses[179] or unrelated businesses.[180]

One of these determinations—the one concerning the organization functioning for the benefit of needy and deserving women[181]—is particularly illustrative of these points of law. As noted, the IRS concluded that the consignment shop was a substantially related business and that the gift shop was a related, but not substantially related, business. The tearoom was found to be an unrelated business.[182]

(b) Size-and-Extent Test

In determining whether an activity contributes importantly to the accomplishment of a tax-exempt purpose, the *size and extent* of the activity must be considered in relation to the nature and extent of the exempt function purportedly served.[183] Thus, when income is realized by an exempt organization from an activity that is generally related to the performance of the organization's exempt functions, but the activity is conducted on a scale that is larger than reasonably

---

[173] La. Credit Union League v. United States, 693 F.2d 525, 534 (5th Cir. 1982).

[174] Reg. § 1.513-1(d)(4)(i).

[175] *Id.*

[176] *E.g.*, Rev. Rul. 67-109, 1967-1 C.B. 136. Certain forms of associate member dues, however, are taxable as unrelated business income. See § 9.4(c).

[177] Reg. § 1.513-1(d)(2).

[178] Hi-Plains Hosp. v. United States, 670 F.2d 528 (5th Cir. 1982). See also Huron Clinic Found. v. United States, 212 F. Supp. 847 (D.S.D. 1962).

[179] *E.g.*, § 9.12.

[180] *E.g.*, § 9.13.

[181] See text accompanied by *supra* notes 165-166.

[182] Tech. Adv. Mem. 200021056. The classification of this tearoom as an unrelated business may be contrasted with the IRS's treatment of museum restaurants. See § 9.3, text accompanied by notes 93-95.

[183] Reg. § 1.513-1(d)(3). One court discussed the point that, in a search for unrelated activity, there should be an examination of the scale on which the activity is conducted. Hi-Plains Hosp. v. United States, 670 F.2d 528 (5th Cir. 1982).

necessary for performance of the functions, the gross income attributable to the portion of the activity that is in excess of the needs associated with exempt functions constitutes gross income from the conduct of an unrelated business.[184] This type of income is not derived from the production or distribution of goods or the performance of services that contribute importantly to the accomplishment of any exempt purpose of the organization.[185]

For example, one of the activities of a tax-exempt trade association, which had a membership of businesses in a particular state, was to supply companies (members and nonmembers) with job injury histories on prospective employees. Despite the association's contention that this service contributed to the accomplishment of its exempt purposes, the IRS ruled that the operation was an unrelated business, in that the activity went "well beyond" any mere development and promotion of efficient business practices.[186] The IRS adopted a similar position in ruling that a retail grocery store operation, formed to sell food in a poverty area at below-market prices and to provide job training for unemployed residents in the area, could not qualify for tax exemption because the operation was conducted on a scale "much larger . . . than reasonably necessary" for the training program.[187] Similarly, the IRS ruled that the provision of private duty nurses to unrelated exempt organizations, by an exempt health care organization that provided nurses to patients of related organizations as related businesses, was an activity performed on a scale "much larger" than necessary for the achievement of exempt functions.[188]

By contrast, a tax-exempt organization formed to provide a therapeutic program for emotionally disturbed adolescents was the subject of a ruling from the IRS, which found that a retail grocery store operation, almost fully staffed by adolescents who were undergoing emotional rehabilitation, was not an unrelated business because it was operated on a scale no larger than reasonably necessary for its training and rehabilitation program.[189] A like finding was made in relation to the manufacture and marketing of toys, which was the means by which an exempt organization accomplished its charitable purpose of training unemployed and underemployed individuals.[190]

(c) Same-State Rule

Ordinarily, gross income from the sale of products created by the performance of tax-exempt functions does not constitute gross income from the conduct of an unrelated business if the item is sold in substantially the *same state* it is in upon completion of the exempt functions. One case involved an exempt charitable organization that rehabilitated disabled individuals: Income from the sale of

---

[184] Reg. § 1.513-1(d)(3).

[185] *Id.* In essence, the size-and-extent test is an application of the fragmentation rule. See § 2.3.

[186] Rev. Rul. 73-386, 1973-2 C.B. 191, 192.

[187] Rev. Rul. 73-127, 1973-1 C.B. 221, 222. Under similar facts, a nonprofit organization that operated restaurants and health food stores in accordance with the tenets of a church was denied tax-exempt status as a charitable entity on the ground that they were operated for substantially commercial purposes. Living Faith, Inc. v. Comm'r, 60 T.C.M. 710 (1990), *aff'd*, 950 F.2d 365 (7th Cir. 1991). See ch. 7.

[188] Priv. Ltr. Rul. 9535023.

[189] Rev. Rul. 76-94, 1976-1 C.B. 171.

[190] Rev. Rul. 73-128, 1973-1 C.B. 222.

articles made by those individuals as part of their rehabilitation training was held not to be gross income from the conduct of an unrelated business. The income in that instance was from the sale of products, the manufacture of which contributed importantly to the accomplishment of the organization's exempt purposes—namely, rehabilitation of the disabled. Conversely, if an item resulting from an exempt function is utilized or exploited in further business endeavors beyond that reasonably appropriate or necessary for disposition in the state it is in upon completion of exempt functions, the gross income derived from these endeavors is from the conduct of an unrelated business.[191]

As an illustration, take the case of an experimental dairy herd maintained for scientific purposes by a tax-exempt research organization. Income from the sale of milk and cream produced in the ordinary course of operation of the project is not gross income from the conduct of an unrelated business. If, however, the organization used the milk and cream in the further manufacture of food items, such as ice cream and pastries, the gross income from the sale of these products would be from the conduct of an unrelated business—unless the manufacturing activities themselves contributed importantly to the accomplishment of an exempt purpose of the organization.[192] Similarly, a charitable organization that operated a salmon research facility as an exempt function was able to sell a portion of its harvested salmon stock, unprocessed, in an untaxed business. By contrast, when this organization converted the fish into salmon nuggets (fish that was seasoned, formed into nugget shape, and breaded), the sale of the fish in that state was an unrelated business.[193] Further, an organization that educates individuals and conducts scientific research on gardening was ruled to be able to sell, without tax, produce grown on-site to visitors and to the general public.[194]

(d) Dual-Use Rule

An asset or facility of a tax-exempt organization that is necessary to the conduct of exempt functions may also be utilized for nonexempt purposes. In these *dual-use* instances, the mere fact of use of the asset or facility in an exempt function does not, by itself, make the income from the nonexempt endeavor gross income from a related business. Rather, the test is whether the activities that produce the income in question contribute importantly to the accomplishment of exempt purposes.[195] For example, an exempt museum may have an auditorium that is designed and equipped for showing educational films in connection with the museum's program of public education in the arts and sciences. The theater is a principal feature of the museum and is in continuous operation during the hours the museum is open to the public. If, however, the museum were to operate the theater as a motion picture theater for public entertainment during the evening hours when the museum is otherwise closed, gross income from that operation would be gross income from the conduct of an unrelated business.[196] Similarly, a

---

[191] Reg. § 1.513-1(d)(4)(ii).
[192] *Id.*
[193] Priv. Ltr. Rul. 9320042.
[194] Priv. Ltr. Rul. 200512025 (the sale of produce grown off-site, however, was not protected by this exception).
[195] Reg. § 1.513-1(d)(4)(iii).
[196] *Id.*

mailing service operated by an exempt organization was ruled to be an unrelated trade or business even though the mailing equipment was also used for exempt purposes.[197]

Another illustration of application of this rule concerns the athletic facilities of a tax-exempt college or university, which, though used primarily for educational purposes, may also be made available for members of the faculty, other employees of the institution, and members of the general public. Income derived from use of the athletic facilities by those who are not students or employees of the institution is likely to be unrelated business income.[198] For example, the IRS ruled that the operation by an exempt school of a ski facility for the general public was the conduct of an unrelated business, whereas use of the facility by the students of the school (both for recreational purposes and through the school's physical education program) were related activities.[199] Likewise, an exempt college that made its facilities and personnel available to an individual not associated with the institution, for the conduct of a summer tennis camp, was ruled to be engaged in the conduct of an unrelated business.[200]

The provision of athletic or other activities by a tax-exempt educational institution to outsiders may be an exempt function, inasmuch as the instruction of individuals on the subject of a sport can be an educational activity.[201] As illustrations, the IRS held that the following were exempt educational activities:

- The conduct of a summer hockey camp for youths by a college[202]

- The conduct of four summer sports camps by a university[203]

- The operation of a summer sports camp by a university-affiliated athletic association[204]

Similarly, the IRS determined that a college may operate a professional repertory theater on its campus that is open to the general public[205] and that a college may make its facilities available to outside organizations for the conduct of conferences[206]—both activities being in furtherance of exempt purposes.

This area of the law intertwines with the exclusion from unrelated income taxation of rent received by tax-exempt organizations.[207] For example, an exempt college may lease its facilities to a professional sports team for the conduct of a summer camp and receive nontaxable lease income, as long as the college does not provide food or cleaning services to the team.[208] By contrast, when the institution

---

[197] Rev. Rul. 68-550, 1968-2 C.B. 249.

[198] *E.g.*, Tech. Adv. Mem. 9645004 (concerning dual use of a university's golf course).

[199] Rev. Rul. 78-98, 1978-1 C.B. 167.

[200] Rev. Rul. 76-402, 1976-2 C.B. 177.

[201] *E.g.*, Rev. Rul. 77-365, 1977-2 C.B. 192. See *Tax-Exempt Organizations,* § 10.2.

[202] Priv. Ltr. Rul. 8024001.

[203] Priv. Ltr. Rul. 7908009.

[204] Priv. Ltr. Rul. 7826003.

[205] Priv. Ltr. Rul. 7840072.

[206] Priv. Ltr. Rul. 8020010.

[207] See § 3.8.

[208] Priv. Ltr. Rul. 8024001.

provides services, such as cleaning, food, laundry, security, and ground maintenance, the exclusion for rent is defeated.[209]

This dichotomy is reflected in the treatment the IRS accorded to a tax-
exempt school that allowed its tennis facilities, which were used during the academic year in the institution's educational program, to be utilized in the summer
as a public tennis club operated by employees of the school's athletic department. Because the school not only furnished the facilities, but also operated the
tennis club through its own employees (who rendered substantial services for
the participants in the club), the IRS held that operation of the club was an unrelated business and that income derived from operation of the club was not sheltered by the exclusion for rental income.[210] The agency also observed, however,
that if the school had furnished its tennis facilities to an unrelated individual
without the provision of services (leaving it to the lessee to hire the club's
administrators) and for a fixed fee not dependent on the income or profits
derived from the leased property, the rental income exclusion would have been
available.[211] In a comparable ruling, the IRS considered a university that leased
its stadium to a professional sports team for several months of the year, and provided the utilities, grounds maintenance, and dressing room, linen, and stadium
security services. The IRS found that the university was engaged in an unrelated
business and was not entitled to the rental income exclusion.[212]

(e) Exploitation Rule

Activities carried on by a tax-exempt organization in the performance of exempt
functions may generate goodwill or other intangibles that are capable of being
exploited in commercial endeavors. When an exempt organization exploits this
type of intangible in commercial activities, the fact that the resultant income
depended in part on the conduct of an exempt function of the organization does
not make that revenue gross income from a related business. In these cases, unless
the activities contribute importantly to the accomplishment of an exempt purpose,
the income they produce will be treated as gross income from the conduct of an
unrelated business.[213]

For example, a tax-exempt scientific organization enjoys an excellent reputation in the field of biological research. It regularly exploits this reputation by
selling endorsements of various items of laboratory equipment to manufacturers. The endorsing of laboratory equipment does not contribute importantly to
the accomplishment of any purpose for which exemption was granted to the
organization. Accordingly, the income derived from the sale of these endorsements is gross income from an unrelated trade or business.[214]

As another example, a tax-exempt university (by definition having a regular faculty and a regularly enrolled student body), sponsors the appearance of

---

[209] Priv. Ltr. Rul. 7840072.

[210] Rev. Rul. 80-297, 1980-2 C.B. 196.

[211] *Id.*

[212] Rev. Rul. 80-298, 1980-2 C.B. 197. The dual-use rule is, in some respects, an application of the fragmentation
rule. See § 2.3.

[213] Reg. § 1.513-1(d)(4)(iv).

[214] *Id.*, Example (1).

professional theater companies and symphony orchestras during the school year; these artists present dramatic and musical performances for the students and faculty members. Members of the general public are also admitted. The university advertises these performances and supervises advance ticket sales at various places, including such university facilities as the cafeteria and university bookstore. The university derives gross income from the conduct of the performances. Presentation of the performances makes use of an intangible generated by the institution's exempt educational functions—the presence of the student body and faculty—and these events also contribute importantly to the overall educational and cultural function of the university. Therefore, the income that the university receives does not constitute gross income from the conduct of an unrelated trade or business.[215]

A third example concerns a tax-exempt business league with a large membership. Pursuant to an arrangement with an advertising agency, the association regularly mails brochures, pamphlets, and other commercial advertising materials to its members, for which service the association charges the agency an agreed amount per enclosure. The distribution of the advertising materials does not contribute importantly to the accomplishment of any of the association's exempt purposes. Accordingly, the payments made to this business league by the advertising agency constitute gross income from an unrelated trade or business.[216]

A fourth example involves a tax-exempt organization that advances public interest in classical music; it owns a radio station and operates the station in a manner that contributes importantly to accomplishment of the organization's exempt purposes. In the course of operation of the station, however, the organization derives gross income from the regular sale of advertising time and services to commercial advertisers, in the manner of a commercial station. Neither the sale of this time nor the performance of these services contributes importantly to the accomplishment of any of the organization's exempt purposes. Notwithstanding the fact that the production of the advertising income depends on the existence of the listening audience resulting from performance of exempt functions, the income is gross income from unrelated business.[217]

A fifth illustration involves a tax-exempt university that provides facilities, instruction, and faculty supervision for a campus newsletter operated by its students. In addition to news items and editorial commentary, the newspaper publishes paid advertising. The solicitation, sale, and publication of the advertising are conducted by students, under the supervision and instruction of the university. Although the services rendered to advertisers are of a commercial character, the advertising business contributes importantly to the university's educational program, through the training of the students involved. Therefore, none of the income derived from publication of the newspaper constitutes gross income from the conduct of an unrelated business. The same result would occur if the newspaper were published by a separately incorporated

---

[215] *Id.*, Example (2).
[216] *Id.*, Example (3). This type of financial arrangement may, however, be structured as an excludable royalty. See
§ 3.7.
[217] *Id.*, Example (4).

charitable organization, qualified under the university's rules for recognition of student activities; even though the organization uses its own facilities, is independent of faculty supervision, and carries out its educational purposes by means of student instruction of other students in the editorial and advertising activities and student participation in those activities.[218]

Another illustration involves a tax-exempt association formed to advance the interests of a profession, and drawing its membership from members of the profession. The organization publishes a monthly journal containing articles and other editorial materials that contribute importantly to accomplishment of the association's exempt purposes. Income from the sale of subscriptions to members and others, in accordance with the organization's exempt purposes, does not constitute gross income from an unrelated trade or business. In connection with the publication of this journal, the association also derives income from the regular sale of space and services for general consumer advertising, including advertising of products such as soft drinks, automobiles, articles of apparel, and home appliances. Neither the publication of these advertisements nor the performance of services for these consumer advertisers contributes importantly to accomplishment of the organization's exempt purposes. Therefore, notwithstanding the fact that the production of income from advertising utilizes the circulation developed and maintained in performance of exempt functions, this income is gross income from an unrelated trade or business.[219]

As a final illustration of this point, assume the facts in the preceding example, except that the advertising in the association's journal promotes only products that are within the general area of its members' professional interests. Following a practice common among for-profit magazines that publish advertising, the association requires advertising to comply with certain general standards of taste, fairness, and accuracy; within these limits, the form, content, and manner of presentation of the advertising messages are governed by the advertisers' basic objective of promoting the sale of the advertised products. Although the advertisements contain certain information of professional interest, the informational function of the advertising is incidental to the controlling aim of stimulating demand for the advertised products, and differs in no essential respect from the informational function of any commercial advertising. Like taxable publishers of advertising, this association accepts advertising only from those who are willing to pay its prescribed rates. Although continuing education of its members in matters pertaining to their profession is one of the association's exempt purposes, the publication of advertising designed and selected in the manner of ordinary commercial advertising is not an educational activity of the kind contemplated by the concept of tax exemption; it differs fundamentally from such an activity both in its governing objective and in its method. Accordingly, this association's publication of advertising does not contribute importantly to the accomplishment of its

---

[218] *Id.*, Example (5).
[219] *Id.*, Example (6).

exempt purposes. Hence, the income it derives from advertising constitutes gross income from an unrelated trade or business.[220]

Thus, the rules with respect to taxation of advertising revenue received by tax-exempt organizations treat advertising as an exploitation of exempt publication activity.[221] Another illustration of this *exploitation rule* is when access by students to an educational institution's athletic facilities is covered by a general student fee. Outside use of the facilities may trigger the exploitation rule: If separate charges for use of the facilities are imposed on students, faculty, and outsiders, any unrelated income is a product of the dual-use rule.[222]

---

[220] *Id.*, Example (7).

[221] See § 6.5.

[222] See, *e.g.*, Priv. Ltr. Rul. 7823062. In general, see Cain, *Marketing Activities in the Nonprofit Sector—Sector Recent Lessons Regarding Tax Implications*, 36 *Amer. Bus. Law J.* 349 (vol. 2, Winter 1999); Hansmann, Kaplan & Jett, *Handling the UBIT Problems of Churches and Religious Organizations*, 6 *J. Tax. Exempt Orgs.* 74 (no. 2, Sept./Oct. 1994); Tesdahl, *Three Easy Ways to Avoid UBIT*, 8 *Exempt Org. Tax Rev.* 937 (no. 5, Nov. 1993); Gallagher III, *The Taxation of Investments by Pension Funds and Other Tax-Exempt Entities*, 67 *Taxes* 981 (no. 12, 1989); Jones, Shortway, & Borhorst, *When Pension Trusts Participate: The Impact of the Unrelated Business Income Rules*, 5 *Real Est. Fin.* 91 (no. 2, 1988); Rosen, *When Will Business Income of an Organization Be Sheltered by Its Tax-Exempt Status?*, 40 *Tax'n for Accts.* 222 (no. 4, 1988); Wittenbach & Gallagher, *The Tax Implications to Exempt Organizations of Six Income-Producing Activities*, 16 *Tax Adv.* 170 (no. 3, 1985); Fant III, *Doing Well While Doing Good, and the Pitfalls of the Unrelated Business Income Tax*, 63 *Taxes* 862 (no. 12, 1985); Walter, *Unrelated Business Income—Division, Characterization and Allocation*, 19 *Univ. of Miami Philip E. Heckerling Inst. on Est. Plan.* 7 (1985); Kennedy, *Considerations in the Determination of Tax on Unrelated Business Income*, 15 *Tax Adv.* 342 (no. 6, 1984).

In recent years, there have been efforts to revise the statutory law concerning the taxation of unrelated business income. In general, see Comment, *Making Tax-Exempts Pay: The Unrelated Business Income Tax and the Need for Reform*, 4 *Admin. L.J. Am. U.* 527 (Winter 1991); Owens, *Current Developments in the Unrelated Business Area—IRS Perspective*, 4 *Exempt Org. Tax Rev.* 923 (no. 7, 1991); Sanders & Cobb, *Impact of Proposals to Revise the Unrelated Business Income Rules*, 2 *Exempt Org. Tax Rev.* 694 (no. 6, 1990); Haley, *The Taxation of the Unrelated Business Activities of Exempt Organizations: Where Do We Stand? Where Do We Seem to Be Headed?*, 7 *Akron Tax J.* 61 (no. 2, 1990); Spitzer, *Reform of the UBIT: An Open Letter to Congress*, 43 *Tax Notes* 195 (no. 2, 1989); Aprill, *Lessons from the UBIT Debate*, 45 *Tax Notes* 1105 (no. 9, 1989); Turner & Lambert, *Why the Furor over UBIT*, 165 *J. Acct.* 78 (no. 5, 1988); Troyer, *Changing UBIT: Congress in the Workshop*, 41 *Tax Notes* 1221 (no. 11, 1988); Kalick, *Reorganizing for the UBIT*, 41 *Tax Notes* 771 (no. 7A, 1988); Hasson, Jr., *An Early Warning: UBIT Changes Ahead*, 127 *Trusts & Ests.* 43 (no. 7, 1988).

CHAPTER THREE

Modifications

Pursuant to the general rules, an activity may constitute an unrelated business that is regularly carried on,[1] yet the income generated by the activity may escape federal taxation as unrelated business income pursuant to one or more statutory exceptions. There are also statutory exceptions for certain forms of income.

There are two basic categories of these exceptions. Some of them appear in the federal tax law concerning a variety of modifications (the subject of this chapter). Others are formally denominated as exceptions.[2]

In determining unrelated business taxable income, gross income derived from an unrelated trade or business is computed with certain *modifications*.[3] These are rules pertaining to dividends, interest, revenue derived from loans of securities, amounts received or accrued as consideration for entering into agreements to make loans, annuities, income from notional principal contracts, royalties, rent, other investment income, capital gains, loan commitment fees, research income,

---

[1] See ch. 2.
[2] See ch. 4.
[3] IRC § 512(b).

foreign source income, member income received by electric companies, gain on the sale of certain brownfield sites, and certain income received by religious orders. Various deductions and losses are also taken into account in this regard.

The facts and circumstances of each case determine whether a particular item of income falls within any of these modifications. For example, a payment termed *rent* by the parties may in fact amount to a return of profits by a person operating the property for the benefit of a tax-exempt organization, or may constitute a share of the profits retained by the organization as a partner or a joint venturer.[4]

§ 3.1 PASSIVE INCOME IN GENERAL

The unrelated business rules were enacted principally to ameliorate the effects of competition between tax-exempt organizations and for-profit (taxable) organizations by generally taxing the net income of exempt organizations from unrelated business activities.[5] The principle underlying this statutory scheme is that the business endeavors must be *active* ones for competitive activity to result. Correspondingly, income derived by a tax-exempt organization in a *passive* manner generally is income that is not acquired as the result of competitive activity; consequently, most forms of passive income paid to exempt organizations are not taxed as unrelated business income.[6] Therefore, passive income—such as dividends, interest, payments with respect to securities loans, annuities, royalties, certain rents (generally of real estate), income from certain option-writing activities, income from interest rate and currency swaps, income from equity and commodity swaps, income from notional principal contracts and the like, and gain from the disposition of capital property—is generally excluded from unrelated business taxable income, taking into account deductions that are directly connected to this type of income.[7]

The legislative history of these provisions indicates that Congress believed that passive income used for exempt purposes should not be taxed under these rules "because investments producing incomes of these types have long been recognized as proper for educational and charitable organizations."[8] Thus, for example, a tax-exempt organization can capitalize a for-profit corporation without endangering the tax exemption of the organization; an exempt organization can own all of the stock of a for-profit corporation without

---

[4] Reg. § 1.512(b)-1, first paragraph.

[5] See § 1.6.

[6] Two significant exceptions to this rule concern income from unrelated debt-financed property (see ch. 5) and income from controlled subsidiaries (see ch. 8).

[7] IRC § 512(b)(1)–(3), (5); Reg. § 1.512(b)-1(a)–(d). In Louis W. Hill Family Found. v. United States, 347 F. Supp. 1225, 1229 (D. Minn. 1972), the court concluded that "conducting a trade or business requires some business activity beyond the mere receipt of profits."

A U.S. Tax Court decision expanded the possibility that what once may have been considered a passive activity will now be treated as an active business enterprise, by holding that nearly any activity engaged in for the production of income (the expenses of which are deductible under IRC § 212) can be converted into a business activity by the intensification of the taxpayer's participation in the activity. Hoopengarner v. Comm'r, 80 T.C. 538 (1983). In general, Hopkins & Kaplan, *Could* Ditumno *and* Hoopengarner *Result in Expanding the Scope of Unrelated Business?*," 60 J. Tax'n 40 (no. 1, 1984).

[8] H.R. Rep. No. 2319, 81st Cong., 2d Sess. 38 (1950). See also S. Rep. No. 2375, 81st Cong., 2d Sess. 30–31 (1950).

endangering its tax exemption;[9] the for-profit corporation can pay dividends to the exempt organization without jeopardizing the tax exemption of the exempt entity, and the dividend income received by the exempt entity will not be taxable as unrelated income.[10]

Tax-exempt organizations may receive forms of passive income that are not strictly within the technical meaning of one of the specific terms referenced in the passive income rules, yet are nonetheless outside the framework of unrelated business income taxation. Occasionally, however, the IRS takes the position that the only items of income that can be regarded as passive income are those specifically listed in the statutory modification rules. This has led to conflict, with the matter usually resolved in favor of tax-exempt organizations by Congress, such as in the instances of the writing of options[11] and the lending of securities.[12]

The legislative history of the unrelated business income tax provisions is clear on the points that (1) Congress, in enacting these rules, did not intend and did not authorize taxation of the passive income of tax-exempt organizations, and (2) a technical satisfaction of the definitional requirements of the terms used in the passive income rules is not required. Thus, for example, the Senate Finance Committee observed in 1950 that the unrelated business income tax was to apply to "so much of . . . [exempt organizations'] income as rises from active business enterprises which are unrelated to the tax exempt purposes of the organizations."[13] This committee added: "The problem at which the tax on unrelated business income is directed is primarily that of unfair competition."[14] Speaking of the exclusion for passive sources of income, the committee stated:

> Dividends, interest, royalties, most rents, capital gains and losses and *similar items* are excluded from the base of the tax on unrelated income because your committee believes that they are "passive" in character and are not likely to result in serious competition for taxable businesses having similar income. Moreover, investment-producing incomes of these types have long been recognized as a proper source of revenue for educational and charitable organizations and trusts.[15]

Therefore, it is unmistakable that passive income, regardless of type, is generally excluded from unrelated business income taxation.[16]

Illustration of the IRS acceptance of this viewpoint is the development of regulations[17] concerning the exclusion of income derived from certain notional

---

[9] There are, however, special rules for private foundations in this regard. See Hopkins, *The Law of Tax-Exempt Organizations, Eighth Edition* (John Wiley & Sons, 2003) [hereinafter *Tax-Exempt Organizations*] § 11.4(c); Hopkins & Blazek, *Private Foundations: Tax Law and Compliance, Second Edition* (John Wiley & Sons, 2003) [hereinafter *Private Foundations*], ch. 7.

[10] See, *e.g.*, Priv. Ltr. Rul. 8244114. See ch. 8.

[11] See text accompanied by *supra* note 7 and *infra* notes § 3.11.

[12] See § 3.4.

[13] S. Rep. No. 2375, 81st Cong., 2d Sess. 27 (1950) (emphasis supplied).

[14] *Id.* at 28.

[15] *Id.* at 30–31 (emphasis supplied).

[16] See also H.R. Rep. No. 2319, 81st Cong., 2d Sess. 36–38 (1950). This topic is pursued further in the context of securities lending transactions (see § 3.4).

[17] Reg. § 1.512(b)-1(a)(2).

principal contracts[18] and other forms of a tax-exempt organization's ordinary and routine investments.[19] This concept is also embedded in the evolution of the rules concerning securities lending.[20]

The foregoing analysis notwithstanding, at least one component of this law rejects the premise that, for an item of income to be excluded from unrelated business income taxation (absent a specific statutory exclusion), it must be passive in nature. That is, there is a view that an item of income, once classified as a royalty or other similar item, is excludable from unrelated income taxation irrespective of whether it is passively derived.

Only the U.S. Tax Court has expressed this view, which arose in the course of consideration of whether payments for the use of mailing lists and payments from the operation of an affinity card program constitute excludable *royalties*. This court held that if the arrangement is properly structured, mailing-list payments are royalties and thus excludable from unrelated business income taxation even if they are not forms of passive income.[21] The court also so held in the case of affinity card program payments.[22] The essence of this view is that although Congress *believed* these types of income to be passive,[23] they need not necessarily always be passive.[24] Stated in the reverse, this view holds that a statutorily classified item of excludable income remains excludable from unrelated business income taxation irrespective of whether the income is passive or is derived from the active conduct of a trade or business. The validity of this view was, however, substantially eroded by a subsequent appellate court opinion.[25]

§ 3.2 DIVIDENDS

Dividends paid to a tax-exempt organization generally are not taxable as unrelated business income.[26] Basically, a *dividend* is a share allotted to each of one or more persons who are entitled to share in the net profits generated by a business undertaking, usually a corporation; it is a payment out of the payor's net profits.

There are some exceptions to this exclusion, principally concerning dividends that are unrelated debt-financed income[27] and those that are from controlled foreign offshore insurance captives.[28] Generally, however, dividends paid to tax-exempt organizations from controlled corporations are not taxable.[29]

---

[18] Reg. § 1.512(b)-1(a)(1).

[19] *Id.* § 3.9

[20] See § 3.4.

[21] Sierra Club, Inc. v. Comm'r, 65 T.C.M. 2582 (1993); Disabled Am. Veterans v. Comm'r, 94 T.C. 60 (1990), *rev'd on other grounds*, 942 F.2d 309 (6th Cir. 1991).

[22] Sierra Club, Inc. v. Comm'r, 103 T.C. 307 (1994). See § 3.7.

[23] See text accompanied by *supra* note 6.

[24] This view is based on additional language in the committee reports indicating that the exception for dividends, interest, annuities, royalties, and the like "applies not only to investment income [a concept broader than passive income], but also to such items as business interest on overdue open accounts receivable." S. Rep. No. 2375, 81st Cong., 2d Sess. 108 (1950); H.R. Rep. No. 2319, 81st Cong., 2d Sess. 110 (1950).

[25] See text accompanied by *infra* notes 78-80.

[26] IRC § 512(b)(1); Reg. § 1.512(b)-1(a)(1).

[27] IRC § 512(b)(4); Reg. § 1.512(b)-1(a)(2), (k). See ch. 5.

[28] See § 3.15.

[29] See § 8.8(b).

§ 3.3 INTEREST

Interest paid to a tax-exempt organization generally is not taxable as unrelated business income.[30] Basically, the term *interest* is defined as compensation that one person (debtor) pays to another person (creditor) for the use or forbearance of money.[31] Similarly, *interest* is defined in the income tax regulations, for personal holding company income purposes, as amounts received for the use of money loaned.[32]

The IRS set forth criteria for use in determining whether a debtor-creditor relationship exists for the purpose of treating as interest certain loan processing fees (commonly known as *points*) paid by a mortgagor-borrower as compensation to a lender solely for the use or forbearance of money. The agency held that when the taxpayer can establish that the fee is paid as compensation to the lender solely for the use or forbearance of money, the fee is considered to be interest. The agency did not find it necessary that the parties to the transaction label a payment made for the use of money as *interest* for that payment to be treated as interest. For these fees to be treated as interest, however, the fees must not have been paid for any specific services that were performed or will be performed in connection with the loan. For example, interest would not include separate charges made for investigating the prospective borrower and the borrower's security, closing costs of the loan, papers prepared in connection with the transaction, or fees paid to a third party for servicing and collecting the loan.[33] Also, even when service charges are not stated separately on a borrower's account, interest cannot include amounts attributable to these services.[34] The IRS applied these principles of law in ruling that services fees received by a tax-exempt organization from mortgage loans do not constitute interest for purposes of the unrelated business income tax exclusion for interest income.[35]

There are some exceptions to this exclusion, principally interest that is unrelated debt-financed income[36] and that is paid by a controlled corporation.[37]

The IRS issues private letter rulings as to what constitutes excludable interest in this context.[38]

§ 3.4 SECURITIES LENDING INCOME

Qualified payments with respect to loans of securities are generally excluded from unrelated business income taxation.[39] These amounts are not excluded from this tax, however, if they constitute unrelated debt-financed income.[40]

---

[30] IRC § 512(b)(1); Reg. § 1.512(b)-1(a)(1).
[31] Deputy v. du Pont, 308 U.S. 488, 498 (1940).
[32] Reg. § 1.543-1(b)(2).
[33] Rev. Rul. 69-188, 1969-1 C.B. 54.
[34] Rev. Rul. 67-297, 1967-2 C.B. 87.
[35] Rev. Rul. 79-349, 1979-2 C.B. 233.
[36] IRC § 512(b)(4); Reg. § 1.512(b)-1(a)(2), (k). See ch. 5.
[37] Reg. § 1.512(b)-1(a)(2). See § 8.8(b).
[38] *E.g.*, Priv. Ltr. Rul. 9108021.
[39] IRC § 512(b)(1); Reg. § 1.512(b)-1(a)(1).
[40] Reg. § 1.512(b)-1(a)(2). See ch. 5.

This exclusion is available for the lending of securities to a broker and the return of identical securities. For this nontaxation treatment to apply, the security loans must be fully collateralized and must be terminable on five business days' notice by the lending organization. Additionally, an agreement between the parties must provide for reasonable procedures to implement the borrower's obligation to furnish collateral to the lender with a fair market value on each business day the loan is outstanding in an amount at least equal to the fair market value of the security at the close of business on the preceding day.[41]

In the typical securities lending transaction involving a tax-exempt organization, the exempt organization lends securities (stocks and bonds) from its investment portfolio to a brokerage house, to enable the broker to effect delivery of the securities to cover either a short sale or a failure to receive equivalent securities. In this type of transaction, the broker receiving the certificates posts cash collateral with the lending institution in an amount equal to or exceeding the then-fair market value of the particular securities. This collateral may be available to the lending organization in the interim for the purpose of short-term investment as it deems appropriate.

Under this arrangement, either the lending tax-exempt organization or the broker can terminate the lending relationship by giving notice. In this instance, the broker becomes obligated to return the identical securities to the exempt organization, which has retained beneficial ownership of them, and the organization becomes obligated to return the collateral to the broker. In the event of default by the broker, the organization is required to use the collateral to purchase replacement securities and has a claim against the borrowing broker for any deficiency. Any excess funds derived in the process of securing replacement securities must be returned to the broker. Thus, the concept is that the exempt organization's portfolio position should not be improved by virtue of any default by a broker-borrower. An amount equivalent to any dividend or interest that comes due during the course of the lending period must be paid by the broker to the organization, whether or not the broker holds the securities. The brokerage house also pays the lending organization compensation for entering into the arrangement, either as a predetermined premium computed as a percentage of the value of the loaned securities or, as noted, by allowing the organization to invest the collateral and retain the income.[42]

A threshold issue in the federal tax context was whether this type of a securities lending arrangement constituted a business.[43] The management of an investment portfolio comprised wholly of the manager's own securities does not constitute the conduct of a trade or business. For example, the U.S. Supreme Court held that the mere keeping of records and collection of interest and dividends from securities, through managerial attention to the investments, is not the operation of a business.[44] On that occasion, the Court sustained the *government's* position that "mere personal investment activities never constitute carrying on a trade

---

[41] IRC § 512(a)(5).

[42] An IRS private letter ruling illustrated a qualified securities lending program involving a private foundation. Priv. Ltr. Rul. 200501017.

[43] See § 2.2.

[44] Higgins v. Comm'r, 312 U.S. 212 (1941).

or business."[45] Subsequently, the Court stated that "investing is not a trade or business."[46] Likewise, a federal court of appeals observed that the "mere management of investments . . . is insufficient to constitute the carrying on of a trade or business."[47] Investment activities by a tax-exempt organization for its own benefit thus do not constitute business undertakings in the unrelated business context.[48] It is settled that mere recordkeeping and income collection for an exempt organization's own investments are not activities regarded as the carrying on of a business.[49]

Until late in 1977, when an IRS private letter ruling was issued to a tax-exempt college, it was not clear whether the agency would regard the practice of securities lending as a trade or business. The IRS's initial position was that the activity was an unrelated business.[50] When it became clear to the agency that the matter was going to be resolved in favor of the tax-exempt organizations community by legislation, the IRS attempted to preclude the legislation by issuing a ruling in 1978 that securities lending by exempt organizations is a form of "ordinary or routine investment activities" and thus not a business.[51] This ploy failed; Congress adopted the legislation[52] notwithstanding promulgation of the favorable ruling.

It seems clear, nonetheless, based on the state of the law before 1978, that the interest earned by the lending organization on the collateral, and the interim dividend and interest payments, were excludable from treatment as unrelated business income.[53] The accepted rule is that the amounts received through independent investment are characterized in accordance with the nature of the investment. Therefore, the income derived from an investment of such collateral by an exempt organization in bank certificates of deposit or a form of short-term investment was without question excludable interest. Similarly, an investment of the collateral by the organization in stocks or bonds unquestionably produced excludable dividends or interest.

The amounts paid by the brokers to a lending tax-exempt organization for any dividends or interest earned by the loaned securities were excludable from unrelated business income. Certainly, the dividends or interest, if paid to the exempt organization while it was in physical possession of the certificates or comparable investment vehicle, were excluded from unrelated business income taxation by virtue of these rules. It would have exalted form over substance to treat the pass-through payments from the broker for dividends and interest any differently. The essence of the transaction should have prevailed[54]—and ultimately it did.

---

[45] *Id.* at 215. The issue in this context was whether the activity was a business for purposes of the business expense deduction rules (IRC § 162).

[46] Whipple v. Comm'r, 373 U.S. 193, 202 (1963).

[47] Continental Trading, Inc. v. Comm'r, 265 F.2d 40, 43 (9th Cir.), *cert. denied*, 361 U.S. 827 (1959).

[48] See § 2.2(d).

[49] *E.g.*, Moller v. United States, 721 F.2d 810 (Fed. Cir. 1983) (holding that investment activities in a home office do not constitute a business).

[50] See Stern & Sullivan, *Exempt Organizations Which Lend Securities Risk Imposition of Unrelated Business Tax*, 45 J. Tax'n 240 (1976).

[51] Rev. Rul. 78-88, 1978-1 C.B. 163.

[52] See *supra* note 41.

[53] See §§ 3.2, 3.3.

[54] McBride v. Comm'r, 44 B.T.A. 273 (1941); Kell v. Comm'r, 31 B.T.A. 212 (1934); Peck v. Comm'r, 31 B.T.A. 87 (1934), *aff'd*, 77 F.2d 857 (2d Cir. 1935), *cert. denied*, 296 U.S. 625 (1935).

As noted, the term *interest* is generally defined as compensation paid for the use or forbearance of money.[55] In a securities lending transaction, the income received by the organization derives from an arrangement involving the use of property. Courts have, however, utilized another definition of *interest*, that being an amount paid that is contingent on having some relationship to an indebtedness.[56] The term *indebtedness* has been defined as something owed in money that a person is unconditionally obligated to repay, the payment of which is enforceable.[57] Therefore, these amounts paid by brokers to an exempt organization constitute interest, inasmuch as they are amounts paid in conjunction with an enforceable indebtedness (namely, the broker's obligation to return the securities or, in lieu thereof, forfeit the collateral).

Even if these payments were not regarded as interest, they nonetheless retained their character as dividends, interest, or another form of passive income for purposes of the exclusion. In the securities lending transaction, the income paid to the lending organization by brokers need not lose its character as dividends or interest. For example, the IRS in a ruling distinguished between *sale-and-purchase transactions* and *loan transactions*. The facts underlying this ruling were that bank customers "sold" securities to a bank in return for loans from the bank, agreeing to "repurchase" the identical securities at the close of the loan period. The agency ruled that this transaction did not amount, in law, to a sale or exchange, but was instead a loan of money upon collateral security (that is, the securities).[58]

The pertinence of this ruling is enhanced by the fact that the securities in question were state or municipal bonds, the interest of which is exempt from federal income taxation.[59] At issue was the appropriate party to have the benefit of this exclusion: the lender-customer or the borrower-bank. Concurrent with its finding that the transaction was a loan and not a sale, the IRS ruled that the tax-exempt interest is the income of the customer who tendered the securities to the bank for collateral and that the bank was not entitled to treat the interest paid by customers as exempt from tax.[60]

The analogy between the facts of this ruling and the securities lending transaction is unmistakable. Just as the bank in that ruling was unable to treat customer-paid interest as tax-exempt income, and had to associate that tax feature with its customers' holdings, so too are the broker-paid amounts to exempt organizations properly treated as dividends or interest (as the case may be) to them, rather than as dividends or interest paid to the broker. This parallel in the transactions was underscored by the IRS's characterization of the transaction as a loan rather than a sale or exchange, which is the correct portrayal to be given

---

[55] See § 3.3, text accompanied by note 31.

[56] Comm'r v. Wilson, 163 F.2d 680 (9th Cir. 1947), *aff'g* 5 T.C.M. 647 (1946), *cert. denied*, 332 U.S. 842 (1947); Comm'r v. Park, 113 F.2d 352 (3d Cir. 1940), *aff'g* 38 B.T.A. 1118 (1938).

[57] Gilman v. Comm'r, 53 F.2d 47 (8th Cir. 1931).

[58] Rev. Rul. 74-27, 1974-1 C.B. 24.

[59] IRC § 103.

[60] In regard to this position, the IRS relied on First Am. Nat'l Bank of Nashville v. United States, 467 F.2d 1098 (6th Cir. 1972), and Am. Nat'l Bank of Austin v. United States, 421 F.2d 442 (5th Cir.), *cert. denied*, 400 U.S. 819 (1970).

the organization's transactions with brokers. It is the exempt organization, not the broker, that retains the debt or equity position in the issuer-corporation.

The courts have recognized the concept of *equivalency payments*, with the result that such payments are regarded as dividends, interest, or the like even though the technical elements of the definitions of those terms may not be wholly satisfied. As an illustration, a federal court of appeals, in characterizing oil and gas lease bonus payments as passive income for personal holding company purposes, concluded that the payments were a "hybrid category of income not expressly provided for in the statute, which, as a matter of semantics, is not clearly either rent or royalty" and decided that, "[b]ecause it seems to us that the type of lease bonus here under consideration is precisely the sort of passive investment income with which the statute is concerned . . . we have no doubt that the lease bonus falls within one category or another."[61] Similarly, the income received by exempt organizations from brokers in securities lending transactions, reflecting dividends or interest paid by the issuer, is properly regarded as dividends or interest for these purposes—even if it is treated as a hybrid category of income that does not fully meet all the semantic definitional requirements.

It was not necessary, however, for unrelated business law purposes, to resolve the question of whether a pass-through theory was pertinent. This is because, irrespective of whether the payments are to be considered dividends or interest by virtue of an equivalency approach, they should nonetheless have been so characterized for purposes of the unrelated business income rules. That is, regardless of the availability of a pass-through rationale, payments by brokers to exempt lending organizations are still appropriately characterized as coming within the exclusion for passive income.

The monies paid by the brokers to exempt organizations perhaps may not satisfy the precise doctrinal requirements of the terms used in these rules, such as *interest* or *dividends*. Nonetheless, these monies clearly constitute passive income to the organization and accordingly warrant treatment as being within the scope of the intentions underlying the exclusions. It may be technically advanced, as noted, that payments by borrowing brokers to a tax-exempt organization cannot qualify as interest, inasmuch as the payments are made for the use of securities, which are property, not money. These payments technically may not constitute *rent*, either, because the securities recovered by an exempt organization are different from those that were borrowed, the right to sell the property becomes vested in the borrower, and the borrower has the authority to sell the securities—features of a transaction usually antithetical to the typical lease arrangement.[62] Nonetheless, the strict definitional classifications of the types of passive income are not dispositive of questions as to their treatment in relation to the unrelated business rules. Rather, "[w]hether a particular item of income falls within any of the modifications . . . shall be determined by all of the facts and circumstances of each case."[63]

---

[61] Bayou Verret Land Co. v. Comm'r, 450 F.2d 840, 855, 854 (5th Cir. 1971), *rev'g & rem'g* 52 T.C. 971 (1970).
[62] See § 3.8(a).
[63] Reg. § 1.512(b)-1. See § 3.1, text accompanied by note 16.

In this factual setting, the income generated by the typical securities lending transaction is clearly passive in nature, thereby warranting treatment as being encompassed by the modifications. That is, from the standpoint of the tax-exempt lending organization, no additional activity is needed to procure the income (the only *activity* is the investment effort in entering into the contracts with brokers) and the amount of income is essentially the same (albeit from a different source).

The validity of the foregoing analysis is borne out by the line of law holding that payments made by a broker-borrower in a securities lending transaction are the functional equivalent of interest paid in connection with a business loan and therefore are deductible by the broker as an ordinary and necessary business expense. Thus, it was held that a taxpayer, which was engaged in extensive short-sales transactions, properly deducted the payments to the lender, which were amounts equal to dividends declared during the period the seller was short, as business expenses.[64] Similarly, on like facts, a court first noted that *interest* is an amount having some relationship to an *indebtedness*, in turn defined as "something owed in money which one is unconditionally obligated or bound to pay, the payment of which is enforceable."[65] Realizing that a securities transaction such as the one under examination necessarily involves a borrower and a lender, the court concluded that "payment of the dividend here represents a sum of money unconditionally owed by the borrower to the lender of stock; it arises out of the relationship of debtor and creditor and is a customary expense in a 'short' sale incident to obtaining and using the stock" and is "ordinary and necessary in this type of transaction."[66]

The IRS's acceptance of this rationale was memorialized in a ruling involving an investor who paid loan premiums and amounts equal to cash dividends to the lenders of securities to the investor. The dividend equivalency and other payments were ruled by the agency to be deductible under these rules.[67]

Therefore, the correct conclusion in this regard—even if securities lending is regarded as a trade or business and even if this matter had not been rectified by statute—would be treatment of the brokers' payments to the lending tax-exempt organization as dividends or interest. Such payments would be excludable from unrelated business income taxation by operation of the rules encompassing passive income, or as income items so functionally equivalent to interest and dividends by virtue of their nature as passive income as to be similarly excludable.

§ 3.5 CERTAIN CONSIDERATION

Amounts received or accrued as consideration for entering into agreements to make loans are excluded from unrelated business income taxation.[68] This exclusion is not available when the income is unrelated debt-financed income.[69]

---

[64] Comm'r v. Wiesler, 161 F.2d 997 (6th Cir. 1947), *aff'g* 6 T.C. 1148 (1946), *cert. denied*, 322 U.S. 842 (1947).
[65] Comm'r v. Wilson, 163 F.2d 680, 682 (9th Cir. 1947).
[66] *Id.*
[67] Rev. Rul. 72-521, 1972-2 C.B. 178.
[68] IRC § 512(b)(1).
[69] IRC § 512(b)(4); Reg. § 1.512(b)-1(k). See ch. 5.

§ 3.6 ANNUITIES

Income received by a tax-exempt organization as an annuity generally is not taxable as unrelated business income.[70] Basically, an *annuity* is an amount of money, fixed by contract between the annuitor and the annuitant, that is paid annually, either in one sum or in installments (such as semiannually or quarterly).

This exclusion is not available when the income is unrelated debt-financed income[71] or is from a controlled corporation.[72]

§ 3.7 ROYALTIES

Generally, a royalty, including an overriding royalty,[73] paid to a tax-exempt organization is excludable from unrelated income taxation.[74]

Basically, a *royalty* is a payment for the use of a valuable intangible right, such as a trademark, trade name, service mark, logo, or copyright, regardless of whether the property represented by the right is used; royalties also include the right to a share of production reserved to the owner of property for permitting another to work mines and quarries or to drill for oil or gas.[75] Royalties have also been characterized as payments that constitute passive income, such as the compensation paid by a licensee to the licensor for use of the licensor's patented invention.[76]

It was the stance of the U.S. Tax Court that a royalty, excludable from unrelated business income taxation, is a payment (income) for the use of valuable intangible property rights, irrespective of whether the income was passive.[77] A federal appellate court, however, is of the view that the Tax Court's definition of the term *royalty* is overly broad, in that a royalty "cannot include compensation for services rendered by the owner of the property."[78] This position, then, is a compromise between the approach of the Tax Court and that of the IRS on the point. Thus, the appellate court wrote that, to the extent the IRS "claims that a tax-exempt organization can do nothing to acquire such fees [to have the income regarded as an excludable royalty]," the agency is "incorrect."[79] Yet, the court continued, "to the extent that . . . [the exempt organization involved] appears to argue that a 'royalty' is any payment for the use of a property right—such as a copyright—regardless of any additional services that are performed in addition to the owner simply permitting another to use the right at issue, we disagree."[80]

Thus, despite the exclusion for royalty income, it is the IRS's position that monies will be taxed, even if they are characterized by the parties as royalties, when the

---

[70] IRC § 512(b)(1); Reg. § 1.512(b)-1(a)(1).

[71] IRC § 512(b)(4); Reg. § 1.512(b)-1(a)(1). See ch. 5.

[72] Reg. § 1.512(b)-1(a)(2); Reg. § 1.512(b)-1(k). See § 8.8(b).

[73] A discussion of the addition of this term appears in J.E. & L.E. Mabee Found., Inc. v. United States, 533 F.2d 521 (10th Cir. 1976), *aff'g* 389 F. Supp. 673 (N.D. Okla. 1975).

[74] IRC § 512(b)(2); Reg. § 1.512(b)-1(b).

[75] *E.g.*, Fraternal Order of Police III State Troopers Lodge No. 41 v. Comm'r, 833 F.2d 717, 723 (7th Cir. 1987).

[76] Disabled Am. Veterans v. United States, 650 F.2d 1178, 1189 (Ct. Cl. 1981).

[77] Sierra Club, Inc. v. Comm'r, 103 T.C. 307, 337 (1994); Sierra Club, Inc. v. Comm'r, 65 T.C.M. 2582, 2586–2588 (1993); Disabled Am. Veterans v. Comm'r, 94 T.C. 60, 70 (1990).

[78] Sierra Club, Inc. v. Comm'r, 86 F.3d 1526, 1532 (9th Cir. 1996).

[79] *Id.* at 1535.

[80] *Id.*

tax-exempt organization is actively involved in the enterprise that generates the revenue, such as through the provision of services.[81] Frequently, the IRS will view the relationship between the parties as that of partners or joint venturers.[82] A common instance of this treatment is the agency's insistence that the funds an exempt organization receives for an endorsement are taxable, whereas the organization asserts that the monies are royalties for the use of its name and logo.[83] An approach to resolution of this issue is to make partial use of the royalty exclusion by means of two contracts: one for the taxable services and one for the royalty arrangement.[84]

Additional litigation has somewhat transformed the IRS's stance in this regard. This process began when an appellate court ruled that a tax-exempt organization could treat income as a royalty even when the organization provided some services.[85] It was furthered when the Tax Court held that revenue was royalty income under this new definition.[86] The IRS's position further eroded when the Tax Court subsequently held, in two decisions, that mailing-list rental payments qualified as royalties.[87] The coup de grace for the government's stance probably came when two other appellate court opinions on the subject of royalty income went against it.[88]

By the close of 1999, the IRS realized that this series of defeats was insurmountable—that the courts were not going to accept its interpretation of the scope of the tax-excludable royalty. The IRS National Office, late that year, communicated with its exempt organizations specialists in the field, essentially capitulating on the point; a memorandum distributed to them stated bluntly that cases should be resolved "in a manner consistent with the existing court cases."[89] This memorandum added that "it is now clear that courts will continue to find the income [generated by activities such as mailing-list rentals and affinity card programs] to be excluded royalty income unless the factual record clearly reflects more than unsubstantial services being provided." The agency highlighted two factors as establishing nontaxable royalty income: when the exempt organization's involvement is "relatively minimal," and

---

[81] *E.g.*, Nat'l Water Well Ass'n, Inc. v. Comm'r, 92 T.C. 75 (1989).

[82] *E.g.*, Tech. Adv. Mem. 9509002.

[83] *E.g.*, Priv. Ltr. Rul. 9450028.

[84] There is support for this approach in Texas Farm Bureau, Inc. v. United States, 53 F.3d 120 (5th Cir. 1995), in which the contracts involved did not expressly cast the revenues at issue as royalties.

[85] See text accompanied by *supra* notes 78–80.

[86] Sierra Club, Inc. v. Comm'r, 77 T.C.M. 1569 (1999). This case was heard on remand; the first decision is the subject of *supra* note 77. In general, Tsilas, Sierra Club, Inc. v. Comm'r: *Why Is the IRS Continuing to Fight a Losing Battle?*, 24 Exempt Orgs. Tax Rev. 487 (no. 3, June 1999); Lauber & Mayer, *Tax Court Rules (Again) on Sierra Club Affinity Card Income*, 24 Exempt Orgs. Tax Rev. 311 (no. 2, May 1999).

[87] Common Cause v. Comm'r, 112 T.C. 332 (1999); Planned Parenthood Fed'n of Am., Inc. v. Comm'r, 77 T.C.M. 2227 (1999). See also Miss. State Univ. Alumni, Inc. v. Comm'r, 74 T.C.M. 458 (1999).

[88] Or. State Univ. Alumni Ass'n, Inc. v. Comm'r, 193 F.3d 1098 (9th Cir. 1999), *aff'g* Alumni Ass'n. of Univ. of Or., Inc. v. Comm'r, 71 T.C.M. 1935 (1996) and 71 T.C.M. 2093 (1996).

[89] Memorandum from Jay H. Rotz, IRS Exempt Organizations Division, National Office, dated Dec. 16, 1999. This is not to say that the government loses every case on this point. When the tax-exempt organization participates in and maintains control over significant aspects of the activities that generate the income, the courts will reject the contention that the revenue is an excludable royalty. See, *e.g.*, Ark. State Police Ass'n, Inc. v. Comm'r, 81 T.C.M. 1172 (2001), *aff'd*, 282 F.3d 556 (8th Cir. 2002). In general, Light, *Denial of the Royalty Exclusion Because of Excessive Participation in* Arkansas State Police Association v. Comm'r, 55 Tax Law. 351 (no. 1, Fall 2001).

when the exempt organization "hired outside contractors to perform most services associated with the exploitation of the use of intangible property."[90]

Earlier, the U.S. Tax Court held that a tax-exempt organization's income from the rental of mailing lists was not taxable, because it was properly characterized as royalties, notwithstanding the extent of activities the organization engaged in to preserve and enhance the list.[91] The court seemed to state that it was irrelevant, in this setting, whether the royalty income was passive. The court apparently acknowledged that the organization's active endeavors were activities to preserve and enhance the asset (maintain the list) rather than the provision of services to others in connection with rental activities. On appeal, however, it was held that the organization was collaterally stopped from bringing the case in the first instance, in that the same issue had been litigated previously.[92]

Mineral royalties, whether measured by production or by gross or taxable income from the mineral property, are excludable by a tax-exempt organization in computing unrelated business taxable income. When however, an exempt organization owns a working interest in a mineral property, and is not relieved of its share of the development costs by the terms of any agreement with an operator, income received from the interest is not excludable from unrelated business income taxation.[93] The holder of a mineral interest is not liable for the expenses of development (or operations) for these purposes when the holder's interest is a net profit interest not subject to expenses that exceed gross profits. Thus, an exempt university was ruled to have excludable royalty interests, because the interests it held in various oil- and gas-producing properties were based on the gross profits from the properties reduced by all expenses of development and operations.[94]

The foregoing reference to development costs is for purposes of illustration. The concept also extends to operating costs because, to be an excludable royalty interest, income received from a mineral lease by an exempt organization must be free of both types of cost.[95]

The IRS ruled that patent development and management service fees, deducted from royalties collected from licensees by a tax-exempt charitable organization for distribution to the beneficial owners of the patents, were not within this exception for royalties. The agency said that "although the amounts

---

[90] An issue under consideration at the IRS is whether there should be an allocation of a single payment between compensation for the use of intangible property and compensation for more than insubstantial services.

[91] Disabled Am. Veterans v. Comm'r, 94 T.C. 60 (1990). In general, see Sperzman & Washlick, *Mailing Lists Revisited: The Disabled American Veterans in Tax Court*, 47 Tax Notes 1377 (no. 11, 1990).

[92] Disabled Am. Veterans v. Comm'r, 942 F.2d 309 (6th Cir. 1991). This previous litigation is reflected in Disabled Am. Veterans v. United States, 650 F.2d 1178 (Ct. Cl. 1981), *aff'd & remanded*, 704 F.2d 1570 (Fed. Cir. 1983). In general, Schadler, *The Courts Point the Way to Royalty Treatment for UBIT Purposes*, 9 J. Tax Exempt Orgs. 244 (no. 6, May/June 1998); Elfenbein & Crigler, Sierra Club *Provides Trailmarks for Royalties*, 8 J. Tax Exempt Orgs. 99 (Nov./Dec. 1996); Cerny & Lauber, *Ninth Circuit Rules on Sierra Club Mailing List and Affinity Card Income*, 14 Exempt Orgs. Tax Rev. 255 (no. 2, Aug. 1996); Desilets, Jr., *Payments Received for Use of an Exempt Organization's Name and Logo: Royalties or UBIT?*, 13 Exempt Orgs. Tax. Rev. 147 (Jan./Feb. 1996); Kirschten & Brown, *The IRS Narrows the UBIT Royalty Exclusion*, 1 J. Tax Exempt Orgs. 20 (Spring 1989).

[93] Reg. § 1.512(b)-1(b).

[94] Priv. Ltr. Rul. 7741004.

[95] Rev. Rul. 69-179, 1969-1 C.B. 158.

paid to the [exempt] organization are derived from royalties, they do not retain the character of royalties in the organization's hands" for these purposes.[96] By Contrast, the IRS decided that income derived by an exempt organization from the sale of advertising in publications produced by an independent firm was properly characterized as royalty income.[97] Likewise, the agency determined that amounts received from licensees by an exempt organization, which was the legal and beneficial owner of patents assigned to it by inventors for specified percentages of future royalties, constituted excludable royalty income.[98] Similarly, federal court of appeals held that income consisting of 100 percent of the net profits in certain oil properties, received by an exempt organization from two corporations controlled by it, constituted income from overriding royalties and thus was excluded from unrelated business income taxation.[99]

A matter of concern to the IRS was the proper tax treatment of payments to a tax-exempt organization, the principal purpose of which is the development of a U.S. team for international amateur sports competition, in return for the right to commercially use the organization's name and logo. The organization entered into licensing agreements that, in consideration of the annual payment of a stated sum, authorized use of the organization's name and logo in connection with the sale of products. The IRS's initial position was that, to be characterized as royalties and thus be excludable from unrelated income taxation, payments must be measured according to the use made of a valuable right be characterized as royalt and. agency became sufficiently persuaded, on the basis of case-law precedent,[100] that fixed-sum payments for the right to use an asset qualify as excludable royalties, although it continues to adhere to the position that absent the statutory exclusion, the income would be taxable as being from an unrelated trade or business.[101]

Subsequently, the IRS ruled that certain payments a labor organization received, from various business enterprises, for the use of its trademark and similar properties were excludable royalties.[102] It reached this conclusion notwithstanding the facts that the organization retained the right to approve the quality or style of the licensed products and services, and that the payments were sometimes set as flat annual amounts.[103]

Of all of the exclusions from unrelated business income taxation that are available by reason of the modifications, the exclusion for royalties is the most

---

[96] Rev. Rul. 73-193, 1973-1 C.B. 262, 263.

[97] Tech. Adv. Mem. 7926003.

[98] Rev. Rul. 76-297, 1976-2 C.B. 178.

[99] United States v. Robert A. Welch Found., 334 F.2d 774 (5th Cir. 1964), aff'g 228 F. Supp. 881 (S.D. Tex. 1963). The IRS refused to follow this decision; Rev. Rul. 69-162, 1969-1 C.B. 158. In general, Holloman, *Are Overriding Royalties Unrelated Business Income?*, 24 *Oil & Gas Tax Q.* 1 (1975).

[100] Comm'r v. Affiliated Enters., Inc., 123 F.2d 665 (10th Cir. 1941), *cert. denied*, 315 U.S. 812 (1942). See also Comm'r v. Wodehouse, 337 U.S. 369 (1949); Rohmer v. Comm'r, 153 F.2d 61 (2d Cir. 1946), *cert. denied*, 328 U.S. 862 (1946); Sabatini v. Comm'r, 98 F.2d 758 (2d Cir. 1938).

[101] Priv. Ltr. Rul. 8006005.

[102] Rev. Rul. 81-178, 1981-2 C.B. 135. By contrast, other payments were held not to be royalties because the personal services of the organization's members were required.

[103] The IRS cited the following authority for its conclusion: Uhlaender v. Henrickson, 316 F. Supp. 1277 (D. Minn. 1970); Cepeda v. Swift & Co., 415 F.2d 1205 (8th Cir. 1969); Comm'r v. Wodehouse, 337 U.S. 369 (1949); Rohmer v. Comm'r, 153 F.2d 61 (2d Cir. 1946); Comm'r v. Affiliated Enters., Inc., 123 F.2d 665 (10th Cir. 1941); Sabatini v. Comm'r, 98 F.2d 758 (2d Cir. 1938).

versatile from a planning standpoint. There is not much flexibility in the terms *dividend, interest,* and *annuity,* but the term *royalty* is sufficiently supple that an exempt organization often can convert what would otherwise be unrelated business income into excludable royalties. For example, instead of publishing and selling a book in a commercial manner directly (an unrelated business that is regularly carried on), an exempt organization can transfer the processes to a publishing company and receive nontaxable royalties.[104]

The IRS issues private letter rulings as to what constitutes excludable royalties in this context.[105]

Unrelated debt-financed income is not subject to this exclusion,[106] nor is royalty income from a controlled corporation.[107]

§ 3.8   RENT

An exclusion from unrelated business income taxation is available with respect to certain rents.[108] The primary exclusion is for rents from real property.[109]

(a) General Rules

Rent is a form of income paid for the occupation or other use of property. In general, this exclusion is available for rental income when the tax-exempt organization is not actively involved in the enterprise that generates the revenue, such as through the provision of services for the convenience of tenants. Payments for the use or occupancy of entire private residences or living quarters in duplex or multiple housing units, of offices in any office building, and the like are generally considered as excludable rent.[110]

The exclusion from unrelated business taxable income for rents is sometimes misunderstood, inasmuch as not all income labeled *rent* qualifies for the exclusion. When a tax-exempt organization carries on activities that constitute an activity carried on for trade or business, even though the activities involve the leasing of real estate, the exclusion will not be available.[111] Thus, payments for the use or occupancy of rooms and other space where services are also rendered to the occupant do not constitute excludable rent. Such disqualifying services include the use or occupancy of rooms or other quarters in hotels, boarding houses, or apartment houses furnishing hotel services; or in tourist camps or tourist homes, motor courts, or motels; or for the use or occupancy of parking lots, warehouses, or storage garages.

Generally, services are considered *rendered to the occupant* if they are primarily for the occupant's convenience and are other than those services usually or

---

[104] Rev. Rul. 69-430, 1969-2 C.B. 129.
[105] *E.g.,* Priv. Ltr. Rul. 8708031.
[106] IRC § 512(b)(4); Reg. § 1.512(b)-1(b); Reg. § 1.512(b)-1(k). See ch. 5.
[107] Reg. § 1.512(b)-1(b). See § 8.8(b). In general, Izuel & Park, *The Application of the Royalty and Volunteer Exceptions to Unrelated Business Taxable Income,* 44 Exempt Orgs. Tax Rev. 299 (no. 3, June 2004).
[108] IRC § 512(b)(3); Reg. § 1.512(b)-1(c)(2).
[109] IRC § 512(b)(3)(A)(i).
[110] Reg. § 1.512(b)-1(c)(5).
[111] In general, the rental of real estate constitutes the carrying on of a trade or business. (*e.g.,* Hazard v. Comm'r, 7 T.C. 372 (1946).

customarily rendered in connection with the rental of rooms or other space for occupancy only. The supplying of maid service, for example, constitutes such service. By contrast, an exempt organization may retain the benefit of the exclusion if it performs normal maintenance services, such as the furnishing of heat, air conditioning, and light; the cleaning of public entrances, exits, stairways, and lobbies; the collection of trash; and the like. When an exempt organization undertakes functions beyond these maintenance services, the payments will not be considered as being from a passive source, but instead are treated as coming from an unrelated trade or business (assuming that the activity is regularly carried on and is not substantially related to the organization's tax-exempt purposes).[112]

Thus, for example, a tax-exempt organization that allowed use of its hall for a fee, and provided only utilities and janitorial services, was held able to utilize this exclusion because the services were minimal; the facts caused the receipts to be characterized as rental income from real property.[113] Conversely, an exempt organization operating to foster public interest in the arts leased studio apartments to artists, provided telephone switchboard and maid services, and operated a dining hall for the tenants. Payments pursuant to these leases were not sheltered by the rental exclusion, because substantial services were rendered to the tenants and the leasing activity was not an exempt function.[114]

The contractual relationship between the parties, from which the ostensible rental income is derived, must be that as reflected in a *lease*, rather than a *license*, for the exclusion for rental income to be available. A lease "confers upon a tenant exclusive possession of the subject premises as against all the world, including the owner."[115] The difference is the conferring of a privilege to occupy the owner's property for a particular use, rather than general possession of the premises. Thus, a tax-exempt organization that permitted an advertising agency to maintain signs and other advertisements on the wall space in the exempt organization's premises was held to be receiving income from a license arrangement, rather than a rental one; hence, the exclusion for rental income was unavailable.[116]

For example, a tax-exempt organization held title to a pipeline system consisting of right-of-way interests in land, pipelines buried in the ground, pumping stations, equipment, and other appurtenant property. The organization leased the system. In concluding that the resultant income constituted rent for purposes of this exclusion, the IRS observed that the basic component of the pipeline system, an easement giving the right-of-way interests, amounted to real property.[117] Thus, income passively received from the rental of real property, such as that from a valid landlord-tenant relationship in which the landlord receives nothing more

---

[112] Reg. § 1.512(b)-1(c)(5).

[113] Rev. Rul. 69-178, 1969-1 C.B. 158. The facts that the use of the hall was for only short periods of time, and that the agreement to use the facility was usually verbal, did not destroy the character of these receipts as qualifying rental income.

[114] Rev. Rul. 69-69, 1969-1 C.B. 159.

[115] Union Travel Assocs., Inc. v. Int'l Assocs., Inc., 401 A.2d 105, 107 (D.C. 1976).

[116] Priv. Ltr. Rul. 9740032.

[117] Rev. Rul. 67-218, 1967-2 C.B. 213.

than net rental payments, is not taxable. The analysis changes, however, if the arrangement is a management contract rather than a lease.[118]

As a general rule, the exclusion for rent is not applicable when the relationship between the parties is a partnership[119] or a joint venture.[120] When the requisite profit motive is absent, even if the arrangement is a partnership or joint venture in the broad sense of ownership of property and sharing of net rents, there presumably is no partnership or joint venture for federal tax purposes, because of the lack of an intent for a return of profits and because the relationship does not involve a working interest or operational control of the "business."[121] Thus, when the income is truly rent and the relationship is a passive one (of investor only), the exclusion for rental income is available.[122]

The rents that are excluded from unrelated business income taxation are all rents from real property[123] and certain rents from personal property[124] leased with real property.[125] The exclusion from unrelated business income for rents of personal property leased with real property is limited to instances in which the rents attributable to the personalty are an incidental amount of the total rents received or accrued under the lease (that is, no more than 10 percent of total rental income).[126] This determination is made at the time the personal property is first placed in service by the lessee.[127] Thus, for example, if rents attributable to personal property leased are $3,000 annually and the total rents from all property leased are $10,000 annually, the $3,000 amount cannot be excluded from the computation of unrelated business income, inasmuch as that amount is not an incidental portion of the total rents.[128]

Moreover, this exclusion is not available, if more than 50 percent of the total rent received or accrued pursuant to the lease is attributable to the personalty leased (determined at the time the personal property is first placed in service by the lessee).[129] When the rent attributable to personalty is between 10 percent and 50 percent of the total, only the exclusion with respect to personalty is lost.[130]

---

[118] State Nat'l Bank of El Paso v. United States, 509 F.2d 832 (5th Cir. 1975), *rev'g & remanding* 75-2 U.S.T.C. ¶ 9868 (W.D. Tex. 1975).

[119] See *Tax-Exempt Organizations*, §§ 32.1, 32.2.

[120] *Id.* § 32.3.

[121] *E.g.*, Rev. Rul. 58-482, 1958-2 C.B. 273 (exempt organization leased real property pursuant to the terms of a lease under which the organization was not a partner or other joint venturer).

[122] United States v. Myra Found., 382 F.2d 107 (8th Cir. 1967) (a private foundation that was a lessor of farmland and received as rent a portion of the crops produced by the tenant was not subject to unrelated business income tax on the rent).

[123] IRC § 512(b)(3)(A)(i). The term *real property* means all real property, including property described in IRC §§ 1245(a)(3)(C) and 1250(c). Reg. § 1.512(b)-1(c)(3)(i).

[124] The term *personal property* means all personal property, including property described in IRC § 1245(a)(3)(B). Reg. § 1.512(b)-1(c)(3)(ii).

[125] If separate leases are entered into with respect to real and personal property, and the properties have an integrated use (for example, one or more leases for real property and another lease or leases for personal property to be used on the real property), all of the leases are treated as one lease. Reg. § 1.512(b)-1(c)(3)(iii).

[126] IRC § 512(b)(3)(A)(ii); Reg. § 1.512(b)-1(c)(2)(ii).

[127] Property is *placed in service* by the lessee when it is first subject to its use in accordance with the terms of the lease. Reg. § 1.512(b)-1(c)(3)(iv).

[128] Reg. § 1.512(b)-1(c)(2)(ii).

[129] IRC § 512(b)(3)(B)(i); Reg. § 1.512(b)-1(c)(2)(iii).

[130] Reg. § 1.512(b)-1(c)(2).

As an illustration, a tax-exempt organization owns a printing facility consisting of a building housing two printing presses and other printing equipment. On January 1, 2006, the exempt organization rents the building and the printing equipment to a person for $100,000 annually. The lease states that $90,000 of the rent is for the building and $10,000 is for the printing equipment. It is determined, however, notwithstanding the terms of the lease, that $40,000 of the rent is in fact attributable to the printing equipment. During 2006, this exempt organization has $30,000 of deductions, all of which are properly allocable to the land and building. The exempt organization need not take into account, in computing its unrelated business taxable income, the $60,000 of rent attributable to the building and the $30,000 of deductions directly connected with that rent. By contrast, the $40,000 of rent attributable to the printing equipment is not excluded from computation of the exempt organization's unrelated business taxable income, because that rent represents more than an incidental portion of the total rents (i.e., 40 percent of the total).[131]

In another example, on January 1, 2006, a tax-exempt organization executed two leases with a person. One lease is for the rental of a computer system, with a stated annual rent of $7,500. The other lease is for the rental of office space in which to use the computer, at a stated annual rent of $72,500. At the time the computer system is first placed in service, taking both leases into consideration, it is determined that, the terms of the leases notwithstanding, $30,000 of the rent is in fact attributable to the computer system. Therefore, for 2006, only $50,000 of the total of $80,000 rent, attributable to rental of the office space, is excludable from the computation of this exempt organization's unrelated business taxable income (37.5 percent of this rent is attributable to the personal property).[132]

If (1) by reason of the placing of additional or substitute personal property in service, there is an increase of 100 percent or more in the rent attributable to all of the personal property leased; or (2) there is a modification of the lease by which there is a change in the rent charged (whether or not there is a change in the amount of personal property rented), the rent attributable to personal property must be recomputed to determine whether the exclusion, or the exception from it, applies. Any change in the treatment of rents attributable to a recomputation under this rule is effective only with respect to rents for the period beginning with the event that occasioned the recomputation.[133]

Another example embellishes the facts of the previous one. The leases to which the computer system and office space are subject provide that the rent may be increased or decreased, depending on the prevailing rental value for similar systems and office space. On January 1, 2007, the total annual rent is increased in the computer system lease to $20,000 and in the office space lease to $90,000. For 2007, it is determined that, notwithstanding the terms of the leases, $60,000 of the total rent (54.5 percent of the total) is in fact attributable to the computer system as of that time. Even though the rent attributable to personal property now exceeds 50 percent of the total rent, the rent attributable to real

---

[131] Reg. § 1.512(b)-1(c)(2)(iv).
[132] Reg. § 1.512(b)-1(c)(4), Example (1).
[133] Reg. § 1.512(b)-1(c)(3)(v).

property will continue to be excluded, because there was no modification of the terms of the leases and because the increase in the rent was not attributable to the placement of new personal property in service. Thus, for 2007, the $50,000 of rent attributable to the office space continues to be excluded from computation of the exempt organization's unrelated business taxable income.[134]

Another example is also based on the first computer/space rental example. On January 1, 2008, the lessee rents additional computer equipment from the exempt organization, and the equipment is placed in service on that date. The total rent is increased to $20,000 for the computer system lease and to $100,000 for the office space lease. It is determined at the time the additional computer equipment is first placed in service that, notwithstanding the terms of the leases, $70,000 of the rent is in fact attributable to all of the computer equipment. Inasmuch as the rent attributable to personal property has increased by more than 100 percent (the increase is 133 percent), a redetermination must be made. As a result, 58.3 percent of the total rent is determined to be attributable to personal property. Accordingly, because more than 50 percent of the total rent the exempt organization receives is attributable to the personal property leased, none of the rents are excludable from computation of the organization's unrelated business taxable income.[135]

A last example is based on the facts of the previous one, except that on June 30, 2010, the lease is modified. The total rent for the computer system is reduced to $15,000 and the total rent for the office space lease is reduced to $75,000. A redetermination is made on June 30, 2010: As of this modification date, it is determined that, notwithstanding the terms of the leases, the rent in fact attributable to the computer system is $40,000 (44.4 percent of the total rent). Because less than 50 percent of the total rent is now attributable to personal property, the rent attributable to real property ($50,000), for periods after June 30, 2010, is excluded from computation of the exempt organization's unrelated business taxable income. However, the rent attributable to personal property ($40,000) is not excluded from unrelated business taxable income for the periods, as it represents more than an incidental portion of the total rent.[136]

Consequently, in a fact situation in which all of the rental income involved is derived from personal property, the exclusion is not available. For example, a tax-exempt employees' trust that owned railroad tank cars leased them to an industrial company. The IRS ruled that this leasing activity was a regularly carried on business of a kind ordinarily carried on for profit, and thus was an unrelated business conducted by the trust. The exclusion for rental income was not available because the rental income was generated solely from the leasing of personal property.[137]

The IRS issues private letter rulings as to what constitutes excludable rent in this context.[138]

---

[134] Reg. § 1.512(b)-1(c)(4), Example (2).
[135] Id., Example (3).
[136] Id., Example (4).
[137] Rev. Rul. 60-206, 1960-1 C.B. 201.
[138] E.g., Priv. Ltr. Rul. 9246032.

Unrelated debt-financed income is not subject to this exclusion,[139] however, nor is royalty income from a controlled corporation.[140]

(b) Profits-Based Income

Notwithstanding these general rules, the exclusion for rent does not apply if the determination of the amount of the rent depends, in whole or in part, on the income or profits derived by any person from the property leased, other than an amount based on a fixed percentage or percentages of receipts of sales.[141] An amount is excluded from consideration as rent from real property if, considering the lease and all of the surrounding circumstances, the arrangement does not conform with normal business practice and is in reality a means of basing the rent on income or profits.[142] This rule is intended to prevent avoidance of the unrelated business income tax when a profit-sharing arrangement would, in effect, make the lessor an active participant in the operation of the property.

As noted, an exception is provided for amounts based on a fixed percentage or percentages of sales. These amounts are customary in rental contracts and are generally considered to be different from the profit or loss of the lessee. Generally, rents received from real property are not disqualified from the exclusion solely by reason of the fact that the rent is based on a fixed percentage of total receipts or sales of the lessee. The fact that a lease is based on a percentage of total receipts, however, would not necessarily qualify the amount received or accrued as rent from real property. For example, an amount would not qualify as rent from real property if the lease provided for an amount measured by varying percentages of receipts and the arrangement did not conform with normal business practices, but was used as a means of basing the rent on income or profits.[143]

This rule can be applied, for example, in determining whether income from sharecrop leasing is excludable rent or taxable rental income.[144] In one of these instances, the IRS argued that even if there was a landlord-tenant relationship, the rents were nonetheless taxable as unrelated business income because they were not in conformance with the passive rent test.[145] The agency contended that, because of the splitting of the expenditures by the tax-exempt organization-landlord, its involvement in the farming operation, and its receipt of a percentage of production as rents, rather than a percentage of receipts, the exempt organization violated the passive rent test. The court disagreed. The exempt organization's rental fee was based solely on a fixed percentage of the crops. The organization shared the costs of some of the expenses related to farming;

---

[139] IRC § 512(b)(4); Reg. § 1.512(b)-1(c)(2)(i); Reg. § 1.512(b)-1(k). See ch. 5.

[140] Reg. § 1.512(b)-1(c)(2)(i). See § 8.8(b). In general, Greif, *Tax Implications of an Exempt Organization Constructing and Operating a Building,* 6 Tax Adv. 354 (1975); Reed, *Exemptions from Unrelated Business Tax—Rental Income,* 21 Cath. Law. 282 (1975); Johnson, *Rental and Investment Income of Many Exempt Organizations May Be Taxable,* 41 J. Tax'n 170 (1974).

[141] IRC § 512(b)(3)(B)(ii); Reg. § 1.512(b)-1(c)(2)(iii)(b).

[142] Reg. §§ 1.512(b)-1(c)(2)(iii)(b), 1.856-4(b)(3), 1.856-4(b)(6) (other than (b)(6)(ii)). The latter set of regulations is part of the rules pertaining to real estate investment trusts.

[143] Reg. § 1.856-4(b)(3).

[144] The law concerning sharecrop leases in the unrelated business income tax context is the subject of § 9.9.

[145] Trust U/W Emily Oblinger v. Comm'r, 100 T.C. 114 (1993).

the tenant, however, bore the entire cost of damages, claims, interest, and other liabilities. The sharecrop lease explicitly exonerated the exempt organization from any liability, claim, and/or damages. Thus, the court held that the crop shares received by the exempt organization were excludable rental income based on a percentage of the receipts of the harvest. This, wrote the court, is the "equivalent of the tenant's reducing the crops to cash and then giving . . . [the exempt organization] its share of the total receipts collected."[146] "It is not," the court continued, a "percentage of profits or net income."[147]

(c) Rental Activity as Related Business

On occasion, rental income is derived by a tax-exempt organization from the operation of a related business; the revenue therefrom is nontaxable for that reason. As an illustration, an exempt museum, having acquired by gift a historically significant and important aircraft, was asked to lease it back to the manufacturer of the airplane for research purposes. The aircraft was returned to the museum repainted and with the engine-test equipment, which enhanced its value as a historical and educational artifact. A court found that this lease "significantly advanced the [m]useum's mission to restore and display historic aircraft" and made the airplane "more conducive to public display," because it was returned to the museum facility rather than a field where it was originally displayed. Thus, there was the requisite substantial causal relationship between the leasing activity and the advancement of exempt purposes,[148] leading to the conclusion that the rental income was exempt function revenue.[149]

In one instance, a public charity with a training program shared office space with a tax-exempt business league that owned the building, in part because the tenants of the league provided volunteer teaching faculty to the charitable organization. The charity accorded the business league the right to allow the tenants use of its research equipment in exchange for maintenance of the equipment. The IRS held that the value of the maintenance services was phantom rent that was not taxable.[150] Similarly, the IRS ruled that an exempt hospital may lease facilities to another exempt hospital, with the leasing activity constituting an exempt function, because of the direct physical connection and close professional affiliation of the institutions.[151] Likewise, the IRS ruled that an exempt charitable organization owning and operating nursing homes could lease, as a related business, a skilled nursing facility to another exempt charitable organization that owned and operated nursing homes.[152]

---

[146] *Id.* at 123.

[147] *Id.* Also Harlan E. Moore Charitable Trust v. United States, 812 F. Supp. 130 (C.D. Ill.), *aff'd*, 9 F.3d 623 (7th Cir. 1993).

[148] See § 3.8(c).

[149] Museum of Flight Found. v. United States, 63 F. Supp. 2d 1257, 1260 (W.D. Wash. 1999). The court was satisfied that "failing to tax this income will not result in a rush of air and space museums clamoring to lease their historic planes."

[150] Priv. Ltr. Rul. 9615045.

[151] Priv. Ltr. Rul. 200314031.

[152] Priv. Ltr. Rul. 200404057.

§ 3.9 OTHER INVESTMENT INCOME

The IRS ruled that the interest earned by a tax-exempt organization pursuant to *interest rate swap agreements* is not taxable as unrelated business income.[153]

A typical transaction of this type proceeds as follows: The tax-exempt organization purchases a debt security; the instrument evidencing the indebtedness provides that the organization will receive interest payments from the issuer that are keyed to the six-month Eurodollar rate; the organization contracts with an unrelated third party to provide it with payments equal to a fixed rate of return on all or a specified part of the principal amount of the debt security; the fixed rate of return is set so as to provide the organization with a return that is a specified spread of basis points over the seven-year U.S. Treasury bill rate; the organization provides the third party with payments equal to a floating rate of return on all or part of the principal amount of the debt security; the floating rate of return is calculated in the same manner as the floating-rate interest payments described in the second stage of the transaction; the funds used to acquire the debt security and the funds used to make the swap payments are not borrowed;[154] and all payments made and received by the organization are in U.S. dollars. The anticipated result of the interest rate swap is to provide the exempt organization with interest payments that are preferable, from its investment standpoint, to those provided for in the floating-rate note.

The IRS concluded that these swap transactions are "ordinary or routine investment activities undertaken in connection with the management of . . . [the tax-exempt organization's] securities portfolio." The agency analogized the exempt organization securities lending practice,[155] finding the swap transaction "similar" in that the "securities will be acquired and the swap agreements will be entered into as part of an investment strategy designed to stabilize the return on the floating rate debt securities."

In addition to the foregoing forms of investment income, income from notional principal contracts,[156] and other substantially similar income from ordinary and routine investments to the extent determined by the IRS, are excluded in computing unrelated business taxable income.[157] This exclusion embraces interest rate and currency swaps, as well as equity and commodity swaps. These exclusions do *not* apply to income derived from (and deductions in connection with) debt-financed property;[158] gains or losses from the sale, exchange, or other disposition of any property;[159] gains or losses from the lapse or termination of options to buy or sell securities;[160] interest and annuities derived from (and deductions in connection with) controlled organizations;[161] or income earned by

---

[153] Priv. Ltr. Rul. 9042038.
[154] This is done to prevent debt-financed income taxation. See ch. 5.
[155] See § 3.4.
[156] Reg. § 1.863-7.
[157] Reg. § 1.512(b)-1(a)(2).
[158] IRC § 512(b)(4); Reg. § 1.512(b)-1(k). See ch. 5.
[159] See § 3.10.
[160] *Id.*
[161] See § 8.8(b).

brokers or dealers (including organizations that make a market in derivative financial products[162]).[163]

§ 3.10 CAPITAL GAINS

Excluded from unrelated business income taxation generally are gains from the sale, exchange, or other disposition of capital gain property.[164]

(a) General Rules

This exclusion for capital gains does not extend to dispositions of inventory or property held primarily for sale to customers in the ordinary course of a business. These transactions cause the seller to be regarded as a *dealer* in the property, which results in ordinary income.[165]

The IRS applies the following factors in determining whether property being or to be sold has been held primarily for investment or for sale to customers in the ordinary course of business (in the latter case the resulting revenue is ordinary income rather than capital gain):

- The purpose for which the property was acquired
- The cost of the property
- The activities of the owner in improving and disposing of the property
- The extent of improvements made to the property
- The proximity of the sale to the purchase
- The purpose for which the property was held
- Prevailing market conditions
- The frequency, continuity, and size of the sales[166]

The general exclusion for capital gains does not apply with respect to the cutting of timber, which is considered[167] a sale or exchange of the timber.[168] The exclusion also does not apply to gain derived from the sale or other disposition of debt-financed property.[169]

The IRS issues private letter rulings as to what constitutes excludable capital gains in this context.[170]

---

[162] Reg. § 1.954-2T(a)(4)(iii)(B).

[163] In general, see Note, *Tax-Exempt Entities, Notional Principal Contracts, and the Unrelated Business Income Tax*, 105 Harv. L. Rev. 1265 (Apr. 1992); Ben-Ami, *UBIT and Portfolio Investments for Exempt Organizations*, 2 J. Tax Exempt Orgs. 12 (Spring 1990).

[164] IRC § 512(b)(5); Reg. § 1.512(b)-1(d)(1). This exclusion applies with respect to "gains and losses from involuntary conversions, casualties, etc." Reg. § 1.512(b)-(d)(1).

[165] IRC § 512(b)(5)(A), (B); Reg. § 1.512(b)-1(d)(1).

[166] *E.g.*, Priv. Ltr. Rul. 9619069. See § 2.2(e).

[167] By application of IRC § 631(a).

[168] Reg. § 1.512(b)-1(d)(1).

[169] IRC § 512(b)(4); Reg. § 1.512(b)-1(d)(1); Reg. § 1.512(b)-1(k). See ch. 5.

[170] *E.g.*, Priv. Ltr. Rul. 9247038.

(b) Exception

Nonetheless, there is an exception from this second limitation[171] that excludes gains and losses from the sale, exchange, or other disposition of certain real property and mortgages acquired from financial institutions that are in conservatorship or receivership.[172] Only real property and mortgages owned by a financial institution (or held by the financial institution as security for a loan) at the time the institution entered conservatorship or receivership are eligible for the exception.

This exclusion is limited to properties designated as *foreclosure property* within nine months of acquisition and disposed of within 2½ years of acquisition.[173] The IRS may extend the 2½-year disposition period if the extension is necessary for the orderly liquidation of the property. No more than one-half by value of properties acquired in a single transaction may be designated as foreclosure property. This exception is not available for properties that are improved or developed to the extent that the aggregate expenditures on development do not exceed 20 percent of the net selling price of the property.[174]

§ 3.11 GAIN FROM LAPSES OR TERMINATIONS OF OPTIONS

There is an exclusion, from the computation of unrelated business income, of gain from the lapse or termination of options to buy or sell securities or real property. This exclusion also covers all gains from the forfeiture of good-faith deposits (that are consistent with established business practice) for the purchase, sale, or lease of real property in connection with the organization's investment activities.[175] Under prior law, the income from the writing of options (premiums) was generally treated as ordinary income, and thus was subject to the unrelated business income tax.[176] (Premiums received for options that are exercised are treated as part of the gain or loss on the sale of the property involved, usually as capital gain or loss.) In the opinion of the Senate Committee on Finance, a change in the law was necessary because taxation of this type of income is "inconsistent with the generally tax-free treatment accorded to exempt organizations' income from investment activities."[177]

An option is considered terminated when the organization's obligation pursuant to the option ceases by any means other than exercise or lapse of the option. If this exclusion is otherwise available, it will apply whether or not the organization owns the securities on which the option is written; that is, irrespective of whether the option is *covered.*

Income from the lapse or termination of an option is, however, excludable only if the option is written in connection with the tax-exempt organization's investment activities. Thus, for example, if the securities on which the options

---

[171] IRC § 512(b)(5)(B).
[172] IRC § 512(b)(16).
[173] IRC §§ 512(b)(16)(B), 514(c)(9)(H)(v).
[174] IRC § 512(b)(16)(A).
[175] IRC § 512(b)(5); Reg. § 1.512(b)-1(d)(2).
[176] Rev. Rul. 66-47, 1966-1 C.B. 137.
[177] S. Rep. No. 1172, 94th Cong., 2d Sess. 3 (1976), accompanying Pub. L. No. 94-396.

are written are held by an organization as inventory or for sale to customers in the ordinary course of a trade or business, the income from the lapse or termination will not be excludable. Similarly, if an organization is engaged in the business of writing options (whether or not the options are covered), the exclusion will not be available.[178]

§ 3.12 LOAN COMMITMENT FEES

The law was unclear as to whether loan commitment fees constitute unrelated business income. A *loan commitment fee* is a nonrefundable charge made by a lender to reserve a sum of money with fixed terms for a specified period of time. This type of charge compensates the lender for the risk inherent in committing to make the loan (such as for the lender's exposure to interest rate changes and for potential lost opportunities). Today, however, an exclusion from such tax treatment applies; the reference is to "amounts received or accrued as consideration for entering into agreements to make loans."[179]

§ 3.13 RESEARCH INCOME

Income derived from research for the United States or any of its agencies or instrumentalities, or a state or political subdivision of a state, and all deductions directly connected with this type of income are excluded in computing unrelated business income.[180] Also excluded from unrelated business income taxation is income derived from research performed for anyone, and all deductions directly connected with the income, when the research is conducted by a tax-exempt college, university, or hospital.[181]

In the case of an organization operated primarily for the purpose of carrying on fundamental research (as distinguished from applied research), the results of which are freely available to the general public, all income derived from research performed for anyone and all deductions directly connected with the income are excluded in computing unrelated business income.[182]

According to the legislative history, the term *research* includes "not only fundamental research but also applied research such as testing and experimental construction and production."[183] With respect to the separate exemption for college, university, or hospital research, "funds received for research by other institutions [do not] necessarily represent unrelated business income," such as a grant by a corporation to a foundation to finance scientific research if the results of the research are to be made freely available to the public.[184] Without defining the term *research*, the IRS was content to find that this rule applied because the studies involved were not "merely quality control programs or

---

[178] Reg. § 1.512(b)-1(d)(2).
[179] IRC § 512(b)(1).
[180] IRC § 512(b)(7); Reg. § 1.512(b)-1(f)(1).
[181] IRC § 512(b)(8); Reg. § 1.512(b)-1(f)(2). See also Rev. Rul. 54-73, 1954-1 C.B. 160; IIT Research Inst. v. United States, 9 Cl. Ct. 13 (1985).
[182] IRC § 512(b)(9); Reg. § 1.512(b)-1(f)(3).
[183] H. Rep. No. 2319, 81st Cong., 2d Sess. 37 (1950).
[184] S. Rep. No. 2375, 81st Cong., 2d Sess. 30 (1950).

ordinary testing for certification purposes, as a final procedural step before marketing."[185]

In employing the term *research* in this context, the IRS generally looks to the body of law defining the term in relation to what is considered tax-exempt scientific research.[186] Thus, the issue is usually whether the activity is being carried on incident to commercial or industrial operations, such as the ordinary testing or inspection of materials or products or the designing or construction of equipment, buildings, and the like.[187] If it is, the activity will almost assuredly be regarded as an unrelated trade or business.[188] In one instance, the IRS found the exclusion for research applicable because the studies undertaken by an exempt medical college, in testing pharmaceutical products under contracts with the manufacturers, were held to be more than "mere quality control programs or ordinary testing for certification purposes, as a final procedural step before marketing."[189] In another instance, the exclusion for research income was held to apply to contract work done by an exempt educational institution for the federal government in the field of rocketry.[190]

College and university audit guidelines issued by the IRS[191] included a section on research activities by these institutions. The auditing agent was directed to:

- Determine whether "purported research is actually the conduct of an activity incident to a commercial enterprise (*e.g.*, testing, sampling or certifying of items to a known standard)"[192]

- Determine whether the research was conducted by the institution or by a separate entity[193]

- Review the institution's safeguards for managing and reporting conflicts of interest and any requirements imposed by any federal agency sponsoring research[194]

- Review the institution's policy regarding ownership of intellectual property[195]

- Review research arrangements with government sponsors and joint venture or royalty-sharing arrangements with industry sponsors[196]

---

[185] Priv. Ltr. Rul. 7936006.
[186] Rev. Rul. 76-296, 1976-2 C.B. 141. *Cf.* IRC § 41 (which provides a tax credit for certain research). In general, see *Tax-Exempt Organizations*, § 9.2; Kertz, *University Research and Development Activities: The Federal Income Tax Consequences of Research Contracts, Research Subsidiaries and Joint Venturers*, 13 J. Coll. & Univ. L. 109 (1986); Kertz, *Tax Exempt Organizations and Commercially Sponsored Scientific Research*, 9 J. Coll. & Univ. L. 69 (1982–1983).
[187] Reg. § 1.512(b)-1(f)(4).
[188] Rev. Rul. 68-373, 1968-2 C.B. 206.
[189] Priv. Ltr. Rul. 7936006.
[190] Priv. Ltr. Rul. 7924009.
[191] See *Tax-Exempt Organizations*, § 24.8(d) (College and University Audit Guidelines).
[192] *College and University Audit Guidelines* § 342(10)(3).
[193] *Id.* § 342(10)(2).
[194] *Id.* § 342(10)(4).
[195] *Id.* § 342(10)(5).
[196] *Id.* § 342(10)(6)(a).

- Determine who holds the patent or right to license technology derived from the research[197]

- Determine whether the institution is investing in licensee firms, either directly or through venture capital funds[198]

- Obtain a list of all publications that discuss the institution's research activities[199]

- Review copies of audit reports from the funding agency, if the institution conducts government-funded research[200]

- Review sample closed research projects[201]

- The term *fundamental research* does not include research carried on for the primary purpose of commercial or industrial application.[202]

§ 3.14 ELECTRIC COMPANIES' MEMBER INCOME

In the case of a tax-exempt mutual or cooperative electric company,[203] there is an exclusion from unrelated business income taxation for income that is treated as member income.[204]

§ 3.15 FOREIGN SOURCE INCOME

A look-through rule characterizes certain foreign source income—namely, income from insurance activities conducted by offshore captives of tax-exempt organizations—as unrelated business income.[205] Generally, U.S. shareholders of controlled foreign corporations must include in income their shares of the foreign entities' income, including certain insurance income.[206] The IRS, before creation of this statutory rule, treated these income inclusions as dividends, with the consequence that the income received by exempt organizations was excludable from tax.[207] This look-through rule, however, overrides the former treatment of this type of income as dividends.

This rule does not apply to amounts that are attributable to insurance of risks of the tax-exempt organization itself, certain of its exempt affiliates,[208] or

---

[197] *Id.* § 342(10)(6)(b).

[198] *Id.* § 342(10)(7).

[199] *Id.* § 342(10)(8).

[200] *Id.* § 342(10)(9).

[201] IRC § 512(b)(1)–(3).

[202] Reg. § 1.512(b)-1(f)(4).

[203] That is, an organization that is exempt from federal income tax by reason of IRC § 501(a) because it is described in IRC § 501(c)(12). See *Tax-Exempt Organizations*, § 18.5(b).

[204] IRC § 512(b)(18).

[205] IRC § 512(b)(17)(A).

[206] IRC §§ 951(a)(1)(A), 953.

[207] See § 3.2. *E.g.*, Priv. Ltr. Rul. 8819034.

[208] The determination as to whether an entity is an affiliate of an organization is made using rules similar to those applied in the context of the tax-exempt leasing rules. See *Tax-Exempt Organizations*, § 29.5(c). Also, two or more organizations generally are regarded as affiliates if the organizations are tax-exempt colleges, universities, hospitals, or other medical entities and they participate in an insurance arrangement whereby any profits from the arrangement are returned to the policyholders in their capacity as such. See *id.*

an officer or director of, or an individual who (directly or indirectly) performs services for, the exempt organization (or certain exempt affiliates), provided that the insurance primarily covers risks associated with the individual's performance of services in connection with the exempt organization (or exempt affiliates).[209]

§ 3.16 BROWNFIELD SITES GAIN

There is an exclusion from unrelated business taxable income for gain or loss from the sale or exchange of certain brownfield properties by a tax-exempt organization, whether the properties are held directly or indirectly through a partnership.[210] For property to qualify for the exclusion, the property must be acquired during a five-year period beginning January 1, 2005, and ending December 31, 2009, although the property may be disposed of after that date. Certain certification requirements must be met. Also, the exempt organization or the partnership of which it is a partner must expend a minimum amount on remediation expenses, which may be determined by averaging expenses across multiple qualifying brownfield properties for a period of as many as eight years.[211]

§ 3.17 RELIGIOUS ORDER RULE

The unrelated business income tax does not apply to a trade or business conducted by a tax-exempt religious or educational institution maintained by a religious order,[212] even if the business is an unrelated one, if: (1) the business consists of the provision of services under a license issued by a federal regulatory agency; (2) less than 10 percent of its net income is used for unrelated activities; and (3) the business has been operated by the order or educational institution since before May 27, 1969.[213]

Also, it must be established to the satisfaction of the IRS that the rates or other charges for these services are fully competitive with rates or other charges levied for the services by entities that are not tax-exempt organizations. Rates or other charges for the services are considered as being fully competitive in this regard if the rates charged in connection with such unrelated businesses are

---

[209] IRC § 512(b)(17)(B). In general, Stretch, Cooper & Snowling, *UBIT Rules Are Expanded to Include Income from Foreign Captives: Congressional Revenue Raisers Pick Another Pocket*, 16 Exempt Orgs. Tax Rev. 29 (no. 16, Jan. 1997).

[210] IRC § 512(b)(19). A *brownfield property* is a parcel of real property where there is a presence of a hazardous substance, pollutant, or contaminant which is complicating the expansion, redevelopment, or use of the property (IRC § 512(b)(19)(C)).

[211] This provision was added to the law in 2004. The Bush administration, in its fiscal year 2006 proposed budget, included among its revenue proposals a proposal to eliminate this exclusion, because of the complexity it added to the Internal Revenue Code; the difficulties of administration; concerns about the effectiveness of the provision, in that there is no limit on the amount of gain that is exempt from the unrelated business income tax; and the possibility that the exclusion could exempt from income tax real estate development considerably beyond mere environmental remediation.

[212] That is, an institution described in IRC § 170(b)(1)(A)(ii). See *Tax-Exempt Organizations*, § 11.3(a).

[213] IRC § 512(b)(15); Reg. § 1.512(b)-1(j)(1)(i)–(iii). It may amuse some aficionados of the federal tax law to know that this rule was enacted solely for the benefit of operation of a radio station by Loyola University in Louisiana; the statute is constructed so that the first letter of the three elements of the exclusion correspond with the station's call letters (WWL).

neither materially higher nor materially lower than the rates charged by similar businesses operating in the same general area.[214]

This exclusion is not available with respect to income from debt-financed property and the deductions attributable thereto.[215]

§ 3.18 CHARITABLE DEDUCTION

Tax-exempt organizations[216] are allowed, in computing their unrelated business taxable income (if any), a federal income tax charitable contribution deduction.[217] This deduction is allowable irrespective of whether the contribution is directly connected with the carrying on of the trade or business. This deduction may not exceed 10 percent of the organization's unrelated business taxable income computed without regard to the deduction.[218]

Trusts[219] are allowed a charitable contribution deduction;[220] the amount that is deductible is basically the same as that allowable pursuant to the rules applicable to charitable gifts by individuals.[221] Again, a deductible charitable gift from a trust need not be directly connected to the conduct of an unrelated business.

Qualification for either of these charitable contribution deductions requires that the payments be made to another organization; that is, the funds may not be used by the organization in administration of its own charitable programs. For example, a tax-exempt university that operates an unrelated business is allowed this charitable deduction for contributions to another exempt university for educational purposes, but is not allowed the deduction for amounts expended in administering its own educational program.[222]

There is no authority on the question as to the deductibility of a charitable gift to a related or affiliated entity, such as a contribution by a tax-exempt business league to its related educational foundation. The outcome should be that, as long as the two organizations are respected as separate entities for tax purposes, the donor entity with unrelated business is entitled to a charitable deduction for the gift inasmuch as the donor entity has contributed to another (albeit controlled) organization, rather than fund its "own" program.

---

[214] IRC § 512(b)(15); Reg. § 1.512(b)-1(j)(1)(iv).

[215] Reg. § 1.512(b)-1(j)(2).

[216] That is, entities described in IRC § 511(a). See § 1.7.

[217] IRC § 512(b)(10); Reg. § 1.512(b)-1(g)(1). This deduction is provided by IRC § 170. See Hopkins, *The Tax Law of Charitable Giving, Third Edition* (John Wiley & Sons, 2005) [hereinafter *Charitable Giving*], ch. 3.

[218] IRC § 512(b)(10); Reg. § 1.512(b)-1(g)(1) (which has not been revised to reflect the increase in this percentage limitation, in 1982, from 5 to 10 percent). *E.g.*, Indep. Ins. Agents of Huntsville, Inc. v. Comm'r, 63 T.C.M. 2468 (1992), *aff'd*, 998 F.2d 898 (11th Cir. 1993) (percentage limitation was applied with respect to the unrelated business income of a business league).

[219] That is, trusts described in IRC § 511(b)(2). See § 11.1, text accompanied by note 8.

[220] IRC § 512(b)(11); Reg. § 1.512(b)-1(g)(2).

[221] In applying the percentage limitations, the contribution base is determined by reference to the organization's unrelated business taxable income (computed with the charitable deduction), rather than by reference to adjusted gross income. See *Charitable Giving*, § 7.2.

[222] Reg. § 1.512(b)-1(g)(3).

§ 3.19 SPECIFIC DEDUCTION

In computing unrelated business taxable income, a specific deduction of $1,000 is available.[223] This deduction, however, is not allowed in computing net operating losses.[224] A diocese, province of a religious order, or a convention or association of churches is allowed, with respect to each parish, individual church, district, or other local unit, a specific deduction equal to the lower of $1,000 or the gross income derived from an unrelated business regularly carried on by such an entity.[225] This deduction is intended to eliminate imposition of the unrelated income tax in cases in which exaction of the tax would involve excessive costs of collection in relation any payments received by the government.[226]

As to this local unit rule, however, a diocese, province of a religious order, or a convention or association of churches is not entitled to a specific deduction for a local unit that, for a tax year, files a separate return. In that instance, the local unit may claim a specific deduction equal to the lower of $1,000 or the gross income derived from any unrelated trade or business that it regularly conducts.[227] For example, a tax-exempt association of churches, on the calendar-year basis, consists of local units A, B, C, and D. During 2006, A, B, C, and D derive gross income from unrelated businesses regularly carried on in the following respective amounts: $1,200, $800, $1,500, and $700. For that year, D files a separate return. The association may claim a specific deduction with respect to A of $1,000, $800 with respect to B, and $1,000 with respect to C. The association cannot claim a specific deduction with respect to D. D, however, may claim a specific deduction of $700 on its return.[228]

§ 3.20 NET OPERATING LOSSES

The net operating loss deduction[229] is allowed in computing unrelated business taxable income.[230] The net operating loss carryback or carryover (from a tax year for which the exempt organization is subject to the unrelated business income tax) is determined under the net operating loss deduction rules without taking into account any amount of income or deduction that is not included under the unrelated business income tax rules in computing unrelated business taxable income. For example, a loss attributable to an unrelated trade or business is not to be diminished by reason of the receipt of dividend income.[231]

For the purpose of computing the net operating loss deduction, any prior tax year for which a tax-exempt organization was not subject to the unrelated

---

[223] IRC § 512(b)(12); Reg. § 1.512(b)-1(h)(1). The IRS rejected the proposition that when a tax-exempt organization is engaged in two or more unrelated businesses, there is a specific deduction with respect to each business. Rev. Rul. 68-536, 1968-2 C.B. 244.
[224] IRC § 512(b)(12); Reg. § 1.512(b)-1(h)(1). See § 3.20.
[225] IRC § 512(b)(12); Reg. § 1.512(b)-1(h)(2).
[226] H.R. Rep. No. 2319, 81st Cong., 2d Sess. 37 (1950); S. Rep. No. 2375, 81st Cong., 2d Sess. 30 (1950).
[227] Reg. § 1.512(b)-1(h)(2)(i).
[228] Reg. § 1.512(b)-1(h)(2)(ii).
[229] IRC § 172.
[230] IRC § 512(b)(6); Reg. § 1.512(b)-1(e)(1).
[231] Reg. § 1.512(b)-1(e)(1).

business income tax may not be taken into account. Thus, if the organization was not subject to this tax for a preceding tax year, the net operating loss is not a carryback to such preceding tax year, and the net operating loss carryover to succeeding tax years is not reduced by the taxable income for such preceding tax year.[232]

A net operating loss carryback or carryover is allowed only from a tax year for which the exempt organization is subject to the unrelated business income tax rules.[233] In determining the span of years for which a net operating loss may be carried for purposes of the net operating loss deduction rules, tax years in which an exempt organization was not subject to the unrelated business income tax regime may be taken into account. For example, if an exempt organization is subject to the unrelated business income tax rules for the tax year 2001 and has a net operating loss for that year, the last tax year to which any part thereof may be carried over is the tax year 2006, irrespective of whether the organization was subject to the unrelated business income tax rules in any of the intervening tax years.[234]

---

[232] Reg. § 1.512(b)-1(e)(2).
[233] Reg. § 1.512(b)-1(e)(3).
[234] Reg. § 1.512(b)-1(e)(4).

CHAPTER FOUR

Exceptions

In addition to the exceptions to the unrelated business income rules provided in the law concerning the myriad of modifications,[1] there are various other exceptions from unrelated business income taxation. These exceptions pertain to convenience businesses, businesses conducted by volunteers, sales of gift items, certain entertainment activities, qualified trade shows, certain services provided by tax-exempt hospitals, certain gambling activities, receipt of certain associate member dues, distribution of low-cost articles, exchange or rental of certain membership or donor mailing lists, certain business activities of employees' associations, holding and sale of S corporation stock, and certain pole rental activities.

Two other categories of activities that may be considered to entail exceptions from the unrelated business rules are discussed elsewhere: corporate sponsorships[2] and travel and tour activities.[3]

§ 4.1 CONVENIENCE BUSINESSES

In the case of a tax-exempt charitable organization or a governmental college or university,[4] a business that is carried on by the organization primarily for the

---

[1] See ch. 3.
[2] See § 6.6.
[3] See §§ 9.1(c), 9.7.
[4] That is, an institution described in IRC § 511(a)(2)(B).

convenience of its members, students, patients,[5] officers, or employees[6] is excluded from treatment as an unrelated business. An example of the application of this exception is a laundry operated by an exempt college for the purpose of laundering dormitory linens and students' clothing.[7] (In contrast, a laundry operated by an exempt college apart from its campus, primarily for the purpose of making a profit from laundering the clothing of the general public, would be an unrelated business and outside the scope of this exception.) Similarly, an exempt university may operate, on its campus, vending machines that provide soft drinks and food, because the activity is carried on for the convenience of the institution's students and employees.[8] As another illustration, the provision by an exempt hospital of mobile services to its patients by means of specially designed vans was ruled to be a convenience business.[9]

A court expanded this concept by holding that physicians on the staff of a teaching hospital were "members" of the hospital, in that the term *members* "refers to any group of persons who are closely associated with the entity involved and who are necessary to the achievement of the organization's purposes."[10] The IRS disagreed with this opinion, however, and took the position that the "hospital's staff physicians are neither 'members' nor 'employees' of the hospital in their capacities as private practitioners of medicine."[11]

The exemption for revenue derived from an activity carried on primarily for the convenience of an organization's members was unsuccessfully invoked in a situation involving advertising in the organization's monthly journal. The lower court rejected the argument, deciding that the primary purpose of the advertising was to raise revenue.[12] On appeal, the higher court wrote that it could not conclude that the finding was clearly erroneous.[13]

Thus, implicit in this rule is the requirement that the convenience business be operated in furtherance of the exempt purposes of the organization; that is, there must be a substantial causal relationship[14] between conduct of the activity and advancement of exempt purposes. This element of the exception was illustrated in the case of a membership organization created to stimulate and foster public interest in the fine arts; it did so by promoting art exhibits, sponsoring cultural events, conducting educational programs, and disseminating information pertaining to the arts. Its activities were carried out in a building containing offices, galleries, music rooms, a library, a dining hall, and studio apartments where artists lived and worked. Though these apartments were rented only to

---

[5] The IRS promulgated criteria as to the meaning of the term *patient* in this context. Rev. Rul. 68-376, 1968-2 C.B. 246.

[6] IRC § 513(a)(2); Reg. § 1.513-1(e)(2). This exception also applies to a college laundry operated primarily for the convenience of the institution's officers and employees. Rev. Rul. 55-676, 1955-2 C.B. 266.

[7] Reg. § 1.513-1(e); S. Rep. No. 2375, 81st Cong., 2d Sess. 108 (1950).

[8] Rev. Rul. 81-19, 1981-1 C.B. 353. An organization that operated a book and supply store, as well as a cafeteria and restaurant, on the campus of an exempt university for the convenience of the student body and faculty was ruled by the IRS to be tax-exempt by reason of IRC § 501(c)(3). Rev. Rul. 58-194, 1958-1 C.B. 240.

[9] Priv. Ltr. Rul. 9841049.

[10] St. Luke's Hosp. of Kan. City v. United States, 494 F. Supp. 85, 92 (W.D. Mo. 1980).

[11] Rev. Rul. 85-109, 1985-2 C.B. 165, 166.

[12] Am. Coll. of Physicians v. United States, 83-2 U.S.T.C. ¶ 9652 (Cl. Ct. 1983).

[13] Am. Coll. of Physicians v. United States, 743 F.2d 1570 (Fed. Cir. 1984), *rev'd*, 475 U.S. 834 (1986).

[14] See § 2.7.

artists, only a few of the tenants were members of the organization. The apartments were not made available to the tenants on the basis of membership in the club, nor were there any other rental criteria that would advance the organization's exempt purposes. The organization provided maid and switchboard services to the tenants; the dining hall was also operated primarily to serve the tenants. The IRS ruled that neither the rental of the studio apartments nor the operation of the dining hall qualified for this exception.[15]

Read literally, this exception pertains only to the classes of individuals who have the requisite relationship directly with the tax-exempt organization; for example, it applies with respect to services carried on by an exempt hospital for the convenience of *its own* patients. Thus, a federal court of appeals refused to permit the convenience doctrine to be applied in a situation in which a for-profit medical clinic provided outpatient diagnostic services for the patients of an exempt health care provider. Rejecting the proposition that the patients of the clinic should be regarded as patients of the hospital for this purpose (so that the sales of pharmaceuticals by an exempt pharmacy to the clinic's patients would not be regarded as unrelated business), this appellate court wrote that the doctrine extends only to situations in which private physicians refer patients to an "outpatient diagnostic facility which is part of a hospital and separate from the physician's private clinic."[16]

This opinion notwithstanding, the IRS ruled that the convenience doctrine was available and applicable when an exempt organization's activities were for the convenience of patients of another, albeit related, exempt entity.[17] At the same time, the agency refused to extend the doctrine to embrace spouses and children of an exempt university's students.[18]

A business carried on by a tax-exempt organization for the convenience or comparable benefit of individuals may inherently be an exempt function and thus not need the protection of this exception. For example, it is common for exempt hospitals to maintain cafeterias and coffee shops on their premises for their medical staff, other employees, and visitors. The IRS is of the view that these are related businesses, because the conduct of them for employees enables the hospitals to operate more efficiently, and the conduct of them for visitors enables visitors to spend more time with the patients (the latter constitutes "supportive therapy that assists in patient treatment and encourages their recovery").[19]

§ 4.2 BUSINESSES CONDUCTED BY VOLUNTEERS

An endeavor in which substantially all of the work required to carry on the business is performed for the tax-exempt organization without compensation is exempt from the scope of the unrelated trade or business rules.[20] An example of

---

[15] Rev. Rul. 69-69, 1969-1 C.B. 159. The exception for rental income (§ 3.8) was not available because substantial services were rendered to the tenants.

[16] Carle Found. v. United States, 611 F.2d 1192, 1196 (7th Cir. 1979), *rev'g* 78-1 U.S.T.C. ¶ 9369 (E.D. Ill. 1978), *cert. denied*, 449 U.S. 824 (1980).

[17] Priv. Ltr. Rul. 9535023.

[18] Tech. Adv. Mem. 9645004.

[19] Rev. Rul. 69-268, 1969-1 C.B. 160.

[20] IRC § 513(a)(1); Reg. § 1.513-1(e)(1).

applicability of this exception is an exempt orphanage that operates a second-hand clothing store, selling to the general public, when substantially all of the work in operating the store is performed for the organization by volunteers.[21] Another illustration of this exception is the production and sale of phonograph records by a medical society, when the services of the performers were provided without compensation.[22] Still another illustration of this exception concerned a trade association that sold advertising in a commercial, unrelated manner, but avoided unrelated income taxation of the activity because the work involved was provided solely by volunteers.[23] Further, an advisory council to an exempt insurance board, serving a municipal board of education, received brokerage commissions that were required to be deposited in a special fund for public purposes. This commission income was not taxable to the board as unrelated business income, inasmuch as all of the council members' work was performed without compensation.[24]

As to the scope of this exception, Congress apparently intended to provide an exclusion from the definition of *unrelated trade or business* only for those unrelated business activities in which the performance of services is a material income-producing factor in carrying on the business and substantially all of the services are performed without compensation.[25] In reliance on the legislative history underlying this rule, the IRS ruled on the rental of heavy machinery under long-term lease agreements that required the lessees to provide insurance, pay the applicable taxes, and make and pay for most repairs; the functions of securing leases and processing rental payments were performed without compensation. The IRS found that this was not an unrelated trade or business excluded under this exception, as "no significant amount of labor [was] regularly required or involved in the kind of business carried on by the organization," and thus the performance of services in connection with the leasing activity was not a material income-producing factor in the business.[26]

A membership entity of a tax-exempt art museum published and sold a book containing recipes, all of which were contributed. Because substantially all of the work of preparing and selling the cookbook was performed by volunteers, the IRS ruled that the activity was not an unrelated business, by reason of this exception.[27]

In another case, a court ruled that this exception was defeated in part because free drinks provided to the collectors and cashiers, in connection with the conduct of a bingo game by a tax-exempt organization, were considered "liquid compensation."[28] This position, however, was rejected on appeal.[29] The same court subsequently held that this exception was not available in the case of an exempt

---

[21] Reg. § 1.513-1(e); S. Rep. No. 2375, 81st Cong., 2d Sess. 108 (1950).

[22] Greene County Med. Soc'y Found. v. United States, 345 F. Supp. 900 (W.D. Mo. 1972).

[23] Priv. Ltr. Rul. 9302023.

[24] Rev. Rul. 56-152, 1956-1 C.B. 56.

[25] H.R. Rep. No. 2319, 81st Cong., 2d Sess. 37 (1950); S. Rep. No. 2375, 81st Cong., 2d Sess. 107–08 (1950).

[26] Rev. Rul. 78-144, 1978-1 C.B. 168.

[27] Tech. Adv. Mem. 8211002. Having reached this conclusion, the IRS declined to apply the exception for contributed merchandise (see § 4.3).

[28] Waco Lodge No. 166, Benevolent & Protective Order of Elks v. Comm'r, 42 T.C.M. 1202 (1981).

[29] Waco Lodge No. 166, Benevolent & Protective Order of Elks v. Comm'r, 696 F.2d 372 (5th Cir. 1983).

organization that regularly carried on gambling activities, because the dealers and other individuals received tips from patrons of the games.[30] In another case, this court found that an exempt religious order that operated a farm was not taxable on the income derived from the farming operations, because the farm was maintained by the uncompensated labor of the members of the order.[31]

For an activity to be eligible for this exception, the activity must be carried on by the tax-exempt organization. This criterion can become an issue when an exempt organization outsources one or more functions.[32]

The matter of substantiality does not arise, of course, when all of the work of conducting the business is performed without compensation.[33] When the exempt organization uses one or more compensated persons (whether as employees or independent contractors), substantiality is generally assessed in terms of time expended. Although the term *substantially all* is not defined in this setting, it is defined in other contexts to mean at least 85 percent, and the IRS follows that rule when applying the volunteer exception.[34]

The volunteer exception was held by a court to be unavailable when 77 percent of the services were provided to a tax-exempt organization without compensation.[35] By contrast, another court ruled that the exception was available when the volunteer services amounted to 94 percent of total hours worked.[36] The IRS ruled that the exception was available when the percentages of volunteer labor were 87 percent,[37] 91 percent,[38] and 97 percent.[39]

This exception references receipt of compensation. Thus, individuals who do not receive any economic benefits in exchange for their services to a tax-exempt organization are uncompensated workers (*volunteers*).[40] Mere reimbursement of expenses incurred by volunteers is not compensation.[41] Economic benefits, however, can be considered compensation, even if not formally cast as a salary or fee for service,[42] unless they are incidental.[43] In some circumstances, nonmonetary benefits can constitute compensation.[44]

---

[30] Executive Network Club, Inc. v. Comm'r, 69 T.C.M. 1680 (1995). A court held that this exception was not available where individuals operating bingo games for a tax-exempt organization were paid a small hourly rate and the payments were subject to tax withholding. Smith-Dodd Businessman's Ass'n, Inc. v. Comm'r, 65 T.C. 620 (1975).

[31] St. Joseph Farms of Indep. Bros. of the Congregation of Holy Cross, S.W. Province, Inc. v. Commissioner, 85 T.C. 9 (1985), *appeal dismissed* (7th Cir. 1986).

[32] *E.g.*, Tech. Adv. Mem. 8041007.

[33] *E.g.*, Rev. Rul. 74-361, 1974-2 C.B. 159.

[34] *E.g.*, Tech. Adv. Mem. 8433010.

[35] Waco Lodge No. 166, Benevolent & Protective Order of Elks v. Comm'r, 696 F.2d 372 (5th Cir. 1983).

[36] St. Joseph Farms of Indep. Bros. of the Congregation of Holy Cross, S.W. Province, Inc. v. Comm'r, 85 T.C. 9 (1985).

[37] Priv. Ltr. Rul. 7806039.

[38] Priv. Ltr. Rul. 9544029.

[39] Tech. Adv. Mem. 8040014.

[40] *E.g.*, Tech. Adv. Mem. 8211002.

[41] *E.g.*, Greene County Med. Soc'y Found. v. United States, 345 F. Supp. 900 (W.D. Mo. 1972).

[42] *E.g.*, Executive Network Club, Inc. v. Comm'r, 69 T.C.M. 1680 (1995).

[43] *E.g.*, Waco Lodge No. 166, Benevolent & Protective Order of Elks v. Comm'r, 696 F.2d 372, 375 (5th Cir. 1983) (free drinks were considered a "trifling inducement").

[44] See, *e.g.*, Shiloh Youth Revival Ctrs. v. Comm'r, 88 T.C. 565 (1987). In general, Izuel & Park, *The Application of the Royalty and Volunteer Exceptions to Unrelated Business Taxable Income*, 44 Exempt Orgs. Tax Rev. 299 (no. 3, June 2004).

§ 4.3 SALES OF GIFT ITEMS

The term *unrelated trade or business* does not include a business, conducted by a tax-exempt organization, that constitutes the selling of merchandise, substantially all of which has been received by the organization by means of contributions.[45] This exception is available for thrift shops operated by tax-exempt organizations that sell donated clothes, books, furniture, and similar items (merchandise) to the general public, with the proceeds going to the exempt organizations.[46]

Despite its origin, however, this exception is not confined to businesses that are thrift shops, either independent stores or thrift shops operated by tax-exempt organizations such as schools. For example, the IRS ruled that an exempt organization could solicit contributions of home heating oil from individuals who had converted to gas heat, extract the oil from fuel tanks, and sell it to the general public, and not be involved in an unrelated business by reason of this exception.[47] Likewise, the agency held that an exempt charitable organization may maintain a property donation program, through which contributed vehicles and other properties are sold to generate funds; such a program is not considered an unrelated business by virtue of this exception.[48]

As noted, substantially all of the merchandise involved must have been contributed. In one instance, the IRS held that the exception was available when less than 5 percent of total sales was of purchased items.[49] For this exception to apply, however, the tax-exempt organization itself must be in the requisite business; it is not enough to have the business owned and operated by an independent contractor that merely uses an exempt organization's name and pays over certain receipts to the exempt organization.[50]

§ 4.4 ENTERTAINMENT ACTIVITIES

Another exception from unrelated business treatment applies to the conduct of entertainment at fairs and expositions.[51] This rule applies to charitable, social welfare, labor, agricultural, and horticultural organizations[52] that regularly conduct, as a substantial tax-exempt purpose, an agricultural and educational fair or exposition.[53]

This type of activity has long been recognized as a tax-exempt function, classified as charitable, educational, and/or agricultural undertakings.[54] For

---

[45] IRC § 513(a)(3); Reg. § 1.513-1(e)(3).
[46] Reg. § 1.513-1(e). The IRS ruled that the operation of a separately incorporated thrift shop to raise funds for a group of specified exempt organizations may qualify for exemption. Rev. Rul. 71-581, 1971-2 C.B. 236.
[47] Priv. Ltr. Rul. 8116095.
[48] Priv. Ltr. Rul. 200230005.
[49] Priv. Ltr. Rul. 8122007.
[50] Tech. Adv. Mem. 8041007. Likewise, when the thrift stores were in a separate corporation, the operation of them was not imputed to a related tax-exempt organization for purposes of this exception. Disabled Am. Veterans Serv. Found., Inc. v. Comm'r, 29 T.C.M. 202 (1970).
[51] IRC § 513(d)(1), (2).
[52] IRC § 501 (c)(3), (4), or (5). See Hopkins, *The Law of Tax-Exempt Organizations, Eighth Edition* (John Wiley & Sons, 2003) [hereinafter *Tax-Exempt Organizations*] chs. 5–10, 12, & 15, respectively.
[53] IRC § 513(d)(2)(C).
[54] For example, the term *educational* pertains to the education of the public on subjects useful to the individual and beneficial to the community. Reg. § 1.501(c)(3)-1(d)(3)(b).

example, decades ago the IRS ruled that an organization with the purpose of instructing individuals on agricultural matters can further that purpose by conducting annual public fairs and exhibitions.[55] These events feature the display of farm equipment, animals, food products, and the like; offer recreational activities, such as midway shows, rodeos, and refreshment stands; and include contests and other competitive events, usually with prizes awarded. The IRS wrote that the overall activities of these fairs are "conducted in such a fashion and on such subjects as will enlighten the viewers and participants on the newest and best techniques of farming, and on other matters useful and beneficial to them and to the community."[56] The agency added that an organization "whose purpose and reason for existence is to educate the public in useful and beneficial subjects does not fail to be operated to educate merely because some entertainment is provided to attract the public."[57] The courts have generally followed this view.[58]

Nevertheless, the IRS and the courts began to regard activities that are collateral to shows and exhibitions as nonexempt functions, perhaps as unrelated businesses. For example, years before this statutory exception was enacted, the IRS ruled regarding a tax-exempt organization that, in conjunction with its annual fair, conducted a two-week horse racing meet featuring parimutuel betting. Finding these races to be regularly carried on in a manner similar to that of commercial race tracks, the IRS concluded that the activity constituted an unrelated business, because the conduct of the races did not contribute importantly to the educational activities of the fair and was not a type of recreational activity intended to attract the public to the fair's educational features.[59]

Likewise, a court, having rejected the argument that rental income received by a tax-exempt organization was excludable from treatment as unrelated business income (because the amount of ostensible rent was tied to profits generated by the ostensible tenant[60]), also rejected the contention that the rental activity was related to horse racing conducted at the fair. The rental agreement provided that the rental activity (auctioning of horses) would take place at times of the year other than during the time the society was carrying on its annual fair; the rental activity was thus held not to be in conjunction with the fair.[61]

To illustrate the difference in approach following enactment of the special rules, a court held that automobile races held by an organization during its annual fair (and arguably those held immediately prior thereto) were qualified public entertainment activities (see below).[62] The organization's other races, held when the fair was not being conducted (some were as much as three months before or after the fair), were found not to warrant treatment as public entertainment activity, because they were not intended to attract the public to the fair.

---

[55] Rev. Rul. 67-216, 1967-2 C.B. 180.

[56] *Id*. at 181.

[57] *Id*.

[58] *E.g.*, Orange County Agric. Soc'y, Inc. v. Comm'r, 893 F.2d 529 (2d Cir. 1990), *aff'g* 55 T.C.M. 1602 (1988).

[59] Rev. Rul. 68-505, 1968-2 C.B. 248.

[60] See § 3.8(b).

[61] Ohio County & Indep. Agric. Societies, Del. County Fair v. Comm'r, 43 T.C.M. 1126 (1982).

[62] Orange County Agric. Soc'y, Inc. v. Comm'r, 55 T.C.M. 1602 (1988), *aff'd*, 893 F.2d 529 (2d Cir. 1990).

Thus, absent this statutory exception, many of these types of activities collateral to fairs and expositions would be taxable as unrelated businesses. One court reviewed the legislative history of these rules and wrote that they exclude from the concept of unrelated business "horse racing at county fairs and renting display space at trade shows."[63]

Pursuant to these statutory rules, the term *unrelated trade or business* does not include *qualified public entertainment activities* of an eligible organization.[64] This latter term is defined to mean any "entertainment or recreational activity of a kind traditionally conducted at fairs or expositions promoting agricultural and educational purposes, including, but not limited to, any activity one of the purposes of which is to attract the public to fairs or expositions or to promote the breeding of animals or the development of products or equipment."[65] Hence, unrelated income taxation is not imposed with respect to the operation of a qualified public entertainment activity that meets one of the following conditions: the public entertainment activity is conducted (1) in conjunction with an international, national, state, regional, or local fair or exposition; (2) in accordance with state law that permits that activity to be conducted solely by an eligible type of tax-exempt organization or by a governmental entity; or (3) in accordance with state law that permits that activity to be conducted under license for not more than 20 days in any year and that permits the organization to pay a lower percentage of the revenue from this activity than the state requires from other organizations.[66]

To qualify under this rule, the tax-exempt organization must regularly conduct, as a substantial exempt purpose, a fair or exposition that is both agricultural and educational. The Senate Finance Committee report that accompanied these rules stated that a book fair held by an exempt university is not sheltered by this provision, inasmuch as this kind of fair is not agricultural in nature.[67]

A charitable, social welfare, labor, agricultural, or horticultural organization is not to be considered as not entitled to tax exemption solely because of its qualified public entertainment activities.

§ 4.5 TRADE SHOWS

Activities that promote demand for industry products and services, like advertising and other promotional activities, generally constitute unrelated businesses if carried on for the production of income. In this context, the federal tax law provides what the IRS termed a "narrow exception"[68] for certain tax-exempt organizations that conduct industry-promotion activities in connection with a convention, annual meeting, or trade show. This exception with respect to trade show activities[69] is available for qualifying organizations: namely,

[63] Clarence LaBelle Post No. 217, Veterans of Foreign Wars v. United States, 580 F.2d 270, 273 (8th Cir. 1978).
[64] IRC § 513(d)(1).
[65] IRC § 513(d)(2)(A).
[66] IRC § 513(d)(2)(B).
[67] S. Rep. No. 94-938, 94th Cong., 2d Sess. 602 (1976).
[68] Rev. Rul. 2004-112, 2004-51 I.R.B. 985.
[69] IRC § 513(d)(1), (3); Reg. § 1.513-3(a)(1), (b).

exempt labor, agricultural, and horticultural organizations; business leagues;[70] and charitable and social welfare organizations[71] that regularly conduct, as a substantial exempt purpose, shows that stimulate interest in and demand for the products of a particular industry or segment of industry or that educate persons in attendance regarding new developments or products or services related to the exempt activities of the organization.[72] This provision overruled contrary IRS determinations.[73]

Under these rules, the term *unrelated trade or business* does not include qualified convention and trade show activities of an eligible organization.[74] The phrase *convention, annual meeting, or trade show* is defined to mean any "activity of a kind traditionally conducted at conventions, annual meetings, or trade shows, including but not limited to, any activity one of the purposes of which is to attract persons in an industry generally (without regard to membership in the sponsoring organization) as well as members of the public to the show for the purpose of displaying industry products or services, or to educate persons engaged in the industry in the development of new products and services or new rules and regulations affecting the industry."[75] This term thus refers to a "specific event at which individuals representing a particular industry and members of the general public gather in person at one location during a certain period of time."[76]

A *qualified convention and trade show activity* is a convention and trade show activity that is: (1) carried on by a qualifying organization; (2) conducted in conjunction with an international, national, state, regional, or local convention, annual meeting, or show; (3) sponsored by a qualifying organization that has as one of its purposes in sponsoring the activity the promotion and stimulation of interest in and demand for the products and services of the industry involved in general or the education of persons in attendance regarding new developments or products and services related to the exempt activities of the organization; and (4) designed to achieve this purpose through the character of the exhibits and the extent of the industry products displayed.[77] It is the nature of the activities and their connection to a specific convention, annual meeting, or trade show that distinguishes qualified convention and trade show activity from other types of advertising and promotional activities conducted for the benefit of an industry.[78] Thus, an example of such qualified activity is an exempt business league that conducted semiannual trade shows at an exhibition facility, with each of the shows occurring over a period of 10 consecutive days.[79]

---

[70] IRC § 501(c)(5), (6). See *Tax-Exempt Organizations*, chs. 15 & 13, respectively.

[71] IRC § 501(c)(3), (4). See *Tax-Exempt Organizations*, chs. 5–10 & 12, respectively.

[72] IRC § 513(d)(3)(C).

[73] Rev. Ruls. 75-516 through 75-520, 1975-2 C.B. 220–226 (holding, *inter alia*, that income received by an exempt business league at its convention or trade show from renting display space may constitute unrelated business income if selling by exhibitors is permitted at the show). Also Rev. Rul. 67-219, 1967-1 C.B. 210; Rev. Rul. 58-224, 1958-1 C.B. 242. Subsequently, these rulings were revoked or rendered obsolete by the IRS. Rev. Rul. 85-123, 1985-2 C.B. 168.

[74] IRC § 513(d)(1).

[75] IRC § 513(d)(3)(A); Reg. § 1.513-3(c)(4).

[76] Rev. Rul. 2004-112, 2004-51 I.R.B. 985.

[77] IRC § 513(d)(3)(B); Reg. § 1.513-3(c)(2).

[78] Rev. Rul. 2004-112, 2004-51 I.R.B. 985.

[79] *Id.*

The income that is excluded from taxation by these rules is derived from the rental of display space to exhibitors. This is so even though the exhibitors who rent the space are permitted to sell or solicit orders, as long as the show is a qualified trade show or a qualified convention and trade show.[80] This exclusion is also available with respect to a supplier's exhibit[81] that is conducted by a qualifying organization in conjunction with a qualified convention or trade show.

As an illustration, an exempt business league, formed to promote the construction industry, had as its membership manufacturers of heavy construction machinery, many of whom owned, rented, or leased one or more digital computers produced by various computer manufacturers. This organization was a qualifying one that regularly held an annual meeting. At this meeting, a national industry sales campaign and methods of consumer financing for heavy construction machinery were discussed. Also, new construction machinery developed for use in the industry was on display, with representatives of the various manufacturers present to promote their machinery. Both members and nonmembers attended this portion of the conference. In addition, computer manufacturers were present to educate the organization's members. Although this aspect of the conference constituted a supplier's exhibit, the income earned from this activity did not constitute unrelated business income to the business league, because the activity was conducted as part of a qualified trade show.[82]

Another illustration is based on the facts in the preceding example, except that the only goods or services displayed are those of suppliers, namely, the computer manufacturers. Order-taking and selling were permitted. Members' exhibits were not maintained. Taken alone, this supplier's exhibit would have constituted a supplier show and not a qualified convention or trade show. In this situation, however, the rental of exhibition space to the suppliers was not an unrelated business. It was conducted by a qualifying organization in conjunction with a qualified convention or trade show. The show (the annual meeting) was a qualified convention or trade show because one of its purposes was the promotion and stimulation of interest in and demand for the products or services of the industry through the character of the annual meeting.[83]

In another example, an exempt business league conducts an annual show at which its members exhibit their products and services in order to promote public interest in the line of business. Potential customers are invited to the show; order-taking and sales are permitted. The organization secures the exhibition facility, undertakes the planning and direction of the show, and maintains exhibits designed to promote the line of business in general. The show is a qualified convention or trade show, and the provision of exhibit space to individual members is a qualified trade show activity, not an unrelated business.[84]

---

[80] Reg. § 1.513-3(d)(1).

[81] A *suppliers' exhibit* is one in which the exhibitors display goods or services that are supplied to, rather than by, the members of the qualifying organization in the conduct of the members' own trades or businesses. Reg. § 1.513-3(d)(2).

[82] Reg. § 1.513-3(e), Example (1).

[83] *Id.*, Example (2).

[84] *Id.*, Example (3).

Another illustration concerns an exempt business league that sponsored an annual show. As the sole activity of the show, suppliers to the members of the organization exhibited their products and services for the purpose of stimulating the sale of these products and services. Order-taking and selling were permitted. This show was a supplier's show and did not meet the definition of a qualified convention or trade show, in that it did not satisfy any of the three alternative bases for qualification. First, the show did not stimulate interest in the members' products through the character of product exhibits; the only products exhibited were those of suppliers, not members. Second, the show did not stimulate interest in members' products through conferences or seminars; these activities were not conducted at the show. Third, the show did not meet the definition of a qualified show on the basis of educational activities; the exhibition of suppliers' products was designed primarily to stimulate interest in and sale of the suppliers' products. Thus, the organization's provision of exhibition space was not a qualified convention or trade show activity, and income derived from the rental of exhibition space to suppliers was unrelated business income.[85] Nonetheless, income from a suppliers' show is not unrelated business income when the displays are educational in nature and soliciting and selling in connection with the displays are prohibited.[86]

Another aspect of this matter may resolve the tax issue for many tax-exempt organizations not expressly covered by these rules. This relates to the fact that an unrelated business must be *regularly carried on* before the revenue from the business can be regarded as unrelated business income.[87] Thus, the net income derived by an exempt organization (irrespective of the statutory basis for its tax exemption) from the conduct of a trade show cannot be taxable as unrelated business income if the trade show is not regularly carried on. A court opinion supports the premise that the conduct of a typical trade show is not an activity that is regularly carried on.[88] This court held that an exempt organization that annually sponsored a vaudeville show did not generate any unrelated business income from the activity because the show was not regularly carried on—rather, it was an "intermittent activity."[89] Consequently, to the extent that an annual trade or similar show of an exempt organization can be regarded as an intermittent activity, it will not give rise to unrelated business income, irrespective of the exempt status of the organization and without regard to invocation of these special rules. It must be noted, however, that in measuring regularity, the IRS sometimes looks not only to the time expended in conducting the activity itself but also to the time expended in preparing for the activity and any time expended afterward that is still related to the activity.[90]

---

[85] *Id.*, Example (4). The legislative history of these statutory rules suggests, however, that the exclusion is applicable with respect to shows that are suppliers' shows in their entirety. S. Rep. No. 94-938, 94th Cong., 2d Sess. 601–603 (1976).

[86] Rev. Rul. 75-516, 1975-2 C.B. 220. In general, see Fones, *Taxation of Trade Shows and Public Entertainment Activities*, 64 A.B.A.J. 913 (1978).

[87] See § 2.5.

[88] Suffolk County Patrolmen's Benevolent Ass'n, Inc. v. Comm'r, 77 T.C. 1314 (1982).

[89] *Id.* at 1321, 1322.

[90] See § 2.5(d).

A tax-exempt organization may sponsor and perform educational and supporting services for a trade show (such as use of its name, promotion of attendance, planning of exhibits and demonstrations, and provision of lectures for the exhibits and demonstrations) without having the compensation for its efforts taxed as unrelated business income, as long as the trade show is not a sales facility.[91] The IRS ruled that this type of activity both stimulates interest in and demand for services of the profession involved (the organization being an exempt business league) and educates the members on matters of professional interest.

The IRS issued guidance as to when Internet activities conducted by qualifying organizations (or at least exempt business leagues) fall within this exception for qualified convention and trade show activity.[92]

§ 4.6 HOSPITAL SERVICES

An exception from classification of an activity as unrelated business is applicable with respect to the performance of certain services for small hospitals. The IRS's position generally is that income that a tax-exempt hospital derives from providing services to other exempt hospitals constitutes unrelated business income to the service-provider hospital, on the theory that the provision of services to other hospitals is not an activity that is substantially related to the exempt purpose of the provider hospital.[93] Congress carved out an exception to this rule for the provision of services to small hospitals.

This special rule[94] applies when a tax-exempt hospital[95] furnishes certain services only to other exempt hospitals, as long as (1) the service is provided solely to hospitals that have facilities to serve no more than 100 inpatients; (2) the service would, if performed by the recipient hospital, constitute an activity consistent with that hospital's tax-exempt purposes; and (3) the service is provided at a fee not in excess of actual cost, including straight-line depreciation and a reasonable rate of return on the capital goods used to provide the service. The services provided must be confined to data processing, purchasing (including the purchasing of insurance on a group basis), warehousing, billing and collection (including the purchase of patron accounts receivable on a recourse basis), food, clinical, industrial engineering, laboratory, printing, communications, record center, and personnel (including selection, testing, training, and education of personnel) services.[96]

This change in the law was implemented to enable a number of small hospitals to receive services from a single institution instead of providing them directly or creating a separate organization to provide the services. Language in

---

[91] Rev. Rul. 78-240, 1978-1 C.B. 170.

[92] See § 10.6, text accompanied by note 64.

[93] Rev. Rul. 69-633, 1969-2 C.B. 121.

[94] IRC § 513(e); Reg. § 1.513-6(a).

[95] That is, an organization described in IRC § 170(b)(1)(A)(iii). Reg. § 1.513(6)(b). See *Tax-Exempt Organizations*, §§ 6.2(a), 11.3(a).

[96] IRC § 501(e)(1)(A); Reg. § 1.501(e)-1(c)(1). See *Tax-Exempt Organizations*, § 10.4. A conspicuous omission in this list of services is the performance of laundry services. Reg. § 1.501(e)-1(c)(2). See *Tax-Exempt Organizations*, § 6.9.

the legislative history, however, is somewhat broader than the specifics of the statutory rule: The Senate Finance Committee explanation stated that a "hospital is not engaged in an unrelated trade or business simply because it provides services to other hospitals if those services could have been provided on a tax-free basis, by a cooperative organization consisting of several tax-exempt hospitals."[97]

Application of this exception requires that the service be provided at a fee not in excess of actual cost, including straight-line depreciation and a reasonable rate of return on the capital goods used to provide the service.[98] The Medicare program formulations are a "safe harbor" for use in complying with the limitations on fees. Thus, a rate of return on capital goods will be considered reasonable as long as it does not exceed, on an annual basis, a percentage that is based on the average of the rates of interest on special issues of public debt obligations issued to the Federal Hospital Insurance Trust Fund for each of the months included in the tax year of the hospital during which the capital goods are used in providing the service. Determinations as to the cost of services and the applicable rate of return are to be in accordance with the Medicare rules,[99] which permit a health care facility to be reimbursed under the Medicare program for the reasonable cost of its services—including, in the case of certain proprietary facilities, a reasonable return on equity capital.[100]

As an illustration, a large metropolitan tax-exempt hospital provided various services to other exempt hospitals. This hospital furnished a purchasing service to hospitals A and B, a data processing service to hospitals C and D, and a food service to hospitals E and F. These hospitals, other than A, had facilities to serve no more than 100 inpatients. The services were furnished at cost to these hospitals, except that hospital C was charged a fee in excess of cost for its use of the data processing service. The purchasing service constituted an unrelated business conducted by the provider hospital, because it was not provided solely to hospitals having facilities to serve no more than 100 inpatients. The data processing service was an unrelated business because it was provided to a hospital at a fee in excess of cost. The food service operation was not an unrelated business, because it satisfied the requirements of this exception.[101]

§ 4.7 GAMBLING ACTIVITIES

In general, gambling activities by tax-exempt organizations will constitute unrelated business. Bingo game income realized by most tax-exempt organizations, however, is not subject to unrelated business income taxation.[102] This exclusion applies only when the bingo game is not conducted on a commercial basis and where the game does not violate state or local laws.[103]

---

[97] S. Rep. No. 94-938 (pt. 2), 94th Cong., 2d Sess. 76 (1976).

[98] IRC § 513(e)(3).

[99] 42 U.S.C. § 1395x(v)(1)(A), (B).

[100] Reg. § 1.513-6(a)(3).

[101] Reg. § 1.513-6(c).

[102] IRC § 513(f); Reg. § 1.513-5(a). The rules pertaining to this exception are inapplicable to a bingo game that is otherwise excluded from consideration as an unrelated business because substantially all of the work is performed without compensation. Reg. § 1.513-5(b).

[103] Reg. § 1.513-5(c); H.R. Rep. No. 95-1608, 95th Cong., 2d Sess 6-7(1978).

More specifically, this exception is not available with respect to a bingo game conducted in a jurisdiction in which bingo games are ordinarily carried out on a commercial basis. Bingo games are "ordinarily carried out on a commercial basis" within a jurisdiction if they are regularly carried on[104] by for-profit organizations in any part of that jurisdiction. Normally, the entire state will constitute the appropriate jurisdiction for determining whether bingo games are ordinarily carried out on a commercial basis. If, however, state law permits local jurisdictions to determine whether bingo games may be conducted by for-profit organizations, or if state law limits or confines the conduct by for-profit organizations to specific local jurisdictions, then the local jurisdiction will constitute the appropriate jurisdiction for determining whether bingo games are ordinarily carried out on a commercial basis.[105]

For example, this exception was held to be unavailable because the bingo game in question was illegal under state law as being a lottery.[106] Absent this exception, then, bingo game operations of exempt organizations would be treated as the conduct of unrelated business.[107] Indeed, the argument that the operation of bingo games does not amount to the conduct of business was rejected by a court.[108]

A *bingo game* is a game of chance played with cards that are generally printed with five rows of five squares each. Participants place markers over randomly called numbers on the cards in an attempt to form a preselected pattern, such as a horizontal, vertical, or diagonal line, or all four corners. The first participant to form the preselected pattern is the winner of the game. The term *bingo game* means any game of bingo in which all wagers are placed, all winners are determined, and all prizes or other property are distributed in the presence of all persons placing wagers in that game.[109] Consequently, the term does not refer to any other game of chance, such as keno games, dice games, card games, and lotteries;[110] the conduct of a "pull-tab operation" is not embraced by the exception.[111] This view as to the scope of the definition of the term was reflected in a court opinion holding that proceeds attributable to an organization's "instant bingo" activities were not protected by the exception, inasmuch as individuals could play and win in isolation.[112]

The reach of this exception is illustrated by the following illustration.[113] A tax-exempt church conducted weekly bingo games in a state where state and local laws provided that bingo games could be conducted by exempt organizations. For-profit businesses did not conduct bingo games in the state. Because

[104] See § 2.5.
[105] Reg. § 1.513-5(c)(2).
[106] Waco Lodge No. 166, Benevolent & Protective Order of Elks v. Comm'r, 42 T.C.M. 1202 (1981).
[107] *E.g.*, Clarence LaBelle Post No. 217, Veterans of Foreign Wars v. United States, 580 F.2d 270 (8th Cir. 1978).
[108] Smith-Dodd Businessman's Ass'n, Inc. v. Comm'r, 65 T.C. 620 (1975).
[109] Reg. § 1.513-5(d).
[110] *Id.*
[111] Tech. Adv. Mem. 8602001.
[112] Julius M. Israel Lodge of B'nai B'rith No. 2113 v. Comm'r, 70 T.C.M. 673 (1995), *aff'd*, 98 F.3d 190 (5th Cir. 1996).
[113] This example and the two that follow assume that the bingo games referred to are operated by individuals who are compensated for their services. See *supra* note 102.

the church's bingo games were not conducted in violation of state or local law, and were not the type of activity ordinarily carried out on a commercial basis in the state, these bingo games were not regarded as unrelated business.[114]

As another illustration, an exempt rescue squad conducts weekly bingo games in a state that has a statute prohibiting all forms of gambling, including bingo games. This law, however, is not generally enforced by state officials against local charitable organizations, such as the rescue squad, that conduct bingo games to raise funds. Nonetheless, because bingo games are illegal under this state's law, these bingo games constitute unrelated business, irrespective of the degree to which the pertinent state law is enforced.[115]

In another example, two exempt veterans' organizations operate in a state that permits the conduct of bingo games by tax-exempt organizations. This state's law also permits bingo games to be conducted by for-profit organizations in a particular city, which is a resort community. Several for-profit organizations conduct nightly bingo games in this city. One of these veterans' organizations also conducts weekly bingo games in this city. The other veterans' organization conducts weekly bingo games in the county in which this city is located. Because state law confines the conduct of bingo games by for-profit organizations to this city, and because bingo games are regularly carried on there by these organizations, the bingo games conducted by the veterans' organization in that city constitute unrelated business. By contrast, the bingo games conducted by the other veterans' organization in the county, and outside of this city, are not regarded as unrelated business.[116]

By virtue of the way the organizations are taxed, the bingo game exception is not available to tax-exempt social clubs, voluntary employees' beneficiary associations, political organizations, and homeowners' associations.[117]

The term *unrelated trade or business* does not include any trade or business that consists of the conduct of games of chance, conducted after June 30, 1981, which, under state law (in effect as of October 5, 1983), can be conducted only by nonprofit organizations.[118] This exception, however, is applicable only with respect to the law of the state of North Dakota.[119]

§ 4.8 ASSOCIATE MEMBER DUES

Some tax-exempt associations may encounter an issue as to the tax treatment of dues derived from associate members (or affiliate or patron members), although the intensity of activity in this area has declined in recent years. In some instances, these dues are treated as forms of unrelated business income, on the

---

[114] Reg. § 1.513-5(c)(3), Example (1).

[115] *Id.*, Example (2).

[116] *Id.*, Example (3).

[117] See ch. 6. As to political organizations, see *Tax-Exempt Organizations*, ch. 17.

[118] Tax Reform Act of 1984, § 311.

[119] Tax Reform Act of 1986, § 1834. This clarification in 1986 would have caused retroactive taxation of this type of revenue derived by tax-exempt organizations in states other than North Dakota. The Technical Corrections and Miscellaneous Revenue Act of 1988 (§ 6201), however, made the 1986 clarification effective for games of chance conducted after October 22, 1986 (the date of enactment of the 1986 technical correction), so that revenue derived by exempt organizations from games of chance conducted prior to the 1986 effective date in any state is governed by the rules enacted in 1984. The IRS issued an explanation of the law on this point in Ann. 89-138, 1989-45 I.R.B. 41.

ground that the associate member is paying for a specific service or to gain access to the regular membership for purposes of selling products or services.[120] Thus, in one instance, the IRS's lawyers recommended taxation of associate members dues, when the associates allegedly joined solely to obtain coverage under the association's automobile, health, dental, and farm owners' insurance programs.[121] In another instance, IRS legal counsel recommended taxation (as advertising income) of the dues paid by associate members for listings in a variety of publications, allegedly to make them accessible to the regular members; the IRS creatively recast the dues as *access fees*.[122] Taxation of dues is more likely when the associate members do not receive exempt function benefits, serve as directors or officers, or vote on association matters, and otherwise lack any meaningful right or opportunity to participate in the affairs of the organization.

The first court opinion on the point held that dues collected by a tax-exempt labor organization from persons who were not regular active members of the organization, who became members so as to be able to participate in a health insurance plan sponsored by the organization, constituted unrelated business income.[123] The court concluded that this special class of members was created to generate revenue and not to contribute importantly to an exempt purpose. The fact that the organization generated substantial net revenues through the sale of these memberships was considered evidence that revenue-raising was the principal intent underlying establishment of this membership category.

In the case of tax-exempt labor, agricultural, and horticultural organizations,[124] the IRS stated that dues payments from associate members will not be regarded as unrelated business income unless, for the relevant period, the membership category was formed or availed of for the principal purpose of producing unrelated income.[125] This aspect of the law was subsequently altered by statute, however, in that certain dues payments to exempt agricultural or horticultural organizations are exempt from unrelated business income taxation.[126] Specifically, if a tax-exempt agricultural or horticultural organization[127] requires annual dues not exceeding $100 (indexed for inflation[128]) to be paid in order to be a member of the organization, no portion of the dues may be considered unrelated business income because of any benefits or privileges to which these members are entitled.[129]

---

[120] This issue is identical to that raised in the context of tax-exempt labor unions (see text accompanied by *infra* notes 124–125).

[121] Tech. Adv. Mem. 9416002.

[122] Tech. Adv. Mem. 9345004.

[123] Nat'l League of Postmasters v. Comm'r, 69 T.C.M. 2569 (1995), *aff'd*, 86 F.3d 59 (4th Cir. 1996).

[124] See *Tax-Exempt Organizations*, ch. 15.

[125] Rev. Proc. 95-21, 1995-1 C.B. 686.

[126] See § 9.4(c).

[127] See *Tax-Exempt Organizations*, §§ 15.2, 15.3.

[128] IRC § 512(d)(2). For years beginning in 1998, this threshold was $109 (Rev. Proc. 97-57, 1997-2 C.B. 584); for years beginning in 1999, this threshold was $110 (Rev. Proc. 98-61, 1998-2 C.B. 811); for years beginning in 2000, this threshold was $112 (Rev. Proc. 99-42, 1999-2 C.B. 568); for years beginning in 2001, this threshold was $116 (Rev. Proc. 2001-13, 2001-1 C.B. 337); for years beginning in 2002, this threshold was $120 (Rev. Proc. 2001-59, 2001-2 C.B. 623); for years beginning in 2003, this threshold was $122 (Rev. Proc. 2002-70, 2002-2 C.B. 845); for years beginning in 2004, this threshold was $124 (Rev. Proc. 2003-85, 203-49 I.R.B. 1184); and for years beginning in 2005, this threshold is $127 (Rev. Proc. 2004-71, 2004-71 I.R.B. 970).

[129] IRC § 512(d)(1).

The term *dues* is defined for this purpose as any "payment required to be made in order to be recognized by the organization as a member of the organization."[130] If a person makes a single payment that entitles the person to be recognized as a member of the organization for more than 12 months, the payment can be prorated for purposes of applying the $100 cap.[131]

Nonetheless, this IRS position continues to be its view with respect to labor organizations (and to agricultural and horticultural entities that do not qualify for the exception). Moreover, the agency indicated that it will follow this approach with respect to associations generally.[132]

§ 4.9 LOW-COST ARTICLES

Another exception from classification as unrelated business is available only to tax-exempt organizations eligible to receive tax-deductible charitable contributions,[133] for activities relating to certain distributions of low-cost articles incidental to the solicitation of charitable contributions.[134] Although this statutory provision generally reflects a similar rule stated in the income tax regulations,[135] there is one important refinement: The term *low-cost article* is defined as any article (or aggregate of articles distributed to a single distributee in a year) that has a cost not in excess of $5 (adjusted for inflation[136]) to the organization that distributes the item or on behalf of which the item is distributed.[137] These rules also require that the distribution of the items be unsolicited and be accompanied by a statement that the distributee may retain the low-cost article irrespective of whether a charitable contribution is made.[138]

---

[130] IRC § 512(d)(3).

[131] H.R. Rep. No. 104-737, 104th Cong., 2d Sess. 14 (1996).

[132] Rev. Proc. 97-12, 1997-1 C.B. 631, *modifying* Rev. Proc. 95-21, 1995-1 C.B. 686. Associate member dues received by an exempt association were found not to be taxable because the associate member category was not formed or availed of for the principal purpose of producing unrelated business income; voting rights were held not to be the sole criterion in this evaluation. Tech. Adv. Mem. 9742001. Associate member dues received by an exempt union were, however, held taxable as unrelated business income, because the membership category was availed of for the principal purpose of producing this type of income. Tech. Adv. Mem. 9751001.

[133] That is, an organization described in IRC § 501, when it qualifies as a charitable donee under IRC § 170(c)(2) or § 170(c)(3) (namely, as a charitable or veterans' organization).

[134] IRC § 513(h)(1)(A).

[135] Reg. § 1.513-1(b).

[136] IRC § 513(h)(2)(C). The IRS calculated that the low-cost article cost threshold was $5.71 for years beginning in 1991; was $6.01 for years beginning in 1992 (Rev. Proc. 92-58, 1992-2 C.B. 410); was $6.20 for years beginning in 1993 (Rev. Proc. 92-102, 1992-2 C.B. 579); was $6.40 for years beginning in 1994 (Rev. Proc. 93-49, 1993-2 C.B. 581); was $6.60 for years beginning in 1995 (Rev. Proc. 94-72, 1994-2 C.B. 811); was $6.70 for years beginning in 1996 (Rev. Proc. 95-53, 1995-2 C.B. 445); was $6.90 for years beginning in 1997 (Rev. Proc. 96-59, 1996-2 C.B. 390); was $7.10 for years beginning in 1998 (Rev. Proc. 97-57, 1997-2 C.B. 584); was $7.20 for years beginning in 1999 (Rev. Proc. 98-61, 1998-2 C.B. 811); was $7.40 for years beginning in 2000 (Rev. Proc. 99-42, 1999-2 C.B. 568); was $7.60 for years beginning in 2001 (Rev. Proc. 2001-13, 2001-1 C.B. 337); was $7.90 for years beginning in 2002 (Rev. Proc. 2001-59, 2001-2 C.B. 623); was $8.00 for years beginning in 2003 (Rev. Proc. 2002-70, 2002-2 C.B. 845); was $8.20 for years beginning in 2004 (Rev. Proc. 2003-85, 2003-49 I.R.B. 1184); and is $8.30 for years beginning in 2005 (Rev. Proc. 2004-71, 2004-50 I.R.B. 970).

[137] IRC § 513(h)(2).

[138] IRC § 513(h)(3).

§ 4.10 MAILING LISTS

Another exception from unrelated business income taxation, available to the category of tax-exempt organizations eligible for the low-cost articles exception,[139] is applicable to the exchange or rental of membership or donor mailing lists with or to others of these exempt organizations.[140]

Absent this exception, however, the rental or exchange of a mailing list by a tax-exempt organization, when regularly carried on, is considered by the IRS to be an unrelated business. This is not a major problem from an economic standpoint when the activity involves a list rental,[141] in that taxes can be paid from the resulting income. When the activity is a list exchange, however, there is no income from the transaction available to pay the tax; it is nonetheless the view of the agency that these exchanges are unrelated businesses.[142] In calculating the amount of "income" of this nature, the IRS advised that the method used should be in accordance with the rules concerning facilities used for related and unrelated purposes; thus, expenses and deductions are to be allocated between the two uses on a reasonable basis.[143] According to the IRS, the "actual calculating of the costs and expenses associated with or allocable to the rental or exchange activities and the income they generate is a factual determination."[144]

If properly structured, however, a mailing-list rental or exchange program involving a noncharitable tax-exempt organization can avoid unrelated business treatment by utilization of the exception for royalties.[145]

§ 4.11 BUSINESSES OF EMPLOYEES' ASSOCIATIONS

If a tax-exempt local association of employees,[146] organized before May 27, 1969, establishes a business to sell items of work-related clothing and equipment and items normally sold through vending machines, through food-dispensing facilities, or by snack bars, for the convenience of its members at their usual places of employment, this business activity is excluded from classification as an unrelated business.[147] This exception does not apply with respect to sales of these items at

---

[139] See § 4.9.

[140] IRC § 513(h)(1)(B). The purpose of this provision is to nullify the decision in Disabled Am. Veterans v. United States, 650 F.2d 1178 (Ct. Cl. 1981). Also Disabled Am. Veterans v. Comm'r, 68 T.C. 95 (1994).

[141] Rev. Rul. 72-431, 1972-2 C.B. 281.

[142] Tech. Adv. Mem. 9502009.

[143] See § 11.2.

[144] In Tech. Adv. Mem. 9502009, the IRS ruled that these exchanges are not a disposition of property causing the realization of gain or loss for tax purposes (IRC § 1001), in that capital assets (IRC § 1222) are not involved. This holding precluded application of the exception from income taxation for capital gains; see § 3.10. The agency also held that the nontaxation rules concerning like-kind exchanges (IRC § 1031) are inapplicable, because the title to the lists does not pass and the rights to the properties acquired by the parties are not perpetual. Koch v. Comm'r, 37 T.C.M. 1167 (1978); Rev. Rul. 55-749, 1955-2 C.B. 295. An earlier technical advice memorandum, concluding that exchanges of mailing lists between tax-exempt organizations did not give rise to unrelated business income (Tech. Adv. Mem. 8128004), was thereafter prospectively revoked by the IRS in Tech. Adv. Mem. 9635001.

[145] E.g., Sierra Club, Inc. v. Comm'r, 86 F.3d 1526 (9th Cir. 1996). Also Am. Acad. of Ophthalmology, Inc. v. Comm'r, Tax Ct. No. 21657-94, in which the IRS abandoned its mailing-list revenue taxation stance in the aftermath of the Sierra Club holding. See the discussion in § 3.7.

[146] IRC § 501(c)(4). See Tax-Exempt Organizations, § 18.3.

[147] IRC § 513(a)(2); Reg. § 1.513-1(e)(2).

locations other than the employees' usual place of employment; hence, sales at such other locations are unrelated businesses (unless otherwise exempt[148]).[149] The IRS ruled that this type of association may change its form, from unincorporated entity to a corporation, without losing its grandfathered status.[150]

§ 4.12 S CORPORATION HOLDINGS AND SALES

Nearly all types of tax-exempt organizations are barred by the federal tax law from holding interests in small business corporations, also known as *S corporations*. There is, however, an exception in this regard for exempt charitable organizations: these entities are allowed to be shareholders in these corporations.[151] The authorization to own this type of a security is a revision of prior law.[152]

This type of interest is considered an interest in an unrelated business.[153] Items of income, loss, or deduction of an S corporation flow through to these exempt organizations as unrelated business income, irrespective of the source or nature of the income.[154] Thus, for example, unlike the partnership rules,[155] passive income of a small business corporation automatically flows to an exempt charitable organization as unrelated business income.

If a charitable organization acquires by purchase stock in a small business corporation (whether the stock was acquired when the corporation was a regular corporation—known as a *C corporation*—or an S corporation) and receives dividend distributions with respect to the stock, the shareholder organization generally must reduce its basis in the stock by the amount of the dividend.[156]

Any gain received on the disposition of S corporation stock also automatically results in unrelated business income.[157]

§ 4.13 POLE RENTAL ACTIVITIES

In the case of a tax-exempt mutual or cooperative telephone or electric company,[158] the term *unrelated trade or business* does not include engaging in qualified pole rental activity.[159] The term *qualified pole rental* means any rental of a pole (or other structure used to support wires) if the pole (or other structure) (1) is used by the telephone or electric company to support one or more wires used by the company in providing telephone or electric services to its members and (2) is

---

[148] For example, the sales activity may not be regularly carried on. See § 2.5.
[149] Reg. § 1.513-1(e).
[150] Priv. Ltr. Rul. 9442013. In so ruling, the IRS relied on Rev. Rul. 54-134, 1954-1 C.B. 88 (holding that an IRS ruling recognizing the tax-exempt status of a corporation, which merely changed in form from unincorporated status, embraces the period of unincorporation as well).
[151] This exception is also available for employee benefit entities described in IRC § 401(a).
[152] IRC § 1361(c)(6).
[153] IRC § 512(e)(1)(A).
[154] IRC § 512(e)(1)(B)(i).
[155] See § 6.4.
[156] IRC § 512(e)(2).
[157] IRC § 512(e)(1)(B)(ii). In general, see Hoyt, *Subchapter S Stock Owned by Tax-Exempt Organizations: Solutions to Legal Issues*, 22 Exempt Orgs. L. Rev. (no. 1) 25 (1998).
[158] See *Tax-Exempt Organizations*, § 18.5.
[159] IRC § 513(g).

used pursuant to the rental to support one or more wires (in addition to the wires previously described) for use in connection with the transmission by wire of electricity or of telephone or other communications.[160] For these purposes, the term *rental* includes any sale of the right to use the pole or other structure.[161]

[160] IRC § 501(c)(12)(D).
[161] *Id.*

CHAPTER FIVE

Unrelated Debt-Financed Income Rules

The unrelated debt-financed income rules can cause income received by tax-exempt organizations holding property (or an interest in property), with respect to which there is debt, to be subject to the unrelated business income tax,[1] even though the income would otherwise be exempt from taxation. It is because of these rules that forms of otherwise excludable income, such as interest and rent, can be taxable as unrelated business income.

§ 5.1 HISTORY AND OVERVIEW OF RULES

Before enactment of the Tax Reform Act of 1969, most charitable organizations and certain other tax-exempt organizations were subject to the unrelated business income tax on rental income from real property, to the extent that the property was acquired with borrowed funds. There was an important exception, however, that excluded rental income from a lease of five years or less; further, the tax was not applicable to all exempt organizations. Moreover, there

---

[1] IRC § 514.

was a question as to whether the tax applied to income received by an exempt organization from the leasing of assets constituting a going business.

In the years immediately preceding enactment of the 1969 Act, some tax-exempt organizations were using their tax privileges to purchase businesses and investments on credit, frequently at more than the market price, while contributing little or nothing themselves to the transaction other than their tax exemption. A typical factual situation in this regard was as follows:

> A sells an incorporated business to B, a charitable foundation, which makes a small (or no) down payment and agrees to pay the balance of the purchase price only out of profits to be derived from the property. B liquidates the corporation and then leases the business assets to C, a new corporation formed to operate the business. A (collectively, the stockholders of the original business) manages the business for C and frequently holds a substantial minority interest in C. C pays 80 percent of its business profits as "rent" to B, which then passes on 90 percent of those receipts to A until the original purchase price is paid in full. B has no obligation to pay A out of any funds other than the "rent" paid by C.[2]

The tax results of this type of transaction provided capital gain to the seller, a rent deduction for the operator, and no tax on the income flowing to the tax-exempt organization.

In this bootstrapping manner, a business was able to realize increased after-tax income and a tax-exempt organization was able to acquire the ownership of a business valued at $1.3 million without investment of its own funds.[3] Immediately prior to adoption of the Tax Reform Act of 1969, a court upheld the acquisition of 24 businesses by a charitable organization in this manner in the period 1945 to 1954.[4]

Congress's response to the problems in this area to enact revamped unrelated debt-financed income rules. In 1969, Congress acted to impose a tax on the investment income of tax-exempt institutions that is traceable in one way or another to borrowed funds. This was done by the addition to the Internal Revenue Code of rules that impose a tax on net unrelated debt-financed income.[5]

§ 5.2   UNRELATED DEBT-FINANCED INCOME

The computation of a tax-exempt organization's unrelated business taxable income must include, with respect to each debt-financed property that is unrelated to the organization's exempt function (as an item of gross income derived from an unrelated trade or business) an amount of income from the property, subject to tax in the proportion in which the property is financed by the debt.[6] Basically, deductions are allowed with respect to each debt-financed property in the same proportion.[7] The allowable deductions are those for expenses that are

---

[2] H.R. Rep. No. 91-413 (pt. 1), 91st Cong., 1st Sess. 45 (1969).

[3] Comm'r v. Brown, 380 U.S. 563 (1965).

[4] Univ. Hill Found. v. Comm'r, 51 T.C. 548 (1969), rev'd, 446 F.2d 701 (10th Cir. 1971), cert. denied, 405 U.S. 965 (1972). See also Anderson Dairy, Inc. v. Comm'r, 39 T.C. 1027 (1963); Shiffman v. Comm'r, 32 T.C. 1073 (1959); Ohio Furnace Co. v. Comm'r, 25 T.C. 179 (1955).

[5] An example of an interpretation of pre-1969 IRC § 514 is in Rev. Rul. 70-132, 1970-1 C.B. 138.

[6] IRC §§ 514(a)(1), 512(b)(4); Reg. § 1.514(a)-1(a)(1)(i).

[7] IRC § 514(a)(2); Reg. § 1.514(a)-1(b).

directly connected with the debt-financed property or income produced there-from, although any depreciation may be computed only on the straight-line method.[8] For example, if a commercial business property is acquired by an exempt organization subject to an 80-percent mortgage, 80 percent of the income and 80 percent of the deductions are taken into account for these tax purposes. As the mortgage is paid, the percentage taken into account usually diminishes. Capital gains on the sale of unrelated debt-financed property are also taxed in the same proportions.[9]

The term *unrelated debt-financed income*,[10] with respect to an item of debt-financed property,[11] is an amount that is the same percentage of the total gross income derived during the tax year from or on account of the property as

1. The average acquisition indebtedness[12] with respect to the property is of

2. The average adjusted basis of the property.[13]

This is known as the *debt-basis percentage*.[14] For example, a tax-exempt association owns an office building that in 2006 produced $100,000 in gross rental income. The average adjusted basis of the building for that year was $1 million and the average acquisition indebtedness with respect to the building for the year was $500,000. Accordingly, the debt-basis percentage for this property for 2006 was 50 percent ($500,000/$1,000,000). Therefore, the unrelated debt-financed income with respect to the building for 2006 was $50,000 (50 percent of $100,000).[15]

§ 5.3 DEBT-FINANCED PROPERTY

(a) General Rules

The term *debt-financed property* means, with certain exceptions including related use,[16] all property (for example, rental real estate, tangible personalty, and corporate stock) that is held to produce income (for example, rents, royalties, interest, and dividends) and with respect to which there is an acquisition indebtedness[17] at any time during the tax year (or during the preceding 12 months, if the property is disposed of during the year).[18]

The extent to which property is used for a particular purpose depends on all of the facts and circumstances. These may include (1) a comparison of the portion of time the property is used for exempt purposes with the total time the property is used, (2) a comparison of the portion of the property that is used for

---

[8] IRC § 514(a)(3).
[9] Reg. § 1.514(a)-1; Reg. § 1.514(a)-1(a)(1)(v).
[10] Reg. § 1.514(a)-1(a)(1)(ii).
[11] See § 5.3.
[12] Reg. § 1.514(a)(3).
[13] Reg. § 1.514(a)(2).
[14] Reg. § 1.514(a)-1(a)(1)(iii).
[15] Reg. § 1.514(a)-1(a)(1)(iv).
[16] See § 5.3(b).
[17] See § 5.4.
[18] IRC § 514(b)(1); Reg. § 1.514(b)-1(a).

exempt purposes with the portion of the property that is used for all purposes, or (3) a blend of the foregoing two elements.[19]

The principles established under the general unrelated income rules[20] are applicable in determining whether there is a substantial relationship between the property and the tax-exempt purposes of the organization. These principles were adversely applied to a tax-exempt organization that was operated for educational purposes in essentially the same manner as a museum, in that it promoted the appreciation of history and architecture by acquiring, restoring, and preserving buildings of historical and/or architectural significance and opening the restored buildings to the general public for a nominal admission fee. The organization acquired certain historically or architecturally significant buildings by assumption of outstanding mortgages and leased them at a fair rental value, subject to a covenant to ensure that the historical architecture of the buildings was maintained by the lessees. The lessees' uses neither bore any relationship to the buildings' historical or architectural significance nor accommodated viewing by the general public. Because this leasing did not contribute importantly to accomplishment of the organization's educational purpose, and had no causal relationship to the achievement of that purpose, the IRS found that substantially all the use of the buildings was not substantially related to the organization's exempt purposes. Thus, the leased buildings constituted debt-financed property.[21]

(b) Related Use Exception

Excepted from the term *debt-financed property* is property of which substantially all use is substantially related to the exercise or performance by the organization of its exempt purpose (aside from the need of the tax-exempt organization for income or funds), or, if less than substantially all use of the property is so related, to the extent that its use is related to the organization's exempt purpose.[22] The term *substantially all* means at least 85 percent.[23]

For example, a tax-exempt organization owns a computer that is used by the organization in the performance of its exempt purpose and with respect to which there is an outstanding principal indebtedness. The organization sells time for use of the computer to a corporation on occasions when the computer is not in full-time use by the organization. The organization uses the computer in furtherance of its exempt purpose more than 85 percent of the time it is in use; the other corporation uses the computer less than 15 percent of the total time the computer is in use. In this situation, substantially all of the use of this computer

---

[19] Reg. § 1.514(b)-1(b)(1)(ii).

[20] See ch. 2.

[21] Rev. Rul. 77-47, 1977-1 C.B. 157.

[22] IRC § 514(b)(1)(A); Reg. § 1.514(b)-1(b)(1)(i). The IRS ruled that proceeds to be received by a private foundation from loans will not constitute income from debt-financed property when the funds will be distributed, as grants, by the foundation to public charities. Priv. Ltr. Rul. 200432026. Unrelated debt-financed income is triggered to the extent that the financing occurred in connection with the acquisition of property used for an exempt purpose, but the loan proceeds were instead invested. S.W. Tex. Elec. Coop., Inc. v. Comm'r, 95-2 U.S.T.C. ¶ 50,565 (5th Cir. 1995), aff'g 68 T.C.M. 285 (1994).

[23] Reg. § 1.514(b)-1(b)(1)(1)(ii).

is related to performance of the exempt organization's exempt purpose; consequently, no portion of the computer is treated as debt-financed property.[24]

Another illustration posits a situation in which property that is debt-financed did not yield unrelated debt-financed income, because use of the property was substantially related to a tax-exempt purpose. In this example, an exempt organization, created to encourage business development in a particular area, constructed a building to lease, at below-market rates, to an industrial tenant for the purpose of attracting new industry to the area. Once the lease was executed, the organization completed the building (which was initially financed by the business community) to suit the needs of the tenant; the completion of the building was financed by subjecting the property to a mortgage. Because the leasing of the building under these circumstances was an activity designed to attract industry to the community, the IRS concluded that the activity contributed importantly to the organization's exempt purpose and hence did not constitute debt-financed property subject to these tax rules.[25] Still another example of this rule was provided by an exempt medical foundation that rented mortgaged property to a medical clinic that had a close working relationship with the foundation; the use of the leased property was held to be related to the foundation's exempt purpose of providing medical training, so the rental income was determined to be nontaxable.[26]

As a further example, a tax-exempt college owns a four-story office building that was purchased with borrowed funds. In 2006, the lower two floors of the building are used to house computers that are used by the college for administrative purposes. The top two stories are rented to the public for $60,000. Expenses total $20,000, allocable equally to both uses of this building. The average adjusted basis of the building for 2006 is $1 million; the outstanding principal indebtedness throughout that year is $60,000. Thus, the average acquisition indebtedness for 2006 is $600,000. Only the upper one-half of this building constitutes debt-financed property;[27] consequently, only the rental income and the deductions directly connected with the income are to be taken into account in computing unrelated business taxable income. The portion of these amounts to be taken into account is determined by multiplying the $60,000 of rental income and $10,000 of deductions directly connected with the rental income by the debt-basis percentage. Here, this percentage is the ratio that $300,000 (one-half of the $600,000) bears to $500,000 (one-half of the $1 million); thus, the debt-basis percentage for 2006 is 60 percent. Therefore, the college has for 2006 rental income, treated as from an unrelated business, in the amount of $36,000 (60% of 60,000), an allowable portion of deductions in the amount of $6,000 (60% of $10,000), and net unrelated business income of $30,000.[28]

Now assume the facts of the foregoing example, except that on December 31, 2006, the college sells the building, realizing a long-term capital gain of $100,000.

---

[24] Reg. § 1.514(b)-1(b)(1)(iii), Example (1).

[25] Rev. Rul. 81-138, 1981-1 C.B. 358, *amplifying* Rev. Rul. 70-81, 1970-1 C.B. 131. *Cf.* Rev. Rul. 58-547, 1958-2 C.B. 275.

[26] Gundersen Med. Found., Ltd. v. United States, 536 F. Supp. 556 (W.D. Wis. 1982). See also Rev. Rul. 69-464, 1969-1 C.B. 132.

[27] This is, in essence, application of the fragmentation rule. See § 2.3.

[28] Reg. § 1.514(b)-1(b)(1)(iii), Example (2).

This is the college's only capital transaction for the year. An allocable portion of this capital gain is subject to tax. This amount is determined by multiplying the gain related to the nonexempt use ($50,000) by the ratio that the allocable part of the highest acquisition indebtedness for the 12-month period preceding the date of sale ($300,000) bears to the allocable part of the average adjusted basis ($500,000). Thus, the debt-basis percentage derived from sale of the building is 60 percent ($300,000/$500,000). Consequently, $30,000 (60% of $50,000) is a net taxable gain for 2006.[29]

As noted, if debt-financed property is sold or otherwise disposed of, a percentage of the total gain or loss derived from the disposition is included in the computation of unrelated business taxable income.[30] The IRS recognizes, however, that the unrelated debt-financed income rules do not render taxable a transaction that would not be taxable by virtue of a nonrecognition provision of the federal tax law if it were carried out by an entity that is not tax-exempt.[31] The occasion for this realization was a transfer, subject to an existing mortgage, of an apartment complex, which had appreciated in value, by an exempt hospital to its wholly owned taxable subsidiary in exchange for additional stock in the subsidiary. Because of the operation of federal tax rules that provide for the nonrecognition of gain or loss in certain circumstances,[32] including those involving this hospital, the transaction did not result in a taxable gain for the hospital.

Substantially all of the use of property is considered substantially related to the exercise or performance of an organization's tax-exempt purpose if the property is real property subject to a lease to a medical clinic, when the lease is entered into primarily for purposes that are substantially related to the lessor's exempt purposes.[33]

Property owned by a tax-exempt organization and used by a related exempt organization, or by an exempt organization related to the owner exempt organization, is not treated as debt-financed property to the extent the property is used by either organization in furtherance of their tax-exempt purpose.[34] Two exempt organizations are *related* to each other if more than 50 percent of the members of one organization are members of the other organization.[35] In one instance, the IRS held that an exempt charitable organization may acquire a building, use a portion of it, and lease the remaining portion to a related charitable organization and a related business league for their offices and activities; in such a case, the building will not be treated as debt-financed property.[36] The organization acquiring the building had as its membership all of the active members of the business league that had contributed to it, and the members of the business league who were elected to and served on the governing body of the business

---

[29] *Id.*, Example (3).
[30] Reg. § 1.514(a)-1(a)(1)(v).
[31] Rev. Rul. 77-71, 1977-1 C.B. 156.
[32] IRC §§ 351, 357.
[33] IRC § 514(b), last sentence; Reg. § 1.514(b)-1(c)(1).
[34] Reg. § 1.514(b)-1(c)(2)(i).
[35] Reg. § 1.514(b)-1(c)(2)(ii)(C).
[36] Priv. Ltr. Rul. 7833055. The IRS cautioned that the charitable organization should charge the business league a fair-market-value rent; if it did not, it would be conferring a financial benefit upon a non-IRC § 501(c)(3) organization, an action that might adversely affect its tax-exempt status.

league. The members of one of the charitable organizations however, need not necessarily be members of the other.

(c) Other Exceptions

To the extent that the gross income from a property is already subject to tax as income from the conduct of an unrelated trade or business, the property is not treated as debt-financed property.[37] Nonetheless, any gain upon disposition of the property is includible as gross income derived from or on account of debt-financed property,[38] unless the gain is properly excludable from treatment as unrelated business income.[39]

There are exceptions in this context for property:

1. To the extent that the income from the property is derived from research activities and therefore is excluded from unrelated business taxable income[40]

2. To the extent that use of the property is in a trade or business exempt from tax because substantially all the work is performed without compensation[41]

3. In connection with a business that is carried on primarily for the convenience of members, students, patients, officers, or employees[42]

4. In connection with a business that constitutes the selling of merchandise, substantially all of which was received as gifts or contributions,[43] or

5. The gain or loss from the sale, exchange, or other disposition of which is excluded[44] from computation of the gross income of any unrelated trade or business.[45]

The *neighborhood land rule* provides an exemption from the debt-financed property rules for interim income from neighborhood real property acquired for a tax-exempt purpose. The tax on unrelated debt-financed income does not apply to income from real property, located in the neighborhood of other property owned by the exempt organization, which it plans to devote to exempt uses within 10 years of the time of acquisition.[46] This rule applies after the first 5 years of the 10-year period only if the exempt organization satisfies the IRS that future use of the acquired land in furtherance of its exempt purposes

---

[37] IRC § 514(b)(1)(B); Reg. § 1.514(b)-1(b)(2).
[38] Reg. § 1.514(b)-1(b)(2).
[39] See § 3.10.
[40] IRC § 514(b)(1)(C); Reg. § 1.514(b)-1(b)(4). See § 3.13.
[41] IRC § 514(b)(1)(D); Reg. § 1.514(b)-1(b)(5). See § 4.2.
[42] IRC § 514(b)(1)(D); Reg. § 1.514(b)-1(b)(5). See § 4.1.
[43] IRC § 514(b)(1)(D); Reg. § 1.514(b)-1(b)(5). See § 4.3.
[44] See § 3.16.
[45] IRC § 514(b)(1)(E).
[46] IRC § 514(b)(3)(A)–(C). In one situation, a tax-exempt organization did not own the original site property in the neighborhood; the property was actually owned by a supporting organization (see Hopkins, *The Law of Tax-Exempt Organizations, Eighth Edition* (John Wiley & Sons, 2003) [hereinafter *Tax-Exempt Organizations*], § 11.3(c)) with respect to the organization. The IRS concluded that the neighborhood land rule nonetheless applied because of the supported organization's "interrelated nature" with the property by means of the supporting organization. Priv. Ltr. Rul. 9603019.

before expiration of the period is reasonably certain.[47] This process is to be initiated by filing a ruling request at least 90 days before the end of the fifth year.[48] A more generous 15-year rule is established for churches; the property need not be in the neighborhood of the church.[49]

(d) Use of Property by Related Organizations

For purposes of the related use exception,[50] the research exception,[51] and the exception for sales of gifted property,[52] the use of property by an exempt organization that is related to an organization is treated as use by the related organization.[53]

Property owned by a tax-exempt organization and used by a related exempt organization, or by an exempt organization that is related to such related exempt organization, is not treated as debt-financed property to the extent the property is used by either organization in furtherance of its exempt purposes. Also, property is not regarded as debt-financed property to the extent the property is used by a related exempt organization in pursuits that are sheltered by the research exception or the exception for sales of gifted property.[54]

For this purpose, an exempt organization is *related* to another exempt organization only in an instance of one of the following circumstances:

1. One organization is an exempt single-member title-holding company and the other organization receives the profits derived by the holding company.

2. One organization has control of the other organization.

3. More than 50 percent of the members of one organization are members of the other organization.

4. Each organization is a local organization that is directly affiliated with a common state, national, or international organization that is also tax-exempt.[55]

As an example, a tax-exempt trade association leases 70 percent of the space of an office building in furtherance of its exempt purpose. The title to the building is held by an exempt holding company that acquired title to the property with borrowed funds. The other 30 percent of the space in this office building is leased to another exempt trade association that uses the space in furtherance of its exempt purposes. The members of the board of directors of the second association serve for fixed terms; the board of directors of the first association selects all of these members. The title-holding company pays to the first of these associations all of the profits it derives from its leasing operations. The title-holding

---

[47] IRC § 514(b)(3)(A).
[48] Reg. § 1.514(b)-1(d)(1)(iii). When an exempt organization failed to seek this ruling, because the IRS was satisfied with the plans the organization had submitted for the future use of the property, the agency granted administrative relief (Reg. § 301.9100-1(a)) by extending the filing period. Priv. Ltr. Rul. 9603019.
[49] IRC § 514(b)(3)(E); Reg. § 1.514(b)-1(e).
[50] See § 5.3(b).
[51] See § 5.3(c).
[52] *Id.*
[53] IRC § 514(b)(2); Reg. § 1.514(b)-1(b)(6).
[54] Reg. § 1.514(b)-1(c)(2)(i).
[55] Reg. § 1.514(b)-1(c)(2)(ii).

company is related to the first association (pursuant to relationship number 1 above), as is the second association (relationship number 2 in the preceding list). Therefore, inasmuch as all of the available space in the office building is leased either to an exempt organization related to the exempt organization holding title to the building or to an exempt organization related to such related exempt organization, no portion of the building is treated as debt-financed property.[56]

As another example, a tax-exempt labor union owns a 10-story office building that was purchased with borrowed funds. Five floors of this building are used by the union in furtherance of its exempt purpose. Four of the other floors are rented to an exempt voluntary employees' association that is operated for the benefit of the union's members; this space is used by the employees' association for its exempt purposes. Seventy percent of the members of the union are also members of the association, so the association is related to the union (relationship number 3 in the preceding list). The remaining floor of the building is rented to the general public (for purposes not protected by any exception to the debt-financed property rules). Under these circumstances, no portion of the building is treated as debt-financed property, because more than 85 percent of the office space available in the building is used either by an exempt organization or by an exempt organization related to the exempt organization in furtherance of their respective exempt purposes.[57]

Assume the facts in the previous example, except that the two entities are each tax-exempt local labor unions without any common membership. Each entity is affiliated with an exempt international labor union. In this instance, no portion of the building is treated as debt-financed property, because more than 85 percent of the office space available in the building is used either by an exempt organization or by a related exempt organization (relationship number 4 in the preceding list).[58]

Assume the facts in the previous example, except that the two local labor unions are directly affiliated with different exempt international labor unions and they are not otherwise affiliated with, nor members of, a common exempt organization, other than an association of international labor unions. Under these circumstances, the portions of the building that are rented to the second union and to the general public are debt-financed property, because the second union is not related to the first union and the first union uses less than 85 percent of the building for its exempt purpose.[59]

§ 5.4   ACQUISITION INDEBTEDNESS

Absent an exception, income-producing property is unrelated debt-financed property, making income from it, less deductions, taxable—when, of course, debt is associated with the property. The formal term is an *acquisition indebtedness* attributable to the property.

---

[56] Reg. § 1.514(b)-1(c)(2)(iii), Example (1).
[57] Reg. § 1.514(b)-1(c)(2)(iii), Example (2).
[58] Reg. § 1.514(b)-1(c)(2)(iii), Example (3).
[59] Reg. § 1.512(b)-1(c)(2)(iii), Example (4).

(a) Definition of *Acquisition Indebtedness*

With respect to debt-financed property, the term *acquisition indebtedness* means the outstanding amount of:

1. The principal indebtedness incurred by the tax-exempt organization in acquiring or improving the property;

2. The principal indebtedness incurred before the acquisition or improvement of the property, if the indebtedness would not have been incurred but for the acquisition or improvement; and

3. The principal indebtedness incurred after the acquisition or improvement of the property, if the indebtedness would not have been incurred but for the acquisition or improvement and the incurring of the indebtedness was reasonably foreseeable at the time of acquisition or improvement.[60]

Whether the incurrence of an indebtedness is *reasonably foreseeable* depends on the facts and circumstances of each situation. The fact that an organization did not actually foresee the need to incur an indebtedness before an acquisition or improvement of property does not necessarily mean that the subsequent incurrence of indebtedness was not reasonably foreseeable.[61]

For example, a tax-exempt organization pledges some of its investment securities with a bank for a loan and uses the proceeds of the loan to purchase an office building, which it leases to the public (for purposes not covered by an exception). The outstanding principal indebtedness with respect to this loan constitutes acquisition indebtedness incurred prior to the acquisition of the property, which indebtedness would not have been incurred but for the acquisition.[62]

As another example, a tax-exempt scientific organization mortgages its laboratory to replace working capital used in remodeling an office building that it rents to an insurance company (for purposes not covered by an exception). This indebtedness is acquisition indebtedness because the indebtedness, although incurred subsequent to the improvement of the office building, would not have been incurred but for the improvement; the indebtedness was reasonably foreseeable when, to make the improvement, the organization reduced its working capital below the amount necessary to continue current operations.[63]

As still another example, a tax-exempt private preparatory school, as its sole educational facility, owns a classroom building that no longer meets the needs of its students. In 2005, the school sells this building for $3 million to a corporation that the school does not control. The school receives $1 million as a down payment and takes back a purchase money mortgage of $2 million that bears interest at 10 percent per annum. At the time the school became the mortgagee, its board of trustees realized that it would have to construct a new classroom building, and knew that it would have to incur indebtedness for the construction of the new classroom building. In 2006, the school builds a new classroom building for a cost

---

[60] IRC § 514(c)(1); Reg. § 1.514(c)-1(a)(1).
[61] Reg. § 1.514(c)-1(a)(1).
[62] Reg. § 1.514(c)-1(a)(2), Example (1).
[63] Reg. § 1.514(c)-1(a)(2), Example (2).

of $4 million. In connection with the construction of this new facility, the school borrows $2.5 million from a bank pursuant to a deed of trust bearing interest at 6 percent per annum. Under these circumstances, $2 million of the $2.5 million borrowed to finance construction of the new classroom building would not have been borrowed but for the retention of the $2 million mortgage. Because such indebtedness was reasonably foreseeable, $2 million of the $2.5 million borrowed to finance construction of the new classroom building is acquisition indebtedness with respect to the mortgage, and the mortgage is debt-financed property.[64]

To continue this example, in 2006, the school receives $200,000 in interest from the buyer corporation and makes a $150,000 interest payment to the bank. The debt-basis percentage for 2006 is 100 percent ($2 million/$2 million). Accordingly, all of the interest and all of the deductions directly connected with the interest income are to be taken into account in computing unrelated business taxable income. Thus, $200,000 of interest income and $120,000 ($150,000 x $2 million/$2.5 million) of deductions directly connected with the interest income are taken into account. Under these circumstances, the school must include net interest income of $80,000 ($200,000 of income less $120,000 of directly connected deductions) in its unrelated business taxable income for 2006.[65]

As a further illustration, in 2006, a tax-exempt organization enters into a partnership with two other persons. The partnership agreement provides that the three partners shall share equally in the profits of the partnership, that they shall each invest $3 million, and that one of these other persons shall be a limited partner.[66] The limited partner invests $1 million of its own funds in the partnership and $2 million of borrowed funds. As its sole asset, the partnership purchases an office building that is leased to the general public (for purposes not covered by an exception). This building costs the partnership $24 million, of which $15 million is borrowed from a bank. This loan is secured by a mortgage on the entire building. The agreement with the bank states that the exempt organization is not liable for payment of the mortgage. The character of any item received by the partnership and included in the partner's distributive share is determined as if the partner had realized the item directly from the source from which it was realized by the partnership, and in the same manner.[67] Therefore, a portion of the exempt organization's income from the building is debt-financed income. Under these circumstances, the $2 million indebtedness incurred by the organization in acquiring its partnership interest was incurred in acquiring income-producing property; so was the $5 million indebtedness: the allocable portion of the partnership's indebtedness incurred in connection with acquisition of the office building which is attributable to the exempt organization in computing the debt-basis percentage (1/3 of $15 million). Thus, the exempt organization has acquisition indebtedness of $7 million. Similarly, the allocable portion of the partnership's adjusted basis in the office building which is attributable to the exempt organization in computing the debt-basis percentage is $8 million (1/3 of $24 million). Assuming no payment with respect to either

---

[64] Reg. § 1.514(c)-1(a)(2), Example (3)(a).
[65] Reg. § 1.514(c)-1(a)(2), Example (3)(b).
[66] See § 8.9(a).
[67] IRC § 702(b).

indebtedness and no adjustments to basis in 2006, the exempt organization's average acquisition indebtedness is $7 million and its average adjusted basis is $8 million for the year. Therefore, the organization's debt-basis percentage with respect to its share of the partnership income for 2006 is 87.5 percent ($7 million/ $8 million).[68]

An interest in a qualified tuition program[69] is not regarded as a debt for purposes of these rules.[70] Trading in commodity futures contracts by a tax-exempt organization does not give rise to acquisition indebtedness.[71]

(b) General Rules

Because property used by an exempt organization can be protected from these rules by an exception, so that the property is not considered debt-financed property,[72] indebtedness with respect to such property is not acquisition indebtedness. If, however, a tax-exempt organization converts the property to a use that is not sheltered by an exception, and the property becomes debt-financed property, the outstanding principal indebtedness with respect to the property will thereafter be treated as acquisition indebtedness. For example, in 2003, a tax-exempt university borrowed funds to acquire an apartment building as housing for married students (a related use). In 2006, the university begins renting the apartment building to the public (for purposes not covered by an exception). The outstanding principal indebtedness is acquisition indebtedness as of the date in 2006 when the building is first rented to the public.[73]

If a tax-exempt organization sells or exchanges property that is subject to an indebtedness covered by these rules, and acquires another property without retiring the indebtedness, and the newly acquired property is otherwise treated as debt-financed property, the outstanding principal indebtedness with respect to the acquired property is acquisition indebtedness, even though the original property was not debt-financed property. For example, to house its administrative offices, an exempt organization purchases a building with $609,000 of its own funds and $400,000 of borrowed funds secured by a pledge of its securities. It later sells the building for $1 million without redeeming the pledge. It uses these proceeds to purchase an apartment building that it rents to the public (for purposes not covered by an exception). The indebtedness of $400,000 is acquisition indebtedness with respect to the apartment building even though the building was not debt-financed property.[74]

(c) Property Acquired Subject to Lien

(i) General Rules. In general, whenever property is acquired by a tax-exempt organization subject to a mortgage, the amount of the outstanding principal

---

[68] Reg. § 1.514(c)-1(a)(2), Example (4).
[69] See *Tax-Exempt Organizations*, § 18.16.
[70] IRC § 529(e)(4).
[71] Gen. Couns. Mem. 39620.
[72] See § 5.3(b), (c).
[73] Reg. § 1.514(c)-1(a)(3).
[74] Reg. § 1.514(c)-1(a)(4).

indebtedness thereby secured is considered acquisition indebtedness incurred by the organization when the property is acquired, even though the organization did not assume or agree to pay the indebtedness.[75] This is so irrespective of whether the property is acquired by purchase, gift, devise, bequest, or other means. For example, a tax-exempt organization pays $50,000 for real property valued at $150,000 and subject to a $100,000 mortgage. This $100,000 of outstanding principal indebtedness is acquisition indebtedness just as though the organization had borrowed $100,000 to acquire the property.[76]

For these purposes, liens similar to mortgages are treated as mortgages. A lien is *similar to* a mortgage if title to property is encumbered by the lien for the benefit of a creditor. Liens similar to mortgages include deeds of trust, conditional sales contracts, chattel mortgages, security interests under the Uniform Commercial Code, pledges, agreements to hold title in escrow, and tax liens (other than those just referenced).[77]

The regulations accompanying the statutory unrelated debt-financed income rules provide, in effect, a special rule for debts for the payment of taxes, stating that "in the case where State law provides that a tax lien attaches to property prior to the time when such lien becomes due and payable, such lien shall not be treated as similar to a mortgage until after it has become due and payable and the organization has had an opportunity to pay such lien in accordance with State law."[78] Before enactment of the Tax Reform Act of 1976, however, the IRS took the position that a lien arising from a special assessment imposed by a state or local government on land for the purpose of making improvements on the land, with the improvements financed by the sale of bonds secured by the lien, constituted acquisition indebtedness, even though (like the property tax lien) the installment payments were due in future periods. In 1976, Congress acted to reverse this position so that, as respects tax years that began after December 31, 1969, when state law provides that a lien for taxes or for assessments made by the state or a political subdivision of the state attaches to property prior to the time the taxes or assessments become due and payable, the indebtedness does not become acquisition indebtedness (that is, the lien is not regarded as similar to a mortgage[79]) until and to the extent that the taxes or assessments become due and payable and the organization has had an opportunity to pay the taxes or assessments in accordance with state law.[80] The Senate Finance Committee noted that "it is not intended that this provision apply to special assessments for improvements which are not of a type normally made by a State or local governmental unit or instrumentality in circumstances in which the use of the special assessment is essentially a device for financing improvements of the sort that normally would be financed privately rather than through a government."[81]

---

[75] IRC § 514(c)(2)(A).
[76] Reg. § 1.514(c)-1(b)(1).
[77] Reg. § 1.514(c)-1(b)(2).
[78] Reg. § 1.514(c)-1(b)(2).
[79] IRC § 514(c)(2)(A).
[80] IRC § 514(c)(2)(C).
[81] S. Rep. No. 94-938 (pt. 2), 94th Cong., 2d Sess. 86 (1976).

(ii) Bequests and Devises. Some relief is available with respect to mortgaged property acquired as a result of a bequest or devise. That is, when property subject to a mortgage is acquired by a tax-exempt organization by bequest or devise, the outstanding principal indebtedness secured by the mortgage is not treated as acquisition indebtedness during the 10-year period following the date of acquisition. The *date of acquisition* is the date the organization receives the property.[82]

(iii) Gifts. A similar rule applies to mortgaged property received by gift. If an exempt organization acquires property by gift subject to a mortgage, the outstanding principal indebtedness secured by the mortgage is not treated as acquisition indebtedness during the 10-year period following the date of the gift, *if* the mortgage was placed on the property more than five years before the date of the gift and the property was held by the donor for more than five years before the date of the gift.[83]

(iv) Limitations. These rules as to property acquired by bequest, devise, or gift are inapplicable, however, if (1) the tax-exempt organization assumes and agrees to pay all or any part of the indebtedness secured by the mortgage, or (2) the organization makes any payment for the equity owned by the decedent or the donor in the property (other than a payment pursuant to a charitable gift annuity arrangement[84]).[85] Whether an exempt organization has assumed and agreed to pay all or any part of an indebtedness in order to acquire a property is determined by the facts and circumstances of each situation.[86]

For example, an individual dies on January 1, 2006. The will devises an office building subject to a mortgage to a tax-exempt organization. The exempt organization never assumes the mortgage. For the period 2006 through 2015, the outstanding principal indebtedness secured by this mortgage is not acquisition indebtedness. Nonetheless, the outstanding principal indebtedness secured by the mortgage is acquisition indebtedness if this building is otherwise treated as debt-financed property.[87] If the exempt organization thereafter assumes the mortgage, the outstanding principal indebtedness secured by the mortgage becomes acquisition indebtedness if the building is otherwise treated as debt-financed property.[88]

A tax-exempt charitable organization acquired an undivided interest in income-producing rental property subject to a mortgage; the property was leased for purposes unrelated to the organization's exempt purposes. To liquidate its share of the mortgage, the organization prepaid its proportionate share of the mortgage indebtedness, thereby receiving releases of liability from the mortgagee and the co-owners. The lien securing payment of the mortgage nonetheless extended to the entire rental property, and the mortgagee was not to release

---

[82] IRC § 514(c)(2)(B); Reg. § 1.514(c)-1(b)(3)(i).
[83] IRC § 514(c)(2)(B); Reg. § 1.514(c)-1(b)(3)(ii).
[84] See § 5.4(e)(ii).
[85] IRC § 514(c)(2)(B).
[86] Reg. § 1.514(c)-1(b)(3)(iii).
[87] Reg. § 1.514(c)-1(b)(3)(iv), Example (1).
[88] *Id.*, Example (2).

the lien until the entire principal of the mortgage was paid by the co-owners. The IRS ruled that the organization, by satisfying the full amount of its indebtedness under the mortgage, did not have any acquisition indebtedness.[89]

By contrast, a tax-exempt charitable organization purchased mineral production payments with borrowed funds to obtain income for its grant-making program. From each payment, it received the difference between the aggregate amount payable to the lender of the borrowed funds and the total amount of the production payment, with the difference generally amounting to 1/16 of 1 percent of each payment purchased. The IRS held that the indebtedness incurred to purchase the production payment was an acquisition indebtedness and that, accordingly, the payments were debt-financed property.[90]

(d) Extensions, Renewals, and Refinancings

An extension, renewal, or refinancing of an obligation evidencing a preexisting indebtedness is considered a continuation of the old indebtedness, to the extent the outstanding principal amount thereof is not increased.[91] When the principal amount of the modified obligation exceeds the outstanding principal amount of the preexisting indebtedness, however, the excess is treated as a separate indebtedness.[92] Any modification or substitution of the terms of an obligation by an exempt organization is treated as an extension or renewal of the original obligation, rather than the creation of a new indebtedness, to the extent that the outstanding principal amount of the indebtedness is not increased. Acts that result in the extension or renewal of an obligation include substitution of liens to secure the obligation; substitution of obligees, whether or not with the consent of the organization; renewal, extension, or acceleration of the payment terms of the obligation; and addition, deletion, or substitution of sureties or other primary or secondary obligors.[93]

In instances in which the outstanding principal amount of the modified obligation exceeds the outstanding principal amount of the unmodified obligation and only a portion of the refinanced indebtedness is to be treated as acquisition indebtedness, payments on the amount of the refinanced indebtedness must be apportioned pro rata (allocated) between the amount of the preexisting indebtedness and the excess amount. For example, a tax-exempt organization has an outstanding principal indebtedness of $500,000 that is treated as acquisition indebtedness. It borrows another $100,000, which is not acquisition indebtedness, from the same lending institution and gives the lender a $600,000 note for its total obligation. In this situation, a payment of $60,000 against the amount of the total obligation would reduce the acquisition indebtedness by $50,000 and the excess indebtedness by $10,000.[94]

---

[89] Rev. Rul. 76-95, 1976-1 C.B. 172.
[90] Rev. Rul. 76-354, 1976-2 C.B. 179.
[91] IRC § 514(c)(3).
[92] Reg. § 1.514(c)-1(c)(1).
[93] Reg. § 1.514(c)-1(c)(2).
[94] Reg. § 1.514(c)-1(c)(3).

(e) Other Exceptions

There are seven additional exceptions from the scope of the term *acquisition indebtedness*.[95]

(i) Exempt Function Debt. The term *acquisition indebtedness* does not include the incurrence of an indebtedness that was necessarily incurred or otherwise inherent in the performance or exercise of an organization's tax-exempt purpose or function.[96] Thus, the term does not include the indebtedness incurred by an exempt credit union[97] in accepting deposits from its members or the obligation incurred by a tax-exempt organization in accepting payments from its members to provide them with insurance, retirement, or other similar benefits.[98] A court held that the purchase of securities on margin and with borrowed funds is not inherent in (meaning essential to) the performance or exercise of a credit union's exempt purposes or function; thus, a portion of the resulting income was taxable as debt-financed income.[99]

The IRS ruled that a tax-exempt employees' trust (which was, in general, subject to tax on unrelated business income[100]), which was a partner in a partnership that was organized to make investments in securities, could experience unrelated debt-financed income.[101] The partnership borrowed money to invest in securities and became primarily liable for repayment of the debt and for payment of interest on the debt, with the partners secondarily liable on a pro rata basis. The IRS held that the indebtedness was an acquisition indebtedness because it was incurred to acquire property for investment purposes, the incurring of the debt was not inherent in the performance of the trust's exempt function (namely, to receive employer and employee contributions and to use them and increments on them to provide retirement benefits to the plan participants[102]), and the investment property was not substantially related to the exercise of the trust's exempt purposes. Thus, whether the trust's investment activity could result in unrelated business taxable income under these rules was determined by whether its share of any partnership income was derived from or on account of debt-financed property.[103] Subsequently, a court held that the income from securities purchased on margin by a qualified profit-sharing plan was unrelated debt-financed income, in that this type of indebtedness was not inherent in the exercise of the trust's exempt function.[104] Similarly, another court concluded that, when an exempt organization withdrew the accumulated cash values in life insurance policies and reinvested the proceeds in income-paying

---

[95] The seventh of these exceptions is the subject of § 5.4(f).
[96] IRC § 514(c)(4); Reg. § 1.514(c)-1(d)
[97] See *Tax-Exempt Organizations*, § 18.7.
[98] IRC § 514(c)(4); Reg. § 1.514(c)-1(d).
[99] Ala. Cent. Credit Union v. United States, 646 F. Supp. 1199 (N.D. Ala. 1986).
[100] Rev. Rul. 71-311, 1971-2 C.B. 184.
[101] Rev. Rul. 74-197, 1974-1 C.B. 143.
[102] Reg. § 1.401-1(a)(2)(i).
[103] Reg. § 1.702-1(a).
[104] Elliot Knitwear Profit Sharing Plan v. Comm'r, 71 T.C. 765 (1979), *aff'd*, 614 F.2d 347 (3d Cir. 1980). Also Ocean Cove Corp. Ret. Plan & Trust v. United States, 657 F. Supp. 776 (S.D. Fla. 1987); Ala. Cent. Credit Union v. United States, 646 F. Supp. 1199 (N.D. Ala. 1986).

investments, it created an acquisition indebtedness and thus unrelated debt-financed income, even though the organization did not have an obligation to repay the funds.[105] Likewise, a court held that the interest earned on certificates of deposit obtained by an exempt organization was taxable as unrelated debt-financed income, because the certificates were acquired using the proceeds of a loan that was collateralized with other certificates of deposit previously purchased by the organization.[106]

By contrast, the IRS examined similar practices engaged in by a trust forming part of a leveraged employee stock ownership plan (ESOP).[107] (An ESOP is a technique of corporate finance designed to build beneficial equity ownership of shares in an employer corporation into its employees substantially in proportion to their relative income without requiring any cash outlay on their part, any reduction in pay or other employee benefits, or the surrender of any rights on the part of the employees.[108]) This type of trust generally acquires stock of the employer with the proceeds of a loan made to it by a financial institution. Consequently, the IRS concluded that a leveraged ESOP's capital growth and stock ownership objectives were part of its tax-exempt function[109] and that "borrowing to purchase employer securities is an integral part of accomplishing these objectives."[110] Thus, the borrowing was not acquisition indebtedness and the securities thereby purchased were not debt-financed property. The agency cautioned, though, that these circumstances are "distinguishable from a situation in which a pension or profit sharing plan that satisfies the requirements of [IRC] section 401(a) borrows money to purchase securities of the employer; in the latter situation the exempt trusts borrowing to purchase employer securities could result in unrelated business income within the meaning of [IRC] section 512."[111]

(ii) Annuities. The term *acquisition indebtedness* does not include an obligation to pay an annuity that:

1. Is the sole consideration (other than a gifted or similarly transferred mortgage[112]) issued in exchange for the property acquired if, at the time of the exchange, the value of the annuity is less than 90 percent of the value of the property received in the exchange;

2. Is payable over the life of one individual who is living at the time the annuity is issued, or over the lives of two individuals living at that time; and

---

[105] Mose & Garrison Siskin Mem'l Found., Inc. v. United States, 603 F. Supp. 91 (E.D. Tenn. 1985), *aff'd*, 790 F.2d 480 (6th Cir. 1986).

[106] Kern County Elec. Pension Fund v. Comm'r, 96 T.C. 845 (1991), *aff'd in unpublished op.* (9th Cir. 1993).

[107] IRC § 4975(e)(7).

[108] S. Rep. No. 94-938, 94th Cong., 2d Sess. 180 (1976).

[109] IRC § 401(a).

[110] Rev. Rul. 79-122, 1979-1 C.B. 204, 206.

[111] *Id. Cf.* Rev. Rul. 79-349, 1979-2 C.B. 233 (IRS ruled that interest income earned from mortgage loans by an exempt employees' trust does not enter into computation of the trust's unrelated business income).

[112] See § 5.4(c).

3. Is payable under a contract that does not guarantee a minimum number of payments or specify a maximum number of payments and does not provide for any adjustment of the amount of the annuity payments by reference to the income received from the transferred property or any other property.[113]

For example, on January 1, 2006, a tax-exempt charitable organization receives property with a value of $100,000 from an individual donor who is 60 years of age. In return, the organization promises to pay this donor $6,000 annually for the balance of the donor's life, with neither a minimum nor a maximum number of payments specified. This annuity is payable on December 31 of each year. The amounts paid pursuant to the annuity arrangement do not depend on the income derived from the property transferred. The value of the annuity is less than 90 percent of the donor's equity in the transferred property. This obligation of the charity to make annuity payments is not acquisition indebtedness.[114]

As another illustration, on January 1, 2006, an individual transfers title to an office building to a tax-exempt university, subject to a mortgage. In return, the university agrees to pay this individual $5,000 annually for the balance of the individual's life, with neither a minimum nor a maximum number of payments specified. The amounts payable pursuant to this annuity arrangement do not depend on the income derived from the building. It is determined that the value of the annuity is less than 90 percent of the value of the donor's equity in the building. The university does not assume the mortgage. During the period 2006 through 2015, the outstanding principal indebtedness secured by the mortgage is not treated as acquisition indebtedness. The university's obligation to make annuity payments to this individual never constitutes acquisition indebtedness.[115]

(iii) Certain Federal Financing. The term *acquisition indebtedness* does not include an obligation to finance the purchase, rehabilitation, or construction of housing for low and moderate income individuals to the extent that the obligation is insured by the Federal Housing Administration.[116]

(iv) Certain Investment Company Indebtedness. The term *acquisition indebtedness* does not include indebtedness incurred by certain small business investment companies if the indebtedness is evidenced by a certain type of debenture.[117]

(v) Securities Lending Arrangements. The term *acquisition indebtedness* does not include a tax-exempt organization's obligation to return collateral security pursuant to a securities lending arrangement. This makes it clear that, in

---

[113] IRC § 514(c)(5); Reg. § 1.514(c)-1(e)(1). The value of an annuity at the time of exchange is computed in accordance with IRC § 1011(b) and Reg. § 1.1011-2(e)(1)(iii)(B)(2). Reg. § 1.514(c)-1(e)(2). See Hopkins, *The Tax Law of Charitable Giving, Third Edition* (John Wiley & Sons, 2005) [hereinafter *Charitable Giving*], § 14.9.

[114] Reg. § 1.514(c)-1(e)(3), Example (1).

[115] *Id.*, Example (2). This example and the previous one are based on the assumption that the property transferred is used for purposes other than those covered by an exception. See § 5.3(b), (c).

[116] IRC § 514(c)(6)(A)(i); Reg. § 1.514(c)-1(f).

[117] IRC § 514(c)(6)(A)(ii), (B).

ordinary circumstances, payments on securities loans are not debt-financed income.[118]

(vi) Charitable Remainder Trusts. A charitable remainder trust[119] does not incur acquisition indebtedness when the sole consideration it is required to pay in exchange for unencumbered property is an annuity interest or a unitrust interest.[120]

(f) Real Property Rules

The term *acquisition indebtedness* generally does not include indebtedness incurred by a qualified organization in acquiring or improving any real property.[121] A *qualified organization* is an operating educational institution,[122] a supporting organization affiliated with an educational institution,[123] or a tax-exempt multiparent title-holding organization,[124] as well as any trust that constitutes a pension trust.[125] In computing the unrelated business taxable income of a disqualified holder of an interest in a multiparent title-holding entity, the holder's pro rata share of the items of income that are treated as gross income derived from an unrelated business (without regard to the exception for debt-financed property) is taken into account as gross income of the disqualified holder derived from an unrelated business; the holder's pro rata share of deductions are likewise taken into account.[126] A *disqualified holder* is a shareholder or beneficiary that is not an educational institution, an affiliated supporting organization, or a pension trust.[127]

   Thus, under this exception, income from investments in real property is not treated as income from debt-financed property and therefore as unrelated business income. An interest in a mortgage is not considered real property for purposes of this exception.[128] Rules govern the allocation of items pertaining to this exception to qualified organizations in partnerships.[129]

---

[118] IRC § 514(c)(8). See § 3.4.

[119] That is, an entity described in IRC § 664. See *Charitable Giving*, ch. 12.

[120] Reg. § 1.514(c)-1(g).

[121] IRC § 514(c)(9)(A).

[122] That is, one described in IRC § 170(b)(1)(A)(ii). See *Tax-Exempt Organization*, § 11.3(a).

[123] That is, one described in IRC § 509(a)(3). See *Tax-Exempt Organizations*, § 11.3(c). When a supporting organization affiliated with an operating educational institution is the sole member of a limited liability company (SMLLC) (see *Tax-Exempt Organizations*, §§ 4.1, 30.7), and the SMLLC receives real property encumbered by debt, both the SMLLC and the supporting organization will be afforded these exemptions for purposes of determining debt-financed income. Priv. Ltr. Rul. 200134025.

[124] That is, one described in IRC § 501(c)(25). See *Tax-Exempt Organizations*, § 18.2(b).

[125] That is, one described in IRC § 401. The definition of *qualified organization* is the subject of IRC § 514(c)(9)(C).

[126] IRC § 514(c)(9)(F)(i), (ii). The purpose of this rule is to prevent the benefits of this exception from flowing through the title-holding company to its shareholders or beneficiaries, unless those organizations themselves are qualified organizations. See *supra* note 123..

[127] IRC § 514(c)(9)(F)(iii). An entity that is this type of shareholder or beneficiary, however, is not a disqualified holder if it otherwise constitutes a qualified organization by reason of being an educational institution, a supporting organization of an educational institution, or a pension trust. *Id.*

[128] IRC § 514(c)(9)(B), last sentence.

[129] IRC § 514(c)(9)(E); Reg. § 1.514(c)-2.

This exception for indebtedness incurred by a qualified organization in acquiring or improving real property is available for investments only if the following restrictions are satisfied:

1. The purchase price for an acquisition or improvement of real property is a fixed amount determined as of the date of the acquisition or completion of the improvement (the *fixed-price restriction*).[130]

2. Neither the amount of the indebtedness, nor any amount payable with respect to the indebtedness, nor the time for making any payment of that amount depends (in whole or in part) on revenues, income, or profits derived from the property (the *participating loan restriction*).[131]

3. The property is not, at any time after the acquisition, leased by the qualified organization to the seller or to a person related[132] to the seller (the *leaseback restriction*).[133]

4. In the case of a pension trust, the seller or lessee of the property is not a disqualified person[134] (the *disqualified person restriction*).[135]

5. The seller or a person related to the seller (or a person related to the plan with respect to which a pension trust was formed) is not providing financing in connection with the acquisition of the property (the *seller-financing restriction*).[136]

6. If the investment in the property is held through a partnership, certain additional requirements are satisfied by the partnership, namely, (a) the partnership satisfies the rules in the foregoing five circumstances, and (b) all of the partners are qualified organizations,[137] each allocation to a partner of the partnership is a qualified allocation,[138] or the partnership meets the rules of a special exception (the *partnership restrictions*).[139]

Nonetheless, the leaseback restriction and the disqualified person restriction are relaxed to permit a limited leaseback of debt-financed real property to

---

[130] IRC § 514(c)(9)(B)(i).
[131] IRC § 514(c)(9)(B)(ii).
[132] As described in IRC § 267(b) or 707(b).
[133] IRC § 514(c)(9)(B)(iii).
[134] As described in IRC § 4975(e)(2)(C), (E), (H).
[135] IRC § 514(c)(9)(B)(iv).
[136] IRC § 514(c)(9)(B)(v).
[137] For this purpose, an organization cannot be treated as a qualified organization if any income of the organization is unrelated business income. IRC § 514(c)(9)(B), penultimate sentence.
[138] A *qualified allocation* is one described in IRC § 168(h)(6). See *Tax-Exempt Organizations*, § 29.5(g), text accompanied by note 130.
[139] IRC § 514(c)(9)(B)(vi). This special exception is the subject of IRC § 514(c)(9)(E). Rules similar to those of this situation also apply in the case of any pass-through entity other than a partnership and in the case of tiered partnerships and other entities. IRC § 514(c)(9)(D).

the seller (or a person related to the seller) or to a disqualified person.[140] The fixed-price restriction and the participating loan restriction are relaxed for certain sales of real property foreclosed on by financial institutions.[141]

(g) Securities Lending Rules

An example of the flexibility of the potential application of the unrelated debt-financed income rules was the suggestion that this type of income is realized by tax-exempt organizations in securities lending transactions.[142] This conclusion was arrived at by way of the contention that the exempt institution is not actually lending the securities, but is "borrowing" the collateral, thereby making the entire interest (and perhaps the dividend or interest equivalent) taxable.

This matter was clarified, however, by enactment of a special rule,[143] and earlier by an IRS ruling that the income from investment of the collateral posted by the broker is not unrelated debt-financed income, inasmuch as the organization did not incur the indebtedness "for the purpose of making additional investments."[144] Thus, the IRS ruled that borrowings pursuant to a line of credit by tax-exempt funds participating in a group trust, for the purpose of facilitating redemptions, did not constitute acquisition indebtedness, because the borrowings allowed the exempt funds to bridge periods of cash shortage rather than make additional investments.[145]

---

[140] This exception applies only when (1) no more than 25 percent of the leasable floor space in a building (or complex of buildings) is leased back to the seller (or related party) or to the disqualified person; and (2) the lease is on commercially reasonable terms, independent of the sale and other transactions. IRC § 514(c)(9)(G). A leaseback to a disqualified person remains subject to the prohibited transaction rules. IRC § 4975.

   The fixed price restriction and the participating loan restriction are not subject to this refinement. Thus, for example, income from real property acquired with seller financing, when the timing or amount of payment is based on revenue, income, or profits from the property, generally continues to be treated as income from debt-financed property, unless another exception applies.

[141] For this purpose, the term *financial institutions* includes financial institutions in conservatorship or receivership, certain affiliates of financial institutions, and government corporations that succeed to the rights and interests of a receiver or conservator. IRC § 514(c)(9)(H)(iv).

   This exception is limited to instances in which (1) a qualified organization obtained real property from a financial institution that acquired the property by foreclosure (or after an actual or imminent default), or the property was held by the selling financial institution when it entered into conservatorship or receivership; (2) any gain recognized by the financial institution with respect to the property is ordinary income; (3) the stated principal amount of the seller financing does not exceed the financial institution's outstanding indebtedness (including accrued but unpaid interest) with respect to the property at the time of foreclosure or default; and (4) the present value of the maximum amount payable pursuant to any participation feature cannot exceed 30 percent of the total purchase price of the property (including contingent payments). IRC § 514(c)(9)(H)(i)–(iii), (v).

   In general, Ferguson & Brown, *More Investment Options Are Available for Tax-Exempt Organizations*, 4 J. Tax. Exempt Orgs. 22 (no. 4, Jan./Feb. 1993); McDowell, *Taxing Leveraged Investments of Charitable Organizations: What Is the Rationale?*, 39 Case W. Res. L. Rev. 705 (no. 3, 1988–1989).

[142] See § 3.4.

[143] See text accompanied by *supra* note 118.

[144] Rev. Rul. 78-88, 1978-1 C.B. 163, 164.

[145] Priv. Ltr. Rul. 200233032.

(h) Additional Considerations

The intent of the unrelated debt-financed income rules is to treat an otherwise tax-exempt organization in the same manner as an ordinary business enterprise to the extent that the exempt organization purchases property through the use of borrowed funds.[146] The IRS recalled this intent in passing on the tax status of indebtedness owed to an exempt labor union by its wholly owned subsidiary title-holding company resulting from a loan to pay debts incurred to acquire two income-producing office buildings. The agency ruled that this *interorganizational indebtedness* was not an acquisition indebtedness, because the "very nature of the title-holding company[,] as well as the parent-subsidiary relationship[,] show this indebtedness to be merely a matter of accounting between the organizations rather than an indebtedness as contemplated by" these rules.[147]

The income of a tax-exempt organization that is attributable to a short sale of publicly traded stock through a broker is not unrelated debt-financed income and thus is not taxable as unrelated business income.[148] This is because, although a short sale creates an obligation, it does not create an indebtedness for tax purposes,[149] and thus there is no acquisition indebtedness. This position of the IRS is not intended to cause any inference with respect to a borrowing of property other than publicly traded stock sold short through a broker. Securities purchased on margin by an exempt organization constitute debt-financed property, which generates unrelated business income.[150]

§ 5.5   COMPUTATION OF UNRELATED DEBT-FINANCED INCOME

Unrelated debt-financed income (the amount subject to tax) is computed by applying to the total gross income (and deductions) attributable to debt-financed property the following fraction: the average acquisition indebtedness for the tax year over the average adjusted basis of the property during the tax year.

For purposes of the numerator of this fraction, acquisition indebtedness is to be averaged over the tax year.[151] This averaging mechanism precludes a tax-exempt organization from avoiding a tax by using other available funds to pay off the indebtedness immediately before any fixed determination date. If debt-financed property is disposed of during the year, *average acquisition indebtedness* means the highest acquisition indebtedness during the preceding 12 months. Absent this rule, a tax-exempt organization could avoid tax by using other

---

[146] H.R. Rep. No. 91-413, 91st Cong., 1st Sess. 46 (1969).

[147] Rev. Rul. 77-72, 1977-1 C.B. 157, 158. This rationale was also applied to avoid the prospect of unrelated business income taxation resulting from the use of joint operating agreements in the health care context. See § 9.8.

[148] Rev. Rul. 95-8, 1995-1 C.B. 107.

[149] Deputy v. du Pont, 308 U.S. 488 (1940).

[150] *E.g.*, Henry E. & Nancy Horton Bartels Trust for the Benefit of the Univ. of New Haven v. United States, 209 F.3d 147 (2d Cir. 2000).

[151] IRC § 514(c)(7).

resources to discharge indebtedness before the end of one tax year and dispose of property after the beginning of the next tax year.

For purposes of the denominator of this fraction, *adjusted basis* is the average adjusted basis for the portion of the year during which the property is held by the tax-exempt organization. The use of average adjusted basis is only for purposes of determining the fraction. When property is disposed of, gain or loss will, as usual, be computed with reference to adjusted basis at the time of disposition.

The essence of the foregoing rules[152] may be illustrated by the following example:

> A tax-exempt organization acquires property for the production of income on July 1, 2006, for $100,000, of which $80,000 is financed (that is, there is an $80,000 acquisition indebtedness). As of December 31, 2006, the organization has satisfied $10,000 of the debt, by one payment (on September 1, 2006) and has claimed $2,500 in straight-line depreciation. For 2006, 75.9 percent of the income (less appropriate deductions) from the property is taxable.
>
> To determine this percentage, the average acquisition indebtedness for 2006 must be computed. This amount is $75,000, ascertained as follows:

(1) Debt	(2) Months Outstanding	(3) (1) × (2)
$80,000	3	$240,000
$70,000	3	$210,000
	6	$450,000

> (3) divided by (2) equals $75,000, which is the weighted average for the six-month period involved.
>
> To determine the average adjusted basis, it is necessary to compute the basis at the beginning of the tax year (here, $100,000) and at the end of the tax year ($97,500, that is, original basis less depreciation). The average adjusted basis ($100,000 divided by $97,500 divided by 2) is $98,750.
>
> The applicable percentage thus becomes 75.9 percent ($75,000/$98,750).

If property is distributed to a tax-exempt organization by a corporation in liquidation, the exempt organization uses the basis of the distributing corporation, with adjustment for any gain recognized on the distribution either to the exempt organization or to the taxable corporation. An example of the former is when an exempt organization had an acquisition indebtedness applicable to its stock in the distributing corporation and an illustration of the latter is an instance of recapture of depreciation.[153] This rule is designed to prevent an exempt organization from acquiring the property in a taxable subsidiary to secure accelerated depreciation during the first several years of the life of the property, enabling the subsidiary to pay off a large part of the indebtedness

---

[152] IRC § 514(a)–(c).
[153] IRC §§ 1245, 1250.

during those years, after which the exempt organization would obtain a stepped-up basis upon liquidation of the subsidiary.[154]

If property is used partly for exempt and partly for nonexempt purposes, the income and deductions attributable to the exempt uses are excluded from the computation of unrelated debt-financed income and allocations are made, as appropriate, for acquisition indebtedness, adjusted basis, and deductions assignable to the property.[155]

---

[154] IRC § 514(d); Reg. § 1.514(d)-1.

[155] IRC § 514(e); Reg. § 1.514(e)-1. Also Florida Farm Bureau Fed'n v. Comm'r, 65 T.C. 1118 (1975). In general, Krasity & Indenbaum, *Tax-Exempt Organizations and Section 514: The Taxation of Income Generated by Bond Reserve Funds and Similar Accounts*, 19 J. Real Estate Tax'n 137 (no. 2, 1992); Indenbaum & Krasity, *Tax-Exempt Entities and Limited Partnerships: Section 514(c)(9)(E)'s Inadequate Response to the Problem of Unrelated Debt-Financed Income*, 18 J. Real Estate Tax'n 37 (no. 1, 1990); Weitz, *Unresolved Issues Remain for Qualified Organizations in Real Estate Partnerships*, 73 J. Tax 332 (1990); Williamson, Duren & Grigorian, *How Exempt Organizations Can Avoid Unrelated Debt-Financed Income on Realty*, 6 J. Tax. Inv. 236 (no. 4, 1989); Larson, *Tax Exempt Organizations and Unrelated Debt Financed Income: Does the Problem Persist?*, 61 N.D. L. Rev. 31 (no. 1, 1985); Beller, *Exempt Organizations: Taxation of Debt-Financed Income*, 24 Tax Law. 489 (1971).

CHAPTER SIX

Special Rules

In addition to a battery of modifications[1] and exceptions,[2] the unrelated business rules include a host of special rules. These laws pertain to tax-exempt social clubs, certain other exempt organizations, private foundations, exempt organizations' involvement in partnerships, and small business corporations; there are also rules pertaining to advertising, periodicals, and corporate sponsorships.

§ 6.1 RULES FOR SOCIAL CLUBS

Social clubs can qualify for a federal income tax exemption when they are organized and operated primarily for pleasure, recreation, and other nonprofitable

---

[1] See ch. 3.
[2] See ch. 4.

purposes, if the doctrine of private inurement is not violated.[3] These clubs, however, are deprived of their exemption when they engage in "business, such as by selling real estate, timber[,] or other products," unless a sale of property is incidental.[4] Nonetheless, in the years leading up to reforms in this area, abuses were prevalent, perhaps fostered by the willingness of some courts to salvage the tax exemption of social clubs. For example, a federal court of appeals held that two golf clubs did not lose their exemptions because of their participation in oil-leasing arrangements on their properties that generated substantial income. The theory was that the leases were incidental to club operations;[5] thus, the profits from the oil leases went untaxed.[6]

In 1969, Congress adhered to the Department of the Treasury's recommendation for reform in this area. The Treasury Department had, in effect, relied on the basic rationale for the tax exemption of social clubs[7] and ran the rationale in reverse, contending that the investment income of these clubs was equivalent to income earned by the club members in their individual capacity. Thus, the Senate Finance Committee stated:

> Since the tax exemption for social clubs and other groups is designed to allow individuals to join together to provide recreational and social facilities or other benefits on a mutual basis, without tax consequences, the exemption operates properly only when the sources of income of the organization are limited to the receipts from the membership. . . . However, where the organization receives income from sources outside the membership, such as income from investments . . . upon which no tax is paid, the membership receives a benefit not contemplated by the exemption in that untaxed dollars can be used by the organization to provide pleasure or recreation (or other benefits) to its membership.[8]

In that year, Congress subjected income unrelated to the normal operation of a social club to the tax on unrelated business income. In the immediate aftermath of this statutory change, the IRS began issuing rulings on the point, such as the criteria the agency uses to determine whether the sale of property by a social

---

[3] IRC § 501(c)(7). See Hopkins, *The Law of Tax-Exempt Organizations, Eighth Edition* (John Wiley & Sons, 2003) [hereinafter *Tax-Exempt Organizations*], ch. 14.

[4] Reg. § 1.501(c)(7)-1(b).

[5] Scofield v. Corpus Christi Golf & Country Club, 127 F.2d 452 (5th Cir. 1942). Also Koon Kreek Klub v. United States, 108 F.2d 616 (5th Cir. 1940); Aviation Country Club, Inc. v. Comm'r, 21 T.C. 807 (1954); Anderson Country Club, Inc. v. Comm'r, 2 T.C. 1238 (1943); Town & Country Club v. Comm'r, 1 T.C.M. 334 (1942). *Cf.* Coastal Club, Inc. v. Comm'r, 43 T.C. 783 (1965), *aff'd*, 368 F.2d 231 (5th Cir. 1966), *cert. denied*, 386 U.S. 1032 (1967).

[6] Cases involving social clubs that were found to be engaged in nonexempt business include Aviation Club of Utah v. Comm'r, 162 F.2d 984 (10th Cir.), *cert. denied*, 332 U.S. 837 (1947); Juniper Hunting Club, Inc. v. Comm'r, 28 B.T.A. 525 (1933).

[7] See *Tax-Exempt Organizations*, § 14.1(a).

[8] S. Rep. No. 91-552, 91st Cong., 1st Sess. 71 (1969); *also* H.R. Rep. No. 91-413, 91st Cong., 1st Sess. 47 (1969) (pt. 1); Rev. Rul. 69-220, 1969-1 C.B. 154. Applying this doctrine, a federal court of appeals held that the regular sale of tickets for lotteries conducted for the public by a Knights of Columbus council (an IRC § 501(c)(8) fraternal society [see *Tax-Exempt Organizations*, § 18.4(a)]) were subject to the wagering excise and occupational taxes. IRC § 4421. The exception from the taxes for activities where there is no inurement of net earnings was ruled not to apply, on the theory that the revenues derived from the gaming are used to preclude dues increases, so that the "subsidization" constituted a form of private inurement to the council's members. Knights of Columbus Council No. 3660 v. United States, 83-2 U.S.T.C. ¶ 16,410 (S.D. Ind. 1983), *aff'd*, 783 F.2d 69 (7th Cir. 1986).

club is an incidental transaction or a transaction intended to produce a profit (the latter being a nonexempt business).[9]

(a) General Rules

For most types of tax-exempt organizations, revenue other than net income from unrelated business activities is nontaxable.[10] Thus, for nearly all exempt organizations, nontaxable revenue embraces gifts, grants, income from the performance of exempt functions, and passive (investment) income. The income of a tax-exempt social club, however, is taxed in a significantly different manner: rather than isolating and taxing unrelated business taxable income (the general rule), the law isolates the exempt function income of social clubs and subjects the balance of its revenue (including investment income) to taxation. (Thus, one of the principal disadvantages of classification as an otherwise tax-exempt social club is that all of the organization's investment income—including passive income—generally is taxable.[11])

Specifically, a tax-exempt social club's *unrelated business taxable income* is defined as "gross income (excluding any exempt function income), less the deductions allowed . . . [for business expenses] which are directly connected with the production of the gross income (excluding exempt function income)."[12] For tax purposes, this income is computed by deducting all expenses directly connected with production of the income and by applying certain of the modifications generally used in determining unrelated business taxable income.[13] Thus, for example, the interest earned by an exempt social club on deposits required for its charter flights was held taxable as unrelated business income.[14] Likewise, investment income that was not set aside for charitable purposes, and thus could not be the subject of an exception,[15] was found to be taxable;[16] the sale of land by an exempt social club, under circumstances in which the transaction did not qualify for an exception,[17] was held to produce unrelated business income.[18] *Exempt function income* is gross income from dues, fees, charges, or similar amounts paid by members of the tax-exempt organization in connection with the purposes constituting the basis for the exemption of the club.[19]

---

[9] Rev. Rul. 69-232, 1969-1 C.B. 154.

[10] See ch. 3.

[11] *E.g.*, Carlson, *The Little Known Repeal of the Income Tax Exemption of Social Clubs*, 26 Tax L. Rev. 45 (1970).

[12] IRC § 512(a)(3)(A). Interest on obligations of a state (see IRC § 103(a)) received by a tax-exempt social club is not included in gross income for purposes of IRC § 512(b)(3). Rev. Rul. 76-337, 1976-2 C.B. 177.

An exempt social club may, in computing its unrelated business taxable income, claim the tax credit for a portion of employer social security taxes paid with respect to employee tips (IRC § 45B) received from members and nonmembers. Rev. Rul. 2003-64, 2003-25 I.R.B. 1036.

[13] IRC §§ 162, 512(b).

[14] Council of British Societies in S. Cal. v. United States, 78-2 U.S.T.C. ¶ 9744 (C.D. Cal.), *aff'd*, 587 F.2d 931 (9th Cir. 1978).

[15] See § 6.1(c).

[16] Confrerie de la Chaine des Rotisseurs v. Comm'r, 66 T.C.M. 1845 (1993).

[17] See § 6.1(d).

[18] Deer Park Country Club v. Comm'r, 70 T.C.M. 1445 (1995).

[19] IRC § 512(a)(3)(B).

The U.S. Tax Court held that a tax-exempt social club, the principal activity of which was to stage an annual mock pirate invasion and a parade, incurred taxable income from the sale of refreshments along the parade route, souvenirs, and advertising, inasmuch as the concession and other income were derived from dealings with nonmembers. The court also held that the expenses of staging the invasion and parade could not be used to offset concession revenue, because the expenses did not have the requisite "direct" relationship with the income.[20]

(b) Profit Motive Requirement

There was a substantial dispute, manifested in different positions by federal appellate courts and eventually resolved by the U.S. Supreme Court[21], as to the extent to which deductions may be taken into account in determining a tax-exempt social club's unrelated business taxable income. This controversy was stimulated by social clubs' practice of deducting from investment income losses incurred in connection with the sale of meals and beverages to nonmembers. Thus, an effort commenced to develop a theory to preclude an exempt social club from generating losses from the performance of nonexempt functions that could be offset against gross investment income.

In 1981, the IRS announced that when a tax-exempt social club operates a food and beverage concession catering to nonmembers, and consistently sells the food and beverages at prices insufficient to recover the cost of sales, the club "may not, in determining its unrelated business taxable income . . . , deduct from its net investment income its losses from such sales to nonmembers."[22] The concept underlying this position was that, when an exempt social club does not endeavor to realize a profit from sales to nonmembers, the expenses cannot be deductible as business expenses under the general rules for that deduction.[23]

This position was tested in the U.S. Tax Court and was upheld, albeit on a different theory. The Tax Court, relying on the statutory language stating that a tax-exempt social club's taxable income is gross nonexempt income less the deductions that are "directly connected" with the production of gross income, held that an exempt social club's expense may be offset only against income it directly helped to generate, thereby precluding a club from deducting the expenses of services to nonmembers against investment income.[24] On appeal, however, it was held that the Tax Court's interpretation of the statute was incorrect and that federal tax law "authorizes deductions to be taken from the sum total of a club's non-exempt gross income, not merely from the portion of the income connected to the particular deduction."[25] This appellate court returned to the IRS position and concluded that exempt social clubs can only deduct the expenses of activities engaged in with the intention of making a profit, thereby precluding the club in the case from reducing its taxable investment income with nonmember service expenses. Thus, an exempt social club was permitted

[20] Ye Mystic Krewe of Gasparilla v. Comm'r, 80 T.C. 755 (1983).
[21] See text accompanied by *infra* notes 34–37.
[22] Rev. Rul. 81-69, 1981-1 C.B. 351, 352.
[23] IRC § 162.
[24] The Brook, Inc. v. Comm'r, 50 T.C.M. 959 (1985) & 51 T.C.M. 133 (1985).
[25] The Brook, Inc. v. Comm'r, 799 F.2d 833 (2d Cir. 1986).

to deduct the donations of the net proceeds of beano games it conducted, where the payments were a condition of its license for the games.[26]

The IRS's stance in this regard was initially upheld in another case,[27] but was rejected on appeal by the Sixth Circuit Court of Appeals. This appellate court's position, which is founded on the difference in tax treatment of social clubs in the unrelated income context,[28] was that a social club has a business expense deduction for outlays associated with activities engaged in with a "basic purpose of economic gain."[29] Under this principle, with which the Second Circuit Court of Appeals expressly disagreed, a club could deduct, as business expenses, all expenses of providing food and beverages to nonmembers against investment income.

The Ninth Circuit Court of Appeals sided with the Second Circuit on this point, holding that a tax-exempt social club must pursue a nonmember activity with a profit motive before it can properly deduct its losses.[30] The appellate court agreed with the IRS that the omission of the term *trade or business* from the definition of *unrelated business taxable income,* as applied to exempt social clubs,[31] does not allow social clubs to deduct losses incurred for nonmember activities that are not businesses; the Ninth Circuit wrote that it is "well-established" that, to qualify as a trade or business, an activity must be "regular and profit-seeking."[32] In the case, the club's nonmember food and bar activity was held not to be profit-seeking, because of consistent losses for six years. Similarly, an exempt association that published a monthly journal for its members was not allowed to offset losses against certain gross unrelated business income, because the organization's "long-standing policy of voluntarily incurring losses evidenced a lack of profit objective."[33]

As noted, this matter was resolved by the U.S. Supreme Court, in 1990, when it held that a tax-exempt social club may use losses incurred in connection with sales to nonmembers to offset investment income only if the sales were motivated by an intent to generate a profit.[34] The Court held that the requisite *profit motive* means an "intent to generate receipts in excess of costs," and concluded that there is "no basis for dispensing with the profit-motive requirement" in these circumstances.[35] The Court explained that elimination of the profit motive standard would create "considerable tension" with the overall statutory scheme of tax treatment of social clubs, in that "Congress intended that the investment income of social clubs (unlike the investment income of most other exempt organizations) should be subject to the same tax consequences as the investment

---

[26] S. End Italian Indep. Club, Inc. v. Comm'r, 87 T.C. 168 (1986).

[27] Cleveland Athletic Club, Inc. v. United States, 588 F. Supp. 1305 (N.D. Ohio 1984).

[28] See text accompanied by *supra* notes 11–13.

[29] Cleveland Athletic Club, Inc. v. United States, 779 F.2d 1160, 1165 (6th Cir. 1986).

[30] N. Ridge Country Club v. Comm'r, 877 F.2d 750 (9th Cir. 1989), *rev'g* 89 T.C. 563 (1987).

[31] IRC § 512(a)(3)(A). See text accompanied by *infra* note 39.

[32] N. Ridge Country Club v. Comm'r, 877 F.2d 750, 753 (9th Cir. 1989), citing Comm'r v. Groetzinger, 480 U.S. 23 (1987) (see § 2.5).

[33] W. Va. State Med. Ass'n v. Comm'r, 882 F.2d 123, 125 (4th Cir. 1989), *aff'g* 91 T.C. 651 (1988), *cert. denied,* 493 U.S. 1044 (1990).

[34] Portland Golf Club v. Comm'r, 497 U.S. 154 (1990), *aff'g* 876 F.2d 897 (9th Cir. 1989), *rev'g & remanding* 55 T.C.M. 212 (1988).

[35] *Id.,* 497 U.S. at 165, 166.

income of any other taxpayer"; thus, allowance of the offset for exempt social clubs "would run counter to the principle of tax neutrality which underlies the statutory scheme."[36] Thereafter, the Tax Court ruled that an exempt social club was not entitled to offset losses from its nonmember activities against investment income, because it did not undertake the activities with the requisite profit motive.[37]

Under the general rules of unrelated income taxation, *unrelated business taxable income* is defined as the "gross income derived by any organization from any unrelated trade or business . . . regularly carried on by it, less the deductions . . . which are directly connected with the carrying on of such trade or business."[38] The *trade or business* requirement is not part of the definition of *unrelated business taxable income* applicable to social clubs. These organizations are thereby subjected to, in the words of the Second Circuit, a "much more far-reaching tax than" are most other categories of tax-exempt organizations.[39]

(c) Set-Asides

As noted, the term *exempt function income* is gross income from dues, fees, charges, or similar amounts paid by members of the tax-exempt organization in connection with the purposes constituting the club's basis for exemption.[40] Also, the passive income of an exempt social club is generally not taxed if it is set aside to be used for charitable and similar purposes.[41]

In the classic court opinion on the subject of set-asides, a court, in noting that the "policy of exempting" charitable and similar organizations from tax is "firmly established," wrote that the set-aside rule (in this instance, embodied in federal tax law) should be read "in such a way as to carry out this policy and not to make the result turn on accidental circumstances or legal technicalities."[42] The tax consequences depend, said the court, "upon who is ultimately entitled to the property constituting [the] income."[43] Thus, the court interpreted the set-aside rule to exempt from taxation the income of an estate that was destined for charitable purposes, even though the representative of the estate held legal title to the underlying property during the period of administration and even though no entry was made on the books of the representative crediting the charitable beneficiaries with the income. This decision was affirmed, with the

---

[36] *Id.* at 165. Confusion has resulted from this Supreme Court opinion concerning the manner in which exempt social clubs demonstrate the necessary profit motive. The Court majority held that the same method of determining "costs" (both direct and indirect) used to ascertain intent to generate a profit must be used in computing actual profit or loss. This holding was criticized, in a partial concurring opinion, on the ground that economic reality and statements of income and expenses for tax purposes may be different. In general, Miller, *U.S. Supreme Court in* Portland Golf Club *Reserves on a Key Profit-Intent Question and Adopts a Pervasive Estoppel-by-Reporting Rule*, 15 Rev. Tax. of Individuals 108 (1991); Falk, Portland Golf Club—*Uncertain Direction from the Supreme Court*, 2 J. Tax Exempt Orgs. 11 (Fall 1990).

[37] Atlanta Athletic Club v. Comm'r, 61 T.C.M. 2011 (1991), *overruled on another issue*, 980 F.2d 1409 (11th Cir. 1993).

[38] IRC § 512(a)(1).

[39] The Brook, Inc. v. Comm'r, 799 F.2d 833, 841 (2d Cir. 1986).

[40] IRC § 512(a)(3)(B).

[41] IRC § 170(c)(4).

[42] Slocum v. Bowers, 15 F.2d 400, 403 (S.D.N.Y. 1926).

[43] *Id.* at 404.

appellate court holding that it was the intent of Congress not to tax income destined for charitable entities and that the designation made by the decedent in the will was the "most effective method" of setting the income aside.[44]

Comparable case law invokes the law of trusts, under which the courts have concluded that the segregated funds of a set-aside are housed in a constructive, implied, or resulting trust. For example, the Tax Court, having found in a set of facts a "reasonable certainty as to the property, the objects, and the beneficiaries," held that funds transferred to an exempt organization for the purpose of carrying out its objectives were "impressed with a trust upon their receipt."[45] "No express words of trust were used, but none are necessary," wrote the court, in concluding that the recipient organization was "merely a designated beneficiary."[46] In finding that the funds did not constitute gross income to the organization, the court focused on the essential criteria for a set-aside: "The organization's books showed the total amount of such fees it received and the unexpended balance thereof at all times."[47] A commingling of the funds with other receipts was held to "not destroy their identity as a trust fund."[48] Nonetheless, a commingling of funds in an organization's general treasury, when there is no earmarking or other dedication of funds, will not give rise to a set-aside.[49]

This type of a set-aside occurs when a tax-exempt fraternity or sorority (classified pursuant to the federal tax law as a social club) transfers income from its investment receipts to a related charitable foundation.[50] In one instance, however, an attempted set-aside failed to immunize net investment income from taxation, because the activity funded by the investment income (publication of a magazine) was found not to be educational.[51]

(d) Sale of Club Assets

Statutory law governs the subject of nonrecurring sales of club assets. A common example of this is a country club that sells land that has become encroached upon by developers, so as to buy land further out in the countryside for new facilities.[52] When the purpose of this type of sale is not profit but facilitation of relocation or a comparable purpose, the law allows a carryover of basis—that is, nonrecognition of gain.[53] Specifically, when property used directly in the performance of the club's tax-exempt function is sold and the proceeds reinvested in

---

[44] Bowers v. Slocum, 20 F.2d 350, 352, 353 (2d Cir. 1927).

[45] Broadcast Measurement Bureau, Inc. v. Comm'r, 16 T.C. 988, 997 (1951).

[46] *Id.* at 997, 1000.

[47] *Id.* at 1001.

[48] *Id.* Also Seven-Up Co. v. Comm'r, 14 T.C. 965 (1950); *Tax-Exempt Organizations*, § 3.4. *Cf.* Reg. § 1.512(a)-4(b)(5); see text accompanied by *infra* note 73.

[49] Confrerie de la Chaine des Rotisseurs v. Comm'r, 66 T.C.M. 1845 (1993).

[50] *E.g.*, Alpha Tau Omega Fraternity v. Comm'r, Dkt. No. 2810-84 (Tax Ct.)(settled).

[51] Phi Delta Theta Fraternity v. Comm'r, 887 F.2d 1302 (6th Cir. 1989), *aff'g* 90 T.C. 1033 (1988).

[52] Rev. Rul. 69-232, 1969-1 C.B. 154; Rev. Rul. 65-64, 1965-1 C.B. 241; Rev. Rul. 58-501, 1958-2 C.B. 262; Santee Club v. White, 87 F.2d 5 (1st Cir. 1936); Mill Lane Club v. Comm'r, 23 T.C. 433 (1954); Anderson Country Club, Inc. v. Comm'r, 2 T.C. 1238 (1943); Juniper Hunting Club, Inc. v. Comm'r, 28 B.T.A. 525 (1933).

[53] IRC § 512(a)(3)(D). The IRS ruled that gain need not be recognized in the case of an exempt club's selling all its real estate in the context of its dissolution. Priv. Ltr. Rul. 200314030.

exempt function property, within a period beginning one year before the sale date and ending three years thereafter, any gain from the sale is recognized only to the extent that the sale price of the old property exceeds the purchase price of the new property.

There can be controversy over the meaning of the term *used directly*. In one case, the government argued that there must be "actual, direct, continuous, and regular usage," and that the property involved must form an "integral part of the exempt functions of a social club"; it lamented the club's "desultory activities" on the property, which it regarded as essentially investment property. The court involved held, however, that these requirements are not in the statute; if they should be, it is the function of Congress, not the courts, to expand the statute.[54] By contrast, when "no part" of a tract of land was ever "physically used" by an exempt social club for recreational purposes, the court found this special rule to be inapplicable and unavailable.[55]

When the sale of tax-exempt social club assets occurs more than once, the IRS is likely to resist application of this special rule, particularly in any case in which the sale transactions substantially deplete the club of its assets and the club evidences no intention to replace the property that is being sold.[56] Also, when a club derives revenue as the result of a grant of an option on the sale of the property, rather than from sale of the property itself, this nonrecognition rule is inapplicable, so the option income is taxable as unrelated income.[57]

In another of these instances, a tax-exempt social club sold a painting that had been prominently displayed in its dining room for decades. The club was of the view that the painting was an important part of its exempt function, because it enhanced a room where exempt activities took place; in fact, the room was named for the painting. Because of concerns over adequate security, the club sold the painting to an unrelated party and used the proceeds in furtherance of its exempt purposes. The IRS ruled that the gain on the sale of the painting qualified for exclusion from unrelated income taxation.[58]

(e) Dividends-Received Deduction

It is the view of the Department of the Treasury that the dividends-received deduction[59] is not allowed in computing the taxable income of social-club organizations.[60] Believing that the reason for this deduction is inapplicable in this context, Congress clarified this point by agreeing to the Treasury Department's position.[61] (A similar change in the law was made for nonexempt membership organizations.[62]) Although this statutory revision took effect in 1976, it was held that tax-exempt social cubs are not entitled to the dividends-recieved deduction

---

[54] Atlanta Athletic Club v. Comm'r, 980 F.2d 1409, 1414 (11th Cir. 1993).

[55] Deer Park Country Club v. Comm'r, 70 T.C.M. 1445, 1449 (1995); Tamarisk Country Club v. Comm'r, 84 T.C. 756 (1985).

[56] *E.g.*, Priv. Ltr. Rul. 8337092.

[57] Framingham Country Club v. United States, 659 F. Supp. 650 (D. Mass. 1987).

[58] Priv. Ltr. Rul. 200051046.

[59] IRC § 243.

[60] Prop. Reg. § 1.512(a)-3(b)(2) (withdrawn).

[61] IRC § 512(a)(3)(A), last sentence; H.R. Rep. No. 1353, 94th Cong., 2d Sess. 6 (1976).

[62] IRC § 277. See *Tax-Exempt Organizations*, § 13.6.

for prior years (back to 1970), because the deduction is not for an expense incurred in the production of income but comes into being as a consequence of the existence of the income.[63]

§ 6.2   RULES FOR CERTAIN OTHER TAX-EXEMPT ORGANIZATIONS

Special rules apply in the unrelated business setting for veterans' organizations, certain employee benefit plans, title-holding companies, and foreign organizations.

(a) Veterans' Organizations

In the case of certain veterans' organizations,[64] the basic unrelated business income rules generally apply.[65] Nonetheless, the term *unrelated business taxable income* does not include any amount attributable to payments for life, illness, accident, or health insurance with respect to members of the organizations or their dependents that is set aside for the purpose of paying insurance benefits or for a charitable purpose.[66] If an amount so set aside is used for any other purpose, it is includable in unrelated business income of the organization, without regard to any of the modifications,[67] in the tax year in which it is withdrawn from the set-aside.[68]

Payments by members (including commissions on the payments earned by the set-aside as agent for an insurance company) into an insurance set-aside must be for the sole purpose of obtaining life, accident, or health insurance benefits from the organization or for the reasonable costs of administration of the insurance program, except that this purpose is not violated when excess funds from an experience gain are utilized for charitable purposes or the reasonable costs of distributing funds for such purposes. Funds for any other purpose may not be set aside in the insurance set-aside.[69]

In addition to these payments by members, only income from amounts in the insurance set-aside (including commissions earned as agent for an insurance company) may be so set aside. Moreover, unless this income is used to provide insurance benefits, for charitable purposes, or for reasonable costs of administration, this income must be set aside within a specific period to avoid being included as an item of unrelated business income.[70] Income from amounts in the insurance set-aside generally must be set aside in the tax year in which it would be includable in gross income but for these rules. However, income set aside on

---

[63] Rolling Rock Club v. United States, 85-1 U.S.T.C. ¶ 9374 (W.D. Pa. 1985), aff'd, 785 F.2d 93 (3d Cir. 1986).

[64] That is, an organization described in IRC § 501(c)(19). See *Tax-Exempt Organizations*, § 18.10(a).

[65] Reg. § 1.512(a)-4(a).

[66] IRC § 512(a)(4); Reg. § 1.512(a)-4(a).

[67] See ch. 3.

[68] Reg. § 1.512(a)-4(a). Amounts are considered to have been withdrawn from an insurance set-aside for an impermissible purpose if they are used in any manner inconsistent with providing insurance benefits, paying the reasonable costs of administering the insurance program for charitable purposes, or distributing funds for charitable purposes. An example of a use of funds that would be considered this type of a withdrawal is use of the funds as security for a loan. *Id.*

[69] Reg. § 1.512(a)-4(b)(1).

[70] Reg. § 1.512(a)-4(b)(2).

or before the date prescribed for filing the organization's unrelated business income tax return (whether or not it had such income) for the year (including any extension of time), may, at the election of the organization, be treated as having been set aside in that year.[71]

Income from amounts in the insurance set-aside may consist solely of items of investment income from, and other gains derived from dealings in, property in the set-aside. The deductions allowed against these items of income or other gains are those amounts that are related to production of this income or other gains. Only the amounts of income or other gain that are in excess of these deductions may be set aside in the insurance set-aside.[72]

An amount is not properly set aside for these purposes if the organization commingles it with any amount that is not to be set aside.[73] Adequate records describing the amount set aside, and indicating that it is to be used for the designated purpose, are sufficient. Amounts that are set aside need not be permanently committed to the use, either under state law or by contract. Thus, for example, it is not necessary that the organization place these funds in an irrevocable trust. Although set-aside income may be accumulated, any accumulation that is unreasonable in amount or duration is considered to be evidence that the income was not accumulated for the purposes set forth. For this purpose, accumulations that are reasonably necessary for the purpose of providing life, illness, health, or accident insurance benefits, judged on the basis of recognized mortality or morbidity tables and assumed rates of interest under an actuarially acceptable method, would not be unreasonable, even though the accumulations are quite large and the time between the organization's receipt of the amounts and the date of benefits payment is quite long. For example, an accumulation of income for 20 years or longer that is determined to be reasonably necessary to pay life insurance benefits to members, their dependents, or designated beneficiaries generally is not an unreasonable accumulation. Income that has been set aside may be invested, pending the action contemplated by the set-aside, without being regarded as having been used for other purposes.[74]

(b) Certain Employee Benefit Plans

Special rules apply to certain types of tax-exempt employee benefit plans, namely, exempt voluntary employees' beneficiary associations[75] (VEBAs) and exempt supplemental unemployment benefit trusts[76] (SUBs). These rules[77] apply the unrelated business income tax to these organizations' net income other than their exempt function income.[78] For example, an exempt VEBA was required to pay the unrelated business income tax on revenue allocable to temporary excess office space, notwithstanding the court's belief that the space was acquired, in

---

[71] Reg. § 1.512(a)-4(b)(3).
[72] Reg. § 1.512(a)-4(b)(4).
[73] Cf. text accompanied by *supra* note 48.
[74] Reg. § 1.512(a)-4(b)(5).
[75] IRC § 501(c)(9). See *Tax-Exempt Organizations*, § 16.3.
[76] IRC § 501(c)(17). See *Tax-Exempt Organizations*, § 16.4.
[77] IRC § 512(a)(3).
[78] IRC § 512(a)(3)(B).

the exercise of sound business judgment, in anticipation of organizational growth.[79]

Exempt function income in this setting is of two types:

1. Gross income from amounts (such as dues or fees) paid by members of the organization as consideration for the provision of goods, facilities, or services in furtherance of tax-exempt purposes

2. Income that is set aside for a charitable purpose or to provide for the payment of life, illness, accident, or other benefits, subject to certain limitations[80]

The amounts set aside in a VEBA or SUB as of a tax year of the organization, to provide for the payment of life, illness, accident, or other benefits, may not be taken into account for purposes of determining exempt function income, to the extent that the amounts exceed the qualified asset account limit[81] for that year.[82] In calculating the qualified asset account for this purpose, a reserve for postretirement medical benefits[83] may not be taken into account.[84]

The exempt function income of a VEBA or SUB for a tax year of the organization includes certain amounts paid by members of the entity[85] and other income of the entity (including earnings on member contributions) that is set aside for the payment of life, illness, accident, or other benefits, to the extent that the total amount set aside in the entity (including member contributions and other income set aside in the entity) as of the close of the tax year for any purpose does not exceed the qualified asset account limit for the organization's year. For these purposes,[86] *member contributions* include both employee contributions and employer contributions to the VEBA or SUB. In calculating the total amount set aside in one of these entities as of the close of a tax year, certain assets with useful lives extending substantially beyond the end of the tax year (such as buildings and licenses) are not to be taken into account, to the extent they are used in the provision of life, illness, accident, or other benefits. For example, cash and securities (and similar investments) held by a VEBA or SUB are not disregarded in calculating the total amount set aside for this purpose, because they are used to pay welfare benefits, rather than merely used in provision of the benefits. Accordingly, the unrelated business income of a VEBA or SUB for a tax year of the organization generally will equal the lesser of two amounts: (1) the entity's income for the year (excluding member contributions), or (2) the excess of the total amount set aside as of the close of the year (including member contributions and excluding certain assets with a useful life extending substantially beyond the end of the tax year, to the extent they are used in the provision of welfare benefits) over the qualified asset account limit (calculated without

---

[79] Uniformed Servs. Benefit Ass'n v. United States, 727 F. Supp. 533 (W.D. Mo. 1990).

[80] IRC § 512(a)(3)(E).

[81] That is, the limit described in IRC § 419A(c), (f)(7).

[82] IRC § 512(a)(3)(E)(i); Reg. § 1.512(a)-5T, A-3(a).

[83] See IRC § 419A(c)(2)(A).

[84] Reg. § 1.512(a)-5T, A-3(a).

[85] That is, amounts within the meaning of the first sentence of IRC § 512(a)(3)(B).

[86] IRC § 512(c)(3)(B).

regard to the otherwise permitted reserve for postretirement medical benefits) for the tax year.[87]

A VEBA's or SUB's income for a tax year includes gain realized by the organization on the sale or disposition of any asset during that year. The gain realized by one of these entities on the sale or disposition of an asset is equal to the amount realized by the organization over the basis of the asset (owned by the organization), reduced by any qualified direct costs attributable to the asset.[88]

A court held that, in determining a VEBA's unrelated business income, the amount of investment income that the VEBA set aside, to provide for the payment of reasonable costs of administration directly connected with the provision and payment of health care benefits, was subject to the above-referenced limitation.[89] The court also held that, in making the calculation, the amount of assets that were set aside may not be reduced by the amount of the reserve[90] for postretirement medical benefits.[91] This decision, however, was reversed, with the appellate court concluding that the limitation does not apply to funds set aside and expended on appropriate administrative costs during the tax year involved; the limit, rather, is on the amount that the organization may accumulate as of year's end.[92]

A VEBA, which provided benefits to a tax-exempt business league and its members, received demutualization proceeds from an insurance company; this is not a form of exempt function revenue. The VEBA avoided unrelated business income taxation of the proceeds by setting them aside for charitable purposes, in the form of transfer to a supporting organization that carried out the charitable and educational purposes of the business league.[93] In another instance, a VEBA avoided taxation of demutualization proceeds by setting the amounts aside for the provision of permissible welfare benefits.[94]

(c) Title-Holding Companies

A title-holding company can be tax-exempt, if it exists for the purpose of holding title to property and collecting the income generated by that property, for the benefit of one or more tax-exempt organizations.[95] There are essentially two types of exempt title-holding entities: those with a single parent[96] and those with two or more parent organizations.[97]

It had been the IRS's position that a title-holding company must lose its tax-exempt status if it generates any amount of certain types of unrelated business

---

[87] Reg. § 1.512(a)-5T, A-3(b).

[88] Reg. § 1.512(a)-5T, A-3(c). The matter of attribution of these costs is the subject of Reg. § 1.419-1T, Q & A-6.

[89] IRC § 512(a)(3)(E)(i).

[90] As defined in IRC § 419A(c)(2)(A).

[91] Sherwin-Williams Co. Employee Health Plan Trust v. Comm'r, 115 T.C. 440 (2000).

[92] Sherwin-Williams Co. Employee Health Plan Trust v. Comm'r, 330 F.3d 449 (6th Cir. 2003). For purposes of the rule that makes this set-aside limitation inapplicable to an organization that receives substantially all of its contributions from tax-exempt employers (IRC § 512(a)(3)(E)(iii)), the term *substantially all* means at least 85 percent. INFO 2003-0225.

[93] Priv. Ltr. Rul. 200223068.

[94] Priv. Ltr. Rul. 200011063. If demutualization proceeds are paid to the employer, which transfers them to a VEBA, the contributions from the employer constitute exempt function revenue to the association. *Id.*

[95] See *Tax-Exempt Organizations*, § 18.2.

[96] That is, an organization described in IRC § 501(c)(2).

[97] That is, an organization described in IRC § 501(c)(25).

taxable income.[98] The federal tax law was amended, however, to permit an exempt title-holding company to receive unrelated business taxable income (that would otherwise disqualify the company for tax exemption) in an amount up to 10 percent of its gross income for the tax year, provided that the unrelated business taxable income is incidentally derived from the holding of real property.[99] For example, income generated from fees for parking or from the operation of vending machines located on real property owned by a title-holding company generally qualifies for the 10 percent *de minimis* rule, but income derived from an activity that is not incidental to the holding of real property (such as manufacturing) does not qualify.[100] Permissible unrelated business income is nonetheless subject to taxation.

Also, a tax-exempt title-holding company will not lose its tax exemption if unrelated business taxable income that is incidentally derived from the holding of real property exceeds the 10-percent limitation, if the organization establishes to the satisfaction of the IRS that the receipt of unrelated business taxable income in excess of the 10-percent limitation was "inadvertent and reasonable steps are being taken to correct the circumstances giving rise to such income."[101]

A tax-exempt organization and a single-parent title-holding corporation[102] may file a consolidated annual information return for a tax year. When this is done, and when the title-holding corporation pays any amount of its net income over the year to the exempt organization (or would have paid the amount but for the fact that the expenses of collecting the income exceeded its income), the corporation is treated as if it was organized and operated for the same purpose(s) as the other exempt organization (in addition to its title-holding purpose).[103] The effect of this rule is to exclude from any unrelated income taxation the income received by the exempt parent organization from the title-holding corporation.

(d) Foreign Organizations

Federal tax law provides a definition of *unrelated business taxable income* specifically applicable to foreign organizations that are subject to the tax on unrelated income.[104] Basically, foreign organizations are taxed on their unrelated business taxable income that is *effectively connected* with the conduct of a trade or business within the United States, and on unrelated income derived from sources within the United States even though not so effectively connected.

---

[98] IRS Notice 88-121, 1988-2 C.B. 457. Indeed, the tax regulations still provide that, because a title-holding corporation cannot be tax-exempt if it engages in any business other than that of holding title to property and collecting income therefrom, it cannot (with certain exceptions) have unrelated business taxable income. Reg. § 1.501(c)(2)-1(a).

[99] IRC § 501(c)(2), last sentence; IRC § 501(c)(25)(G).

[100] H.R. Rep. No. 103-111, 103d Cong., 1st Sess. 618 (1993).

[101] IRC § 501(c)(2), last sentence; IRC § 501(c)(25)(G)(ii).

[102] See § 8.2.

[103] IRC § 511(c).

[104] IRC § 512(a)(2); Reg. § 1.512(a)-1(g).

§ 6.3 PRIVATE FOUNDATION RULES

A *private foundation* is a charitable organization that is not a public charity.[105] A standard private foundation essentially has the following characteristics (in addition to being charitable in nature): It is funded from one source (usually an individual, married couple, family, or corporation), its ongoing funding is in the form of investment income (rather than from a flow of charitable contributions), and it makes grants to advance the charitable endeavors of other persons (rather than conducting its own programs).

Private foundations have minimal entanglement with the unrelated business rules. The principal reason for this, from a law standpoint, is the limitation on excess business holdings.[106] Generally, it is common for a tax-exempt organization itself to conduct an unrelated business as one of its many activities. When an exempt organization does that, it is conducting the business function as a *sole proprietorship*; the exempt organization is the sole owner of the business enterprise.[107] A private foundation cannot, however, own 100 percent of a business operated as a sole proprietorship.[108] Therefore, because of this restriction, a private foundation generally cannot actively engage in an unrelated business activity.[109]

(a) Business Enterprises

The concept of the *business enterprise* is integral to the excess business holdings rules. In general, that term means the active conduct of an unrelated trade or business, including any activity that is regularly carried on for the production of income from the sale of goods or the performance of services.[110] When an activity carried on for profit constitutes an unrelated business, no part of the business may be excluded from classification as a business enterprise merely because it does not result in a profit.[111]

There are several ways in which a private foundation can, without adverse tax consequences, engage in an unrelated business (or business-like) activity. These ways are founded on the concept that the activity fails to constitute a business enterprise.

---

[105] See *Tax-Exempt Organizations*, §§ 11.1, 11.3.

[106] IRC § 4943. See Hopkins & Blazek, *Private Foundations: Tax Law and Compliance, Second Edition* (John Wiley & Sons, 2003) [hereinafter *Private Foundations*], ch. 7.

[107] A *sole proprietorship* is any business enterprise (see text accompanied by *infra* note 110) that is actually and directly owned by a private foundation, in which the foundation has a 100 percent equity interest, and that is not held by a corporation, trust, or other business entity for the foundation. Reg. § 53.4943-10(e).

[108] IRC § 4943(c)(3)(B); Reg. § 53.4943-3(c)(3).

[109] Some tax-exempt organizations participate in unrelated business activity by means of partnerships. See §§ 8.9(a), 8.11. The principles of the excess business holdings rules apply, however, to holdings by a private foundation by means of a partnership, joint venture, or other business enterprise that is not incorporated. IRC § 4943(c)(3).

As noted (see text accompanied by *supra* note 108), for a proprietorship owned by a private foundation to be a sole proprietorship, the foundation must have a 100 percent interest in the equity of the business enterprise. Thus, if a private foundation sells an interest in a sole proprietorship, the business enterprise becomes treated as a partnership. Reg. § 53.4943-10(e).

[110] Reg. § 53.4943-10(a)(1).

[111] *Id.* This language, and that of the previous sentence, is identical to that defining a *trade or business* in the unrelated business setting generally. See § 2.2.

The principal way for a private foundation to engage in allowable and non-taxable unrelated business is to engage in an activity in which at least 95 percent of the gross income of the business is derived from passive sources.[112] Gross income from *passive sources* includes the items excluded pursuant to the modification rules for dividends, interest, payments with respect to securities loans, amounts received as consideration for entering into agreements to make loans, annuities, royalties, rent, capital gains, and gains from the lapse or termination of options to buy or sell securities.[113] For example, a private foundation held, as an investment, a fee ownership interest in several thousand acres of timberland and received capital gains pursuant to timber-cutting contracts; the IRS ruled that the foundation's ownership of the timberland was not a business enterprise, inasmuch as at least 95 percent of the gross income from the property was in the form of capital gain.[114]

There are two refinements to these rules:

1. A bond or other evidence of indebtedness does not constitute a holding in a business enterprise, unless the evidence of indebtedness is otherwise determined to be an equitable interest in an enterprise.[115]

2. A leasehold interest in real property does not constitute an interest in a business enterprise, even though the rent payable under the lease depends, in whole or in part, on the income or profits derived by another person from the property, unless the leasehold interest constitutes an interest in the income or profits of an unrelated business.[116]

Thus, as long as the income is generated as one or more forms of these or other types of passive income, the income will not—as a general rule—be taxed as unrelated business income. This exception consequently usually shields most forms of investment income from unrelated income taxation.

Therefore, as a general proposition, a private foundation may invest in (or receive as a contribution and retain) securities without becoming subject to the unrelated business income rules. The same is generally true with respect to rental property, although the income may be taxed if the rental property is used in an active business operation, if the rent is based on the lessee's net income or profits, or if the property is indebted. As to royalties, as long as the income is passive in nature or the organization's involvement in the income-producing process is insubstantial, the income is not taxable.

Gross income from passive sources also includes income from the sale of goods (including charges or costs passed on at cost to purchasers of the goods or income received in settlement of a dispute concerning or in lieu of the exercise of the right to sell the goods) if the seller does not manufacture, produce,

---

[112] IRC § 4943(d)(3)(B); Reg. § 53.4943-10(c)(1). A charitable remainder trust's wholly owned foreign subsidiary's distributive share of a U.S. partnership's income was found not to be unrelated business income; conversely, gain from the sale of an interest in a partnership that held indebted real estate was treated as gain subject to the unrelated business income tax. Priv. Ltr. Rul. 199952086.

[113] IRC § 4943(d)(3), last sentence; Reg. § 53.4943-10(c)(2). See ch. 3.

[114] Priv. Ltr. Rul. 9252028.

[115] Reg. § 53.4943-10(a)(2).

[116] *Id.*

physically receive or deliver, negotiate sales of, or maintain inventories in the goods.[117] If in a year less than 95 percent of the income of a trade or business is from passive sources, a private foundation may, in applying this 95-percent test, substitute for the passive source gross income in the year the average gross income from passive sources for the 10 years immediately preceding the year involved.[118] Thus, stock in a passive holding company is not considered a holding in a business enterprise even if the company is controlled by a private foundation; instead, the foundation is treated as owning the proportionate share of any interests in a business enterprise held by the company.[119]

A private foundation should be cautious when attempting to maximize the value of real property that it holds, whether the property was originally invested in by the foundation or acquired by gift. A private foundation can own or have an expectancy interest in this type of property for years, then be tempted to improve it, sell it, or otherwise generate maximum value from the holding. A plan of maximizing value may have been initiated while the property was held by a prior owner, such as a donor, or was in an estate that was protected by the estate administration exception.[120] The private foundation may want to continue that plan or initiate one of its own; its trustees may believe that, as a matter of prudent asset management, that is the proper course of conduct. Nonetheless, unless the property is being or will be used for exempt purposes, the foundation should be wary about being classified, for tax purposes, as a dealer in the property. This outcome can entail both excess business holdings and unrelated business issues.

(b) Permitted Businesses

There are two other ways in which a private foundation can, without adverse tax consequences, actively engage in a business activity:

1. A foundation can operate a *functionally related business* that accomplishes its exempt purposes, such as a research institute or publication program.[121]

2. Business holdings do not include *program-related investments*, which are related undertakings.[122]

Passive income derived from a subsidiary is generally taxable as unrelated business income.[123] Generally, a private foundation cannot own a subsidiary, because of the excess business holdings rules. A private foundation may, however, be able to own a controlled organization that generates passive income.

These exceptions may be obviated when a private foundation incurred debt to acquire or improve a property.[124] That is, the resulting income may be taxed, in whole or in part, as unrelated business income, notwithstanding the fact that

---

[117] IRC § 4943(d)(3), last sentence.
[118] Reg. § 53.4943-10(c)(2).
[119] *Id.*
[120] See *Private Foundations*, § 5.12(a).
[121] IRC § 4943(d)(3)(A); Reg. § 53.4943-10(b). See *Private Foundations*, § 7.3.
[122] Reg. § 53.4943-10(b). See *Private Foundations*, § 8.3.
[123] See § 8.8(b).
[124] See ch. 5.

it is passive in nature. (This type of income nonetheless retains its character as passive income for purposes of the excess business holdings rules.[125])

(c) Partnerships and S Corporations

A private foundation's share of income from a partnership, whether or not distributed to the foundation, flows through to the foundation and retains its character as rent, interest, business, or other type of income.[126] If the partnership conducts a trade or business that is unrelated to the foundation's exempt purpose, the foundation's share of the business income, less associated deductions, must be reported as unrelated business income. The modifications pertaining to passive income[127] apply to exclude the foundation's share of interest or other passive income distributed by the partnership. This rule applies with respect to foundations that are general or limited partners. Partnerships are required to provide sufficient information to tax-exempt partners to enable them to correctly report any items of unrelated business income.[128]

Financial advisors to institutional investors have created sophisticated forms of investment vehicles in recent years. Some trade securities, some purchase rental properties, some buy security hedges, and some invest in venture capital. Entities that invest in real estate (partnerships and real estate investment trusts) commonly distribute income attributable to indebted property, which may be taxable. A partnership that elects to use the mark-to-market rules for securities trading[129] reports the income on the information return provided to partners[130] as "ordinary income from trade or business," although it actually has realized short-term capital gain. This type of income is not, however, treated as unrelated business income to tax-exempt organizations, including private foundations.[131] Dividends, interest, payments with respect to securities loaned, annuities, income from notional principal contracts, or other substantially similar income from ordinary and routine investment[132] are generally excluded from treatment as unrelated business income.[133] Income from the sale of property "other than stock in trade or other property of a kind which would properly be included in the inventory of the organization if on hand at the close of the tax year" is also excluded from such taxation.[134] Thus, the gain or loss is excluded from the computation of unrelated business income unless the partnership is a dealer in securities. Additionally, gain from the lapse or termination (sale) of options to buy or sell securities written in connection with an exempt organization's investment activity is excluded from consideration as unrelated business income.[135]

---

[125] Reg. § 53.4943-10(c)(2).
[126] IRC § 513(c)(1). See § 8.10.
[127] See ch. 3.
[128] Instructions to Form 1065 (partnership information return).
[129] IRC § 475.
[130] Form K-1.
[131] Reg. § 1.512(b)-1(d)(1), (2).
[132] Reg. § 1.512(b)-1(a)(1).
[133] See ch. 3.
[134] Reg. § 1.512(b)-1(d)(1).
[135] IRC § 512(b)(5); Reg. § 1.512(b)-1(d)(2). See § 3.11.

Tax-exempt charitable organizations are eligible to be shareholders in S corporations.[136] Stock in this type of a corporation, however, represents an interest in an unrelated trade or business.[137] Unlike the situation with partnerships, all of the income distributed to an exempt organization by an S corporation (including passive income excluded under the general rule) flows through to the exempt organization as unrelated business income. Gain or loss on the sale of S corporation shares are also subject to unrelated business taxation. Thus, whenever possible, a private foundation's investment in an entity that will produce significant amounts of passive income should be confined to instances in which the entity is a partnership.

§ 6.4 PARTNERSHIP RULES

A trade or business regularly carried on by a partnership, of which a tax-exempt organization is a member, may be an unrelated trade or business with respect to the organization. If so, in computing its unrelated business taxable income, the exempt organization must include its share of the gross income of the partnership from the unrelated trade or business (whether or not distributed, and subject to certain modifications[138]) and its share of the partnership deductions directly connected with the gross income.[139] This rule—known as the *look-through rule*—applies irrespective of whether the exempt organization is a general or limited partner.[140] The courts reject the thought that income derived by an exempt organization from a limited partnership interest is, for that reason alone, not taxable on the ground that a limited partnership interest is a passive investment by which the organization lacks any ability to actively engage in the management, operation, or control of the partnership.[141]

An illustration of this rule was provided when the IRS ruled that income from utility services, to be provided in the context of the provision of telecommunications services, will be treated as rental income to tax-exempt organizations and excluded from unrelated business income taxation.[142] This income will flow to the exempt organizations from partnerships and limited liability companies.[143]

The look-through rule also applies when a partnership, of which a tax-exempt organization is a member, engages in activities that are related to the exempt purposes of the exempt organization. In this situation, any income generated by the related business is not subject to taxation as unrelated business income.[144]

---

[136] IRC § 512(e).

[137] See § 4.12.

[138] See ch. 3.

[139] IRC § 512(c)(1), Reg. § 1.512(c)-1. See, *e.g.*, Priv. Ltr. Rul. 7934008.

[140] Rev. Rul. 79-222, 1979-2 C.B. 236.

[141] See, *e.g.*, Service Bolt & Nut Co. Profit Sharing Trust v. Comm'r, 724 F.2d 519 (6th Cir. 1983), *aff'g* 78 T.C. 812 (1982).

[142] See § 3.8.

[143] Priv. Ltr. Rul. 200147058.

[144] See, *e.g.*, Priv. Ltr. Rul. 9839039. Oddly, in finding income to be from a related business, the IRS applied the look-through rule to income derived by a tax-exempt organization from a partnership—but the exempt organization was not a member of the partnership. Tech. Adv. Mem. 9847002.

§ 6.5 ADVERTISING

Generally, the net income derived by a tax-exempt organization from the sale of advertising is taxable as unrelated business income.[145]

(a) Advertising and Unrelated Business in General

Despite the extensive body of regulatory and case law concerning when and how advertising revenue may be taxed, there is little law on the question of what constitutes *advertising*. In one instance, a court considered the publication of "business listings," consisting of "slogans, logos, trademarks, and other information which is similar, if not identical in content, composition and message to the listings found in other professional journals, newspapers, and the 'yellow pages' of telephone directories," and found them to qualify as advertising.[146]

Under the rules defining what is a *trade or business*,[147] income from the sale of advertising in publications of tax-exempt organizations generally constitutes unrelated business income, taxable to the extent it exceeds the expenses directly related to the advertising (even when the content of the publications is related to the exempt purpose of the organization). If, however, the editorial aspect of the publication is carried on at a loss, the editorial loss may be offset against the advertising income from the publication. Thus, there will be no taxable unrelated trade or business income because of advertising when the publication as a whole is published at a loss. This rule embodies a preexisting regulation[148] that was promulgated in an effort to carve out (and tax) income from advertising and other activities in competition with taxpaying business, even though the advertising may appear in a periodical related to the educational or other tax-exempt purpose of the organization.

These rules are not intended to encompass the publication of a magazine with little or no advertising, which is distributed free or at a nominal charge not intended to cover costs. This type of publication would likely be published basically as a source of public information and not for the production of income. For a publication to be considered an activity carried on for the production of income, it must be contemplated that the revenues from advertising in the publication or the revenues from sales of the publication, or both, will result in net income (although not necessarily in a particular year). Nonetheless, for the tax on unrelated business income to apply, the advertising activity must

---

[145] IRC § 513(c). In one instance, the IRS concluded that an association did not receive any unrelated business income from a newspaper advertising program, because the association did not conduct the activity and there was no basis for attribution of the advertising activities of its members. Tech. Adv. Mem. 200102051.

[146] Fraternal Order of Police, Ill. State Troopers Lodge No. 41 v. Comm'r, 87 T.C. 747, 754 (1986), *aff'd*, 833 F.2d 717 (7th Cir. 1987).

[147] IRC § 513(c). See § 2.2.

[148] Reg. § 1.513-1(b). This regulation became effective on December 13, 1967. IRC § 513(c) became effective on December 31, 1969. With respect to tax years beginning between these dates, the regulation was of no effect, as an impermissible administrative enlargement of the scope of the statutory unrelated business income law. Mass. Med. Soc'y v. United States, 514 F.2d 153 (1st Cir. 1975); Am. Coll. of Physicians v. United States, 530 F.2d 930 (Ct. Cl. 1976).

also constitute a trade or business that is regularly carried on. Further, the tax is inapplicable when the advertising activity is a tax-exempt function.[149]

As an example, a tax-exempt association of law enforcement officials published a monthly journal containing conventional advertising featuring the products or services of a commercial enterprise. The IRS ruled that the regular sale of space in the journal for the advertising was carried on for the production of income and constituted the conduct of a trade or business not substantially related to the organization's exempt functions.[150] The "controlling factor in this case," the agency wrote, was that the "activities giving rise to the income in question constitute the sale and performance of a valuable service on the part of the publisher, and the purchase of that service on the part of the other party to the transaction."[151]

In a similar situation, the IRS ruled that income derived by a tax-exempt membership organization from the sale of advertising in its annual yearbook was unrelated business income.[152] Preparation of the editorial materials in the yearbook was largely done by the organization's staff, which also distributed it. An independent commercial firm was used, under a full-year contract, to conduct an intensive advertising solicitation campaign in the organization's name; the firm was paid a percentage of the gross advertising receipts for selling the advertising, collecting from advertisers, and printing the yearbook. The IRS stated that by "engaging in an extensive campaign of advertising solicitation, the organization is conducting competitive and promotional efforts typical of commercial endeavors."[153]

Initially, it appeared that the courts were willing to accede to this approach by the IRS. In the leading case, a tax-exempt medical organization was found to be engaging in an unrelated business by selling advertising in its scholarly journal. The court rejected the contention that the purpose of the advertising was to educate physicians, holding instead that its primary purpose was to raise revenue. In reaching this conclusion, the court reviewed the content, format, and positioning of the advertisements, and concluded that they were principally commercial in nature. The court, however, set forth some standards as to when journal advertising might be an exempt function, such as advertising that comprehensively surveys a particular field or otherwise makes a systematic presentation on an appropriate subject.[154]

These findings were reversed on appeal, with the appellate court holding that the content of the advertisements was substantially related to the organization's educational purpose.[155] The court noted that the advertisements appeared only in bunches, at the beginning and end of the publications; were screened with respect to subject matter, with the contents controlled; and were indexed by advertiser.

---

[149] *E.g.*, Priv. Ltr. Rul. 7948113 (holding that proceeds from the sale of advertising in a program published in promotion of a postseason all-star college football game were not unrelated business income).

[150] Rev. Rul. 74-38, 1974-1 C.B. 144, clarified by Rev. Rul. 76-93, 1976-1 C.B. 170.

[151] Rev. Rul. 74-38, 1974-1 C.B. 144, 145.

[152] Rev. Rul. 73-424, 1973-2 C.B. 190.

[153] *Id.* at 191.

[154] Am. Coll. of Physicians v. United States, 83-2 U.S.T.C. ¶ 9652 (Ct. Cl. 1983).

[155] Am. College of Physicians v. United States, 743 F.2d 1570 (Fed. Cir. 1984).

Also, only advertisements directly relevant to the practice of internal medicine were published. This decision, then, established the principle that advertising is like any other trade or business, in that it is not automatically an unrelated activity but may serve an information dissemination (educational) function.

This dispute as to the tax treatment of advertising revenue in the unrelated income context—specifically, whether the IRS is correct in asserting that all net income from advertising in tax-exempt publications is always taxable—was resolved by the U.S. Supreme Court in 1986. After reviewing the history of the regulations promulgated in 1967[156] and of the statutory revisions authored in 1969,[157] the Court held that it is possible to have related advertising.[158] The Court said that the standard is whether the conduct of the exempt organization in selling and publishing the advertising is demonstrative of a related function, rather than a determination as to whether the advertising is inherently educational.

The Supreme Court observed that, in ascertaining relatedness, it is not sufficient to merely cluster the advertising in the front and back of the tax-exempt publication. Other facts that tend to militate against relatedness are that all advertising is paid, the advertising is for established products or services, advertising is repeated from month to month, or the advertising concerns matters having "no conceivable relationship" to the exempt purpose of the sponsoring exempt organization.[159] The test, said the Court, quoting from the trial court's opinion, is whether the organization uses the advertising to "provide its readers a comprehensive or systematic presentation of any aspect of the goods or services publicized." As the Court put it, an exempt organization can "control its publication of advertisements in such a way as to reflect an intention to contribute importantly to its . . . [exempt] functions."[160] This can be done, said the Court, by "coordinating the content of the advertisements with the editorial content of the issue, or by publishing only advertisements reflecting new developments."[161]

The foregoing may be contrasted with the situation involving a tax-exempt charitable organization that raised funds for an exempt symphony orchestra. As part of this effort, the organization published an annual concert book that was distributed at the orchestra's annual charity ball. The IRS ruled that the solicitation and sale of advertising by volunteers of the organization was not an unrelated taxable activity, because the activity was not regularly carried on and

---

[156] See *supra* note 148.

[157] IRC § 513(c).

[158] United States v. Am. Coll. of Physicians, 475 U.S. 834 (1986). A court found the advertising of a tax-exempt trade association to be taxable as unrelated business income because the advertising was not substantially related to the organization's exempt purposes and no "systematic effort" was made to "advertise products that related to the editorial content of the magazine, [nor] . . . to limit the advertisements to new products." Fla. Trucking Ass'n, Inc. v. Comm'r, 87 T.C. 1039 (1986). Displays and listings in a yearbook published by a tax-exempt labor organization (see *Tax-Exempt Organizations,* § 15.1) were found to be the result of unrelated business. State Police Ass'n of Mass. v. Comm'r, 97-2 U.S.T.C. ¶ 50,627 (1st Cir. 1997).

[159] United States v. Am. Coll. of Physicians, 475 U.S. 834, 849 (1986).

[160] *Id.*

[161] *Id.* at 849–50. Subsequently, a court found that a tax-exempt organization's advertising did not contribute importantly to the carrying out of any of its exempt purposes, although it was willing to explore the argument to the contrary and found that the subject matter of some of the advertising was related to the organization's exempt purpose. Minn. Holstein-Friesian Breeders Ass'n v. Comm'r, 64 T.C.M. 1319 (1992). The court concluded that the primary purposes underlying the advertising were commercial: stimulating demand for the advertised products and raising revenue for the exempt organization.

because it was conducted as an integral part of the process of fundraising for charity.[162] Thus, part of a successful contention that the unrelated income tax should not apply in the advertising context would seem to be a showing that the advertising activity ties in with other organization activity. Yet the same type of organization that engaged in the sale of advertising over a four-month period by its paid employees, for publication in concert programs distributed free at symphony performances over an eight-month period, was found by the IRS to be carrying on an unrelated business.[163] In that ruling, the IRS observed:

> It is a matter of common knowledge that many non-exempt organizations make a regular practice of publishing and distributing a seasonal series of special interest publications covering only a portion of each year with a format that includes substantial amounts of advertising matter. It would not be unusual for such an organization to concentrate its efforts to sell the advertising space thus made available during similar periods of intensive activity that would frequently last for no more than three or four months of each year. Since it is likewise further apparent that the activities giving rise to the advertising income here in question do not otherwise substantially differ from the comparable commercial activities of nonexempt organizations, those activities of the subject organization are regularly carried on within the meaning of section 512 of the Code.[164]

Similarly, a tax-exempt business league that sold a membership directory only to its members was held not to be engaged in an unrelated trade or business.[165] The directory was considered to contribute importantly to the achievement of the organization's exempt purposes, by facilitating communication among its members and encouraging the exchange of ideas and expertise, thus resulting in greater awareness of collective and individual activities of the membership. The principal aspect governing the outcome of this matter, however, was the fact that sale of the directory, undertaken in a noncommercial manner, did not confer any private benefit on the members of the organization.

(b) Advertising in Periodicals

In general, amounts realized by a tax-exempt organization from the sale of advertising in a periodical constitute gross income from an unrelated trade or business activity involving the exploitation of an exempt activity[166] : namely, the circulation and readership of the periodical developed through the production and distribution of the readership content of the periodical.[167]

(i) Income and Costs. Total income attributable to a tax-exempt organization periodical is regarded either as circulation income or (if any) as gross advertising income.[168] *Circulation income* is the income attributable to the production, distribution, or circulation of a periodical (other than gross advertising income), including amounts realized from or attributable to the sale or distribution of the readership content of the periodical. This type of income includes

---

[162] Rev. Rul. 75-201, 1975-1 C.B. 164.
[163] Rev. Rul. 75-200, 1975-1 C.B. 163.
[164] *Id.* at 164.
[165] Rev. Rul. 79-370, 1979-2 C.B. 238.
[166] In general, see § 2.7(e).
[167] Reg. § 1.512(a)-1(f)(1).
[168] Reg. § 1.512(a)-1(f)(3)(i).

amounts realized from charges made for reprinting articles and special items in the periodical and amounts realized from sales of back issues.[169] *Gross advertising income* is the amount derived from the unrelated advertising activities of an exempt organization periodical.[170]

Likewise, the costs attributable to a tax-exempt organization periodical are characterized as readership costs and direct advertising costs.[171] A reasonable allocation may be made between cost items attributable both to an exempt organization periodical and to the organization's other activities (such as salaries, occupancy costs, and depreciation).[172] *Readership costs* of an exempt organization periodical are the cost items directly connected with the production and distribution of the readership content of the periodical, and that would otherwise be allowable as deductions in determining unrelated business income, other than the items properly allocable to direct advertising costs.[173] *Direct advertising costs* of an exempt organization periodical include items directly connected with the sale and publication of advertising (such as agency commissions and other selling costs, artwork, and copy preparation), the portion of mechanical and distribution costs attributable to advertising lineage, and any other element of readership costs properly allocable to the advertising activity.[174]

As noted, a tax-exempt organization is not taxable on its advertising income when its direct advertising costs for its periodical equal such (gross) income.[175] Even if gross advertising income of an exempt organization periodical exceeds direct advertising costs, costs attributable to the readership content of the publication qualify as costs that are deductible in computing (unrelated) income from the advertising activity, to the extent that the costs exceed the income attributable to the readership content.[176] There are limitations on this rule, however, including the conditions that its application may not be used to realize a loss from the advertising activity nor to give rise to a cost deductible in computing taxable income attributable to any other unrelated activity.[177] If the circulation income of the periodical exceeds its readership costs, any unrelated business taxable income attributable to the publication is the excess of gross advertising income over direct advertising costs.[178]

An illustration of these rules concerns a tax-exempt trade association, which publishes a single periodical that carries advertising. During 2006, the association realizes $40,000 from the sale of advertising in the periodical (gross advertising income) and $60,000 from sales of the periodical to members and nonmembers (circulation income). The total periodical costs are $90,000, of which $50,000 is

---

[169] Reg. § 1.512(a)-1(f)(3)(iii).
[170] Reg. § 1.512(a)-1(f)(3)(ii).
[171] Reg. § 1.512(a)-1(f)(6)(i)
[172] *Id.* Once a reasonable method of allocation is adopted, it must be used consistently. Reg. § 1.512(a)-1(f)(6)(i). A court held that the application of a ratio used in previous years for this purpose is not a *method*; it is the output of a method that cannot be automatically applied each year. Nat'l Ass'n of Life Underwriters, Inc. v. Comm'r, 94-2 U.S.T.C. ¶ 50,412 (D.C. Cir. 1994), *rev'g* 64 T.C.M. 379 (1992).
[173] Reg. § 1.512(a)-1(f)(6)(iii).
[174] Reg. § 1.512(a)-1(f)(6)(ii).
[175] Reg. § 1.512(a)-1(f)(2)(i).
[176] Reg. § 1.512(a)-1(f)(2)(ii), (d)(2).
[177] Reg. § 1.512(a)-1(f)(2)(ii).
[178] *Id.*

directly connected with the sale and publication of advertising (direct advertising costs) and $40,000 is attributable to the production and distribution of the readership content (readership costs). The production and distribution of the readership content of the periodical is related to the association's exempt purpose. Inasmuch as the direct advertising costs of the periodical ($50,000) exceed gross advertising income ($40,000), the unrelated business taxable income attributable to advertising is determined solely on the basis of the income and deductions directly connected with the production and sale of the advertising. Gross advertising revenue of $40,000 and direct advertising costs of $50,000 result in a loss of $10,000 attributable to advertising. This loss is an allowable deduction in computing the association's unrelated business taxable income derived from any other unrelated trade or business activity.[179]

Now assume the facts as stated in the foregoing example, except that the circulation income of the association's periodical is $100,000 (instead of $60,000) and that, of the total periodical costs, $25,000 are direct advertising costs and $65,000 are readership costs. Because the circulation income ($100,000) exceeds the total readership costs ($65,000), the unrelated business taxable income attributable to the advertising activity is $15,000: the excess of gross advertising income ($40,000) over direct advertising costs ($25,000).[180]

Assume the facts as stated in the first of these two examples, except that, of the total periodical costs, $20,000 are direct advertising costs and $70,000 are readership costs. Because the readership costs of the periodical exceed the circulation income ($60,000), pursuant to the second of the rules listed above, the unrelated business income attributable to advertising is the excess of the total income attributable to the periodical over the total periodical costs. Thus, the association has unrelated business income attributable to the advertising activity in the amount of $10,000 ($100,000 total income attributable to the periodical less $90,000 total periodical costs).[181]

Further, assume the facts as stated in the first example, except that the total periodical costs are $120,000, of which $30,000 are direct advertising costs and $90,000 are readership costs. Because the readership costs of the periodical ($90,000) exceed the circulation income ($60,000), pursuant to the second of the rules listed above, the unrelated business income attributable to advertising is the excess, if any, of the total income attributable to the periodical over the total periodical costs. Inasmuch as the total income of the periodical ($100,000) does not exceed the total periodical costs ($120,000), the association has not derived any unrelated business income from the advertising activity. Moreover, only $70,000 of the $90,000 of readership costs may be deducted in computing unrelated business taxable income, because the costs may be deducted, to the extent they exceed circulation income, only to the extent they do not result in a loss from the advertising activity. Thus, there is no loss from this activity and no amount may be deducted on this account in computing the association's unrelated business income derived from any other unrelated business activity.[182]

---

[179] Reg. § 1.512(a)-1(f)(2)(iii), Example (1).
[180] Id., Example (2).
[181] Id., Example (3).
[182] Id., Example (4).

(ii) Dues Allocation.   Another set of rules requires an allocation of membership dues to circulation income when the right to receive the periodical is associated with membership status in the tax-exempt organization for which dues, fees, or other charges are received.[183] The portion of membership dues that constitute a part of circulation income (*allocable membership receipts*) is determined in one of three ways:

1. If 20 percent or more of the total circulation of a periodical consists of sales to nonmembers, the subscription price charged to the nonmembers is the amount allocated from each member's dues to circulation income. The term *total circulation* means paid circulation; that is, it does not include distribution of a periodical without charge to those who are not members of the tax-exempt organization.[184] This term means the actual number of copies of the periodical distributed for compensation, without regard as to how the copies were purchased. In one case, members of an exempt association, who paid for subscriptions by means of dues, designated nonmember recipients of the periodical; the nonmember recipients were considered part of the total circulation base.[185]

2. If rule 1 does not apply, and if the membership dues from 20 percent or more of the members of the organization are less than the dues received from the remaining members because the former category of members does not receive the periodical, the amount of dues reduction is the amount used in allocating membership dues to circulation income.

3. Otherwise, the portion of membership receipts allocated to the periodical is an amount equal to the total amount of the receipts multiplied by a fraction, the numerator of which is the total costs of the periodical and the denominator of which is these costs plus the costs of the other exempt activities of the organization.[186]

---

[183] Reg. § 1.512(a)-1(f)(4). The IRS initially took the position that the requirement that membership receipts be allocated on a pro rata basis to circulation income of a tax-exempt organization's periodical (Reg. § 1.512(a)-1(f)(4)(iii)) means that the "cost of other exempt activities of the organization" must be offset by the income produced by the activities (the "net cost" rule). Gen. Couns. Mem. 38104. The IRS subsequently concluded that the gross cost of the other exempt activities must be used in computing the denominator of the formula. Gen. Couns. Mems. 38205, 38168.

[184] Am. Hosp. Ass'n v. United States, 654 F. Supp. 1152 (N.D. Ill. 1987).

[185] N.C. Citizens for Bus. & Indus. v. United States, 89-2 U.S.T.C. ¶ 9507 (Cl. Ct. 1989).

[186] The reference to the "costs of the other exempt activities" means the total costs or expenses incurred by an organization in connection with its other tax-exempt activities, not offset by any income earned by the organization from the activities. Rev. Rul. 81-101, 1981-1 C.B. 352.

An organization, such as a business league (see *Tax-Exempt Organizations*, ch. 13), may have within it an integral fund that is a charitable organization. The costs of such a fund can be included in the formula used to calculate the organization's net unrelated business taxable income derived from advertising, thereby reducing the entity's tax liability. Am. Bar Ass'n v. United States, 84-1 U.S.T.C. ¶ 9179 (N.D. Ill. 1984).

These regulations, particularly the third pro rata allocation method rule, were challenged in court on substantive and procedural grounds. Although the challenge was initially successful, it essentially failed on appeal. Am. Med. Ass'n v. United States, 887 F.2d 760 (7th Cir. 1989), *aff'g & rev'g* 608 F. Supp. 1085 (N.D. Ill. 1987), 668 F. Supp. 1101 (N.D. Ill. 1987), 668 F. Supp. 358 (N.D. Ill. 1988), *and* 691 F. Supp. 1170 (N.D. Ill. 1988). The basic assertion, which was ultimately rejected, was that a tax-exempt organization can deduct, as direct advertising costs, the readership content costs of periodicals distributed for the purpose of generating advertising revenue.

Three illustrations illuminate these rules. These examples assume that the tax-exempt organization periodical contains advertising, and that the production and distribution of the readership content of the periodical is related to the organization's exempt purpose.

In the first of these examples, a tax-exempt scientific organization has 10,000 members who each pay annual dues of $15. One of this organization's activities is publication of a monthly periodical that is distributed to all its members. The organization also distributes 5,000 copies of its periodical to nonmember subscribers at a cost of $10 per year. Pursuant to the first of the above three rules, because the nonmember circulation of the organization's periodical represents one-third of its total circulation, the subscription price charged to nonmembers will be used to determine the portion of the organization's membership receipts allocable to the periodical. Thus, the organization's allocable membership receipts will be $100,000 ($10 x 10,000 members), and its total circulation income for the periodical will be $150,000 ($100,000 from members + $50,000 from sales to nonmembers).[187]

The second example is based on the facts of the first, except that the exempt organization sells 500 copies of its periodical to nonmembers. The organization's members may elect not to receive this periodical, in which case their annual dues are reduced to $6 a year; 3,000 members elect to receive the periodical and pay the $15 annual dues. The organization's stated subscription price to members of $9 consistently results in an excess of total income (including gross advertising income) attributable to the periodical over total costs of the periodical. Because the 500 copies of the periodical distributed to nonmembers represent only 14 percent of the 3,500 copies distributed, pursuant to the first of the above rules, the $10 subscription price charged to nonmembers will not be used in determining the portion of membership receipts allocable to the periodical. Because 70 percent of the members elect not to receive the periodical and pay $9 less per year in dues, pursuant to the second of the above rules, the $9 price will be used in determining the subscription price charged to members. Thus, the allocable membership receipts will be $9 per member, or $27,000 ($9 x 3,000 copies); the exempt organization's total circulation income will be $32,000 ($27,000 + $5,000).[188]

In the third example, a tax-exempt trade association has 800 members who pay annual dues of $50. The association publishes a monthly journal, the editorial content and advertising of which are directed to the business interests of its own members. The journal is distributed to all of the association's members; there are no receipts from nonmembers. The association has total receipts of $100,000, of which $40,000 ($50 x 800) are membership receipts and $60,000 are gross advertising income. The organization's total costs for the journal and other exempt activities is $100,000. It has total periodical costs of $76,000, of which $41,000 are direct advertising costs and $35,000 are readership costs.

The first of the above three rules does not apply, inasmuch as copies of the publication are not made available to nonmembers. Therefore, the allocation of membership receipts must be made in accordance with the third of these rules. Based on pro rata allocation of membership receipts ($40,000) by a fraction, the

---

[187] Reg. § 1.512(a)-1(f)(5), Example (1).
[188] Id., Example (2).

numerator of which is total periodical costs ($76,000) and the denominator of which is the total costs of the journal and the other exempt activities ($100,000), $30,400 ($76,000/$100,000 x $40,000) of membership receipts is circulation income.[189]

These rules become more intricate when a tax-exempt organization publishes more than one periodical for the production of income. (A periodical is published *for the production of income* if the organization generally receives gross advertising income from the periodical equal to at least 25 percent of its readership costs and the periodical activity is engaged in for profit.) In this instance, the organization may treat the gross income from all (but not just some) of the periodicals and the deductible items directly connected with the periodicals on a consolidated basis in determining the amount of unrelated business taxable income derived from the sale of advertising. (Thus, an organization cannot consolidate the losses of a periodical not published for the production of income with the profit of other periodicals that are so published.[190]) This treatment must be followed consistently and, once adopted, is binding, unless the organization obtains the requisite permission from the IRS to change the method.[191]

It is the position of the IRS, as supported by the Tax Court, that the specific rules concerning the computation of net unrelated income derived from advertising are inapplicable when the "issue of whether the . . . [organization's] publication of the readership content of the magazines is an exempt activity has not been decided, stipulated to, or presented for decision," and when the IRS "has not sought to apply such regulations, maintaining that they cannot be applied due to the . . . [organization's] failure to produce credible evidence of its advertising and publishing expenses."[192]

---

[189] *Id.*, Example (3).

[190] Reg. § 1.512(a)-1(f)(7).

[191] IRC § 466(e); Reg. § 1.446-1(e).

[192] CORE Special Purpose Fund v. Comm'r, 49 T.C.M. 626, 630 (1985). Notwithstanding the differences in the manner in which tax-exempt social clubs are treated for purposes of unrelated taxation (see § 6.1), the rules concerning taxation of advertising revenue apply to them. Chicago Metro. Ski Council v. Comm'r, 104 T.C. 341 (1995). In general, Reap, *Getting the Most from Periodical Advertising Income*, 4 *Exempt Orgs. Tax Rev.* 1065 (no. 8, 1991); Geske, *Unrelated Business Taxable Income and Advertising Revenue of Exempt Organization Periodicals*, 4 *Exempt Orgs. Tax Rev.* 311 (no. 3, 1991); Schnee & Brock, *Opportunities Exist to Reduce Unrelated Business Income from Advertising Revenue*, 74 *J. Tax'n* 240 (no. 4, 1991); Littman, *Advertising and the Unrelated Business Income Tax after* United States v. American College of Physicians, 49 *Ohio St. L.J.* 625 (no. 2, 1988); Gallagher, *"Substantially Related": The Magic Words for Nonprofit Organizations:* United States v. American College of Physicians, 21 *U.S.F.L. Rev.* 795 (no. 4, 1987); Huffaker & Gut, *Supreme Court Holds Advertising Revenue Was Not Substantially Related Income*, 65 *J. Tax'n* 2 (no. 1, July 1986); Gross, *New Developments Regarding Advertising Income of Tax-Exempt Organizations*, 24 *Am. Bus. L.J.* 116 (no. 1, 1986); Shillingburg, American College of Physicians v. United States: *An Ending—A Beginning—Or?*, 64 *Taxes* 539 (no. 9, 1986); Simpson, *Taxation of Income from Advertising in Exempt Organizations' Publications*, 10 *Est., Gifts, & Trs. J.* 184 (no. 6, 1985); Weinberg & Nixon, *What Are the Implications of the Federal Circuit's Holding in* American College?," 62 *J. Tax'n* 242 (no. 4, 1985); Gregory, Jr., *Federal Circuit Holds ABE Insurance Program Does Not Constitute Unrelated Business Income*, 63 *J. Tax'n* 244 (no. 4, 1985); Kannry, *Taxing Advertising*, 9 *Philanthropy Monthly* 26 (no. 5, 1976); Kannry, *How to Mitigate the Impact of New Regulations on Exempt Organizations' Advertising Income*, 45 *J. Tax'n* 304 (1976); Sugarman & Vogt, *The New Advertising Regulations and Their Application to Exempt Organizations*, 54 *Taxes* 196 (1976); Spevack, *Taxation of Advertising Income of Exempt Organizations' Publications*, 21 *Cath. Law.* 268 (1975); Endicott, *Proposed Changes in the Taxation of Advertising Income of Exempt Organization Publications*, 2 *Tax Adv.* 710 (1971); Lehrfeld, *The Unfairness Doctrine: Commercial Advertising Profits as Unrelated Business Income*, 23 *Tax Law.* 349 (1970); Weithorn & Liles, *Unrelated Business Income Tax: Changes Affecting Journal Advertising Revenues*, 45 *Taxes* 791 (1967).

§ 6.6 CORPORATE SPONSORSHIPS

A payment made by a corporation to sponsor an event or activity of a tax-exempt organization may be a contribution or may be taxable as unrelated business income. This type of payment usually is a transfer of a relatively large amount of money by a for-profit business to a charitable organization. If sponsorship payments received by an exempt organization are *qualified* payments, those amounts are not subject to unrelated business income taxation. That is, the activity of soliciting and receiving these payments is not an unrelated business.[193]

This being a safe-harbor rule, a corporate sponsorship payment that is not a qualified one is not necessarily taxable. Rather, the tax treatment of it is evaluated under the unrelated business rules generally. Thus, the transaction would be assessed as to whether it is a business,[194] whether it is regularly carried on,[195] whether it is subject to an exception for income or activities,[196] and the like.

(a) Qualified Sponsorship Payments

A *qualified sponsorship payment* is a payment made by a person, engaged in a trade or business, to a tax-exempt organization, with respect to which there is no arrangement or expectation that the person will receive from the exempt organization a substantial return benefit.[197] It is irrelevant whether the sponsored activity is related or unrelated to the recipient tax-exempt organization's exempt purpose. It is also irrelevant whether the sponsored activity is temporary or permanent. The word *payment* means the payment of money, transfer of property, or performance of services.[198]

A *substantial return benefit* is a benefit, other than certain uses or acknowledgments and other than certain disregarded benefits.[199] Benefits are disregarded if the aggregate fair market value of all the benefits provided to the payor or persons designated by the payor in connection with the payment during the organization's tax year is not more than 2 percent of the amount of the payment.[200] If the aggregate fair market value of the benefits exceeds 2 percent of the amount of the payment, then the entire fair market value of the benefits is a substantial return benefit, unless it is a shielded use or acknowledgment.[201]

Benefits provided to the payor or a designated person may include advertising; an exclusive provider arrangement; goods, facilities, services, or other privileges; and/or exclusive or nonexclusive rights to use an intangible asset (such as a trademark, patent, logo, or destination) of the exempt organization.[202]

An illustration of these rules features a national corporation and a tax-exempt charitable organization that, on June 30, 2006, enter into a five-year,

---

[193] IRC § 513(i)(1); Reg. § 1.513-4(a).
[194] See § 2.2.
[195] See § 2.5.
[196] See chs. 3, 4.
[197] IRC § 513(i)(2)(A); Reg. § 1.513-4(c)(1).
[198] Reg. § 1.513-4(c)(1).
[199] Reg. § 1.513-4(c)(2)(i).
[200] Reg. § 1.513-4(c)(2)(ii).
[201] *Id.*
[202] Reg. § 1.513-4(c)(2)(iii).

binding, written contract effective for the years 2007 to 2012. This contract provides that the corporation will make an annual payment of $5,000 to the charity; in return, the corporation will not receive any benefit other than advertising. On June 30, 2006, the fair market value of the advertising to be provided to the corporation in each year covered by the agreement is $75, which is less than the disregarded benefit amount (2 percent of $5,000 is $100).[203] In 2007, pursuant to the sponsorship contract, the corporation pays the charitable organization $5,000 and receives the advertising benefit. As of January 1, 2007, the fair market value of the advertising to be provided by the charity each year increases to $110. For purposes of this rule, however, the fair market value of the advertising benefit is determined on June 30, 2006, the date the parties entered into the sponsorship contract. Therefore, the entire $5,000 payment received in 2007 is a qualified sponsorship payment.[204]

As another example, the facts are the same as in the previous illustration, except that the contract provides that the corporation will make an initial payment to the charitable organization of $5,000 in 2007, followed by annual payments of $1,000 during each of the years 2008 to 2012. In 2008, pursuant to the sponsorship contract, the corporation pays the charity $1,000 and receives the advertising benefit. In 2008, the fair market value of the benefit provided ($75, as determined on June 30, 2006) exceeds 2 percent of the total payment received (2 percent of $1,000 is $20). Therefore, only $925 of the $1,000 payment received in 2008 is a qualified sponsorship payment.[205]

A substantial return benefit does not include the use or acknowledgement of the name, logo, or product lines of the payor's trade or business in connection with the exempt organization's activities. Although a use or acknowledgment does not include advertising, it may include an exclusive sponsorship arrangement; logos and slogans that do not contain qualitative or comparative descriptions of the payor's products, services, facilities, or company; a list of the payor's locations, telephone numbers, or Internet address; value-neutral descriptions, including displays or visual depictions, of the payor's product line or services; and/or reference to the payor's brand or trade names and product or service listings.[206]

Logos or slogans that are an established part of a payor's identity are not considered to contain qualitative or comparative descriptions. Mere display or distribution, whether for free or remuneration, of a payor's product by the payor or the exempt organization to the general public at the sponsored activity is not considered an inducement to purchase, sell, or use the payor's product and thus will not affect the determination of whether a payment is a qualified sponsorship payment.[207]

The term *advertising* means any message or other programming material that is broadcast or otherwise transmitted, published, displayed, or distributed, and that promotes or markets any trade or business, or any service, facility, or

---

[203] See text accompanied by *supra* note 200.
[204] Reg. § 1.513-4(d)(1)(iv), Example (1).
[205] *Id.*, Example (2).
[206] Reg. § 1.513-4(c)(2)(iv).
[207] *Id.*

product.[208] The term includes messages containing qualitative or comparative language, price information or other indications of savings or value, an endorsement, or an inducement to purchase, sell, or use any company, service, facility, or product.[209] A single message that contains both advertising and an acknowledgement constitutes advertising.[210]

These rules do not apply to activities conducted by a payor on its own. For example, if a payor purchases broadcast time from a television station to advertise its product during commercial breaks in a sponsored program, the activities of the tax-exempt organization are not thereby converted to advertising.[211]

(b) Exclusivity Arrangements

An arrangement that acknowledges the payor as the exclusive sponsor of a tax-exempt organization's activity, or the exclusive sponsor representing a particular trade, business, or industry, generally does not, by itself, result in a substantial return benefit.[212] For example, if in exchange for a payment, an exempt organization announces that its event is sponsored exclusively by the payor (and does not provide any advertising or other substantial return benefit to the payor), the payor has not received a substantial return benefit. An arrangement that limits the sale, distribution, availability, or use of competing products, services, or facilities in connection with an exempt organization's activity generally results in a substantial return benefit.[213] For example, if, in exchange for a payment, an exempt organization agrees to allow only the payor's products to be sold in connection with an activity, the payor has received a substantial return benefit.[214]

An illustration of these rules concerns a tax-exempt liberal arts college. A soft-drink manufacturer enters into a binding, written contract with this college that provides for a large payment to be made to the college's department of English in exchange for the college agreeing to name a writing competition after the soft-drink manufacturer. The contract also provides that the college will allow the manufacturer to be the exclusive seller/provider of all soft drinks on the college's campus. The fair market value of the exclusive provider component of the contract exceeds 2 percent of the total payment. The college's use of the manufacturer's name in the writing competition constitutes acknowledgment of the sponsorship. The exclusive provider arrangement, however, is a substantial return benefit. Only that portion of the payment, if any, that the college can demonstrate exceeds the fair market value of the exclusive provider arrangement is a qualified sponsorship payment.[215]

---

[208] Reg. § 1.513-4(c)(2)(v).
[209] IRC § 513(i)(2)(A).
[210] *Id.*
[211] *Id.*
[212] Reg. § 1.513-4(c)(2)(vi)(A).
[213] Reg. § 1.513-4(c)(2)(vi)(B).
[214] In general, Irvine, *Does Exclusivity Create Liability for UBIT?*, 14 *J. Tax'n Exempt Orgs.* 19 (no. 1, July/Aug. 2002).
[215] Reg. § 1.513-4(c)(2)(vi)(B), Example (6).

(c) Allocations

To the extent that a portion of a payment would be a qualified sponsorship payment if made as a separate payment, that portion of the payment and the other portion of the payment are treated as separate payments.[216] Thus, if there is an arrangement or expectation that the payor will receive a substantial return benefit with respect to any payment, then only the portion, if any, of the payment that exceeds the fair market value of the substantial return benefit is a qualified sponsorship payment.[217] If, however, the exempt organization does not establish that the payment exceeds the fair market value of a substantial return benefit, then no portion of the payment constitutes a qualified sponsorship payment.[218] To the extent necessary to prevent avoidance of the rules concerning determination of substantial return benefits and allocation of payments, when a tax-exempt organization fails to make a reasonable and good-faith valuation of a substantial return benefit, the IRS may determine the portion of a payment allocable to the substantial return benefit and/or may treat two or more related payment as a single payment.[219]

(d) Treatment of Other Payments

Again, the unrelated business treatment of a payment, or portion of a payment, that is not a qualified sponsorship payment is determined by application of the general rules. For example, payments related to the provision of facilities, services, or other privileges by a tax-exempt organization to a payor, or designated person; advertising; exclusive provider arrangements; a license to use intangible assets of an exempt organization; or other substantial return benefits, are evaluated separately in determining whether the exempt organization realizes unrelated business income therefrom.[220]

(e) Valuation

The *fair market value* of a substantial return benefit provided as part of a sponsorship arrangement is the price at which the benefit would be provided between a willing recipient and a willing provider of the benefit, neither being under any compulsion to enter into the arrangement and both having reasonable knowledge of relevant facts, and without regard to any other aspect of the sponsorship arrangement.[221] In general, the fair market value of a substantial return benefit is determined when the benefit is provided. If the parties enter into a binding, written sponsorship contract, however, the fair market value of any substantial return benefit provided pursuant to that contract is determined as of the date the parties enter into the sponsorship contract. If the parties make a material change to a sponsorship contract, it is treated as a new sponsorship contract as of the date the material change becomes effective. A *material change*

---

[216] IRC § 513(i)(3).
[217] Reg. § 1.513-4(d)(1).
[218] *Id.*
[219] Reg. § 1.513-4(d)(2).
[220] Reg. § 1.513-4(d)(1)(i).
[221] Reg. § 1.513-4(d)(1)(ii).

includes an extension or renewal of the contract, or a more-than-incidental change to any amount payable (or other consideration) pursuant to the contract.[222]

(f) Special Rules

The existence of a written sponsorship agreement does not, in itself, cause a payment to fail to be a qualified sponsorship payment. The terms of the agreement, not its existence or degree of detail, are relevant to the determination of whether a payment is a qualified sponsorship payment. Similarly, the terms of the agreement, rather than the title or responsibilities of the individuals negotiating the agreement, determine whether a payment, or a portion of a payment, made pursuant to the agreement is a qualified sponsorship payment.[223]

The term *qualified sponsorship payment* does not include any payment the amount of which is contingent, by contract or otherwise, on the level of attendance at one or more events, broadcast ratings, or other factors indicating the degree of public exposure to the sponsored activity. The fact that a payment is contingent on sponsored events or activities actually being conducted does not, by itself, cause the payment to fail to be a qualified sponsorship payment.[224]

Qualified sponsorship payments in the form of money or property—but not services—are contributions received by the tax-exempt organization involved. For organizations that are required to or need to compute public support,[225] these payments are contributions for that purpose.[226] The fact that a payment to an exempt organization constitutes a qualified sponsorship payment, which is treated as a contribution to the payee organization, does not determine whether the payment is deductible by the payor.[227] The payment may be deductible as a charitable contribution[228] or as a business expense.[229]

As an example, a tax-exempt local charity organizes a marathon and walka-thon at which it serves to participants drinks and other refreshments provided free by a national corporation. The corporation also gives the charity prizes to be awarded to winners of the event. The charity recognizes the assistance of the corporation by listing the corporation's name in promotional flyers, in newspaper advertisements of the event, and on shirts worn by the participants. The charity changes the name of its event to include the name of the corporation. The drinks, refreshments, and prizes provided by the corporation constitute qualified sponsorship payments.[230]

As another example, a tax-exempt art museum organizes an exhibition and receives a large payment from a corporation to help fund the exhibition. The museum recognizes the corporation's support by using the corporate name and

---

[222] Reg. § 1.513-4(d)(1)(iii).
[223] Reg. § 1.513-4(e)(1).
[224] IRC § 513(i)(2)(B)(i); Reg. § 1.513-4(e)(2).
[225] See *Tax-Exempt Organizations*, § 11.3(b).
[226] Reg. § 1.513-4(e)(3).
[227] *Id.*
[228] IRC § 170.
[229] IRC § 162.
[230] Reg. § 1.513-4(f), Example (1).

established logo in materials publicizing the exhibition (banners, posters, brochures, and public service announcements). The museum also hosts a dinner for the corporation's executives. The fair market value of the dinner exceeds 2 percent of the total payment. The museum's use of the corporate name and logo in connection with the exhibition constitutes acknowledgment of the sponsorship. Because the fair market value of the dinner exceeds 2 percent of the total payment, however, the dinner is a substantial return benefit. Only that portion of the payment, if any, that the museum can demonstrate exceeds the fair market value of the dinner is a qualified sponsorship payment.[231]

In another illustration, a tax-exempt organization coordinates sports tournaments for local charities. A manufacturer of automobiles agrees to underwrite the expenses of the tournaments. The exempt organization recognizes the automobile manufacturer by including the manufacturer's name and logo in the title of each tournament, as well as featuring the name on signs, scoreboards, and other printed material. The automobile manufacturer receives complimentary admission passes and pro-am playing spots for each tournament that have a combined fair market value in excess of 2 percent of the total payment. Additionally, the organization displays the latest models of the manufacturer's premier luxury cars at each tournament. The organization's use of the manufacturer's name and logo, and its display of cars, in the tournament constitute acknowledgment of the sponsorship. The admission passes and pro-am playing spots, however, are a substantial return benefit. Only that portion of the payment, if any, that the organization can demonstrate exceeds the fair market value of the admission passes and pro-am playing spots is a qualified sponsorship payment.[232]

In still another example, a tax-exempt organization conducts an annual college football bowl game. It sells to commercial broadcasters the right to broadcast this game on television and radio. A major corporation agrees to be the exclusive sponsor of the game. The detailed contract between the organization and the corporation provides that, in exchange for a $1 million payment, the name of the bowl game will include the name of the corporation. In addition, the contract provides that the corporation's name and logo will appear on the players' helmets and uniforms, on the scoreboard and stadium signs, on the playing field, on cups used to serve drinks at the game, and on all related printed material distributed in connection with the game. The organization also agrees to give the corporation a block of game passes for its employees and to provide advertising in the bowl game program book. The fair market value of the passes is $6,000; the fair market value of the program advertising is $10,000. The agreement is contingent on the game being broadcast on television and radio, but the amount of the payment is not contingent on the number of individuals attending the game or on the television ratings. The contract provides that television cameras will focus on the corporation's name and logo on the field at certain intervals during the game. The exempt organization's use of the corporation's name and logo in connection with the bowl game constitutes

---

[231] *Id.*, Example (2).
[232] *Id.*, Example (3).

acknowledgment of the sponsorship. The exclusive sponsorship arrangement is not a substantial return benefit. Because the fair market value of the game passes and program advertising ($16,000) does not exceed 2 percent of the total payment (2 percent of $1 million is $20,000), these benefits are disregarded; hence, the entire payment is a qualified sponsorship payment.[233]

In still another example, a tax-exempt organization organizes an amateur sports team. A major pizza chain gives uniforms to players on the organization's team and also pays some of the team's operational expenses. The uniforms bear the name and logo of the pizza chain. During the final tournament series, the organization distributes without charge souvenir flags bearing its name to employees of the pizza chain who come out to support the team. The flags are valued at less than 2 percent of the combined fair market value of the uniforms and operational expenses paid. The organization's use of the name and logo of the pizza chain in connection with the tournament constitutes acknowledgment of the sponsorship. Because the fair market value of the flags does not exceed 2 percent of the total payment, the entire amount of the funding and the value of the supplied uniforms are a qualified sponsorship payment.[234]

Another illustration concerns a tax-exempt broadcast station that airs a program funded by a local music store. In exchange for the funding, the exempt organization broadcasts the following message: "This program has been brought to you by the Music Shop, located at 123 Main Street. For your music needs, give them a call today at 615-555-1234. This station is proud to have the Music Shop as a sponsor." Because this single broadcast message contains both advertising and an acknowledgment, the entire message is considered advertising. The fair market value of the advertising exceeds 2 percent of the total payment. Thus, the advertising is a substantial return benefit. Unless the organization establishes that the amount of the payment exceeds the fair market value of the advertising, none of the payment is a qualified sponsorship payment.[235]

As another example, a tax-exempt symphony orchestra performs a series of concerts. A program guide that contains notes on guest conductors and other information concerning the evening's program is distributed by the exempt organization at each concert. The Music Shop makes a $1,000 payment to the organization in support of the concert series. As a supporter of the event, the Music Shop receives complimentary tickets having a fair market value of $85; it is also recognized in the program guide and on a poster in the lobby of the concert hall. The lobby poster states: "The [organization's] concert is sponsored by the Music Shop, located at 123 Main Street, telephone number 615-555-1234." The program guide contains the same information and also states: "Visit the Music Shop today for the finest selection of music CDs and cassette tapes." The fair market value of the advertisement in the program guide is $15. The organization's use of the Music Shop's name, address, and telephone number in the lobby poster constitutes acknowledgment of the sponsorship. The combined fair market value of the advertisement in the program guide and complimentary tickets, however, is $100 ($15 plus $85), which exceeds 2 percent

---

[233] *Id.*, Example (4).
[234] *Id.*, Example (5).
[235] *Id.*, Example (7).

of the total payment (2 percent of $1,000 being $20). The fair market value of the advertising and complimentary tickets, therefore, constitutes a substantial return benefit, so only that portion of the payment that exceeds the fair market value of the substantial return benefit ($900) is a qualified sponsorship payment.[236]

As another example, a national charitable organization dedicated to the promotion of health organizes a campaign to inform the public about potential cures to combat a serious disease. As part of this campaign, the organization sends representatives to community health fairs around the country to answer questions about this disease and inform the public about recent developments in the search for a cure. A pharmaceutical company makes a payment to the organization to fund the organization's booth at a health fair. The organization places a sign in the booth displaying the company's name and slogan, "Better Research, Better Health," which is an established part of the company's identity. In addition, the organization grants the pharmaceutical company a license to use the organization's logo in marketing its products to health care providers around the country. The fair market value of the license exceeds 2 percent of the total payment received from the company. The organization's display of the pharmaceutical company's name and slogan constitutes acknowledgment of the sponsorship. The license granted to the company to use the organization's logo, however, is a substantial return benefit. Only that portion of the payment, if any, that the organization can demonstrate exceeds the fair market value of the license granted to the pharmaceutical company is a qualified sponsorship payment.[237]

(g) Website Links

One of the many issues in the context of use of the Internet by tax-exempt organizations and application of the unrelated business rules is the import of website hyperlinks. In this setting, the matter concerns links between exempt organizations and their corporate sponsors. The tax regulations address the significance of website links by two examples. The essence of these examples is that the mere existence of a link, from the website of the sponsored exempt organization to the website of the corporate sponsor, does not cause a payment to fail to be a qualified sponsorship payment; however, material on the linked site can cause the payment to entail a substantial return benefit.

In one of these examples, a tax-exempt symphony orchestra maintains a website containing its performance schedule and other pertinent information. The Music Shop makes a payment to the orchestra to fund a concert series; the orchestra organization posts a list of its sponsors on its website, including the Music Shop's name and Internet address. The exempt organization's website does not promote the Music Shop or advertise its merchandise. The Music Shop's Internet address appears as a hyperlink from the organization's website to the Music Shop's website. The organization's posting of the Music Shop's name and Internet address on its website constitutes acknowledgment of the sponsorship. The entire payment is a qualified sponsorship payment.[238]

---

[236] *Id.*, Example (8).
[237] *Id.*, Example (9).
[238] *Id.*, Example (11).

In the second of these examples, a tax-exempt health-based charitable organization sponsors a year-long initiative to educate the public about a particular medical condition. A large pharmaceutical company, which manufactures a drug that is used in treating this medical condition, provides funding for the initiative that helps the organization produce educational materials for distribution and post information on its website. The exempt organization's website contains a link to the pharmaceutical company's website. On the company's website, this statement appears: "[The charitable organization] endorses the use of our drug, and suggest that you ask your doctor for a prescription if you have this medical condition." The organization reviewed this endorsement before it was posted on the pharmaceutical company's website and gave permission for the endorsement to appear. The endorsement constitutes advertising. The fair market value of the advertising exceeds 2 percent of the total payment received from the pharmaceutical company. Therefore, only the portion of the payment, if any, that the organization can demonstrate exceeds the fair market value of the advertising on the pharmaceutical company's website is a qualified sponsorship payment.[239]

(h) Exceptions

This safe-harbor rule does not apply to payments made in connection with qualified convention and trade show activities.[240] It also does not apply to income derived from the sale of an acknowledgment or advertising in the periodical of a tax-exempt organization.[241] The term *periodical* means regularly scheduled and printed material published by or on behalf of an exempt organization that is not related to and primarily distributed in connection with a specific event conducted by the exempt organization.[242] For purposes of the corporate sponsorship rules, at least, the term *printed material* includes material that is published electronically.[243]

An example of this rule concerns a trade association that publishes a monthly scientific magazine for its members, containing information about current issues and developments in the field. A textbook publisher makes a large payment to the association to have its name displayed on the inside cover of the magazine each month. Because the monthly magazine is a periodical,[244] this safe harbor for qualified sponsorship payments is inapplicable.[245]

[239] *Id.*, Example (12).
[240] IRC § 513(i)(2)(B)(ii)(II); Reg. § 1.513-4(b). See § 4.5.
[241] IRC § 513(i)(2)(B)(ii)(I); Reg. § 1.513-4(b). See § 6.5(b).
[242] *Id.*
[243] Reg. § 1.513-4(b). A history of the law leading to these rules is in Hopkins, *The Law of Fundraising, Third Edition* (John Wiley & Sons, 2002), § 5.16; Henderson; *The Tax Treatment of Corporate Sponsorship Payments and the Aftermath of the Cotton Bowl Ruling*, 13 *Exempt Orgs. Tax Rev.* 789 (no. 5, May 1996). In general, Woods, *Tax Treatment of Corporate Sponsorship Payments to Exempt Organizations: Final Regulations*, 38 *Exempt Orgs. Tax Rev.* 205 (no. 2, Nov. 2002).
[244] See text accompanied by §6.5(b).
[245] Reg. § 1.513-4(f), Example (10).

CHAPTER SEVEN

Commercial Activities

Occasionally, as part of the evolution of the law of tax-exempt organizations, courts will create or develop law that is grafted onto statutory criteria. This phenomenon is most obvious and extensive in connection with the evolution and application of the commerciality doctrine. These principles are affecting the law concerning qualification for tax exemption and, in the process, helping shape the law of unrelated business. Over the decades of development of the commerciality doctrine, it has been applied by the courts only with respect to charitable organizations. Recently, however, the IRS has begun taking the position that social welfare organizations[1] are also subject to this doctrine.[2]

Despite its enormous effect to date, the commerciality doctrine is somewhat of an enigma. In writing the law of tax-exempt organizations over the decades, Congress did not create the doctrine. With one exception,[3] the word *commercial* does not appear in the federal statutory law concerning exempt organizations. Nor, with one exception,[4] is the term to be found in the applicable income tax regulations. The IRS has not issued formal guidance concerning the commerciality doctrine, although reference to the doctrine appears in private letter rulings. It is, then, a doctrine largely created and advanced by courts.

---

[1] See Hopkins, *The Law of Tax-Exempt Organizations, Eighth Edition* (John Wiley & Sons, 2003) [hereinafter *Tax-Exempt Organizations*], ch. 12.

[2] See text *infra* accompanied by notes 118–122.

[3] IRC. § 501(m), denying tax exemption to certain organizations that provide commercial-type insurance (see *infra* §§ 7.1(b), 7.3).

[4] See § 7.1(c).

§ 7.1 COMMERCIALITY DOCTRINE: ORIGINS

The commerciality doctrine, as it relates to the activities of tax-exempt organizations, is an overlay body of law that the courts have integrated with the statutory and regulatory rules.

(a) Nature of Doctrine

The *commerciality doctrine* is essentially this: A tax-exempt organization is engaged in a nonexempt activity when the manner in which that activity is engaged in is considered commercial. An act is a *commercial* one if it has a direct counterpart, or is conducted in the same manner as, in the realm of for-profit organizations. (Having stated the essence of the doctrine, it must also be said that the doctrine is unevenly applied.)

The doctrine appears to be born of the basic fact that United States society is composed of three sectors: the business (for-profit) sector, the governmental sector, and the nonprofit sector. Generally, the governmental sector is not viewed as an operator of businesses—though there are, of course, exceptions to this—so that sector is not a factor in this analysis other than as the source of regulation.

The United States is essentially a capitalist society, so the business sector is, in several ways, the preferred sector. Although entities in the business sector are seen as being operated for private ends (for example, profits to shareholders), with the overall result a capitalist (albeit rather regulated) economy for the society, the nonprofit sector is seen as being operated for public ends (the general good of society).[5] Many today still perceive nonprofit organizations as entities that do not and should not earn a profit, are operated largely by volunteers, and are not to be "run like a business."[6]

Out of these precepts (some of which are false) emanates the view that organizations in the nonprofit sector should not compete with organizations in the business sector. Thus, over recent years, the nonprofit community has heard much about competition between for-profit organizations (usually, small business) and nonprofit organizations—with the word *competition* almost always preceded by the word *unfair*.[7]

This doctrine thus involves a *counterpart test*. When a court sees an activity being conducted by a member of the business sector and the same activity being conducted by a member of the nonprofit sector, it often concludes that the nonprofit organization is conducting that activity in a commercial manner, motivated by some form of intuitive offense at the thought that a nonprofit organization is doing something that "ought to" be done or is being done by a for-profit-organization. This conclusion then leads to a finding that the commercial activity is a nonexempt function, with adverse consequences in law for the nonprofit organization with respect to either unrelated income taxation or tax exemption. Consequently, the federal tax law pertaining to nonprofit organizations is being shaped by a doctrine that rests in part on untrue premises

---

[5] See *Tax-Exempt Organizations*, § 1.1(b).
[6] See *id.* § 4.9.
[7] See § 1.8.

and that has crept into the law by actions of courts—courts that, consciously or unconsciously, have ignored the Internal Revenue Code and the underlying regulations, and developed law with these premises in mind.

The long-simmering and contentious debate over whether credit unions should continue to be tax-exempt[8] is a classic illustration of the counterpart test. A report from the Congressional Research Service, a division of the Library of Congress, issued in 1990, supported repeal of the exemption and referred to the fact that "many believe that an economically neutral tax system requires that financial institutions engaged in similar activities should have the same tax treatment."[9] Fifteen years later, another study concluded that there is "no good policy argument based on equity or efficiency for maintaining the tax exemption" for credit unions, and opined that "[r]emoving the credit unions' tax exemption would create a more equitable tax system and help level the playing field with other financial institutions."[10] Citing differences between credit unions and other financial institutions, organizations like the National Credit Union Administration argue for the ongoing exemption, while organizations like the American Bankers Association disagree.[11]

A second illustration of this point is the question of the ongoing tax exemption for fraternal beneficiary societies.[12] A study conducted by the Department of the Treasury, which culminated in a report in early 1993,[13] found that the insurance functions of these organizations are income-producing activities that are similar in "nature and scope" to those provided by for-profit commercial insurance companies. Although the study concluded that the insurance policies of these societies "appear to serve the same markets as those served by commercial insurers," and that the large societies charge prices "that are not significantly less than those charged by comparable large mutual life insurers," it did not advocate repeal of the tax exemption for these organizations. Rather, it concluded that the "benefits of society from [their] charitable services . . . may justify continuation of tax exemption" for the insurance activities of fraternal beneficiary societies. The report thus dismissed this aspect of commerciality, stating that the societies "do

---

[8] See *Tax-Exempt Organizations*, § 18.7.

[9] *Should Credit Unions Be Taxed?*, *CRS Analysis* No. I B 89066 (Sept. 18, 1990).

[10] Tax Foundation, *Competitive Advantage: A Study of the Federal Tax Exemption for Credit Unions* (2005), released by the Independent Community Bankers Association on February 28, 2005.

[11] The banking industry is consolidating resources to push for repeal of the tax-exempt status of credit unions. The emerging term in this quarter is *bank-like credit unions*. The group leading this campaign is the Inter-Trade Credit Union Coordinating Council, the purpose of which is to "call congressional and public attention to the activities of bank-like credit unions, their exemption from taxes, their exemption from Community Investment Act requirements, and their proposals to expand credit unions' powers and fields of membership." The council was formed by the American Bankers Association (ABA), the Independent Community Bankers Association, and America's Community Bankers. The chairman of the ABA spoke of "aggressive credit unions" that are the "elephant in the room . . . trying to blend in with the furniture while gobbling up the hors d'oeuvres at taxpayers' expense." The president of the Credit Union National Association responded: "[W]e take this as a sign that the banking trade groups are going to continue their behavior of recklessly attacking credit unions, despite the facts that they have made record profits, continue to enjoy unequaled prosperity and dominate the financial services market. Just as assuredly, credit unions must be prepared to defend themselves—and we will be."

[12] See *Tax-Exempt Organizations*, § 18.4(a).

[13] *Id.*, n. 96 (Department of the Treasury, *Report to the Congress on Fraternity Beneficiary Societies* (Jan. 15, 1993)).

not use their exemption to compete unfairly with commercial insurers in terms of price or to operate inefficiently."[14]

A dozen years later, however, a new view emerged concerning fraternal beneficiary societies' qualification for tax-exempt status, when the staff of the Joint Committee on Taxation issued a report concluding that these societies that provide insurance are engaged in an activity the nature and scope of which is "inherently commercial" and that tax-exempt status for them is inappropriate.[15] The staff proposed that a fraternal beneficiary society, order, or association be exempt from federal income taxation only if no substantial part of its activities consists of providing commercial-type insurance. If the organization is exempt under the proposal, the activity of providing commercial-type insurance would be treated as an unrelated business and taxed pursuant to the rules applicable to insurance companies.[16] This report stated that the provision of exempt status for organizations that engage in insurance activities gives these organizations an "unfair competitive advantage," especially as the "rationale for providing the exemption for an organization (i.e., that the organization provides benefits exclusively to members that share a common, fraternal bond) has been eroded, and fraternal features are incidental to the insurance activity such that the organization is indistinguishable from a taxable insurance company."[17] The report concluded: "The original fraternal purpose of the organization has been lost if it can effectively provide insurance to any person."[18]

A third example is the debate over the criteria for tax exemption for hospitals. This issue raises the question of whether the basis for this exemption should continue to be the community benefit standard,[19] or whether it should be revised to reflect a charity care standard.[20]

(b) Internal Revenue Code

Usually, when endeavoring to understand a point of federal tax law, one turns first to the Internal Revenue Code. In searching for the law embodied by the commerciality doctrine as it applies to tax-exempt organizations, however, a perusal of the Code is basically futile. That is, articulation of the commerciality doctrine, as a general standard of law, is not to be found there.

Nonetheless, a significant aspect of the doctrine was added to the Internal Revenue Code in 1986, as a consequence of Congress's decision to deprive organizations that are providers of health care insurance, such as Blue Cross and

---

[14] This conclusion is wholly inconsistent with contemporary court opinions and IRS ruling policy. In those quarters, commercial practices are automatically considered unrelated activities, leading to denial or revocation of exemption or to a finding of unrelated business. This report concluded that, for these outcomes to occur, there must be more than commerciality; there must also be unfair competition. See § 1.8.

[15] Joint Committee on Taxation, *Options to Improve Tax Compliance and Reform Tax Expenditures* 323 (JCS-02-05, Jan. 27, 2005).

[16] *Id.* at 324. This proposal is thus based on IRC. § 501(m); see § 7.3.

[17] Joint Committee on Taxation, *Options to Improve Tax Compliance and Reform Tax Expenditures* 324 (JCS-02-05, Jan. 27, 2005).

[18] *Id.* at 325. This analysis stated that in 2004, the largest of these exempt fraternal organizations had assets of $62.5 billion, with an increase in asset size of 38 percent from 1999 to 2003.

[19] See *Tax-Exempt Organizations,* § 6.2(a).

[20] See Hopkins & Hyatt, *The Law of Tax-Exempt Healthcare Organizations* (John Wiley & Sons, 2001) [hereinafter *Tax-Exempt Healthcare Organizations*], ch. 26.

Blue Shield organizations, of tax-exempt status. The rationale for this decision was that this type of insurance is being provided by the for-profit sector, that these types of nonprofit organizations look like and compete with for-profit organizations, and that tax exemption for insurance providers is no longer appropriate.[21] This legislation is a classic illustration of the points made above, concerning the for-profit business sector preference and the counterpart test.

Thus, Congress devised a rule providing that an entity cannot be tax-exempt as a charitable organization[22] or a social welfare organization[23] if a substantial part of its activities consists of the provision of *commercial-type insurance*.[24] This term is not defined in the Internal Revenue Code; its legislative history stated that "commercial-type insurance generally is any insurance of a type provided by commercial insurance companies."[25] This is, of course, an application of the counterpart test: If the activity is found in the for-profit business sector, it is inappropriate for such activity to be conducted in the nonprofit organization sector.

Organizations that seek to be tax-exempt must meet an *operational test*, a body of law that evaluates activities in relation to the requirement that tax-exempt functions be conducted.[26] The operational test is most refined in the body of law concerning charitable organizations.[27] The regulations also amplify the Internal Revenue Code use of words such as *charitable* and *educational*.[28]

The Internal Revenue Code taxes the net income derived by nearly all tax-exempt organizations from *unrelated business activities*.[29] These activities are those that are not substantially related to the exercise or performance by the exempt organization of its exempt purpose or function.[30] Neither the organization's need for the revenue derived from a business nor the use it makes of the profits derived from the business can be used as a basis for demonstrating relatedness in the unrelated business context.[31]

Absent an applicable statutory exception, an activity is taxable as an unrelated one when the activity is a trade or business, the business is regularly carried on, and the conduct of the business is not substantially related (other than through the production of funds) to the organization's performance of its exempt function.[32] Pursuant to the statutory law, the *fragmentation rule* provides that an "activity does not lose identity as trade or business merely because it is carried on within a larger aggregate of similar activities or within a larger complex of

---

[21] This is precisely the same argument being advanced for the repeal of tax exemption for certain fraternal beneficiary societies. See text accompanied by *supra* notes 13–14).

[22] That is, an organization described in IRC. § 501(c)(3). See *Tax-Exempt Organizations*, pt. 2.

[23] That is, an organization described in IRC. § 501(c)(4). See *Tax-Exempt Organizations*, ch. 12.

[24] IRC. § 501(m).

[25] H.R. Rep. No. 841, 99th Cong., 2d Sess. II-345 (1986).

[26] See *Tax-Exempt Organizations*, § 4.5.

[27] Reg. § 1.501(c)(3)-1(c).

[28] Reg. § 1.501(c)(3)-1(d)(2), (3).

[29] See § 1.7.

[30] See § 2.7.

[31] See § 2.6. This rule may be contrasted with the IRS's view that tax-exempt status can be preserved, even when a majority of an organization's activities consists of unrelated business, if the purpose of conducting the unrelated activities is to generate revenue to support related activities. Tech. Adv. Mem. 200021056.

[32] See §§ 2.2, 2.5–2.7.

other endeavors that may, or may not, be related to the exempt purposes of the organization."[33]

(c) Tax Regulations

The tax regulations exist to explain, illustrate, and, in some instances, amplify the rules as stated in the statutory law. Yet, when it comes to the commerciality doctrine, as it is being conceived and interpreted by the courts today, is nowhere to be found in the regulations.

The income tax regulations are silent on the matter of commercial operations in relation to a determination of whether an activity is substantially related to the accomplishment of exempt purposes.[34] With one minor exception (concerning commercial advertising), the same is true with respect to the definition of the term *trade or business*.[35]

The term *commercial* is used in the tax regulations as part of the elements for determining whether a business is regularly carried on.[36] Thus, the regulations state that specific business activities of an exempt organization are ordinarily deemed to be regularly carried on if they "manifest a frequency and continuity, and are pursued in a manner, generally similar to comparable commercial activities of nonexempt organizations."[37]

To determine whether an activity is substantially related to an organization's exempt purposes, it is necessary to examine the "relationship between the business activities which generate the particular income in question—the activities, that is, of producing or distributing the goods or performing the services involved—and the accomplishment of the organization's exempt purposes."[38]

A business is *related to exempt purposes* when the conduct of the business activity has a causal relationship to the achievement of exempt purposes, and it is *substantially related* when the causal relationship is a substantial one.[39] For a business to be substantially related to exempt purposes, the production or distribution of the goods or the performance of the services from which the gross income is derived must "contribute importantly to the accomplishment of those purposes."[40] Whether activities productive of gross income contribute importantly to the accomplishment of one or more exempt purposes "depends in each case upon the facts and circumstances involved."[41]

As noted, this regulatory definition of relatedness does not make any reference to the commerciality doctrine. Rather, this definition of relatedness is a causal relationship test. Thus, under the regulations, a business may be regularly carried on (that is, be commercially conducted) and not be taxed, when there is a substantial causal relationship between the activity and the accomplishment of

---

[33] See § 2.3.
[34] Reg. § 1.513-1(d).
[35] Reg. § 1.513-1(b).
[36] See § 2.5.
[37] Reg. § 1.513-1(c)(1), (2)(ii).
[38] Reg. § 1.513-1(d)(1).
[39] Reg. § 1.513-1(d)(2).
[40] *Id.*
[41] *Id.*

exempt purposes. In other words, the IRS regulations contemplate a nontaxable, related business that is commercially carried on.

(d) Beginnings of Doctrine

The commerciality doctrine is not the consequence of some grand pronounce-ment by the Supreme Court—or, for that matter, of any court. The doctrine merely chanced upon the scene and evolved, growing from flaccid language in court opinions, which in turn seems to have reflected judges' personal views as to what the law ought to be (rather than what it is). The commerciality doctrine appears to be the product of what is known in the law as *dictum:* a gratuitous remark by a judge that need not have been uttered to resolve the case. The term stems from the Latin *simplex dictum,* meaning an "assertion without proof," and later *obiter dictum,* which means a statement "lacking the force of an adjudica-tion." Over the years, however, the commerciality doctrine has very much taken on the force of an adjudication.

The doctrine was initiated a quarter of a century before Congress enacted the unrelated income rules in 1950. It was first mentioned, at the federal level, in 1924, by the U.S. Supreme Court.[42] The case concerned a tax-exempt religious order that was operated for religious purposes, but also engaged in other activi-ties that the government alleged destroyed the basis for its exemption: The order had extensive investments in real estate and stock holdings that returned a profit, as well as some incidental sales of wine, chocolate, and other articles. The Court found that the order was exempt as a religious entity, justifying the order's investment and business efforts with the indisputable assertion that "[s]uch [religious] activities cannot be carried on without money."[43]

In this case, the Court did not articulate a commerciality doctrine. To the contrary: the Court, characterizing the government's argument as being that the order was "operated also for business and *commercial* purposes,"[44] rejected this portrayal, writing that there was no "competition" and that although the "trans-actions yield some profit[, it] is in the circumstances a negligible factor."[45] Thus, in this case, rather than enunciating the commerciality doctrine, the Court, by merely uttering the word in describing the government's position, inadvertently gave birth to the commerciality doctrine.

The principles that flowed out of this Supreme Court opinion are embod-ied in today's operational test, which is stated in the tax regulations.[46] The opinion laid down the rule that a charitable organization can engage in busi-ness activities for profit, without loss of exemption, if its net income is des-tined for charitable uses. This rule, known as the *destination of income test,* was terminated by Congress in 1950, when it enacted the body of law pertaining to feeder organizations.[47] An analysis of the cases applying the destination of

---

[42] Trinidad v. Sagrada Orden de Predicadores de la Provincia del Santisimo Rosario de Filipinas, 263 U.S. 578 (1924).

[43] *Id.* at 581.

[44] *Id.* at 581 (emphasis added).

[45] *Id.* at 582.

[46] Reg. § 1.501(c)(3)-1(c)(1). See *Tax-Exempt Organizations,* § 4.5.

[47] IRC. § 502. See *Tax-Exempt Organizations,* § 28.6.

income test, and of that test's transition out of existence, was provided in a 1957 appellate court opinion.[48]

Repeal of the destination of income test, however, did not extinguish what has been termed the *activities standard*.[49] This standard is used when a nonprofit organization engages in activities that, though commercial, further the organization's exempt purposes.[50] Today, the activities standard survives as the operational test.

The 1924 Supreme Court opinion established another point: When an organization's activities are a negligible factor (as was the order's sale of wine and chocolate), they are considered incidental in relation to exempt purposes, and thus have no adverse effect on the entity's tax exemption.[51] This aspect of the law is reflected in the contemporary rule that a charitable organization must be operated exclusively for exempt purposes, with today's understanding that the word *exclusively* actually means *primarily*. The word *exclusively* is in the Internal Revenue Code; in the tax regulations the word is *primarily*.[52]

The Supreme Court edged up to an announcement of the commerciality doctrine in 1945, when reviewing a case concerning the tax exemption of a chapter of the Better Business Bureau, which was seeking exempt status as an educational organization.[53] On this occasion, the Court said that the exclusivity requirement "plainly means that the presence of a single non-educational purpose, if substantial in nature, will destroy the exemption regardless of the number or importance of truly educational purposes."[54] The Court found a noneducational purpose in the promotion of a community of profitable businesses. In the closest it has come to expressly articulating the commerciality doctrine, the Court said that the organization had a "commercial hue" and that its "activities are largely animated by this commercial purpose."[55]

(e) Focus on Publishing

The commerciality doctrine flourished during a period in the early 1960s, in the context of the courts' scrutiny of nonprofit publishing organizations. This focus is understandable given that publishing occurs in both the for-profit and nonprofit sectors, and thus facilitates easy application of the counterpart doctrine.

An early case invoking the commerciality doctrine, along with the counterpart test, was decided in 1961.[56] The organization published and sold religious literature in furtherance of its purpose of upgrading the quality of teaching materials for Bible instruction in Sunday schools; it generated what the court termed "very

---

[48] Lichter Found. v. Welch, 247 F.2d 431 (6th Cir. 1957).

[49] Fides Publishers Ass'n v. United States, 263 F. Supp. 924 (N.D. Ind. 1967).

[50] *Id.* at 933–34.

[51] Trinidad v. Sagrada Orden de Predicadores de la Provincia del Santisimo Rosario de Filipinas, 263 U.S. 578, 582 (1924).

[52] Reg. § 1.501(c)(3)-1(c)(1). See *Tax-Exempt Organizations*, § 4.6.

[53] Better Bus. Bureau of Wash., D.C. v. United States, 326 U.S. 279 (1945).

[54] *Id.* at 283.

[55] *Id.* at 283–84.

[56] Scripture Press Found. v. United States, 285 F.2d 800 (Ct. Cl. 1961).

substantial" profits.[57] The court rejected the argument that profits alone preclude tax exemption, writing: "If the defendant [IRS] seeks by this distinction ["slight" versus "very substantial" profits] to suggest that where an organization's profits are very large a conclusion that the organization is non-charitable must follow, we reject such a suggestion."[58] The court then added these fateful words: "If, however, defendant means only to suggest that it is at least some evidence indicative of a *commercial* character[,] we are inclined to agree."[59]

This court found the organization to be directly involved in the conduct of a trade or business for profit, with religious objectives "incidental."[60] Application of the counterpart test was articulated in a footnote, with the court observing "that there are many commercial concerns which sell Bibles, scrolls, and other religious and semi-religious literature which have not been granted exemption as to that part of their businesses."[61] Consequently, the court found that the organization's activities were of a "nonexempt character."[62] The court declined to apply the unrelated income tax rules to these facts, though; thus, this 1961 opinion is devoid of any discussion of related and unrelated activities. The court obviously thought that the organization's primary activities were unrelated ones, inasmuch as its tax exemption was revoked, but the word *commercial* was used rather than the word *unrelated*. The opinion offers no definition of the word *commercial* and contains no indication as to why the court employed it.

In one of these cases, decided in 1956, a court held that an organization that sold religious publications and charged admission fees to conclaves was tax-exempt because the "activities bear an intimate relationship to the proper functioning of" the organization.[63] The court made no mention of a commerciality doctrine. Earlier, in 1954, this court held that an organization organized to prepare and publish a widely accepted system for indexing library collections (the Dewey Decimal Classification System) was exempt.[64] Again, there was no mention of any commerciality doctrine. The commerciality doctrine appears, on the basis of this 1961 opinion, to take into account at least three elements: the scope of an organization's net profits, the extent of accumulated surplus revenue (capital), and amounts expended for what the court deems to be exempt functions.

As it turned out, a different court had another nonprofit publishing organization before it the next year. This organization disseminated publications (principally newsletters and books) containing investment advice to subscribers and other purchasers. Rejecting the argument that the organization was engaged in educational activities, the court held that the organization was not entitled to tax exemption because "its purpose is primarily a business one."[65] Once again, the court did not discuss whether the business was related or unrelated.

---

[57] *Id.* at 803.
[58] *Id.*
[59] *Id.* (emphasis added).
[60] Scripture Press Found. v. United States, 285 F.2d at 805.
[61] *Id.* at 806, n.11.
[62] *Id.* at 807.
[63] Saint Germain Found. v. Comm'r, 26 T.C. 648, 658 (1956).
[64] Forest Press, Inc. v. Comm'r, 22 T.C. 265 (1954).
[65] Am. Inst. for Econ. Research v. United States, 302 F.2d 934, 938 (Ct. Cl. 1962).

This court did not need to use the word *commercial*; the proper terminology would have been *unrelated business*. Instead, in this 1962 opinion, the court wrote passages such as the organization was "in competition with other commercial organizations providing similar services"[66]; the organization's "investment service in all its ramifications may be educational, but its purpose is primarily a business one"[67]; and the "totality of these activities is indicative of a business, and . . . [the organization's] purpose is thus a commercial purpose and nonexempt."[68] With that, the commerciality doctrine, and its counterpart test and the concern about competition between the sectors, was irrevocably launched. The doctrine was becoming a material part of the law of tax-exempt organizations.

In 1963, a court rejected the federal government's contention that publication and sale of religious magazines, books, pamphlets, Bibles, records, tape recordings, and pictures amounted to commercial activity.[69] In 1964, this court was faced with another case involving the operation of alleged commercial enterprises, this time concerning a religious organization that conducted training projects. The court rejected application of the commerciality doctrine, stating that "we regard consistent nonprofitability as evidence of the absence of commercial purposes."[70]

Still another case involving a religious publishing organization was considered by a federal district court in 1967. This court refined the commerciality doctrine by distinguishing between organizations that have commercial activities as a part of their overall activities and those that have commercial activities as their sole activity.[71] Organizations that retained their tax exemption in the prior cases fell into the first category;[72] the other organizations were placed in the second category. The court thus relied on the other cases[73] in concluding that the publishing company was not exempt. The nonexempt purpose[74] was portrayed as the "publication and sale of religious literature at a profit."[75] The court said that its conclusion could not be otherwise: "If it were, every publishing house would be entitled to an exemption on the ground that it furthers the education of the public."[76]

In 1968, another federal district court reached the identical result. A publisher of religious materials was denied tax exemption because it was "clearly engaged primarily in a business activity, and it conducted its operations, although on a small scale, in the same way as any commercial publisher of religious books for

---

[66] *Id.* at 938.

[67] *Id.* at 938.

[68] *Id.* at 937.

[69] A.A. Allen Revivals, Inc. v. Comm'r, 22 T.C. 1435 (1963).

[70] Golden Rule Church Ass'n v. Comm'r, 41 T.C. 719, 731 (1964).

[71] Fides Publishers Ass'n v. United States, 263 F. Supp. 924 (N.D. Ind. 1967).

[72] This includes cases such as Saint Germain Found. v. Comm'r, 26 T.C. 648 (1956); Golden Rule Church Ass'n v. Comm'r, 41 T.C. 719 (1964); A.A. Allen Revivals, Inc. v. Comm'r, 22 T.C. 1435 (1963).

[73] Scripture Press Found. v. United States, 285 F.2d 800 (Ct. Cl. 1961); Am. Inst. for Econ. Research v. United States, 302 F.2d 934 (Ct. Cl. 1962).

[74] Following the rationale in Better Bus. Bureau of Wash., D.C. v. United States, 326 U.S. 279 (1945).

[75] Fides Publishers Ass'n v. United States, 263 F. Supp. 924, 935 (N.D. Ind. 1967).

[76] *Id.*

profit would have done."[77] The fact that the organization's ultimate purpose was a religious one was not, for that court, sufficient to confer exemption.

The next year, however, this opinion was reversed; the organization prevailed before the appellate court on the ground that the entity did not have "operational profits."[78] The court of appeals concluded that the "deficit operation reflects not poor business planning nor ill fortune but rather the fact that profits were not the goal of the operation."[79] Although the nonprofit organization involved in the case prevailed, this opinion went a long way toward establishment of the point that the existence of profit is evidence of commerciality.

Thus, the 1960s witnessed court cases that invoked and solidified the commerciality doctrine. After this flurry of activity involving publishing organizations, not much happened with the doctrine for over a decade. Then, in 1978, came the first of the court opinions articulating the contemporary commerciality doctrine.

In 1978, a court had occasion to review the previous cases discussing the commerciality doctrine. Once again, it had before it an organization the sole activity of which was religious publishing. Essentially, the purpose of the organization under review was to disseminate sermons to ministers to improve their religious teachings. The court allowed the organization a tax exemption on the ground that the sale of religious literature was an "integral part of and incidental to" the entity's religious purpose.[80]

That same year, the court was called upon to determine whether an organization that purchased, imported, and sold artists' crafts could be tax-exempt. The IRS contended that the organization was a "commercial import firm."[81] The organization argued that its purpose was to help disadvantaged artisans in poverty-stricken countries to subsist and preserve their craft and to furnish services to exempt museums by providing museum stores with representative handicrafts from disadvantaged countries. Once again, the court came down on the side of exemption, concluding that the organization engaged in the purchase, import, and sale activities, not as an end unto themselves, but as a means of accomplishing exempt purposes. This organization thus escaped characterization as a commercial organization.

In early 1979, this court went the other way on the point, concluding that the primary purpose of the organization involved was the publication and sale of books written by its founder. In concluding that the principal purpose served by this organization was commercial in nature, the court focused on the fact of annual profits and the organization's distribution and marketing practices. Although the conclusion reached was that the organization was principally commercial, the case had considerable overtones of private inurement.[82]

Later that same year, the court analyzed the facts involving an organization operated to purchase and sell products manufactured by blind individuals. The court found that the principal purpose of the organization was to provide

---

[77] Elisian Guild, Inc. v. United States, 292 F. Supp. 219, 221 (D. Mass. 1968).
[78] Elisian Guild, Inc. v. United States, 412 F.2d 121, 125 (1st Cir. 1969).
[79] *Id.* at 125.
[80] Pulpit Res. v. Comm'r, 70 T.C. 594, 611 (1978).
[81] Aid to Artisans, Inc. v. Comm'r, 71 T.C. 202, 208 (1978).
[82] Christian Manner Int'l v. Comm'r, 71 T.C. 661 (1979).

employment for the blind, thereby alleviating the hardship these disabled individuals experience in securing and holding regular employment. The fact that the organization generated a profit was disregarded.[83]

Early in 1980, the same court considered the case of an organization that benefited the poor of the Navajo Nation by assisting in the organization and operation of businesses that employ or are owned by residents of the Navajo reservation. Its most substantial source of revenue was the leasing of oil well drilling equipment. The court, in denying the organization tax exemption on the ground that it was operated primarily for commercial purposes, articulated the commerciality doctrine as follows:

> Profits may be realized or other nonexempt purposes may be necessarily advanced incidental to the conduct of the commercial activity, but the existence of such nonexempt purposes does not require denial of exempt status so long as the organization's dominant purpose for conducting the activity is an exempt purpose, and so long as the nonexempt activity is merely incidental to the exempt purpose."[84]

The organization's activities were found to be in violation of the operational test.

The next year, a federal district court concluded that an organization that published religious literature should lose its tax exemption on the ground that it had evolved into a commercial entity. Though originally formed as a missionary organization, the court ruled that it had become an organization with a "commercial hue" and a "highly efficient business venture."[85] In reaching this conclusion, the court noted that the organization adhered to publishing and sales practices followed by comparable commercial publishers, had shown increasing profits in recent years, had experienced a growth in accumulated surplus, and had been paying substantially increased salaries to its top employees.

Late in 1982, this court issued an opinion concerning still another religious publishing house, again concluding that its exemption should be revoked because the court felt that the organization had become too profitable and thus commercial.[86] Once again, the court found a "commercial hue," derived from profits, wide profit margins, development of a professional staff, and competition with commercial publishers.[87] The opinion was reversed, though, with the appellate court "troubled by the inflexibility of the Tax Court's approach."[88] The court of appeals afforded no clarity; although it was bothered by the facts, it could not bring itself to revoke the organization's exemption. Thus, the appellate court said that "success in terms of audience reached and influence exerted, in and of itself, should not jeopardize the tax-exempt status of organizations which remain true to their stated goals."[89] Still, the court also wrote that if an

---

[83] Indus. Aid for the Blind v. Comm'r, 73 T.C. 96 (1979).

[84] Greater United Navajo Dev. Enters., Inc. v. Comm'r, 74 T.C. 69, 79 (1980).

[85] Inc. Trustees of Gospel Worker Soc'y v. United States, 510 F. Supp. 374, 381 (D.D.C.), aff'd, 672 F.2d 894 (D.C. Cir.), cert. denied, 456 U.S. 944 (1981).

[86] Presbyterian & Reformed Publ'g Co. v. Comm'r, 79 T.C. 1070 (1982).

[87] Id. at 1083.

[88] Presbyterian & Reformed Publ'g Co. v. Comm'r, 743 F.2d 148, 152 (3d Cir. 1984).

[89] Id. at 158.

exempt "organization's management decisions replicate those of commercial enterprises, it is a fair inference that at least one purpose is commercial."[90]

In 1983, a court concluded that an ostensibly religious organization could not qualify for tax exemption because its principal purpose was "tax avoidance" counseling.[91] The court was clearly displeased at that element of the facts, so, in a sense, the case has more to do with private benefit[92] than with commerciality. The court noted that the information provided by the organization "is no different from that furnished by a commercial tax service."[93]

About three years went by before a court considered another commerciality case. Before this court was an organization that had been formed to assist in the process of technology transfer, which is the transfer of technology from universities and research institutions to for-profit industry.[94] The court concluded that the organization's major activity was the provision of patenting and licensing services, and that the activity was primarily commercial in nature.[95]

In 1986, a court held that a religious retreat center was not an organization that is commercial in nature, because it did not compete with commercial entities.[96] The entity was held to be an integral part of a conference of the United Methodist Church. The organization was portrayed as a general contractor for the construction of housing, on its own property, to promote increased religious activity. The fact that the organization charged fair market prices was held to necessary to avoid charges of private inurement.

The latter half of the 1980s brought little attention to the commerciality doctrine. The focus, particularly with respect to religious organizations, was on unrelated business activities, rather than loss of tax exemption. In only one instance did courts discuss the commerciality doctrine; the case concerned a nonprofit organization that operated an adoption agency.[97] It was held that this organization could not qualify as an exempt charitable or educational entity because adoption services are not inherently exempt functions. The organization was cast as operating in a manner not "distinguishable from a commercial adoption agency," because it generated substantial profits, accumulated capital, was funded entirely by fees, had no plans to solicit contributions, and had a paid staff.[98]

(f) Recent Applications of Doctrine

(i) Court Opinions.   The 1990s continued to spawn cases involving the commerciality doctrine. In the first of these, the court concluded that the commerciality doctrine was the basis for denial of tax-exempt status, as a charitable and religious

---

[90] *Id.* at 155.

[91] Ecclesiastical Order of the Ism of Am, Inc. v. Comm'r, 80 T.C. 833, 843 (1983).

[92] See § 1.10.

[93] Ecclesiastical Order of the Ism of Am, Inc. v. Comm'r, 80 T.C. at 839.

[94] See *Tax-Exempt Organizations*, § 9.5.

[95] Wash. Research Found. v. Comm'r, 50 T.C.M. 1457 (1985). This opinion was "overturned" by Congress when it enacted § 1605 of the Tax Reform Act of 1986. See H.R. Rep. No. 841, 99th Cong., 2d Sess. II-827 (1986).

[96] Junaluska Assembly Hous., Inc. v. Comm'r, 86 T.C. 1114 (1986).

[97] Easter House v. United States, 846 F.2d 78 (Fed. Cir. 1988), *aff'g* 87-1 U.S.T.C. ¶ 9359 (Ct. Cl. 1987), *cert. denied*, 488 U.S. 907 (1988).

[98] *Id.*, 87-1 U.S.T.C. ¶ 9359 at 87,864.

entity, to an organization associated with the Seventh-day Adventist Church that operated, in advancement of church doctrine, vegetarian restaurants and health food stores.[99] The court wrote that the organization's "activity was conducted as a business and was in direct competition with other restaurants and health food stores."[100] The court added: "Competition with commercial firms is strong evidence of a substantial nonexempt purpose."[101]

When this case was considered on appeal, the appellate court affirmed the lower court's decision.[102] The appellate court opinion specified the factors to be utilized in finding commerciality, thus becoming the best contemporary explication of the commerciality doctrine:

1. The organization sold goods and services to the public. This factor alone was said to make the operations "presumptively commercial."

2. The organization was in "direct competition" with for-profit restaurants and food stores.

3. The prices set by the organization were based on pricing formulas common in the retail food business. The "profit-making price structure loom[ed] large" in the court's analysis, and the court criticized the organization for not having "below-cost pricing."

4. The organization used promotional materials and "commercial catch phrases" to enhance sales.

5. The organization advertised its services and food.

6. The organization's hours of operation were basically the same as those of for-profit enterprises.

7. The guidelines by which the organization operated required that its management have "business ability" and six months' training.

8. The organization did not use volunteers; instead, it paid salaries.

9. The organization did not receive charitable contributions.[103]

Subsequently, a court concluded that an organization's principal activity was the "operation of a number of canteen-style lunch trucks," which is a commercial activity, and upheld revocation of the organization's tax exemption.[104] Likewise, a nonprofit organization, the activities of which were the same as those of a temporary service agency, was denied exempt status because it was

---

[99] Living Faith, Inc. v. Comm'r, 60 T.C.M. 710 (1990).

[100] *Id.* at 713.

[101] *Id.*

[102] Living Faith, Inc. v. Comm'r, 950 F.2d 365 (7th Cir. 1991).

[103] It should be noted that some of these elements, principally those that appear toward the end of the list, do not make any sense in the modern era. It is obvious that, today, many tax-exempt organizations (including health care providers, educational institutions, and theaters) advertise their services and products; utilize promotional materials (the travel tour regulations [see § 9.7] contain three examples of the use of these materials in the conduct of related activities [Reg. § 1.513-7(b), Examples (2), (5), and (6)]; have hours of operation that are comparable to those of for-profit entities; and have personnel who have training. It is also clear that an organization can be charitable without receiving charitable gifts. See, *e.g.*, IRC. § 509(a)(2); *Tax-Exempt Organizations*, § 11.3(b)(iv).

[104] New Faith, Inc. v. Comm'r, 64 T.C.M. 1050 (1992).

"essentially a commercial venture."[105] Further, it was held that an organization selling religious tapes was a nonexempt commercial organization,[106] and that an organization operating prisoner rehabilitation programs was not eligible for exemption because of its commercial activities.[107]

A federal court denied tax-exempt status to an organization that had as its principal purpose the operation of a conference center, on the ground that there was a distinctly commercial hue associated with those operations.[108] The commerciality doctrine as applied in this case was based on a close following of the foregoing appellate court decision.[109] The court stated that among the "major factors" courts have considered in "assessing commerciality" are competition with for-profit entities, the extent and degree of low-cost services provided, pricing policies, and the reasonableness of financial reserves.[110] Additional factors were said to include whether the organization uses "commercial promotional methods (*e.g.*, advertising)" and the extent to which the organization receives charitable contributions.[111] The conference center was portrayed as being operated in a commercial manner, in part because its patrons were not confined to tax-exempt organizations and use of the facility was partially for weddings and similar events.

(ii) IRS Private Rulings.   Some years ago, the IRS tentatively applied the commerciality doctrine in the context of ascertaining whether a tax-exempt charitable organization should lose its exempt status because its fundraising costs were too "high."[112] Today, however, the agency openly, enthusiastically, and expansively embraces the commerciality doctrine. For example, it issued a private ruling asserting that commerciality was to be found in the facts that the organization involved will "place advertisements in the telephone yellow pages and other local media" and will "develop its own website"; these undertakings were cast as methods of promoting the sale of the organization's services "in ways that are typical for any for-profit business."[113] Also, the IRS held that an organization that facilitates charitable contributions of boats and other items of tangible personal property to charitable organizations cannot be recognized as an exempt charitable entity because it functions as agent for the donors and all of its activities are "common commercial" activities.[114] In the second of these

---

[105] At Cost Servs., Inc. v. Comm'r, 80 T.C.M. 573, 576 (2000).

[106] United Missionary Aviation, Inc. v. Comm'r, 60 T.C.M. 1152 (1990), *rev'd & remanded,* 985 F.2d 564 (8th Cir. 1989), *cert. denied,* 506 U.S. 816 (1992).

[107] Public Indus., Inc. v. Comm'r, 61 T.C.M. 1626 (1991).

[108] Airlie Found. v. IRS, 283 F. Supp. 2d 58 (D.D.C. 2003).

[109] See *supra* note 102.

[110] Airlie Found. v. IRS, 283 F. Supp. 2d 58, 63 (D.D.C. 2003).

[111] *Id.*

[112] See, *e.g.*, United Cancer Council, Inc. v. Comm'r, 109 T.C. 326 (1997), *rev'd & remanded,* 165 F.3d 1173 (7th Cir. 1999).

[113] Exemption Denial and Revocation Letter (Ex. Den. & Revoc. Ltr.) 20044045E. See § 7.4. One may contemplate the magnitude of the notion that maintenance of a Web site by a tax-exempt organization is evidence of commerciality. This is, of course, a wholly nonsensical conclusion. In one minor illustration of how inconsistent this idea is with law and reality, the IRS's regulations concerning the conduct of travel tours by tax-exempt organizations (see § 9.7) observe that an exempt organization can promote its tours, as related businesses, on its Internet site. Reg. § 1.513-7(b), Example (5).

[114] Priv. Ltr. Rul. 200512027.

rulings, the agency did not state, as it usually does, that the activities were non-exempt functions; it held that the organization was being operated for the primary purpose of carrying on an unrelated business.[115] Further, the IRS examined nine discrete businesses of a tax-exempt organization and concluded that two of them were unrelated businesses carried on in a commercial manner: a conferences and catering activity, and operation of a golf course.[116]

The IRS held that the operation of a miniature golf course by a charitable organization, the purpose of which was to provide for the welfare of young people, constituted an unrelated business because the course was operated in a commercial manner.[117] Its exempt function was maintenance of services and facilities that would contribute to youth's physical, social, mental, and spiritual health, at minimum or no cost. Membership in, and the services and facilities of, the organization were available for payment of nominal annual dues. The operation of the course, which was open to the general public and managed by salaried employees, was found by the IRS to be substantially similar to that of for-profit miniature golf courses, in that the admission fees were comparable and designed to return a profit.

Indeed, the IRS has now adopted the view that the commerciality doctrine applies beyond charitable entities and extends to the realm of tax-exempt social welfare organizations. In what is believed to be the agency's first ruling on the point, the assertion was made without any explanation of the underlying facts or analysis of law.[118] Thereafter, the IRS issued a private letter ruling denying exempt status to an entity as a social welfare organization because it operated as a facilitator for the sale of health insurance to participating employers, by insurance companies with which it contracted. and because it provided various services for these insurance companies for a fee; the organization was found to be operating in a commercial manner.[119] Although this latter organization did not in fact qualify as a social welfare organization,[120] the authorities relied on by the IRS[121] do not support invocation of the commerciality doctrine in this setting.[122]

The commerciality doctrine is being applied in some of the cases involving the provision of commercial-type insurance.[123] For example, in one of these cases, the court wrote that the "various factors to consider in determining whether an organization promotes a forbidden nonexempt purpose," under

---

[115] In this ruling, the IRS also referenced the rarely invoked commensurate doctrine (see *Tax-Exempt Organizations*, § 4.7), observing that this organization does not carry on a charitable program that is commensurate in scope with its financial resources.

[116] Priv. Ltr. Rul. 200512025.

[117] Rev. Rul. 79-361, 1979-2 C.B. 237.

[118] Priv. Ltr. Rul. 200501020.

[119] Priv. Ltr. Rul. 200512023.

[120] See *Tax-Exempt Organizations*, § 12.1.

[121] The two court opinions cited by the IRS (Am. Ass'n of Christian Schs. Voluntary Employees' Beneficiary Ass'n Welfare Plan Trust v. United States, 850 F.2d 1510 (11th Cir. 1988); and Mut. Aid Ass'n of the Church of the Brethren v. United States, 759 F.2d 792 (10th Cir. 1985)), as well as a revenue ruling (Rev. Rul. 86-98, 1986-2 C.B. 74), say nothing about application of the commerciality doctrine; they involve substantial nonexempt purposes and furtherance of private ends.

[122] Consequently, it seems that the appearance of the commerciality doctrine in the IRC. § 501(c)(4) context is on an even shakier basis than its launch in the IRC. § 501(c)(3) context.

[123] See § 7.3.

the rules concerning charitable organizations, include the "manner in which an organization conducts its activities; the commercial hue or nature of those activities; the competitive nature of the activities; the existence of accumulated profits; and the provision of free or below cost services."[124] The organization, the tax status of which was at issue in the case, was characterized by the court as existing "solely for the purpose of selling insurance to nonprofit exempt organizations at the lowest possible cost on a continued, stable basis"; the court continued with the observation that "[s]elling insurance undeniably is an inherently commercial activity ordinarily carried on by a commercial for-profit company."[125] The court added that although the organization "may not possess every attribute characteristic of a mutual insurance company, it possesses a majority of the qualifying characteristics, which only further enhances the determination that . . . [it] is presumptively commercial in nature."[126] In another of these cases, a court concluded that a group of self-insurance pools had a "commercial hue."[127]

The commerciality doctrine, as a court-founded rule of law, has come to be widely accepted in the courts. This phenomenon has occurred, and is occurring, even as other judicial and administrative theories and doctrines are coming to the fore. These other doctrines include competition between nonprofit and for-profit organizations,[128] the private benefit doctrine,[129] the commensurate test,[130] and the unrelated business rules.[131]

§ 7.2 CONTEMPORARY PERSPECTIVE ON DOCTRINE

One of the requirements for qualification as a tax-exempt charitable organization is that the entity be operated exclusively for one or more exempt purposes.[132] This is, in essence, a *primary purpose* rule.[133]

Pursuant to the exclusively doctrine, the IRS or a court may conclude that an organization is not operated exclusively for a tax-exempt purpose because its operation is similar to that of a commercial enterprise operated on a for-profit basis. In many of the court opinions focusing on this point, the courts have expressed concern about the "commercial hue" of the organization.

There is more to the commerciality doctrine than generation of profits. It partakes, as well, of other elements discussed throughout, such as the matter of competition with for-profit organizations, the private inurement and private benefit rules, and the commensurate test (as previously noted). The IRS may, however, use the existence of a profit to characterize the activity as being

---

[124] Nonprofits' Ins. Alliance of Cal. v. United States, 94-2 U.S.T.C. ¶ 50,593 (Fed. Cl. 1994).

[125] *Id.*

[126] *Id.*

[127] Paratransit Ins. Corp. v. Comm'r, 102 T.C. 745, 754 (1994). Subsequently, Congress enacted a limited tax exemption for certain charitable risk pools. See *Tax-Exempt Organizations*, § 10.6.

[128] See *supra* note 7.

[129] See *Tax-Exempt Organizations*, § 19.10.

[130] See *id.* § 4.7.

[131] See § 7.3.

[132] See *Tax-Exempt Organizations*, § 4.6.

[133] See *id.* § 4.4.

commercial in nature, thus placing at issue the question of whether the organization's activities are devoted exclusively to tax-exempt purposes.

The competition issue is the most troublesome, particularly as the lines of demarcation between nonprofit and for-profit organizations are, in some instances, blurring. Nonprofit organizations are becoming increasingly reliant on revenue in the form of fees for services. For-profit organizations are entering domains of goods production and service provision that were once the sole province of nonprofit organizations. Laws are changed to promote greater parity between the sectors, such as the Office of Management and Budget regulations requiring tax-exempt organizations that pursue government contracts to calculate tax revenues foregone. Management of nonprofit organizations is becoming more sophisticated.

Two categories of charitable organizations continue to evolve: those that are supported largely by gifts (*donative organizations*),[134] and those that are supported principally by exempt function revenue (*service provider organizations*).[135] As this trend continues, it will exert new pressures on the concept of tax exemption. New rationales for exemption may emerge. The battles that are building over the ground rules for exemptions for hospitals[136] and credit unions[137] may be appreciated from this perspective. A sort of domino theory may be in the works in this setting. One commentator was of the view that "if nonprofit hospitals lose their exemption, federal corporate tax exemption for most or all of the second [commercial] nonprofit sector may then be in doubt."[138]

The undermining effect of the commerciality doctrine on the future of the nonprofit sector cannot be underestimated. Recall the underlying premise of the commerciality doctrine, which is that there are two sectors that can engage in commercial activities. The bias, however, is that commercial activities should be conducted only in the for-profit sector—the United States being a capitalist society. The business sector is, in several ways, the preferred sector. This view is that of the Treasury Department, as expressed in 1987, when an assistant secretary testified before the House Subcommittee on Oversight that the "role of the quasi-governmental, not-for-profit sector should . . . be restricted to that of supplementing, and not supplanting, the activities of for-profit businesses."[139]

The commerciality doctrine is a backdrop against which the unrelated business laws can be viewed. This is in part because, in the view of some, the concept of relatedness and unrelatedness is outmoded, and should be replaced by a commerciality test.[140] Even if the commerciality doctrine does not cause denial or loss of

---

[134] See *Tax-Exempt Organizations*, § 11.3(b)(i).

[135] See *id*. § 11.3(b)(iv).

[136] See text accompanying *supra* notes 19–20.

[137] See text accompanying *supra* notes 8–11.

[138] Hansmann, *The Two Nonprofit Sectors: Fee for Service Versus Donative Organizations*, in *The Future of the Nonprofit Sector* 95 (Jossey-Bass, 1989).

[139] "Unrelated Business Income Tax," Statement of O. Donaldson Chapeton, Deputy Assistant Secretary (Tax Policy), Department of the Treasury, Hearings before the Subcommittee on Oversight, House Committee on Ways and Means, House of Representatives, 100th Cong., 1st Sess. 35 (1987).

[140] Bennett & Rudney, *A Commerciality Test to Resolve the Commercial Nonprofit Issue*, 36 *Tax Notes* 1065 (no. 14, 1987).

tax-exempt status, the doctrine remains a significant force in determining what is an unrelated trade or business.[141]

§ 7.3 COMMERCIAL-TYPE INSURANCE RULES

An otherwise tax-exempt charitable organization or social welfare organiza-tion[142] will lose or be denied tax exemption if a substantial part of its activities consists of the provision of commercial-type insurance.[143] Otherwise, the activ-ity of providing commercial-type insurance is treated as the conduct of an unrelated trade or business, and the income from it is taxed under the rules pertaining to taxable insurance companies.[144] These exempt organizations are subject to tax on the income from these insurance activities (including invest-ment income that might otherwise be excluded from unrelated business income taxation[145]) according to the rules by which for-profit insurance companies are taxed.[146]

The term *commercial-type insurance* generally means any insurance of a type provided by commercial insurance companies.[147] For example, an organization was held not to qualify as a tax-exempt social welfare organization because its sole activity was the provision of certain benefits to students in a school who were injured in the course of school-related activities; the coverage it offered was similar to contingent or excess insurance coverage.[148] This term does not, however, include insurance provided at substantially below cost to a class of charitable recipients, incidental health insurance provided by a health mainte-nance organization (HMO) of a kind customarily provided by these organiza-tions,[149] property or casualty insurance provided (directly or through a qualified employer[150]) by a church or convention or association of churches for the church or convention or association of churches, or the provision of retire-ment or welfare benefits (or both) by a church or a convention or association of churches (directly or through a qualified organization[151]) for the employees of the church or convention or association of churches or the beneficiaries of these

---

[141] In general, Columbo, *Regulating Commercial Activity by Exempt Charities: Resurrecting the Commensu-rate-in-Scope Doctrine*, 39 *Exempt Orgs. Tax Rev.* 341 (no. 3, Mar. 2003); Washlick, *The Commerciality Standard Changes the Rules of UBIT Planning*, 4 *J. Tax. Exempt Orgs.* 15 (Nov./Dec. 1992); Hopkins, *Is the Rationale for Tax-Exempt Organizations Changing?*, 4 *J. Tax'n Exempt Orgs.* 13 (Spring 1992); Hopkins, *The Most Important Concept in the Law of Tax-Exempt Organizations Today: The Commerciality Doctrine*, 5 *Exempt Orgs. Tax Rev.* 459 (no. 3, 1992); Brown, *Religious Nonprofits and the Commercial Manner Test*, 99 *Yale L.J.* 1631 (no. 7, 1990).
[142] See *Tax-Exempt Organizations*, ch. 12.
[143] IRC. § 501(m).
[144] IRC. subch. L. The application of these rules may require organizations affected by them to change their accounting methods; the process for doing so is the subject of Rev. Proc. 87-51, 1987-2 C.B. 650.
[145] See ch. 3.
[146] IRC. § 501(m)(2).
[147] H.R. Rep. No. 99-841, 99th Cong., 2d Sess. II-345 (1986).
[148] Gen. Couns. Mem. 39703.
[149] See, *e.g.*, Priv. Ltr. Rul. 9246004.
[150] That is, an organization described in IRC. § 414(e)(3)(B)(ii.).
[151] That is, an organization described in IRC. § 414(e)(3)(A) or 414(e)(3)(B)(ii).

employees.[152] This rule is also inapplicable to income from an insurance activity conducted by a political subdivision of a government.[153]

The IRS endeavored to define the term *commercial-type insurance*, as the phrase is undefined in the statute. Following a review of tax cases defining the term *insurance*, the agency's Chief Counsel's office concluded that the definition of *commercial-type insurance* "should include some form of risk-sharing and risk-distribution."[154] The IRS's lawyers also said that, despite the statutory exception for HMO insurance, "it is our opinion that in certain circumstances a health maintenance organization may be found to provide" commercial-type insurance.[155]

Of course, for these rules to apply, the underlying activity must be the provision of *insurance* in the first instance. (The essence of the concept of insurance is that the risk of liability is shifted to at least one third party [the insurer], and that the risk is shared and distributed across a group of persons.[156]) For these purposes, the issuance of annuity contracts is considered the provision of insurance.[157] These rules do not, however, apply to a *charitable gift annuity*, which is defined for this purpose as an annuity under which a portion of the amount paid in connection with the issuance of the annuity is allowable as a charitable deduction for federal income or estate tax purposes, when the annuity is described in the special rule for annuities in the unrelated debt-financed income provisions[158] (determined as if any amount paid in cash in connection with the issuance were property).[159]

A court ruled as to a nonprofit organization established to create and administer a group self-insurance pool for the benefit of tax-exempt social service paratransit providers and to provide the necessary financing for comprehensive automobile liability, risk management, and related services for pool members. The court held that this organization did not qualify for exemption as a charitable organization because it provided commercial-type insurance.[160] The court observed that the purpose of the insurance pool was to "shift the risk of potential tort liability from each of the individual insured paratransit organizations" to the entity, which "diversifies the risk of liability for each individual member."[161] It

---

[152] IRC. § 501(m)(3). The IRS ruled that the management of regulated investment companies by supporting organizations (*see* Tax-Exempt Organizations, § 11.3(c)) for a church, to provide benefits for church employees, would not cause loss of the organizations' tax-exempt status by reason of IRC. § 501(m). Priv. Ltr. Rul. 9645007.

[153] Priv. Ltr. Rul. 8836038.

[154] Gen. Couns. Mem. 39828.

[155] The IRS held that a supporting organization's global capitation agreements with unrelated insurance companies and individuals did not entail the provision of commercial-type insurance (and thus did not generate unrelated business income). Priv. Ltr. Rul. 200044039.

[156] *E.g.*, Sears, Roebuck & Co. v. Comm'r, 96 T.C. 61 (1991); Harper Group v. Comm'r, 96 T.C. 45 (1991); Americo & Subsidiaries v. Comm'r, 96 T.C. 18 (1991); Humana, Inc. v. Comm'r, 88 T.C. 197 (1987), *aff'd in part, rev'd in part*, 881 F.2d 276 (7th Cir. 1989); Beech Aircraft Corp. v. United States, 797 F.2d 920 (10th Cir. 1986); Clougherty Packing Co. v. Comm'r, 84 T.C. 948 (1985), *aff'd*, 811 F.2d 1297 (9th Cir. 1987); Stearns-Roger Corp. v. United States, 774 F.2d 414 (10th Cir. 1985); Carnation Co. v. Comm'r, 71 T.C. 400 (1978), *aff'd*, 640 F.2d 1010 (9th Cir.), *cert. denied*, 454 U.S. 965 (1981); Helvering v. LeGierse, 312 U.S. 531 (1941).

[157] IRC. § 501(m)(4).

[158] IRC. § 514(c)(5); see § 5.3.

[159] IRC. §§ 501(m)(3), (5). *See* Hopkins, *The Tax Law of Charitable Giving, Third Edition*, ch. 14 (John Wiley & Sons, 2005)

[160] Paratransit Ins. Corp. v. Comm'r, 102 T.C. 745 (1994).

[161] *Id.* at 754.

added that the type of insurance offered was "basic automobile liability insurance, a type of insurance provided by a number of commercial insurance carriers."[162] The court, writing that the phrase *commercial-type insurance* encompasses "every type of insurance that can be purchased in the commercial market," rejected the contention that the rules as to commercial-type insurance apply only when the insurance is offered to the general public. As to substantiality, the court, having found claims expenses to be as high as 75 percent, held that these insurance activities of the organization were "unquestionably a substantial part of its operations."[163]

This court subsequently held that three types of hospital membership funds could not qualify as tax-exempt because they provided forms of commercial-type insurance. One fund enabled hospitals to self-insure on a group basis against hospital professional liability; this fund and another provided centralized cooperative insurance services to its member hospitals through the employment of actuaries, risk managers, underwriters, accountants, and other insurance consultants. The third fund was created as a vehicle for member hospital employers to self-insure on a group basis against workers' compensation claims. Finding the commercial-type insurance rules applicable, the court observed that the funds "provide actuarial, accounting, underwriting, claims payment, and similar services . . . "essential to the administration of the insurance programs."[164] The court said that there was "no dispute that hospital professional liability and workers' compensation insurance are normally offered by commercial insurers."[165]

Another case concerned an organization that administered a group self-insurance risk pool for a membership of nearly 500 charitable organizations that operated to fund or provide health or human services. The risk pool was formed to provide its membership, which had endured periods of large premium increases, coverage reductions, and cancellations, with affordable insurance. The organization also developed educational materials and made educational presentations, provided loss control and risk management services without charge, and served as a resource for insurance-related questions. As to the insurance coverage, the organization provided commercial general liability, automobile liability, employer's nonowned and hired automobile liability, and miscellaneous professional liability. Observing that the organization "exists solely for the purpose of selling insurance to nonprofit exempt organizations at the lowest possible cost on a continued, stable basis," the court wrote that "[s]elling insurance undeniably is an inherently commercial activity ordinarily carried on by commercial for-profit compan[ies]."[166] Despite the facts that the insurance was provided on a low-cost basis, and that loss control and risk management services were provided without charge, the court said that the "nature and operation" of the organization were commercial in nature.[167] It noted that the organization engaged in the actual underwriting of insurance policies, contracted with other firms to secure reinsurance for

---

[162] *Id.*

[163] *Id.*

[164] Fla. Hosp. Trust Fund v. Comm'r, 103 T.C. 140 (1994).

[165] *Id.* at 158. This opinion was affirmed at 71 F.3d 808 (11th Cir. 1996).

[166] Nonprofits' Ins. Alliance of Cal. v. United States, 94-2 U.S.T.C. ¶ 50,593 (Fed. Cl. 1994).

[167] *Id.*

high claims, and ceased membership benefits when a member failed to timely pay the required premium payments.

The foregoing body of case law has,[168] however, been somewhat supplanted by statutory law providing tax-exempt status for charitable risk pools.[169]

As noted,[170] these rules do not apply to the provision of insurance by a non-profit organization at substantially below cost to a class of charitable recipients.[171] The courts are placing great emphasis on a ruling by the IRS, issued in a different context, that the phrase *substantially below cost* denotes a subsidy of at least 85 percent.[172] Thus, in one case, although the court declined to "draw a bright line" defining that phrase, it rejected the proposition that a subsidy of about 35 percent qualified.[173] In another instance, this exception was ruled not applicable when member contributions for one year were in excess of 80 percent.[174]

§ 7.4 CREDIT COUNSELING ORGANIZATIONS

The IRS has always resisted the notion that nonprofit consumer credit counseling agencies are, in general, eligible for tax-exempt status as charitable and/or educational organizations. The most the agency was willing to concede was that these entities are so exempt when they confine provision of their services to financially troubled low-income individuals (who are members of a charitable class[175]), provide debt counseling without charge,[176] and provide the public with information on budgeting, buying practices, and the sound use of consumer credit.[177] Otherwise, the IRS was of the view that these agencies, if they are to be exempt at all, are properly classified as social welfare organizations, in that their activities contribute to the betterment of the community as a whole.[178]

The IRS experienced a setback in this regard in 1978, when a court ruled that the agency could not condition a consumer credit counseling organization's tax status solely on the extent to which it provided assistance to the indigent.[179] This court held that the classification of these organizations as exempt charitable entities cannot be made dependent on whether they confine their assistance to low-income individuals or provide their services without charge. Consumer credit counseling organizations were found to be entitled to recognition as charitable and educational organizations as long as they can demonstrate that they satisfy at least

---

[168] See text accompanied by *supra* notes 143–155.
[169] See *Tax-Exempt Organizations*, § 10.6.
[170] See *supra* note 152.
[171] IRC. § 501(m)(3)(A).
[172] Rev. Rul. 71-529, 1971-2 C.B. 234.
[173] Nonprofits' Ins. Alliance of Cal. v. United States, 94-2 U.S.T.C. ¶ 50,593 (Fed. Cl. 1994).
[174] Paratransit Ins. Corp. v. Comm'r, 102 T.C. 745 (1994). In general, Shill, *Revocation of Blue Cross & Blue Shield's Tax-Exempt Status an Unhealthy Change? An Analysis of the Effect of the Tax Reform Act of 1986 on the Taxation of Blue Cross & Blue Shield and Health Insurance Activities*, 6 B.U. J. Tax L. 147 (1988); McGovern, *Federal Tax Exemption of Prepaid Health Care Plans*, 7 Tax Adviser 76 (Feb. 1976).
[175] *Tax-Exempt Organizations*, § 5.5(a).
[176] *Id.* §§ 6.1, 6.2.
[177] *Id.* §§ 7.4, 7.5; Rev. Rul. 69-441, 1969-2 C.B. 115.
[178] Rev. Rul. 65-299, 1965-2 C.B. 165. These organizations are the subject of *Tax-Exempt Organizations*, ch. 12.
[179] Consumer Credit Counseling Serv. of Ala., Inc. v. United States, 78-2 U.S.T.C. ¶ 9660 (D.D.C. 1978).

one of the definitions of the term *charitable*[180] *or qualify as educational organizations.*[181] *The IRS decided not to pursue this matter in the courts, being of the view that "further litigation of this issue would be futile."*[182]

Twenty-five years later, however, the IRS revisited the matter of tax exemption for consumer credit counseling organizations, on the theory that these entities in their contemporary iteration are substantially different from their predecessors. The agency portrayed these organizations as a "new breed," focused on marketing debt management plans, and charging high fees, rather than providing charitable or educational services. The IRS went so far as to cast some of these organizations as fronts for for-profit businesses, because of outsourcing of functions and use of for-profit management companies. The IRS began working with state attorneys general and the Federal Trade Commission to alert consumers about the pernicious activities of these new types of credit counseling entities.[183]

The lawyers advising the IRS exempt organizations policymakers concluded that many of the new types of credit counseling agencies arguably fail the requirements for tax exemption as charitable and educational organizations.[184] These contentions included the charges that such counseling organizations are being operated for substantial nonexempt purposes, and that they are violating the doctrines of private inurement and private benefit.[185] The essence of this advocacy conclusion, however, was that these credit counseling agencies are commercial-type organizations, with debt management plans cast as a commercial service, and with the agencies receiving excessive fees from consumers and nothing in the form of contributions and grants.

On this occasion, the IRS's lawyers wrote that "we will want to argue that today's credit-counseling organizations have departed so far from the facts in the cases and rulings that they no longer serve an exempt purpose." Credit counseling was said not to be "inherently charitable"; the purpose of these organizations was seen as generating fees for for-profit entities, which was a basis for concluding that the organizations are being operated in a commercial manner. One of the elements reviewed was whether the counseling organization competes with commercial businesses "using similar advertising, pricing, and business methods." A credit counseling organization that "budgets no money for public educational activities, apart from advertising," was said to be "signaling a possible nonexempt purpose." Further investigation was urged, to ferret out evidence that these agencies are "primarily commercial profit centers."[186]

---

[180] For example, a consumer credit counseling organization may be exempt as a charitable entity because it advances education or promotes social welfare. See *Tax-Exempt Organizations*, §§ 6.6, 6.7.

[181] Also Credit Counseling Ctrs. of Okla., Inc. v. United States, 79-2 U.S.T.C. ¶ 9468 (D.D.C. 1979).

[182] Gen. Couns. Mem. 38881.

[183] *E.g.*, IR-2004-81, consisting of the prepared statement of the Internal Revenue commissioner's testimony before a hearing conducted by the Senate Finance Committee on June 22, 2004, concerning charitable giving problems and charities' best practices. Also IR-2003-120 (Oct. 14, 2003), which is a "consumer alert" for those seeking assistance from tax-exempt consumer credit counseling organizations.

[184] Chief Counsel Adv. Mem. 200431023.

[185] See *Tax-Exempt Organizations*, ch. 19; § 1.9.

[186] Indeed, the IRS essentially reverted to its original stance on this matter, with its lawyers writing that the factors to be looked at include whether the organization serves an exclusively charitable class and offers some of its services free or below cost. Another factor was whether the organization is "making a lot of money."

The IRS's lawyers observed that the "marketing" of debt management plans "is by far the most successful activity" of these "new breed" consumer credit counseling organizations, and this forms the basis for revocation of tax exemption. The lawyers noted, however, that when the selling of these plans is not a substantial activity, "it is likely that we would want to assert" that the resulting income is unrelated business income.

Shortly after the IRS's lawyers rendered this advice, private determinations from the agency denying or revoking tax-exempt status for nonprofit consumer credit counseling entities began to appear. In what apparently was the first of the rulings denying tax-exempt status to a credit counseling organization, the IRS held that the entity:

1. Was operated for the private benefit of the company that processed its debt management plans

2. Substantially benefited the credit card companies to which its clients owed money, because it functioned as a "collection agent"

3. Did not restrict its activities for the benefit of the poor

4. Failed to engage in public education

5. Charged "significant" fees

6. Accumulated revenue

7. Functioned by means of a paid staff

8. In recruiting clients, operated in a manner "indistinguishable from a commercial phone solicitor"[187]

Indeed, this entity was said to conduct its activities akin to a "common for-profit business enterprise." Another credit counseling organization was denied exemption in part because its "revenue is derived entirely from fees received in return for services, an important characteristic of a commercial enterprise."[188] Evidence of commerciality was found in the fact that another organization will "place advertisements in the telephone yellow pages and other local media" and will "develop its own website"; these undertakings were cast as ways of promoting the sale of the organization's services "in ways that are typical for any for-profit business"[189]

§ 7.5 SOCIAL ENTERPRISE MOVEMENT

One of the principal contemporary forces with the potential for meaningfully shaping the law of tax-exempt organizations is what is known as *entrepreneurialism*: the open and accepted conduct of businesses by exempt organizations, on a for-profit basis, to the end of supplementing or even supplanting charitable contributions and grants. The unabashed aim of organizations undertaking entrepreneurial activities

---

[187] Ex. Den. & Revoc. Ltr. 20044044E.
[188] Priv. Ltr. Rul. 200450037.
[189] Ex. Den. & Revoc. Ltr. 20044045E. In general, Tenenbaum, Constantine, & Epperly, *Characteristics of a Tax-Exempt Credit Counseling Agency*, 47 *Exempt Orgs. Tax Rev.* 161 (no. 2, Feb. 2005).

is to make money for the mission, upgrade the quality of staff and other resources, and become self-sufficient (that is, not dependent on external funders).

The nomenclature surrounding this phenomenon is illuminating: *social enterprises, business ventures, corporate partnerships, strategic partnerships,* and *cause-related marketing.* This parlance is decorated with verbs such as *leverage, develop* (the mission), *license, capitalize,* and *invest.*

Community Wealth Ventures, Inc., in Washington, D.C., has published a fascinating study on entrepreneurialism by public charities (available at www.communitywealth.com), replete with essays on nonprofit ventures and case studies. The analysis also includes the results of a 2002 survey of 72 tax-exempt organizations conducting 105 social enterprises. Some of the findings are as follows:

- Tax-exempt organizations that engage in business ventures tend to offer some type of social service (such as employment training programs) to at-risk populations in their communities, as contrasted with educational, arts, and religious organizations.

- Eighty percent of the organizations had been in existence at least nine years, suggesting that business ventures are not normally part of organizations' initial plans.

- Business ventures are not confined to large exempt organizations. One-third of the organizations surveyed had annual operating budgets of less than $1 million and another third had budgets of $1 million to $5 million.

- Nearly one-half (46 percent) of these organizations are community-based, 38 percent operate on a regional basis, and 14 percent have on a national basis.

- Nearly one-half (46 percent) of these organizations operate multiple ventures; 25 percent of them manage at least 3 ventures.

- Eighty-nine percent of these organizations indicated that their ventures were related (or nearly so) to their exempt purpose.

- Most of these business ventures generate modest revenue. About one-third of these organizations generate annual gross revenue in the range of $100,000 to $500,000.

- Sixty-nine percent of these organizations reported that their ventures had either made a profit or broken even. Of the 42 percent that were profitable, 16 percent netted less than $25,000 and 13 percent generated more than $50,000.

- It took organizations with profitable ventures an average of 2.5 years to break even.

- Initial capitalization for these ventures averaged $200,000 (with a mean of $90,000).

- Eighty-nine percent of these exempt organizations operated their ventures as a department or division of the entity. Only 10 percent established the venture using a for-profit corporation, partnership, limited liability company, other joint venture, or other structure.

- Tax-exempt organizations that are interested in social enterprise tend to believe that planning and research are important.

- The greatest impact of operating a social enterprise was the creation of a "more entrepreneurial culture," although many organizations were of the view that it helped to attract and retain staff and contributors, and enabled the organization to achieve greater self-sufficiency.

The thinking and actions of today's entrepreneurialism clash dramatically with the commerciality doctrine. That body of law holds that a charitable organization's tax-exempt status is endangered when the entity takes elements such as focus on the wants and needs of the general public, profits, and marketing into account—not to mention the use of trained employees and decreased reliance on gifts and grants.

Social entrepreneurialism tends, as the survey indicates, to eschew the use of for-profit subsidiaries and formal joint venture vehicles such as limited liability companies. Rather, the attraction is to partnerships—not in the sense of discrete legal entities, but rather direct interrelationships with for-profit businesses, where the entities function in-tandem ("partner" or form a "strategic alliance") to advance charitable causes ("missions"), rely on in-kind gifts, engage in unique fundraising promotions, utilize technical assistance, and operate using other forms of "mission alignment."

Proponents of this form of social enterprise disregard concern about traditional federal tax law constraints. Rarely in the literature of entrepreneurialism does one see much about the effect of these business ventures on organizations' tax-exempt status or susceptibility to unrelated business income taxation. Indeed, in this study, the "reluctance to engage in commerce" by public charities was said to range from "lack of interest to suspicion and downright disdain."

§ 7.6 COMMERCIALITY AND UNRELATED BUSINESS RULES

Traditionally, the unrelated business rules and the commerciality doctrine have developed along parallel, rather than intersecting, lines. More recently, however, the IRS has begun integrating the law of the commerciality doctrine into its analyses as to whether an activity is a related or unrelated business.

A striking example of this approach was provided the case of an organization that functioned to "establish and maintain . . . a place for the reception, exhibition and sale of articles, [which are] the product and manufacture of industrious and meritorious women." Another of its purposes was to "assist needy and deserving women in their efforts to earn an honest livelihood by their own industry."[190] This organization had three activities, each approximately the same size. One was a consignment shop, operated by volunteers and employees, where goods made by needy women were displayed and sold. Another was a gift shop, operated by volunteers and employees; the organization purchased decorative items at wholesale

---

[190] Tech. Adv. Mem. 200021056.

from for-profit vendors for sale to the public. The third function was a tearoom, operated by volunteers and employees, which was a luncheon facility (dining area and kitchen) serving to the general public.

The consignment shop was held by the IRS to be a related business, in that it provided necessary services to members of a charitable class.[191] The gift shop was found to be a regularly carried on business that did not have a substantial causal relationship to the advancement of the organization's exempt purposes.

The organization contended that the tearoom was a related business because it served to attract to the organization's facilities the type of individuals who would be willing to purchase items from the consignment shop and the gift shop. There was considerable merit to this argument; entities such as museums have relied on it for years.[192] For example, the operation of an eating facility that helped to attract visitors to a museum, and enhanced the efficient operation of the museum by enabling its staff to remain on the premises throughout the work-day, was held by the IRS to contribute importantly to the accomplishment of the museum's exempt purposes and thus to constitute a related business.[193] In the instance of the tearoom, however, the IRS relied on the principal case articulating the commerciality doctrine,[194] concluding that "where the operation of an eating facility is presumptively commercial, competes directly with other restaurants, uses profit-making pricing formulas, engages in advertising, has hours of operation competitive with commercial enterprises, and the underlying organization does not have plans to solicit donations," the facility is a nonexempt function.

---

[191] Rev. Rul. 68-167, 1968-1 C.B. 255.
[192] See § 9.3.
[193] Rev. Rul. 74-399, 1974-2 C.B. 172.
[194] Living Faith, Inc. v. Comm'r, 950 F.2d 365 (7th Cir. 1991).

CHAPTER EIGHT

Use of Separate Entities

The unrelated business rules include considerable law on the subject of the tax treatment of income flows to tax-exempt organizations from separate (including controlled) entities. These other entities are likely to be for-profit subsidiaries, partnerships, and other joint ventures.

§ 8.1 NECESSITY OF SEPARATE ENTITY

There is little law concerning the amount of unrelated business income a tax-exempt organization may receive, and/or the amount of unrelated business activity in which an exempt organization may engage, without jeopardizing its exempt status. The general principle is that unrelated business activities must be confined to something less than a substantial portion of an exempt organization's overall activities.[1]

Measuring allowable unrelated business essentially is done on the basis of application of an often elusive facts-and-circumstances test. Practitioners use various percentages as guides in this regard, dependent in part on personality (aggressive or not) and mood of the day; some prefer a 15-percent maximum, others can tolerate up to one-third, and still others push the limit to just less than 50 percent.[2]

Whatever the limit selected, at some point a tax-exempt organization may find that its exempt status is about to be, or is being, jeopardized because of too much unrelated business. It is at that stage of an exempt organization's development that it is well advised to spin off some or all of its unrelated activity into a separate organization. There may be other reasons why a separate entity—perhaps another exempt organization—is needed. Overall, a tax-exempt organization may be affiliated with other entities, both tax-exempt and taxable. Thus, an exempt organization may be a parent of one or more organizations, a subsidiary of another organization, or an organization that is under the common control of another organization. In general, an exempt organization is treated as separate from its related entities as long as the purposes for which the related entity was formed are carried out by means of its activities and certain formalities as to the relationship are adhered to.[3]

Related organization structures involving tax-exempt organizations are often used by these organizations to:

- Isolate potential state law liability (*e.g.*, tort or contract) in a separate entity
- Isolate actual or potential income tax attributes (such as unrelated business income) in a separate entity
- Conduct for-profit or dissimilar nonprofit activities in a separate entity for management, administrative, reporting, or other reasons
- Participate in an investment
- Satisfy a requirement (or an encouragement) of state or federal law, or of another party (such as a lender), for use of a separate entity for the particular type of arrangement.[4]

§ 8.2 CHOICE OF FORM

The nature of the taxation of unrelated business income, if any, may depend on the form of the entity generating the income for the tax-exempt organization. Thus, from a planning perspective, an exempt organization contemplating

---

[1] See § 1.10.

[2] *E.g.*, Hopkins, *650 Essential Nonprofit Law Questions Answered*, 261 (John Wiley & Sons, 2005).

[3] *E.g.*, Hopkins, *The Law of Tax-Exempt Organizations, Eighth Edition* (John Wiley & Sons, 2003) [hereinafter *Tax-Exempt Organizations*], §§ 30.1, 31.1.

[4] *Historical Development and Present Law of the Federal Tax Exemption for Charities and Other Tax-Exempt Organizations* (JCX-29-05) (Apr. 19, 2005); see § 1.9, n.156.

establishment of a separate entity to house one or more unrelated businesses should take this element of entity form into consideration.

Usually, the entity chosen to conduct unrelated business is a standard for-profit corporation—the *C corporation*. These corporations are taxable entities that, are treated as entities separate from the exempt organization involved, as long as the corporate form is respected for federal tax law purposes. From the perspective of tax-exempt organizations, this form of corporation preserves their exempt status and permits them to control the amount (and in some instances the nature[5]) of income flowing from the for-profit entity. This feature of separateness is often what for-profit organizations seek to avoid when establishing a subsidiary, because of the prospect of double taxation. In situations in which a corporation is owned in part by an exempt organization and in part by one or more for-profit entities, interests can clash on this point.

Consideration may be given to creation of the separate entity as a partnership, limited liability company, or other form of joint venture. This often is inadvisable from the standpoint of exempt organizations, inasmuch as these other entities are *flow-through entities;* that is, these organizations are not taxable and net unrelated business income is automatically attributed to the exempt organization involved.[6] Thus, with this approach, there is no opportunity to modulate the flow of unrelated business income to the exempt organization, as can be done with a C corporation. Again, when a for-profit owner is involved, a flow-through entity may be preferable so as to avoid double taxation.

An unlikely candidate for the separate organization housing unrelated business is the type of small business corporation that is classified for federal tax purposes as an *S corporation*. Tax-exempt charitable organizations are allowed to be shareholders in these corporations, which are forms of flow-through entities and generally are treated for tax purposes the same as partnerships. From the viewpoint of exempt charitable organizations, however, these entities are unattractive because distributions from them to the exempt organizations are treated as unrelated business income, irrespective of the source or nature of the income.[7]

The one type of entity that is unusable in this regard is the single-member limited liability company. These entities are generally disregarded for federal tax purposes, so all of their economic activity is regarded as conducted by the member. When the member is a tax-exempt organization, unrelated business in this form of limited liability company would be treated (and taxed) as if it had been undertaken directly by the exempt organization member.[8]

On rare occasions, the separate entity can be a nonprofit, albeit taxable, organization, usually a corporation. Even more rare is the situation in which the other entity is a tax-exempt organization, because the problem of excessive unrelated business is likely to be merely transferred to the other entity.

---

[5] That is, this type of income is likely to be dividends, interest, rent, or royalties.
[6] See § 8.10.
[7] See § 6.4.
[8] See § 8.12(b).

§ 8.3 ELEMENT OF CONTROL

Presumably, when it forms a taxable subsidiary, a tax-exempt organization intends to maintain control over the subsidiary. Certainly, after capitalizing the enterprise,[9] nurturing its growth and success, and desiring to enjoy profits from the business, the prudent exempt organization parent usually would not want to place the activity in a vehicle over which it cannot exercise ongoing control.

When the taxable subsidiary is structured as a business corporation, the tax-exempt organization parent can own the entity and ultimately control it simply by owning the stock received in exchange for the capital contributed. Thereafter, the exempt organization parent, as the stockholder, can select the board of directors of the corporation and, if desired, its officers.

If the taxable subsidiary is structured as a nonprofit corporation, three choices are available. The tax-exempt organization parent can control the subsidiary by means of interlocking directorates. Alternatively, the subsidiary can be a membership corporation, with the parent entity the sole member. In the third— and least utilized—approach, the entity can be structured as a nonprofit organization that can issue stock, in which case the exempt organization parent would control the subsidiary by holding its stock. If the latter course is chosen, and if the nonprofit subsidiary is to be headquartered in a (foreign) state in which stock-based nonprofit organizations are not authorized, the subsidiary can be incorporated in a state that allows nonprofit organizations to issue stock and thereafter be qualified to do business in the home (domestic) state.

§ 8.4 ATTRIBUTION CONSIDERATIONS

For federal income tax purposes, a parent corporation and its subsidiary are respected as separate entities as long as the purposes for which the subsidiary was formed are reflected in authentic business activities.[10] In other words, when an organization is established with the bona fide intention that it will have some real and substantial business function, its existence will generally not be disregarded for tax purposes.[11]

Nonetheless, if the parent organization so controls the affairs of the subsidiary that it is merely an extension of the parent, the subsidiary may not be regarded as a separate entity.[12] In an extreme situation (such as when the parent is directly involved in day-to-day management of the subsidiary), the establishment and operation of an ostensibly separate subsidiary may be regarded as a sham

---

[9] See § 8.5.

[10] *E.g.*, Comm'r v. Bollinger, 485 U.S. 340 (1988); Moline Props., Inc. v. Comm'r, 319 U.S. 436 (1943); Nat'l Carbide Corp. v. Comm'r, 336 U.S. 422 (1949); Britt v. United States, 431 F.2d 227 (5th Cir. 1970). Also Sly v. Comm'r, 56 T.C.M. 209 (1988), Universal Church of Jesus Christ, Inc. v. Comm'r, 55 T.C.M. 143, 153 (1988) (debt collection business was said to be "operating under the thinnest of veils in an attempt to give itself the appearance of a religious enterprise").

[11] Britt v. United States, 431 F.2d 227 (5th Cir. 1970).

[12] *E.g.*, Krivo Indus. Supply Co. v. Nat'l Distillers & Chem. Corp., 483 F.2d 1098 (5th Cir. 1973); Orange County Agric. Soc'y, Inc. v. Comm'r, 55 T.C.M. 1602 (1988), *aff'd*, 893 F.2d 647 (2d Cir. 1990).

perpetrated by the parent and thus ignored for tax purposes (*collapsed*); with this outcome, the tax consequences are the same as if the two "entities" were one.[13]

The IRS's position on this subject can be traced through three pronouncements from its Office of Chief Counsel. In 1968, the IRS was advised by its lawyers that an attempt to attribute the activities of a subsidiary to its parent "should be made only where the evidence clearly shows that the subsidiary is merely a guise enabling the parent to carry out its . . . [disqualifying] activity or where it can be proven that the subsidiary is an arm, agent, or integral part of the parent."[14] In 1974, the IRS Chief Counsel advised that to "disregard the corporate entity requires a finding that the corporation or transaction involved was a sham or fraud without any valid business purpose, or the finding of a true agency or trust relationship between the entities."[15] In 1984, the IRS's lawyers reviewed a situation in which a separate for-profit corporation provided management and operations services to several tax-exempt hospitals. Although the IRS rulings division was inclined otherwise, the agency's lawyers advised that the activities of a subsidiary cannot be attributed to the parent, for purposes of determining the parent's exempt status, when the subsidiary is organized for a bona fide business purposes and the exempt parent is not involved in the day-to-day management of the subsidiary.[16] In the third instance, this was the outcome irrespective of the fact that the parent exempt organization owned all of the stock of the subsidiary corporation.

Thus, the IRS's current posture in this regard can be distilled to two tests. First, for the legitimacy of a for-profit subsidiary to be respected, the subsidiary must engage in an independent, bona fide function and not be a mere instrumentality of the tax-exempt parent. As to this requirement, the IRS's lawyers wrote that

> The first aspect [in determining the authenticity of a for-profit subsidiary] is the requirement that the subsidiary be organized for some bona fide purpose of its own and not be a mere sham or instrumentality of th0e [exempt] parent. We do not believe that this requirement that the subsidiary have a bona fide business purpose should be considered to require that the subsidiary have an inherently commercial or for-profit activity. The term "business" . . . is not synonymous with "trade or business" in the sense of requiring a profit motive.[17]

As to the second requirement, the IRS's lawyers observed that

> The second aspect of the test is the requirement that the parent not be so involved in, or in control of, the day-to-day operations of the subsidiary that the relationship between parent and subsidiary assumes the characteristics of the relationship of principal and agent, i.e., that the parent not be so in control of the affairs of the subsidiary that it is merely an instrumentality of the parent.[18]

---

[13] Gen. Couns. Mem. 39598. In a similar set of circumstances, courts are finding nonprofit organizations to be the alter ego of the debtor, with the result that the assets of the organization are made available to IRS levies. See the cases collected in *Tax-Exempt Organizations*, § 4.1, n. 22.

In the reverse situation, when a for-profit entity controls a tax-exempt organization (such as by day-to-day management of it), the exemption of the controlled entity may be jeopardized. *E.g.*, United Cancer Council, Inc. v. Comm'r, 109 T.C. 326 (1997), *rev'd & remanded*, 165 F.3d 1173 (7th Cir. 1999). Nonetheless, management of an exempt organization by a for-profit company generally does not raise these concerns. *E.g.*, Priv. Ltr. Rul. 9715031.

[14] Gen. Couns. Mem. 33912.

[15] Gen. Couns. Mem. 35719.

[16] Gen. Couns. Mem. 39326.

[17] Gen. Couns. Mem. 39598.

[18] *Id.*

At one point, the IRS demonstrated some proclivity to treat two organizations in this context as one when the entities' directors and officers are the same. For example, the IRS ruled that the activities of a for-profit subsidiary are to be attributed to its exempt parent for purposes of determining the parent's ongoing tax exemption, when the officers and directors of the two organizations are identical.[19]

The rationale underlying this ruling rests on the premise that, when the tax-exempt parent is involved in the day-to-day management of the subsidiary, the activities of the subsidiary are imputed to the parent. In this ruling, the IRS stated that an exempt parent is "necessarily" involved in the day-to-day management of the subsidiary simply because the officers and directors of the parent serve as the officers and directors of the subsidiary. Thus, because of this structural overlap, the IRS attributed the activities of the subsidiary to the parent. Once this attribution occurs, the impact of the attribution must be ascertained to determine whether the parent will remain exempt.

In the subject case, the attribution to the tax-exempt parent of the activities of the for-profit subsidiary was not fatal to the parent's tax exemption, because the parent's involvement was deemed insubstantial. (The exempt parent was a scientific research organization; the subsidiary developed and manufactured products that were derived from patentable technology generated by the parent's research activities. The parent's average annual income was $50 million; the subsidiary's was $10,000 to $70,000.) The for-profit subsidiary was capitalized by the parent (for between $10,000 to $100,000). The parent maintained a controlling interest in the subsidiary, and the two shared facilities and equipment. These relationships were evidenced by employment contracts and lease agreements. Separate books and records of the two entities were maintained.

The principles of law do not, however, support the IRS's conclusion in this ruling, which was that an overlap of directors and officers of two organizations automatically results in an attribution of the subsidiary's activities to the parent. The case law is instructive, in that this can be the consequence when the facts show that the arrangement is a sham; still, this cannot be a mechanical and inexorable outcome. Indeed, in subsequent rulings, the IRS's rulings division has been guided by this advice from its lawyers:

> Control through ownership of stock, or power to appoint the board of directors, of the subsidiary will not cause the attribution of the subsidiary's activities to the parent. We do not believe that [a prior general counsel memorandum] should be read to suggest, by negative inference, that when the board of directors of a wholly owned subsidiary is made up entirely of board members, officers, or employees of the parent there must be attribution of the activities of the subsidiary to the parent.[20]

Contemporary rulings from the IRS evidence an abandonment of this earlier approach.[21] Indeed, the IRS subsequently summarized the law on the point as follows: "The activities of a separately incorporated subsidiary cannot ordinarily be attributed to its parent organization unless the facts provide clear and

---

[19] Priv. Ltr. Rul. 8606056.
[20] Gen. Couns. Mem. 39598.
[21] *E.g.*, Priv. Ltr. Rul. 9245031 (the "activities of [the] subsidiary cannot be attributed to [the] [p]arent").

convincing evidence that the subsidiary is in reality an arm, agent or integral part of the parent."[22] In that instance, the agency offered a most munificent application of this aspect of the law, concluding that the activities of a for-profit subsidiary were not to be attributed to the tax-exempt organization that was its parent, notwithstanding extensive and ongoing in-tandem administrative and programmatic functions. That is, the IRS observed that the two entities will "maintain a close working relationship," they will be "sharing investment leads," they will co-invest in companies, the subsidiary will rent office space from the exempt parent, the subsidiary will purchase administrative and professional services from the parent, and the subsidiary will reimburse its parent for the services of some of the parent's employees.

There was somewhat of an aberration in these areas, in a situation involving a legal issue concerning tax-exempt cooperatives. To be exempt, these entities must receive at least 85 percent of their income from amounts collected from members for the sole purpose of meeting losses and expenses.[23] The IRS initially ruled that the gross receipts of a wholly owned subsidiary of such a cooperative must be aggregated with the receipts of the parent for purposes of calculating the 85-percent-member-income test.[24] The rationale for this approach was based on cooperative principles, according to which a subsidiary must be created to perform a function that the parent cooperative might engage in as an integral part of its operations without adversely affecting its exempt status.[25] This ruling was met with intense opposition from the industry and members of Congress; the IRS subsequently ruled, using conventional analysis, that the income of a subsidiary is not included for purposes of determining whether the parent cooperative satisfied the member-income test.[26] In this latter ruling, the IRS reiterated the point that a corporation is a separate taxable entity for federal income tax purposes if the corporation is formed for valid business purposes, and is not a sham, agency, or instrumentality.[27]

Thus, the IRS is highly unlikely to attribute the activities of a for-profit subsidiary of a tax-exempt organization to the parent entity, by reason of the foregoing elements of law. The use of for-profit subsidiaries in the contemporary exempt organizations setting has become too customary for this form of attribution to occur, absent the most egregious of facts.[28]

§ 8.5 CAPITALIZATION

Assets of a tax-exempt organization that are currently being used in an unrelated business activity may, with little (if any) legal constraint, be spun off into an

---

[22] Priv. Ltr. Rul. 200132040.

[23] See *Tax-Exempt Organizations*, § 18.5, text accompanied by n. 109.

[24] Priv. Ltr. Rul. 9722006.

[25] *E.g.*, Rev. Rul. 69-575, 1969-2 C.B. 134.

[26] Rev. Rul. 2002-55, 2002-37 I.R.B. 529.

[27] For this proposition, the IRS cited Comm'r v. Bollinger, 485 U.S. 340 (1988); Moline Props., Inc. v. Comm'r, 319 U.S. 436 1943).

[28] This does not mean that revenue from a for-profit subsidiary to an exempt parent is not taxable; in fact, just the opposite is often the case. See § 8.8(b).

affiliated for-profit organization. The extent to which a for-profit corporation can be capitalized using exempt organization assets (particularly charitable ones), however, is a matter involving far more strict confines.

A tax-exempt organization can invest a portion of its assets and engage in a certain amount of unrelated activities. At the same time, the governing board of an exempt organization must act in conformity with basic fiduciary responsibilities, and the organization cannot (without jeopardizing its exemption) contravene the prohibitions on private inurement and private benefit.[29]

IRS private letter rulings suggest that only a small percentage of a tax-exempt organization's resources ought to be transferred to controlled for-profit subsidiaries.[30] The percentages approved by the IRS are usually low and, in any event, probably pertain only to cash. (Many of the agency's rulings in this area do not state the amount of capital involved.[31]) In some cases, though, a specific asset may—indeed, perhaps must—best be utilized in an unrelated activity, even though its value represents a meaningful portion of the organization's total resources.[32] Also, the exempt parent may want to make subsequent advances or loans to the subsidiary.

The best guiding standard in this regard is that of prudence. In capitalizing a subsidiary, a tax-exempt organization should only part with an amount of resources that is reasonable under the circumstances and that can be rationalized in relation to amounts devoted to programs and invested in other fashions. Relevant to all of this is the projected return on the investment, in terms of income and capital appreciation. If a contribution to a subsidiary's capital seems unwise, the putative parent should consider a loan (albeit one bearing a fair rate of interest and accompanied by adequate security).[33]

In all instances, it is preferable that the operation of the subsidiary further (if only by providing funds for) the tax-exempt purposes of the parent.[34] Indeed, the IRS's lawyers wrote that an exempt organization with a successful for-profit subsidiary has a "continuing obligation" to "translate this valuable asset into funds, and use these funds for the expansion" of its exempt activities.[35] Certainly, circumstances in which exempt purposes are thwarted by the operation of a for-profit subsidiary are to be avoided.

---

[29] See § 1.10.

[30] E.g., Priv. Ltr. Rul. 8505044.

[31] E.g., Priv. Ltr. Rul. 9305026.

[32] In one instance, the IRS characterized the amount of capital transferred as "substantial," although the exempt parent was not a charitable entity; it was a tax-exempt social welfare organization. Priv. Ltr. Rul. 9245031.

[33] Payments by a tax-exempt organization to its subsidiary for services provided, with the payments coming from revenues generated by the services, are likely to be considered by the IRS to be compensation for services rather than contributions to capital. Priv. Ltr. Rul. 200227007.

[34] E.g., Priv. Ltr. Rul. 8709051.

[35] Tech. Adv. Mem. 200437040. These lawyers suggested that some of the subsidiary's assets be sold or that a portion of the subsidiary's stock be sold, with the proceeds used to fund programs. They added that an exempt organization "cannot be allowed to focus its energies on expanding its subsidiary's commercial business and assets, and neglect to translate that financial success into specific, definite and flexible plans for the expansion of" its exempt activities.

§ 8.6 SHARING OF RESOURCES

Generally, as a matter of the law of tax-exempt organizations, a tax-exempt organization and its for-profit subsidiary may share resources without adverse consequences to the exempt entity. That is, the two organizations may share office facilities, equipment, supplies, and the like. Particularly where the exempt entity is a charitable one, however, all relevant costs should be allocated on the basis of actual use, and each organization should pay fair market value for the resources used.[36]

It is generally preferable for the tax-exempt organization to reimburse the for-profit entity for the exempt organization's use of resources, to avoid the perception that the funds of an exempt organization are being used to subsidize a for-profit organization. Nonetheless, this approach often is impractical when the exempt organization is the parent company.

§ 8.7 LIQUIDATIONS

The federal tax law causes recognition of gain or loss by a for-profit corporation in an instance of a liquidating distribution of its assets (as if the corporation had sold the assets to the distributee at fair market value) and in the event of liquidating sales. There is an exception for liquidating transfers within an affiliated group (which is regarded as a single economic unit), so that the basis in the property is carried over from the distributor to the distributee in lieu of recognition of gain or loss.

This nonrecognition exception is modified for eligible liquidations in which an 80-percent corporate shareholder receives property with a carryover basis, to provide for nonrecognition of gain or loss with respect to any property actually distributed to that shareholder. Nonetheless, this nonrecognition rule under the exception for 80-percent corporate shareholders is generally not available when the shareholder is a tax-exempt organization. That is, any gain or loss generally must be recognized by the subsidiary on the distribution of its assets in liquidation as if the assets had been sold to the exempt parent at fair market value.[37] (Gain or loss is not recognized by the parent entity on its receipt of the subsidiary's assets pursuant to the liquidation.[38]) This nonrecognition treatment is available in the tax-exempt organizations context, however, when the property distributed is used by the exempt organization in an unrelated business immediately after the distribution. If the property subsequently ceases to be used in an unrelated business, the exempt organization will be taxed on the gain at that time.[39]

---

[36] *E.g.*, Priv. Ltr. Rul. 9308047. When the charitable organization is a private foundation, however, caution is required in this regard, in that this type of resource-sharing is likely to constitute self-dealing. See *Tax-Exempt Organizations*, § 11.4(a); Hopkins & Blazek, *Private Foundations: Tax Law and Compliance, Second Edition*, ch. 5 (John Wiley & Sons, 2003).

[37] IRC § 337(b)(2)(A).

[38] IRC § 332(a).

[39] IRC § 337(b)(2)(B)(ii). *Cf.* Centre for Int'l Understanding v. Comm'r, 62 T.C.M. 629 (1991) (applying the liquidation rules of IRC § 337(c)(2)(A)). Regulations were issued in final form, under authority of IRC § 337(d), concerning the liquidation of for-profit entities into tax-exempt organizations, when the relationship is not that of parent and subsidiary. The rules in this regard are essentially the same as those that apply to liquidations of subsidiaries, although they also apply when a for-profit corporation converts to an exempt entity. See *Tax-Exempt Organizations*, §§ 33.4(b), (c), 33.5.

In one instance, a tax-exempt home health and hospice agency formed a wholly owned, for-profit subsidiary to provide home companion services and operate an assisted living facility. Years later, the parent organization expanded its programs and facilities, and determined that the activities conducted by the subsidiary could be undertaken by the parent without adversely affecting the parent's exempt status. The parent organization proceeded to liquidate the subsidiary and transfer to itself all of the assets, which had appreciated in value, of the subsidiary. The IRS ruled that the gain attributable to the distribution of the subsidiary's assets to the parent organization, upon liquidation, would be excludable from taxation as unrelated business income by reason of the exclusion from taxation of capital gains.[40] This ruling was silent on the tax consequences of transfer of the appreciated assets by the subsidiary.[41]

In another instance, one of the functions of a charitable entity was the publication and circulation of religious materials. This organization had a for-profit subsidiary that engaged in both exempt and commercial printing activities. Once it decided to discontinue the commercial printing operations, the exempt parent proposed to liquidate the subsidiary and distribute its assets to the parent organization. The IRS ruled that any gain or loss must be recognized by the subsidiary on the distribution of its assets in liquidation (as if they had been sold to the exempt parent at fair market value), to the extent the assets were to be used in related business activities.[42]

§ 8.8 CONTROLLED ORGANIZATIONS

(a) General Rules

Though such is not always the case, most tax-exempt organizations develop an unrelated business with the idea or anticipation that it will serve as a source of revenue. Thus, the development within, or shifting of unrelated business to, a taxable subsidiary should be done in a way so as not to preclude or inhibit the flow of income from the subsidiary to the parent.

The staff and other resources of an affiliated business are usually those of the tax-exempt organization parent. Thus, the headquarters of the taxable subsidiary are likely to be the same as those of its parent. This means that the taxable subsidiary may have to reimburse the exempt organization parent for the subsidiary's occupancy costs, share of employees' time, and use of the parent's equipment and supplies. Therefore, one way for dollars to flow from the subsidiary to the parent is as this form of reimbursement, which would include an element of rent.

---

[40] Priv. Ltr. Rul. 9438029.

[41] In general, this ruling did not utilize the liquidation rules of IRC §§ 332 and 337. It is not clear from this ruling whether the assets in the subsidiary were to be used in related or unrelated activities by the exempt parent after the liquidation. If the assets were to be used in related activities, the gain should have been recognized and taxable to the subsidiary. IRC § 337(b)(2)(A).

[42] Priv. Ltr. Rul. 9645017. This ruling expressly addressed the point that, to the extent the assets were to be used by the parent in unrelated activities, any gain would not be recognized during the pendency of that type of use. IRC § 337(b)(2)(B)(ii).

Another type of relationship between a tax-exempt organization parent and a taxable subsidiary is that of lender and borrower. That is, in addition to funding its subsidiary by means of a capital contribution (resulting in a holding of equity by the parent), the parent may find it appropriate to lend money to its subsidiary. Inasmuch as a no-interest loan to a for-profit subsidiary by a tax-exempt organization parent may endanger the exempt status of the parent, and trigger problems under the below-market interest rules,[43] it would be appropriate for a loan to bear a fair market rate of interest. Therefore, another way for dollars to flow from the subsidiary to the parent is in the form of interest.

The business activity of a for-profit subsidiary may be to market and sell a product or service. When done in conformity with its tax-exempt status, the parent can license the use of its name, logo, acronym, and/or some other feature that would enhance the sale of the product or service by the subsidiary. For this license, the subsidiary would pay the parent a royalty—another way of transferring dollars from a for-profit subsidiary to a tax-exempt parent.

A conventional way of transferring money from a corporation to its stockholders is for the corporation to distribute its earnings and profits to them. These distributions are *dividends* and represent yet another way in which a taxable subsidiary can transfer dollars to its tax-exempt parent.

Certain types of income are exempted from taxation as unrelated income—principally the various forms of passive income.[44] Were it not for a special rule of federal tax law, a tax-exempt organization could have it both ways: avoid taxation of the exempt organization on unrelated income by housing the activity in a subsidiary, and thereafter receive passive, nontaxable income from the subsidiary. Congress, however, became mindful of this potential double benefit, and thus legislated a rule that is an exception to the general body of law exempting passive income from taxation: Otherwise passive nontaxable income that is derived from a controlled taxable subsidiary is generally taxed as unrelated income. Thus, when a tax-exempt organization parent receives rent, interest, or most other forms of passive income from a controlled taxable subsidiary, those revenues will generally be taxable.[45]

There is no tax deduction, however, for the payment of dividends. Consequently, when a for-profit subsidiary pays a dividend to its tax-exempt organization parent, the dividend payments are not deductible by the subsidiary. Therefore, Congress determined that it would not be appropriate to tax revenue to an exempt organization parent when that payment is not deductible by the taxable subsidiary.

(b) Tax Rules

Payments of interest, annuities, royalties, and/or rent by a controlled organization to a tax-exempt controlling organization can be taxable as unrelated business

---

[43] IRC § 7872.
[44] *E.g.*, §§ 3.1–3.3, 3.6–3.8.
[45] See § 8.8(b).

income,[46] notwithstanding the fact that these types of income are generally otherwise nontaxable as forms of passive income.[47] The purpose of this body of law is to preclude an exempt organization from housing an unrelated business in a separate but controlled organization and receiving nontaxable income by reason of the passive income rules (such as an exempt organization renting unrelated income property to a subsidiary).[48] The law in this regard was changed significantly in 1997 because its purpose had been frustrated under prior law, in that it was too narrowly written and easily circumvented.[49]

The rule for determining control in this context is a more-than-50-percent standard. Thus, in the case of a corporation, *control* means ownership by vote or value of more than 50 percent of the stock in the corporation.[50] If the entity is a partnership, control is ownership of more than 50 percent of the profits interest or capital interests in the partnership.[51] In the case of a trust, or in any other circumstance, control is measured in terms of more than 50 percent of the beneficial interests in the entity.[52]

Preexisting constructive ownership rules are engrafted onto this area of law for purposes of determining ownership of stock in a corporation.[53] For example, if 50 percent or more in value of the stock in a corporation is owned, directly or indirectly, by or for any person, that person is considered as owning any stock owned, directly or indirectly, by or for the corporation, in the proportion that the value of the stock the person so owns bears to the value of all of the stock in the corporation.[54] Likewise, if 50 percent or more in value of the stock in a corporation is owned, directly or indirectly, by or for any person, the corporation is considered the owner of the stock owned, directly or indirectly, by or for that person.[55] Similar principles apply in determining ownership of interests in any other type of entity.[56] Attribution rules apply with respect to stock owned by members of a family, partnerships, estates, and trusts.[57]

Thus, when a controlling organization receives, directly or indirectly, a specified payment from a controlled entity (whether or not tax-exempt), the controlling entity may have to treat that payment as unrelated business

---

[46] IRC § 512(b)(13).

[47] See, *e.g.*, §§ 3.1, 3.3, 3.6–3.8.

[48] S. Rep. No. 91-552, 91st Cong., 1st Sess. 73 (1969). In general, J.E. & L.E. Mabee Found., Inc. v. United States, 533 F.2d 521 (10th Cir. 1976), *aff'g* 389 F. Supp. 673 (N.D. Okla. 1975); Crosby Valve & Gauge Co. v. Comm'r, 380 F.2d 146 (1st Cir. 1967); United States v. Robert A. Welch Found., 334 F.2d 774 (5th Cir. 1964), *aff'g* 228 F. Supp. 881 (S.D. Tex. 1963); Campbell v. Carter Found. Prods. Co., 322 F.2d 827 (5th Cir. 1963), *aff'g in part* 61-2 U.S.T.C. ¶ 9630 (N.D. Tex. 1961).

[49] H.R. Rep. No. 105-148, 105th Cong., 1st Sess. 491 (1997). Under prior law, for example, control was not present when the classes of stock issued by a subsidiary were split between related tax-exempt organizations. For example, an exempt trade association with a related foundation was not considered to control a for-profit subsidiary when the association held all of the subsidiary's voting stock and the foundation held all of its nonvoting stock. Likewise, a control element was not found when a second-tier subsidiary paid income to an exempt organization.

[50] IRC § 512(b)(13)(D)(i)(I).

[51] IRC § 512(b)(13)(D)(i)(II).

[52] IRC § 512(b)(13)(D)(i)(III).

[53] IRC §§ 512(b)(13)(D)(ii), 318.

[54] IRC § 318(a)(2)(C).

[55] IRC § 318(a)(3)(C).

[56] IRC § 512(b)(13)(D)(ii).

[57] IRC § 318(a)(1), (2)(A), (2)(B), (3)(A), (3)(B).

income.[58] The term *specified payment* means interest, annuities, royalties, and/or rent.[59] A specified payment must be treated as unrelated business income of the controlling entity to the extent the payment reduced the net unrelated income of the controlled entity or increased any net unrelated loss of the controlled entity.[60] The controlling organization may deduct expenses that are directly connected with amounts treated as unrelated business income pursuant to this rule.[61]

With respect to a controlled entity that is not tax-exempt, the term *net unrelated income* means the portion of the entity's taxable income that would be unrelated business taxable income if the entity were exempt and had the same exempt purposes as the controlling organization.[62] When the controlled entity is tax-exempt, the term *net unrelated income* means the amount of the unrelated business taxable income of the controlled entity.[63] The term *net unrelated loss* means the net operating loss adjusted under rules similar to those pertaining to net unrelated income.[64]

§ 8.9 PARTNERSHIPS AND JOINT VENTURE BASICS

The use of joint venture vehicles is one of the most predominant forms of planning and operations in the law of tax-exempt organizations today. Over past years, this law has focused on the involvement of exempt organizations in partnerships.[65] More recently, however, the emphasis has shifted to use of other types of joint ventures, most notably those structured using limited liability companies. Almost all of the developments to date in this regard concern public charities. The principal issues are the ongoing exempt status of the nonprofit organization or organizations involved and the potential generation of unrelated business income. The legal doctrines underlying the exemption issue tend to cover private inurement or private benefit.[66] The intermediate sanctions rules[67] may also be implicated in this setting.

A *partnership* is a form of business entity, recognized in the law as a separate legal entity, as is a corporation or trust. It is usually evidenced by a document (*partnership agreement*). The term *joint venture* is broader than, and subsumes, the concept of a partnership. There can be a joint venture without establishment of an entity and without a document signifying it; in fact, the joint venture form can be

---

[58] IRC § 512(b)(13)(A). Examples of such indirect payments are in J.E. & L.E. Mabee Found., Inc. v. United States, 533 F.2d 521 (10th Cir. 1976), *aff'g* 389 F. Supp. 673 (N.D. Okla. 1975), and Gen. Couns. Mem. 38878.

[59] IRC § 512(b)(13)(C). This term thus does not include dividends. It also does not include capital gain, which fact enables a controlling organization to sell property that has appreciated in value to a controlled entity without generating unrelated business income. *Cf.* IRC § 4940(c).

[60] IRC § 512(b)(13)(A).

[61] *Id.*

[62] IRC § 512(b)(13)(B)(i)(I).

[63] IRC § 512(b)(13)(B)(i)(II).

[64] IRC § 512(b)(13)(B)(ii). In general, Nagel, *The Use of For-Profit Subsidiaries by Non-Profit Corporations,* 17 *Colo. Law.* 1293 (no. 7, 1998); Bird, *Exempt Organizations and Taxable Subsidiaries,* 4 *Prac. Tax Law.* 53 (no. 2, 1990); Heinlen, *Commercial Activities of Exempt Organizations—Joint Ventures and Taxable Subsidiaries,* 16 *N. Ky. L. Rev.* 285 (no. 2, 1989).

[65] See *Tax-Exempt Organizations,* ch. 32.

[66] See § 1.10.

[67] See *Tax-Exempt Organizations,* § 19.11.

imposed on parties in particular factual circumstances, even contrary to their intent and wish.[68] A joint venture can, however, be a formal legal entity other than a partnership; the best example of this is the limited liability company.

The parties to a partnership are *partners*. Parties to a joint venture arrangement, including a limited liability company, are *members*.

(a) Partnerships

Partnerships come in two basic types. This delineation turns largely on the nature of the partners, which can be *general* or *limited*. Normally, liability for the consequences of a partnership's operations rests with the general partner or partners, whereas the limited partners' exposure to liability for the functions of the partnership is confined to the amount of their contribution(s) to the partnership.

The partnership that has only general partners is a *general partnership*. In this type of partnership, the interests of the general partners may or may not be equal. These partners are usually equally liable for satisfaction of the obligations of the partnership, and can be called on to make additional capital contributions to the entity.

Capital in a partnership can come from investors, that is, limited partners. A limited partner is not in the venture to control and administer the underlying business; rather, it intends to obtain a return on the investment and perhaps to procure some tax advantages. A partnership with both general and limited partners is a *limited partnership*.[69]

(b) Joint Ventures in General

A *joint venture*, conceptually, is an association of two or more persons with intent to carry out a business enterprise for joint profit, for which purpose they combine their efforts, property, money, skill, and knowledge. Often, as noted, this arrangement is something less than a formal legal entity such as a partnership.[70] There are three types of joint ventures:

1. One or more of the venturers places itself, in its entirety, in the venture.

2. One or more of the venturers places a primary portion of its operations in the venture.

3. One or more of the venturers places a small portion of its operations in the venture.

The first type of these joint ventures is the *whole entity joint venture*, started in the health care context (and thus known in that setting as the *whole hospital joint venture*[71]). The third of these joint ventures is the *ancillary joint venture*.[72]

---

[68] See § 8.16.
[69] In general, see *Tax-Exempt Organizations*, § 32.1.
[70] *Id.* § 32.3.
[71] *Id.* § 32.4.
[72] *Id.* § 32.5.

(c) Limited Liability Companies

A *limited liability company* is a legal entity that has some of the attributes of a corporation (*e.g.*, limitations as to legal liability for persons other than the entity) and (by means of an election) some of the characteristics of a partnership (principally, taxation as a partnership). A limited liability company is evidenced by a document forming the entity.[73]

§ 8.10 FLOW-THROUGH ENTITIES

Partnerships and the other joint venture entities are, for federal tax purposes, *flow-through entities*. This means that these entities are not taxpaying organizations; rather, they are conduits of net revenue (and other items) to the partners, which bear the responsibility for the payment of tax on their net income.

For tax-exempt organizations, the receipt of income from a joint venture vehicle raises issues as to unrelated business income taxation (and, in some instances, ongoing eligibility for tax-exempt status). In resolving these issues, a *look-through rule* is used. Pursuant to that rule, if a business regularly carried on by a partnership or other joint venture, of which an exempt organization is a member, is an unrelated business with respect to the organization, the organization must include its share of the gross income of the venture when computing unrelated business income. Likewise, if the business in the venture is a related one as to the organization, the resulting income is treated as exempt function revenue. Thus, in application of the look-through rule, the business conducted by the joint venture is evaluated to determine what the outcome would be if the exempt organization directly conducted the business.[74]

§ 8.11 PARTNERSHIPS—DETAILS

The law as to the involvement by public charities as general partners in limited partnerships, once one of the most controversial aspects of the law of tax-exempt organizations, has stabilized. The IRS's concern in this regard has always been, and continues to be, that the resources of a charitable organization are being used to provide substantial benefits to for-profit participants in the partnership (usually the limited partners) when the exempt organization is a general partner in the partnership. It remains the view of the IRS that there is an inherent tension between a charitable organization's ability to function exclusively in furtherance of its exempt functions and a general partner's obligation to operate the partnership for the economic benefit of the limited partners. Indeed, the IRS's original position was that a public charity would lose its tax-exempt status if it became a general partner in a limited partnership; that stance was predicated on application of the private inurement or private benefit doctrine.[75]

The IRS's posture changed over the years as it lost all but one of the court cases on the point.[76] The prevailing models in the area of partnerships involving

---

[73] *Id.* §§ 4.1(b), 30.7, 32.4.
[74] *Id.* § 28.4.
[75] *Id.* § 32.2(a).
[76] *Id.* § 32.2(a).

tax-exempt organizations thus are partnerships with only general partners and partnerships consisting of both general and limited partners.

Today, the criteria to be applied are far more refined, and a three-step analysis is used:

1. Does the partnership further a charitable purpose?

2. If so, does the partnership agreement reflect an arrangement that permits the exempt organization to act primarily in furtherance of its exempt (charitable) purposes? That is, does the organization's role as general partner preclude or deter it from advancing its charitable ends?

3. If the primary purpose of the organization is not being thwarted, does the arrangement cause the exempt organization to provide an impermissible private benefit to the limited partners?

There should be no undue difficulty in assessing the first and third of these criteria. Indeed, as the following examples indicate, involvement in a limited partnership by a public-charity general partner is almost always undertaken in furtherance of charitable ends. The principal rationales the planner may use in applying the first criterion are: the raising of needed capital,[77] the creation of new programs, the sharing of a risk inherent in a new exempt activity, and the pooling of diverse areas of expertise.

The second criterion is more troublesome. Here, the IRS looks to means by which the organization may, under the particular facts and circumstances, be insulated from the day-to-day responsibilities of a general partner. This element of the equation is conceptually difficult: once an entity is a general partner in a partnership, it cannot escape the responsibility and potential liability of that position.

Here are the favorable factors that the IRS takes into consideration in evaluating a tax-exempt charitable organization's involvement as a general partner in a limited partnership:

- Limited contractual liability of the exempt partner

- Limited (that is, reasonable) rate of return on the capital invested by the limited partners

- The exempt organization's right of first refusal on the sale of partnership assets

- The presence of additional general partners that are obligated to protect the interest of the limited partners

- Lack of control over the venture or the exempt organization by the for-profit limited partners

---

[77] Involvement of a charitable organization in a partnership is often a means to an end: raising of capital for one or more projects that advance the organization's exempt purposes. A partnership is, for the most part, a fundraising vehicle. The major problem in the federal tax setting is that, in its zeal to raise needed capital, the charitable organization may run afoul of the private inurement or private benefit doctrines. *E.g.*, Redlands Surgical Servs. v. Comm'r, 113 T.C. 47 (1999), *aff'd*, 242 F.3d 904 (9th Cir. 2001); Rev. Rul. 98-15, 1998-1 C.B. 718. In general, *Tax-Exempt Organizations*, § 32.4.

- Absence of any obligation to return the limited partners' capital from the exempt organization's funds

- Absence of profit as a primary motivating factor for the exempt organization's involvement in the partnership

- All transactions with partners are at arm's length

- A management contract terminable for cause by the venture, with a limited term, renewal subject to approval of the venture, and preferably with an independent entity

- Effective control in the exempt organization over major decisions involving the venture

- Written commitment in the joint venture governing document to the fulfillment of charitable purposes in the event of a conflict with a duty to maximize profit

Not all of these criteria need be met, and not all are of equal weight. For example, as to the fifth element, the IRS has approved of an arrangement whereby all of the limited partners in a limited partnership are members of the board of the charitable organization that is the general partner.[78] As another illustration, the last of these elements has taken on enormous importance; in one instance, the case largely turned (in favor of the exempt organization) on this point.[79]

The IRS looks at certain unfavorable factors as well:

- Disproportionate allocation of profits and/or losses in favor of the limited partners

- Commercially unreasonable loans by the exempt organization to the partnership

- Inadequate compensation received by the exempt organization for services it provides or excessive compensation paid by the exempt organization in exchange for services it receives

- Control of the exempt organization by the limited partners (see above) or lack of sufficient control by the exempt organization to ensure that it is able to carry out its charitable activities

- Abnormal or insufficient capital contributions by the limited partners

- Profit motivation on the part of the exempt partner

- Guarantee of the limited partner's projected tax credits or return on investment, to the detriment of the exempt general partner

The state of the law in this regard is illuminated by IRS private letter rulings, almost all of them in the health care context:

---

[78] *E.g.*, Tech. Adv. Mem. 200151045; Priv. Ltr. Rul. 8541108.
[79] St. David's Health Care Sys., Inc. v. United States, 2002-1 U.S.T.C. ¶ 50,452 (W.D. Tex. 2002), *vacated & remanded*, 349 F.3d 242 (5th Cir. 2003). Thereafter, the trial court conducted a trial before a jury, which voted that the corporation should retain its tax-exempt status. No. 101CV-046 (W.D. Tex., Mar. 4, 2004).

- The IRS ruled that the tax-exempt status of a charitable organization should not be revoked; the issue was its participation as a general partner in seven limited partnerships.[80]

- The IRS ruled that a charitable organization created by 10 unrelated hospitals could remain exempt, even though its only function was to become a sole general partner in a limited partnership that included individuals as limited partners. The purpose of the partnership was furtherance of exempt purposes (operation of a lithotripsy center) and the benefit to nonexempt limited partners (including physicians) was incidental.[81]

The planner should consider two other relevant aspects of the law as well:

1. *Aggregate approach rule.* The IRS and the courts apply an *aggregate approach rule* in this setting.[82] This means that when the nonprofit organization's eligibility for tax-exempt status is being evaluated (anew or on an ongoing basis), the activities of the organization *and* the activities of a joint venture in which the organization is a member are taken into consideration.

2. *Involvement of subsidiary.* Some tax-exempt organizations, rather than becoming directly involved in a joint venture, will participate indirectly. This is accomplished by causing a subsidiary (controlled entity) to be a member in the parent's stead. Depending on the circumstances, the subsidiary may be a for-profit organization or a tax-exempt organization (the latter is often a supporting organization).

§ 8.12 LIMITED LIABILITY COMPANIES—DETAILS

Just as legal attention to the involvement of public charities in partnerships is subsiding, developments in the law concerning the use of limited liability companies by charitable and other tax-exempt organizations is on the increase. It appears today that the limited liability company is the joint venture vehicle of choice in the exempt organizations context.

Limited liability companies (LLCs) are of two varieties: the multimember limited liability company and the single-member limited liability company.[83]

(a) Multimember LLC

A limited liability company can have two or more members. One or more of the members may be tax-exempt organizations; there may be for-profit co-venturers as well. All of the members of the LLC may be exempt organizations.

In assessing whether a charitable organization's participation as a member of a multimember LLC, consisting of one or more nonexempt persons, will have an adverse impact on the charitable organization's tax-exempt status, the planner

---

[80] Priv. Ltr. Rul. 8938001.
[81] Priv. Ltr. Rul. 200151045.
[82] Rev. Rul. 98-15, 1998-1 C.B. 718. One of the principal decisions on the aggregate approach rule is Butler v. Comm'r, 36 T.C. 1097 (1961).
[83] State law needs to be checked on this point, as the law may not permit single-member limited liability companies.

should extrapolate from the criteria used by the IRS in making the same determination when the vehicle involved is a partnership (see the preceding section).

Again, private letter rulings illustrate this use of the multimember LLC (and, again, many of these rulings are in the health care context):

- An institution of higher education operated two neonatal intensive care units in its role as a component of an academic medical center. A hospital also operated a neonatal intensive care unit. The two organizations formed an LLC for the purpose of administering the hospital's existing facility and a new and expanded neonatal intensive care unit.[84]

- A tax-exempt organization that provides supportive services to a health care provider and an exempt long-term health care facility formed an LLC for the purpose of providing rehabilitation services in a community.[85]

- A tax-exempt health care system and a group of physicians formed an LLC for the purpose of owning and operating an ambulatory surgery center.[86]

- A tax-exempt hospital owned and operated six cardiac catheterization laboratories; these facilities were in the hospital building. The hospital wanted to develop a seventh cardiac catheterization laboratory as an outpatient facility and wanted to involve the physicians who have staff privileges at the institution. The hospital created an LLC consisting of its supporting organization and the physicians.[87]

- Private colleges and universities can maintain their own qualified prepaid tuition plans.[88] A single plan has been established, structured for use by private colleges and universities throughout the nation; this program is stitched together by means of a "consortium agreement." The vehicle for this plan is an LLC that has the colleges and universities as its members.[89]

- Three trade associations (business leagues) having comparable (but not similar) exempt purposes, and members with congruent interests, operated their own trade shows in years past. To reduce the administrative costs of the shows, the associations created an LLC for the purpose of conducting a single trade show.[90]

The principal problem facing the planner in this context may be the ongoing tax-exempt status of the charitable organization that is a member of a limited liability company. This issue will likely arise if the charitable organization has lost control (or is perceived to have lost control) of its resources to one or more of the for-profit members. The extreme in this regard is the *whole entity joint venture*, detailed in the companion volume.[91]

---

[84] Priv. Ltr. Rul. 200044040.
[85] Priv. Ltr. Rul. 200102052.
[86] Priv. Ltr. Rul. 200118054.
[87] Priv. Ltr. Rul. 200304041.
[88] See *Tax-Exempt Organizations*, § 18.16.
[89] Priv. Ltr. Rul. 200311034.
[90] Priv. Ltr. Rul. 200333031.
[91] *Tax-Exempt Organizations*, § 32.4.

Again, as the fourth of these examples illustrates, a charitable organization may cause a related entity to be the member of the LLC in lieu of itself. In that example, the form of the related entity was a tax-exempt supporting organization. The aggregate approach rule applies in this context as well.

(b) Single-Member LLC[92]

A limited liability company may be formed with only one member. This type of entity is likely to be disregarded for federal tax purposes.[93] This means that although the company has the limitation-of-liability feature afforded pursuant to state law, the federal tax law regards the economic activity in the tax-exempt organization and in the LLC as conducted in one entity (the exempt organization). Consequently, the exempt organization in this situation must report on its annual information return[94] the economic activity, assets, and/or liabilities of the LLC.[95]

(i) Separateness of Entities. Whether an organization is an entity separate from its owner or owners for federal tax purposes is a matter of federal tax law, and does not depend on whether the organization is recognized as an entity under state law.[96] Certain organizations that have a single owner can choose to be recognized or disregarded as entities separate from their owners.[97]

A *business entity* is any entity recognized for federal tax purposes (including an entity with a single owner that may be disregarded as an entity separate from its owner) that is not properly classified as a trust[98] or otherwise subject to special treatment pursuant to federal tax law. A business entity with two or more owners is classified for federal tax purposes as either a corporation or a partnership. A business entity with only one owner is classified as a corporation or is disregarded; if the entity is disregarded, its activities are treated in the same manner as a sole proprietorship, branch, or division of the owner.[99] In general, a business entity that has a single owner and is not a corporation is disregarded as an entity separate from its owner.[100]

A business entity that is not classified as a corporation[101]—an *eligible entity*—can elect its classification for federal tax purposes.[102] An eligible entity with at least two owners can elect to be classified as either an association (and thus a corporation[103]) or a partnership, and an eligible entity with a single owner can elect to be classified as an association or to be disregarded as an entity separate from its owner.

---

[92] In general, see *Tax-Exempt Organizations*, § 30.7.
[93] *Id.* § 4.1(b).
[94] See § 11.3.
[95] Ann. 99-102, 1999-43 I.R.B. 545.
[96] Reg. § 301.7701-1(a)(1).
[97] Reg. § 301.7701-1(a)(4).
[98] Reg. § 301.7701-4.
[99] Reg. § 301.7701-2(a).
[100] Reg. § 301.7701-2(c)(2)(i).
[101] Reg. § 301.7701-2(b)(1), (3), (4), (5), (6), (7), or (8).
[102] Reg. § 301.7701-3(a).
[103] Reg. § 301.7701-2(b)(2).

Generally, in the absence of an election otherwise, a domestic eligible entity is a partnership if it has at least two members, and is disregarded as an entity separate from its owner if it has a single owner.[104] As noted, a disregarded limited liability company is regarded as a branch or division of its member owner. Thus, although the single-member LLC is a separate legal entity for nontax purposes, it is treated as a component of its owner for federal income tax purposes; thus, in that sense, it is not a subsidiary of the member. The IRS observed that when the sole member of an LLC is a tax-exempt organization, the function of the LLC is treated as an "activity" of the exempt organization.[105]

Usually, the single-member LLC is deliberately created with the tax feature of being disregarded. It is possible, however, for a multimember LLC to be treated for tax purposes as a single-member LLC. For example, the IRS ruled that an LLC with two members was nonetheless a disregarded entity, because one of the members did not have any economic interest in the company and thus failed to qualify as a member for tax purposes.[106]

(ii) Exempt Organizations' Use of Single-Member LLCs.   Tax-exempt organizations are making creative use of the single-member limited liability company. Here are some examples:

- A public charity was working with a city government to transform the older, downtown sections of the city into a center of industry, commerce, housing, transportation, government services, and cultural and educational opportunities. These sections lacked adequate parking due to the completion of several major development projects. The charity organized a single-member LLC to address the need for affordable downtown parking; it was to acquire a parking garage and two parking lots by means of a bond issue. The IRS ruled that the LLC was a disregarded entity and that its operations would not jeopardize the charity's tax-exempt status, because the charity, by means of the LLC, was lessening the burdens of government[107] (i.e., the city).[108]

- A charitable organization may accept a gift of property that carries with it exposure of the donee to legal liability (such as environmental or premises tort liability). Before the advent of the single-member LLC, a charitable organization could attempt to shield its other assets from liability by placing the gift property in a separate exempt entity, such as a supporting organization or a title-holding company. Among the difficulties with this approach was the need or desire to file an application for recognition of tax exemption for the new entity and/or file annual information returns on its behalf. As an alternative, however, a charitable organization can utilize a single-member LLC as the vehicle to receive and hold a contribution of

---

[104] Reg. § 301.7701-3(b)(1). An eligible entity may elect to be classified other than as provided under this rule, or to change its classification, by filing Form 8832. Reg. § 301.7701-3(c).

[105] Priv. Ltr. Rul. 200134025.

[106] Priv. Ltr. Rul. 200201024.

[107] For a discussion of lessening the burdens of government as a charitable purpose, see *Tax-Exempt Organizations*, § 6.4.

[108] Priv. Ltr. Rul. 200124022.

this nature. Each of these contributed properties can be placed in a separate single-member LLC, thereby offering protection in relation to each of the other properties and providing the charity with overall liability protection.[109]

- A tax-exempt museum, organized as a private operating foundation,[110] owned and operated a racetrack and a campground, with these activities in a single-member LLC. The IRS ruled[111] that these activities were functionally related businesses.[112]

- A public charity, the objective of which was to construct, own, and lease student housing for the benefit of a tax-exempt college, developed and operated the project through a single-member LLC. In this fashion it issued taxable and tax-exempt bonds, and provided temporary construction jobs and permanent employment opportunities in the community.[113]

- A charitable organization that provided educational opportunities (and housing) to low-income and other students provided facilities for various colleges. The ownership and operation of each facility were placed in a separate LLC.[114]

- A tax-exempt trade association had its trade shows conducted by an independent company, although the association set the standards for the shows and was perceived by exhibitors as responsible for them. The association sought to assume control over the exhibits to assure their quality, for the benefit of its industry, and wanted to enforce contracts directly. Rather than conduct the shows itself (because of concerns about legal liability), the association operated the shows by means of a single-member LLC, which qualified as an entity disregarded for federal tax purposes. The IRS ruled that income resulting from the LLC's activities would not be unrelated business income to the association, because the LLC entity was disregarded and the trade shows qualified for the statutory exception for such shows.[115]

In the unrelated business setting, a supporting organization affiliated with an operating educational institution[116] was the sole member of a limited liability company. The IRS ruled that when the single-member LLC received real property encumbered by debt, it and the supporting organization would be afforded an exemption from the rules concerning acquisition indebtedness[117] for purposes of determining debt-financed income.[118]

---

[109] Priv. Ltr. Rul. 200134025.
[110] *Tax-Exempt Organizations*, § 11.1(b).
[111] Priv. Ltr. Rul. 200202077.
[112] *Tax-Exempt Organizations*, § 11.3(c).
[113] Priv. Ltr. Rul. 200249014.
[114] Priv. Ltr. Rul. 200304036.
[115] Priv. Ltr. Rul. 200510030. The statutory exception is that provided by IRC § 513(d); see § 4.5.
[116] *Id.* § 11.3(a).
[117] *Tax-Exempt Organizations*, § 29.3.
[118] Priv. Ltr. Rul. 200134025.

§ 8.13   OTHER JOINT VENTURES

Tax-exempt organizations may be involved in relationships or arrangement with other entities (exempt or nonexempt) that constitute joint ventures, even when there is no formal joint venture vehicle (namely, a partnership or limited liability company). Often, however, these arrangements are not viewed by the parties as joint ventures at all—although the law may see things differently.

One of the issues the planner may have to face in this context is the filing of a partnership return.[119] The law is unclear as to when an arrangement becomes sufficiently "formal" to trigger this reporting requirement.

§ 8.14   WHOLE ENTITY JOINT VENTURES

The U.S. Tax Court has heard only one case in the whole entity joint venture setting; this momentous decision, issued in 1999 and affirmed in 2001,[120] is still having a major impact on the operation of health care entities. From a larger perspective, however, it is fascinating to speculate on what this opinion means for public charities in general. The case is one in a series of cases (more assuredly will follow) involving a variety of major law doctrines in the exempt organizations field: private inurement, private benefit, intermediate sanctions, involvement in partnerships and other joint ventures, and the commerciality doctrine.

From a health law perspective, the case is seen as an example of the whole hospital joint venture, which it obviously is. The case provides judicial underpinning for the IRS's position as to these ventures.[121] The fundamental principle is that when a public charity (in the *Redlands* case, a surgical center) cedes authority over its operations to a related for-profit organization, the charity will quite likely lose its tax-exempt status.

From the larger perspective, however, this case is a private benefit case; indeed, it is a significant private benefit case. In the past, some advisors would evaluate a set of facts involving a transaction between a public charity and a for-profit person and determine if that person was an insider (for private benefit purposes) or a disqualified person (for excess benefit transaction purposes). If the answer to both questions was no, the analysis ended. Clearly, this can no longer be the practice, because of the sudden emergence of the private benefit doctrine as a major force. This is because private benefit can occur even when the person being benefited is not an insider or a disqualified person. In *Redlands*, the Tax Court wrote that impermissible private benefit can be conferred on "unrelated or disinterested" persons.[122]

Another reason the private benefit doctrine has not received much attention until fairly recently is that it is somewhat hidden. It is not part of the Code, nor is it in the regulations. Until recently, there have been few court opinions on the subject. As the Tax Court nicely stated in *Redlands*, the private benefit proscription

---

[119] See *Tax-Exempt Organizations*, § 32.6.
[120] Redlands Surgical Servs. v. Comm'r, 113 T.C. 47 (1999), *aff'd*, 242 F.3d 904 (9th Cir. 2001).
[121] *Id.*
[122] Redlands Surgical Servs. v. Comm'r, 113 T.C. 47, 74 (1999).

"inheres in the requirement that an organization operate exclusively [primarily] for exempt purposes."[123]

Also until recently, most of the private benefit cases concerned public charities' relationships with individuals. The leading case had been one involving a school, which failed to gain exemption because it conferred private benefit (other than insubstantially) on individuals in their private capacities.[124] The whole entity joint venture case, however, should force public charities to face another application of the private benefit doctrine: their relationships with for-profit organizations.

The *Redlands* joint venture case teaches that a fundamental concept in this context is *control*. The opinion stands as a warning to all public charities to examine their relationships with for-profit entities to see if they have lost or ceded control of their resources to a for-profit entity. Examples are the relationships established in management agreements, leases, fundraising contracts, and, of course, partnership or other joint venture agreements. The scary aspect of all this is that it is irrelevant if the public charity is in fact engaging in exempt activities and if the fees paid by the exempt organization to the for-profit entity are reasonable (traditional private inurement analysis). There still can be private benefit.

That rule of law is the essence of a case decided by the Tax Court in 1979.[125] The point has been made subsequently, however. In a case decided by the U.S. Court of Appeals for the Ninth Circuit in 1985, the court wrote: "The critical inquiry is not whether particular contractual payments to a related for-profit organization are reasonable or excessive, but instead whether the entire enterprise is carried on in such a manner that the for-profit organization benefits substantially from the operation of" the nonprofit organization.[126]

The case in this area that has been regarded as being on the outer reaches is the Tax Court's 1979 decision. That case—20 years of age at the time of the whole entity joint venture decision—had almost been forgotten . . . until now. One of the underdiscussed aspects of the whole hospital joint venture case is its resurrection of the law embodied in the 1979 case. The problem is that the 1979 case involved extreme facts and the Tax Court took a hard line.

In the 1979 case, several for-profit organizations that did not have any formal structural control over the nonprofit entity in question nevertheless exerted "considerable control" over its activities.[127] The for-profit entities set fees that the nonprofit organization charged the public for training sessions, required the nonprofit organization to carry on certain types of educational activities, and provided management personnel paid for and responsible to one of the for-profit organizations. Under a licensing agreement with the for-profit organizations, the nonprofit entity was allowed to use certain intellectual property for 10 years; at the end of the licensing period, all copyrighted material, including new material developed by the nonprofit organization, had to be turned back to the for-profit

---

[123] *Id.*

[124] Am. Campaign Acad. v. Comm'r, 92 T.C. 1053 (1989).

[125] Est of Haw. v. Comm'r, 71 T.C. 1067 (1979), *aff'd*, 647 F.2d 170 (9th Cir. 1981).

[126] Church by Mail v. Comm'r, 48 T.C.M. 471 (1984), *aff'd*, 765 F.2d 1387 (9th Cir. 1985).

[127] Est of Haw. v. Comm'r, 71 T.C. 1067, 1080 (1979).

organizations. The nonprofit organization was required to use its excess funds for the development of related research. The for-profit organizations also required that trainers and local organizations sign agreements not to compete with the nonprofit entity for two years after terminating their relationships with comparable organizations.

The Tax Court concluded in 1979 that the nonprofit organization was "part of a franchise system . . . is operated for private benefit and [that] . . . its affiliation with this system taints it with a substantial commercial purpose."[128] The "ultimate beneficiaries" of the nonprofit organization's activities were found to be the for-profit corporations; the nonprofit organization was "simply the instrument to subsidize the for-profit corporations and not vice versa."[129] The nonprofit organization was held not to be operating exclusively for charitable purposes.

This 1979 case has (to date, anyway) framed the borders of this analysis. Even without formal control over the ostensible tax-exempt organization by one or more for-profit entities, the ostensible exempt organization can be seen as merely the instrument to subsidize a for-profit organization. The nonprofit organization's "affiliation" with a for-profit entity or a "system" involving one or more for-profit entities can taint the nonprofit organization with a substantial commercial purpose. The result is private benefit that causes the nonprofit organization to lose or be denied tax-exempt status.

Matters worsen within these boundaries when there is actual control. This is the message sent by the whole hospital joint venture decision. In that case, the public charity became a co-general partner with a for-profit organization in a partnership that owned and operated the surgery center. The arrangement was managed by a for-profit management company that was affiliated with the for-profit co-general partner. Participation in the partnership was the public charity's sole activity (hence the name *whole hospital joint venture*). The court termed this "passive participation in a for-profit health-service enterprise."[130]

The Tax Court concluded that it was "patently clear" that the partnership was not being operated in an exclusively charitable manner.[131] The income-producing activity of the partnership was characterized as "indivisible."[132] No "discrete part" of these activities was "severable from those activities that produce income to be applied to the other partners' profit."[133]

The heart of the whole hospital joint venture case is this: To the extent that a public charity "cedes control over its sole activity to for-profit parties [by, in this case, entering into the joint venture] having an independent economic interest in the same activity and having no obligation to put charitable purposes ahead of profit-making objectives," the charity cannot be assured that the partnership will in fact be operated in furtherance of charitable purposes.[134] The consequence is the conferring of "significant private benefits" on the for-profit parties.[135]

---

[128] *Id.* at 1080.
[129] *Id.* at 1082.
[130] Redlands Surgical Servs. v. Comm'r, 113 T.C. 47, 77 (1999).
[131] *Id.*
[132] *Id.*
[133] *Id.*
[134] Redlands Surgical Servs. v. Comm'r, 113 T.C. at 78.
[135] *Id.*

This matter of control is not always so stark as in the whole hospital joint venture case. For example, the litigation involving the United Cancer Council[136] shows how courts can differ as to whether a nonprofit organization is controlled by a for-profit one. This issue also arises in the definitions of *disqualified person* in the intermediate sanctions context.[137]

Further, it would be a mistake for a public charity to disregard the whole hospital joint venture case on the basis that the charity is not involved in a partnership. As discussed below, there need not be a formal partnership agreement for the rules to apply. The law can characterize the relationship between two organizations as a joint venture even though neither organization has an intent or desire to be in a joint venture. (In some of the cases that the IRS lost on the issue of whether revenue constitutes a royalty, the IRS asserted that the exempt organizations involved were effectively participating in a joint venture.[138])

The IRS exempt organization continuing professional education technical instruction program textbook for fiscal year 2001 contains an article discussing the private benefit doctrine. Therein, the IRS concedes that "in reality it is difficult to apply the private benefit analysis." The doctrine is applied in the IRS's discussion to charter schools and organizations providing low-income housing.

What can a public charity do to protect itself against allegations of this type of private benefit? Obviously, the main strategy is not to lose control over program activities. Another element is documentation: The agreements and other documents involved should stress the powers and functions of the nonprofit organization. Contracts should be negotiated at arm's length. Contracts for services should not have long terms. (The management agreement in the whole hospital joint venture case had the partnership, and thus the charity, locked in for at least 15 years.) If a partnership is involved, the public charity should try to have assets and other resources apart from those invested in the partnership. The public charity should try to receive gifts and grants on an ongoing basis, and not rely solely on exempt function revenue. (This consideration is prompted by the commerciality doctrine.) Overall, the exempt organization should not be operated so as to provide to a for-profit entity a nonincidental "advantage; profit; fruit; privilege; gain; [or] interest."[139]

§ 8.15 ANCILLARY JOINT VENTURES

A pending issue is the extent to which the principles of law being developed in the whole entity joint venture setting are applicable to the operations of ancillary joint ventures. An *ancillary joint venture* is a joint venture involving a public charity (or other tax-exempt organization[140] in which less than the entirety of the charity's resources are placed in the venture. The ancillary joint venture is sometimes called a *programmatic joint venture*.

---

[136] United Cancer Council, Inc. v. Comm'r, 109 T.C. 326 (1997), *rev'd*, 165 F.3d 1173 (7th Cir. 1999).

[137] IRC § 4958(f)(1).

[138] *Tax-Exempt Organizations*, § 27.1(g).

[139] Am. Campaign Acad. v. Comm'r, 92 T.C. 1053, 1065–1066 (1989).

[140] In mid-2005, the IRS ruled (for the first time) that these joint venture rules also apply to organizations other than public charities; the entity involved was a tax-exempt business league. Priv. Ltr. Rul. 200528029.

The law on this point is evolving. In one instance, the IRS approved a proposed joint venture to operate an ambulatory surgery center.[141] This joint venture, which involved a public charity and nonexempt entities (physicians), serves as an illustration of the type of these ventures.

(a) Initial IRS Guidance

The charitable organization involved was a supporting organization (SO) that operated a community-based health care system. SO and its affiliates provided hospital, physician, home health, hospice, nursing home, and other health care services. Other functions, however constituted SO's primary activities.

To better serve community needs, SO and a group of local physicians formed a limited liability company (LLC) to own and operate an ambulatory surgery center. The ruling stated that SO formerly owned and operated the center, but somehow the center became owned by a for-profit subsidiary of SO (FP). Inasmuch as involvement in the center was not the primary activity of SO, this was an *ancillary joint venture.*

SO acquired a 70-percent ownership interest in LLC. The physicians acquired the remaining 30-percent interest. SO was to reduce its percentage interest in LLC by selling membership interests to board-approved purchasers until its percentage interest was 51 percent. Profits and losses were to be allocated to the members based on membership percentage.

LLC leased the center from FP. It also leased the equipment used in the center pursuant to a separate lease agreement. SO represented to the IRS that both of the lease agreements were negotiated at arm's length, and that they reflected the fair market rental value of the facilities and the fair market purchase value of the equipment.

LLC's operations were conducted pursuant to the terms of an operating agreement. That agreement provided that the purpose of LLC was to lease and/ or own and operate an ambulatory surgery center in furtherance of charitable purposes by promoting health for a broad cross-section of the community. It further provided that LLC and its board of directors would at all times cause LLC to be operated for these purposes and that this duty overrode any duty to operate LLC for the benefit of its members. SO represented that this override was enforceable under state law.

LLC was managed on a day-to-day basis by a board made up of six directors. SO appointed two of the directors; the physician members elected four of the directors. Each director appointed by SO had three votes on all matters coming before the board. Each of the other directors had one vote. Board decisions were by majority vote. The directors appointed by SO were community leaders experienced in health care matters, were not on the medical staff of the hospital or the center, and were not otherwise engaged in business transactions with SO, LLC, or the surgery center.

LLC had a charity care policy consistent with SO's charity care policy, and this policy was made known to potential patients. Charity care was not

---

[141] Priv. Ltr. Rul. 200118054.

included in bad debt. The percentages of patients that were expected to be served by LLC, as to indigents, Medicare and Medicaid patients, self-pay patients, and the like, were approximately equivalent to the percentages of patients served at the center when it was owned by SO.

Physician privileges at LLC's facility were not dependent on ownership of a membership interest in LLC. Medical staff members applied for and were granted privileges at the facility based on credentialing criteria. LLC had no employees and no plans to hire any; SO provided support services to LLC. SO leased nursing, clinical, administrative, clerical, and other personnel to LLC. Medical staff members were independent practitioners. Professional services were billed separately by the independent practicing medical staff members who provided the services.

The IRS began its analysis of these facts by emphasizing three fundamental points of law:

1. The promotion of health is a charitable purpose.[142]

2. Whether a health care organization promotes health in a charitable manner is determined under the community benefit standard.[143]

3. The activities of a partnership are attributed to a tax-exempt member for purposes of application of the operational test.[144]

As discussed, this third element of the law is known as the *aggregate principle*; it was articulated in the IRS revenue ruling concerning whole hospital joint ventures.[145] In the ruling in this case, the IRS wrote that "[a]ggregate treatment is also consistent with the treatment of partnerships for purposes of the unrelated business income tax."

The IRS observed that a charitable organization may form and participate in a partnership, including a limited liability company, and meet the operational test if (1) participation in the partnership furthers a charitable purpose and (2) the partnership arrangement permits the exempt organization to act exclusively in furtherance of its exempt purposes and only incidentally for the benefit of for-profit partners. The agency also said that, based on its revenue ruling, whether a nonprofit organization, the principal activity of which is the ownership of a membership interest in an LLC that is engaged in health care activities, satisfies the community benefit standard depends on all the facts and circumstances.

In this case, the IRS ruled that, following the formation and operation of LLC, SO would continue to be primarily involved in furthering the needs of the exempt hospital system and its tax-exempt entities. Also, its participation in this venture was ruled to further its exempt purposes. SO's participation in LLC and operation of the ambulatory surgery center were said to promote health for the community. The structure of LLC and the operation of the center were portrayed by the IRS as allowing SO to act exclusively in furtherance of charitable purposes, with no undue private benefit to the physician members.

---

[142] *Tax-Exempt Organizations,* § 6.3.

[143] Hyatt & Hopkins, *The Law of Tax-Exempt Healthcare Organizations* 2nd Edition, ch. 6 (John Wiley & Sons, 2001).

[144] See text accompanied by *supra* note 82.

[145] Rev. Rul. 98-15, 1998-1 C.B. 718.

As with other joint ventures, the IRS focused on control. As noted, SO owned at least 51 percent of LLC. It had 6 of the 10 votes on LLC's board of directors. Because a majority of votes was needed to approve decisions, SO exercised effective control over the major decisions of LLC and over the operations of the center. This control ensured that the assets SO owned through LLC, and the activities it conducted through LLC at the center, would be used primarily to further tax-exempt purposes. Also, the IRS reiterated that the operating agreement of LLC provided that the duty of its members and board was to operate LLC in a manner that furthers charitable purposes and that this duty overrode any duty to operate LLC for the financial benefit of its members.

(b) Formal IRS Guidance

The IRS ruled that a public charity involved in a partnership arrangement with a for-profit entity will not lose its exempt status if the involvement is an insubstantial part of its total operations and will not be subject to unrelated business income taxation if the charity retains control over the partnership arrangement and operations which constitute one or more related businesses.

A tax-exempt university offered, as part of its educational programs, summer seminars to enhance the skill level of elementary and secondary school teachers. To expand the reach of these seminars, the university, along with a for-profit company, formed a limited liability company (LLC). The for-profit company specialized in the conduct of interactive video training programs. Its governing instruments provided that the sole purpose of LLC is to offer teacher training seminars at locations off the university's campus using interactive video technology.

The university and the for-profit company each held a 50 percent interest in LLC, which is proportionate to the value of their respective capital contributions to LLC. The governing documents of LLC provided that all returns of capital, allocations, and distributions are to be made in proportion to the members' respective ownership interests.

Its governing documents provided that LLC will be managed by a governing board comprised of three directors selected by the university and three directors selected by the for-profit company. LLC arranged and conducted all aspects of the video teacher training seminars, including advertising, enrolling participants, arranging for the necessary facilities, distributing the course materials, and broadcasting the seminars to various locations. LLC's teacher training seminars covered the same content that is covered in the seminars that the university conducts on its campus. School teachers participated through an interactive video link at various locations, rather than in person.

LLC's governing documents granted the university the exclusive right to approve the curriculum, training materials, and instructors, and to determine the standards for successful completion of the seminars. The for-profit company was granted the exclusive right to select the locations where participants can receive a video link to the seminars and to approve other personnel (such as camera operators) necessary to conduct the video seminars. All other actions required the mutual consent of the university and the for-profit company.

The governing documents required that the terms of all contracts and transactions entered into by LLC, with the university, the for-profit company, or any other party, be at arm's length and that all contract and transaction prices be at fair market value determined by reference to the prices for comparable goods or services. These documents limited LLC's activities to the conduct of the teacher training seminars and also required that LLC not engage in any activities that would jeopardize the tax-exempt status of the university. LLC operated, in all respects, in accordance with its governing documents.

The university's participation in LLC was an insubstantial part of its activities. LLC was classified as a partnership for federal tax purposes. Inasmuch as LLC was treated as a partnership for federal tax purposes, its activities were attributed to the university for the purpose of determining whether it continues to qualify for exemption (that is, whether it was operating primarily for charitable and educational purposes) and whether it was engaging in an unrelated business.

The activities that the university was conducting through LLC were merely an insubstantial part of its activities. Therefore, the university's participation in LLC, taken alone, did not adversely affect its continuing qualification for exemption.

The university's activities conducted through LLC constituted a business that was substantially related to the exercise and performance of the university's purposes and functions. Even though LLC arranged and conducted all aspects of the teacher training seminars, the university alone approved the curriculum, training materials and instructors, and determined the standards for successful completion of the seminars. The fact that the for-profit entity selected the seminar locations and approved the other personnel did not change the conclusion that the seminars were a related business.

The teacher training seminars were conducted using interactive video technology and embraced the same content as the seminars conducted by the university on its campus. LLC's activities expanded the reach of the university's teacher training seminars. Therefore, the IRS concluded that the manner in which LLC conducted the seminars contributed importantly to the accomplishment of the university's educational purposes; the activities of LLC were substantially related to the university's educational purposes. Thus, the university was not required to pay any unrelated business income tax on its distributive share of LLC's income.

§ 8.16 LAW-IMPOSED JOINT VENTURES

In some instances, the law will treat an arrangement as a general partnership (or other joint venture) for tax purposes, even though the parties involved intended (or insist they intended) that their relationship be something else. The ostensible true relationship may be that of landlord and tenant, parties pursuant to a management agreement, or payor and payee of royalties. As discussed in the companion volume, the law is unclear as to the criteria used in making these assessments.[146]

---

[146] Rev. Rul. 2004-51, 2004-22 I.R.B. 974.

Case law on this point, concerning landlord-tenant relationships, is summarized in the companion volume.[147] As another illustration, the IRS asserted there was a joint venture relationship involving a volunteer fire company and taverns in a county in which the organization placed "tip jars." This was a fundraising program conducted by the fire company; the court declined to find the presence of a joint venture.[148]

§ 8.17 LOOK-THROUGH RULE—DETAILS

As noted, when a tax-exempt organization is a member of a joint venture, the look-through principle applies in determining whether any resulting income is unrelated business income. The planner must evaluate the nature of the business in the venture in relation to the purposes of the exempt organization, and assess what the tax outcome would be if the exempt organization conducted the business directly. That evaluation will lead to the conclusion as to whether the revenue from the venture is taxable.

The same unrelated business rules apply in this setting as apply generally. This includes the modifications rules for passive and other income. Here are some examples of this point:

- A tax-exempt group trust arrangement has as its principal purpose serving as a medium for the collective investment of the funds of pension, profit-sharing, and other qualified benefit trusts in real estate and real estate interests. This entity has interests in partnerships and limited liability companies; the properties owned therein are held for leasing purposes. The IRS ruled that, to the extent that the organization receives income from a partnership or an LLC, the character of the income as rent from real property[149] is retained and its flow through the partnerships and LLCs does not preclude the income from being received by the organization tax-free.[150]

- Three trade associations (business leagues) having comparable (but not similar) exempt purposes, and members with congruent interests, operated their own trade shows for years. To reduce the administrative costs of the shows, the associations create an LLC for the purpose of conducting a single trade show. The IRS ruled that the trade show income is protected by the special trade show rules in the unrelated business setting[151] and thus that the income is received by each of these associations free of tax.[152]

---

[147] *Id.*, text accompanied by notes. 17–18.
[148] Vigilant Hose Co. of Emmitsburg v. United States, 2001-2 U.S.T.C. ¶ 50,458 (D. Md. 2001).
[149] *Tax-Exempt Organizations*, § 27.1(h).
[150] Priv. Ltr. Rul. 200147058.
[151] *Tax-Exempt Organizations*, § 27.2(f).
[152] Priv. Ltr. Rul. 200333031.

CHAPTER NINE

Contemporary Applications of the Unrelated Business Rules

Myriad activities undertaken by various types of tax-exempt organizations illustrate contemporary applications of the unrelated business rules. Traditionally, colleges and universities raised the most issues as to related and unrelated business endeavors, although in recent years health care institutions have achieved the dubious distinction of being first in this regard. Other exempt organizations that are currently generating significant unrelated business issues are museums, associations, and labor, agricultural, and horticultural organizations.

§ 9.1 EDUCATIONAL INSTITUTIONS

The principal business of tax-exempt colleges, universities, and schools[1] is the education of students; monies generated by this endeavor in the form of tuition, fees, assessments, dormitory rent, and food service revenue are related business income. Consequently, the IRS ruled that when an institution of higher education receives a distribution from a qualified tuition plan[2] of proceeds reflecting a tuition certificate, in consideration for the provision of educational services to a qualified beneficiary, the proceeds are revenue from a related business.[3] Another major exempt function at these institutions is research; this activity is not normally taxed, either because it is inherently an exempt function or because it is sheltered from tax by statute.[4]

The legislative history of the unrelated business income rules states that a wheat farm operated by a tax-exempt agricultural college as part of its educational program is a related business. Similarly, income from a university press is exempt "in the ordinary case" because it is derived from an activity that is substantially related to the purposes of the university.[5]

Educational organizations can engage in activities that are exempt functions because they facilitate or otherwise support accomplishment of the institutions' educational purposes and major functions, such as student housing. Thus, a public charity that constructed, owned, and leased an exempt college's student housing project was ruled to be engaged in related business (that is, operated to advance education[6]).[7] Likewise, a public charity was held to be engaging in related business when it commenced establishment of student housing facilities in college communities, with emphasis on housing for low-income students.[8]

Conversely, an activity such as the manufacture and sale of automobile tires by a tax-exempt college ordinarily is an unrelated business; this type of activity does not become substantially related simply because some students performed minor clerical or bookkeeping functions as part of their educational program.[9]

---

[1] Essentially, these are institutions referenced in IRC § 170(b)(1)(A)(ii). See Hopkins, *The Law of Tax-Exempt Organizations, Eighth Edition* (John Wiley & Sons, 2003) [hereinafter *Tax-Exempt Organizations*], § 11.3(a).

[2] See *Tax-Exempt Organizations*, § 18.16.

[3] Priv. Ltr. Rul. 200313024.

[4] See § 3.13.

[5] S. Rep. No. 2375, 81st Cong., 2d Sess. 107 (1950).

[6] See *Tax-Exempt Organizations*, § 6.6.

[7] Priv. Ltr. Rul. 200249014.

[8] Priv. Ltr. Rul. 200304036.

[9] S. Rep. No. 2375, 81st Cong., 2d Sess. 107 (1950). A college or university may operate a health and physical fitness center, with many of its programs qualifying as related business activities. *E.g.*, Priv. Ltr. Rul. 9732032.

By contrast, the IRS determined that the sale of handicraft articles by an exempt vocational school, made by its students as part of their regular courses of instruction, was a related trade or business.[10] Likewise, the IRS held that an exempt university may publish, as a related business, scholarly works written by its faculty and students.[11]

(a) Bookstore Operations

For colleges, universities, and some schools, operation of bookstores raises several potential unrelated business income issues.[12] Although the operation of these stores generally is a tax-exempt function,[13] some sales can be subject to the tax on unrelated business income. There are three categories of business activities in this context: related business, business activities that are protected from taxation by a statutory exception, and unrelated business.

Related business activities include the sale of items such as course books, supplies, tapes, compact discs, athletic wear necessary for participation in the institution's athletic and physical education programs, computer hardware and software,[14] and items that induce school spirit, such as t-shirts, tote bags, pennants, and mugs.

Another category of sales that are not taxable are those within the ambit of the *convenience doctrine*, when the business activity is engaged in for the benefit (convenience) of the students.[15] Items protected from taxation by this doctrine include sundry articles, film, cards, health and beauty aids, and novelty items.

For the most part, all other sales are unrelated business transactions. It is the view of the IRS that items that have a useful life of more than one year cannot be the subject of the convenience doctrine.[16] Sales of articles such as wearing apparel, appliances, stuffed animals, wall posters, wristwatches, and plants can thus be taxable.[17] Sales of items to the general public, as opposed to students and faculty, can also constitute unrelated business activity.

(b) Athletic Events

It is an understatement to say that preparation for and participation in athletic events is a major function of today's tax-exempt educational institution. The revenue that a college, university, or school derives from charges for admission

---

[10] Rev. Rul. 68-581, 1968-2 C.B. 250.

[11] Priv. Ltr. Rul. 9036025.

[12] Some institutions lease the bookstore operation to unrelated parties; the resulting rent is nontaxable. See § 3.8(a).

[13] Squire v. Students Book Corp., 191 F.2d 1018 (9th Cir. 1951); Rev. Rul. 58-194, 1958-1 C.B. 240.

[14] The IRS, in its college and university examination guidelines (see *Tax-Exempt Organizations*, § 24.8(d)), stated that "[a]lthough the sale of one computer to a student or faculty member may be substantially related to exempt purposes, the sale of multiple computers, in a single year, to a single student or the sale of a computer to someone who is not a student, officer or employee of the institution may result in unrelated business income." § 342.(13)(5).

[15] See § 4.1.

[16] Gen. Couns. Mem. 35811.

[17] *E.g.*, Priv. Ltr. Rul. 8025222.

to athletic events is income from a related business, inasmuch as the activities are substantially related to the institution's educational program.[18]

Revenue generated by the televising, and radio and cable broadcasting, of these events also is not taxable, in that this activity is related to the institutions' educational mission.[19] As the IRS observed, an "audience for a game may contribute importantly to the education of the student-athlete in the development of his/her physical and inner strength." Also, "[a]ttending the game enhances student interest in education generally and in the institution because such interest is whetted by exposure to the school's athletic activities." Further, the "games (and the opportunity to observe them) foster those feelings of identification, loyalty, and participation typical of a well-rounded educational experience."[20]

The IRS ruled that a tax-exempt organization that sponsored a postseason all-star college football game for the benefit of a state university did not jeopardize its exempt status because of, nor realize unrelated business income from the sale of, television broadcasting rights to the games. Broadcasting of the games "contributes importantly" to the accomplishment of its exempt purposes.[21] The agency also ruled that:

- Payments received by a state university for the sale of radio and television broadcasting rights to its basketball and football games were not unrelated business income, because carrying on the sporting events was substantially related to the university's exempt purposes.[22]

- Income received by an exempt organization, which promoted professional automobile racing, from the sale of television broadcasting rights to the races it sanctioned did not constitute unrelated income, because the television coverage effectively popularized automobile racing.[23]

- Income derived from the sale by an exempt organization, which sponsored and sanctioned amateur athletics, of television rights to broadcast its athletic events was not unrelated income, because the television medium was used to disseminate the organization's goals and purposes to the public.[24]

- An exempt organization promoting interest in a particular sport, which sold television rights to championship golf tournaments that it sponsored, did not thereby incur unrelated business income, because the grant of the rights was directly related to the organization's exempt purposes.[25]

---

[18] H.R. Rep. No. 2319, 81st Cong., 2d Sess. 37, 109 (1950); S. Rep. No. 2375, 81st Cong., 2d Sess. 107 (1950). A university "would not be taxable on income derived from a basketball tournament sponsored by it, even where the teams were composed of students from other schools." H.R. Rep. No. 2319, *supra*, at 37; S. Rep. No. 2375, *supra*, at 29).

[19] Tech. Adv. Mem. 7851004.

[20] Priv. Ltr. Rul. 7930043.

[21] Priv. Ltr. Rul. 7948113 (which also held that the proceeds from admissions to the game, sales of game programs, and sales of advertising in the program were not taxable as unrelated business income).

[22] Priv. Ltr. Rul. 7930043.

[23] Priv. Ltr. Rul. 7922001.

[24] Priv. Ltr. Rul. 7851003.

[25] Priv. Ltr. Rul. 7845029.

- The income received by an exempt amateur sports organization for the licensing of television broadcasting rights was not unrelated business income, because the broadcast of the sports events was substantially related to the organization's exempt purpose of promoting international goodwill.[26]
- Payments to be received from the sale of radio and television broadcasting rights to an athletic event were not items of unrelated business income, because promotion of the event (the organization's exempt purpose) was furthered by the broadcast of the event.[27]

The IRS held that the sale to an independent producer of exclusive television and radio broadcasting rights to athletic events, by a tax-exempt national governing body for amateur athletics, was not an unrelated business, because the "broadcasting of the organization's sponsored, supervised, and regulated athletic events promotes the various amateur sports, fosters widespread public interest in the benefits of its nationwide amateur athletic program, and encourages public participation." Therefore, the sale of the broadcasting rights and the broadcast of the events were exempt functions.[28] The agency issued a similar ruling with respect to the sale of broadcasting rights, to a national radio and television network, by an organization created by a regional collegiate athletic conference and composed of exempt universities, the purpose of which was to hold an annual athletic event.[29]

The IRS asserted that the payment, by a for-profit corporation, of a sponsorship fee to a college, university, or bowl association in connection with the telecasting or radio broadcast of an athletic event, was unrelated business income, because the package of "valuable services" received by the corporation was not substantially related to exempt purposes and amounted to advertising services.[30] This matter was generally resolved by the enactment of legislation concerning the qualified sponsorship payment.[31]

(c) Travel Tours

The IRS is concerned that a college, university, or school, or alumni or alumnae association, will offer a travel tour as an ostensible educational experience, when in fact it is a social, recreational, or other form of vacation opportunity and thus an unrelated business. In a 1977 unpublished technical advice memorandum, the IRS ruled that a travel tour program conducted by an alumni association of a university was an unrelated trade or business. The program was available to all

---

[26] Priv. Ltr. Rul. 8303078.

[27] Priv. Ltr. Rul. 7919053.

[28] Rev. Rul. 80-295, 1980-2 C.B. 194.

[29] Rev. Rul. 80-296, 1980-2 C.B. 195. These two public rulings, along with Rev. Rul. 80-294, 1980-2 C.B. 187, capture the essence of the foregoing (notes 20–27) and similar private letter rulings. In general, Jensen, *Taxation, the Student Athlete, and the Professionalization of College Athletics*, 1987 *Utah L. Rev.* 35 (no. 1, 1987); Thompson & Young, *Taxing the Sale of Broadcast Rights to College Athletics—An Unrelated Trade or Business?*, 8 *J. Coll. & Univ. L.* 331 (1981–1982); Kaplan, *Intercollegiate Athletics and the Unrelated Business Income Tax*, 80 *Colo. L. Rev.* 1430 (1980); Note, *University TV Receipts Not Unrelated Business Income*, 50 *J. Tax'n* 184 (1979).

[30] Tech. Adv. Mem. 9147007.

[31] See § 6.6. The taxation of advertising revenue is the subject of § 6.5.

members of the association and their families; in the year at issue, the association sent 4 mailings announcing 9 tours to between 27,500 and 34,900 individuals. The memorandum stated that "[al]though the tours include sightseeing, there is no formal educational program conducted in connection with them; nor is there any program for contacting and meeting with alumni in the countries visited." The IRS determined that: (1) the activities of the alumni association, in working with commercial travel agencies in the planning and preparation of the tours, mailing out the tour announcements, and receiving reservations, constituted a trade or business; (2) the travel tours were inherently recreational, not educational,[32] and thus did not contribute importantly to a tax-exempt (educational) purpose; (3) the unrelated business was regularly carried on; and (4) this commercial endeavor exploited an intangible asset, namely, the association's membership.[33]

An alumni association travel tour program that is structured as an authentic educational activity is not an unrelated trade or business.[34] The IRS's policy with respect to travel tours generally is that some are related and some are unrelated, depending on how they are structured, what they consist of, and what they accomplish. Tours that feature "bona fide educational methodologies"—such as organized study, reports, lectures, library access, and reading lists—are likely to be considered educational in nature. Pursuant to a primary purpose test, tours that devote a significant amount of time to endeavors such as sightseeing are not usually exempt functions. Tours that are "not significantly different from commercially sponsored" tours are probably unrelated businesses, as are extension (or add-on) tours.[35]

The law in this regard has evolved in the form of regulations on the unrelated business tax aspects of travel and tour activities of tax-exempt organizations generally.[36]

(d) Rental of Facilities

A tax-exempt educational institution may provide athletic facilities, dormitories, and other components of the campus to persons other than its students, such as for seminars or the training of professional athletes. The IRS is likely to regard revenue derived from the provision of the facilities in these circumstances as unrelated business income, particularly when the institution is providing collateral services such as meals or maintenance. A mere leasing of facilities would likely generate passive rental income that is excluded from taxation.[37] The provision of dormitory space may be an activity that is substantially related to an exempt purpose, however, as the IRS ruled in an instance of rental of dormitory rooms. The

---

[32] Rev. Rul. 67-327, 1967-2 C.B. 187. See also Rev. Rul. 84-55, 1984-1 C.B. 29, holding that the travel expenses incurred by an alumnus for participation in a university's continuing education program in foreign countries were not deductible because they were personal outlays. Cf. IRC § 170(k).

[33] This technical advice memorandum is the basis of Rev. Rul. 78-43, 1978-1 C.B. 164. The IRS revoked the tax-exempt status of a charitable organization, because of the extent of its conduct of golf and tennis tours, ostensibly undertaken in furtherance of exempt purposes. Tech. Adv. Mem. 9540002.

[34] Rev. Rul. 70-534, 1970-2 C.B. 113.

[35] Tech. Adv. Mem. 9702004.

[36] See § 9.7.

[37] See § 3.8(a).

rooms were rented primarily to individuals under the age of 25 by an exempt organization, the purpose of which was to provide for the welfare of young people.[38]

§ 9.2 HEALTH CARE PROVIDERS

Hospitals and other health care providers[39] have as their principal purpose the promotion of health. Income generated by this related activity in the form of revenue from patients (whether by means of Medicare, Medicaid, insurance, or private pay) is not subject to federal income tax.[40]

(a) Various Related Businesses

Tax-exempt hospitals operate many businesses that are necessary to achievement of their exempt purposes. Thus, an exempt hospital may operate a gift shop, which is patronized by patients, visitors making purchases for patients, and its employees, without incurring unrelated business income tax.[41] The IRS observed: "By providing a facility for the purchase of merchandise and services to improve the physical comfort and mental well-being of its patients, the hospital is carrying on an activity that encourages their recovery and therefore contributes importantly to its exempt purposes."[42] The same rationale is extended to a hospital's operation of a cafeteria and coffee shop primarily for its medical staff, other employees and visitors. In this context, maintenance of these food-service businesses for employees "enables the hospital to operate more efficiently" and "enables [visitors] to spend more time with patients," which "constitutes supportive therapy that assists in patient treatment and encourages their recovery."[43] Likewise, related businesses include an exempt hospital's operation of a parking lot for its patients and visitors,[44] and an exempt hospital's operation of a guest accommodation facility.[45]

In one instance, a tax-exempt hospital had as its primary activity the operation of a clinic that provided various rehabilitation services to handicapped individuals, including those with hearing deficiencies. The hospital tested and evaluated the hearing of its patients with the deficiencies and recommended types of hearing aids as necessary in each case. The hospital also sold hearing

---

[38] Rev. Rul. 76-33, 1976-1 C.B. 169. In general, Keeling, *Property Taxation of Colleges and Universities: The Dilemma Posed by the Use of Facilities for Purposes Unrelated to Education*, 16 J. Coll. & Univ. L. 623 (1990); Behrsin, *College and University Leasing Activities Evoke IRS Scrutiny*, 57 Taxes 431 (1979).

[39] Essentially, these are institutions referenced in IRC § 170(b)(1)(A)(iii). See *Tax-Exempt Organizations*, § 11.3(a).

[40] S. Rep. No. 2375, 81st Cong., 2d Sess. 107 (1950).

[41] Rev. Rul. 69-267, 1969-1 C.B. 160.

[42] *Id.*

[43] Rev. Rul. 69-268, 1969-1 C.B. 160.

[44] Rev. Rul. 69-269, 1969-1 C.B. 160. Also Ellis Hosp. v. Fredette, 279 N.Y.S. 925 (N.Y. 1967); Rev. Rul. 81-29, 1981-1 C.B. 329.

[45] Priv. Ltr. Rul. 9404029. In holding that the operation of a motel by a supporting organization of a university's medical center (including a hospital), for the benefit of patients and their relatives and friends, was a related business, the IRS observed that "[p]roviding a temporary living facility for patients and their friends or family members . . . advances one of the purposes of the hospital which is to provide health care for members of the community." Tech. Adv. Mem. 9847002.

aids and fitted them to ensure maximum assistance to the patients in the correction or alleviation of their hearing deficiencies. The IRS ruled that the sale of hearing aids as an integral part of the hospital's program was not an unrelated business, because it "contributes importantly to the organization's purpose of promoting the health of such persons."[46] Likewise, the IRS determined that a hospital was not conducting an unrelated business when it allowed its physicians and facilities to be used in reading and diagnosing electrocardiogram tests for an exempt hospital that lacked the physicians and facilities to provide the service.[47] Similarly, an exempt health care provider was held not to be engaging in an unrelated trade or business when it provided supplemental staffing services to hospitals and nursing homes.[48] Further, an exempt hospital was ruled to be operating outpatient clinics (faculty physician practices) as a related business.[49]

The *convenience doctrine*—applicable with respect to businesses that are conducted for the benefit of a tax-exempt organization's patients—is of considerable import in the health care setting.[50] The IRS has defined the term *patient* of a health care provider.[51]

A tax-exempt hospital may be able to develop real estate by constructing condominium residences, to be used as short-term living quarters by its patients, as a related business.[52] The provision of ancillary health care services by charitable health care providers, by means of a health maintenance organization (an exempt social welfare entity[53]), and with income in the form of capitated payments for the services of employee-physicians and independent-contractor physicians, was ruled to be a related business.[54]

(b) Sales of Pharmaceuticals

The sale of pharmaceutical supplies, by a tax-exempt hospital, to private patients of physicians who have offices in a medical building owned by the hospital is considered by the IRS to constitute the conduct of an unrelated business.[55] The agency also outlined circumstances in which an exempt hospital derives unrelated business income from the sale of pharmaceutical supplies to the general public.[56] In contrast, the sale of pharmaceutical supplies by a hospital pharmacy to the hospital's patients is not the conduct of an unrelated trade or business.

A federal court of appeals considered this issue and concluded that sales of pharmaceuticals by a tax-exempt hospital to members of the general public gave

---

[46] Rev. Rul. 78-435, 1978-2 C.B. 181.
[47] Priv. Ltr. Rul. 8004011.
[48] Tech. Adv. Mem. 9405004.
[49] Priv. Ltr. Rul. 200211051.
[50] See § 4.1.
[51] Rev. Rul. 68-376, 1968-2 C.B. 246.
[52] Priv. Ltr. Rul. 8427105.
[53] See *Tax-Exempt Organizations*, ch. 12.
[54] Priv. Ltr. Rul. 9837031.
[55] Rev. Rul. 68-375, 1968-2 C.B. 245. *Cf.* Rev. Rul. 69-463, 1969-2 C.B. 131 (holding that a lease, by an exempt hospital, of some of its facilities to an association of physicians to use as a clinic was a related activity. See § 3.8(c).
[56] Rev. Rul. 68-374, 1968-2 C.B. 242.

rise to unrelated business income.[57] The concept of the *general public* encompassed the private patients of the hospital-based physicians, on the rationale that sales by the pharmacy to the patients were related to the purchaser's visit to his or her private physician at offices rented from the hospital and were not related to the use of services provided by the hospital. Another consideration was that exempt hospital-operated pharmacies unfairly compete with commercial pharmacies.

By contrast, another appellate court concluded that sales of pharmaceuticals, by a tax-exempt hospital, to nonhospital private patients of physicians located in the hospital did not produce unrelated business income; the sales were important in attracting and retaining physicians in a community that had lacked any medical services for eight years before the establishment of the hospital.[58] This appellate court ruled that the trial court was in error in defining the organization's function solely as that of providing a hospital, and held that another purpose was to attract physicians to the community and provide facilities to retain them. Thus, this appellate court concluded that the "availability of the hospital's pharmacy for use by the doctor's private patients is causally related to inducing doctors to practice" at the hospital.[59] The court distinguished this case from the holding of the other court of appeals, stating that the facts in the previous case "give no indication that the hospital had any difficulty in attracting doctors to its staff."[60]

(c) Testing Services

The IRS regards the performance of diagnostic laboratory testing, by a tax-exempt hospital, on specimens from private patients of the hospital's staff physicians, generally constitutes unrelated business, if such services are otherwise available in the community.[61] The agency concluded that there was no substantial causal relationship between achievement of a hospital's exempt purposes and provision of the testing to nonpatients, and that there were commercial laboratories that could perform the testing services on a timely basis. Nonetheless, the IRS noted that "unique circumstances" may exist that would cause the testing to be a related activity: Such circumstances could include emergency laboratory diagnosis of blood samples from nonpatient drug overdose or poisoning victims, in order to identify specific toxic agents, when referral of these specimens to other locations would be detrimental to the health of hospital nonpatients; or situations in which other laboratories are not available within a reasonable distance from the area served by the hospital or are clearly unable or inadequate to conduct the tests needed by hospital nonpatients.[62]

---

[57] Carle Found. v. United States, 611 F.2d 1192 (7th Cir. 1979), *cert. denied*, 449 U.S. 824 (1980).

[58] Hi-Plains Hosp. v. United States, 670 F.2d 528 (5th Cir. 1982), *rev'g & remanding* 81-1 U.S.T.C. ¶ 9214 (N.D. Tex. 1981).

[59] *Id.* at 531.

[60] *Id.* at 533.

[61] Rev. Rul. 85-110, 1985-2 CB. 166.

[62] *Id.* at 168. Laboratory testing services provided by a tax-exempt university's dental school were ruled to be related activities because a unique type of diagnostic dental service and testing was provided, and no commercial laboratories provided a comparable service. Priv. Ltr. Rul. 9739043.

A court held that income received by a tax-exempt teaching and research hospital for the performance of pathological diagnostic tests on samples submitted by physicians associated with the hospital was not unrelated business income.[63] The court found that the performance and interpretation of these outside pathology tests by the hospital's pathology department were substantially related to the hospital's performance of its exempt functions, because the tests contributed importantly to the hospital's teaching activities. Further, the court concluded that the testing was a related activity because it increased the physicians' confidence in the quality of the work performed by the pathology department and it was convenient in the event of surgery, in that the pathologist who interpreted the test could interpret the biopsy.[64]

From time to time, the IRS rules that analysis and testing activities conducted by tax-exempt hospitals and other exempt health care entities in laboratories are the conduct of exempt functions.[65]

(d) Fitness Centers and Health Clubs

Another area of controversy is whether fitness centers and health clubs, operated as a program of a tax-exempt hospital, are unrelated businesses. In this context, the IRS looks to the breadth of the group of individuals being served. If the fees for use of a health club are sufficiently high to restrict use of the club's facilities to a limited segment of a community, operation of the club will not be exempt—that is, it will constitute an unrelated business.[66] By contrast, when the health club provides a community-wide benefit for the community the organization serves, operation of the club will be an exempt function (related business).[67] This latter position is predicated on the rule in the general law of charity that promotion of the happiness and enjoyment of members of the community is considered to be a charitable purpose.[68] In one instance, the IRS blended these two definitions of *charity* in finding that a health club was exempt because its "operations promote health in a manner which is collateral to the providing of recreational facilities which advances the well-being and happiness of the community in general."[69] Similarly, a fitness center was held to be exempt because it furthered accomplishment of certain other programs of the health organization that operated it (including an occupational and physical therapy program); its facilities and programs were specially designed for the needs of the handicapped and the treatment plans of patients in other programs; its fee structure

---

[63] St. Luke's Hosp. of Kan. City v. United States, 494 F. Supp. 85 (W.D. Mo. 1980). The IRS agreed to follow this aspect of the decision. Rev. Rul. 85-109, 1985-2 C.B. 165.

[64] Also Anateus Lineal 1948, Inc. v. United States, 366 F. Supp. 85 (W.D. Ark. 1973). In general, see Mancino, *The Unrelated Business Income Taxation of Nonprofit Hospitals,* 4 *Exempt Orgs. Tax Rev.* 35 (no. 1, 1991); Kannry, *How Hospitals Can Minimize Their Potential Exposure to the Unrelated Business Income Tax,* 43 *J. Tax'n* 166 (1975).

[65] *E.g.,* Priv. Ltr. Rul. 9851054.

[66] Rev. Rul. 79-360, 1979-2 C.B. 236.

[67] Tech. Adv. Mem. 8505002.

[68] *Restatement (Second) of Trusts* § 374 (1959); 4 Scott, *The Law of Trusts* § 374.10 (3d ed. 1967).

[69] Tech. Adv. Mem. 8505002. A similar facility operated by a university was ruled to constitute related business activities. Priv. Ltr. Rul. 9732032.

was designed to make it available to the general public; and it offered a range of programs and activities that focused on wellness.[70]

In another instance, a health care provider of rehabilitative services developed a full-service preventive health care and rehabilitation facility. It consisted of health resources, physical development and rehabilitation, outpatient services, physician offices, and a chapel. The facilities included a gymnasium, track, warm-water hydrotherapy pool, lap pool, natatorium, racquetball and squash courts, health resources library, physical development equipment, aerobic studio rooms, exercise areas, massage therapy area, and several areas dedicated to education classes, including a demonstration kitchen. The facility further included a pro shop and a café. The organization provided rehabilitation services to its patients, offered extensive community education and prevention programs, and had a pricing policy that enabled all segments of the community to be represented in its membership. The IRS ruled that these operations consisted of charitable and educational undertakings.[71]

(e) Physical Rehabilitation Programs

Organizations that maintain physical rehabilitation programs often provide housing and other services that are available commercially. Nevertheless, the IRS ruled that an organization that provided specially designed housing to physically handicapped individuals at the lowest feasible cost, and maintained in residence those tenants who subsequently became unable to pay the monthly fees, was a tax-exempt charitable entity.[72] The agency similarly ruled that rental to individuals under the age of 25, and low-income individuals of all ages, of dormitory rooms and similar residential accommodations was a related business.[73] The IRS likewise ruled that a halfway house, organized to provide room, board, therapy, and counseling for individuals discharged from alcoholic treatment centers, was an exempt charitable organization; its operation of a furniture shop to provide full-time employment centers for its residents was considered a related business.[74] Also, the IRS ruled that an organization that provided a residence facility and therapeutic group living program for individuals recently released from a mental institution was an exempt charitable organization.[75] An organization with the purpose of providing rehabilitative and prevocational counseling to the handicapped and developmentally disabled received an IRS ruling that its residential and day care facilities were related activities.[76] Another entity, a charitable organization that maintained nursing homes and ancillary health facilities, was ruled to be engaged in the following related businesses: programs offering physical therapy, occupational therapy, speech therapy, injury

---

[70] Priv. Ltr. Rul. 9329041.
[71] Priv. Ltr. Rul. 200101036.
[72] Rev. Rul. 79-19, 1979-1 C.B. 195.
[73] Rev. Rul. 76-33, 1976-1 C.B. 169.
[74] Rev. Rul. 75-472, 1975-2 C.B. 208.
[75] Rev. Rul. 72-16, 1972-1 C.B. 143.
[76] Priv. Ltr. Rul. 9335061.

prevention, pediatric services, and adult care, as well as the provision of day care for the organization's employees.[77]

Lifestyle rehabilitation programs can also present this dichotomy. For example, the IRS ruled that the operation of a miniature golf course in a commercial manner by a tax-exempt organization, the purpose of which was to provide for the welfare of young people, constituted an unrelated trade or business.[78] The agency also ruled, however, that an exempt organization, formed to improve the lives of abused and otherwise disadvantaged children by means of the sport and business of golf, did not conduct an unrelated activity in operation of a golf course, because the opportunity to socialize and master skills through playing the game were "essential to the building of self-esteem and the ultimate rehabilitation of the young people" in the organization's programs.[79]

(f) Other Health Care Activities

In other instances, the IRS ruled that the rental of pagers to staff physicians by a tax-exempt hospital is not an unrelated business;[80] the sale by an exempt hospital of silver recovered from x-ray film is not an unrelated activity;[81] and the leasing of space and the furnishing of services to practitioners is not an unrelated undertaking by the exempt lessors.[82] Still other related businesses in the health care setting are operation of mobile cancer screening units;[83] sales and rentals of durable medical equipment to patients of an exempt health care organization;[84] the provision by an exempt hospital of services such as ultrasound and general radiology, outpatient dialysis, acute dialysis, critical life support, home health, occupational health, electrocardiogram computer, wellness and prevention, employee physicals, and storage of medical and administrative records;[85] the operation of home care services;[86] the operation of an adult foster care home;[87] the transfer to and operation of blood-related clinical service programs by a charitable organization;[88] and the operation of an assisted living facility.[89]

The provision of services by and among organizations within a tax-exempt hospital system, such as the leasing of property and the sale of services, generally will not give rise to unrelated business income.[90] Designation of an exempt health care provider as the preferred provider of services for patients of another charitable organization and its statewide affiliates is not the creation of an

---

[77] Priv. Ltr. Rul. 9241055.
[78] Rev. Rul. 79-361, 1979-2 C.B. 237.
[79] Priv. Ltr. Rul. 8626080.
[80] Tech. Adv. Mem. 8452011.
[81] Tech. Adv. Mem. 8452012.
[82] Priv. Ltr. Rul. 8452099.
[83] Priv. Ltr. Rul. 8749085.
[84] Priv. Ltr. Rul. 8736046.
[85] *E.g.*, Priv. Ltr. Rul. 8736046.
[86] *E.g.*, Priv. Ltr. Rul. 9822039. In general, see Hyatt & Hopkins, *The Law of Tax-Exempt Healthcare Organizations* (John Wiley & Sons, 2001) [hereinafter *Tax-Exempt Healthcare Organizations*], ch. 10.
[87] Priv. Ltr. Rul. 199943053.
[88] Priv. Ltr. Rul. 199946036.
[89] Priv. Ltr. Rul. 199946037.
[90] *E.g.*, Priv. Ltr. Rul. 8822065.

unrelated business.[91] The operation of a call center by an exempt ambulance service provider was ruled to be a related business.[92]

§ 9.3 MUSEUMS

Tax-exempt museums operate related businesses when they maintain collections and make them accessible to the general public. Admissions fees and the like are income from related business.

(a) General Operations

Some exempt museum business operations are nontaxable by reason of the lines of law concerning exempt health care organizations, pertaining to parking lots, snack bars, and the like.[93] The operation of a dining room, cafeteria, and snack bar by an exempt museum, for use by its staff, employees, and members of the public, usually are related activities.[94] The elements the IRS prefers to find in this context are eating facilities that are of a size commensurate with accommodation of only the museum's patrons, facilities that are accessible from the galleries but not directly from the street, no solicitation of patronage of the facilities by the general public, and dedication of any profits to the museum's exempt purposes. Food-service operations of this nature are considered related businesses when they are merely "convenient eating places" for visitors (to enable them to devote maximum time and attention to the collection) and employees (to enable efficient operation of the museum), as opposed to endeavors "designed to serve as a public restaurant."[95]

The IRS ruled that a tax-exempt museum may operate an art conservation laboratory, and perform conservation work for other institutions and collectors for a fee, without incurring unrelated business income.[96] Likewise, the agency ruled that a museum store may sell items in furtherance of the exempt museum's exempt purpose, other than those that have utilitarian purposes.[97]

(b) Retail Sales Activities

One of the most difficult issues presented by tax-exempt museum operations in the unrelated trade or business context concerns sales to the general public. For example, when an exempt museum sells to the public greeting cards displaying reproductions of works from the museum's collection and from other art collections, the sales activity is substantially related to the museum's exempt purpose. This is so even if a large volume of cards is sold at a significant profit. The rationale for this

---

[91] Priv. Ltr. Rul. 9839040.
[92] Priv. Ltr. Rul. 200222031. In general, *Tax-Exempt Healthcare Organizations*, particularly ch. 24.
[93] See § 9.2.
[94] Rev. Rul. 74-399, 1974-2 C.B. 172. *Cf.* Rev. Rul. 69-268, 1969-1 C.B. 160 (holding that an exempt hospital may operate a cafeteria and coffee shop, primarily for the medical staff and other employees, without engaging in unrelated business).
[95] *E.g.*, Priv. Ltr. Rul. 200222030. The IRS, however, is not this tolerant outside the museum setting. *E.g.*, Tech. Adv. Mem. 200021056, holding that a gift shop and tearoom operated in conjunction with an exempt craft and foodstuff business were unrelated activities.
[96] Priv. Ltr. Rul. 8432004.
[97] Tech. Adv. Mem. 8605002.

conclusion is that (1) sale of the cards "contributes importantly to the achievement of the museum's exempt educational purposes[,] by stimulating and enhancing public awareness, interest, and appreciation of art"; and (2) a "broader segment of the public may be encouraged to visit the museum itself to share in its educational functions and programs as a result of seeing the cards."[98]

The IRS applies the fragmentation rule[99] to segment the retailing activities of tax-exempt museums.[100] For example, exempt museums traditionally sell greeting cards, slides, instructional literature, and metal, wood, and ceramic copies of artworks. Some museums sell souvenirs, novelty items, clothing, and the like; these items usually have no causal relationship to art.[101] To the extent that the items being sold are "expensive," "lavish," or otherwise "luxury" items, there is a greater likelihood that the IRS will presume the sales activity to be an unrelated business.

When an item sold by a tax-exempt museum is priced at a "low cost,"[102] and bears the museum's logo, the IRS generally finds the sales activity to be related, because these items enhance public awareness of and encourage greater visitation to the museum. Again, however, as the price of items bearing a museum's logo increases, so too will the likelihood that the agency will find the sales activity to be substantially unrelated to the museum's exempt purposes. The sale of, for example, clothing bearing a reference to one or more items in a museum's collection is substantially related to the museum's exempt purposes, irrespective of the price paid for the clothing, as it publicizes the museum and attracts visitors. By contrast, sales at a price mre than "low" of clothing bearing only the museum's logo are regarded by the IRS as unrelated business.

The IRS draws a distinction between museum *reproductions* and *adaptations*. For the most part, the agency considers sales of reproductions to be sales that are related to the museum's tax-exempt purposes, although the IRS may resist reaching that conclusion when the items, though copies of items originally created by master period craftsmen, are not contemporaneously made in a manner commensurate with the period. The IRS is more likely to question the relatedness of sales of *adaptations*, which are items that may incorporate or reflect original art but differ significantly in form from the original work. Nonetheless, an adaptation may have intrinsic artistic merit or historical significance in its adaptive form (so that a sale of it by an exempt museum is a related activity), or it may feature an exempt museum's logo or otherwise reference the museum (so that it enhances public awareness of the museum and encourages the public to visit the museum, thereby making the sale of it a related activity).

In applying the fragmentation rule, the IRS may attempt to determine the motivation underlying a tax-exempt museum's sale of an item. For example, the agency's general counsel advised the IRS that it should apply a test to determine

---

[98] Rev. Rul. 73-104, 1973-1 C.B. 263.

[99] See § 2.3.

[100] Rev. Rul. 73-105, 1973-1 C.B. 264.

[101] The fact that some of these items may, in a different context, be related to another organization's educational purposes does not change the conclusion that the sales do not contribute importantly to a museum's exempt purposes.

[102] Reg. § 1.513-1(b). See § 4.9.

whether the primary purpose of the article sold is utilitarian.[103] According to this test, if the "primary purpose of the article is utilitarian and the utilitarian aspects are the predominant reasons for the production and sale of the article, it should not be considered related." Conversely, if the "utilitarian or ornamental aspects are merely incidental to the article's relation to an exempt purpose, then the article should be considered related." In most instances, the IRS will conclude that a tax-exempt museum regularly sells both related and unrelated items. The agency's counsel readily admitted that application of the utilitarian standard is easiest when "reproductions or adaptations of items contained in the [m]useum's collection" are considered (sales of them are clearly related), or when "items of a souvenir, trivial, or convenience nature" are considered (sales of these are clearly unrelated). "The difficult task," conceded the IRS counsel, "lies in identifying those items that raise classification problems, such as those that are arguably reproductions with utilitarian, ornamental, or decorative aspects and those that present an interpretation of some theme related to an exempt purpose."

The museum evaluated by the IRS counsel and the IRS agreed that the items sold in the museum could be classified as follows: (1) replicas or reproductions of items or artifacts in the collections or exhibitions; (2) reproductions, adaptations, or examples of items that are not on exhibit, but that are representative of, and designed to encourage interest in, historical periods or artistic, scientific, or technological developments featured in the museum collections, or that are related to areas of museum involvement; (3) artworks and craft works by artists, or by native and/or foreign groups, whose works are in the collections or have been included in museum exhibitions; (4) arts and crafts items representing similar forms that can be found in the various museum collections and designed to illustrate the techniques and historical development of these forms; (5) arts and crafts kits, tools, and instruments designed to encourage a personal experience of various arts and crafts forms; (6) books and records relating to art, science, history, and other areas of museum involvement; (7) educational toys and games for children, based on museum exhibits or relating to areas of museum involvement; (8) scientific and aviation models, tools and specimens, and other educational items that encourage interest and personal participation in the sciences; (9) posters, postcards, note cards, and calendars, with photographs, drawings, or depictions relating to areas of museum involvement; (10) souvenirs of the museum; and (11) convenience items. The IRS counsel did not attempt to classify the sale of each of these categories of items as related or unrelated business, but instead observed that "[t]hese judgments are not, of course, easy to make."

Thus, the IRS, in application of the fragmentation rule, also applies a primary purpose test. If the article sold by a tax-exempt museum is predominantly utilitarian, sales of that article produce unrelated income, as is the case with items sold primarily to generate income. If an article is primarily related to the museum's exempt function and any utilitarian aspects are incidental, sales income is related business income. This guideline was provided: "If the primary purpose of an article that interprets some facet of the [m]useum's collection is to

---

[103] Gen. Couns. Mem. 38949.

encourage personal learning experiences about the [m]useum's collection[,] even though not an accurate depiction of an item in the collection, the article should be considered related."

The IRS's current emphasis in this regard is on the primary purpose for the production and sale of each item by the museum. As noted, the sale of reproductions of items found in the collection is not an unrelated business, as are sales of adaptations of artistic utilitarian items in the collection (particularly when the items are sold with descriptive literature illustrating their artistic, cultural, or historic connections with the museum's collections or exhibits). Museum sales of original art or craft may, however, be unrelated business, as these activities are inconsistent with the purpose of exhibiting art for the public benefit.[104]

The IRS again addressed the tax treatment of retail sales of items by a tax-exempt museum in 1986.[105] In that instance, the IRS inventoried the various items sold by the museum, fragmenting them into categories such as furniture, china, fabrics, wallpaper, lamps, note cards, cooking accessories, handicrafts, and gift items. The IRS observed that, to be exempt from the tax on unrelated business income, items sold in museum gift shops must be substantially related to accomplishment of the museum's exempt purpose. This relationship, said the agency, "must extend specifically to the particular subject matter of the museum in which the items are sold[,] as contrasted to being educational generally." The IRS added: "The characterization of a sales activity as an unrelated trade or business does not hinge on whether the activities may have a commercial hue or are in competition with for-profit entities such as furniture stores, or roadside gift stands offering souvenir items with a regional flavor."

In this instance, the IRS said that the museum's retail sales inventory should be evaluated in the context of its tax-exempt purpose (which was to preserve and protect the cultural and historical heritage unique to a particular city in the seventeenth through nineteenth centuries). The agency analyzed the various categories of items, finding the sale of nearly all of them related. All of the furniture sales were held to be related activities because of the items' educational value, despite the fact that the "items are sturdy enough for practical use in the home." The sales of china were found related because of the design of the items and accompanying descriptive literature. The sales of fabric and wallpaper were deemed related because of the original designs and derivations from documented research. Lamp sales were related, despite the "utilitarian adaptation of the modern electric lamps from various artifacts," because the original design was not distorted. Most of the sales of the other items were held related because of authenticated design motifs, decorations portraying historical scenes, and/or accompanying literature. This rationale embraced chandeliers, artwork, kitchen accessories, cookbooks, lawn furniture, toys, and games. The only sales found to be unrelated were those of a cast iron trivet (merely bearing the museum's logo), soaps, colognes, and bath oils.

---

[104] Priv. Ltr. Rul. 8326008. On this last point, *cf.* Goldsboro Art League v. Comm'r, 75 T.C. 337 (1980) (art sales activities of an arts organization were found to be incidental and secondary in relation to overall exempt purposes).

[105] Tech. Adv. Mem. 8605002.

(c) Catalog and Off-Site Sales

The just-referenced museum did more than sell at retail from its store; it also engaged in catalog sales. Applying the fragmentation rule, the IRS found that the catalog operation itself was a tax-exempt function, in that it was of educational value because it featured articles and illustrations generally supportive of the museum's exempt purpose. The IRS rejected the view that income from catalog sales should be divided into related and unrelated income on an allocable basis in relation to the listing of related and unrelated items.

In technical advice made public thereafter, the IRS once again (in 1995) had occasion to review the tax treatment of sales of items by a tax-exempt museum.[106] As before, the agency stated that a museum's primary purpose for selling a particular item is determinative of whether the sale is a related or unrelated activity. Thus, when the primary purpose behind the production and sale of an item is to further the organization's exempt purpose, the sale is a related one. In a departure from previous pronouncements, however, the IRS added that this is the case even though the item has a utilitarian function or value.[107] By contrast, when the primary purpose underlying production and sale of an item is to generate income, the activity is an unrelated business. On this occasion, the IRS listed various factors to be considered in ascertaining this primary purpose, including (1) the degree of connection between the item and the museum's collection, (2) the extent to which the item relates to the form and design of the original item, and (3) the overall impression conveyed by the article. If the "dominant impression" individuals gain from viewing or using the article relates to the subject matter of the original article, picture, or likeness, substantial relatedness would be established. If the noncharitable use or function predominates, however, the sale is an unrelated business activity.

In this case, the IRS addressed the fact that many of the museum's sales are off-site. The agency wrote that the museum has "many outlets and utilizes many vehicles to advertise and sell its wares, namely, retail stores, gift shops, an outlet located in another city, mail order catalogues, advertisements in various publications, a corporate/conference program," and more. The IRS held, however, that the sole fact that sales are off-site does not make them unrelated; this is true even when the sales are made in a commercial manner and in competition with for-profit companies. The reason: The off-site sales enhance a broader segment of the public's understanding of the collection and may encourage more individuals to visit the museum.

In another of these instances, a tax-exempt museum that sponsored programs for children also maintained a shop. The IRS found that the sales of certain tots' and children's items constituted unrelated businesses. Nonetheless, items that were reproductions or adaptations of articles displayed in the museum's collections and exhibits were held salable in related business. The agency reiterated its general stand that when the primary purpose behind production and sale of an

---

[106] Tech. Adv. Mem. 9550003.
[107] See text accompanied by *supra* note 103.

item is utilitarian, or the item is an ornamental souvenir in nature, or only generally educational, the sale constitutes unrelated business.[108]

§ 9.4 ASSOCIATIONS

A tax-exempt association (or, technically, business league[109]) is subject to the unrelated business rules. The basic related business function of an exempt association is the provision of services to its members in exchange for dues; thus, income in the form of members' dues and similar assessments is related revenue.

(a) Services to Members

The IRS ruled that a variety of services performed by tax-exempt associations for their members are unrelated businesses.[110] Illustrations of this rule include the sale of equipment by an exempt association to its members;[111] the management of health and welfare plans for a fee by an exempt business league;[112] the provision of insurance to members of an exempt association;[113] the operation of an executive referral service;[114] the publication of ordinary commercial advertising for products and services used by the legal profession in an exempt bar association's journal;[115] the conduct of a language translation service by an exempt trade association that promoted international trade relations;[116] the publication and sale, by an exempt association of credit unions to its members, of a consumer-oriented magazine designed as a promotional device for distribution to the members' depositors;[117] the provision of mediation and arbitration services by an exempt business league;[118] advertising and administrative services provided by an exempt business league with respect to a for-profit discount purchasing service;[119] and the operation by an exempt association of members in the trucking industry of an alcohol and drug testing program for both members and nonmembers.[120]

Nonetheless, the IRS is not always successful in this regard, as illustrated by a court's finding that the sales of preprinted lease forms and landlord's manuals by a tax-exempt association of apartment owners and managers was a related activity.[121] By contrast, the agency concluded that the sale, at a discount, of television time to governmental and nonprofit organizations by an exempt association of television stations was a related business.[122]

---

[108] Tech. Adv. Mem. 9720002.

[109] See *Tax-Exempt Organizations*, ch. 13.

[110] *Id.* § 13.4.

[111] Rev. Rul. 66-338, 1966-2 C.B. 226.

[112] Rev. Rul. 66-151, 1966-1 C.B. 152.

[113] Rev. Rul. 74-81, 1974-1 C.B. 135.

[114] Tech. Adv. Mem. 8524006.

[115] Rev. Rul. 82-139, 1982-2 C.B. 108. In this ruling, the IRS also held that the publication of legal notices by an exempt bar association was not an unrelated trade or business.

[116] Rev. Rul. 81-75, 1981-1 C.B. 356.

[117] Rev. Rul. 78-52, 1978-1 C.B. 166.

[118] Priv. Ltr. Rul. 9408002.

[119] Tech. Adv. Mem. 9440001.

[120] Tech. Adv. Mem. 9550001.

[121] Tex. Apartment Ass'n v. United States, 869 F.2d 884 (5th Cir. 1989).

[122] Priv. Ltr. Rul. 9023081.

Sometimes there is a conflict between the IRS and the courts in this area. For example, the sale of standard legal forms by a local bar association to its member lawyers, which purchased the forms from the state bar association, was ruled by the IRS to be an unrelated business, because the activity did not contribute importantly to accomplishment of the association's exempt functions.[123] A court held, however, that the sale of standard real estate legal forms to lawyers and law students by an exempt bar association was an exempt function, because it promoted the common business interests of the legal profession and improved the relationship among the bench, bar, and public.[124]

In one instance, the IRS examined seven activities of a tax-exempt trade association and found all of them to be productive of unrelated income. These activities were the sale of vehicle signs to members, the sale to members of embossed tags for inventory control purposes, the sale to members of supplies and forms, the sale to members of kits to enable them to retain sales tax information, the sale of price guides, the administration of a group insurance program, and the sale of commercial advertising in the association's publications. Moreover, because the majority of the organization's income was derived from these activities, and the majority of the time of the organization's employees was devoted to them, the agency revoked the association's tax exemption.[125]

(b) Insurance Programs

It is common for a tax-exempt association to be involved in the provision of various forms of insurance for its members. The state of the law on this point is that nearly any form of insurance program of an association—endorsement or otherwise—is an unrelated activity.

A tax-exempt association can become involved in insurance programs in several ways. An association may have little relationship to an insurance offering other than making its name and membership records available to the insurer. It may endorse a particular insurance policy or have a role in the processing of claims. By contrast, the exempt association may be directly involved in the management of an insurance program, or it may operate a self-insurance fund. The insurance coverage (on a group basis or otherwise) may range over life, health, disability, legal liability, workers' compensation, product liability, and similar areas. The insureds may be the association's employees, members, and/or employees of members.

At the outset of the evolution of the law on this issue, an insurance company's provision of insurance coverage for a tax-exempt association's members (and/or its employees), when the association was the mere sponsor, appeared to be minimal involvement of the association in the insurance process that did not amount to an unrelated trade or business. In one instance, an exempt association provided an insurance company with information about its membership, mailed a letter about the insurance coverage, and allowed the insurer to use the association's name and insignia on brochures. For this, the association received

---

[123] Rev. Rul. 78-51, 1978-1 C.B. 165.
[124] San Antonio Bar Ass'n v. United States, 80-2 U.S.T.C. ¶ 9594 (W.D. Tex. 1980).
[125] Priv. Ltr. Rul. 7902006.

a percentage of the premiums paid by its members to the insurance company. When the matter was litigated, the court concluded that the association was merely passively involved and thus that the activity did not become a trade or business.[126] Another court concluded that this type of remuneration, sometimes euphemistically termed an *administrative allowance*, paid to an exempt association for its efforts in administering an accident and health insurance program for its members, did not constitute unrelated income, because the association's activities in this regard did not rise to the level of a business; this holding, however, was reversed.[127] Similar logic was applied in a decision regarding fees received by an exempt business league in return for its sponsorship of a bank payment plan made available to its members.[128]

Today, however, it is clear that when a tax-exempt association actively and regularly manages an insurance program for its members, for a fee, and a substantial portion of its income and expenses is traceable to the activity, the IRS will regard the management undertaking as an unrelated business. This has essentially been the IRS's position from the beginning.[129] The agency initially permitted exempt associations to escape taxation of insurance income by structuring the payments as royalties,[130] but subsequently reversed its position and ruled that such payments are taxable income for the rendering of unrelated services.[131] If the provision of insurance is an association's sole or principal activity, the IRS will deny recognition of, or deprive the association of, tax exemption, as illustrated by the denial of exemption to an organization that provided group workers' compensation insurance to its members[132] and to an organization that provided insurance and similar plans for its members.[133]

The approach of the courts in this area is essentially the same as that of the IRS. The Court of Claims, for example, found that a significant portion of an association's income was derived from the performance of services to members, including billing and collecting insurance premiums and distributing claim forms (with the association's income set as a percentage of premiums collected); it therefore held that the association did not qualify for tax exemption.[134] The Tax Court adopted a like rationale, combining insurance activities with the sale of educational materials, jewelry, emblems, and supplies to conclude that an association failed to qualify for tax exemption because of substantial unrelated

---

[126] Okla. Cattlemen's Ass'n, Inc. v. United States, 310 F. Supp. 320 (W.D. Okla. 1969).

[127] Carolinas Farm & Power Equip. Dealers Ass'n, Inc. v. United States, 541 F. Supp. 86 (E.D.N.C. 1982), *aff'd*, 699 F.2d 167 (4th Cir. 1983).

[128] San Antonio Dist. Dental Soc'y v. United States, 340 F. Supp. 11 (W.D. Tex. 1972).

[129] *E.g.*, Rev. Rul. 66-151, 1966-1 C.B. 152. Also Rev. Rul. 60-228, 1960-1 C.B. 200 (holding that an exempt agricultural organization engaged in unrelated business when it rendered services to insurance companies and performed certain property management services).

[130] See § 3.1. This IRS position was stated in Priv. Ltr. Rul. 8828011.

[131] Priv. Ltr. Rul. 9029047. In reaching this conclusion, the IRS took into consideration not only the insurance-related activities of the association, but also the activities of its agent, which the IRS attributed to the association under the authority of National Water Well Ass'n, Inc. v. Commissioner, 92 T.C. 75 (1989). Further, the IRS held that the membership list exception (see § 4.10) governed the tax consequences of the transaction, in that the payments for services were inseparable from payments for use of the association's membership list; however, the IRS held that the exception was unavailable.

[132] Rev. Rul. 76-81, 1976-1 C.B. 156.

[133] Rev. Rul. 67-176, 1967-1 C.B. 140.

[134] Ind. Retail Hardware Ass'n v. United States, 366 F.2d 998 (Ct. Cl. 1966).

business.[135] This decision was followed by a holding that the promotional and administrative fees received by an exempt association of independent insurance agents, for the promotion of group insurance programs for its members, constituted unrelated business income.[136]

One of the first courts to rule directly on the point upheld the IRS position. The court determined that a commission paid to a tax-exempt organization on the writing of new and renewal insurance policies by an insurance company, the coverage plans of which the organization endorsed, was unrelated business income.[137] Subsequently, the Tax Court echoed that decision, holding that the promotional and administrative fees received by an exempt business league from insurance companies, for the sponsorship of insurance programs for the benefit of its members, were taxable as unrelated income.[138] In so holding, the Tax Court rejected the reasoning of the two decisions finding that this type of income is merely passively derived and thus not taxable.[139] The court held that because the activity was engaged in with the intent to earn a profit, the activity must be considered a trade or business.[140] Also, the court was of the view that the enactment in 1969 of a statutory definition of the term *trade or business* overruled the passive income concept utilized in the other cases.[141] An appellate court agreed, holding that an organization was engaged in a taxable business because it "engaged in extensive activity over a substantial period of time with intent to earn a profit."[142]

Thus, the remaining major substantive issue in this area is no longer whether a tax-exempt association can have its tax status adversely affected by, or must treat as an unrelated trade or business, the active conduct of an insurance program; the issue is whether there is a way for an association to be only passively involved in an insurance activity. The IRS does not believe the court decision finding this passive involvement[143] to be correct. Rather, the agency is of the view that initiation of an insurance program by an association, negotiation with the broker, and general support of and promotion of the program are services provided to the association's members, in their private capacities, and thus is an unrelated business.[144] Consequently, in the view of the IRS, once the insurance

---

[135] Associated Master Barbers & Beauticians of Am., Inc. v. Comm'r, 69 T.C. 53 (1977).

[136] Prof'l Ins. Agents of Mich. v. Comm'r, 78 T.C. 246 (1982), *aff'd*, 726 F.2d 1097 (6th Cir. 1984). Also Prof'l Ins. Agents of Wash. v. Comm'r, 53 T.C.M. 9 (1987); Long Island Gasoline Retailers Ass'n, Inc. v. Comm'r, 43 T.C.M. 815 (1982).

[137] La. Credit Union League v. United States, 501 F. Supp. 934 (E.D. La. 1980), *aff'd*, 693 F.2d 525 (5th Cir. 1982).

[138] Prof'l Ins. Agents of Mich. v. Comm'r, 78 T.C. 246 (1982).

[139] See *supra* notes 126–127.

[140] See § 2.2.

[141] *Id.*

[142] Prof'l Ins. Agents of Mich. v. Comm'r, 726 F.2d 1097, 1102 (6th Cir. 1984). Also Prof'l Ins. Agents of Wash. v. Comm'r, 53 T.C.M. 9 (1987); Tex. Farm Bureau v. United States, 822 F. Supp. 371 (W.D. Tex. 1993), *aff'd in part, rev'd in part*, 95-1 U.S.T.C. ¶ 50,297 (5th Cir. 1995); Indep. Ins. Agents of Huntsville, Inc. v. Comm'r, 63 T.C.M. 2468 (1992), *aff'd*, 998 F.2d 898 (11th Cir. 1993); Ill. Ass'n of Prof'l Ins. Agents, Inc. v. Comm'r, 49 T.C.M. 924 (1985).

[143] See *supra* note 126.

[144] *E.g.*, Priv. Ltr. Rul. 7840014.

activity rises to the level of a business,[145] it is an unrelated activity, and all association insurance activities constitute more than mere passive involvements.[146]

One solution may be to have the insurance program conducted by a separate entity, such as a trust or corporation, albeit controlled by the parent tax-exempt association. This approach requires care to ensure that the separate entity is in fact a true legal entity, with its own governing instruments, governing board, and separate tax return filing obligation.[147] If it is a mere trusteed bank account (or the like) of the association, the IRS will regard the program as an integral part of the association.[148] If it is an authentic separate legal entity, any tax liability will be confined to that imposed on the net income of the entity, which presumably would have no basis for securing tax exemption.[149] If the entity transfers funds to the parent association, however, the funds may be taxable to the association as unrelated business income.[150] Likewise, the funds may be taxable to the association if the separate entity is regarded as an agent of the association.[151]

A court recognized that the acquisition and provision of insurance can be an exempt function of a tax-exempt business league.[152] In this case, the organization's purposes included counseling governmental agencies with regard to insurance programs, accepting and servicing insurance written by those agencies, and otherwise acting as an insurance broker for the governmental agencies. Finding this function to be an "important public service" (because the activity resulted in the best comprehensive insurance program for each agency and eliminated political corruption in the procurement of insurance), the court held that the net brokerage commissions received by the business league were not taxable as income from an unrelated trade or business. In so holding, the court relied on an IRS ruling that the provision for equitable distribution of high-risk insurance policies among member insurance companies is an exempt undertaking.[153]

If a tax-exempt association provides insurance for its own employees, it can do so without adverse tax consequences by contracting with an insurance provider or by establishing a voluntary employees' beneficiary association that is itself exempt.[154] This type of organization provides "for the payment of life, sick,

---

[145] See § 2.2.

[146] In the first appellate court decision following the Supreme Court's pronouncement in the *American Bar Endowment* case (Am. Bar Endowment v. United States, 84-1 U.S.T.C. ¶ 9204 (Ct. Cl. 1984)), a court concluded that the performance of promotional and administrative services by an exempt association in connection with the sale of insurance to its members was an unrelated activity. Ill. Ass'n of Prof'l Ins. Agents, Inc. v. Comm'r, 86-2 U.S.T.C. ¶ 9702 (7th Cir. 1986), *aff'g* 49 T.C.M. 925 (1985). See also Nat'l Water Well Ass'n, Inc. v. Comm'r, 92 T.C. 75 (1989).

[147] See *Tax-Exempt Organizations, supra* note 1, § 24.3.

[148] Priv. Ltr. Rul. 7847001.

[149] N.C. Oil Jobbers Ass'n, Inc. v. United States, 78-2 U.S.T.C. ¶ 9658 (E.D.N.C. 1978); N.Y. State Ass'n of Real Estate Bds. Group Ins. Fund v. Comm'r, 54 T.C. 1325 (1970).

[150] See § 8.8(a).

[151] See § 9.14.

[152] Indep. Ins. Agents of N. Nev., Inc. v. United States, 79-2 U.S.T.C. ¶ 9601 (D. Nev. 1979). This IRS position extends to insurance programs maintained by tax-exempt social welfare membership organizations. *E.g.*, Priv. Ltr. Rul. 9441001.

[153] Rev. Rul. 71-155, 1971-1 C.B. 152.

[154] See *Tax-Exempt Organizations, supra* note 1, § 16.3.

accident, or other benefits to the members of such association or their dependents or designated beneficiaries."[155]

Separate consideration must be given to the insurance programs of tax-exempt fraternal beneficiary societies,[156] as their exempt purpose is to provide for the payment of qualified benefits to their members and members' dependents.[157] The IRS recognized that these benefits are in the nature of insurance, in the course of holding that a society may not, as an exercise of an exempt function, provide additional insurance for terminated members.[158]

(c) Associate Member Dues

The tax treatment of dues derived from associate members (or affiliate or patron members) may become an issue for tax-exempt associations, although this matter has largely been resolved by statute.[159]

(d) Other Association Business Activity

The IRS takes the view that a tax-exempt business league can engage in charitable activities, without conducting unrelated business, even though the activities are technically unrelated to the business league's purposes.[160]

The IRS's position is that the operation of an employment service by a tax-exempt association is an unrelated activity.[161] This approach embraces registry programs[162] but not job training programs.[163]

Tax-exempt associations are encountering a conflict in the federal tax law with regard to the classification of an activity as being a related service for members or an unrelated business. In the absence of statutory or administrative regulatory authority on the point, the courts are formulating their own standards. For example, a federal court of appeals applied three factors in resolving the issue of whether an activity is substantially related to an association's exempt purposes: whether (1) the fees charged are directly proportionate to the benefits received; (2) participation is limited to members and thus is of no benefit to those in the industry who are nonmembers; and (3) the service provided is one commonly furnished by for-profit entities.[164] In subsequent application of these criteria, a court found that an association's administration of vacation pay and guaranteed annual income accounts for its members, under a collective bargaining agreement, was unrelated to its exempt negotiation and arbitration activities, because each member benefited in proportion to its participation in the activity,

---

[155] In general, Greif & Goldstein, *Rulings Holding Insurance Plans of Exempt Organizations Taxable May Threaten Exemptions*, 50 *J. Tax'n* 294 (1979); Claytor, *When Will Business Activities Cause Trade Associations to Forfeit Their Exempt Status?*, 49 *J. Tax'n* 104 (1978).
[156] See *Tax-Exempt Organizations*, § 18.4(a).
[157] *Id.*
[158] Priv. Ltr. Rul. 7937002.
[159] See § 4.8.
[160] Tech. Adv. Mem. 8418003.
[161] Rev. Rul. 61-170, 1961-2 C.B. 112.
[162] Priv. Ltr. Rul. 8503103.
[163] Rev. Rul. 67-296, 1967-2 C.B. 22.
[164] Carolinas Farm & Power Equip. Dealers Ass'n, Inc. v. United States, 699 F.2d 167, 171 (4th Cir. 1983).

only the association's members were eligible to participate in the service, and the functions could have been performed by for-profit entities.[165]

§ 9.5 LABOR AND AGRICULTURAL ORGANIZATIONS

One of the principal issues in the unrelated income context for tax-exempt labor unions[166] is the taxation of revenue (dues) derived from associate members (sometimes termed *limited benefit members*) who joined the organization solely to be able to participate in the organization's health insurance plans. The settled view is that this dues revenue is taxable.[167] When this issue was initially litigated, the government did not prevail, basically on the ground that the courts lacked the authority to define the bona fide membership of exempt labor unions.[168] The current view, however, is that the same rules that apply with respect to tax-exempt associations[169] also apply to exempt labor organizations.

In other applications of the unrelated income rules to tax-exempt labor organizations, the IRS found revenue derived by an exempt labor organization, from the operation of semiweekly bingo games[170] and from the performance of accounting and tax services for some of its members,[171] to be unrelated business income.

Tax-exempt agricultural organizations are likewise subject to the tax on unrelated business income. As an illustration, the IRS ruled that the following is taxable: income received by an exempt agricultural organization from the sale of supplies and equipment to members,[172] commissions from the sale of members' cattle,[173] income from the sale of supplies to seedspersons,[174] and income from the operation of club facilities for the organization's members and their guests.[175]

Federal tax law provides an exclusion from the unrelated business rules for income received by a tax-exempt organization that is used to establish, maintain, or operate a retirement home, hospital, or similar facility for the exclusive use and benefit of the elderly and infirm members of the organization, provided that the income is derived from agricultural pursuits and conducted on grounds contiguous to the facility and further provided that the income does not constitute more than 75 percent of the cost of maintaining and operating the facility.[176]

---

[165] S.S. Trade Ass'n of Baltimore, Inc. v. Comm'r, 757 F.2d 1494 (4th Cir. 1985), in which the court endorsed Rev. Rul. 66-151, 1966-1 C.B. 152. *Cf.* Rev. Rul. 82-138, 1982-2 C.B. 106 (IRS ruled that a trust created pursuant to collective bargaining agreements between an exempt labor union and several exempt business leagues was an exempt business league); Rev. Rul. 65-164, 1965-1 C.B. 238 (IRS ruled that an organization that negotiated collective bargaining contracts, interpreted these contracts, and adjusted labor disputes was an exempt business league).

[166] See *Tax-Exempt Organizations, supra* note 1, § 15.1.

[167] Am. Postal Workers Union, AFL-CIO v. United States, 925 F.2d 480 (D.C. Cir. 1991); Nat'l Ass'n of Postal Supervisors v. United States, 90-2 U.S.T.C. ¶ 50,445 (Ct. Cl. 1990), *aff'd*, 944 F.2d 859 (Fed. Cir. 1991).

[168] Am. Postal Workers Union, AFL-CIO v. United States, 90-1 U.S.T.C. ¶ 50,013 (D.D.C. 1989), *rev'd*, 925 F.2d 480 (D.C. Cir. 1991).

[169] See § 9.4 (c).

[170] Rev. Rul. 59-330, 1959-2 C.B. 153. *Cf.* § 4.7.

[171] Rev. Rul. 62-191, 1962-2 C.B. 146.

[172] Rev. Rul. 57-466, 1957-2 C.B. 311.

[173] Rev. Rul. 69-51, 1969-1 C.B. 159.

[174] Priv. Ltr. Rul. 8429010.

[175] Rev. Rul. 60-86, 1960-1 C.B. 198.

[176] Pre-1976 IRC § 512(b)(4). Although this provision was removed from the Internal Revenue Code as one of the "deadwood" provisions of the Tax Reform Act of 1976, it remains preserved in the law.

§ 9.6 FUNDRAISING ACTIVITIES

Fundraising practices of charitable organizations and the unrelated business rules have endured a precarious relationship for decades. For this purpose, the term *fundraising* means the solicitation of contributions, grants, and other forms of financial support, usually by charitable organizations.[177] Fundraising activities, which are almost always distinct from program activities, are often businesses.

(a) Fundraising as Unrelated Business

The type of fundraising undertaking that is most likely to be considered a business is the *special event*. These events include functions such as auctions, dinners, sports tournaments, dances, theater events, fairs, car washes, and bake sales.[178] A court may apply the statutory definition of the term *business*[179] in concluding that the event is an unrelated endeavor; on other occasions, a court will utilize other criteria, such as competition[180] or commerciality,[181] to find that the event is or is not an unrelated business.

Conventional fundraising—namely, the solicitation and collection of contributions and grants—technically is a business (or, perhaps, two or more businesses). Nevertheless, neither the IRS nor a court has yet characterized these practices as business, let alone unrelated business.

A case concerned a tax-exempt school that solicited charitable contributions by mailing packages of greeting cards as inducements to prospective donors. The IRS asserted that the school was actually involved in the unrelated business of selling greeting cards. The tax regulations, however, provide that an "activity does not possess the characteristics of a trade or business . . . when an organization sends out low cost articles incidental to the solicitation of charitable contributions."[182] The government asserted that this rule did not apply in this instance because the funds involved were not gifts, but the court disagreed, writing that to read the law in that narrow manner would "completely emasculate the exception."[183] The court found that the case turned on the fact that the unrelated business rules were designed to prevent exempt organizations from unfairly competing with for-profit

---

[177] The federal tax law does not generally define the term *fundraising*. The tax regulations promulgated in connection with the expenditure test (see *Tax-Exempt Organizations, supra* note 1, § 20.2(c)), however, provide that the term embraces three undertakings: (1) solicitation of dues or contributions from members of the organization, from persons whose dues are in arrears, or from the general public; (2) solicitation of gifts from businesses or gifts or grants from other organizations, including charitable entities; or (3) solicitation of grants from a governmental unit or any agency or instrumentality of the unit. Reg. § 56.4911-4(f)(1). See Hopkins, *The Law of Fundraising, Third Edition* (John Wiley & Sons, 2002) [hereinafter *Fundraising*], § 5.10.

[178] The IRS, in the instructions that accompany the annual information return filed by most tax-exempt organizations (see *Tax-Exempt Organizations, supra* note 1, § 24.3), states: "These activities [fundraising special events] only incidentally accomplish an exempt purpose. Their sole or primary purpose is to raise funds that are other than contributions to finance the organization's exempt activities."

[179] See § 2.2.

[180] See § 1.8.

[181] See ch. 7.

[182] Reg. § 1.513-1(b). See § 4.9.

[183] Hope Sch. v. United States, 612 F.2d 298, 302 (7th Cir. 1980).

entities,[184] and held that the school's fundraising program did not give it an "unfair competitive advantage over taxpaying greeting card businesses."[185]

Greeting cards and similar items, when used in conjunction with the solicitation of charitable contributions, are termed *premiums*. This fundraising practice has spawned considerable litigation and IRS ruling activity. An unrelated business may be present when the value of the premium approximates the amount of the ostensible gift. Also, if the premiums are mailed with the gift solicitation, the result probably is charitable giving; if the premiums are made available following the alleged gifts, there may be commercial activity. Thus, a court wrote, in a case involving a greeting card program of a tax-exempt national veterans' organization, that "when premiums are advertised and offered only in exchange for prior contributions in stated amounts," the activity is commercial, but if the organization "had mailed the premiums with its solicitations and had informed the recipients that the premiums could be retained without any obligation arising to make a contribution," the activity is not a business because it is not a competitive practice.[186] Another court ruled that the revenue derived by an exempt veterans' organization from the distribution of cards to its members constituted unrelated business income; the court concluded that the organization was acting with a profit motive and that the card program was the "sale of goods."[187] IRS rulings likewise reflect this approach.[188] Nevertheless, another court held, without referencing the other two opinions, that the revenue generated by a veterans' organization from the dissemination of greeting cards was not income from an unrelated business, but rather contributions resulting from a fundraising program.[189]

One of the earliest examples of a fundraising event cast as a business was an IRS ruling, issued in 1979, holding that a religious organization was engaged in an unrelated business by conducting, as its principal fundraising activity, thrice-weekly bingo games and related concessions.[190] The agency concluded that the games "constitute a trade or business with the general public, the conduct of which is not substantially related to the exercise or the performance by the organization of the purpose for which it was organized other than the use it makes of the profits derived from the games."[191]

A court ruled that the conduct by a charitable organization of weekly and monthly lotteries was activity regularly carried on, and thus was an unrelated business, because the gambling activities were not substantially related to the organization's charitable purposes.[192]

---

[184] See § 1.6.

[185] Hope Sch. v. United States, 612 F.2d 298, 304 (7th Cir. 1980).

[186] Disabled Am. Veterans v. United States, 650 F.2d 1179, 1187, 1186 (Ct. Cl. 1981).

[187] Veterans of Foreign Wars, Dep't of Mich. v. Comm'r, 89 T.C. 7, 38 (1987). *Cf.* Veterans of Foreign Wars, Dep't of Mo., Inc. v. United States, 852 U.S.T.C. ¶ 9605 (W.D. Mo. 1984).

[188] *E.g.*, Priv. Ltr. Rul. 8203134.

[189] Am. Legion Dep't of N.Y. v. United States, 93-2 U.S.T.C. ¶ 50,417 (N.D.N.Y. 1993).

[190] Priv. Ltr. Rul. 9746001. Also P.L.L. Scholarship Fund v. Comm'r, 82 T.C. 196 (1984); Piety, Inc. v. Comm'r, 82 T.C. 193 (1984).

[191] This organization was unable to utilize the exemption from unrelated income taxation accorded to bingo games (see § 4.7) because, under the law of the state in which it was organized, the games at that time constituted an illegal lottery.

[192] United States v. Auxiliary to Knights of St. Peter Claver, Charities of Ladies Court No. 97, 92-1 U.S.T.C. ¶ 50,176 (S.D. Ind. 1992).

Another court case concerned the tax status of an organization of citizens'-band radio operators, which used insurance, travel, and discount plans to attract new members.[193] The organization contended that it was only doing what many tax-exempt organizations do to raise contributions, analogizing these activities to fundraising events. The court rejected this argument, defining a *fundraising event* as a "single occurrence that may occur on limited occasions during a given year and [the] purpose [of which] is to further the exempt activities of the organization."[194] These events were contrasted with activities that are "continuous or continual activities which are certainly more pervasive a part of the organization than a sporadic event and [that are] . . . an end in themselves."[195]

When a nonprofit school consulted with a tax-shelter investment firm in search of fundraising methods, the result was a program in which individuals purchased various real properties from the school, which the school would simultaneously purchase from third parties; both the sellers and the buyers were clients of the investment firm. There were about 22 of these transactions during the years at issue, from which the school received income reflecting the difference between the sales prices and the purchase prices. Finding the "simultaneous purchase and sale of real estate . . . not substantially related to the exercise or performance of [the school's] . . . exempt function," a court held that the net income from the transactions was unrelated business income.[196]

At issue before a court was whether income, received by a charitable organization as the result of assignments to it of dividends paid in connection with insurance coverage purchased by members of a related professional association at group rates, was taxable as unrelated business income. The trial court wrote that, when the tax-exempt organization involved in an unrelated business case is a charitable one, the court must "distinguish between those activities that constitute a trade or business and those that are merely fundraising."[197] The court said that this distinction is not always readily apparent, in that charitable activities are "sometimes so similar to commercial transactions that it becomes very difficult to determine whether the organization is raising money 'from the sale of goods or the performance of services' [the statutory definition of a *business*[198]] or whether the goods or services are provided merely as an incident to a fundraising activity." Nonetheless, the court held that the test is whether the activity in question is "operated in a competitive, commercial manner," which is a "question of fact and turns upon the circumstances of each case."[199] "At bottom," the court wrote, the "inquiry is whether the actions of the participants conform with normal assumptions about how people behave in a commercial context"; "[i]f they do not, it may be because the participants are engaged in a charitable fundraising activity."[200]

---

[193] U.S. CB Radio Ass'n No. 1, Inc. v. Comm'r, 42 T.C.M. 1441 (1981).
[194] *Id.* at 1444.
[195] *Id.*
[196] Parklane Residential Sch., Inc. v. Comm'r, 45 T.C.M. 988, 992 (1983).
[197] Am. Bar Endowment v. United States, 84-1 U.S.T.C. ¶ 9204 (Ct. Cl. 1984).
[198] See § 2.2.
[199] Am. Bar Endowment v. United States, 84-1 U.S.T.C. ¶ 9204 (Ct. Cl. 1984).
[200] *Id.*

In this case, the court stressed the following elements: the pioneering nature of the idea at inception of the activity; the original creation and subsequent presentation of the activity as a fundraising effort; the "staggering amount of money" and "astounding profitability" that were generated by the activity; the degree of the organization's candor toward its members and the public concerning the operation and revenue of the program; and the fact that the activity was operated with the consent and approval of the organization's membership.[201] Concerning the third element, substantial profits and consistently high profit margins are usually cited as reasons for determining that the activity involved is a business. In this instance, however, the amounts of money involved were so great that they could not be rationalized in conventional business analysis terms; the only explanation that was suitable to the court was that the "staggering amount" of money was the result of successful charitable fundraising.

Notwithstanding this rational analysis, the U.S. Supreme Court overturned the opinion.[202] The Court found of consequence the facts that the organization negotiated premium rates with insurers, selected the insurers that provided the coverage, solicited the membership of the association, collected the premiums, transmitted the premiums to the insurer, maintained files on each policyholder, answered members' questions concerning insurance policies, and screened claims for benefits. In deciding that this bundle of activities amounted to an unrelated business, the Court observed that the charitable organization "prices its insurance to remain competitive with the rest of the market," that the Court "can easily view this case as a standard example of monopoly pricing," and that the case "presents an example of precisely the sort of unfair competition that Congress intended to prevent."[203]

The Court in this case concluded that the "only valid argument in the charitable organization's favor, therefore, is that the insurance program is billed as a fundraising effort."[204] But the Court summarily rejected this contention—in language that highlights why most fundraising efforts are unrelated businesses—writing that such "fact, standing alone, cannot be determinative, or any exempt organization could engage in a tax-free business by 'giving away' its product in return for a 'contribution' equal to the market value of the product."[205]

Contemporary fundraising techniques that raise questions as to application of the unrelated business rules are forms of *commercial co-venturing* and *cause-related marketing*. The former involves situations in which a charitable organization consents to be a recipient of funds from a commercial business that agrees to make payments to the organization, with the understanding that the agreement will be advertised, and the amount of the payment is predicated on the extent of products sold or services provided by the business to the public during a particular time period. The latter involves the public marketing of products or services by or on behalf of a tax-exempt organization, or some other similar use of an

---

[201] *Id.*
[202] United States v. Am. Bar Endowment, 447 U.S. 105 (1986).
[203] *Id.* at 112–14.
[204] *Id.* at 115.
[205] *Id.* Revisions in this program led the IRS to conclude that it was no longer an unrelated business. Priv. Ltr. Rul. 8725056.

exempt organization's resources. A manifestation of the latter is the participation by exempt organizations in affinity card programs, through which an exempt organization is paid a portion of the revenues derived from the marketing of credit cards to its members or other constituency. The IRS's initial position was that although participation (the licensing of mailing lists) is an exploitation of the organization's exempt function,[206] the resultant revenues are not taxable because they constitute passive royalty income.[207] The agency subsequently determined that an affinity card program is an unrelated business, that the payments are not exempt royalty income, and that the resulting revenue is taxable as income from a third party's use of the organization's membership mailing lists.[208]

Nonetheless, the U.S. Tax Court, following its stance with respect to the exclusion for royalty income,[209] ruled that affinity card revenue is excludable from unrelated income taxation when the arrangement is structured, through a pertinent agreement with one or more for-profit participants, so as to produce royalties.[210] The court rejected the government's arguments that the exempt organization involved participated in a joint venture with regard to the affinity card program or that it was engaged in the business of selling financial services to its members. Finding that the organization made available its name, marks, and mailing list for use by the for-profit participant, and that those items were intangible property, the court ruled that the "financial consideration received by . . . [the organization] under the agreement was in consideration of such use" and thus that the resulting revenue was excludable royalty income.[211]

On appeal, however, the appellate court crafted a different definition of the term *royalty*,[212] and reversed the Tax Court as to the affinity card revenue holding, remanding the case.[213] Nonetheless, applying this revised definition of the term *royalty*, the Tax Court again concluded that the organization's affinity card revenue was excludable as royalty income.[214]

The IRS held that the regular sales of membership mailing lists by a tax-exempt educational organization to colleges and business firms for the production of income was an unrelated business.[215] By contrast, the agency ruled that the exchange of mailing lists by an exempt organization with similar exempt organizations does not give rise to unrelated business income (namely, barter income of an amount equal to the value of the lists received).[216] In this ruling, the IRS concluded

---

[206] See § 2.7(e).

[207] Priv. Ltr. Rul. 8747066.

[208] Gen. Couns. Mem. 39727. Priv. Ltr. Rul. 8747066 (see *supra* note 207) was revoked by Priv. Ltr. Rul. 8823109. As to the mailing-list approach, the IRS determined that the statutory exception (see § 4.7) was not available because the lists were provided to noncharitable organizations. In general, Cerny & Lauber, *Logos, UBIT, and a Strict IRS Approach to Affinity Card Programs*, 2 *J. Tax Exempt Orgs.* 9 (Winter 1991).

[209] See § 3.7.

[210] Sierra Club, Inc. v. Comm'r, 103 T.C. 307 (1994). Also Miss. State Univ. Alumni, Inc. v. Comm'r, 74 T.C.M. 458 (1997); Or. State Univ. Alumni Ass'n, Inc. v. Comm'r, 71 T.C.M. 1935 (1996), *aff'd*, 99-2 U.S.T.C. ¶ 50,879 (9th Cir. 1999); Alumni Ass'n of Univ. of Or., Inc. v. Comm'r, 71 T.C.M. 2093 (1996), *aff'd*, 99-2 U.S.T.C. ¶ 50,879 (9th Cir. 1999).

[211] Sierra Club, Inc. v. Comm'r, 103 T.C. 307, 344 (1994).

[212] See § 3.7, text accompanied by notes 78–80.

[213] Sierra Club, Inc. v. Comm'r, 86 F.3d 1526 (9th Cir. 1996).

[214] Sierra Club, Inc. v. Comm'r, 77 T.C.M. 1569 (1999).

[215] Rev. Rul. 72-431, 1972-2 C.B. 281.

[216] Priv. Ltr. Rul. 8127019.

that the activity was not a business because it was not carried on for profit, but rather to obtain the names of potential donors. Likewise, this exchange function was held to be substantially related to the organization's exempt function as being a "generally accepted method used by publicly supported organizations to assist them in maintaining and enhancing their active donor files."[217] Nonetheless, when an exempt organization exchanges mailing lists so as to produce income, it is the position of the IRS that the transaction is economically the same as a rental arrangement and thus is an unrelated business.[218]

(b) Application of Exceptions

Many fundraising endeavors of charitable and other tax-exempt organizations are businesses and are not related activities. Nonetheless, they often escape unrelated business taxation because of one or more exceptions.

The exception most frequently utilized to shelter fundraising activities from this taxation is the one for business activities that are not regularly carried on.[219] The typical special event, for example, is usually not regularly carried on,[220] although on occasion the inclusion of preparatory time will convert the activity into an unrelated business.[221] The IRS ruled, for example, that the net proceeds resulting from the annual conduct by a charitable organization of a dance and a golf tournament were not taxable because the events were not regularly carried on.[222]

In one case, a court concluded that the annual fundraising activity of a tax-exempt charitable organization, consisting of the presentation and sponsoring of a professional vaudeville show, conducted one weekend per year, was a business that was not regularly carried on.[223] The court concluded: "The fact that an organization seeks to insure the success of its fundraising venture by beginning to plan and prepare for it earlier should not adversely affect the tax treatment of the income derived by the venture."[224]

Conventional fundraising (the solicitation and collection of gifts and grants), however, is usually regularly carried on, yet there have been no assertions that these activities are taxable, even though they may be businesses and are not related to exempt purposes.

Other exceptions may be available in the fundraising setting. For example, a business, albeit regularly carried on, in which substantially all of the work is

---

[217] *Id.*

[218] Priv. Ltr. Rul. 8216009.

[219] See § 2.5. A charitable organization may, however, be found to be engaged in an unrelated business for conducting this type of fundraising event when it is done for the benefit of another charity. Rev. Rul. 75-201, 1975-1 C.B. 164.

[220] *E.g.*, Priv. Ltr. Rul. 200128059 (concerning an annual charity ball and annual golf tournament).

[221] See § 2.5(d).

[222] Priv. Ltr. Rul. 200128059.

[223] Suffolk County Patrolmen's Benevolent Ass'n, Inc. v. Comm'r, 77 T.C. 1314, 1323 (1981). The court took this opportunity to observe that the IRS "apparently believes that all fundraisers of exempt organizations are conducted by amateurs in an amateurish manner"; that "[w]e do not believe that this is, nor should be, the case"; and that it is "entirely reasonable for an exempt organization to hire professionals in an effort to insure the success of a fundraiser [i.e., fundraising event]."

[224] *Id.* at 1324.

performed for the organization by volunteers is not taxable.[225] The same is true of the sale of merchandise substantially all of which has been received by the organization as gifts.[226] Activities carried on primarily for the convenience of the organization's members, students, patients, officers, or employees are not taxable as unrelated businesses.[227] The receipts from certain gambling activities (bingo games) are exempted from related business income taxation.[228]

(c) Tax Planning Consulting

It is common for charitable organizations that engage in fundraising efforts to provide financial and tax planning information to prospective donors. This may entail modest amounts of information, such as direction as to valuation of property or the extent of the charitable deduction. In other settings, by contrast, the financial and tax information supplied may be substantial and complex. This is particularly so with respect to planned giving, where charities are directly involved in charitable gift planning and preparation of documents, such as charitable remainder trusts, other trust arrangements, and wills.[229]

A fundamental precept of the federal tax law concerning charitable organizations is that they may not, without jeopardizing their tax-exempt status, be operated in a manner that causes persons to derive a private benefit from their operations.[230] Occasionally, these elements conflict, in that the provision of tax planning information and services by charitable organizations to prospective contributors is considered the provision of impermissible private benefit. It might seem nearly inconceivable to seriously contend that, when a charitable organization works with a prospective donor to effect a sizable gift that will generate significant tax and other advantages for the donor, by reason of a charitable contribution deduction and other benefits, the organization is imperiling its tax exemption because it is conferring a private benefit—but this is the import of three court opinions.

One case concerned the tax-exempt status of an organization that engaged in financial counseling by providing tax planning services, including charitable giving counseling, to wealthy individuals referred to it by subscribing exempt religious organizations. The counseling given by the organization consisted of advice as to how a contributor may increase current or planned gifts to these religious organizations, including the development of a financial plan that, among other objectives, resulted in a reduction in federal income and estate taxes. The IRS's position was that this organization could not qualify for federal income tax exemption because it served the private interests of individuals by enabling them to reduce their tax obligations. The organization's position was that it was engaging in activities that exempt charitable organizations may generally undertake without loss of the tax exemption. A court agreed with the government, holding that the organization's "sole financial planning activity,

---

[225] See § 4.2.
[226] See § 4.3.
[227] See § 4.1.
[228] See § 4.7.
[229] See Hopkins, *The Tax Law of Charitable Giving, Third Edition* chs. 8, 12 (John Wiley & Sons, 2005)
[230] See *Tax-Exempt Organizations*, ch. 19.

albeit an exempt purpose furthering . . . [exempt] fundraising efforts, has a nonexempt purpose of offering advice to individuals on tax matters that reduces an individual's personal and estate tax liabilities."[231] The court dryly stated that "[w]e do not find within the scope of the word charity that the financial planning for wealthy individuals described in this case is a charitable purpose."[232]

In this opinion, the court singled out this organization's planned giving techniques for portrayal as methods that give rise to unwarranted private benefit. The example given was of the creation of a charitable remainder trust, under which the donor receives "considerable lifetime advantages," such as the flow of income for life, reduced capital gain taxes in instances involving property that has appreciated in value, and lower probate costs.[233] (The court could have recited other benefits, such as the charitable contribution deduction, the calculation of the deduction based on the full fair market value of property, and the benefits of [free to the donor] professional money and property management.) These were cast as "real and substantial benefits" that inure to contributors as the consequence of the organization's activities, with these benefits "substantial enough to deny exemption."[234]

In another case, this court held that a religious organization could not be tax-exempt because it engaged in a substantial nonexempt purpose: namely, the counseling of individuals on the purported tax benefits accruing to those who become ministers of the organization.[235] The court decided that the organization was akin to a "commercial tax service, albeit within a narrower field (i.e., tax benefits to ministers and churches) and a narrower class of customers (i.e., . . . [the organization's] ministers)," and thus found that the organization served private purposes.[236] The many detailed discussions by the organization in its literature of ways to maximize tax benefits led the court to observe that, although the organization "may well advocate belief in the God of Am [the deity worshipped by the members of the organization], it also advocates belief in the God of Tax Avoidance."[237] In words with considerable implications for fundraising for charitable purposes generally, the court wrote that a "substantial nonexempt purpose does not become an exempt purpose simply because it promotes the organization in some way."[238] The court apparently grasped the larger portent of its opinion and attempted to narrow its scope by noting that "[w]e are not

---

[231] Christian Stewardship Assistance, Inc. v. Comm'r, 70 T.C. 1037, 1041 (1978).

[232] *Id.* at 1043.

[233] *Id.* at 1044.

[234] *Id.* This was, indeed, a sweeping conclusion for the court to reach, at least without noting that charitable organizations continuously engage in these practices. (The problem in this case, apparently, was that the financial and tax planning functions were in a separate organization.) Congress provided the benefits to donors who make contributions by means of charitable remainder trusts. IRC § 664. It was unusual for the court to suggest that, when charities make their supporters aware of, and donors elect to avail themselves of, these benefits, the donee charitable organization should in turn lose its tax exemption. Indeed, the court subsequently somewhat circumscribed the reach of this conclusion. See text accompanying *infra* note 244.

[235] Ecclesiastical Order of the Ism of Am, Inc. v. Comm'r, 80 T.C. 833 (1983), *aff'd*, 740 F.2d 967 (6th Cir. 1984), *cert. denied*, 471 U.S. 1015 (1985).

[236] *Id.*, 80 T.C. at 839. See also Universal Life Church v. United States, 87-2 U.S.T.C. ¶ 9617 (Ct. Cl. 1987).

[237] Ecclesiastical Order of the Ism of Am, Inc. v. Comm'r, 80 T.C. at 840.

[238] *Id.* at 841.

holding today that any group which discusses the tax consequences of donations to and/or expenditures of its organization is in danger of losing or not
acquiring tax-exempt status."[239] That, of course, was the essence of its holding
in the prior case.

The court thereafter held that an organization, the membership of which
was "religious missions," was not entitled to tax-exempt status as a religious
organization, because it engaged in the substantial nonexempt purpose of providing financial and tax advice.[240] The court was heavily influenced by a caval-
cade of cases before it concerning, in the court's words, "efforts of taxpayers to
hide behind the cover of purported tax-exempt religious organizations for significant tax avoidance purposes."[241] As the court saw the facts of this case, each
member mission was the result of individuals attempting to create churches
involving only their families so as to convert after-tax personal and family
expenses into deductible charitable contributions. The central organization provided sample incorporation papers, tax seminars, and other forms of tax advice
and assistance to those creating the missions. Consequently, the court was persuaded that the "pattern of tax avoidance activities which appears to be present
at the membership level, combined with . . . [the organization's] admitted role as
a tax advisor to its members," justified the conclusion that the organization was
ineligible for tax exemption.[242]

These three court opinions can be read as meaning that, when an organization's only function is the provision of financial and tax planning services, it cannot constitute a tax-exempt charitable organization, even when its only
"customers" are other charitable, educational, and religious entities. At the same
time, particularly when read out of context, some of the court's pronouncements
on this point make little sense, and are hardly synchronous with real-world
fundraising practices. In light of this expansive interrelationship of the unrelated
business rules and the private benefit doctrine in this aspect of the fundraising
setting, the court's disclaimer in the second of these cases[243] looms large.[244]

§ 9.7   TRAVEL OPPORTUNITIES

Travel tour activities that constitute a trade or business not substantially related
to an organization's tax-exempt purpose constitute one or more unrelated businesses. Whether travel tour endeavors conducted by an exempt organization are
substantially related to the organization's exempt purpose depends on an analysis of the relevant facts and circumstances, including how a travel tour is developed, promoted, and operated.[245]

---

[239] *Id.* at 842. This decision was affirmed at 740 F.2d 967 (6th Cir. 1984), *cert. denied*, 471 U.S. 1015 (1985).
[240] Nat'l Ass'n of Am. Churches v. Comm'r, 82 T.C. 18 (1984).
[241] *Id.* at 29–30.
[242] *Id.* at 32.
[243] See text accompanied by *supra* note 235.
[244] In general, see *Fundraising*, 77, § 5.7.
[245] Reg. § 1.513-7(a).

(a) General Rules

The balance of the law on this topic, generally confined to tax regulations, must be extracted from examples provided in the regulations. These illustrations tend to swing one from one extreme to the other, so one must draw cautiously from them in striving to design related travel opportunities. In the seven examples that follow, the travel tours are priced to produce a profit for the exempt organization.

In the first of these examples, a tax-exempt university educational alumni association operates, as part of its activities, a travel tour program that is available to all current members of the association and their guests. The association works with travel agencies to schedule approximately 10 tours annually to various destinations around the world. The association members pay a fee to the organizing travel agency to participate in a tour; the travel agency pays the association a per-person fee for each participant. Although the literature advertising the tours encourages the association's members to continue their "lifelong learning" by joining the tours, and a faculty member of the university frequently joins the tour as a guest of the association, none of the tours includes any "scheduled instruction or curriculum related to the destinations being visited." The travel tours made available to this association's members do not contribute importantly to the accomplishment of the organization's educational purpose. Rather, this program is designed to generate revenue for the association by "regularly offering its members travel services." Accordingly, this tour program is an unrelated trade or business.[246]

As a second example, a tax-exempt educational and cultural organization formed for the purpose of educating individuals about the geography and culture of the United States engages in a number of activities to accomplish its purposes, including offering courses and publishing periodicals and books. As one of its activities, this organization conducts study tours to national parks and other locations; the tours are conducted by teachers and other personnel certified by a state's board of education. The tours are directed toward students enrolled in degree programs at educational institutions in this state, as reflected in the promotional materials, but are open to all who agree to participate in the required study program. Each tour's study program consists of "instruction on subjects related to the location being visited on the tour." During the tour, five or six hours per day are devoted to "organized study, preparation of reports, lectures, instruction, and recitation by the students"; a "library of material related to the subject being studied" is available; examinations are given at the end of the tour; and academic credit is offered for participation in the tour. Because these tours include a "substantial amount of required study, lectures, report preparation, [and] examinations, and qualify for academic credit, the tours are a related business with respect to this organization.[247]

As a third example, a tax-exempt membership organization fosters cultural unity and educates eligible Americans about their common country of origin; membership in this entity is open to all Americans interested in this particular heritage. As part of its activities, the organization sponsors a program of travel

---

[246] Reg. § 1.513-7(b), Example (1).
[247] Reg. § 1.513-7(b), Example (2).

tours to this country. One set of these tours are trips that are designed to "immerse participants in [the country's] history, culture and language." Substantially all of the daily itinerary includes "scheduled instruction" on the country's language, history, and cultural heritage, and destinations for visits are selected because of their historical or cultural significance or because of the instructional resources they offer. A second set of tours also entails trips to this country but, rather than offering "scheduled instruction," participants are given the option of taking guided tours of various locations in the country; there is no "instruction or curriculum." Destinations of principally recreational interest, rather than historical or cultural interest, are regularly included in the second type of tour. The sponsorship of the first set of tours is a related trade or business with respect to this organization, whereas sponsorship of the second set of tours does not contribute importantly to the organization's accomplishment of exempt purposes and thus is an unrelated trade or business.[248]

Another example concerns a tax-exempt scientific organization engaged in environmental research, including a long-term study of how agricultural pesticide and fertilizer use affects the populations of various bird species. The organization collects data at several bases located in an important agricultural region in a country. The minutes of a meeting of this organization's board of directors state that, after study, the board determined that nonscientists can reliably perform needed data collection in the field, under the supervision of the organization's biologists. These minutes also reflect that the board approved the offering of one-week trips to the organization's bases in this country, where participants will assist the biologists in collecting data for the study. Tour participants collect data during the same hours as the organization's biologists. Normally, data collection occurs during the early morning and evening hours, although the work schedule varies by season. Although each base has "rustic accommodations and few amenities," this country is renowned for its beautiful scenery and abundant wildlife. The organization promotes the trips in its newsletter, on its Internet site, and through various conservation organizations. The promotional materials describe the work schedule and emphasize the valuable contribution made by trip participants in the organization's research activities. This type of activity is a related trade or business with respect to this organization.[249]

In another illustration, a tax-exempt educational organization is devoted to the study of ancient histories and cultures. It conducts archaeological expeditions around the world, including in a particular region of a country. In cooperation with the National Museum of this country, the organization presents an exhibit on ancient civilizations of this region, including artifacts from the collection of the museum. The organization institutes a program of travel tours to its archaeological sites located in this region. The tours are initially proposed by the organization's staff members as a means of educating the public about ongoing field research conducted by it. The organization engages a travel agency to handle logistics such as accommodations and transportation. In

---

[248] Reg. § 1.513-7(b), Example (4).
[249] Reg. § 1.513-7(b), Example (5).

preparation for the tours, the organization develops educational materials relating to each archaeological site to be visited on the tour, describing in detail the layout of the site, the methods used by the organization's researchers in exploring the site, the discoveries made at the site, and the historical significance of those discoveries. The organization also arranges special guided tours of its exhibit on the region for individuals registered for the travel tours. Two archaeologists from the organization (who participated in prior archaeological expeditions in the region) accompany the tours; these experts lead guided tours of each site and explain the significance of the sites. At several of the sites, tour participants meet with a working team of archaeologists from the organization and the museum, who share their experiences. The organization prepares promotional materials describing the educational nature of the tours, including the daily trips to the archaeological sites and the educational background of the tour leaders, and provides a recommended reading list. These materials do not refer to any recreational or sightseeing activities. These activities are found to be part of a "coordinated educational program" that constitutes a related trade or business.[250]

In another illustration on this topic, a tax-exempt educational organization is devoted to the study of the performing arts; it presents public performances of musical and theatrical works. Individuals become members of this organization by making annual contributions to it. Annually, the organization offers its members an opportunity to travel to one or more major cities in the United States or other countries. In each city, tour participants are provided with tickets for a public performance of a play, concert, or dance program each evening. The organization also arranges a sightseeing tour of each city and provides evening receptions for tour participants. The organization views its tour programs as an important means to develop and strengthen bonds between it and its members, and to increase their financial and volunteer support. It engages a travel agency to handle logistics such as accommodations and transportation. No educational materials are prepared by the organization or provided to tour participants in connection with the tours. Apart from attendance at the evening cultural events, the tours do not offer any scheduled instruction, organized study, or group discussion. Although several members of the organization's administrative staff accompany each tour group, their role is to facilitate member interaction. The staff members do not have special expertise in the performing arts and do not play an educational role in the tours. The organization does prepare promotional materials describing the sightseeing opportunities on the tours and emphasizing the opportunity for members to socialize informally and interact with one another and the staff, while pursuing shared interests. Although these tours may foster goodwill among the organization's members, they do not contribute importantly to its educational purposes. This tour program is "primarily social and recreational in nature," with sightseeing and attendance at cultural events not part of a "coordinated educational program." This tour program is an unrelated trade or business.[251]

---

[250] Reg. § 1.513-7(b), Example (6).
[251] Reg. § 1.513-7(b), Example (7).

(b) Advocacy Travel

Advocacy travel can qualify as related business. For example, travel tours for a tax-exempt social welfare organization's members to Washington, D.C., where the participants spend substantially all of their time during normal business hours over several days attending meetings with legislators and government officials, and receiving briefings on policy developments related to issues that are the organization's focus, are related businesses. "Bringing members to Washington to participate in advocacy on behalf of the organization and learn about developments relating to the organization's principal focus is [activity that is] substantially related to [its] social welfare purpose." This is so even though the participants have some time in the evenings to engage in social and recreational activities.[252]

(c) Summary of Law

As these examples indicate, for a travel opportunity to constitute a related trade or business, there must be some form of formal, scheduled instruction or curriculum, involving use of substantive educational materials. The greater the number of hours each day devoted to instruction the better, although it is not always necessary that there be daily recitations, examinations, and availability of academic credit. The formal involvement of college and university faculty, and/or other experts in the field, is preferred if the activity is to amount to a related business. Relatedness is more likely to attach if the physical attractiveness of the facilities and other surroundings is low, and the participants have to provide meaningful services to the organization; the IRS views ocean cruises and similar outings with suspicion. Factors such as optional activities, free time, sightseeing and recreational activities, and other socializing opportunities tend to lead the IRS to conclude that the undertaking is an unrelated trade or business. The use of a travel agency is not automatically fatal to a casting of a travel opportunity sponsored by a tax-exempt organization as a related activity, but the organization needs to do more than be a provider of travel services.

§ 9.8   PROVISION OF SERVICES

In general, income from the provision of services by a tax-exempt organization to another organization, including another exempt organization, is unrelated business income. This is because it is not automatically an exempt function for one exempt organization to provide services to another, even when both organizations have the same category of exempt status. For example, the IRS ruled that the provision of administrative services by an exempt association to an exempt voluntary employees' beneficiary association, where the latter entity provided a health and welfare benefit plan for the former entity's members' employees, was an unrelated business.[253] Likewise, the provision of management services by an exempt association to a charitable organization it founded was ruled by the IRS to be an unrelated business.[254] Indeed,

---

[252] Reg. § 1.513-7(b), Example (3).
[253] Tech. Adv. Mem. 9550001.
[254] Tech. Adv. Mem. 9811001.

the provision of management services by a nonprofit organization to unaffiliated charitable organizations led to the revocation of the organization's exemption as a charitable entity.[255] Management, administrative, fundraising, and similar services generally are termed *corporate services*.

There are two exceptions to this general rule. One is that, under certain circumstances, it can be a related business for a tax-exempt organization to provide services to another exempt entity. As an illustration, an exempt business association with an aggressive litigation strategy placed the litigation function in a separate exempt organization, because of a substantial risk of counterclaims and other retaliatory actions against the association and its members. The IRS concluded that the association's provision of management and administrative services to the other exempt organization was in furtherance of the provider association's exempt purposes.[256] Likewise, the IRS ruled that a national charitable organization engaged in related business activities when it provided certain coordination services for its chapters in connection with a new program it was implementing.[257] Additionally, an exempt organization that was an arm of an association of public school boards, which administered the association's cash/ risk management funds, was found to be engaged in the charitable activity of lessening the burdens of government.[258]

The provision of professional, managerial, and administrative services among a group of interrelated health care organizations, directly or by means of a partnership, was ruled to be a bundle of related businesses.[259] Similarly, the lease and management of a computer system to a partnership, by a supporting organization of a university's medical center, which system was used for billing, collection, and recordkeeping of the partners, was found to be a related business because the partners were physicians who constituted the faculty of the university's medical school and teaching hospital.[260] Further, the IRS ruled that a graduate educational institution engaged in a related business when it provided "central services" (such as campus security, a central steam plant, accounting services, and a risk and property insurance program) to a group of affiliated colleges.[261] From time to time, the IRS issues other rulings on this point.[262]

The other exception is when the tax-exempt organizations are related entities, usually parent and subsidiary. In the health care context, for example, the IRS has a ruling policy that the provision of services by and to related entities is not an unrelated business. This policy is being articulated in rulings concerning the tax consequences of creation of a health care delivery system by means of a joint operating agreement. The arrangement entails what the IRS terms the provision of corporate services by and among exempt organizations (in this type of system, several hospitals and a parent supporting organization). The IRS stated that if the participating

---

[255] Tech. Adv. Mem. 9822004.
[256] Tech. Adv. Mem. 9608003.
[257] Priv. Ltr. Rul. 9641011.
[258] Tech. Adv. Mem. 9711002.
[259] Priv. Ltr. Rul. 9839039.
[260] Tech. Adv. Mem. 9847002.
[261] Priv. Ltr. Rul. 9849027.
[262] *E.g.*, Priv. Ltr. Rul. 199910060.

exempt organizations are in a parent and subsidiary relationship, corporate services provided between them that are necessary to accomplishment of their exempt purposes are treated as other than an unrelated business, and the financial arrangements between them are viewed as "merely a matter of accounting."[263] Indeed, in some of these rulings, the IRS extended the matter-of-accounting rationale to relationships analogous to parent-subsidiary arrangements.

This outcome obviously was welcome news for tax-exempt health care organizations desiring to utilize joint operating agreements. From the larger perspective, though, the development was a transformative one for many other exempt organizations as well. The tax law rationale underlying these agreements cannot be confined to the health care context; this means that, in any situation in which an exempt organization has a parent-subsidiary relationship with another exempt organization, the provision of corporate services may be protected from unrelated business taxation by this rationale. It also means that the matter-of-accounting reasoning can be extended to any arrangement in which the relationship between two exempt organizations is analogous to that of parent and subsidiary.

The first time this parent-subsidiary rationale was used outside the health care setting was in a typical situation: a tax-exempt social welfare organization provided corporate services to its related foundation.[264] This arrangement was held not to generate unrelated business income, because of the "close structural relationship" between the two organizations. The IRS subsequently ruled on this point.[265]

As to arrangements in which the relationship is analogous to that of parent and subsidiary, the first illustration was provided in the case of a vertically, horizontally, and geographically integrated charitable health care system that used two supporting organizations. The IRS ruled that the affiliation agreements involved established relationships analogous to that of parent and subsidiary.[266] A subsequent case concerned two charitable organizations that managed health care facilities and entered into a management agreement with a third such organization. Although each of these entities was independent of the others, the IRS found that, by reason of the agreement, these two charitable organizations had ceded to the third organization "significant financial, managerial and operational authority over their affairs, including exclusive authority over capital and operating budgets, strategic plans, managed care contracting, the ability to allocate or reallocate services among the health care facilities [they] manage, and the ability to monitor and audit compliance with directives." The agency ruled that these two organizations were "effectively under the common control" of the third organization. Therefore, the IRS held that these organizations were "within a relationship analogous to that of a parent and subsidiary"; hence, the provision of these corporate services would not result in unrelated business income.[267]

---

[263] *E.g.*, Priv. Ltr. Rul. 9651047. In constructing this rationale, the IRS utilized an accounting concept heretofore reserved to the feeder organization rules (see *Tax-Exempt Organizations*, § 28.6, n. 73) and the unrelated debt-financed income rules (see §5.4(h) text accompanied by note 147.)

[264] Priv. Ltr. Rul. 200022056.

[265] *E.g.*, Priv. Ltr. Rul. 200037050.

[266] Priv. Ltr. Rul. 200101034.

[267] Priv. Ltr. Rul. 200108045. In general, Prescott, Jr., *Management and Consulting Services: The Impact on Exempt Status and UBIT*, 42 *Exempt Orgs. Tax Rev.* 209 (no. 2, Nov. 2003).

Another instance, involving the leasing of facilities by a tax-exempt hospital to another exempt hospital, further illustrated this approach. The IRS ruled that the leasing activity was an exempt function, because of the direct physical connection and close professional affiliation of the institutions.[268] As to the latter factor, however, the lessor and lessee hospitals were closely associated with an exempt medical school; thus, the agency could have ruled that the two hospitals were in a relationship analogous to that of parent and subsidiary.

§ 9.9 SHARECROP LEASING

An unrelated business tax issue that is of concern to the IRS, and that is being addressed in the courts, is the proper tax treatment to be accorded sharecrop revenue received by tax-exempt organizations. This subject is informed by two bodies of law: the existence or nonexistence of a general partnership or joint venture for tax purposes,[269] and the interpretation of the passive rent rules.[270]

A sharecrop lease arrangement may involve land that is owned by a tax-exempt organization and leased by the organization to a farmer. Under the terms of a typical lease, the tenant is exclusively responsible for managing and operating the farm property. The tenant is also required to prepare a farm operating plan, including a schedule of crops to be grown on the land, seeding or planting rates, chemicals and fertilizers to be used, conservation practices and tillage plans, livestock breeding and market schedules, nutrition and feeding schedules, and harvesting and storage plans. After the operating plan is complete, the tenant is usually required to submit the plan to the exempt organization for review.[271]

Operation of all aspects of the farm is the sole responsibility of the tenant, including cultivation of the land, planting, fertilizing, harvesting and marketing crops, and all aspects of livestock husbandry. The tax-exempt organization is generally responsible for all of the costs associated with the land and fixed improvements, including the costs of wells and pumps, irrigation equipment, and initially required limestone and rock phosphate applications. Either the tenant or the landlord may provide the equipment and tools required to farm the land. The allocation of the proceeds of the sale of any crops and/or livestock raised on the property between the exempt organization and the tenant is negotiated between them and is generally comparable to percentage crop rents negotiated between other landlords and farm operators in the community.[272]

Under the terms of the typical sharecrop lease, the tenant farmer is required to submit a detailed farm operating plan to the tax-exempt organization for review, which provides an opportunity for the exempt organization to exert some control over the farming operations. The IRS is of the view, however, that "it does not follow that under the terms of such a farm lease that the exempt

---

[268] Priv. Ltr. Rul. 200314031.

[269] See *Tax-Exempt Organizations*, ch. 32.

[270] See § 3.8(a).

[271] The final college and university examination guidelines omitted a discussion of crop leasing, because of the litigation throughout 1993. See text accompanied by *infra* notes 281–295. The proposed guidelines (Ann. 93-2, 1993-2 I.R.B. 39), however, contained this analysis in § 342.12(2); the text is based on that summary.

[272] Ann. 93-2, 1993-2 I.R.B. 39, § 342.12(2).

organization manages and directs the operation of the property to a significant extent."[273] The agency also stated that, even if the requirement of a farm operating plan provides control over how a tenant conducts the farming activity, "it does not rise to a level of control that would require treating crop shares as other than rental from real property."[274] The IRS observed that it is "significant that under such a farm lease there is no sharing of expense and the exempt organization does not provide financing for its tenants."[275]

The determination of whether an amount received pursuant to a sharecrop lease constitutes excludable rent[276] is a two-step process. First, there must be a determination as to whether the sharecrop arrangement constitutes a lease or some other arrangement. It is necessary to compare the particular sharecrop arrangement with standard sharecrop arrangements in a particular locality to determine whether the agreement constitutes a lease under local law and whether an amount received according to the agreement constitutes rent. Most sharecrop arrangements, however, are in the nature of leases that produce rental income. There are cases in which the IRS found that a particular sharecrop agreement created a joint venture rather than a lease; in these circumstances, the agency will assert that the income under the agreement does not constitute rent[277] and that the income is therefore unrelated business income. Second, if it is found that a sharecrop agreement constitutes a lease producing rental income, a determination must be made as to whether the exclusion for rental income applies. In cases in which the IRS asserts that the underlying agreement is not a lease, it generally will also assert (as a backup argument) that the exclusion for rent does not apply because the rent is in any event based on the profit from the farm.[278]

When a tax-exempt organization shares the crop produced by a tenant farmer, the rent is in fact based on a percentage of receipts or sales, though this fact does not bar it from treatment as rent from real property for these purposes. When the sharing is combined with a substantial sharing of farm costs with the tenant, however, the rent is in effect based on the profit from the farm, and the income is not protected by the exclusion.[279]

A federal district court was the first to issue an opinion grappling with the question of whether income received by a tax-exempt organization, as rent from a sharecrop lease, was a form of passive income (and thus is not unrelated business income) or revenue from participation in a joint venture that is not in furtherance of an exempt purpose (and thus is unrelated business income). The court concluded that the income was "true rent" that was based on a fixed percentage of receipts from the farm production within the scope of the statutory exclusion,[280] and thus was not unrelated business income.[281]

---

[273] Id.

[274] Id.

[275] Id.

[276] See § 3.8(a).

[277] Ann. 93-2, 1993-2 I.R.B. 39, § 342.12(3)(a).

[278] Id. § 342.12(3)(b).

[279] Id. § 342.12(4).

[280] IRC § 512(b)(3)(A)(i), (B)(ii).

[281] Harlan E. Moore Charitable Trust v. United States, 812 F. Supp. 130, 135 (C.D. Ill.), aff'd, 9 F.3d 623 (7th Cir. 1993).

The tax-exempt organization in this case owned a farm that was managed by a bank. The organization entered into a sharecrop agreement with two individuals, and their rent was set at 50 percent of farm production after the crop was divided at the grain elevator. The tenants made the farming decisions; they and the bank were billed separately for the shared expenses and never assumed one another's debts. The parties to the lease did not share in each other's profits or losses. The court reviewed applicable state law and concluded that there was no evidence that this relationship was a partnership or other form of joint venture.

The government's alternative argument was that the rent from the share-crop agreement was based on a percentage of income or profits and thus was not exempt from treatment as unrelated business income pursuant to a special exception.[282] This assertion led the court to review the legislative history of this provision and conclude that, in enacting it, Congress sought to tax property rentals that are measured by reference to the net income from the property. The court again reviewed the terms of the lease and state law, which recognized that rent may be paid as a portion of crops. The pertinent state law said that if the farm were leased on a cash-rent basis, the rent would be excludable from tax.[283] The court wrote that it "seems anomalous that identical activities undertaken on a share-crop lease should be taxable."[284] The court, noting the "long history" of sharecrop leases in the particular state and the absence of a "clear directive from Congress to the contrary," held that division of the crops under this share-crop lease was a receipt of rent and not a division of profits.[285]

In a subsequent case, another court held that rents received under sharecrop leases by a charitable trust were excluded from consideration as unrelated business income.[286] The trust, by means of a bank that managed the property, oper-ated farmland, paid necessary expenses, made necessary improvements, and rented the farmland under sharecrop leases. Thus, the trust supplied the farm and the buildings on it, materials necessary for repairs and improvements on the farm, and skilled labor for making permanent improvements. The trust was responsible for 50 percent of the cost of seed, fertilizer, limestone, herbicides, and insecticides. These leases obligated the tenant to be responsible for all machinery, equipment, power, and labor necessary to farm the land. The parties were to confer for the purpose of planning land use and sharing certain costs. Liability for all accidents relative to farming was conferred on the tenant. The amount of rent payable to the trust under these leases was fixed at 50 percent of the harvested corn, oats, soybean, and wheat.

Generally, to be excluded from treatment as unrelated business income, rent must be passive income. Thus, rent is regarded as unrelated business income if the "determination of the amount of such rent depends in whole or in part on the income or profits derived by any person from the property leased."[287] Nonetheless, rent may be excluded from classification as unrelated business income when the amount of rent is based on a "fixed percentage or

---

[282] IRC § 512(b)(3)(B)(ii). See § 3.8(b).
[283] IRC § 512(b)(3)(A)(i).
[284] Harlan E. Moore Charitable Trust v. United States, 812 F. Supp. 130, 135 (C.D. Ill. 1993).
[285] Id.
[286] Trust U/W Emily Oblinger v. Comm'r, 100 T.C. 114 (1993).
[287] IRC § 512(b)(3)(B)(ii).

percentages of receipts or sales."[288] These two provisions were termed by the court the "passive rent test."[289] The court wrote that, to "exclude rents from . . . [treatment as unrelated business income], rents must in substance qualify as rent, as opposed to actually representing a return of profits by the tenant or a share of profits retained by the landlord as either a partner or joint venturer . . . and not violate the . . . passive income test."[290]

The IRS contended that these arrangements were either general partnerships or joint ventures and that the payments under the leases represented a return of profits that were a form of unrelated business income. This contention rested largely on the lease provisions concerning land use planning and cost-sharing.

The court disagreed with the IRS's characterization of the facts. It found that the trust "did not itself or through its managing agent participate in the day-to-day operations of the farm to a degree which would support the existence of a joint venture or partnership with the tenant."[291] The court singled out the provision concerning liability for farming accidents as evidence that the arrangement was not a partnership or other joint venture. Also, the court noted that the trust was not required to contribute to losses, there were no provisions to carry over losses from one year to reduce payments to the trust in later years, and the leases were typical of sharecrop leases used in the region. The court then found that the specified rent did not violate the passive rent test. The tax regulations state that an amount is excluded from "rents from real property" if, considering the lease and the surrounding circumstances, the arrangement does not conform with normal business practice and is in reality used as a means of basing the rent on income or profits.[292] The court wrote that this test is "intended to prevent avoidance of unrelated business income tax where a profit-sharing arrangement will, in effect, make the lessor an active participant in the operation of the property."[293]

As noted, an exception from treatment as unrelated business income is provided for amounts based on a fixed percentage or percentages of receipts or sales. In asserting that the arrangements violated the passive rent test, the IRS emphasized the trust's splitting of the expenses, its involvement in the farming operations, and its receipt of a percentage of production as rent, rather than a percentage of receipts. The court disagreed, finding the leases to amount to the "equivalent of the tenant's reducing the crops to cash and then giving . . . [the trust] its share of the total receipts collected."[294] In conclusion, wrote the court, the "passive rent test was not violated since . . . [the trust's] rent was not determined, in whole or in part, on the net profits or income derived from the property."[295]

---

[288] *Id.*
[289] Trust U/W Emily Oblinger v. Comm'r, 100 T.C. 114, 121 (1993).
[290] *Id.* at 117.
[291] *Id.* at 120.
[292] Reg. § 1.512(b)-1(c)(2)(iii)(b).
[293] Trust U/W Emily Oblinger v. Comm'r, 100 T.C. 114, 122 (1993).
[294] *Id.* at 123.
[295] *Id.* In so holding, the court favorably cited the opinion in Harlan E. Moore Charitable Trust v. Comm'r, 812 F. Supp. 130 (C.D. Ill.), *aff'd*, 9 F.3d 623 (7th Cir. 1993). Indep. Order of Odd Fellows Grand Lodge of Iowa v. United States, 93-2 U.S.T.C. ¶ 50,448 (S.D. Iowa 1993); White's Iowa Manual Labor Inst. v. Comm'r, 66 T.C.M. 389 (1993).

§ 9.10 RETIREMENT PLAN REVERSIONS

A tax-exempt organization may maintain a qualified pension or other retire-ment plan to provide retirement benefits to its employees.[296] Generally, the assets of the plan must be used exclusively for the employees and their benefi-ciaries,[297] and the contributions of an employer to a qualified plan are deduct-ible in the year in which the contributions are paid.[298] This type of plan may be terminated; in that instance, all benefits accrued to the date of termination must become completely vested and nonforfeitable, and either plan benefits must be distributed to the participants in the plan or annuities providing for the payment of comparable benefits must be purchased and distributed to the participants. When a plan is terminated and assets remain after the satisfaction of all liabilities to plan participants and other beneficiaries, and if the excess of assets is attributable to actuarial error, the employer is permitted to recover the excess assets.[299] Generally, this excess must be included in the employer's gross income.

When the employer organization is a tax-exempt entity subject to the rule that all income other than exempt function income is regarded as unrelated busi-ness income,[300] such as a social club,[301] the amount of the reversion generally is includable in the organization's unrelated business income, because it cannot qualify as exempt function income.[302] This body of law does not contain the gen-eral requirement that be a *trade or business* before the income can be characterized as unrelated business income.[303]

Income of a tax-exempt organization with these characteristics may, how-ever, be excluded from taxation by reason of the *tax benefit rule.* Under the exclusionary portion of this rule, gross income does not include income attrib-utable to the recovery during a tax year of any amount deducted in any prior tax year, to the extent that amount did not reduce the amount of income tax for that year.[304] By contrast, under the inclusionary aspect of this rule, when the amount previously deducted from gross income generated a tax benefit and is then recaptured in a subsequent year, the recaptured amount is includable in gross income in the year of recapture.[305] Consequently, to the extent that this type of tax-exempt organization deducted contributions to a defined benefit plan in determining its taxable nonexempt function income, the inclusionary aspect of the tax benefit rule would apply.[306]

When the employer organization is a tax-exempt entity that is not subject to this rule concerning treatment of nonexempt function income, the tax conse-quences of a reversion of plan assets are different. Because (1) the operation of

---

[296] See *Tax-Exempt Organizations,* § 16.1.
[297] IRC § 401(a)(2).
[298] IRC § 401(a)(1)(A).
[299] Reg. § 1.401-2(b)(1).
[300] See §§ 6.1, 6.2(b).
[301] See *Tax-Exempt Organizations,* ch. 14.
[302] Gen. Couns. Mem. 39717.
[303] See § 2.2.
[304] IRC § 111(a).
[305] IRC § 61; Rev. Rul. 68-104, 1968-1 C.B. 361; Gen. Couns. Mem. 39744.
[306] Gen. Couns. Mem. 39717.

the plan is not a business,[307] but rather an administrative function that is part of the exempt organization's overall operations; and (2) the funds that revert on termination of the plan are a one-time source of income rather than income from an activity that is regularly carried on,[308] the reverted funds are generally not treated as unrelated business income.[309] Thus, for example, the IRS ruled that the reversion of assets from a defined benefit pension plan to a tax-exempt charitable organization employer, as part of termination of the plan, did not give rise to unrelated business income.[310]

The tax benefit rule can apply in this setting as well. In general, an organization that is not subject to this special rule of unrelated business income treatment is usually exempt from taxation and thus would not derive any tax benefit from the making of contributions to a qualified pension plan. This is another application of the exclusionary aspect of the tax benefit rule. This type of organization could, however, receive a tax benefit from a contribution to a qualified plan if it deducted the amount of the contribution in calculating unrelated business taxable income. In that situation, by operation of the inclusionary aspects of the tax benefit rule, the recovery of the previously deducted amounts would be unrelated business income taxable to the tax-exempt organization.[311]

§ 9.11 EXEMPT FUNCTIONS AS UNRELATED BUSINESS

It is possible for an activity that is a related business when conducted by one type of tax-exempt organization to be an unrelated business when conducted by another type of exempt organization. For example, the IRS ruled that a certification program conducted by a tax-exempt educational and scientific organization was an unrelated business, because it primarily advanced the interests of individuals in a particular profession and only incidentally served the interests of the public.[312] The agency said that the activity was appropriate when conducted by an exempt business league,[313] but became an activity promoting nonexempt (unrelated) purposes when conducted by a charitable organization.[314]

§ 9.12 OTHER INSTANCES OF RELATED BUSINESS

There are many determinations by the courts and the IRS that activities by tax-exempt organizations are related businesses. For example, a furniture shop operated by an exempt halfway house and staffed by its residents was found to be a related business.[315] An organization that promoted professional automobile racing was held not to receive unrelated business income from the conduct of a product certification program, because the program was part of the organization's

---

[307] See § 2.2.
[308] See § 2.5.
[309] Gen. Couns. Mem. 39806.
[310] Priv. Ltr. Rul. 200131034.
[311] Gen. Couns. Mem. 39806.
[312] Priv. Ltr. Rul. 200439043.
[313] See *Tax-Exempt Organizations*, § 13.1(c).
[314] *Id.* §§ 6.3(g), 7.6A.
[315] Rev. Rul. 75-472, 1975-2 C.B. 208.

regulatory activities designed to prevent trade abuses in the automobile racing business.[316] Certification of the accuracy and authenticity of export documents by an exempt chamber of commerce, for the purpose of providing independent verification of the origin of exported goods, was ruled to be a related business, because the activity "stimulate[d] international commerce by facilitating the export of goods and, thus, promote[d] and stimulate[d] business conditions in the community generally."[317]

The IRS rules that a tax-exempt national conservation education organization was engaging in related business activities by selling stationery items, serving items, desk accessories, nature gift items, emblem items, toys, and wearing apparel, because each of the product lines served to stimulate public interest in wildlife preservation.[318] The operation of a members' restaurant and cocktail lounge by certain exempt organizations, such as social clubs and veterans' organizations, is an activity in furtherance of their exempt purposes.[319]

Other court opinions and IRS rulings illustrate *related* business activities conducted by tax-exempt organizations: the sponsorship of championship tournaments by an association organized to promote a sport;[320] the charging of activity fees to libraries of for-profit organizations for computer-stored library cataloging services;[321] the operation of a beauty shop and barber shop by a senior citizens' center;[322] the sale of members' horses by a horse breeders' association;[323] the conduct of weekly dances by a volunteer fire company;[324] tax collection activities by a social welfare organization on behalf of its member municipalities;[325] sponsorship of a bank payment plan for the membership of a professional society;[326] gambling receipts from members of social and fraternal organizations;[327] loan organization and servicing activities;[328] the conduct of an employment program providing training and work experience for the disabled;[329] a project to facilitate court proceedings by telephone;[330] the operation of a lawyer referral service by a bar association;[331] the performance of management services for a charitable organization;[332] the provision of group insurance and workers' compensation self-insurance for member counties by a social welfare organization;[333] the provision

---

[316] Priv. Ltr. Rul. 7922001.

[317] Rev. Rul. 81-127, 1981-1 C.B. 357, 358.

[318] Priv. Ltr. Rul. 8107006.

[319] Priv. Ltr. Rul. 8120006.

[320] Rev. Rul. 58-502, 1958-2 C.B. 271, as clarified by Rev. Rul. 80-294, 1980-2 C.B. 187. *Cf.* Mobile Arts & Sports Ass'n v. United States, 148 F. Supp. 315 (S.D. Ala. 1957).

[321] Priv. Ltr. Rul. 7816061.

[322] Rev. Rul. 81-61, 1981-1 C.B. 355.

[323] Priv. Ltr. Rul. 8112013.

[324] Rev. Rul. 74-361, 1974-2 C.B. 159. Also Rev. Rul. 68-225, 1968-1 C.B. 283; Rev. Rul. 67-296, 1967-2 C.B. 212; Rev. Rul. 67-219, 1967-2 C.B. 210; Rev. Rul. 64-182, 1964-1 (pt. 1) C.B. 186; Md. State Fair & Agric. Soc'y, Inc. v. Chamberlin, 55-1 U.S.T.C. ¶ 9399 (D. Md. 1955).

[325] Ky. Mun. League v. Comm'r, 81 T.C. 156 (1983).

[326] San Antonio Dist. Dental Soc'y v. United States, 340 F. Supp. 11 (W.D. Tex. 1972).

[327] Gen. Couns. Mem. 39061.

[328] Priv. Ltr. Rul. 8349051.

[329] Priv. Ltr. Rul. 8349072.

[330] Priv. Ltr. Rul. 8351160.

[331] Priv. Ltr. Rul. 8417003.

[332] Priv. Ltr. Rul. 8422168.

[333] Priv. Ltr. Rul. 8442092.

of worker's compensation insurance coverage to county government employees by a social welfare organization;[334] the provision of veterinary services by a tax-exempt humane society;[335] a low-cost animal neutering service;[336] the operation of a health club for individuals reflective of the community;[337] the conduct of research and counseling activities for the purpose of promoting business in foreign countries;[338] the sales of products in connection with the conduct of educational programs;[339] the sale of computer software by an organization formed to make new scientific technology widely available for the benefit of the public;[340] the sale of life memberships in a rural lodge used only for religious and educational purposes;[341] the performance of art conservation services for private collectors;[342] the operation of an arena (including concessions and leases);[343] the construction and operation of a recreational complex and ancillary activities;[344] the operation of golf courses to promote rehabilitation of disadvantaged youth;[345] the management of a project to restore historic property;[346] the sale of posters and other promotional items carrying the organization's program message;[347] the operation of a secondhand store;[348] the conduct of teleconferencing activities;[349] the publication and sale of common tariffs by a shipowners' and operators' organization;[350] the operation of a medical malpractice peer review program by a medical society;[351] the operation of a mobile cancer screening program;[352] the activities of a trade association as a "certified frequency coordinator" (as designated by the Federal Communications Commission) for its industry;[353] the leasing of a theater by a performing arts organization for musical productions;[354] a charitable organization's sale of insurance on the lives of donors;[355] the licensing of an educational institution's curriculum to other colleges and universities;[356] the teaching of computer programming courses for employees of a corporation;[357] the operation of nursing homes by a health care organization;[358] the operation of physical, occupational, and speech therapy, injury prevention, pediatric services,

[334] Tech. Adv. Mem. 8443009.
[335] Tech. Adv. Mem. 8450006.
[336] Tech. Adv. Mem. 8501002.
[337] Tech. Adv. Mem. 8505002.
[338] Priv. Ltr. Rul. 8505047.
[339] Priv. Ltr. Rul. 8512084.
[340] Priv. Ltr. Rul. 8518090.
[341] Priv. Ltr. Rul. 8523072.
[342] Priv. Ltr. Rul. 8606074.
[343] Priv. Ltr. Rul. 8623081.
[344] Priv. Ltr. Rul. 8624127.
[345] Priv. Ltr. Rul. 8626080.
[346] Priv. Ltr. Rul. 8628049.
[347] Priv. Ltr. Rul. 8633034.
[348] Priv. Ltr. Rul. 8643049.
[349] Priv. Ltr. Rul. 8643091.
[350] Priv. Ltr. Rul. 8709072.
[351] Priv. Ltr. Rul. 8730060.
[352] Priv. Ltr. Rul. 8749085.
[353] Priv. Ltr. Rul. 8802079.
[354] Gen. Couns. Mem. 39715.
[355] Priv. Ltr. Rul. 8820061.
[356] Priv. Ltr. Rul. 8824018.
[357] Priv. Ltr. Rul. 9137002.
[358] Priv. Ltr. Rul. 9237090.

and adult day care programs;[359] the cleanup of spills of oil and oil products;[360] the conduct of services relating to use of an organization's mailing list;[361] the operation of a birthing center by a church;[362] the sponsorship of gospel concerts by a broadcast ministry;[363] the receipt of income from Medicare, Medicaid, or private insurance programs for the operation of intermediate care facilities;[364] the operation by a charitable organization of a parking garage for the benefit of its member charities;[365] the performance of preacquisition student loan services by a public charity;[366] health care entity's provision of temporary nurses to a related exempt organization;[367] a religious organization's sale of books written by the organization's founder;[368] the provision of services by a community development organization to a community development bank;[369] the conduct by an agricultural organization of activities promoting cooperative programs among farmers in a state;[370] the development and operation by a business league of a tracking system for alimony and support payments;[371] the conduct by a public charity of market development and investment programs intended to promote investment in foreign countries;[372] the operation of a center for regional economic development and for educational and cultural activities;[373] the sale of caskets by an exempt cemetery company;[374] the conduct of national amateur athletic contests;[375] the sale of medical diagnostic literature and equipment;[376] the rental of office space and rooms, and the provision of food service, with respect to an educational facility operated by a charity;[377] lease of the assets of a hospital district to a charitable organization that was to operate the hospital;[378] the sale of a corporate charter, licenses to conduct an insurance business, and deposits with state regulatory departments by an exempt property and casualty insurance company;[379] the administration of state education assistance programs by a state-controlled charity;[380] the provision of lobbying services by a business league for the benefit of its member health care providers;[381] the provision of services by a community development organization as the managing member of a limited liability

---

[359] Priv. Ltr. Rul. 9241055.
[360] Priv. Ltr. Rul. 9242035.
[361] Priv. Ltr. Rul. 9249001.
[362] Priv. Ltr. Rul. 9252037.
[363] Priv. Ltr. Rul. 9325062.
[364] Priv. Ltr. Rul. 9335061.
[365] Priv. Ltr. Rul. 9401031.
[366] Priv. Ltr. Rul. 9403022.
[367] Priv. Ltr. Rul. 9535023.
[368] Priv. Ltr. Rul. 9535050.
[369] Priv. Ltr. Rul. 9539015.
[370] Ohio Farm Bureau Fed'n, Inc. v. Comm'r, 106 T.C. 222 (1996).
[371] Priv. Ltr. Rul. 9633044.
[372] Priv. Ltr. Rul. 9651046.
[373] Priv. Ltr. Rul. 9810038.
[374] Priv. Ltr. Rul. 9814051.
[375] Priv. Ltr. Rul. 9821049.
[376] Priv. Ltr. Rul. 9821063.
[377] Priv. Ltr. Rul. 9824048.
[378] Priv. Ltr. Rul. 9825030.
[379] Priv. Ltr. Rul. 9853026.
[380] Priv. Ltr. Rul. 199905027.
[381] Priv. Ltr. Rul. 199905031.

company used as a financing vehicle;[382] the provision of office automation training services by a charitable organization for job seekers with vocational disadvantages;[383] the participation by a charitable organization in homebuyer assistance
programs for low- and moderate-income families;[384] the operation by a charitable
organization of a mushroom-growing and -processing facility predominantly to
employ poor and drug-addicted individuals;[385] the sale of a commodity code by
an organization of federal and state purchasing agencies;[386] the provision of credit
enhancement services to developers of, and predevelopment and construction
lending to projects that result in, affordable housing;[387] the conduct by a library of
a remote access project, fee-based services, research assistance for library users,
business information collection, and library management training;[388] the operation by a charitable organization of a rural health infrastructure loan program;[389]
the operation by a private operating foundation of a guest house in conjunction
with its conference center;[390] the construction and operation by a charitable organization of an office complex for the promotion of African-American businesses;[391] the sale of cat-related merchandise by an organization that educates the
public about the ownership of cats;[392] the reorganization of an educational institution;[393] the operation of a fee-for-services plan by an exempt retirement home;[394] a
public charity's operation of noncommercial television and radio stations;[395] a
charitable organization's use of a vessel to provide ferry service for a limited time
in the context of an emergency;[396] the leasing of industrial buildings by a charitable organization to promote development of an economically distressed
county;[397] payments to a pension plan trust to induce it to lend its securities;[398] the
renovation of a conference center and redevelopment of commercial rental property;[399] the addition of a warehouse facility to a charitable organization's manufacturing program for the development of disabled individuals;[400] the carrying
out of student loan securitization transactions by a supporting organization for
the benefit of the supported organization, which undertakes a variety of student
loan programs;[401] the earnings received by a federally chartered charitable organization under a funding and trust agreement with government agencies;[402] and

---

[382] Priv. Ltr. Rul. 199909056.
[383] Priv. Ltr. Rul. 199910053.
[384] Priv. Ltr. Rul. 199910061.
[385] Priv. Ltr. Rul. 199920041.
[386] Tech. Adv. Mem. 199922055.
[387] Priv. Ltr. Rul. 199929049.
[388] Priv. Ltr. Rul. 199945062.
[389] Priv. Ltr. Rul. 199949045.
[390] Priv. Ltr. Rul. 200030027.
[391] Priv. Ltr. Rul. 200030033.
[392] Priv. Ltr. Rul. 200126033.
[393] E.g., Priv. Ltr. Rul. 200150032.
[394] Priv. Ltr. Rul. 200150038.
[395] Priv. Ltr. Rul. 200151047.
[396] Priv. Ltr. Rul. 200204051(time limit extended by Priv. Ltr. Rul. 200301048).
[397] Priv. Ltr. Rul. 200213027.
[398] Priv. Ltr. Rul. 200220028.
[399] Priv. Ltr. Rul. 200225044.
[400] Priv. Ltr. Rul. 200241050.
[401] Priv. Ltr. Rul. 200345041.
[402] Priv. Ltr. Rul. 200349008.

the receipt by a charitable organization of "phantom" income in the form of investment income accruing to charitable remainder trusts and charitable lead trusts it controlled as trustee.[403]

Private letter rulings from the IRS provide additional illustrations of related business activity.[404]

§ 9.13 OTHER INSTANCES OF UNRELATED BUSINESS

There are many determinations by the courts and the IRS that activities by tax-exempt organizations are unrelated businesses. For example, the presentation of commercial programs and the sale of air time were ruled to be activities not substantially related to the exempt purposes of an exempt broadcasting station.[405] The operation of a miniature golf course in a commercial manner, by a charitable organization operating to promote the welfare of young individuals, was determined to constitute an unrelated business.[406] The operation of dining facilities for the general public by an exempt social club or exempt veterans' organization is an unrelated business.[407]

Other court opinions and IRS rulings illustrate unrelated business activities: the provision of pet boarding and grooming services, for pets owned by the general public, by an organization operated to prevent cruelty to animals;[408] carrying on of commercially sponsored research, when the organization withheld or significantly delayed publication of the research beyond the time reasonably necessary to establish ownership rights;[409] weekly operation of a bingo game by a social welfare organization;[410] sale of membership lists to commercial companies by educational organizations;[411] publication of academic works;[412] receipt of commissions from an agricultural organization's sales of cattle for its members;[413] a blood bank's sale of certain blood and blood components to commercial laboratories;[414] a business league's management of health and welfare plans for a fee;[415] a religious organization's furnishing of laborers (usually its members) to forest owners to plant seedlings on cleared

---

[403] Priv. Ltr. Rul. 200352017.

[404] *E.g.*, Priv. Ltr. Rul. 8640007.

[405] Rev. Rul. 78-385, 1978-2 C.B. 174.

[406] Rev. Rul. 79-361, 1979-2 C.B. 237.

[407] Rev. Rul. 68-46, 1968-1 C.B. 260.

[408] Rev. Rul. 73-587, 1973-2 C.B. 192.

[409] Rev. Rul. 76-296, 1976-2 C.B. 141.

[410] Clarence LaBelle Post No. 217 v. United States, 580 F.2d 270 (8th Cir. 1978); Smith-Dodd Businessman's Ass'n, Inc. v. Comm'r, 65 T.C. 620 (1975). Also Rev. Rul. 59-330, 1959-2 C.B. 153.

[411] Rev. Rul. 72-431, 1972-2 C.B. 281.

[412] Priv. Ltr. Rul. 7839042. See also Okla. Dental Ass'n v. United States, 75-2 U.S.T.C. ¶ 9682 (W.D. Okla. 1975); W. Catholic Church v. Comm'r, 73 T.C. 196 (1979), *aff'd*, 631 F.2d 736 (7th Cir. 1980), *cert. denied*, 450 U.S. 981 (1981).

[413] Rev. Rul. 69-51, 1969-1 C.B. 159.

[414] Rev. Rul. 66-323, 1966-2 C.B. 216, *as modified by* Rev. Rul. 78-145, 1978-1 C.B. 169.

[415] Rev. Rul. 66-151, 1966-1 C.B. 152. Also Cooper Tire & Rubber Co., Employees' Ret. Fund v. Comm'r, 306 F.2d 20 (8th Cir. 1962); Rev. Rul. 69-633, 1969-2 C.B. 121; Rev. Rul. 69-69, 1969-1 C.B. 159; Rev. Rul. 68-505, 1968-2 C.B. 248; Rev. Rul. 68-267, 1968-1 C.B. 284; Duluth Clinic Found. v. United States, 67-1 U.S.T.C. ¶ 9226 (D. Minn. 1967); Rev. Rul. 66-47, 1966-1 C.B. 149; Rev. Rul. 62-191, 1962-2 C.B. 146; Rev. Rul. 60-228, 1960-1 C.B. 200; Rev. Rul. 60-86, 1960-1 C.B. 198; Rev. Rul. 58-482, 1958-2 C.B. 273; Rev. Rul. 57-466, 1957-2 C.B. 311; Rev. Rul. 57-313, 1957-2 C.B. 316; Rev. Rul. 55-449, 1955-2 C.B. 599.

forest land;[416] the sale of heavy-duty appliances to senior citizens by a senior citizens' center;[417] administrative services performed by a business league in connection with vacation pay and guaranteed annual income accounts established by a collective bargaining agreement;[418] a labor union's operation of a commuting program for its members;[419] the provision of veterinary services, for a fee, by an animal cruelty prevention society;[420] the distribution of business directories to new residents in a community;[421] the sale of work uniforms by a union;[422] the operation of a central payroll and records system;[423] the sale of printing services to other persons (including exempt organizations);[424] the provision of commercial hospitalization review services by a professional standards review organization;[425] sales of liquor by a veterans' organization;[426] the sale of a computer-based information retrieval and message service provided by a for-profit business;[427] the sale of information about real estate used to prepare market evaluations and house appraisals;[428] the provision of arbitration and mediation, and other alternative dispute resolution services, for the benefit of consumers;[429] the conduct of utilization review services and drug-free workplace programs for private businesses by a professional standards review organization;[430] an exempt scientific research organization's sale of herbs and herb products to private practitioners and the general public;[431] a low-income housing corporation's operation of a temporary storage business open to the general public;[432] an agricultural organization's storage of trailers, campers, motor homes, boats, and automobiles;[433] a business league's operation of a recycling facility;[434] and the public use of a golf course maintained by an exempt planned community.[435]

Private letter rulings from the IRS provide additional illustrations of unrelated business activity.[436]

---

[416] Rev. Rul. 76-341, 1976-2 C.B. 307. Also Shiloh Youth Revival Ctrs v. Comm'r, 88 T.C. 565 (1987).
[417] Rev. Rul. 81-62, 1981-1 C.B. 355.
[418] Steamship. Trade Ass'n of Baltimore, Inc. v. Comm'r, 757 F.2d 1494 (4th Cir. 1985).
[419] Tech. Adv. Mem. 8226019.
[420] Priv. Ltr. Rul. 8303001.
[421] Priv. Ltr. Rul. 8433010.
[422] Tech. Adv. Mem. 8437014.
[423] Tech. Adv. Mem. 8446004.
[424] Priv. Ltr. Rul. 8452074.
[425] Priv. Ltr. Rul. 8511082.
[426] Priv. Ltr. Rul. 8530043.
[427] Priv. Ltr. Rul. 8814004.
[428] Priv. Ltr. Rul. 9043001.
[429] Priv. Ltr. Rul. 9145002.
[430] Priv. Ltr. Rul. 9436002.
[431] Tech. Adv. Mem. 9550001.
[432] Tech. Adv. Mem. 9821067.
[433] Tech. Adv. Mem. 9822006.
[434] Tech. Adv. Mem. 9848002.
[435] Tech. Adv. Mem. 200047049.
[436] E.g., Priv. Ltr. Rul. 9128003.

§ 9.14 AGENCY RULE

Occasionally, a situation will arise in which monies paid to an agent of a tax-exempt organization, who in turn pays the monies over to the organization, are taxable as unrelated business income. This situation occurs, for example, in connection with an exempt religious order, which requires its members to provide services for a component of the supervising church and to turn over their remuneration to the order under a vow of poverty. Under these circumstances, the payments for services are income to the order and not to the member.[437] When the individual is not acting as agent for the order and is performing services (as an employee) of the type ordinarily required by members of the religious order, however, the income is to the individual, and the unrelated income tax is avoided, because the monies are received by the order as charitable contributions.

Likewise, amounts received from a tax-exempt hospital, by a registered nurse who was a member of an exempt religious organization, were held excludable from the nurse's gross income, rather than wages subject to withholding, when the nurse performed services in the hospital as an agent of the religious entity to which the nurse remitted the amounts.[438] By contrast, trust income, the assignment of which was prohibited by the trust instrument and state law, was held includable in the gross income of a trust income beneficiary who joined a religious order, took a vow of poverty, and turned over all payments from the trust to the order.[439]

---

[437] Rev. Rul. 76-323, 1976-2 C.B. 18, *clarified by* Rev. Rul. 77-290, 1977-2 C.B. 26.

[438] Rev. Rul. 68-123, 1968-1 C.B. 35.

[439] Rev. Rul. 77-436, 1977-2 C.B. 25. Some solace was provided by the IRS in this case, in that the amounts transferred to the order were ruled to be deductible charitable contributions.

CHAPTER TEN

Unrelated Business and the Internet

Unrelated business is conducted by tax-exempt organizations on the Internet, with products and services advertised and sold by means of this medium. The Internet, being an instrument of communication, offers to exempt organizations (and, of course, nearly everyone else) a magnificent opportunity to create business, market goods and services, and sell these goods and services to the general public. As in other contexts, however, federal tax law does not provide any unique treatment to transactions or activities of tax-exempt organizations involving related or unrelated business simply because the Internet is the communication medium.

§ 10.1 STATE OF THE "LAW"

Recent years have seen increasingly extensive use of the Internet by tax-exempt organizations; this use has several implications for development of the federal tax law pertaining to related and unrelated business activities. There is little federal tax or other law, however, concerning tax-exempt organizations' use of the Internet—in the unrelated business setting or otherwise. There is no Internal Revenue Code provision; other than two examples, there are no tax regulations; there are no court opinions. Nonetheless, the IRS has by no means been silent on these matters. The agency addressed the subject of Internet use by exempt organizations and the tax law on the following occasions:

- In its tax-exempt organizations continuing professional education technical instruction program textbook for the federal government's fiscal year 1999, issued in the fall of 1998, the IRS included an article titled "Internet Service Providers Exemption Issues under IRC 501(c)(3) and 501(c)(12)."[1]

- In its tax-exempt organizations continuing professional education technical instruction program textbook for the federal government's fiscal year 2000, issued in the fall of 1999, the IRS included an article titled "Tax-Exempt Organizations and Worldwide Web Fundraising and Advertising on the Internet."[2]

- In the preamble accompanying the proposed regulations on the subject of corporate sponsorships, which appeared in 2000, the IRS requested comments on such sponsorships in the Internet context.[3]

- Also in 2000, the IRS requested comments on a series of questions posed by the agency concerning Internet communications by tax-exempt organizations.[4]

- In 2002, the IRS issued final regulations to accompany the corporate sponsorship rules;[5] these regulations include two significant examples.[6]

- In 2004, the IRS issued a revenue ruling concerning virtual trade shows conducted by tax-exempt organizations.[7]

Though not law in the formal (precedential) sense, the IRS has issued a few private determinations on the subject.[8]

The coming months and years will bring much extrapolation from existing law concerning offline activities of tax-exempt organizations, for the purpose of creating comparable law in the Internet setting. This process is already under way, as illustrated by three IRS private determinations on the subject of tax-exempt organizations and the Internet.

In one of these rulings, the agency pondered the question of whether a non-profit organization that functioned as an Internet service provider, serving the general public, could qualify as a tax-exempt organization on the ground that it was advancing charitable and educational purposes. The answer to this question

---

[1] Referred to in this chapter as "IRS FY 1999 CPE Text on Internet Service Providers."
[2] Referred to in this chapter as "IRS FY 2000 CPE Text on Exempt Organizations and Internet Use."
[3] 65 Fed. Reg. 11,013, 11,015 (Mar. 1, 2000).
[4] Ann. 2000-84, 2000-2 C.B. 385 (hereinafter Announcement). See § 10.14.
[5] See § 6.6.
[6] See § 10.2, text accompanied by notes 41–44.
[7] See § 10.6, text accompanied by note 64.
[8] *E.g.*, Priv. Ltr. Ruls. 9723046, 200303062. Also see *infra* notes 9,10,12,16, and 19.

was no; provision of Internet service is a nonexempt commercial undertaking, and the IRS ruled accordingly.[9] In so doing, the IRS engaged in extrapolation by analogizing these activities to those of a nonprofit lawyer referral service, which was ruled to be a nonexempt entity.[10]

The IRS considered the international operations of a business league[11] that has a program for the maintenance of collections of standard master agreements, legal memoranda and opinions, and legislation of many countries; the association is the only entity providing this service. The organization has formed a partnership to make use of and deliver an online legal information service to its members. This information is available to the members by means of a password-protected Web site maintained by the association. The IRS ruled that this service is substantially related to the organization's exempt purposes of promoting practices conducive to the efficient conduct of its members' businesses and informing members of legislative and administrative developments affecting the industry.[12] The agency added that this is not an instance of an association's provision of "individualized advice or services tailored to the specific needs of individual members." In this instance, the IRS relied on an appellate court opinion, finding the online service analogous to the compilation and maintenance of a loose-leaf library service.[13] The agency also cited another court of appeals opinion, which held that the compilation of a manual and sale of forms were substantially related businesses.[14]

The IRS ruled that a tax-exempt rural electric cooperative[15] can, on a cooperative basis, provide its members with Internet service in addition to electric power, and retain its exemption.[16] The organization was restructured into two divisions and amended its governing instruments accordingly. The IRS concluded that the organization will continue to qualify as a "like" organization for exemption purposes. In this situation, the IRS decided that the Internet service was comparable to a two-way radio system that was found to be an exempt function of cooperatives nearly 50 years ago.[17]

Also, the IRS ruled that creation by a for-profit corporation, engaged in a particular business, of a Web site on which the corporation will conduct that business is an expansion of the corporation's business rather than the acquisition of a new or different business.[18] Furthermore, it held that a public charity may conduct a portion of its health care provider services via a Web site.[19]

---

[9] Tech. Adv. Mem. 200203069.

[10] Rev. Rul. 80-287, 1980-2 C.B. 185. The IRS also ruled that the fact that a tax-exempt organization will "develop its own website" is evidence of commerciality (see ch. 7), thus threatening tax-exempt status. Ex. Den. & Revoc. Ltr. 20044045E. That view would destroy the tax exemption of countless organizations and is, of course, not the law. See § 7.1(f), note 113.

[11] That is, an organization described in IRC § 501(c)(6). See Hopkins, *The Law of Tax-Exempt Organizations, Eighth Edition* (John Wiley & Sons, 2003) [hereinafter *Tax-Exempt Organizations*], ch. 13.

[12] Priv. Ltr. Rul. 200506025.

[13] La. Credit Union League v. United States, 693 F.2d 525 (5th Cir. 1982).

[14] Tex. Apartment Ass'n v. United States, 869 F.2d 884 (5th Cir. 1989).

[15] That is, an organization described in IRC § 501(c)(12). See *Tax-Exempt Organizations*, § 18.5(b).

[16] Priv. Ltr. Rul. 200504035.

[17] Rev. Rul. 57-420, 1957-2 C.B. 308.

[18] Rev. Rul. 2003-38, 2003-17 I.R.B. 811.

[19] Priv. Ltr. Rul. 200307094.

§ 10.2 TWO OVERARCHING ISSUES

Two overarching issues, from a law standpoint, permeate the interaction of Internet use by tax-exempt organizations and the law that affects their operations. They are the costs associated with functions carried out by means of the Internet and the inherent qualities to be assigned to website links.

(a) Costs of Internet Operations

Traditionally, from a federal tax law perspective, the activities of a tax-exempt organization are assessed and quantified in terms of the amount of money expended in the conduct of those activities.[20] (Sometimes the amount of time involved is also a factor.[21]) This is so, irrespective of whether the issue is ongoing eligibility for tax-exempt status pursuant to application of the primary purpose test,[22] ascertainment of an amount of lobbying or political activity,[23] or measurement of the extent of unrelated business.[24] The conduct of the activity usually has been stated in terms of staff expense and the cost of communication by modes such as travel, U.S. mail, radio, television, and various forms of print media.

This approach does not work very well (indeed, often not at all) in the context of activities conducted by tax-exempt organizations via the Internet. Important lobbying, fundraising, political campaign, and unrelated business undertakings can be transacted by exempt organizations on the Internet at a fraction of the expense that would have been incurred had traditional means of communication been used. It is by no means clear—to exempt organizations, the IRS, or the courts—which basis to utilize in quantifying these Internet activities.

There are three basic options in this regard. One is to simply disregard Internet communications of this nature for purposes of applying the federal law of tax-exempt organizations; this is an unlikely outcome. The second approach is to apply some form of safe-harbor test. The third alternative is an ephemeral facts-and-circumstances test, which would take into account the factor of influence; there is no law directly on point for this.

(b) Essence of Links

A definition of a *link* (technically, a *hyperlink*) is that it is a "connection between two hypertext documents," by means of which users can "travel freely in any direction throughout a document series [with text files formatted by Hypertext

---

[20] In general, to be tax-exempt, an organization must devote a substantial or primary amount of its efforts to the furtherance of exempt purposes and the conduct of exempt activities; this is the *primary purpose test*. See *Tax-Exempt Organizations*, § 4.4. Often, this test is applied by assessing the amount of funding devoted to programs.

[21] In the context of charitable (IRC § 501(c)(3)) organizations, the IRS occasionally applies a *commensurate test* to determine whether an organization is entitled to tax exemption. *See Tax-Exempt Organizations*, § 4.7. This test, which assesses entitlement to exemption in terms of the amount of an organization's resources that are being devoted to program, can take into account the amount of time expended, particularly if that amount is greater than the amount of expenditures for program activities.

[22] See *supra* note 20.

[23] See *Tax-Exempt Organizations*, chs. 20, 21.

[24] See § 1.6.

Markup Language] or Web site."[25] Another, fuller explanation of a link[26] observed that a link can be incorporated into an e-mail message or a Web site; it can appear as a displayed address for another site or as a graphic message. "Clicking on the link," as this explanation noted, "causes the routine built into the link to run, issuing a request to see the Web site whose address is built into the link." A key point: "The link does not function until the user clicks on it."

This latter explanation also noted that a link "can carry the user directly to the new site, with no way to return to the original site other than to use the 'back' function of the Web browser." Alternatively, the link "can function as a 'framing link,' causing a new copy of the Web browser to start running on top of the existing copy, leaving the existing copy of the Web browser and the original site still visible in the background." Moreover, "[s]ites can also have a frame of their own," so that "[c]licking on a link may leave the original site's frame in place but change the content that appears inside the frame to be that of a new site."

The Web site of a tax-exempt organization can—and often does—contain one or more links to other Web sites. These other sites may be those maintained by other tax-exempt organizations, government agencies, and/or for-profit organizations. When an exempt organization's website link is to that on a site maintained by another exempt organization, that other entity may have the same exempt status as the linking organization, a different exempt status, or perhaps no true exempt status.

The law is a long way from sorting out the inherent qualities of these links. The meaning in law of the very presence of a link is unclear. The most serious aspect of this is the prospect of *attribution* of a Web site (or particular content on the site) of a linked organization to a tax-exempt organization, principally for federal tax law purposes. In the Announcement, for example, the IRS asked whether the provision of a link by an exempt charitable organization to the Web site of another organization that engages in lobbying or political campaign activity constitutes lobbying or political campaign activity by the charitable organization.

As to the matter of a link's inherent quality, it was observed that links "do not create an identity between the sites on either side of the link." That is, they "are nothing more than a communications tool and are completely independent of the content they bridge."[27] This observation is not, however, entirely accurate; this characterization of links overstates the case and accords too much sterility to links. Links do not simply materialize; they are put in place for one or more reasons.

To this commentator's credit, the article also stated that the IRS "should look only to what the charity [or other type of exempt organization] intends when it affirmatively establishes a connection, as demonstrated by the context created for the link."[28] Though this observation is also somewhat overstated, it is much closer to what the emerging standard seems to be. Intent clearly is far more important than the mere fact of the existence of a link. Thus, for example, if an exempt charitable organization controls another entity, there is a link between

---

[25] Johnson, *The Nonprofit Guide to the Internet, Second Edition,* 229 (John Wiley & Sons, 1999).

[26] Livingston, *Tax-Exempt Organizations and the Internet: Tax and Other Legal Issues,* 31 *Exempt Orgs. Tax Rev.* 420 (no. 3, Mar. 2001) (hereinafter Livingston).

[27] *Id.* at 426.

[28] *Id.*

the Web sites of the two organizations, and there is a political campaign message on the Web site of the other entity, the charitable organization is likely to have some difficulty contending that it is not engaged in political campaign activity because it did not intend to be associated with the message.[29]

This observer advanced another argument, this one based on the thought that links "function entirely at the user's discretion."[30] The article used the example of an individual reading educational material on the Web site of a charitable organization, who thereafter uses a link in that material to move to educational material on a Web site created by a noncharitable entity, and then links to a third site that contains a political campaign message. The point presumably was that the charitable organization created the first link but not the second one, so the political message should not be attributed to it. The observation was that the charitable organization "did not connect that series of events even though it invited the reader to take the first step."[31] To the extent that this is all the argument connotes, the conclusion is correct. But there is danger in assigning too much neutrality to links; the argument can border on disingenuity. If, in this example, the charitable organization knew that the link to the political message would be created once it initiated the first link, the outcome would be different. In these circumstances, it will not do to blandly assert that the political message should not be attributed to the charity because the visitor to the Web sites exercised discretion in getting to the third site. If the charity builds it, the charity has the resulting responsibility when users come. Again, the matter ultimately is that of the intent of one or more human beings, not some inherent characteristic of a link or Web site user discretion.

Another element to be taken into account in this setting is identity of interests. In determining whether the content of an organization's Web site should be attributed to a tax-exempt organization because of a link between the two entities, one should explore whether there is an identity of interests between them. In a private letter ruling issued in the context of the political activities rules,[32] the IRS emphasized that certain political action committees were sponsored by unions, which, on labor issues, may have political interests differing from those of a related charitable organization. The IRS relied on this fact in concluding that there was no identity of interest between the charitable entity and the political action committees; thus, the charity was not considered to have violated the political campaign activity constraint,[33] and did not thereby endanger its tax-exempt status.[34]

As to the law on identity of interests, the IRS relied on a Supreme Court decision, holding that partnerships formed to develop apartment complexes were the owners of the complexes for federal tax purposes, even though each

---

[29] See *Tax-Exempt Organizations*, ch. 21.
[30] Livingston, at 426.
[31] *Id.*
[32] Priv. Ltr. Rul. 200151060.
[33] See *Tax-Exempt Organizations*, ch. 21.
[34] The IRS subsequently overruled itself on this point, concluding that the administration of a payroll-deduction plan by a public charity, in support of a political action committee, constituted prohibited participation or intervention in political campaigns. Tech. Adv. Mem. 200446033.

partnership caused a corporation to hold legal title to the property for the purpose of securing financing, inasmuch as the relationship between the parties was that of agent and principal, with the partnerships as the principals.[35]

Thus, if there is no identity of interests between two organizations with linked sites, that fact should go a long way—perhaps even give rise to a presumption—in showing that the content of the Web site of an organization is not attributable to the other organization. (At the same time, just because there is an identity of interests between two entities, attribution of views because of a link should not be automatic.)

The state of the federal tax law is not such that a link alone constitutes a ground for attributing a statement posted by one organization on its Web site to another organization that is linked to that Web site. Indeed, the federal tax consequences of automatic attribution of content in this manner are sobering to contemplate.[36] Currently, a link from the Web site of one organization to the Web site of another does not, by itself, cause any activity of the linked organization to be attributed to the linking organization.

Another factor in this regard is the content of the linked message. In many instances in the tax-exempt organizations setting, a link will be in place in advance of one or more programs, as charitable, educational, and like organizations link to similar organizations. Matters become more complex, however, when exempt organizations with differing tax-exempt statuses link. As an illustration, a tax-exempt trade association is not likely to endanger its exempt status by linking to the Web site of its related foundation, but the foundation may have an exemption problem if it is perceived as linking to the association, because of message content (such as lobbying[37]) on the association's Web site. Not surprisingly, this aspect of linkage will be even more problematic when a tax-exempt organization maintains a Web site link with a for-profit company; the federal tax issues here are manifold, such as the unrelated business rules (if there is an income flow), as well as the private inurement doctrine,[38] the private benefit doctrine,[39] and the intermediate sanctions rules.[40]

Considerable insight into the emerging law on these points was provided by the IRS in the tax regulations pertaining to the tax treatment of corporate sponsorships,[41] which were issued in final form in 2002. In that body of law, the sponsorship revenue is not regarded as unrelated business income as long as the recipient tax-exempt organization merely *acknowledges* the financial support, by referencing only the sponsor's name, logo, product lines, and similar items; services provided in the nature of *advertising* may cause the sponsorship payments to be taxable. The question thus arose in this context as to whether, or under what circumstances, the exempt organization receiving the payment goes beyond the bounds of gift acknowledgment by providing a link to the Web site

---

[35] Comm'r v. Bollinger, 485 U.S. 340 (1988).
[36] One commentator found the prospect of automatic attribution "breathtaking." Livingston, at 426.
[37] See *Tax-Exempt Organizations*, ch. 20.
[38] See *Tax-Exempt Organizations*, ch. 19.
[39] *Id.* at § 19.10.
[40] *Id.* at § 19.11.
[41] See § 6.6.

of the sponsor, thereby raising the prospect of taxation of the payment on the ground that provision of the link is a substantial return benefit.

By means of two examples in these regulations, the IRS took the position—thereby greatly relieving the tax-exempt community on the point[42] —that the mere presence of a Web site link by a tax-exempt organization to the site of a corporate sponsor does not defeat characterization of the payment as a nontaxable sponsorship. In one of these examples, a music shop is the sponsor of a concert series presented by an exempt organization that has as its function the operation of a symphony orchestra. Although the exempt organization posts the music shop's Internet address on the organization's Web site, and the address links the exempt organization's Web site to the shop's site, the organization does not promote the shop or advertise its merchandise. This payment in its entirety is said to be a qualified sponsorship payment, which means that it is not considered unrelated business income.[43]

In the other example, by contrast, a tax-exempt, health-based charitable organization has a link to its corporate sponsor, a pharmaceutical company that funds an educational initiative of the charitable entity. The company manufactures a drug that is used in treating the medical condition that is the focus of the charity's programs. The company's Web site contains a statement that the charity "endorses the use of our drug" and "suggests that you ask your doctor for a prescription if you have this medical condition." The charitable organization reviews the endorsement before it is posted and gives the company permission to use it. This payment may be taxable as unrelated business income.[44]

These examples show how a message on another entity's Web site can be attributed to a tax-exempt organization for unrelated business law (and other federal tax law) purposes. This analysis clearly took into account not only the content of the message but also the intent of the parties in posting it. Had the exempt organization posted the communication on its Web site, it would have been advertising there; the posting of it on the sponsor's site, coupled with the link, led to the same result by reason of attribution. Thus, this aspect of the law of tax-exempt organizations is headed toward the vagaries of another facts-and-circumstances test, where the factors to take into account will include intent (of both organizations and users), the content of the message, which organization created and/or initiated the link, why the link was created, and who clicked on it and why.

Lack of attribution of this type, however, does not mean that a link does not have inherent value or benefit. A link is not some inanimate thing passively reposing on a Web site, of no consequence unless and until an individual clicks on it. "Many argue," the IRS wrote as part of a discussion of Web site links and the exclusion from taxation for eligible corporate sponsorships, where the exempt organization's Web site is linked to the sponsor's site, "that the payment should

---

[42] At a much earlier point, it appeared that the IRS was leaning toward ruling the other way; the agency wrote that "[a]dvertising spots differ from mere expressions of recognition in that they may contain additional information about an advertiser's product, services, or facilities, or function as a hypertext link to the advertiser." Priv. Ltr. Rul. 9723046.

[43] Reg. § 1.513-4(f), Example 11.

[44] *Id.*, Example 12.

retain its character as a mere acknowledgment since the Web site visitor must take an affirmative action to reach the donor's Web site." The IRS thus was (and remains) of the view that a link generally retains the "passive character" associated with most forms of corporate sponsorship (and thus does not constitute advertising).

This is a most helpful interpretation of the rules, to be sure, dictated in no small part by the widespread and growing nature of the practice, and the fact that the IRS would have been awash in controversy had it decreed that the mere presence of a Web site link destroys the tax shield otherwise accorded to a corporate sponsorship. Nonetheless, the provision of a link can be a valuable service or benefit; its existence certainly goes beyond the mere utilization of a corporation's name or logo. Consequently, this matter of tax-exempt organizations and Internet links will persist as a contentious area of the law.

§ 10.3 WEB-BASED BUSINESS: TAX LAW PERSPECTIVE

As the IRS saliently observed, the "use of the Internet to accomplish a particular task does not change the way the tax laws apply to that task." The agency continued: "Advertising is still advertising and fundraising is still fundraising."[45] The IRS also could have written: "Unrelated business activity is still unrelated business activity." Indeed, the agency stated in 1999 that "it is reasonable to assume that as the Service position [on tax-exempt organization Web merchandising, advertising, and publishing] develops[,] it will remain consistent with our position with respect to advertising and merchandising and publishing in the off-line world."[46] Thus, the rules as to unrelated business activity by exempt organizations embrace this type of activity engaged in by means of the Internet.

There are four forms of Internet communications in this setting:

1. A communication published on a publicly accessible Web site

2. A communication posted on a password-protected portion of a Web site

3. A communication on a listserv (or using similar methods, such as a newsgroup, chat room, and/or forum)

4. A communication by means of e-mail

The IRS observed that "[m]any tax-exempt organizations now have a web page that describes their purpose, discusses their activities, provides lists of upcoming events, lists local affiliates, provides contact information, and more." The IRS also noted that, "[b]y publishing a webpage on the Internet, an exempt organization can provide the general public with information about the organization, its activities, and issues of concern to the organization, as well as immediate access to Web sites of other organizations."[47]

---

[45] IRS FY 2000 CPE Text on Exempt Organizations and Internet Use, at 64.
[46] *Id.* at 74.
[47] *Id.* at 70.

(a) Business Activities

By application of the fragmentation rule, the federal tax law views a tax-exempt organization as a cluster of businesses, with each discrete activity evaluated independent of the others.[48] The fundamental statutory definition of the term, in the unrelated business setting, is that a *business* includes "any activity which is carried on for the production of income from the sale of goods or the performance of services."[49] Thus, nearly every activity that an exempt organization engages in by means of the Internet is a business. Indeed, use of the Internet by an exempt organization constitutes the conduct of one or more businesses, is a component of one or more businesses, or (in rare instances) does not rise to the level of a business.

The Web site of a typical tax-exempt organization primarily, if not exclusively, contains information concerning the organization's programs. The organization's operations and purposes are thus described, often in some detail. In some instances, substantive information is provided pertaining to its area or areas of interest. Some collateral information may be on the site; photographs, maps, membership lists, and staff directories are common. Many charitable organizations include information about giving opportunities. Some exempt organizations discuss their advocacy activities. Rarely, however, are unrelated business endeavors openly pursued on an exempt organization's Web site.

It is not common for a Web site to function wholly as one or more discrete businesses. Rather, the various components and postings are extensions of offline programs and other activities. A university's site, for example, summarizes its undergraduate and graduate programs, describes its various schools, and offers information as to how and when to apply for admission. A scientific research institution's site inventories the research projects in process and perhaps highlights the work of particular scientists. An association's site enumerates its various programs; perhaps contains information about its advocacy efforts; and includes information about its other activities, such as certification and enforcement of its code of ethics. Usually all of this information is also available elsewhere.

As noted, in some instances, Web site use by tax-exempt organizations does not amount to business activity. In one case, an exempt agricultural membership association, with the exempt functions of providing educational information to its members regarding agricultural issues and promoting the sharing of information among members regarding common agricultural problems and concerns, operated a Web site through which it provided its members and the public with information on its activities and programs, and on current issues affecting agriculture. This association had arrangements with various third-party service providers that offered special or discounted services and benefits to the organization's members. The association provided these programs to attract and retain members, who are interested in and support the organization's purposes, and to create a strong membership base that actively participates in the organization's exempt activities. Consistent with these goals, the organization publicized the availability of these

---

[48] See § 2.3.
[49] IRC § 513(c). See § 2.2.

services and benefits to its members and potential members by describing the services and benefits and by providing the contact information for each service provider. The organization did not charge service providers a fee for the listings, nor did it charge a fee for a link from its Web site to the Web sites of the service providers. These services and benefits were available only to the association's members (rather than the general public). The IRS ruled that the association's listing of information about service providers in its publications and on its Web site, and its provision of a link from its Web site to the service providers' Web sites did not amount to business.[50]

One of the major difficulties in this regard is the allocation of time and expenditures to Web site offerings.[51] There are, of course, the expenses of building and maintaining a Web site. The costs of posting the information, however, are negligible. Thus, an unanswered question is: How are Web site establishment and maintenance costs allocated to a tax-exempt organization's various programs and other activities?

There may be an alternative approach. The fragmentation rule could be applied in such a way that Web site establishment and maintenance itself is a business, or perhaps two or more businesses. Certainly the matter of determination and allocation of expenses would be simplified if this were so. For most tax-exempt organizations, this approach would mean that Web site creation and maintenance is wholly a related business. For other exempt organizations, however, even with this approach, the expenses of activities such as fundraising, advocacy, and unrelated business would have to be factored out for reporting and other purposes.

(b) Regularly Carried On

For the most part, activities reflected on a tax-exempt organization's Web site are regularly carried on. Organizations change the content of the site from time to time, of course, but usually the categories of information (programs, directories, fundraising, advocacy, certification, ethics enforcement, and the like) remain the same.

(c) Substantially Related

As noted, nearly everything on a tax-exempt organization's Web site—often, *everything*—consists of information and material related to the organization's exempt purposes. The biggest exception for charitable organizations is likely to be fundraising activities. Many organizations that are involved in unrelated businesses do not, as noted, openly disclose or flaunt that fact on their Web sites. Likewise, an exempt organization's participation in a joint venture (such as a partnership or limited liability company)[52] usually is not mentioned on the site; the same is true of the use of a for-profit subsidiary.[53]

---

[50] Priv. Ltr. Rul. 200303062.
[51] See § 10.2(a).
[52] See §§ 8.2, 8.3, 8.9.
[53] See § 8.1.

§ 10.4 WEB SITE ADVERTISING

One of the major uses of the Internet by tax-exempt organizations is for advertising—of themselves. Today, one of the principal purposes of an exempt organization's Web site is advertising of its programs: services, products, and facilities. Visits to Web sites lead to invitations to apply to a college, join an association, explore a museum, tour a scientific research facility, and much more. Some Web sites are entire bastions of advertising, with headings such as "Who we are," "What we do," "FAQs about us," and so forth. In some cases, by contrast, there is Web site advertising (or ostensible advertising) of the goods and/or services of others, such as by means of displays, a link, or a "moving banner" (a graphic advertisement, usually a moving image, measured in pixels).

(a) Advertising in General

Usually, advertising[54] by tax-exempt organizations of the products or services of other persons is considered an unrelated activity. Before the advent of the Internet, rare was the situation in which advertising was considered a related function.

The huge growth of Internet use has not changed the rules as to commercial advertising, however. From this perspective, three categories of information dissemination are in the realm of advertising: related advertising, commercial (unrelated) advertising, and acknowledgments in the context of corporate sponsorships.[55] As between related and unrelated advertising, the Supreme Court instructed that a tax-exempt organization can "control its publication of advertisements in such a way as to reflect an intention to contribute importantly to its . . . [exempt] functions."[56] This can be done, wrote the Court, by "coordinating the content of the advertisements with the editorial content of the issue, or by publishing only advertisements reflecting new developments."[57]

(b) Compensation for Advertising

The IRS observed that the advertising rates charged by a tax-exempt organization "will vary considerably based on its area of concern, the quality of its Web site and the user traffic it generates."[58] The IRS includes as advertising the display of a "banner, graphic, or statement of sponsorship." The agency noted that exempt organizations generally favor "less obtrusive" sponsorship statements over banner advertisements, in that the latter are "perceived as more appropriate to commercial sites and potentially more offensive to potential donors." Also, a moving banner is "probably more likely" to be considered taxable advertising than other approaches.[59]

---

[54] See § 6.5.

[55] As to the latter, see §§ 6.6, 10.5.

[56] United States v. Am. Coll. of Physicians, 475 U.S. 834, 849 (1986).

[57] Id. at 849–50.

[58] IRS FY 2000 CPE Text on Exempt Organizations and Internet Use, at 74. All quotations of the IRS in this section and §§ 10.5–10.11 are from this text.

[59] In one situation, the exempt organization stipulated that income it derived from the sale of banner advertising was unrelated business income. Priv. Ltr. Rul. 200303062.

One way for a tax-exempt organization to be compensated for Web site advertising is by means of a flat fee. An organization may offer pay-per-view advertisements, whereby it earns a credit each time a visitor to the site views the advertisement. A related form of compensation is the click-through charge, whereby the advertiser pays only when an individual clicks through the banner or corporate logo and visits the advertiser's site.

The IRS addressed the fact that many exempt organization Web sites include links to related, affiliated, or similarly recommended sites. Some organizations exchange banners or links. The IRS wrote that it is presently "unclear" as to whether it will treat link or banner exchanges as "similar to a mailing list exchange[,] or whether an organization that participates in such a program may incur liability for unrelated business income." The agency added that, in analyzing these exchange mechanisms, their *purpose* is critical, in that it must be determined "whether the link [or banner] exchange is an exchange of advertising or rather merely an attempt to refer the site visitor to additional information in furtherance of the organization's exempt purposes and activities."

§ 10.5 WEB SITE CORPORATE SPONSORSHIPS

The IRS recognized that the "differences between an advertisement and corporate sponsorship is [*sic*] further complicated in the Internet environment."[60] The agency noted that it is "not uncommon" for a tax-exempt organization to have all or part of its Web site sponsored by a corporation. This financial support may be acknowledged through display of a corporate logo, a notation of the sponsor's Web site address and/or 800 number, a moving banner, or a hypertext link.

In an understatement, the IRS declared that, "[g]enerally, exempt organizations prefer to view payments as corporate sponsorship rather than advertising income, which is more likely to be subject to unrelated business income tax." The agency wrote that the "use of promotional logos or slogans that are an established part of a sponsor's identity" is not, alone, advertising. It also noted that display or sale of a sponsor's product by an exempt organization in connection with a sponsored event is an acknowledgment, not advertising.

A payment cannot be a qualified sponsorship payment if the amount is contingent, by contract or otherwise, on the level of attendance at one or more events, broadcast ratings, or other factors indicating the degree of public exposure to an activity. Although the IRS did not say so, this rule seems to preclude pay-per-view or click-through arrangements from constituting qualified corporate sponsorship arrangements.

Because of the evolution of this aspect of the law, tax-exempt organizations now have their first inkling as to the IRS's position on the tax law import of links. It came in the final regulations concerning corporate sponsorships, in which the agency considered whether the use of a link, in what would otherwise be an acknowledgment, changes the character of a payment from a qualified (nontaxable) corporate sponsorship to taxable advertising. The essence of the IRS's position is

---

[60] The corporate sponsorship rules in general are the subject of § 6.6.

that the mere presence of a link from the Web site of a tax-exempt organization to the site of a corporate sponsor does not defeat characterization of the payment as a nontaxable sponsorship.[61] If, however, the sponsor's Web site contains advertising in the nature of an endorsement of a product or service by the exempt organization, the protections of the qualified corporate sponsorship rules may fall away, at least in part.[62]

§ 10.6 TRADE SHOWS

Application of the trade show rules[63] in connection with what the IRS referred to as the "trade show in the virtual reality format" was originally unclear. The agency initially signaled that the answer was that the rules are inapplicable, writing that it is "highly questionable whether income from a year round virtual trade show would be accorded exclusion from unrelated business income tax" (and it should not).

The IRS noted that some of these trade shows "merely consist of a listing of HyperText links to industry suppliers' Web sites for which remuneration is received by the Web site host trade association." Others have "displays including educational information related to issues of interest to industry members." Virtual trade shows are "sometimes timed to coincide with the sponsoring organization's annual meeting or regular trade show in order to increase participation by industry members who are unable to attend the actual events."

The IRS subsequently provided guidance in this regard, holding that activities conducted on the premises of a tax-exempt business league's trade shows, and on a special section of the organization's Web site that allows members and the interested public to access the same information available at the show, constituted qualified convention and trade show activity. Each show occurred over a consecutive 10-day period; the special section of the Web site was available online during that period, as well as during a 3-day period prior to the show and a 3-day period following the show. The IRS cast these Web site sections, each of which thus lasted 16 days, as an "alternative medium," and characterized these online activities as being carried out in conjunction with, ancillary to, and as an extension of each show. If, however, this type of Internet activity does not overlap or coincide with an exempt organization's international, national, regional, state, or local convention, annual meeting, or trade show, or augment or enhance such a show—such as a Web site posting trade-show-type information available to the general public 24 hours a day, 7 days a week, for a 2-week period—the Internet activity will be ineligible for the trade show activity exception. Moreover, this type of site itself is not a convention, annual meeting, or trade show, because it is not a "specific event" at which an exempt organization's members,

---

[61] In one instance, the IRS ruled that an exempt organization's provision of a link to a sponsor's Web site, in connection with a sponsorship payment, was an acknowledgment rather than advertising. Priv. Ltr. Rul. 200303062.

[62] See § 10.2(b).

[63] See § 4.5.

suppliers, and potential customers gather in person at a physical location during a certain period of time and have face-to-face interaction.[64]

§ 10.7 MERCHANDISING

The IRS has mused about the proper tax treatment of "[o]nline storefronts complete with virtual shopping carts." Not surprisingly, the agency is relying on its "traditional" assessment of sales activities by tax-exempt organizations, particularly museum shop sales.[65]

Once again, the determination of ultimate causal relationship and its importance[66] is based on the facts and circumstances of each case. As with museums, the IRS will determine relatedness of sales based on the tax-exempt organization's primary purpose for selling the item. If the purpose underlying the production and/or sale of the item is furtherance of the organization's exempt purposes, the sale will be considered a related one. If, however, the primary purpose of an item for sale is utilitarian, ornamental, or only generally educational in nature, or amounts to a souvenir, the sales activity is not likely to be regarded as related. The IRS considers various factors in analyzing this primary purpose, as the agency probes the "nature, scope, and motivation" for these sales. The factors include the degree of connection between the item being sold, the purpose of the exempt organization, and the "overall impression" conveyed by the article; if the "dominant impression" leads to the conclusion that "noncharitable use or function predominates," the sale will be categorized as an unrelated one. The fact that an item could, in a different context, be held related to the exempt purpose of another tax-exempt organization does not make the sale by the organization under review a related activity.

Thus, the IRS is comparing Internet merchandising to sales made in stores and through catalogs and similar vehicles. Merchandise will be evaluated on an item-by-item basis—the fragmentation rule[67] again—to determine whether the sales activity furthers accomplishment of an organization's exempt purposes or is "simply a way to increase revenues."

§ 10.8 AUCTIONS

The IRS is looking at online auctions, in part, from the standpoint as to the manner in which they are conducted. Some tax-exempt organizations conduct their own auctions; others use outside service providers. Some online auction Web sites provide services for exempt organizations only; other sites and search engines also operate auctions for individuals and for-profit organizations. Two obvious advantages to use of an outside auction service provider are the availability of a larger auction audience than might be available if the exempt organization conducted the auction itself, and avoidance of credit card fraud problems.

---

[64] Rev. Rul. 2004-112, 2004-51 I.R.B. 985. Because this type of Web site activity is usually conducted over what this ruling referred to as a "relatively short period of time," it is likely to avoid unrelated business taxation because it is not regularly carried on. See § 2.5.

[65] See § 9.3.

[66] See §§ 2.6, 2.7.

[67] See § 2.3.

Yet, as the IRS delicately phrased the matter, "entering into an agreement with an outside service provider might have tax implications."

One of the factors considered by the IRS is the degree of control (if any) the tax-exempt organization will exercise over the marketing and conduct of the auction. The IRS wants the event to be "sufficiently segregated from other, particularly non-charitable auction activities" and expects the exempt organization to retain "primary responsibility" for publicity and marketing. Otherwise, the agency "may be more likely to view income from such auction activities as income from classified advertising rather than as income derived from the conduct of a fundraising event."

Also, the IRS has characterized these service providers as "essentially professional fundraisers." One may expect that the IRS will scrutinize service providers' functions and fees "using traditional [private] inurement and private benefit principles."[68] The intermediate sanctions rules[69] also are applicable in this setting.

§ 10.9 CHARITY MALLS

Internet sites of tax-exempt organizations may permit online shoppers to purchase items from affiliated vendors through links on the site. For each purchase, the vendor agrees to remit, through a charity mall operator, an agreed-upon percentage of the purchase price to a designated charity. A few charity mall operators represent that they use volunteers and pass on all of the funds raised to the designated charities; others retain a percentage of the proceeds for site maintenance and development. Some malls solicit paid advertisements. The mall operator credits the charity with the contribution upon receipt of the rebate from the vendor.[70]

An organization that operates one of these malls as its primary purpose probably cannot qualify as a tax-exempt charitable organization, "since the marketing and operation of the virtual mall is a trade or business ordinarily [regularly] carried on for profit." Among the IRS's concerns about virtual charity mall operations are that (1) the beneficiary organizations "do not appear to have any agreement with the virtual mall operators and do not appear to be entitled to any record of member designations or transactions;" and (2) the exempt organization "has little recourse if it finds its name used in association with such mall operators, who may or may not prove reputable."

§ 10.10 MERCHANT AFFILIATE PROGRAMS

Affiliate and other co-venture programs are growing in popularity, both online and off, and are spawning many variations. Probably the most ubiquitous of these programs on the Internet involves co-ventures with large, online booksellers, although art galleries, toy merchants, and even credit-report providers also have these programs. Organizations are offered the options of making book

---

[68] See *Tax-Exempt Organizations*, ch. 19.
[69] *Id.* § 19.11.
[70] See Hopkins, *The Tax Law of Charitable Giving, Third Edition* (John Wiley & Sons, 2005) §§ 3.1(h), 6.10 for a discussion of the deductibility of these rebates.

recommendations that may be "displayed" or listed on the organization's Web site, or simply using a logo or other link to the bookseller. The exempt organization earns a percentage of sales of recommended materials, as well as a commission on other purchases sold as a result of use of the referring link. The exempt organization receives a periodic report detailing link activity. The IRS noted that a "distinct advantage that these programs have over the virtual mall type operations from the point of view of the charity is that the exempt organization itself enters into an agreement with the merchant and is provided an activity report in order to ensure that it [is] credited with the appropriate royalty."

The controversy over the tax treatment of income received by tax-exempt organizations from affinity card programs[71] may have an impact on the taxation of income generated by these ventures. In this context, then, the IRS seems to have conceded that these payments qualify as tax-excludable royalties.[72] Indeed, the payments discussed in some of the preceding sections also constitute excludable royalties.

§ 10.11   ASSOCIATIONS

Many professional and trade associations have Web sites accessible by the general public, along with material that is restricted to members. These member-only sections often "provide access to research services, continuing education opportunities, employment listings, membership directories, links to various organization benefit programs, legislative alerts, publications, etc." The IRS issued this caution: "Organizations and web designers must be aware that the traditional rules with respect to prohibitions on providing particular services, treatment of advertising income, [and] sales activity, as well as lobbying restrictions[,] still apply to Web site activities."[73]

§ 10.12   WEB SITE MATERIAL AS PERIODICAL

The corporate sponsorship rules intertwine with the general unrelated business rules, as applicable in the Internet communications context, in several instances. Again, the fundamental issue is whether the communication by the sponsored organization, in response to receipt of the corporate support, is merely an acknowledgment of the support or is a communication that amounts to advertising.[74]

This dichotomy between acknowledgments and advertising becomes irrelevant if the communication involved appears in a periodical. In this circumstance, the exception for corporate sponsorship payments is not available. Technically, the exception for a qualified corporate sponsorship does not apply to a payment that entitles the payor (sponsor) to the use or acknowledgment of

---

[71] See § 3.7.

[72] *Id.*

[73] As to these bodies of law, see *Tax-Exempt Organizations*, § 13.4.

[74] See §§ 6.6, 10.5. The term *advertising* means any message or other programming material that is broadcast or otherwise transmitted, published, displayed, or distributed, and that promotes or markets any trade or business, or any service, facility, or product. Reg. § 1.513-4(c)(2)(v).

the name or logo (or product line) of the payor's business in a periodical of a tax-exempt organization.[75]

A *periodical* is regularly scheduled and printed material published by or on behalf of the payee (sponsored) organization that is not related to and primarily distributed in connection with a specific event conducted by the payee organization.[76] Thus, the corporate sponsorship exception does not apply to payments that lead to acknowledgments in a monthly journal,[77] but it does apply if a sponsor receives an acknowledgment in a program or brochure distributed at a sponsored event. The tax regulations provide that the term *printed material* includes material that is published electronically.[78]

If a Web site is considered a periodical, the rules for determining unrelated business taxable income from the publishing of advertising in periodicals apply.[79] Amounts realized by an exempt organization from the sale of advertising in a periodical constitute gross income from an unrelated business activity involving the exploitation of an exempt function: namely, the circulation and readership of the periodical developed through the production and distribution of the readership content of the periodical.[80]

In one instance, the IRS considered whether a tax-exempt organization's Web site was a periodical for these purposes. The agency observed that the periodical advertising rules would apply to the organization's sale of advertising on its Web site "only where such advertising is part of a periodical that appears on-line." By contrast, if the advertising "appears on [the organization's] Web site generally, and not as part of an on-line periodical, [the periodical advertising rules] would not apply."[81] The IRS advised that if an advertiser pays an exempt organization an amount that is attributable to both periodical advertising and advertising that appears on the organization's Web site generally, an allocation will have to be made between periodical and nonperiodical advertising.

An observer pointed out that the IRS took an "interesting, and perhaps controversial, position" concerning this matter of Web-site-as-periodical.[82] In 1999, the agency wrote that "[m]ost of the materials made available on exempt organization Web sites are clearly prepared in a manner that is distinguishable from the methodology used in the preparation of periodicals."[83] This means that the IRS will not consider most Web sites maintained by exempt organizations as periodicals, which in turn means that the corporate sponsorship payment rules will be available to shelter the income from taxation—as long as all of the other requirements of these rules are met (basically, no advertising).

The IRS continued in this analysis, however, to say that, in considering how to treat potential income from Web site materials for unrelated business income tax purposes, the agency "will look closely at the methodology used in the

---

[75] IRC § 513(i)(2)(B)(ii)(I).
[76] *Id.*
[77] Reg. § 1.513-4(b).
[78] *Id.*
[79] See § 6.6(b).
[80] Reg. § 1.512(a)-1(f).
[81] Priv. Ltr. Rul. 200303062.
[82] Livingston, at 422.
[83] IRS FY 2000 CPE Text on Exempt Organizations and Internet Use, at 77.

preparation of" Web site materials. It added that the IRS "will be unwilling to allow the exempt organization to take advantage of the specialized rules available to compute unrelated business income from periodical advertising income unless the exempt organization can clearly establish that the on-line materials are prepared and distributed in substantially the same manner as a traditional periodical." This means that, if there is advertising, the special rules for calculating unrelated business taxable income from periodicals will not be available.

The observer astutely pointed out a "leap" in reasoning by the IRS.[84] The corporate sponsorship payment rules refer to "regularly scheduled and printed material."[85] This usage led this commentator to offer some useful guidelines and distinctions:

- "Bulletins distributed by e-mail on an occasional but unscheduled basis should not be considered periodicals any more than they would be if they were in hard copy distributed by U.S. mail."

- The "fact that a Web site may contain certain discrete factual information, like the date or key news items, that are [*sic*] updated on a regularly scheduled basis should not cause the site to be treated as a periodical to the extent the bulk of the site's content does not change on any regular scheduled basis."

- "That the technology makes it possible to make frequent updates to what functions effectively as a brochure, overview, or educational text, should not dictate the characterization of the site as a periodical."

- This analysis "may be a bit complicated for certain Internet-based publications that change chunks of content on a rolling but regularly scheduled basis."

- "If the intent is to revise all of the content on a regularly scheduled basis, then it seems likely the publication will be characterized as a periodical."[86]

As Livingston noted, the statutory "definition" of the word *periodical* does not contain any "reference to the process,"[87] yet the IRS analysis emphasizes the "methodology used in the preparation of periodicals."[88] This observer also noted, in decrying this methodology test, that the "process of writing, editing, and producing publications, in hard copy or electronic form, varies greatly from organization to organization"; that "[c]ontent come from staff, professional writers, members, volunteers, unsolicited submissions, and other sources"; and that some materials "are heavily revised and edited," whereas other organizations "simply go through the mechanical process of laying out and printing submissions as the author has written them." Therefore, this observer concluded, "no one can say what methodology an organization must show the Service to prove [that] a Web-based item is or is not a periodical."[89]

---

[84] Livingston, at 422.
[85] IRC § 513(i)(2)(B)(ii)(I).
[86] Livingston, at 423.
[87] *Id.* at 422.
[88] IRS FY 2000 CPE Text on Exempt Organizations and Internet Use, at 77.
[89] Livingston, at 422.

In fact, the operative element in the definition of the word *periodical* is the scheduling of the publication; these materials are regularly compiled and distributed to the public on a *periodical* basis. This observer opined that the IRS "should rethink its view on this point."[90] Indeed, it was reported that a representative of the IRS subsequently acknowledged that this agency view "may be in error."[91]

Unrelated business taxable income earned from advertising on a Web site that is not a periodical is determined by the general rules[92]: namely, by adding the gross income from the advertising to the gross income generated from any other unrelated business activity (other than advertising in periodicals) and subtracting the expenses that are directly connected with carrying on the unrelated business or businesses.[93] The reference to an expense that is *directly connected* to the conduct of unrelated business means an expense (to be deductible) that is an item of deduction that has a "proximate and primary relationship" to the carrying on of an unrelated business.[94]

If the "facility" is used both to carry on exempt activities and to conduct unrelated activities, the expenses attributable to these activities (as, for example, items of overhead) are to be allocated between the two uses on a basis that is reasonable.[95] The same rule applies with respect to the expenses associated with personnel (such as, for example, salaries). It is common to make these allocations on the basis of time expended on the various activities.[96]

If the unrelated activity involved constitutes an exploitation of an exempt activity, the allocation rule is different. For expenses to be deductible, the unrelated business activity must have a "proximate and primary relationship" to the exempt purpose activity.[97]

§ 10.13 ROYALTY ARRANGEMENTS

In the context of Internet use by tax-exempt organizations for unrelated business purposes, the applicable exceptions from unrelated business income taxation are likely to be those pertaining to corporate sponsorships[98] and royalty arrangements.[99] As a general proposition, royalty income received by an exempt organization is excluded from unrelated business income taxation.[100]

In one instance, a tax-exempt organization received, from two entities, licensing revenue that was properly treated as royalties. The exempt organization proposed to list information about these two entities in its publications and on its Web site, and to provide links to the entities' Web sites as part of the listings. The organization represented to the IRS that the proposed listings and links would be

---

[90] *Id.* at 422–23.
[91] *Id.* at 423.
[92] See § 6.5(a).
[93] Reg. § 1.512(a)-1(a).
[94] *Id.*
[95] Reg. § 1.512(a)-1(c).
[96] *E.g.*, Rensselaer Polytechnic Inst. v. Comm'r, 732 F.2d 1058 (2d Cir. 1984).
[97] Reg. § 1.512(a)-1(d).
[98] See § 10.5.
[99] See § 3.7.
[100] IRC § 512(b)(2).

mechanisms through which it would communicate the availability of services and benefits offered by the entities to its members. It also represented to the IRS that it did not provide personal or other services to the two entities in connection with its licensing arrangements. The IRS ruled that these listings and links would not cause any portion of the exempt organization's licensing revenues from the two entities to be treated other than as excludable royalties.[101]

A tax-exempt organization may have parallel arrangements with another entity, such as an advertising arrangement and a licensing arrangement with the same entity. The IRS ruled that when the amounts of the royalty and advertising payments will be determined on separate and independent bases, and licensees will not be treated more (or less) favorably than other organizations wishing to purchase advertising space in the exempt organization's periodicals or on its Web site, the sale of advertising will not adversely affect the treatment of the licensing revenue as excludable royalties.[102]

§ 10.14 QUESTIONS POSED BY IRS ANNOUNCEMENT

In the Announcement, the IRS observed that tax-exempt organizations "use the Internet to carry on activities that otherwise can be conducted through other media, such as radio or television broadcasts, print publications, or direct mailings." The emphasis was thus placed on types of media rather than types of activities. Hence, one of the major issues as to Internet communications by exempt organizations is whether advertising by means of that medium is related or unrelated business.

In this context, the determination as to the type of business—related (nontaxable) or unrelated (taxable)—must be made in light of the fundamental purpose of the unrelated business rules.[103] In part, this means ascertaining whether the advertising activity is regularly carried on.[104] The tax regulations provide that, for purposes of determining regularity of advertising activity, the "manner of conduct of the activities must be compared with the manner in which commercial activities are normally pursued by nonexempt organizations."[105] If the advertising activity is infrequent, the net income involved is not taxable even if the advertising content is unrelated to exempt purposes.

(a) General Issues

The first of the general questions posed by the Announcement was whether a Web site maintained by a tax-exempt organization "constitute[s] a single publication or communication." A Web site presumably can be considered a single *publication*, in that a single publication can encompass many subjects and messages.

---

[101] Priv. Ltr. Rul. 200303062. Although the IRS did not expressly so rule, this arrangement can be seen as one in which the listing and links activity did not rise to the level of business and was separated or fragmented (see § 2.3) from the activity generating the royalties.

[102] Priv. Ltr. Rul. 200303062.

[103] See § 1.6.

[104] See § 2.5.

[105] Reg. § 1.513-1(c)(2)(ii).

A college's catalog, an association's journal, or a charity's newsletter is a single publication, notwithstanding the variety of its content.

That point notwithstanding, it is highly unlikely that a Web site would be regarded as a single communication. If the word *communication* is defined simply as the act of imparting or transmitting information, then a Web site could be treated as a single communication. If, however, prominence is accorded the content of the communication—as it should be—a Web site is revealed as a myriad of communications. As noted, the IRS correlated Internet communications to other media, such as television broadcasts. A television channel may be thought of as a single unit, but its programming is a series of communications. The same is true of a Web site. Thus, for example, a visitor to an exempt association's site is able to access a host of communications about the organization's programs, members, staff, and other matters, such as certification, ethics, and perhaps its related foundation and/or political action committee. Consequently, the answer to this question should be that a tax-exempt organization's Web site may constitute a single publication, but only rarely should be considered a single communication.

The IRS then asked, perhaps suggesting its view as to the answer to the first question, if a Web site is not a single publication or single communication, "how should it be separated into distinct publications or communications?" Inasmuch as application of the fragmentation rule[106] is conceptually limitless (or bottomless), one approach would be to separate the communications by category, such as program, fundraising, advocacy, related activities, and the like. For larger organizations, the category of program could be fragmented, so that there would be communications as to program A, program B, program C, certification, ethics enforcement, and so on. These exercises will generate new and interesting applications of the fragmentation rule.

This question and the next one have a meaningful relationship. When a Web site is fragmented into multiple publications or multiple communications, each of these functions presumably carries with it maintenance expenses. The amount of taxable unrelated business income (if any) that results will be affected by the number of these functions and the expenses associated with or assigned to each of them.

The third of the IRS questions inquired as to the proper methodology to use when allocating expenses for a Web site. Again, simply by referencing the subject of allocation, the agency must be thinking that a Web site is comprised of, if not more than one publication, then certainly more than one communication. Before allocating expenses of a Web site, however, the expenses themselves must be determined. There are the costs of establishing the site and the costs of maintaining the site. Usually, much of the material on a Web site was previously created for offline use, such as articles, directories, and information about charitable giving, certification, and ethics. Thus, it appears that there must be allocation of expenses as between offline and online material and information. There may not be that much left over to allocate in the context of Internet communications.

The question presupposes that allocation is required. That, however, may not always be the case. A tax-exempt organization that uses its Web site for

[106] See § 2.3.

related purposes (that is, nothing on the site pertains to fundraising or unrelated business) and not for advocacy purposes may see no reason to allocate expenses among programs. In that case, the organization may simply have a line item for Web site expenses.

When allocation is required or desired, the simplest of answers to the IRS question would be to separate a Web site into discrete communications on the basis of the amount of space each communication occupies on the site. As the agency noted, expense allocation could be based on Web pages. This approach is often taken in the case of print publications. In some instances, however, a primary purpose test is applied (or at least advocated): If the primary purpose of a publication is to communicate a particular message, the entire publication is deemed to have communication of that message as its purpose.

The IRS observed that, "[u]nlike other publications of an exempt organization, a Web site may be modified on a daily basis." The IRS then asked: "To what extent and by what means should an exempt organization maintain the information from prior versions of the organization's Web site?" It would be impractical, to say the least, to require an exempt organization to maintain the information posted on every prior version of its Web site, whether the agency is in search of unrelated activity or otherwise.

This matter of expense allocation can be considered in light of these last two questions combined. Isolating the costs of various Web site communications is difficult enough, without taking into account the many changes in site content that occur in the course of a year. When the changes are factored in, expense isolation and allocation may become nearly impossible—or, in any event, more expensive than the Web site expenses themselves.[107]

An additional complicating factor is that the time and expense involved in preparing a Web site communication may be elements that the tax-exempt organization would incur in any event. The same messages may be used in other forms of communication, such as print and broadcast media. That aspect of various activities, then, may well be accounted for already, leaving the cost in connection with the Web site only that of posting the material, which is negligible. As has been suggested elsewhere, the answer to this dilemma may lie in the development of a safe-harbor rule or de minimis exception to a general rule.[108]

(b) Specific Questions

In the Announcement, the IRS asked three questions specifically pertaining to unrelated business activities on the Web sites of tax-exempt organizations. The agency is of the unassailable view that a "number of exempt organizations use the Internet as another outlet for their own sales activity."

---

[107] In discussing this point in the context of lobbying by tax-exempt organizations, a commentator observed that the "cost[s] for adding the Web as a tool for lobbying communication are likely to be quite modest, and could in fact be dwarfed by the cost of accounting for them." Livingston, at 425.

[108] Following up on *supra* note 107, this commentator continued: "It would be highly problematic if charities were deterred from using the most efficient tool available for participating in legislative debates because all of the resources gained from the increased efficiency were being consumed by the burdens of an accounting rule. To prevent that from happening, charities may consider proposing to the IRS adoption of some form of de minimis rule or safe harbor for this kind of expense allocation." *Id.*

The first of these questions was: "To what extent are business activities conducted on the Internet regularly carried on?" The answer to this question should be that regularity of business operations on a tax-exempt organization's Web site is determined using the same criteria as are applied in any other context.[109] This assessment is generally made on the basis of the particular year of the tax-exempt organization.

As a follow-up question, the IRS asked: "What facts and circumstances are relevant in determining whether these activities on the Internet are regularly carried on?"

This determination has two parts. First, it is necessary to ascertain whether the business activities manifest the requisite frequency and continuity. Business undertakings that are intermittent or discontinuous are not regularly carried on. Thus, business activities that are reflected on a tax-exempt organization's Web site only occasionally are not regularly carried on. By contrast, a business undertaking that is always represented on a site is regularly carried on. It is unlikely, however, that an exempt organization would conduct an unrelated business on its Web site under circumstances in which the business is not regularly carried on.

The fact is that most unrelated businesses are not carried on by means of the Internet. This state of affairs is likely to change, however. Still, research has uncovered no tax-exempt organization that openly offers "unrelated business activities" as one of its selectable web pages

If income-producing activities are of a kind normally undertaken by nonexempt commercial organizations only on a seasonal basis, the conduct of those activities by a tax-exempt organization during a significant portion of the season ordinarily constitutes the regular conduct of a business.[110] Particular problems lurk in this setting when fundraising activities are conducted by means of the Internet. If services or products are being sold in a business undertaking that is not related, it is likely that the business is being regularly carried on. Even if the actual business activity on the Internet is not continuous, the matter of the preparatory time involved[111] may be an adverse factor.

The second part of this determination looks to the manner in which the business activities are pursued. Thus, a business activity of a tax-exempt organization is likely to be considered regularly carried on if it is pursued in a manner generally similar to comparable commercial activities of nonexempt organizations. In this setting, then, a determination should be made as to how the comparable activity would be conducted on the Internet by for-profit companies.

Another IRS question was whether there are "any circumstances under which the payment of a percentage of sales from customers referred by the exempt organization to another Web site would be substantially related." That question was prefaced with the observation that some tax-exempt organizations "receive payments based upon a percentage of sales for referring customers to another Web site, while others receive payments based upon the number of persons who use the hyperlink to go to the other webpage." Presumably, at least

[109] See § 2.5.
[110] Id., text accompanied by notes 140–142.
[111] Id., §2.5(d).

one of the fact patterns that the IRS has in mind is the relationship between an exempt organization and a commercial bookselling company, in the course of which the exempt organization refers potential customers to the bookseller to purchase books on subjects that relate to the organization's exempt purposes.

Generally, fees of this nature are unrelated income. The fact that the books purchased may pertain to the tax-exempt organization's exempt purpose is too tenuous a basis to sustain a claim that the payment is being made within the confines of exempt functions. If the two organizations are programmatically related, however, the referrals and bookselling may be a related activity.

Even if a payment of this nature is deemed to be unrelated income, that does not necessarily mean that the payment is taxable. Generally, it would seem that payments of this nature are excludable from taxation as royalties.[112] Also, if the two organizations with linked Web sites are related, as in a parent-subsidiary relationship or a relationship that is analogous to that of parent and subsidiary, the payments may be disregarded for tax purposes as being merely a matter of accounting if the referral function is viewed as a corporate service.[113]

The IRS observed that some tax-exempt organizations operate "virtual trade shows," in an "attempt to replicate trade shows on the Internet." This led the IRS to ask: "Are there any circumstances under which an online 'virtual trade show' qualifies as an activity of a kind 'traditionally conducted' at trade shows" pursuant to the exception for trade show operations?[114] The IRS subsequently provided guidance on this point.[115] In writing this exception, Congress had in mind the type of show conducted as part of an association's annual convention and thus lasting only a few days each year. The typical virtual trade show is conducted on a year-round basis. Also, as the IRS noted, some of these virtual trade shows "simply consist of hyperlinks to industry suppliers' websites." This is unrelated activity.

Oddly, the IRS, in the Announcement, did not ask any questions concerning advertising. Generally, advertising income received by a tax-exempt organization is taxable income.[116] Nonetheless, the Announcement noted that "[m]any exempt organizations receive payment from companies to display advertising messages on the organization's website." Stated that way, those payments would be unrelated business income, absent the unlikely circumstance that the advertising is a related activity (such as advertising by another tax-exempt organization with a similar mission) or is not regularly carried on.

The IRS also observed in the Announcement that some exempt organizations "have banners on their websites containing information about and a link to other organizations in exchange for a similar banner on the other organization's website(s)." Banners on Web sites generally are forms of advertising; thus, unless these banners constitute program activities (related advertising), it is inescapable that the regular running of them is unrelated activity.

---

[112] See § 3.7.
[113] See § 9.8.
[114] See § 4.5.
[115] See § 10.6.
[116] See § 6.5.

Tax-exempt organizations also, said the IRS in the Announcement, "provide hyperlinks on their Web sites to companies that sponsor their activities." The tax consequences of this practice are governed, at least initially, by the rules pertaining to corporate sponsorships.[117]

§ 10.15 SUMMARY

The law as to unrelated business activities will prove to be the most difficult of the components of the law of tax-exempt organizations to apply in the Internet communications context. Fragmentation of Web site activities into discrete businesses will frequently be difficult, as will the allocation of costs to them. These activities will usually be regularly carried on. Saving this area from even worse catastrophes is the fact that most of this activity will consist of related endeavors. The commerciality doctrine[118] may be a problem, however, in that nonprofit Web sites are being operated in essentially the same fashion as for-profit Web sites.[119]

The rules as to advertising will cause difficulties for many tax-exempt organizations, inasmuch as the IRS is likely to concentrate its efforts in this area. Directly tied to this will be application of the corporate sponsorship rules, where distinction between qualified and nonqualified payments will be exacerbated by Internet communications. Creative uses of the royalty exception should be anticipated in this setting. Related tax-exempt organizations will, however, be able to provide Web site-based services to each other without fear of unrelated business income taxation.[120]

---

[117] See §§ 6.6, 10.5.
[118] See ch. 7.
[119] See 10.3(a).
[120] In general, Hopkins, *The Nonprofits' Guide to Internet Communications Law* (John Wiley & Sons, 2003).

CHAPTER ELEVEN

Reporting Requirements

Nearly every organization that is exempt from federal income taxation must, as required by statute,[1] file an annual information return with the IRS. The form of the return varies depending on the nature and size of the tax-exempt organization. For most exempt organizations, the return that must be annually filed is Form 990. Small organizations[2] file Form 990-EZ; private foundations[3] file Form 990-PF.

---

[1] IRC § 6m033(a)(1).

[2] That is, organizations that have gross receipts that are less than $100,000 and total assets that are less than $250,000 in value at the end of the reporting year.

[3] IRC § 509(a). See Hopkins, *The Law of Tax-Exempt Organizations*, *Eighth Edition* (John Wiley & Sons, 2003) [hereinafter *Tax-Exempt Organizations*], § 11.1.

Form 990, which consists of six pages plus two schedules comprising another 14 pages, calls for considerable information, some of it financial and some of it narrative.[4] This document, being an information return rather than a tax return, is available for public review.[5] The Form 990 is structured in part to ferret out a tax-exempt organization's unrelated income. Thereafter, the exempt organization is usually required to report its unrelated business income, and related information, on Form 990-T.[6] This form, being a tax return, is not open to public inspection.

§ 11.1 TAX STRUCTURE

The unrelated income tax rates payable by most tax-exempt organizations are the corporate rates.[7] Some organizations, such as trusts, are subject to the individual income rates.[8] The tax law features the following three-bracket structure for corporations:

Taxable Income	Rate (percent)
$50,000 or less	15
$50,000–$75,000	25
More than $75,000	34

An additional 5-percent surtax is imposed on corporations' taxable income between $100,000 and $335,000, pushing the marginal tax rate to 39 percent on taxable income in that range.[9] This tax structure is inapplicable to the taxation of insurance companies,[10] which is the tax law paradigm used to figure tax for organizations that cannot qualify as charitable organizations or social welfare organizations because a substantial part of their activities consists of the provision of commercial-type insurance.[11]

Tax-exempt organizations must make quarterly estimated payments of the tax on unrelated business income, under the same rules that require quarterly estimated payments of corporate income taxes.[12]

---

[4] A copy of the Form 990 is reproduced in Appendix D.
[5] IRC § 6104(b). See *Tax-Exempt Organizations*, § 24.4.
[6] IRC § 6012(a); Reg. § 1.6012-(e).
[7] IRC § 11; Also IRC § 12(1).
[8] IRC § 1(E). A court discussed the applicability of the corporate and trust rates in this context, in holding that a tax-exempt voluntary employees' beneficiary association is taxable at the trust, not the corporate, rates. Sherwin-Williams Co. Employee Health Plan Trust v. United States, 2002-2 U.S.T.C. ¶ 50,721 (N.D. Ohio 2002), *aff'd*, 2005 U.S. App. LEXIS 6003 (6th Cir. 2005).
[9] IRC § 11(b).
[10] IRC § 11(c)(2). See IRC § 801 *et seq.* (IRC subch. L).
[11] IRC § 501(m)(2)(B). See § 7.3.
[12] IRC § 6655(a)–(d). See § 11.5(e). A tax-exempt organization is generally subject to an addition to tax for any underpayment of estimated tax on its unrelated business income. IRC § 6655(a), (g)(3). An exempt organization does not have an underpayment of estimated tax if it makes four timely estimated tax payments that total at least 100 percent of the tax liability shown on its return for the current taxable year. IRC § 6655(d)(1)(B). An exempt organization may determine its estimated unrelated income tax payments (filed by means of Form 990-W) under one of three annualized income installment methods: a standard option, option 1, or option 2. Form 8842 must be filed annually to elect option 2.

§ 11.2 DEDUCTION RULES

Generally, the term *unrelated business taxable income* means the gross income derived by a tax-exempt organization from one or more unrelated trades or businesses, regularly carried on by the organization and not protected by an exception, less business deductions that are directly connected with the carrying on of the trade or business.[13] For purposes of ascertaining unrelated business taxable income, both gross income and business deductions are computed with certain modifications.[14]

Generally, to be *directly connected with* the conduct of an unrelated business, an item of deduction must have a proximate and primary relationship to the carrying on of that business. In the case of a tax-exempt organization that derives gross income from the regular conduct of two or more unrelated business activities, unrelated business taxable income is the aggregate of gross income from all unrelated business activities, less the aggregate of the deductions allowed with respect to all unrelated business activities.[15] Expenses, depreciation, and similar items attributable solely to the conduct of unrelated business are approximately and primarily related to that business and therefore qualify for deduction to the extent that they meet the requirements of relevant provisions of the federal income tax law.[16] A loss incurred in the conduct of an unrelated activity may be offset against the net gain occasioned by the conduct of another unrelated activity only when the loss activity was conducted with a profit motive.[17]

When facilities and/or personnel are used to carry on both tax-exempt activities and an unrelated trade or business, the expenses, depreciation, and similar items attributable to the facilities and/or personnel, such as overhead or items of salary, must be allocated between the two uses on a reasonable basis.[18] Despite the statutory rule that an expense must be directly connected with an unrelated business to be deductible, the regulations merely state that the portion of the expense allocated to the unrelated business activity must be apportioned on a reasonable basis and be proximately and primarily related to the business activity.[19] Once an item is proximately and primarily related to a business undertaking, it is allowable as a deduction in computing unrelated business income in the manner and to the extent permitted by federal income tax law generally.[20]

Two courts found these regulations to conform to the statutory requirements, in a case concerning the proper allocation of fixed expenses of a tax-exempt university's operation of a fieldhouse, when the facility was used for both exempt and unrelated purposes.[21] Therefore, the critical question in this context is whether a

---

[13] IRC § 512(a)(1).

[14] See ch. 3. A tax-exempt organization is not entitled to an expense deduction for funds transferred from one internal account to another. Women of Motion Picture Indus. v. Comm'r, 74 T.C.M. 1217 (1997).

[15] Reg. § 1.512(a)-1(a).

[16] *E.g.*, IRC §§ 162, 167; Reg. § 1.512(a)-1(b).

[17] *E.g.*, W. Va. State Med. Ass'n v. Comm'r, 91 T.C. 651 (1988), *aff'd*, 882 F.2d 123 (4th Cir. 1989), *cert. denied*, 493 U.S. 1044 (1990). See § 2.4.

[18] Reg. § 1.512(a)-1(c). In Disabled Am. Veterans v. United States, 704 F.2d 1570 (Fed. Cir. 1983), *aff'g & remanding* 82-2 U.S.T.C. ¶ 9440 (Cl. Ct. 1982), the appellate court approved an allocation of expenses proposed by the lower court whereby the tax-exempt organization was permitted to allocate its fundraising expenses between the taxable and exempt portions of its solicitation program.

[19] Reg. § 1.512(a)-1(c).

[20] *Id.*

[21] Rensselaer Polytechnic Inst. v. Comm'r, 732 F.2d 1058 (2d Cir. 1984), *aff'g* 79 T.C. 967 (1982).

particular method of allocation is reasonable. The university contended that fixed expenses should be allocated on the basis of relative times of actual use, so that the portion of the deductible expenses is determined by means of a ratio, the numerator of which is the total number of hours the facility is used for unrelated purposes and the denominator of which is the total number of hours the fieldhouse is used for both related and unrelated activities. By contrast, the IRS argued that the allocation should be on the basis of total time available for use, so that the denominator of the fraction should be the total number of hours in the tax year. These courts found for the university.

The IRS's argument essentially was that the allocation was not reasonable, because the outcome was a deductible expense that was not directly connected with the unrelated activity. The appellate court reasoned, however, that it was merely following the government's own regulations. A dissent took the position that the regulation must be read in conjunction with the statute, so that the "directly connected with" language is a requirement in addition to those expressly contained in the regulations.[22]

Gross income may be derived from an unrelated trade or business that exploits a tax-exempt function.[23] Generally, in these situations, expenses, depreciation, and similar items attributable to conduct of the exempt function are not deductible in computing unrelated business taxable income. Because the items are incident to a function of the type that it is the chief purpose of the organization to conduct, they do not possess a proximate and primary relationship to the unrelated trade or business. Therefore, they do not qualify as being directly connected with that business.[24]

A tax-exempt organization will be denied business expense deductions in computing its unrelated business taxable income if it cannot adequately substantiate that the expenses were incurred or that they were directly connected with the unrelated activity. In one instance, an exempt organization derived unrelated business income from the sale of advertising space in two magazines, and incurred expenses in connection with solicitation of the advertising and publication of the magazines. A court basically upheld the position of the IRS, which disallowed all of the claimed deductions (other than those for certain printing expenses) because the organization failed to establish the existence or relevance of the expenses.[25] The court found that this organization did not maintain adequate books and records, failed to accurately allocate expenses among accounts, and had insufficient accounting practices. During pretrial discovery, the organization failed to provide the requisite documentation. This led to a court order to produce the material, the response to which was labeled by the court as "evasive and incomplete."[26] Consequently, the court imposed sanctions, which essentially prevented the organization from introducing at trial any documentary evidence embraced by the government's request in discovery. The court rejected the organization's effort to prove its expenses at trial by testimony and to use its accountant's audit as evidence of the facts stated in the report. Thus, most of the claimed expenses were not

---

[22] *Id.*, 732 F2d at 1063–66.
[23] See § 2.7(e).
[24] Reg. § 1.512(a)-1(d).
[25] CORE Special Purpose Fund v. Comm'r, 49 T.C.M. 626 (1985).
[26] *Id.* at 629.

allowed; those that were allowed over the government's objection were ascertained by the court by approximation.[27]

§ 11.3   ANNUAL INFORMATION RETURN

The annual information return filed by most tax-exempt organizations—Form
990—reflects aspects of the unrelated business rules.

(a) Parts VII and VIII

Parts VII and VIII of this annual information return are the principal portions of
the return concerning the unrelated business rules. Part VII is titled "Analysis of
Income-Producing Activities." This part of the return requires the reporting
exempt organization to list amounts (usually gross amounts) received from a
variety of income sources, including:

- Program service revenue—revenue derived from the conduct of one or
  more activities by an exempt organization that comprise or include the
  organization's exempt function(s) (also known as *exempt function revenue*
  or *related business income*)

- Fees and contracts from government agencies—payments by government
  agencies to an exempt organization for a service, facility, or product that
  primarily benefited the agency, either economically or physically (as
  opposed to government *grants* that enabled the organization to conduct
  exempt activities)

- Membership dues and assessments

- Dividends and interest

- Rental income—including net rental income from investment property and
  passive rental income from unaffiliated exempt organizations (as opposed
  to rental income generated from the conduct of an exempt function, which
  is a form of program service revenue)[28]

- Other investment income

- Gain from sales of assets

- Special event income (net)

- Other revenue

Following the tally of types of income received, the organization is required
to indicate whether the income item is:

- Related business (exempt function) income, in which case the filing organization must explain, in Part VIII, how each activity for which the

---

[27] In general, Lyons & Hall, *Allocating and Substantiating Income and Expenses for Tax-Exempt Organizations*,
8 *J. Tax'n Exempt Orgs.* 107 (Nov./Dec. 1996); Bloom, *Offsetting Expenses Against UBI Can Be an Allocation
Headache for Tax-Exempts*, 8 *J. Tax'n Exempt Orgs.* 33 (July/Aug. 1996); Blazek, *Accentuate the Negative:
Maximizing Deductions on Form 990-T*, 4 *J. Tax'n Exempt Orgs.* 24 (May/June 1993).

[28] If the rental property is debt-financed, different rules apply. See ch. 5.

income is so reported contributed importantly to accomplishment of the organization's exempt purposes[29]

- Unrelated business income. A *business code* (found in the unrelated business return instructions) must be assigned to each such entry
- Income received by an exempt organization that is excluded from taxation by an exception.[30] An *exclusion code* (found in the annual information return instructions) must be assigned to each such entry; if more than one exclusion code applies to a particular revenue item, the organization should use the lowest-numbered applicable code; if nontaxable revenues from several sources are reportable on the same line, the organization should use the exclusion code that applies to the largest revenue source.

(b) Exclusion Codes

The following are the exclusion codes assigned to income that is nontaxable by virtue of an exception (including a modification or an exclusion) for a function or type of income, the Internal Revenue Code provision involved, and the section of this book that summarizes the law pertaining to the exception.

Exception	Exclusion Code	IRC Section	Book Section
Activity not regularly carried on	01	512(a)(1)	2.5
Business conducted primarily by volunteers	02	513(a)(1)	4.2
Convenience doctrine	03	513(a)(2)	4.1
Certain activities of local association of employees	04	513(a)(2)	4.11
Sale of gift items	05	513(a)(3)	4.3
Public entertainment activity	06	513(d)(2)	4.4
Trade shows	07	513(d)(3)	4.5
Certain hospital services	08	513(e)	4.6
Certain bingo games	09	513(f)	4.7
North Dakota games of chance	10	N/A	4.7
Pole rental income	11	513(g)	4.13
Distribution of low-cost articles	12	513(h)	4.9
Certain rentals or exchanges of donor lists	13	513(h)	4.10
Forms of passive income	14	512(b)(1)	3.1–3.3
Royalties	15	512(b)(2)	3.7
Rental income—real property	16	512(b)(3)	3.8
Rental income—personal property	17	512(b)(3)	3.8
Capital gain or loss	18	512(b)(5)	3.10
Financial institutions' property	18	512(b)(16)(A)	—
Lapse or termination of options	19	512(b)(5)	3.11

---

[29] See § 2.7.
[30] See chs. 3, 4.

Exception	Exclusion Code	IRC Section	Book Section
Government research	20	512(b)(7)	3.13
College, university, hospital research	21	512(b)(8)	3.13
Fundamental research	22	512(b)(9)	3.13
Certain activities of religious order	23	512(b)(15)	3.17
Foreign organizations	24	512(a)(2)	3.15
Certain set-asides	25	512(a)(3)(B)(i)	6.1(c)
Sales of exempt function property	26	512(a)(3)(D)	—
Benefits set-asides	27	512(a)(3)(B)(ii)	6.1(c)
Veterans' set-asides	28	512(a)(4)	6.2(a)
Insurance or charitable set-asides	29	N/A	6.1(c)
Exempt debt-financed income	30	514(b)(1)(A)	5.3
Mortgaged research property	31	514(b)(1)(C)	5.3
Other mortgaged property	32	514(b)(1)(D)	5.3
Neighborhood land	33	514(b)(3)	5.3
Mortgaged property acquired by bequest or devise	34	514(c)(2)(B)	5.3
Mortgaged property acquired by gift	35	514(c)(2)(B)	5.3
Gift annuity	36	514(c)(5)	5.3
FHA-insured mortgaged property	37	514(c)(6)	5.3
Certain mortgaged real property	38	514(c)(9)	5.3
Retirement homes, hospitals, etc.	39	N/A	5.3
Certain dues	40	512(d)	4.8
Absence of profit motive	41	N/A	2.4
Corporate sponsorship	42	513(i)	6.7

(c) Other Parts of Return

The items listed in Part VII of Form 990 should also be reported in Part I, which includes revenue in the form of contributions and grants (line 1d). The total amount in Part VII (line 105), plus the amount of contributions and grants, should equal the total amount in Part I (line 12).

Part III of the return requires a description of the exempt organization's exempt purpose (program service) accomplishments, with emphasis on measurable outcomes. This part and Part VII reflect the fragmentation rule.[31]

In Part VI, the organization must answer the question as to whether it had unrelated business gross income of $1,000[32] or more during the year involved (line 78a). If the answer to that question is yes, the organization is required to indicate whether it filed an exempt organization unrelated business income tax return[33] for the year (line 7b).

---

[31] See § 2.3.
[32] See § 3.19.
[33] See § 11.4.

§ 11.4 UNRELATED BUSINESS INCOME TAX RETURN

A tax-exempt organization that has unrelated business gross income in excess of $1,000 is required to file an exempt organization business income tax return, which is, as noted, Form 990-T.[34] Among the items to be provided at the outset is a description of the exempt organization's primary unrelated business activity (line H).

(a) Overview of Return

Part I of this return consists of a listing of the organization's items of unrelated business gross income. Many of these items relate to information that must be provided on a schedule (see below). Part II of the return is a listing of expenses that are deductible in computing unrelated business taxable income (line 34) because they are directly connected with the unrelated business income (other than in the case of charitable contributions (line 20)).[35] Part III of the return is used to compute the tax.[36] In Part IV, the organization reports any applicable tax credits, estimated tax payments, and any tax due.

The schedules that are part of, or otherwise filed with, the Form 990-T are:

- Schedule A—cost of goods sold
- Schedule C—rental income[37]
- Schedule D—capital gain[38]
- Schedule E—unrelated debt-financed income[39]
- Schedule F—interest, annuities, royalties, and rent from controlled organizations[40]
- Schedule G—investment income of certain types of exempt organizations[41]
- Schedule I—exploited exempt activity income (other than advertising income)[42]
- Schedule J—advertising income and certain costs[43]
- Schedule K—compensation of officers, directors, and trustees

---

[34] IRC § 6012(a)(2), (4); Reg. § 1.6012-2(e). The Form 990-T on which this analysis is based is the return for 2004, reproduced in Appendix E. The reader will find it helpful to have a copy of the return at hand in connection with this summary.

　　This book, like *Tax-Exempt Organizations*, focuses on organizations that are conventionally thought of as *tax-exempt organizations* (usually nonprofit entities). There are, however, other types of tax-exempt organizations that may be required to file Form 990-T: qualified pension, profit-sharing, and stock bonus plans (IRC § 501(a)); individual retirement accounts, SEPs, or SIMPLEs (IRC § 408(e)(1)); Roth IRAs (IRC § 408A); Archer MSAs (IRC § 220(e)(1)); Coverdell education savings account (IRC § 530(a)); and qualified tuition programs (IRC § 529(a)).

[35] See § 11.2.
[36] See § 11.1.
[37] See § 3.8.
[38] See § 3.10.
[39] See ch. 5.
[40] See § 8.8(b).
[41] See §§ 6.1, 6.2(b).
[42] See § 2.7(e).
[43] See § 6.5.

(b) Initial Information

The organization should ensure that its name and address, as shown on its unrelated business income tax return, are the same as those shown on the corresponding annual information return. If the organization has changed its name, it should check the box following "Name of organization" and provide the following with the return:

- If it is a corporation, a copy of the amendment to the articles of incorporation, along with proof of filing with the state

- If it is a trust, a copy of the amendment to the trust agreement, along with the signature of the trustee or trustees

- If it is an unincorporated association, a copy of the amendment to the articles of association, constitution, bylaws, or other organizing document, along with signatures of at least two officers and/or members

The organization is required to enter, in block E, the applicable unrelated business activity code(s) that specifically describes the organization's unrelated business activity. If a specific activity code does not accurately describe the organization's activities, the organization should select a general code that best describes its activity. These codes are listed in the instructions to the unrelated business income tax return.[44]

The organization is required to describe, in block H, its primary unrelated business activity, based on unrelated business income. A schedule may be used if more space is needed.

The organization should check the "Yes" box in block I if it is a corporation and either:

- the corporation is a subsidiary in an affiliated group[45] but is not filing a consolidated return for the tax year with that group, or

- the corporation is a subsidiary in a parent-subsidiary controlled group.[46]

(c) Form 990-T, Part I

A tax-exempt organization that files an unrelated business income tax return is required to complete column A of Part I of the return, lines 1–13. If the amount on line 13 does not exceed $10,000, the organization may complete only line 13 for columns B and C; these entities do not have to complete Schedules A through K.

Generally, the installment sales method cannot be used for dealer dispositions of property. A *dealer disposition* is (1) any disposition of personal property by a person who regularly sells or otherwise disposes of personal property of the same type on the installment plan, or (2) any disposition of real property held for sale to customers in the ordinary course of the taxpayer's trade or business. These restrictions on use of the installment method do not apply to dispositions of property

---

[44] See also Appendix F.
[45] See § 11.5(i).
[46] IRC § 1563. If the corporation is an excluded member of a controlled group (IRC § 1563(b)(2)), it is nonetheless a member of a controlled group for purposes of answering the block I question.

used or produced in a farming business or sales of timeshares and residential lots for which the organization elects to pay interest.[47] For sales of timeshares and residential lots reported under the installment method, the organization's income tax is increased by the interest amount.[48]

The organization should enter on line 1a (and carry to line 3) the gross profit on collections from installment sales for dealer dispositions of property before March 1, 1986; dispositions of property used or produced in the trade or business of farming; and certain dispositions of timeshares and residential lots reported under the installment method. The organization should attach a schedule showing the following information for the current and three preceding years: gross sales, cost of goods sold, gross profits, percentage of gross profits to gross sales, amount collected, and gross profit on amount collected.

On line 1a, the filing exempt organization enters its gross income from any unrelated trade or business regularly carried on that involves the sale of goods or performance of services,[49] other than income that is the subject of a modification[50] or an exception.[51] Distinctions may have to be made in this context, such as a tax-exempt social club's reporting of its restaurant and bar receipts from nonmembers on line 1a and its investment income on line 9.[52]

In general, advance payments are reported in the year of receipt. Special rules apply with respect to reporting income from long-term contracts.[53] Other rules apply to the reporting of certain advance payments for goods and long-term contracts.[54] There are rules concerning permissible methods for reporting advance payments for services by an accrual method organization.[55]

Organizations that qualify to use the nonaccrual experience method[56] should attach a schedule showing total gross receipts, amounts not accrued as a result of the application of certain rules,[57] and the net amount accrued. This net amount is entered on line 1a.

As to line 4a, generally, tax-exempt organizations that are required to file an unrelated business income tax return are not taxed on the net gains from the sale, exchange, or other disposition of property.[58] Net gains from debt-financed property are taxed,[59] however, as are capital gains on cutting timber and ordinary gains on sections 1245, 1250, 1252, 1254, and 1255 property. Capital gain or loss passed through from an S corporation, and any gain or loss on the disposition of S corporation stock by an organization qualified to own such stock, are taxed as a capital gain or loss.[60]

---

[47] This election is the subject of IRC § 453(l)(3).
[48] See Form 990-T, pt. IV, line 42.
[49] See §§ 2.2, 2.5.
[50] See ch. 3.
[51] See ch. 4.
[52] See § 6.1.
[53] IRC § 460.
[54] Reg. § 1.451-5.
[55] Rev. Proc. 2004-34, 2004-22 I.R.B. 991.
[56] See § 11.5(a).
[57] IRC § 448(d)(5).
[58] See § 3.10. Special rules for social clubs and other organizations are the subject of sections 6.1 and 6.2.
[59] See ch. 5.
[60] See § 4.12.

Also as to line 4a, the amount of gain or loss to be reported on the sale, exchange, or other disposition of debt-financed property[61] is the same percentage as the highest acquisition indebtedness[62] for the property for the 12-month period before the date of disposition bears to the average adjusted basis of the property.

If the tax-exempt organization is a partner in a partnership that is carrying on an unrelated trade or business, the organization's share of the partnership's income or loss from the unrelated trade or business (whether or not distributed) should be entered on line 5.[63] The partnership's gross income and deductions are to be determined in the same manner in which the exempt organization determines unrelated business income that it earns directly.

Tax-exempt charitable organizations can own stock in S corporations. All items of income, loss, or deduction are taken into account in ascertaining unrelated business income.[64] Any income or loss from S corporations is reported on line 5; gain or loss from the disposition of S corporation stock is reported on line 4.

(d) Form 990-T, Part II

If the amount on line 13, column A, of Part I of the unrelated business income tax return is no more than $10,000, the exempt organization does not have to complete lines 14–28 of Part II of the return. Nonetheless, the organization is required to complete lines 29–34 of Part II of the return.

Only expenses that are directly connected with unrelated trade or business income may be deducted in Part II.[65] This limitation does not, however, apply with respect to charitable contributions (line 20).[66]

Generally, an accrual basis taxpayer[67] may only deduct business expenses and interest owed to a related party in the year the payment is included in the income of the related party.[68] Corporations may be required to adjust deductions for depletion of iron ore and coal; intangible drilling, exploration, and development costs; and the amortizable basis of pollution control facilities.[69]

(i) **Absence of Profit Motive.** If income is attributable to an activity lacking a profit motive, a loss from the activity may not be claimed on the unrelated business income tax return. Generally, an activity *lacking a profit motive* is one that is not conducted for the purpose of producing a profit, or one that has consistently produced losses when direct and indirect expenses are taken into account.[70] Therefore, in Part I, column B, and Part II, the total of deductions for expenses directly connected with income from an activity lacking a profit motive is limited to the amount of that income.

---

[61] See ch. 5.
[62] See § 5.4.
[63] See § 4.12.
[64] See § 6.4.
[65] See § 11.2.
[66] See § 3.18.
[67] See § 11.5(a).
[68] IRC §§ 163(e)(3), 163(j), 267.
[69] IRC § 291.
[70] See § 2.4.

(ii) Uniform Capitalization Requirements.   Uniform capitalization rules require organizations to capitalize or include as inventory cost certain costs incurred in connection with the production of real property and tangible personal property held in inventory or held for sale in the ordinary course of business; real property or personal property (tangible and intangible) held in inventory acquired for resale; and the production of real property and tangible personal property by the organization for use in its trade or business or in an activity engaged in for profit.[71] Tangible personal property produced by an organization includes a film, sound recording, videotape, book, or similar property.

Organizations subject to these uniform capitalization rules are required to capitalize direct costs and an allocable portion of most indirect costs (including taxes) that benefit the assets produced or acquired for resale or are incurred by reason of the performance of production or resale activities. For inventory, some of the indirect expenses that must be capitalized are administrative expenses; taxes; depreciation; insurance; compensation paid to officers attributable to services; rework labor; and contributions to pension, stock bonus, and certain profit-sharing, annuity, or deferred compensation plans. Other indirect costs that relate to production or resale activities must be capitalized or may be currently deductible.[72] Interest expense paid or incurred during the production period of designated property must be capitalized and is governed by special rules.[73] The costs required to be capitalized under these rules are not deductible until the property to which the costs relate is sold, used, or otherwise disposed of by the organization.

The uniform capitalization rules do not apply to personal property acquired for resale if the organization's average annual gross receipts for the three prior tax years were no more than $10 million; timber; most property produced under long-term contract; certain property produced in a farming business; certain research and experimental costs;[74] mining exploration and development costs; inventory of an organization that accounts for inventories in the same manner as materials and supplies that are not incidental; and intangible drilling costs for oil, gas, and geothermal property.

(iii) Travel.   Generally, in computing unrelated business taxable income, a tax-exempt organization can deduct ordinary and necessary travel expenses paid or incurred in connection with a trade or business.[75] An exempt organization cannot deduct travel expenses of any individual accompanying the organization's officer or employee, including a spouse or dependent, unless that individual is an employee of the organization and his or her travel is for a bona fide business purpose and would otherwise be deductible by that individual.

(iv) Meals and Entertainment.   Generally, in computing unrelated business taxable income, a tax-exempt organization can deduct ordinary and necessary

---

[71] IRC § 263A.

[72] Reg. § 1.263A-1(e)(3).

[73] Reg. § 1.263A-8 through -15.

[74] IRC § 174.

[75] IRC §§ 162 (business expense deduction), 212 (production of income expenses), 274(d) (substantiation rules).

meals and entertainment expenses paid or incurred in connection with a trade or business.[76] Usually, the organization can deduct only 50 percent of the amount otherwise allowable for these meals and entertainment expenses.[77] Meals must not be lavish or extravagant; a bona fide business discussion must occur during, immediately before, or immediately after the meal; and an employee of the organization must be present at the meal.[78] Special rules apply with respect to gifts, skybox rentals, luxury water travel, convention expenses, and entertainment tickets.[79] An exempt organization cannot deduct an expense paid or incurred for use of a facility, such as a yacht or hunting lodge, for an activity usually considered entertainment, amusement, or recreation.

An organization generally may be able to deduct otherwise nondeductible travel, meals, and entertainment expenses if the amounts are treated as compensation of an employee or independent contractor. If the recipient is an officer or director, the deduction for otherwise nondeductible meals, travel, and entertainment expenses is limited to the amount treated as compensation.[80]

(v) Membership Dues.   An exempt organization may deduct amounts paid or incurred for membership dues in civic or public service organizations, professional organizations (such as bar and medical associations), business leagues, trade associations, chambers of commerce, boards of trade, and real estate boards.[81] A deduction is not allowed, however, if a principal purpose of the organization is to entertain or provide entertainment facilities for members or their guests. Also, organizations may not deduct membership dues in any club organized for business, pleasure, recreation, or other social purpose, including country clubs, golf and athletic clubs, airline and hotel clubs, and clubs operated to provide meals under conditions favorable to business discussion.[82]

(vi) Tax Credits.   For the following tax credits, an exempt organization must reduce the otherwise allowable deductions for expenses used to compute the credit by the amount of the current-year credit: the credit for increasing research activities, the enhanced oil recovery credit, the disabled access credit, the employer credit for social security and Medicare taxes paid on certain employee tips, the credit for employer-provided child care, and the orphan drug credit.[83]

(vii) Business Startup Expenses.   Business startup and organizational costs must be capitalized unless an election is made to amortize them. The organization can elect to deduct up to $5,000 of such costs for the year the organization begins business operations. This deduction is reduced by the amount by which the total costs exceed $50,000. If this election is made, any costs that are not deductible must be amortized ratably over a 180-month period beginning with

---

[76] IRC § 162.
[77] IRC § 274(n).
[78] IRC § 274(k).
[79] IRC § 274(b), (h), (l), (m).
[80] IRC § 274(e)(2).
[81] IRC § 162.
[82] IRC § 274(a)(3).
[83] IRC § 26.

the month the organization begins business operations.[84] The deductible amount of these costs and any amortization are reported on line 28.

(viii) Interest. In connection with the line 18 interest deduction, if the proceeds of a loan were used for more than one purpose (such as to purchase a portfolio investment and to acquire an interest in a passive activity), an interest expense allocation must be made.[85] Generally, an organization may not include interest on indebtedness incurred or continued to purchase or carry obligations on which the interest income is exempt from income tax.[86] In general, a cash basis taxpayer cannot deduct prepaid interest allocable to years following the current tax year.[87] Also, the interest and carrying charges on straddles usually cannot be deducted; they must be capitalized.[88] Special rules apply in connection with the disqualified portion of original issue discount on a high-yield discount obligation.[89] Certain interest paid or accrued by the organization, directly or indirectly, to a related person may be limited if tax is not imposed on the interest.[90] An organization cannot deduct interest on debt allocable to the production of designated property; interest that is allocable to this type of property produced by the organization for its own use or for sale must be capitalized. Also, an organization must capitalize any interest on debt allocable to an asset used to produce the property.[91] Special rules are applicable concerning the deductibility of forgone interest on certain below-market-rate loans.[92]

(ix) Taxes and License Fees. On line 19, an exempt organization enters taxes and license fees paid or incurred during the year. It cannot include federal income taxes; foreign or U.S. possession income taxes if a tax credit is claimed; taxes not imposed on the organization; taxes, including state or local sales taxes, paid or incurred in connection with an acquisition or disposition of property;[93] taxes assessed against local benefits that increase the value of the property assessed; or taxes deducted elsewhere on the return, such as those reflected in cost of goods sold. Rules apply with respect to apportionment of taxes on real property between a buyer and seller.[94]

(x) Charitable Contributions. On line 20, exempt organizations enter the amount of contributions made to or for the use of one or more charitable or governmental entities within the tax year. This includes any unused contributions carried over from prior years. This deduction is allowed whether or not directly connected with the carrying on of a trade or business.

---

[84] IRC §§ 195, 248.
[85] Reg. § 1.163-8T.
[86] IRC § 265.
[87] IRC § 461(g).
[88] IRC § 263(g).
[89] IRC § 163(e)(5).
[90] IRC § 163(j).
[91] IRC § 263A(f).
[92] IRC § 7872.
[93] These taxes must be treated as part of the cost of the acquired property or, in the case of a disposition, as a reduction in the amount realized on the disposition.
[94] IRC § 164(d).

The total amount claimed by a tax-exempt corporation cannot be more than 10 percent of unrelated business taxable income determined without regard to this charitable deduction.[95] Contributions in excess of this limitation are not deductible, but may be carried over for up to five subsequent tax years.[96] In computing the charitable contribution deduction, if the tax-exempt corporation has a net operating loss carryover to the tax year, the 10-percent limit is applied using the taxable income, after taking into account any deduction for the net operating loss. In determining any remaining net operating loss carryover to later years, taxable income must be modified.[97] To the extent charitable contributions are used to reduce taxable income for this purpose, or to increase a net operating loss carryover, a contributions carryover is not allowed.[98]

If the reporting entity is a tax-exempt trust, for contributions to public charities and certain other charitable entities,[99] the amount claimed may not be more than 50 percent of the unrelated business taxable income computed without this deduction.[100] As to contributions to other charitable organizations, the amount claimed may not be more than the smaller of (1) 30 percent of unrelated business taxable income computed without the charitable deductions, or (2) the amount by which 50 percent of the unrelated business taxable income exceeds the contribution allowed in conjunction with gifts to public charities.[101]

If the contribution is of property other than money and the claimed deduction is in excess of $500, the exempt organization must attach a schedule describing the kind of property contributed and the method used to determine its fair market value. If the total claimed deduction for all property contributed is more than $5,000, the filing organization will have to attach a Form 8283 to the return, and it may have to satisfy certain appraisal requirements.[102] If the organization made a qualified conservation contribution,[103] it must also include the fair market value of the underlying property before and after the contribution, the type of legal interest contributed, and a description of the conservation purpose furthered by the gift; if a contribution carryover is included, the organization should show the amount and how it was determined. There are special rules for certain contributions of ordinary income and capital gain property.[104]

If a charitable contribution deduction is taken for property sold to a charitable organization, in a transaction known as a *bargain sale*, the adjusted basis for determining gain from the sale is an amount that is in the same ratio to the adjusted basis as the amount realized bears to the fair market value of the property.[105]

---

[95] IRC § 170(b)(2). See Hopkins, *The Tax Law of Charitable Giving, Third Edition* (John Wiley & Sons, 2005) [hereinafter *Charitable Giving*], § 7.18(a).

[96] IRC § 170(d)(2)(A). See *Charitable Giving*, § 7.18(b).

[97] IRC § 172(b).

[98] IRC § 170(d)(2)(B).

[99] That is, to organizations described in IRC § 170(b)(1)(A).

[100] In other words, the rules pertaining to charitable contributions by individuals apply. See *Charitable Giving*, § 7.5(a).

[101] IRC § 170(b)(1)(B). See *Charitable Giving*, § 7.6.

[102] See *Charitable Giving*, § 21.2.

[103] IRC § 170(h). See *Charitable Giving*, § 9.7.

[104] IRC § 170(e). See *Charitable Giving*, §§ 4.3–4.5.

[105] See *Charitable Giving*, § 9.19.

Tax-exempt corporations on the accrual basis of accounting[106] may elect to deduct contributions paid by the fifteenth day of the third month following the close of the tax year, if the contributions are authorized by the board of directors during the tax year.[107] The organization should attach a declaration to the return stating that the resolution authorizing the contributions was adopted by the board of directors during the tax year; this declaration must include the date the resolution was adopted.

Generally, the federal income tax charitable contribution deduction is not allowed to a tax-exempt organization (or other donor) for a gift of $250 or more unless the organization receives a written acknowledgment from the charitable donee by the earlier of the due date (including extensions) for filing the unrelated business income tax return or the date the return is filed.[108] This written acknowledgment must reflect the amount of money contributed, a description of any property contributed, whether the charitable donee provided any goods or services to the donor, and a description and good-faith estimate of the value of any goods or services provided to the donor in exchange for the contribution. These rules do not apply, however, if the goods or services have insubstantial value, a statement is included that the goods or services consist wholly of intangible religious benefits, or certain types of benefits are received that are customarily provided in exchange for membership payments of $75 or less annually.

Generally, if a tax-exempt organization makes a charitable contribution of more than $75 and receives something in return—a transaction known as a *quid pro quo contribution*—the amount of the contribution that is deductible for federal income tax purposes is limited to the amount by which the contribution exceeds the value of the goods or services received.[109] The charitable organization that solicits or receives the contribution must inform the donor of this by written statement and must provide the donor with a good-faith estimate of the value of the goods or services provided in exchange for the contribution.

Charitable contributions made to an organization conducting lobbying activities are not deductible if the lobbying activities relate to matters of direct financial interest to the donor's trade or business and the principal purpose of the contribution was to avoid federal income tax by obtaining a deduction for activities that would have been nondeductible under the lobbying expense rules[110] if conducted directly by the donor.[111]

(xi) Specific Deduction.   Line 33 references the *specific deduction*,[112] which is a $1,000 deduction allowed in computing unrelated business taxable income, except for computing net operating loss and the net operating loss deduction.[113]

---

[106] See § 11.5(a).

[107] IRC § 170(a)(2). See *Charitable Giving*, § 6.13.

[108] IRC § 170(f)(8). See *Charitable Giving*, § 21.1(b). This acknowledgment should not be attached to the return, but should be maintained as part of the organization's records.

[109] IRC § 6115. See *Charitable Giving*, § 22.2.

[110] IRC § 162(e).

[111] IRC § 170(f)(9). See *Charitable Giving*, § 10.8.

[112] See § 3.19.

[113] IRC § 172.

(e) Form 990-T, Part III

Federal tax law provides tax computation rules for organizations taxable as corporations and for trusts.[114] Organizations liable for tax on unrelated business taxable income may be liable for alternative minimum tax on certain adjustments and tax preference items (line 28).

(f) Form 990-T, Part IV

Domestic tax-exempt organizations owing less than $500 of unrelated business income tax, and foreign organizations that do not have an office or place of business in the United States, should enclose a check or money order (payable in U.S. funds), made payable to the United States Treasury, with the unrelated business income tax return. Domestic organizations owing $500 or more of tax and foreign organizations with an office or place of business in the United States should use the depository method of tax payment.[115]

(g) Form 990-T, Schedule A

Generally, inventories are required at the beginning and end of each tax year (lines 1 and 6) if the production, purchase, or sale of merchandise is an income-producing factor.[116] If, however, the organization is a qualifying taxpayer or a qualifying small business taxpayer, it may adopt or change its accounting method to account for inventoriable items in the same manner as materials and supplies that are not incidental (unless the business is a tax shelter). A *qualifying taxpayer* is a taxpayer that, for each prior tax year, has average annual gross receipts of $1 million or less for the three-tax-year period ending with that prior tax year. A *qualifying small business taxpayer* is a taxpayer (1) that, for each prior tax year, has average annual gross receipts of $10 million or less for the three-tax-year period ending with that prior tax year, and (2) whose principal business activity is not an ineligible activity.

Pursuant to this accounting method, inventory costs for raw materials purchased for use in producing finished goods and merchandise purchased for resale are deductible in the year the finished goods or merchandise are sold (but not before the year the organization paid for the raw materials or merchandise, if it is also using the cash basis method of accounting). The organization should enter amounts paid for all raw materials and merchandise during the tax year on line 2. The amount the organization can deduct for the tax year is determined on line 7. A filing tax-exempt organization not using the cash method of accounting should review the uniform capitalization rules before completing this schedule.

Inventories can be valued at cost,[117] lower of cost or market,[118] or any other method approved by the IRS that conforms to certain requirements. If, however, an organization is using the cash method of accounting, it is required to use the

---

[114] See § 11.1.
[115] See § 11.5(f).
[116] Reg. § 1.471-1.
[117] Reg. § 1.471-3.
[118] Reg. § 1.471-4.

cost inventory valuation method. Organizations that use erroneous valuation methods must change to a method permitted for federal income tax purposes. This is accomplished by filing Form 3115.

A *small producer* is one whose average annual gross receipts are $1 million or less. Small producers that account for inventories in the same manner as materials and supplies that are not incidental may currently deduct expenditures for direct labor and all indirect costs that would otherwise be included in inventory costs.

Inventory may be valued below cost when the merchandise is unsalable at normal prices or unusable in the normal way because the goods are damaged, imperfect, shopworn, or the like.[119] The goods may be valued at the current bona fide selling price, minus the direct cost of disposition (but not less than scrap value) if such a price can be established.

If the exempt organization is changing its method of accounting so that it no longer accounts for inventories, it must recompute its prior year's closing inventory using the new accounting method and enter the result on line 1. If there is a difference between last year's closing inventory and the redetermined amount, the organization is required to attach a statement explaining the difference.

An entry is required on line 4a only for exempt organizations that have elected a simplified method of accounting. For organizations that have elected the simplified production method, *additional 263A costs* generally are those costs, other than interest, that are now required to be capitalized but that were not capitalized under the method of accounting the organization used immediately prior to the effective date of that provision.[120]

For exempt organizations that have elected the simplified resale method, *additional 263A costs* generally are those costs incurred with respect to the following categories: off-site storage or warehousing; purchasing; handling, such as processing, assembling, repackaging, and transporting; and general and administrative costs (*mixed service costs*).[121]

(h) Form 990-T, Schedule C

Schedule C concerns most tax-exempt organizations' rental income. This schedule, however, is not to be used by exempt social clubs,[122] voluntary employees' beneficiary associations,[123] or supplemental unemployment benefit trusts.[124] Unless the rent is exempt function income, these three categories of organizations enter gross rents on Part I, line 6, and applicable expenses on Part II, lines 14–28.

All tax-exempt organizations with rental income, other than those in the foregoing three categories, should complete this schedule and report the following rent as taxable income (Part I, line 6):

- Rents from personal property leased with real property, if the rents from the personal property are more than 10 percent of the total rents received

---

[119] Reg. § 1.471-2(c).
[120] Reg. § 1.263A-2(b).
[121] Reg. § 1.263A-3(d).
[122] That is, organizations described in IRC § 501(c)(7). See *Tax-Exempt Organizations*, ch. 14.
[123] That is, organizations described in IRC § 501(c)(9). See *Tax-Exempt Organizations*, § 16.3.
[124] That is, organizations described in IRC § 501(c)(17). See *Tax-Exempt Organizations*, § 16.4.

or accrued under the lease, determined at the time the personal property is placed in service

- Rents from real and personal property, if:
  - more than 50 percent of the total rents received or accrued under the lease are for personal property, or
  - the amount of the rent depends on the income or profits derived by any person from the property leased (except an amount based on a fixed percentage of receipts or sales)[125]

A redetermination of the percentage of rent for personal property is required when an increase of 100 percent or more is caused by the placement of additional or substitute personal property into service, or the lease is modified to change the amount of the rent charged.

Rents from both real and personal property not reportable on Part I, line 6, may be reportable (taxable) on line 8 if the income is from a controlled organization,[126] or on line 7 if the property is debt-financed.[127] Taxability of rents must be considered in that order: rents not taxed on line 6 may be taxed on line 8; rents not taxed on lines 6 or 8 may be taxed on line 7.

Rents from personal property that is not leased with real property should be reported on Part I, line 12.

(i) Form 990-T, Schedule E

Schedule E, pertaining to unrelated debt-financed income, is applicable to all tax-exempt organizations except social clubs, voluntary employees' beneficiary associations, and supplemental unemployment benefit trusts.[128] When debt-financed property is held for exempt purposes and other purposes, the exempt organization must allocate the basis, debt, income, and deductions among the purposes for which the property is held. Amounts allocated to exempt purposes are not to be reflected in Schedule E.

For purposes of column 1, any property held to produce income is *debt-financed property* if, at any time during the tax year, acquisition indebtedness was outstanding for the property. Also, when a property held by an exempt organization for the production of income is disposed of at a gain during a tax year, and acquisition indebtedness was outstanding for that property at any time during the 12-month period before the date of disposition, the property is debt-financed property.

Acquisition indebtedness is the outstanding amount of principal debt incurred by a tax-exempt organization to acquire or improve a property:

- before the property was acquired or improved, if the debt was incurred because of the acquisition or improvement of the property, or

---

[125] See § 3.8(b).
[126] See § 8.8(b).
[127] See ch. 5; § 11.4(i).
[128] See *supra* notes 122–124.

- after the property was acquired or improved, if the debt was incurred because of the acquisition or improvement, and the organization could reasonably foresee the need to incur the debt at the time the property was acquired or improved

With exceptions, acquisition indebtedness does not include debt incurred by:

- A qualified[129] trust in acquiring or improving real property[130]

- A tax-exempt school[131] and its affiliated supporting organization[132] for indebtedness

- A multiparent title-holding company[133]

- An obligation, to the extent that the obligation is insured by the Federal Housing Administration, to finance the purchase, rehabilitation, or construction of housing for low- and moderate-income individuals, or indebtedness incurred by a small business investment company licensed under the Small Business Investment Act if the indebtedness is evidenced by a debenture issued by the company under that Act[134] and held or guaranteed by the Small Business Administration[135]

Concerning column 2, income is not unrelated debt-financed income if it is otherwise included in unrelated business taxable income. For example, rental income from personal property shown in Schedule C, or rents and interest from controlled corporations shown in Schedule F, should not be reflected in column 2.

Column 4 requires determination of the amount of average acquisition debt on or allocable to debt-financed property. *Average acquisition indebtedness* for a tax year is the average amount of the outstanding principal debt during the part of the tax year the property is held by the tax-exempt organization. Calculation of the average amount of acquisition debt requires determination of the amount of the outstanding principal debt on the first day of each calendar month during the part of the tax year that the organization holds the property, addition of these amounts, and division of the result by the total number of months during the tax year that the organization held the property.

Column 5 requires determination of the average adjusted basis of, or basis allocable to, debt-financed property, which is the average of the adjusted basis of the property on the first and last days during the tax year that the organization held the property. The exempt organization, having ascertained the adjusted basis of the property,[136] is required to further adjust the basis of the property by the depreciation for all earlier tax years, whether or not the organization was exempt from tax for any of these years. Similarly, for tax years during which the organization was subject to tax on unrelated business taxable income, the basis

---

[129] IRC § 401.
[130] IRC § 514(c)(9).
[131] See *Tax-Exempt Organizations*, § 11.3(a).
[132] *Id.*, § 11.3(c).
[133] That is, an organization described in IRC § 501(c)(25).
[134] Specifically, under § 303(a) of that Act.
[135] IRC § 514(c)(6)(B).
[136] IRC § 1011.

of the property must be adjusted by the entire amount of allowable depreciation, even though only a part of the deduction for depreciation is taken into account in computing unrelated business taxable income.

If there are no adjustments to the basis of an item of property, the basis of the property is its cost amount.

As to column 7, the amount of income from debt-financed property included in unrelated trade or business income is determined by multiplying the property's gross income by the percentage obtained from dividing the property's average acquisition indebtedness for the tax year by the property's average adjusted basis during the period it is held in the tax year.

Concerning column 8, for each debt-financed property, the organization must deduct this percentage of the total deductions that are directly connected to the income, including the dividend-received deductions.[137] If the debt-financed property is depreciable property, the depreciation deduction is determined by the straight-line method only; that amount is entered in column 3(a). For each debt-financed property, the organization should attach to the return schedules showing separately a computation of the depreciation deduction (if any) reported in column 3(a) and a breakdown of the expenses included in column 3(b).

When a capital loss for the tax year may be carried back or carried over to another tax year, the amount to carry over or back is determined by using the above percentage. In the year to which the amounts are carried, however, the organization may not apply the debt-basis percentage to determine the deduction for that year.

The foregoing procedure may be illustrated with an example of a tax-exempt organization that owns a four-story building. Two of the floors are used for exempt purposes; two floors are rented (as an unrelated business) for $10,000. The expenses are $1,000 for depreciation and $5,000 for other expenses that relate to the entire building. The average acquisition indebtedness is $6,000 and the average adjusted basis is $10,000, both of which apply to the entire building. Completion of Schedule E in this instance entails the following:

- Enter the description of the property in column 1.

- Enter $10,000 in column 2 (the entire amount of rent is for the debt-financed property).

- Enter $500 and $2,500 in columns 3(a) and 3(b), respectively (one-half of the expenses is for the debt-financed property).

- Enter $3,000 and $5,000 in columns 4 and 5, respectively (one-half of the acquisition indebtedness and the average adjusted basis is for the debt-financed property).

- Enter 60 percent in column 6.

- Enter $6,000 in column 7.

- Enter $1,800 in column 8.

---

[137] IRC §§ 243–245.

Now assume that the facts are the same, except that the entire building is rented as an unrelated business for $20,000. Schedule E would be completed as follows:

- Enter the description of the property in column 1.
- Enter $20,000 in column 2.
- Enter $1,000 and $5,000 in columns 3(a) and 3(b), respectively (the entire amount is for debt-financed property).
- Enter $6,000 and $10,000 in columns 4 and 5 (the entire amount is for debt-financed property).
- Enter 60 percent in column 6.
- Enter $12,000 in column 7.
- Enter $3,600 in column 8.

(j) Form 990-T, Schedule F

Interest, annuities, royalties, and rents received or accrued, directly or indirectly, by a controlling organization from a controlled organization are subject to the unrelated business income tax, irrespective of whether the activity conducted by the controlling organization to earn these amounts is a trade or business or is regularly carried on.[138] These revenues are reported on Schedule F.

An entity is a *controlled organization* if the controlling organization owns: (1) by vote or value, more than 50 percent of a corporation's stock (for an organization that is a corporation); (2) more than 50 percent of a partnership's profits or capital interests (for an organization that is a partnership); or (3) more than 50 percent of the beneficial interests in an organization (for an organization other than a corporation or parstnership). Constructive ownership rules are applied to determine the ownership of stock in a corporation.[139] Similar principles are applied to ascertain the ownership of interests in a partnership or other organization.

The term *specified payment* means any payment of interest, annuity, royalty, or rent. A tax-exempt organization includes a specified payment in gross unrelated business income to the extent that the payment reduces the net unrelated income, or increases the net unrelated loss, of the controlled organization. The term *net unrelated income* means: (1) when the controlled organization is a tax-exempt entity,[140] the unrelated business taxable income of the controlled organization; and (2) when the controlled organization is not exempt, the part of the controlled organization's taxable income that would be unrelated business taxable income if the controlled organization was tax-exempt and had the same exempt purpose as the controlling organization. The term *net unrelated loss* means the net operating loss determined using comparable rules.

---

[138] See § 8.8(b).
[139] IRC § 318.
[140] That is, an organization that is exempt from tax under IRC § 501(a).

(k) Form 990-T, Schedule G

Schedule G concerns investment income received by tax-exempt social clubs, voluntary employees' beneficiary associations, and supplemental unemployment benefit trusts.[141] For most tax-exempt organizations, investment income is not taxable as unrelated business income,[142] but for these categories of exempt organizations generally, unrelated trade or business income includes all gross income from nonmembers. These organizations report on this schedule all income from investments in securities and other similar investment income from nonmembers, including all income and directly connected expenses from debt-financed property.

All exempt organizations in one of these three categories determine their investment income using Schedule G. Interest on state and local governmental obligations,[143] however, is not included. Only expenses that are directly connected to the investment income are deductible. When necessary, deductions must be allocated between exempt activities and other activities.[144] These organizations may not take the dividends-received deductions[145] in computing net investment income, because those deductions are not considered to be directly connected with the production of gross income.

These organizations may set aside income that would otherwise be taxable under these rules. Income derived from an unrelated trade or business may not be set aside, however. Also, any income set aside and subsequently expended for other purposes must be included in income. Net investment income set aside must be specifically earmarked as such, or placed in a separate account or fund (except for an exempt employees' association, which, by the terms of its governing instrument, must use its net investment income for its exempt purposes).

These rules apply to a tax-exempt title-holding company the income of which is payable to one of these three types of exempt organizations, if it files a consolidated return with the parent organization. If one of these four types of exempt organizations sells property that was used for the exempt function of the parent organization, and purchases other property used for the organization's exempt function within a period beginning one year before the date of the sale and ending three years after the date of the sale, the gain from the sale will be recognized only to the extent that the sales price of the old property is more than the cost of the other property. The other property need not be similar in type or use to the old property. The organization must notify the IRS of the sale, by means of a statement attached to the return or other written notice.

---

[141] See *supra* notes 122–124.

[142] See ch. 3.

[143] IRC § 103(a).

[144] *E.g.*, Inter-Com Club, Inc. v. United States, 721 F. Supp. 1112 (D. Neb. 1989) (concerning the deduction by an exempt social club, that operated a restaurant and lounge, of losses incurred on the sale of food and beverages to nonmembers from investment income in computing unrelated business taxable income). In general, Chiechi & Munk, *When Can Social Clubs Offset Investment Income with Losses from Nonmember Activities?*, 73 J. Tax'n 184 (no. 3, 1990).

[145] See §6.1(E).

(l) Form 990-T, Schedule I

A tax-exempt social club, voluntary employees' beneficiary association, or supplemental unemployment benefit trust[146] should not report exploited exempt activity income on Schedule I. Rather, this income is reported in Part I, line 1a, or the appropriate line for the particular kind of income.

Other types of tax-exempt organizations that have gross income from an unrelated trade or business activity that exploits an exempt activity[147] (other than advertising income[148]) are required to complete Schedule I.

An exempt organization may take all deductions directly connected with the gross income from the unrelated trade or business activity. In addition, an exempt organization may take into account all deductible items attributable to the exploited exempt activity, with the following limitations:

1. It must reduce the deductible items of the exempt activity by the amount of income from the activity.

2. It must limit the net amount of deductible items arrived at in step 1 for the exempt activity to the net unrelated business income from the exploited exempt activity.

3. It must exclude income and expenses of the exempt activity in computing a loss carryover or carryback from the unrelated trade or business activity exploiting the exempt activity.

4. It must exclude deductible items of the exempt activity in computing unrelated trade or business income from an activity that is not exploiting the same exempt activity.

Therefore, the net includable exploited exempt activity income is the unrelated business taxable income less the excess of the exempt activity expenses over the exempt activity income. If the income from the exempt activity exceeds the exempt activity expenses, the organization may not add that profit to the net income from the unrelated business activity. If two or more unrelated trade or business activities exploit the same exempt activity, the organization should treat the activities as one on Schedule I. A separate schedule, showing the computation, should be attached to the return.

(m) Form 990-T, Schedule J

Schedule J pertains to advertising income.[149] A tax-exempt social club, voluntary employees' beneficiary association, or supplemental unemployment benefit trust[150] does not report advertising income on Schedule J. Rather, they report that income on Part I, line 1a.

---

[146] See *supra* notes 122–124.
[147] See § 2.7(e).
[148] See §§ 6.5, 11.4(m).
[149] See §§ 6.5, 11.4(m).
[150] See *supra* notes 122–124.

All other tax-exempt organizations that earned gross income from the sale of advertising in an exempt organization periodical must complete Schedule J. The part of the advertising income taken into account is determined as follows:

- If direct advertising costs (expenses directly connected with advertising income) are more than advertising income (unrelated business income), the exempt organization must deduct that excess in computing unrelated business taxable income from any other unrelated trade or business activity carried on by the organization.

- If advertising income is more than direct advertising costs, and circulation income (exempt activity income) equals or exceeds readership costs (exempt activity expenses), then unrelated business taxable income is the excess of advertising income over direct advertising costs.

- If advertising income is more than direct advertising costs, and readership costs are more than circulation income, then unrelated business taxable income is the excess of total income (advertising income and circulation income) over total periodical costs (direct advertising costs and readership costs).

- If the readership costs are more than the circulation income, and the net readership costs are more than the excess of advertising income over direct advertising costs, there is no allowable loss.

If an exempt organization publishes two or more periodicals, to determine its unrelated business taxable income, it may elect to treat the gross income for all (but not less than all) periodicals, and deductions directly connected with those periodicals (including excess readership costs), as if the periodicals were one periodical. This rule applies only to periodicals published for the production of income. A periodical is considered *published for the production of income* if gross advertising income of the periodical is at least 25 percent of the readership costs, and the periodical is an activity engaged in for profit.

(n) Form 990-T, Schedule K

A tax-exempt organization is required to complete columns 1–4 of Schedule K for those trustees, directors, and officers the salaries or other compensation of which are allocable to unrelated business gross income. Column 4 should not include compensation that is deducted on lines 15, 28, or Schedules A through J.

An exempt organization should include on Schedule K (or elsewhere on the return) only compensation that is directly attributable to its unrelated trade or business activities. If personnel are used both to carry on exempt activities and to conduct unrelated trade or business activities, the salaries and wages of those individuals must be allocated between the activities. For example, assume that a tax-exempt organization derives gross income from the conduct of unrelated trade or business activities. This organization pays its president a salary of $195,000 annually; 10 percent of the president's time is devoted to the unrelated business activity. On its unrelated business income tax return, the organization enters $19,500 (10 percent of $195,000) on Schedule K for the part of the president's salary allocable to the unrelated trade or business activity. The remaining $175,500 cannot, however, be deducted, because it is not directly attributable to the organization's unrelated trade or business activities.

If taxable fringe benefits, such as personal use of an automobile, are provided to an exempt organization's employees, the organization may not deduct as salaries and wages the amounts it deducted for depreciation and other deductions.

(o) Recordkeeping and Preparing Return

The IRS estimates that the average time consumed in preparing and maintaining the records needed for preparation of the 2004 unrelated business income tax return is 67 hours, 26 minutes. The estimated average time required to learn about the applicable law or the return is 27 hours, 10 minutes. The estimated average time to prepare the return is 43 hours, 25 minutes. The time required to photocopy, assemble, and send the return to the IRS is 4 hours, 1 minute.

§ 11.5 OTHER RULES CONCERNING PREPARATION AND FILING OF RETURN

Preparation and filing of the unrelated business income tax return requires some knowledge of accounting methods, the establishment and change of an accounting method, filing due dates and process, tax deposit rules, and the law concerning interest and penalties.

(a) Accounting Methods

An *accounting method* is a set of rules used to determine when and how income and expenses are reported. Tax-exempt organizations are expected to compute taxable unrelated business income using the method of accounting that is regularly used in keeping their books and records.

Permissible accounting methods are the cash basis method, the accrual method, or any other accounting method authorized by the federal tax law. In all instances, however, the method used must clearly reflect taxable income.

Under the accrual method of accounting, an amount is includable in income when (1) all the events have occurred that fix the right to receive the income, which is the earliest of the dates the required performance takes place, payment is due, or payment is received; and (2) the amount can be determined with reasonable accuracy.[151]

Generally, an organization must use the accrual method of accounting if its average annual gross receipts exceed $5 million.[152] An organization engaged in farming operations generally must use the accrual method, though there are exceptions to this requirement.[153]

If inventories are required, the accrual method generally must be used for sales and purchases of merchandise. Qualifying taxpayers and eligible businesses of

---

[151] Reg. § 1.451-1(a).
[152] IRC § 448(c).
[153] IRC § 447.

qualifying small business taxpayers, however, are excepted from the requirement of use of the accrual method of accounting for eligible trades or businesses; they may account for inventoriable items as materials and supplies that are not incidental.

Generally, an accrual basis taxpayer can deduct accrued expenses in the tax year when all events that determine the liability have occurred, the amount of the liability can be determined with reasonable accuracy, and economic performance takes place with respect to the expense. There are exception to the economic performance rule for certain items, including recurring expenses.[154]

Accrual method organizations are not required to accrue certain amounts to be received from the performance of services that, on the basis of the organizations' experience, will not be collected, if (1) the services are in the fields of health, law, engineering, architecture, accounting, actuarial science, performing arts, or consulting; or (2) the organization's average annual gross receipts for the three prior tax years does not exceed $5 million. This rule does not apply to any amount if interest must be paid on the amount or if there is any penalty for failure to pay the amount.[155]

To change the method of accounting used to report taxable income (for income in its entirety or for the treatment of any material item), the organization must file with the IRS either an advance consent request for a ruling or an automatic change request for certain specific changes in accounting method. The filing of Form 3115 is required.

(b) Accounting Period

The unrelated business income tax return must be filed using the tax-exempt organization's established annual accounting period. If the organization lacks such a period, the return should be filed on the calendar-year basis.

To change an accounting period, some exempt organizations may make a notation on a timely filed annual information return or unrelated business income tax return. Other organizations, however, may be required to file Form 1128.[156] If an exempt organization changes its accounting period, it should file its unrelated business income tax return for the short period that begins with the first day after the end of the old tax year and ends on the day before the first day of the new tax year. For this short-period return, the organization should compute the tax by placing the organization's taxable income on an annual basis.[157]

(c) Filing Due Dates

The unrelated business income tax return filed by a tax-exempt organization generally is due by the fifteenth day of the fifth month following the close of the organization's tax year.[158] If this due date falls on a Saturday, Sunday, or legal holiday, the due date is the next business day.

---

[154] IRC § 461(h).
[155] IRC § 448(d)(5); Reg. § 1.448-2T.
[156] See Rev. Proc. 85-58, 1985-2 C.B. 740.
[157] IRC § 443.
[158] IRC § 6072(e).

A corporation may request an automatic six-month extension of time to file the return; such a request is made by filing Form 8868. A trust may request an automatic three-month extension of time to file; such a request is made by means of the same form. If more time is needed, trusts may file another form to request that an additional (but not automatic) three-month extension of time be granted by the IRS.

When a tax-exempt organization files an amended return to correct errors or otherwise change a previously filed return, the IRS recommends that the organization write "Amended Return" at the top of the return. The organization should include with the submission a statement that indicates the line number(s) on the original return that are being changed and summarizes the reason for each change. Generally, an amended return must be filed within three years after the date the original return was due or three years after the date the organization filed the original, whichever is later.

(d) Filing Process

A tax-exempt organization can file the unrelated business income tax return by mailing it or delivering it to the Internal Revenue Service Center in Ogden, UT 84201-0027. Also, an exempt organization can use certain private delivery services in filing the return.

(e) Estimated Taxes

Generally, a tax-exempt organization filing an unrelated business income tax return must make installment payments of estimated tax if its estimated tax (the tax less any allowable credits) is expected to be at least $500. The computation and payment of this tax, by corporations and trusts, is by means of Form 990-W.

(f) Electronic Deposit Requirements

A tax-exempt organization may be required to deposit its unrelated business income tax payments electronically. The organization is required to make electronic deposits of the tax, using the Electronic Federal Tax Payment System, in 2005 if the total deposits in 2003 were more than $200,000 or if the organization was required to deposit electronically in 2004.

If an exempt organization is required to use this electronic tax payment system and fails to do so, it may be subject to a 10-percent penalty. An organization that is not required to use this system may do so voluntarily. For deposits using this system to be made on a timely basis, the organization must initiate the transaction at least one business day before the date the deposit is due.

(g) Deposits with Form 8109

If a tax-exempt organization does not use the electronic tax payment system, it must deposit unrelated business income tax payments and estimated tax payments with Form 8109. This form is to be mailed or delivered, with the payment, to an authorized depositary (namely, a commercial bank or other financial institution authorized to accept federal tax deposits). The form and payment should not be sent to an IRS office.

Checks or money orders should be made payable to the depositary. To help ensure proper crediting, the organization should write its federal identification number, the tax period to which the deposit applies, and "Form 990-T" on the check or money order. The organization may mail the form and payment to Financial Agent, Federal Tax Deposit Processing, P.O. Box 970030, St. Louis, MO 63197. The check or money order should be made payable to "Financial Agent."

(h) Interest and Penalties

A tax-exempt organization may be subject to interest and penalty charges if it files a return late or fails to pay tax when due. Generally, an exempt organization is not required to include the interest and penalty charges on the return, because the IRS will compute the amount and bill the organization for it.

(i) Interest. Interest is charged on taxes not paid by the due date, even if an extension of time to file was granted. Interest is also charged on penalties imposed for failure to file, negligence, fraud, substantial valuation misstatements, and substantial understatements of tax; interest is calculated from the due date (including extensions) to the date of payment. The interest charge is computed at the underpayment rate.[159]

(ii) Penalty for Late Filing. An exempt organization that fails to file its unrelated business income tax return when due (including extensions of time for filing) is subject to a penalty of 5 percent of the unpaid tax for each month or part of a month the return is late, up to a maximum of 25 percent of the unpaid tax. The minimum penalty for a return that is more than 60 days late is an amount equal to the smaller of the tax due or $100. This penalty will not be imposed if the organization can show that the failure to timely file was due to reasonable cause. An organization filing late should attach a statement explaining the basis for the reasonable-cause claim.

(iii) Penalty for Late Payment of Tax. The penalty for late payment of taxes usually is an amount equal to 0.5 percent of the unpaid tax for each month or part of a month the tax is unpaid. This penalty cannot exceed 25 percent of the unpaid tax. The penalty will not be imposed if the organization can show that the failure to pay on time was due to reasonable cause.

(iv) Estimated Tax Penalty. An exempt organization that fails to make estimated tax payments when due may be subject to an underpayment penalty for the period of underpayment. Generally, an organization is subject to this penalty if its tax liability is at least $500 and it did not make estimated tax payments of an amount equal to at least the smaller of its tax liability for the year or 100 percent of the prior year's tax.[160]

---

[159] IRC § 6621.
[160] IRC § 6655.

(v) Form 2220. Form 2220 is used by corporations and trusts filing an unrelated business income tax return to determine if the organization owes a penalty and to compute the amount of the penalty. Generally, the organization is not required to file this form, because the IRS can compute the amount of any penalty and bill the organization for it. Nonetheless, even if an organization does not owe a penalty, it is required to complete and attach this form if the annualized income or adjusted seasonal installment method is used, or if the organization is a large organization computing its first required installment based on the prior year's tax.

(i) Consolidated Returns

The consolidated return rules[161] do not apply to tax-exempt organizations, except in the case of an exempt organization with a title-holding company. If a title-holding corporation pays any amount of its net income for a tax year to a tax-exempt organization[162] (or would have, except that the expenses of collecting its income exceeded that income), and the corporation and exempt organization file a consolidated return, the exempt organization should treat the title-holding corporation as being organized and operated for the same purposes as the other exempt organization (in addition to its title-holding purposes).

Two tax-exempt organizations, one a title-holding company and the other earning income from it, will be includable corporations for purposes of the consolidated return rules.[163] If the organizations meet the definition of an affiliated group and certain other rules, they may file a consolidated return. The parent organization must attach Form 851 to the consolidated return. For the first year a consolidated return is filed, the title-holding company must attach Form 1122.

---

[161] IRC § 1501.
[162] That is, an organization that is exempt from federal income tax by reason of IRC § 501(a).
[163] IRC § 1504(a).

APPENDIX A

Sources of the Law

The law as described in this book is derived from many sources. For those not familiar with these matters and wishing to understand what "the law" regarding unrelated business is, the following explanation should be of assistance.

FEDERAL LAW

At the federal (national) level in the United States, there are three branches of government, as provided for in the U.S. Constitution. Article 1 of the Constitution established the U.S. Congress as a bicameral legislature, consisting of the House of Representatives and the Senate. Article II of the Constitution established the presidency. Article III of the Constitution established the federal court system.

Congress

The legal structure underlying the federal law for nonprofit organizations in the United States has been created by Congress. Most of this law is manifested in the tax law and thus appears in the Internal Revenue Code (which is officially codified in Title 26 of the United States Code and referenced throughout the book as the "IRC" (see § 1.1, note 4)).

Tax laws for the United States must originate in the House of Representatives (U.S. Constitution, art. I, § 7). Consequently, most of the nation's tax laws are initially written by the members and staff of the House Committee on Ways and Means. Frequently, these laws are generated by work done at the subcommittee level, usually the Subcommittee on Oversight or the Subcommittee on Select Revenue Measures.

Committee work in this area within the Senate is undertaken by the Committee on Finance. The Joint Committee on Taxation, consisting of members from both the House of Representatives and the Senate, also provides assistance in this regard. Nearly all of this legislation is finalized by a House-Senate conference committee, consisting of senior members of the House Ways and Means Committee and the Senate Finance Committee.

A considerable amount of the federal tax law for charitable organizations and charitable giving is found in the legislative history of these statutory laws. Most of this history is in congressional committee reports. Reports from committees in the House of Representatives are cited as "H. R. Rep. No." (see, e.g., § 1.4,

n. 50); reports from committees in the Senate are cited as "S. Rep. No." (see, e.g., § 1.6, n. 113), conference committee reports are cited as "H. R. Rep. No." Transcripts of the debate on legislation, formal statements, and other items are printed in the *Congressional Record* (Cong. Rec.). The *Congressional Record* is published every day one of the houses of Congress is in session and is cited as "[number] Cong. Rec. [number] (daily ed., [date of issue])." The first number is the annual volume number, the second number is the page in the daily edition on which the item begins. Periodically, the daily editions of the *Congressional Record* are republished as a hardbound book, which is cited as "[number] Cong. Rec. [number] ([year])." As before, the first number is the annual volume number and the second is the beginning page number. The bound version of the *Congressional Record* then becomes the publication that contains the permanent citation for the item.

A Congress sits for two years, each of which is termed a *session*. Each Congress is sequentially numbered. For example, the 109th Congress will meet during the calendar years 2005–2006. A legislative development that took place in 2005 is referenced as occurring during the 109th Congress, 1st Session (109th Cong., 1st Sess. (2005)).

A bill introduced in the House of Representatives or Senate during a particular Congress is given a sequential number in each house. For example, the thousandth bill introduced in the House of Representatives in 2005 is cited as "H.R. 1000, 109th Cong., 1st Sess. (2005)"; the five-hundredth bill introduced in the Senate in 2005 is cited as "S. 500, 109th Cong., 1st Sess. (2005)."

Executive Branch

A function of the executive branch in the United States is to administer and enforce the laws enacted by Congress. This executive function is performed by departments and agencies, and "independent" regulatory commissions (such as the Federal Trade Commission or the Securities and Exchange Commission). One of these functions is the promulgation of regulations, which are published by the U.S. government in the *Code of Federal Regulations* (C.F.R.). When adopted, regulations are printed in the *Federal Register* (Fed. Reg.). The federal tax laws are administered and enforced by the Department of the Treasury.

One of the ways in which the Department of the Treasury executes these functions is by the promulgation of regulations (Treas. Reg. or simply Reg.), which are designed to interpret and amplify the related statute (see, e.g., § 1.6, n. 111). These regulations (like rules made by other departments, agencies, and commissions) have the force of law, unless they are overly broad in relation to the accompanying statute or are unconstitutional, in which case they can be rendered void by a court.

Within the Department of the Treasury is the Internal Revenue Service (IRS). The IRS is, among its many roles, a tax-collecting agency. The IRS, though headquartered in Washington, D.C. (its "National Office"), has regional and field offices throughout the country.

The IRS (from its National Office) prepares and disseminates guidelines interpreting tax statutes and tax regulations. These guidelines have the force of law, unless they are overbroad in relation to the statute and/or Treasury regulation involved, or are unconstitutional. IRS determinations on a point of law are termed *revenue rulings* (Rev. Rul.); those that are rules of procedure are termed *revenue procedures* (Rev. Proc.).

Revenue rulings (which may be based on one or more court opinions) and revenue procedures are sequentially numbered every calendar year, with that number preceded by a four-digit number reflecting the year of issue. For example, the fiftieth revenue ruling issued in 2005 is cited as "Rev. Rul. 2005–50." Likewise, the twenty-fifth revenue procedure issued in 2005 is cited as "Rev. Proc. 2005–25."

These IRS determinations are published each week in the *Internal Revenue Bulletin* (I.R.B.). In the foregoing examples, when the determinations are first published, the revenue ruling is cited as "Rev. Rul. 2005–50, 2005–_____ I.R.B. _____," with the number after the hyphen being the number of the particular issue of the weekly *Bulletin* and the last number being the page number within that issue on which the item begins. Likewise, the revenue procedure is cited as "Rev. Proc. 2005–25, 2005–_____ I.R.B. _____." Every six months, the *Internal Revenue Bulletins* are republished as hardbound books; these publications are termed the *Cumulative Bulletin* (C.B.). The *Cumulative Bulletin* designation then becomes the permanent citation for the determination. Thus, the permanent citations for these two IRS determinations are "Rev. Rul. 2005–50, 2005–1 C. B. _____" (see, e.g., § 3.4, n. 33) and "Rev. Proc. 2005–25, 2005–1 C. B. _____" (see, e.g., § 4.8 n. 125), with the first number being the year of issue, the second number (after the hyphen) indicating whether the determination is published in the first six months of the year ("1," as in the example, or the second six months of the year ("2")), and the last number being the page number within that semiannual bound volume at which the determination begins.

The IRS considers itself bound by its revenue rulings and revenue procedures. These determinations are the "law," particularly in the sense that the IRS regards them as precedential, although they are not binding on the courts. Indeed, the courts generally treat an IRS revenue ruling as merely the position of the IRS with respect to a specific factual situation.

By contrast to these forms of "public" law, the IRS (again, from its National Office) also issues private or nonprecedential determinations. These documents principally are private letter rulings (Priv. Ltr. Rul.), technical advice memoranda (Tech. Adv. Mem.), and chief counsel advice memoranda (Chief Counsel Adv. Mem.). These determinations may not be cited as legal authority (I.R.C. § 6110(j)(3)). Nonetheless, these pronouncements can be valuable in understanding IRS thinking on a point of law and, in practice (the statutory prohibition notwithstanding), these documents are cited in court opinions, articles, and books as IRS positions on issues.

The IRS issues private letter rulings in response to written questions (termed *ruling requests*) submitted to the IRS by individuals and organizations. An IRS district office may refer a case to the IRS National Office for advice (termed *technical advice*); the resulting advice is provided to the IRS district office in the form of a technical advice memorandum. In the course of preparing a revenue ruling, private letter ruling, or technical advice memorandum, the IRS National Office may seek legal advice from its Office of Chief Counsel; the resulting advice is provided in the form of a chief counsel advice memorandum. These documents are eventually made public, albeit in redacted form.

Private letter rulings and technical advice memoranda for years were identified by seven-digit numbers, as in "Priv. Ltr. Rul. 9826007" (see, e.g., § 1.6, n. 146). (A reference to a technical advice memorandum appears in § 1.6, n. 136.) Beginning in 1999, however, the IRS began using a nine-digit numbering system, as in "Priv. Ltr. Rul. 199926007 (e.g., § 2.2(d), n. 61). The first four numbers are for the year involved (here, 1999), the second two numbers reflect the week of the calendar year involved (here, the twenty-sixth week of 1999), and the remaining three numbers identify the document as issued sequentially during the particular week (here, this private letter ruling was the seventh one issued during the week involved). General counsel memoranda (now Chief Counsel Adv. Mem.) are numbered sequentially in the order in which they are written (e.g., Gen. Couns. Mem. 39457 is the thirty-nine thousand, four hundred fifty-seventh general counsel memorandum ever written by the IRS's Office of Chief Counsel.) A reference to a general counsel memorandum appears in § 1.6, n. 127.

The IRS also issues technical expedited advice memoranda, which will replace some technical advice memoranda; these are intended to produce requested advice within a shorter period. In the tax-exempt organizations area, the IRS was ordered by a federal court of appeals in 2004 to release rulings denying or revoking exempt status; these are termed exemption denial and revocation letters (Ex. Den. & Revoc. Ltr.). An example appears in § 7.1(f), n. 113.

The Judiciary

The federal court system has three levels: trial courts (including those that initially hear cases when a formal trial is not involved), courts of appeal (*appellate courts*), and the U.S. Supreme Court. The trial courts include the various federal district courts (at least one in each state, the District of Columbia, and the U.S. territories), the U.S. Tax Court, and the U.S. Court of Federal Claims (formerly the U.S. Claims Court). There are 13 federal appellate courts: the U.S. Courts of Appeals for the First through the Eleventh Circuits, the U.S. Court of Appeals for the District of Columbia, and the U.S. Court of Appeals for the Federal Circuit.

Cases concerning the tax law of charitable giving at the federal level can originate in any federal district court, the U.S. Tax Court, or the U.S. Court of Federal Claims. Under a special declaratory judgment procedure available only to charitable organizations (I.R.C. § 7428), cases can originate only with the U.S. District Court for the District of Columbia, the U.S. Tax Court, or the U.S. Court of Federal Claims. Cases involving tax-exempt organizations are considered by the U.S. courts of appeal and the U.S. Supreme Court.

Most opinions emanating from a U.S. district court are published by the West Publishing Company in the Federal Supplement series (F. Supp.). Thus, a citation to one of these opinions appears as "[number] F. Supp. [number]," followed by an identification of the court and the year of the opinion. The first number is the annual volume number; the second number is the page in the book on which the opinion begins (see, e.g., Chapter § 2.2(d), n. 55). (In early 1998, West began publishing the Federal Supplement Second series (once volume 999 of the Federal Supplement series was published); thus, citations to subsequent opinions from the U.S. courts of appeal appear as "[number] F. Supp. 2d [number].") Some district court opinions appear sooner in Commerce Clearing House or Prentice-Hall publications (see, e.g., § 1.2, n.12); occasionally, these publications will contain opinions that are never published in the Federal Supplement reporter.

Most opinions emanating from a U.S. court of appeals are published by the West Publishing Company in the Federal Reporter Second series (F.2d). Thus, a citation to one of these opinions appears as "[number] F.2d [number]," followed by an identification of the court and the year of the opinion. The first number is the annual volume number, the second number is the page in the book on which the opinion begins (see, e.g., § 1.2, n.12). (In early 1994, the Federal Reporter Third series was started (once volume 999 of the Federal Reporter Second series was published); thus, citations to subsequent opinions from the U.S. courts of appeal appear as "[number] F.3d [number].") Appellate court opinions appear sooner in Commerce Clearing House or Prentice-Hall publications; occasionally, these publications will contain opinions that are never published in the Federal Reporter series. Opinions from the U.S. Court of Federal Claims are also published in Federal Reporter Second (and Third) series.

Opinions from the U.S. Tax Court are published by the U.S. government and are usually cited as "[number] T.C. [number]," followed by the year of the opinion (see, e.g., § 1.2, n.12). As always, the first number of these citations is the annual volume number; the second number is the page in the book on which the opinion begins.

U.S. district court and Tax Court opinions may be appealed to the appropriate U.S. court of appeals. For example, cases in the states of Maryland, North Carolina, South Carolina, Virginia, and West Virginia, and the District of Columbia, are appealable (from either court) to the U.S. Court of Appeals for the Fourth Circuit. Cases from any federal appellate or district court, the U.S. Tax Court, and the U.S. Court of Federal Claims may be appealed to the U.S. Supreme Court.

The U.S. Supreme Court usually has discretion as to whether to accept a case. This decision is manifested as a "writ of certiorari." When the Supreme Court agrees to hear a case, it grants the writ ("*cert. granted*"); otherwise, it denies the writ ("*cert. denied*").

In this book, citations to Supreme Court opinions are to the United States Reports series published by the U.S. government, when available ("[number] U.S. [number]," followed by the year of the opinion) (see, *e.g.*, § 1.2, n.15). When the United States Reports series citation is not available, the Supreme Court Reporter series, published by the West Publishing Company, reference is used ("[number] S. Ct. [number]," followed by the year of the opinion). As always, the first number of these citations is the annual volume number; the second number is the page in the book on which the opinion begins. There is a third way to cite Supreme Court cases, which is by means of the United States Supreme Court Reports—Lawyers' Edition series, published by the Lawyers

Co-Operative Publishing Company and the Bancroft-Whitney Company, but that form of citation is not used in this book. Supreme Court opinions appear earlier in the Commerce Clearing House or Prentice-Hall publications.

STATE LAW

The Legislative Branches

Statutory laws in the various states are created by the state legislatures.

The Executive Branches

The rules and regulations published at the state level emanate from state departments, agencies, and the like. For charitable organizations, these departments are usually the office of the state's Attorney General and the state's Department of State. There are no references to state rules and regulations in this book.

The Judiciary

Each of the states has a judiciary system, usually a three-tiered one modeled after the federal system. Cases involving charitable organizations are heard in all of these courts. There are a few references to state court opinions in this book.

State court opinions are published by the governments of each state, and the principal ones are also collected and published by the West Publishing Company. The latter sets of opinions (referenced in this book) are published in "reporters" covering court developments in various regions throughout the country. For example, the *Atlantic Reporter* contains court opinions issued by the principal courts in the states of Connecticut, Delaware, Maine, Maryland, New Hampshire, New Jersey, Pennsylvania, Rhode Island, and Vermont, and the District of Columbia; the *Pacific Reporter* contains court opinions issued by the principal courts of Arizona, California, Colorado, Idaho, Kansas, Montana, Nevada, New Mexico, Oklahoma, Oregon, Utah, Washington, and Wyoming.

PUBLICATIONS

Articles, of course, are not forms of "the law." However, they can be cited, particularly by courts, in the development of the law. Also, as research tools, they contain useful summaries of the applicable law. In addition to the many law school "law review" publications, the following (which is not an exclusive list) periodicals contain material that may be helpful in following developments concerning charitable organizations and giving to them:

Bruce R. Hopkins' Nonprofit Counsel (John Wiley & Sons)

The Chronicle of Philanthropy (The Chronicle of Higher Education. Inc.)

Daily Tax Report (Bureau of National Affairs)

Exempt Organization Tax Review (Tax Analysts)

Foundation News (Council on Foundations)

The Journal of Taxation (Warren, Gorham & Lamont)

The Journal of Taxation of Exempt Organizations (Faulkner & Gray)

The Philanthropy Monthly (Non-Profit Reports, Inc.)

Tax Law Review (Rosenfeld Launer Publications)

The Tax Lawyer (American Bar Association)

Tax Notes (Tax Analysts)

Taxes (Commerce Clearing House)

APPENDIX B

Internal Revenue Code Sections

Following are the provisions of the Internal Revenue Code of 1986, as amended, that constitute the statutory framework for the law of unrelated business. Each is coupled to references (by chapter or section) to the portion(s) of this book where the provision is discussed.

Section 170—income tax deduction for charitable contributions [3.18, 11.4]

Section 501(a)—source of tax exemption for nearly all exempt organizations [1.2]

Section 501(b)—tax-exempt organizations subject to tax on unrelated business income [1.2]

Section 501(c)(1)—tax exemption for instrumentalities of the United States [1.5]

Section 501(c)(2)—tax exemption for single-parent title-holding corporations [1.5]

Section 501(c)(3)—tax exemption for charitable, educational, religious, scientific, and similar entities [1.5]

Section 501(c)(4)—tax exemption for social welfare organizations [1.5]

Section 501(c)(5)—tax exemption for agricultural, horticultural, and labor organizations [1.5]

Section 501(c)(6)—tax exemption for business leagues, including trade, business, and professional associations [1.5]

Section 501(c)(7)—tax exemption for social clubs [1.5]

Section 501(c)(8)—tax exemption for certain fraternal beneficiary societies [1.5]

Section 501(c)(9)—tax exemption for voluntary employees' beneficiary associations [1.5]

Section 501(c)(10)—tax exemption for certain domestic fraternal societies [1.5]

Section 501(c)(11)—tax exemption for teachers' retirement fund associations [1.5]

Section 501(c)(12)—tax exemption for benevolent or mutual organizations [1.5]

Section 501(c)(13)—tax exemption for certain cemetery companies [1.5]

Section 501(c)(14)—tax exemption for certain credit unions and mutual reserve funds [1.5]

Section 501(c)(15)—tax exemption for certain insurance companies or associations [1.5]

Section 501(c)(16)—tax exemption for crop operations finance corporations [1.5]

Section 501(c)(17)—tax exemption for supplemental unemployment benefit trusts

Section 501(c)(18)—tax exemption for certain pension plan trusts [1.5]

Section 501(c)(19)—tax exemption for veterans' organizations [1.5]

Section 501(c)(21)—tax exemption for black lung benefit trusts [1.5]

Section 501(c)(22)—tax exemption for multiemployer benefit trusts [1.5]

Section 501(c)(23)—tax exemption for certain veterans' organizations [1.5]

Section 501(c)(24)—tax exemption for certain employee benefit trusts [1.5]

Section 501(c)(25)—tax exemption for multiparent title-holding corporations or trusts [1.5]

Section 501(c)(26)—tax exemption for high-risk individuals health care coverage organizations [1.5]

Section 501(c)(27)—tax exemption for workers' compensation reinsurance organizations [1.5]

Section 501(m)—rules concerning issuance of commercial-type insurance [7.3]

Section 511—imposition of tax on unrelated business income [1.7]

Section 512—definition of unrelated business income [6]

Section 512(b)—various modifications in computing unrelated business income [3]

Section 512(c)—special unrelated business rules for partnerships [6.4]

Section 512(d)—nontaxation of certain associate member dues [9.4]

Section 512(e)—taxation of interests in S corporations [4.12]

Section 513—general unrelated business rules [2.3]

Section 513(c)—definition of *trade or business* [2.2, 2.3]

Section 513(d)—trade show and like activities rules [4.5]

Section 513(e)—rules as to certain hospital services [4.6]

Section 513(f)—rules as to bingo games [4.7]

Section 513(g)—rules as to certain pole rentals [4.13]

Section 513(h)—rules as to rentals of lists and distribution of low-cost articles [4.9, 4.10]

Section 513(i)—rules as to unrelated debt-financed income [5]

Section 521—tax-exempt farmers' cooperatives [1.5]

Section 526—tax-exempt shipowners' protection and indemnity associations [1.5]

Section 527—tax-exempt political organizations [1.5]

Section 528—tax-exempt homeowners' associations [1.5]

Section 529—tax exemption for qualified state tuition programs [1.5]

Section 4943—private foundation excess business holdings rules [6.3]

Section 6012—requirement of income tax returns [11.4]

Section 6031—requirement of partnership tax returns [6.4]

Section 6033—requirement of filing of annual information returns [11.3]

Section 6072(e)—time for filing returns [11.5]

Section 6154(h)—estimated unrelated income quarterly tax payments [11.5]

Section 6651(a)(1)—addition to tax for failure to timely file unrelated business income tax (and other tax) return [11.5]

Section 6655(g)(3)—penalties for failure by a tax-exempt organization to pay estimated unrelated business income taxes [11.5]

APPENDIX C

Glossary

Throughout this book, reference is made to various types of organizations, most of them tax-exempt entities. For ease of understanding, here is a brief summary of selected terms used in this book.

business league An organization generically known as a trade, business, or professional association; an entity described in IRC § 501(c)(6).[1] This type of organization is an association of persons that have a common business interest; its purpose is to promote that common business interest. Its activities should be directed to the improvement of business conditions of one or more lines of business, as distinguished from the performance of particular services for individual persons. An exempt business league usually provides various services to its members.

C corporation A for-profit entity, the federal tax status of which is derived from the fact that the tax treatment of these corporations is the subject of IRC Subtitle A, Chapter 1, subchapter C.[2]

charitable organization A term often used to encompass all entities referenced in IRC § 501(c)(3).[3] The term also has a more specific definition, referring to a variety of organizations, including those that relieve the poor or distressed; promote health; lessen the burdens of government; advance religion, education, or science; promote social welfare; or promote the arts.[4]

educational organizations Certain types of entities referenced in IRC § 501(c)(3), such as universities, colleges, schools, museums, and organizations that instruct individuals and the public on a multitude of subjects.[5]

labor organization An entity, such as a union, that has as its primary purpose the betterment of the working conditions of its members; an entity that is tax-exempt by virtue of the provisions of IRC § 501(c)(5).[6]

private foundation A tax-exempt, *charitable organization* that is usually funded on an ongoing basis by investment income and makes grants for charitable purposes; an entity described in IRC § 501(c)(3) that is not a *public charity*.[7]

---

[1] Hopkins, *The Law of Tax-Exempt Organizations, Eighth Edition* (John Wiley & Sons, 2003) [hereinafter *Tax-Exempt Organizations*], ch. 13.

[2] IRC §§ 301–385.

[3] *Tax-Exempt Organizations*, ch. 5.

[4] *Id.*, ch. 6.

[5] *Id.*, ch. 7.

[6] *Id.*, § 15.1.

[7] *Id.*, § 11.1; Hopkins & Blazek, *Private Foundations: Tax Law and Compliance, Second Edition* (John Wiley & Sons, 2003) [hereinafter *Private Foundations*], § 1.2.

public charity   An exempt institution, such as a house of worship, university, college, school, health care provider, or governmental unit; a publicly supported charity; or a supporting organization.[8]

religious organizations   Certain types of entities referenced in IRC § 501(c)(3), such as churches, synagogues, mosques, integrated auxiliaries of churches, religious orders, and apostolic organizations.[9]

S corporation   A for-profit entity, the federal tax status of which is derived from the fact that the tax treatment of these corporations is the subject of IRC Subtitle A, Chapter 1, subchapter S.[10]

scientific organizations   Certain types of entities referenced in IRC § 501(c)(3), such as research institutions and entities that publish scientific material.[11]

social club   An organization that provides social and recreational services to its members; described in IRC § 501(c)(7).[12] In general, the tax exemption extends to social and recreational clubs that are supported solely by membership fees, dues, and assessments.

social welfare organization   Originally, an entity such as a civic league or a homeowners' association; today, often an advocacy organization. These entities are described in IRC § 501(c)(4).[13] The general rule remains that an organization is operated primarily for the promotion of social welfare if it is primarily engaged in promoting, in some way, the common good and general welfare of the people of a community. This includes entities that are operated primarily for the purpose of bringing about civic betterments and social improvements.

supporting organization   A type of *public charity* that is organized and operated exclusively for the benefit of, to perform the functions of, or to carry out the purposes of one or more qualified supported organizations.[14]

title-holding company (multimember)   A company that has as its function the holding of title to property for the benefit of two or more other types of tax-exempt organizations; described in IRC § 501(c)(25).[15]

title-holding company (single-member)   A company that has as its function the holding of title to property as a subsidiary of another type of tax-exempt organization; described in IRC § 501(c)(2).[16] A title-holding company may also serve related members.

voluntary employees' beneficiary association (VEBA)   An association that provides for the payment of life, illness, accident, or other benefits to its members, their dependents, and other designated beneficiaries; described in IRC § 501(c)(9).

---

[8] *Tax-Exempt Organizations*, § 11.3; *Private Foundations*, ch. 15.
[9] *Private Foundations*, ch. 8.
[10] IRC §§ 1361–1363.
[11] *Tax-Exempt Organizations*, ch. 9.
[12] *Id.*, ch. 14.
[13] *Id.*, ch. 12.
[14] *Id.*, § 11.3(c); *Private Foundations*, § 15.7.
[15] *Id.*, § 18.2(b).
[16] *Tax-Exempt Organizations*, § 18.2(a).

A P P E N D I X   D

Form **990**

Return of Organization Exempt From Income Tax

Under section 501(c), 527, or 4947(a)(1) of the Internal Revenue Code (except black lung benefit trust or private foundation)

Department of the Treasury
Internal Revenue Service

▶ The organization may have to use a copy of this return to satisfy state reporting requirements.

OMB No. 1545-0047

2004

Open to Public Inspection

A For the 2004 calendar year, or tax year beginning _____ , 2004, and ending _____ , 20____

B Check if applicable:	Please use IRS label or print or type. See Specific Instructions.	**C** Name of organization		**D** Employer identification number
☐ Address change				⋮
☐ Name change		Number and street (or P.O. box if mail is not delivered to street address)	Room/suite	**E** Telephone number
☐ Initial return				( )
☐ Final return		City or town, state or country, and ZIP + 4		**F** Accounting method: ☐ Cash ☐ Accrual
☐ Amended return				☐ Other (specify) ▶

☐ Application pending

● **Section 501(c)(3) organizations and 4947(a)(1) nonexempt charitable trusts must attach a completed Schedule A (Form 990 or 990-EZ).**

G Website: ▶

J Organization type (check only one) ▶ ☐ 501(c) ( ) ◀ (insert no.) ☐ 4947(a)(1) or ☐ 527

K Check here ▶ ☐ if the organization's gross receipts are normally not more than $25,000. The organization need not file a return with the IRS; but if the organization received a Form 990 Package in the mail, it should file a return without financial data. **Some states require a complete return.**

H and **I** are not applicable to section 527 organizations.
H(a) Is this a group return for affiliates? ☐ Yes ☐ No
H(b) If "Yes," enter number of affiliates ▶ _____
H(c) Are all affiliates included? ☐ Yes ☐ No
(If "No," attach a list. See instructions.)
H(d) Is this a separate return filed by an organization covered by a group ruling? ☐ Yes ☐ No
I Group Exemption Number ▶
M Check ▶ ☐ if the organization is **not** required to attach Sch. B (Form 990, 990-EZ, or 990-PF).

L Gross receipts: Add lines 6b, 8b, 9b, and 10b to line 12 ▶

Part I Revenue, Expenses, and Changes in Net Assets or Fund Balances (See page 18 of the instructions.)

1	Contributions, gifts, grants, and similar amounts received:			
a	Direct public support	**1a**		
b	Indirect public support	**1b**		
c	Government contributions (grants)	**1c**		
d	**Total** (add lines 1a through 1c) (cash $ _____ noncash $ _____) .		**1d**	
2	Program service revenue including government fees and contracts (from Part VII, line 93)		**2**	
3	Membership dues and assessments		**3**	
4	Interest on savings and temporary cash investments		**4**	
5	Dividends and interest from securities		**5**	
6a	Gross rents	**6a**		
b	Less: rental expenses	**6b**		
c	Net rental income or (loss) (subtract line 6b from line 6a)		**6c**	
7	Other investment income (describe ▶)		**7**	
8a	Gross amount from sales of assets other than inventory	(A) Securities **8a**	(B) Other	
b	Less: cost or other basis and sales expenses.	**8b**		
c	Gain or (loss) (attach schedule) . . .	**8c**		
d	Net gain or (loss) (combine line 8c, columns (A) and (B))		**8d**	
9	Special events and activities (attach schedule). If any amount is from **gaming**, check here ▶ ☐			
a	Gross revenue (not including $ _____ of contributions reported on line 1a)	**9a**		
b	Less: direct expenses other than fundraising expenses .	**9b**		
c	Net income or (loss) from special events (subtract line 9b from line 9a)		**9c**	
10a	Gross sales of inventory, less returns and allowances . .	**10a**		
b	Less: cost of goods sold	**10b**		
c	Gross profit or (loss) from sales of inventory (attach schedule) (subtract line 10b from line 10a).		**10c**	
11	Other revenue (from Part VII, line 103)		**11**	
12	**Total revenue** (add lines 1d, 2, 3, 4, 5, 6c, 7, 8d, 9c, 10c, and 11)		**12**	
13	Program services (from line 44, column (B))		**13**	
14	Management and general (from line 44, column (C))		**14**	
15	Fundraising (from line 44, column (D))		**15**	
16	Payments to affiliates (attach schedule)		**16**	
17	**Total expenses** (add lines 16 and 44, column (A))		**17**	
18	Excess or (deficit) for the year (subtract line 17 from line 12)		**18**	
19	Net assets or fund balances at beginning of year (from line 73, column (A)) . . .		**19**	
20	Other changes in net assets or fund balances (attach explanation).		**20**	
21	Net assets or fund balances at end of year (combine lines 18, 19, and 20)		**21**	

(Left margin labels: Revenue, Expenses, Net Assets)

For Privacy Act and Paperwork Reduction Act Notice, see the separate instructions. Cat. No. 11282Y Form **990** (2004)

Part II — Statement of Functional Expenses

All organizations must complete column (A). Columns (B), (C), and (D) are required for section 501(c)(3) and (4) organizations and section 4947(a)(1) nonexempt charitable trusts but optional for others. (See page 22 of the instructions.)

Do not include amounts reported on line 6b, 8b, 9b, 10b, or 16 of Part I.		(A) Total	(B) Program services	(C) Management and general	(D) Fundraising
22 Grants and allocations (attach schedule) (cash $ _____ noncash $ _____)	22				
23 Specific assistance to individuals (attach schedule)	23				
24 Benefits paid to or for members (attach schedule)	24				
25 Compensation of officers, directors, etc.	25				
26 Other salaries and wages	26				
27 Pension plan contributions	27				
28 Other employee benefits	28				
29 Payroll taxes	29				
30 Professional fundraising fees	30				
31 Accounting fees	31				
32 Legal fees	32				
33 Supplies	33				
34 Telephone	34				
35 Postage and shipping	35				
36 Occupancy	36				
37 Equipment rental and maintenance	37				
38 Printing and publications	38				
39 Travel	39				
40 Conferences, conventions, and meetings	40				
41 Interest	41				
42 Depreciation, depletion, etc. (attach schedule)	42				
43 Other expenses not covered above (itemize): a	43a				
b	43b				
c	43c				
d	43d				
e	43e				
44 Total functional expenses (add lines 22 through 43). *Organizations completing columns (B)-(D), carry these totals to lines 13—15*	44				

Joint Costs. Check ▶ ☐ if you are following SOP 98-2.
Are any joint costs from a combined educational campaign and fundraising solicitation reported in **(B)** Program services? ▶ ☐ Yes ☐ No
If "Yes," enter **(i)** the aggregate amount of these joint costs $_____ ; **(ii)** the amount allocated to Program services $_____ ;
(iii) the amount allocated to Management and general $_____ ; and **(iv)** the amount allocated to Fundraising $_____

Part III — Statement of Program Service Accomplishments (See page 25 of the instructions.)

What is the organization's primary exempt purpose? ▶ --

All organizations must describe their exempt purpose achievements in a clear and concise manner. State the number of clients served, publications issued, etc. Discuss achievements that are not measurable. (Section 501(c)(3) and (4) organizations and 4947(a)(1) nonexempt charitable trusts must also enter the amount of grants and allocations to others.)

Program Service Expenses (Required for 501(c)(3) and (4) orgs., and 4947(a)(1) trusts; but optional for others.)

a ....
....
....
(Grants and allocations $)

b ....
....
....
(Grants and allocations $)

c ....
....
....
(Grants and allocations $)

d ....
....
....
(Grants and allocations $)

e Other program services (attach schedule) (Grants and allocations $)

f Total of **Program Service Expenses** (should equal line 44, column (B), Program services). ▶

Form **990** (2004)

Part IV Balance Sheets (See page 25 of the instructions.)

Note: *Where required, attached schedules and amounts within the description column should be for end-of-year amounts only.*

			(A) Beginning of year		**(B)** End of year
Assets	45	Cash—non-interest-bearing		45	
	46	Savings and temporary cash investments		46	
	47a	Accounts receivable	**47a**		
	b	Less: allowance for doubtful accounts .	**47b**	47c	
	48a	Pledges receivable	**48a**		
	b	Less: allowance for doubtful accounts .	**48b**	48c	
	49	Grants receivable		49	
	50	Receivables from officers, directors, trustees, and key employees (attach schedule)		50	
	51a	Other notes and loans receivable (attach schedule)	**51a**		
	b	Less: allowance for doubtful accounts .	**51b**	51c	
	52	Inventories for sale or use		52	
	53	Prepaid expenses and deferred charges		53	
	54	Investments—securities (attach schedule) . . ▶ ☐ Cost ☐ FMV		54	
	55a	Investments—land, buildings, and equipment: basis	**55a**		
	b	Less: accumulated depreciation (attach schedule)	**55b**	55c	
	56	Investments—other (attach schedule)		56	
	57a	Land, buildings, and equipment: basis .	**57a**		
	b	Less: accumulated depreciation (attach schedule)	**57b**	57c	
	58	Other assets (describe ▶ _____)		58	
	59	**Total assets** (add lines 45 through 58) (must equal line 74) . . .		59	
Liabilities	60	Accounts payable and accrued expenses		60	
	61	Grants payable		61	
	62	Deferred revenue		62	
	63	Loans from officers, directors, trustees, and key employees (attach schedule)		63	
	64a	Tax-exempt bond liabilities (attach schedule)		64a	
	b	Mortgages and other notes payable (attach schedule)		64b	
	65	Other liabilities (describe ▶ _____)		65	
	66	**Total liabilities** (add lines 60 through 65)		66	
Net Assets or Fund Balances		**Organizations that follow SFAS 117, check here ▶ ☐ and complete lines 67 through 69 and lines 73 and 74.**			
	67	Unrestricted		67	
	68	Temporarily restricted		68	
	69	Permanently restricted		69	
		Organizations that do not follow SFAS 117, check here ▶ ☐ and complete lines 70 through 74.			
	70	Capital stock, trust principal, or current funds.		70	
	71	Paid-in or capital surplus, or land, building, and equipment fund .		71	
	72	Retained earnings, endowment, accumulated income, or other funds		72	
	73	**Total net assets or fund balances** (add lines 67 through 69 **or** lines 70 through 72; column (A) **must** equal line 19; column (B) **must** equal line 21) . .		73	
	74	**Total liabilities and net assets / fund balances** (add lines 66 and 73)		74	

Form 990 is available for public inspection and, for some people, serves as the primary or sole source of information about a particular organization. How the public perceives an organization in such cases may be determined by the information presented on its return. Therefore, please make sure the return is complete and accurate and fully describes, in Part III, the organization's programs and accomplishments.

Form 990 (2004)   Page **4**

Part IV-A Reconciliation of Revenue per Audited Financial Statements with Revenue per Return (See page 27 of the instructions.)

a   Total revenue, gains, and other support per audited financial statements . ▶ | a |

b   Amounts included on line **a** but not on line 12, Form 990:

(1) Net unrealized gains on investments . . $_____

(2) Donated services and use of facilities $_____

(3) Recoveries of prior year grants . . . $_____

(4) Other (specify):

.... $_____

Add amounts on lines (1) through (4) ▶ | b |

c   Line **a** minus line **b** . . . . . ▶ | c |

d   Amounts included on line 12, Form 990 but not on line **a**:

(1) Investment expenses not included on line 6b, Form 990. . . $_____

(2) Other (specify):

.... $_____

Add amounts on lines (1) and (2) ▶ | d |

e   Total revenue per line 12, Form 990 (line **c** plus line **d**). . . . . . ▶ | e |

Part IV-B Reconciliation of Expenses per Audited Financial Statements with Expenses per Return

a   Total expenses and losses per audited financial statements . . ▶ | a |

b   Amounts included on line **a** but not on line 17, Form 990:

(1) Donated services and use of facilities $_____

(2) Prior year adjustments reported on line 20, Form 990. . . . $_____

(3) Losses reported on line 20, Form 990 . $_____

(4) Other (specify):

.... $_____

Add amounts on lines (1) through (4) ▶ | b |

c   Line **a** minus line **b** . . . . . ▶ | c |

d   Amounts included on line 17, Form 990 but not on line **a**:

(1) Investment expenses not included on line 6b, Form 990 . . $_____

(2) Other (specify):

.... $_____

Add amounts on lines (1) and (2) ▶ | d |

e   Total expenses per line 17, Form 990 (line **c** plus line **d**) . . . . . ▶ | e |

Part V List of Officers, Directors, Trustees, and Key Employees (List each one even if not compensated; see page 27 of the instructions.)

(A) Name and address	(B) Title and average hours per week devoted to position	(C) Compensation (If not paid, enter -0-.)	(D) Contributions to employee benefit plans & deferred compensation	(E) Expense account and other allowances
--				
--				
--				
--				
--				
--				
--				
--				
--				
--				
--				

75   Did any officer, director, trustee, or key employee receive aggregate compensation of more than $100,000 from your organization and all related organizations, of which more than $10,000 was provided by the related organizations? ▶ ☐ **Yes** ☐ **No**   If "Yes," attach schedule—see page 28 of the instructions.

Form **990** (2004)

APPENDIX D

Form 990 (2004)   Page **5**

Part VI	**Other Information** (See page 28 of the instructions.)		Yes	No

76	Did the organization engage in any activity not previously reported to the IRS? If "Yes," attach a detailed description of each activity.	**76**		
77	Were any changes made in the organizing or governing documents but not reported to the IRS? . . .	**77**		
	If "Yes," attach a conformed copy of the changes.			
78a	Did the organization have unrelated business gross income of $1,000 or more during the year covered by this return?	**78a**		
b	If "Yes," has it filed a tax return on **Form 990-T** for this year?	**78b**		
79	Was there a liquidation, dissolution, termination, or substantial contraction during the year? If "Yes," attach a statement	**79**		
80a	Is the organization related (other than by association with a statewide or nationwide organization) through common membership, governing bodies, trustees, officers, etc., to any other exempt or nonexempt organization? . .	**80a**		
b	If "Yes," enter the name of the organization ▶ _____ _____ and check whether it is ☐ exempt **or** ☐ nonexempt.			
81a	Enter direct and indirect political expenditures. See line 81 instructions . . |81a|			
b	Did the organization file **Form 1120-POL** for this year?	**81b**		
82a	Did the organization receive donated services or the use of materials, equipment, or facilities at no charge or at substantially less than fair rental value?	**82a**		
b	If "Yes," you may indicate the value of these items here. Do not include this amount as revenue in Part I or as an expense in Part II. (See instructions in Part III.) . |82b|			
83a	Did the organization comply with the public inspection requirements for returns and exemption applications?	**83a**		
b	Did the organization comply with the disclosure requirements relating to quid pro quo contributions? . .	**83b**		
84a	Did the organization solicit any contributions or gifts that were not tax deductible?	**84a**		
b	If "Yes," did the organization include with every solicitation an express statement that such contributions or gifts were not tax deductible?	**84b**		
85	*501(c)(4), (5), or (6) organizations.* **a** Were substantially all dues nondeductible by members?	**85a**		
b	Did the organization make only in-house lobbying expenditures of $2,000 or less?	**85b**		
	If "Yes" was answered to either 85a or 85b, **do not** complete 85c through 85h below unless the organization received a waiver for proxy tax owed for the prior year.			
c	Dues, assessments, and similar amounts from members. . . . . |85c|			
d	Section 162(e) lobbying and political expenditures. . . . . |85d|			
e	Aggregate nondeductible amount of section 6033(e)(1)(A) dues notices . . . |85e|			
f	Taxable amount of lobbying and political expenditures (line 85d less 85e) . . |85f|			
g	Does the organization elect to pay the section 6033(e) tax on the amount on line 85f?	**85g**		
h	If section 6033(e)(1)(A) dues notices were sent, does the organization agree to add the amount on line 85f to its reasonable estimate of dues allocable to nondeductible lobbying and political expenditures for the following tax year?	**85h**		
86	*501(c)(7) orgs.* Enter: **a** Initiation fees and capital contributions included on line 12. |86a|			
b	Gross receipts, included on line 12, for public use of club facilities . . . . |86b|			
87	*501(c)(12) orgs.* Enter: **a** Gross income from members or shareholders . . . |87a|			
b	Gross income from other sources. (Do not net amounts due or paid to other sources against amounts due or received from them.) . . . . |87b|			
88	At any time during the year, did the organization own a 50% or greater interest in a taxable corporation or partnership, or an entity disregarded as separate from the organization under Regulations sections 301.7701-2 and 301.7701-3? If "Yes," complete Part IX	**88**		
89a	*501(c)(3) organizations.* Enter: Amount of tax imposed on the organization during the year under: section 4911 ▶_____ ; section 4912 ▶_____ ; section 4955 ▶			
b	*501(c)(3) and 501(c)(4) orgs.* Did the organization engage in any section 4958 excess benefit transaction during the year or did it become aware of an excess benefit transaction from a prior year? If "Yes," attach a statement explaining each transaction	**89b**		
c	Enter: Amount of tax imposed on the organization managers or disqualified persons during the year under sections 4912, 4955, and 4958 . . . . ▶ _____			
d	Enter: Amount of tax on line 89c, above, reimbursed by the organization . . . . ▶ _____			
90a	List the states with which a copy of this return is filed ▶ _____			
b	Number of employees employed in the pay period that includes March 12, 2004 (See instructions.) |90b| _____			
91	The books are in care of ▶ _____ Telephone no. ▶ (____)_____			
	Located at ▶ _____ ZIP + 4 ▶ _____			
92	*Section 4947(a)(1) nonexempt charitable trusts filing Form 990 in lieu of **Form 1041**—*Check here. . . . . . . ▶ ☐			
	and enter the amount of tax-exempt interest received or accrued during the tax year . . . ▶ |92|			

Form **990** (2004)

APPENDIX D

Part VII   Analysis of Income-Producing Activities (See page 33 of the instructions.)

Note: *Enter gross amounts unless otherwise indicated.*

	Unrelated business income		Excluded by section 512, 513, or 514		(E) Related or exempt function income
	(A) Business code	(B) Amount	(C) Exclusion code	(D) Amount	
93 Program service revenue:					
a					
b					
c					
d					
e					
f Medicare/Medicaid payments					
g Fees and contracts from government agencies					
94 Membership dues and assessments					
95 Interest on savings and temporary cash investments					
96 Dividends and interest from securities					
97 Net rental income or (loss) from real estate:					
a debt-financed property					
b not debt-financed property					
98 Net rental income or (loss) from personal property					
99 Other investment income					
100 Gain or (loss) from sales of assets other than inventory					
101 Net income or (loss) from special events					
102 Gross profit or (loss) from sales of inventory					
103 Other revenue: a					
b					
c					
d					
e					
104 Subtotal (add columns (B), (D), and (E))					

105 **Total** (add line 104, columns (B), (D), and (E)) . . . . ▶

Note: *Line 105 plus line 1d, Part I, should equal the amount on line 12, Part I.*

Part VIII   Relationship of Activities to the Accomplishment of Exempt Purposes (See page 34 of the instructions.)

Line No.
▼   Explain how each activity for which income is reported in column (E) of Part VII contributed importantly to the accomplishment of the organization's exempt purposes (other than by providing funds for such purposes).

Part IX   Information Regarding Taxable Subsidiaries and Disregarded Entities (See page 34 of the instructions.)

(A) Name, address, and EIN of corporation, partnership, or disregarded entity	(B) Percentage of ownership interest	(C) Nature of activities	(D) Total income	(E) End-of-year assets
	%			
	%			
	%			
	%			

Part X   Information Regarding Transfers Associated with Personal Benefit Contracts (See page 34 of the instructions.)

(a) Did the organization, during the year, receive any funds, directly or indirectly, to pay premiums on a personal benefit contract? ☐ Yes ☐ No
(b) Did the organization, during the year, pay premiums, directly or indirectly, on a personal benefit contract? ☐ Yes ☐ No
Note: *If "Yes" to (b), file Form 8870 and Form 4720 (see instructions).*

Please Sign Here
Under penalties of perjury, I declare that I have examined this return, including accompanying schedules and statements, and to the best of my knowledge and belief, it is true, correct, and complete. Declaration of preparer (other than officer) is based on all information of which preparer has any knowledge.

▶ Signature of officer   Date

▶ Type or print name and title.

Paid Preparer's Use Only

Preparer's signature ▶	Date	Check if self-employed ▶ ☐	Preparer's SSN or PTIN (See Gen. Inst. W)
Firm's name (or yours if self-employed), address, and ZIP + 4 ▶		EIN ▶	
		Phone no. ▶ ( )	

Form **990** (2004)

Form **990-T**	**Exempt Organization Business Income Tax Return** **(and proxy tax under section 6033(e))**	OMB No. 1545-0687
Department of the Treasury Internal Revenue Service	For calendar year 2004 or other tax year beginning .... , 2004, and ending .... , 20 ..... ▶ **See separate instructions.**	**2004**

A ☐ Check box if address changed		Name of organization (☐ check box if name changed and see instructions)		**D Employer identification number** (Employees' trust, see instructions for Block D on page 7.)
B Exempt under section ☐ 501( )( ) ☐ 408(e) ☐ 220(e) ☐ 408A ☐ 530(a) ☐ 529(a)	**Please Print or Type**	Number, street, and room or suite no. (If a P.O. box, see page 7 of instructions.)		**E New unrelated bus. activity codes** (See instructions for Block E on page 7.)
		City or town, state, and ZIP code		
C Book value of all assets at end of year	**F** Group exemption number (see instructions for Block F on page 7) ▶			
	G Check organization type ▶ ☐ 501(c) corporation ☐ 501(c) trust ☐ 401(a) trust ☐ Other trust			

H Describe the organization's primary unrelated business activity. ▶

I During the tax year, was the corporation a subsidiary in an affiliated group or a parent-subsidiary controlled group? ▶ ☐ Yes ☐ No
If "Yes," enter the name and identifying number of the parent corporation. ▶

J The books are in care of ▶ _____ Telephone number ▶ ( )

Part I	**Unrelated Trade or Business Income**		**(A) Income**	**(B) Expenses**	**(C) Net**
1a	Gross receipts or sales _____				
b	Less returns and allowances _____ **c** Balance ▶	**1c**			
2	Cost of goods sold (Schedule A, line 7)	**2**			
3	Gross profit (subtract line 2 from line 1c)	**3**			
4a	Capital gain net income (attach Schedule D)	**4a**			
b	Net gain (loss) (Form 4797, Part II, line 17) (attach Form 4797)	**4b**			
c	Capital loss deduction for trusts	**4c**			
5	Income (loss) from partnerships and S corporations (attach statement)	**5**			
6	Rent income (Schedule C)	**6**			
7	Unrelated debt-financed income (Schedule E)	**7**			
8	Interest, annuities, royalties, and rents from controlled organizations (Schedule F)	**8**			
9	Investment income of a section 501(c)(7), (9), or (17) organization (Schedule G)	**9**			
10	Exploited exempt activity income (Schedule I)	**10**			
11	Advertising income (Schedule J)	**11**			
12	Other income (see page 9 of the instructions—attach schedule)	**12**			
13	**Total** (combine lines 3 through 12)	**13**			

Part II	**Deductions Not Taken Elsewhere** (See page 9 of the instructions for limitations on deductions.) (Except for contributions, deductions must be directly connected with the unrelated business income.)		
14	Compensation of officers, directors, and trustees (Schedule K)	**14**	
15	Salaries and wages	**15**	
16	Repairs and maintenance	**16**	
17	Bad debts	**17**	
18	Interest (attach schedule)	**18**	
19	Taxes and licenses	**19**	
20	Charitable contributions (see page 11 of the instructions for limitation rules)	**20**	
21	Depreciation (attach Form 4562) **21**		
22	Less depreciation claimed on Schedule A and elsewhere on return . **22a**	**22b**	
23	Depletion	**23**	
24	Contributions to deferred compensation plans	**24**	
25	Employee benefit programs	**25**	
26	Excess exempt expenses (Schedule I)	**26**	
27	Excess readership costs (Schedule J)	**27**	
28	Other deductions (attach schedule)	**28**	
29	**Total deductions** (add lines 14 through 28)	**29**	
30	Unrelated business taxable income before net operating loss deduction (subtract line 29 from line 13)	**30**	
31	Net operating loss deduction	**31**	
32	Unrelated business taxable income before specific deduction (subtract line 31 from line 30) . .	**32**	
33	Specific deduction (Generally $1,000, but see line 33 instructions for exceptions)	**33**	
34	**Unrelated business taxable income** (subtract line 33 from line 32). If line 33 is greater than line 32, enter the smaller of zero or line 32.	**34**	

For Privacy Act and Paperwork Reduction Act Notice, see instructions. Cat. No. 11291J Form **990-T** (2004)

Part III	Tax Computation

35 **Organizations Taxable as Corporations** (see instructions for tax computation on page 12). Controlled group members (sections 1561 and 1563)—check here ☐ . **See instructions** and:

a Enter your share of the $50,000, $25,000, and $9,925,000 taxable income brackets (in that order):

(1) |$ | (2) |$ | (3) |$ |

b Enter organization's share of: **(1)** additional 5% tax (not more than $11,750) |$ |

(2) additional 3% tax (not more than $100,000). . . . . |$ |

c Income tax on the amount on line 34 . . . . ► | 35c |

36 **Trusts Taxable at Trust Rates** (see instructions for tax computation on page 13). Income tax on the amount on line 34 from: ☐ Tax rate schedule or ☐ Schedule D (Form 1041). . . . ► | 36 |

37 **Proxy tax** (see page 13 of the instructions) . . . . ► | 37 |

38 Alternative minimum tax . . . . | 38 |

39 **Total** (add lines 37 and 38 to line 35c or 36, whichever applies) . . . . | 39 |

Part IV	Tax and Payments

40a Foreign tax credit (corporations attach Form 1118; trusts attach Form 1116) . | 40a |

b Other credits (see page 14 of the instructions) . . . . | 40b |

c General business credit—Check here and indicate which forms are attached: ☐ Form 3800 ☐ Form(s) (specify) ► .... | 40c |

d Credit for prior year minimum tax (attach Form 8801 or 8827). . . | 40d |

e **Total credits** (add lines 40a through 40d). . . . . | 40e |

41 Subtract line 40e from line 39 . . . . | 41 |

42 Other taxes. Check if from: ☐ Form 4255 ☐ Form 8611 ☐ Form 8697 ☐ Form 8866 ☐ Other (attach schedule) | 42 |

43 **Total tax** (add lines 41 and 42) . . . . | 43 |

44a Payments: A 2003 overpayment credited to 2004. . . . . | 44a |

b 2004 estimated tax payments. . . . . | 44b |

c Tax deposited with Form 8868 . . . . | 44c |

d Foreign organizations—Tax paid or withheld at source (see instructions) | 44d |

e Backup withholding (see instructions) . . . . | 44e |

f Other credits and payments: ☐ Form 2439 _____ ☐ Form 4136 _____ ☐ Other _____ Total ► | 44f |

45 **Total payments** (add lines 44a through 44f). . . . . | 45 |

46 Estimated tax penalty (see page 4 of the instructions). Check ► ☐ if Form 2220 is attached . | 46 |

47 **Tax due**—If line 45 is less than the total of lines 43 and 46, enter amount owed. . . . . ► | 47 |

48 **Overpayment**—If line 45 is larger than the total of lines 43 and 46, enter amount overpaid . ► | 48 |

49 Enter the amount of line 48 you want: **Credited to 2005 estimated tax** ► _____ Refunded ► | 49 |

Part V	Statements Regarding Certain Activities and Other Information (See instructions on page 15.)

		Yes	No
1	At any time during the 2004 calendar year, did the organization have an interest in or a signature or other authority over a financial account in a foreign country (such as a bank account, securities account, or other financial account)? If "Yes," the organization may have to file Form TD F 90-22.1. If "Yes," enter the name of the foreign country here ► --		
2	During the tax year, did the organization receive a distribution from, or was it the grantor of, or transferor to, a foreign trust? If "Yes," see page 15 of the instructions for other forms the organization may have to file.		
3	Enter the amount of tax-exempt interest received or accrued during the tax year ► $		

Schedule A—Cost of Goods Sold — Enter method of inventory valuation ►

1	Inventory at beginning of year.	1		6	Inventory at end of year . . .	6	
2	Purchases	2		7	**Cost of goods sold.** Subtract line 6 from line 5. (Enter here and on line 2, Part I.)	7	
3	Cost of labor	3					
4a	Additional section 263A costs (attach schedule)	4a		8	Do the rules of section 263A (with respect to property produced or acquired for resale) apply to the organization?	Yes	No
b	Other costs (attach schedule).	4b					
5	**Total**—Add lines 1 through 4b	5					

Sign Here ►

Under penalties of perjury, I declare that I have examined this return, including accompanying schedules and statements, and to the best of my knowledge and belief, it is true, correct, and complete. Declaration of preparer (other than taxpayer) is based on all information of which preparer has any knowledge.

Signature of officer	Date	Title	May the IRS discuss this return with the preparer shown below (see instructions)? ☐ Yes ☐ No

Paid Preparer's Use Only

Preparer's signature ►		Date	Check if self-employed ☐	Preparer's SSN or PTIN
Firm's name (or yours if self-employed), address, and ZIP code ►			EIN	
			Phone no. ( )	

Form **990-T** (2004)

Schedule C—Rent Income (From Real Property and Personal Property Leased With Real Property)
(See instructions on page 16.)

1 Description of property

(1)
(2)
(3)
(4)

2 Rent received or accrued		**3** Deductions directly connected with the income in columns 2(a) and 2(b) (attach schedule)
(a) From personal property (if the percentage of rent for personal property is more than 10% but not more than 50%)	**(b)** From real and personal property (if the percentage of rent for personal property exceeds 50% or if the rent is based on profit or income)	
(1)		
(2)		
(3)		
(4)		
Total	Total	

Total income (Add totals of columns 2(a) and 2(b). Enter here and on line 6, column (A), Part I, page 1.) . . ▶

Total deductions. Enter here and on line 6, column (B), Part I, page 1. . ▶

Schedule E—Unrelated Debt-Financed Income (See instructions on page 17.)

1 Description of debt-financed property	**2** Gross income from or allocable to debt-financed property	**3** Deductions directly connected with or allocable to debt-financed property	
		(a) Straight line depreciation (attach schedule)	**(b)** Other deductions (attach schedule)
(1)			
(2)			
(3)			
(4)			

4 Amount of average acquisition debt on or allocable to debt-financed property (attach schedule)	**5** Average adjusted basis of or allocable to debt-financed property (attach schedule)	**6** Column 4 divided by column 5	**7** Gross income reportable (column 2 × column 6)	**8** Allocable deductions (column 6 × total of columns 3(a) and 3(b))
(1)		%		
(2)		%		
(3)		%		
(4)		%		
			Enter here and on line 7, column (A), Part I, page 1.	Enter here and on line 7, column (B), Part I, page 1.

Totals. . . . . ▶

Total dividends-received deductions included in column 8 . . . . ▶

Schedule F—Interest, Annuities, Royalties, and Rents From Controlled Organizations (See instructions on page 18.)

		Exempt Controlled Organizations			
1 Name of Controlled Organization	**2** Employer Identification Number	**3** Net unrelated income (loss) (see instructions)	**4** Total of specified payments made	**5** Part of column (4) that is included in the controlling organization's gross income	**6** Deductions directly connected with income in column (5)
(1)					
(2)					
(3)					
(4)					

Nonexempt Controlled Organizations

7 Taxable Income	**8** Net unrelated income (loss) (see instructions)	**9** Total of specified payments made	**10** Part of column (9) that is included in the controlling organization's gross income	**11** Deductions directly connected with income in column (10)
(1)				
(2)				
(3)				
(4)				
			Add columns 5 and 10. Enter here and on line 8, Column (A), Part 1, page 1.	Add columns 6 and 11. Enter here and on line 8, Column (B), Part 1, page 1.

Totals . . . . ▶

Form **990-T** (2004)

Form 990-T (2004)   Page **4**

Schedule G—Investment Income of a Section 501(c)(7), (9), or (17) Organization
(See instructions on page 18.)

1 Description of income	**2** Amount of income	**3** Deductions directly connected (attach schedule)	**4** Set-asides (attach schedule)	**5** Total deductions and set-asides (col. 3 plus col. 4)
(1)				
(2)				
(3)				
(4)				
Totals . . . . ▶	Enter here and on line 9, column (A), Part I, page 1.			Enter here and on line 9, column (B), Part I, page 1.

Schedule I—Exploited Exempt Activity Income, Other Than Advertising Income
(See instructions on page 18.)

1 Description of exploited activity	**2** Gross unrelated business income from trade or business	**3** Expenses directly connected with production of unrelated business income	**4** Net income (loss) from unrelated trade or business (column 2 minus column 3). If a gain, compute cols. 5 through 7.	**5** Gross income from activity that is not unrelated business income	**6** Expenses attributable to column 5	**7** Excess exempt expenses (column 6 minus column 5, but not more than column 4).
(1)						
(2)						
(3)						
(4)						
Totals. . . . . ▶	Enter here and on line 10, col. (A), Part I, page 1.	Enter here and on line 10, col. (B), Part I, page 1.				Enter here and on line 26, Part II, page 1.

Schedule J—Advertising Income (See instructions on page 19.)

Part I   Income From Periodicals Reported on a Consolidated Basis

1 Name of periodical	**2** Gross advertising income	**3** Direct advertising costs	**4** Advertising gain or (loss) (col. 2 minus col. 3). If a gain, compute cols. 5 through 7.	**5** Circulation income	**6** Readership costs	**7** Excess readership costs (column 6 minus column 5, but not more than column 4).
(1)						
(2)						
(3)						
(4)						
Totals (carry to Part II, line (5)) . . . . ▶						

Part II   Income From Periodicals Reported on a Separate Basis (For each periodical listed in Part II, fill in columns 2 through 7 on a line-by-line basis.)

(1)						
(2)						
(3)						
(4)						
(5) **Totals from Part I**						
Totals, Part II (lines 1-5) . . . ▶	Enter here and on line 11, col. (A), Part I, page 1.	Enter here and on line 11, col. (B), Part I, page 1.				Enter here and on line 27, Part II, page 1.

Schedule K—Compensation of Officers, Directors, and Trustees (See instructions on page 19.)

1 Name	**2** Title	**3** Percent of time devoted to business	**4** Compensation attributable to unrelated business
		%	
		%	
		%	
		%	
Total—Enter here and on line 14, Part II, page 1 . . . . ▶			

Form **990-T** (2004)

APPENDIX F

Codes for Unrelated Business Activity

(If engaged in more than one unrelated business activity, select up to two codes for the principal activities. List first the largest in terms of gross unrelated income, then the next largest. Be sure to classify your unrelated activities, rather than your related activities. For example, code income from advertising in publications as 541800, Advertising and related services, rather than selecting a code describing a printing or publishing activity. Also, if possible, select a code that more specifically describes your unrelated activity, rather than a code for a more general activity.)

AGRICULTURE, FORESTRY, HUNTING, AND FISHING
Code
110000 Agriculture, forestry, hunting, and fishing
111000 Crop production

MINING
Code
211110 Oil and gas extraction
212000 Mining (except oil and gas)

UTILITIES
Code
221000 Utilities

CONSTRUCTION
Code
230000 Construction
236000 Construction of buildings

MANUFACTURING
Code
310000 Manufacturing
323100 Printing and related support activities
339110 Medical equipment and supplies manufacturing

WHOLESALE TRADE
Code
423000 Merchant wholesalers, durable goods
424000 Merchant wholesalers, nondurable goods

RETAIL TRADE
Code
441100 Automobile dealers
442000 Furniture and home furnishings stores
443120 Computer and software stores
444100 Building materials and supplies dealers
445100 Grocery stores
445200 Specialty food stores
446110 Pharmacies and drug stores
446199 All other health and personal care stores
448000 Clothing and clothing accessories stores
451110 Sporting goods stores
451211 Book stores
452000 General merchandise stores
453000 Miscellaneous store retailers
453220 Gift, novelty, and souvenir stores
453310 Used merchandise stores
454110 Electronic shopping and mail-order houses

TRANSPORTATION AND WAREHOUSING
Code
480000 Transportation
485000 Transit and ground passenger transportation
493000 Warehousing and storage

INFORMATION
Code
511110 Newspaper publishers (except Internet)
511120 Periodical publishers (except Internet)
511130 Book publishers (except Internet)
511140 Directory and mailing list publishers (except Internet)
511190 Other publishers (except Internet)
512000 Motion picture and sound recording industries
515100 Radio and television broadcasting (except Internet)
516110 Internet publishing and broadcasting
517000 Telecommunications (including paging, cellular, satellite, cable, and other telecommunications)
518111 Internet service providers
518112 Web search portals

518210 Data processing, hosting, and related services
519100 Other information services

FINANCE AND INSURANCE
Code
522100 Depository credit intermediation (including commercial banking, savings institutions, and credit unions)
522200 Nondepository credit intermediation (including credit card issuing and sales financing)
523000 Securities, commodity contracts, and other financial investments and related activities
524113 Direct life insurance carriers
524114 Direct health and medical insurance carriers
524126 Direct property and casualty insurance carriers
524292 Third-party administration of insurance and pension funds
524298 All other insurance-related activities
525100 Insurance and employee benefit funds
525920 Trusts, estates, and agency accounts
525990 Other financial vehicles

REAL ESTATE AND RENTAL AND LEASING
Code
531110 Lessors of residential buildings and dwellings
531120 Lessors of nonresidential buildings (except miniwarehouses)
531190 Lessors of other real estate property
531310 Real estate property managers
531390 Other activities related to real estate
532000 Rental and leasing services
532420 Office machinery and equipment rental and leasing
533110 Lessors of nonfinancial intangible assets (except copyrighted works)

PROFESSIONAL, SCIENTIFIC, AND TECHNICAL SERVICES
Code
541100 Legal services
541200 Accounting, tax preparation, bookkeeping, and payroll services
541300 Architectural, engineering, and related services
541380 Testing laboratories
541511 Custom computer programming services
541519 Other computer-related services
541610 Management consulting services
541700 Scientific research and development services
541800 Advertising and related services
541860 Direct mail advertising
541900 Other professional, scientific, and technical services

MANAGEMENT OF COMPANIES AND ENTERPRISES
Code
551111 Offices of bank holding companies
551112 Offices of other holding companies

ADMINISTRATIVE AND SUPPORT AND WASTE MANAGEMENT AND REMEDIATION SERVICES
Administrative and Support Services
Code
561000 Administrative and support services
561300 Employment services
561439 Other business service centers (including copy shops)
561499 All other business support services
561500 Travel arrangement and reservation services
561520 Tour operators
561700 Services to buildings and dwellings
Waste Management and Remediation Services
Code
562000 Waste management and remediation services (sanitary services)

EDUCATIONAL SERVICES
Code
611600 Other schools and instruction (other than elementary and secondary schools or colleges and universities, which should select a code to describe their unrelated activities)
611710 Educational support services

HEALTHCARE AND SOCIAL ASSISTANCE
Code
621110 Offices of physicians
621300 Offices of other health practitioners
621400 Outpatient care centers
621500 Medical and diagnostic laboratories
621610 Home health care services
621910 Ambulance services
621990 All other ambulatory health care services
623000 Nursing and residential care facilities
623990 Other residential care facilities
624100 Individual and family services
624200 Community food and housing, and emergency and other relief services
624310 Vocational rehabilitation services
624410 Child day care services

ARTS, ENTERTAINMENT, AND RECREATION
Code
711110 Theater companies and dinner theaters
711120 Dance companies
711130 Musical groups and artists
711190 Other performing art companies
711210 Spectator sports (including sports clubs and racetracks)
711300 Promoters of performing arts, sports, and similar events
713110 Amusement and theme parks
713200 Gambling industries
713910 Golf courses and country clubs
713940 Fitness and recreational sports centers
713990 All other amusement and recreation industries (including skiing facilities, marinas, and bowling centers)

ACCOMMODATION AND FOOD SERVICES
Code
721000 Accomodation
721110 Hotels (except casino hotels) and motels
721210 RV (recreational vehicle) parks and recreational camps
721310 Rooming and boarding houses
722100 Full-service restaurants
722210 Limited-service eating places
722320 Caterers
722410 Drinking places (alcoholic beverages)

OTHER SERVICES
Code
811000 Repair and maintenance
812300 Drycleaning and laundry services
812900 Other personal services
812930 Parking lots and garages

OTHER
Code
900000 Unrelated debt-financed activities other than rental of real estate
900001 Investment activities of section 501(c)(7),(9), or (17) organizations
900002 Rental of personal property
900003 Passive income activities with controlled organizations
900004 Exploited exempt activities

355

Table of Cases

Table of IRS Revenue Rulings and Revenue Procedures

Revenue Rulings	Book Sections	Revenue Rulings	Book Sections	Revenue Rulings	Book Sections
54-73	3.13	67-297	3.3	71-581	4.3
54-134	4.11	67-327	9.1(c)	72-16	9.2(e)
55-449	9.13	68-46	9.13	72-124	2.2(c)
55-676	4.1	68-104	9.10	72-431	4.10, 9.6(a),
55-749	4.10	68-123	9.14		9.13
56-152	4.2	68-167	7.6	72-521	3.4
56-511	2.2(d)	68-225	9.12	73-45	2.2(c)
57-313	9.13	68-267	9.13	73-104	9.3(b)
57-420	10.1	68-373	3.13	73-105	9.3(b)
57-466	9.5, 9.13	68-374	9.2(b)	73-127	2.7(b)
58-194	4.1, 9.1(a)	68-375	9.2(b)	73-128	2.7(b)
58-224	4.5	68-376	4.1, 9.2(a)	73-193	3.7
58-482	3.8(a), 9.13	68-505	2.5(a), 4.4, 9.13	73-386	2.7(b)
58-501	6.1(d)	68-536	2.4, 3.19	73-424	2.5(a), 6.5(a)
58-502	9.12	68-550	2.7(d)	73-587	9.13
58-547	5.3(b)	68-581	9.1	74-27	3.4
59-91	2.2(e)	69-51	9.5, 9.13	74-38	6.5(a)
59-330	9.5, 9.13	69-69	3.8(a), 4.1, 9.13	74-81	9.4(a)
60-86	9.5, 9.13	69-162	3.7	74-197	5.4(e)(i)
60-206	3.8(a)	69-178	3.8(a)	74-361	4.2, 9.12
60-228	9.4(b), 9.13	69-179	3.7	74-399	7.6, 9.3(a)
61-170	9.4(d)	69-188	3.3	74-614	2.2(c)
62-191	9.5, 9.13	69-220	1.6, 6.1	75-200	6.5(a)
64-182	9.12	69-232	6.1, 6.1(d)	75-201	6.5(a), 9.6(b)
65-64	6.1(d)	69-267	9.2(a)	75-472	9.2(e), 9.12
65-164	9.4(d)	69-268	4.1, 9.2(a),	75-516	4.5
65-299	7.4		9.3(a)	75-517	4.5
66-47	3.11	69-269	9.2(a)	75-518	4.5
66-47	9.13	69-430	3.7	75-519	4.5
66-151	9.4(a), 9.4(b),	69-441	7.4	75-520	4.5
	9.4(d), 9.13	69-463	9.2(b)	76-33	9.1(d), 9.2(e)
66-221	§ 1.6	69-464	5.3(b)	76-81	9.4(b)
66-323	2.2(c), 9.13	69-574	2.2(d)	76-93	6.5(a)
66-338	9.4(a)	69-575	8.4	76-94	2.7(b)
67-109	2.7(a)	69-633	4.6, 9.13	76-95	5.4(c)(iv)
67-176	9.4(b)	70-81	5.3(b)	76-296	3.13, 9.13
67-216	4.4	70-132	5.1	76-297	3.7
67-218	3.8(a)	70-534	9.1(c)	76-323	9.14
67-219	4.5, 9.12	71-155	9.4(b)	76-337	6.1(a)
67-296	9.4(d)	71-311	5.4(e)(i)	76-341	9.13
67-296	9.12	71-529	2.2(c), 7.3	76-354	5.4(c)(iv)

TABLE OF IRS REVENUE RULINGS AND REVENUE PROCEDURES

Revenue Rulings	Book Sections
76-402	2.7(d)
77-47	5.3(a)
77-71	5.3(b)
77-72	5.4(h)
77-290	9.14
77-365	2.7(d)
77-436	9.14
78-43	9.1(c)
78-51	9.4(a)
78-52	9.4(a)
78-88	2.2(d), 3.4, 5.4(g)
78-98	2.7(d)
78-144	4.2
78-145	2.2(c), 2.3, 9.13
78-240	4.5
78-385	9.13
78-428	2.2(c)
78-435	9.2(a)
79-17	2.2(c)

Revenue Rulings	Book Sections
79-18	2.2(c)
79-19	2.2(c), 9.2(e)
79-31	2.3
79-122	5.4(e)(i)
79-222	6.4
79-349	3.3, 5.4(e)(i)
79-360	9.2(d)
79-361	7.1(f)(ii), 9.2(e), 9.13
79-370	6.5(a)
80-287	10.1
80-294	9.1(b), 9.12
80-295	9.1(b)
80-296	9.1(b)
80-297	2.7(d)
80-298	2.7(d)
81-19	4.1
81-29	2.2(c), 9.2(a)
81-61	9.12
81-62	9.13

Revenue Rulings	Book Sections
81-69	6.1(b)
81-75	9.4(a)
81-101	6.5(b)(i)
81-127	9.12
81-138	5.3(b)
81-178	3.7
82-138	9.4(d)
82-139	9.4(a)
84-55	9.1(c)
85-109	4.1, 9.2(c)
85-110	9.2(c)
85-123	4.5
86-98	7.1(f)(ii)
95-8	5.4(h)
98-15	8.11, 8.15(b)
2002-55	8.4
2003-38	10.1
2003-64	
2004-51	8.15(b)
2004-112	4.5, 10.6

Revenue Procedures	Book Sections
85-58	11.5(b)
87-51	7.3
92-58	4.9
92-102	4.9
93-49	4.9
94-72	4.9
95-21	4.8

Revenue Procedures	Book Sections
95-53	4.9
96-59	4.9
97-12	4.8
97-57	4.8, 4.9
98-61	4.8, 4.9
99-42	4.8, 4.9
2001-13	4.8, 4.9

Revenue Procedures	Book Sections
2001-59	4.8, 4.9
2002-70	4.8, 4.9
2003-85	4.8, 4.9
2004-34	11.4(c)
2004-71	4.8, 4.9

Table of IRS Private Determinations Cited in Text

Chief Counsel Advice Memorandum	Book Sections
200431023	7.4

Exemption Denial and Revocation Letters	Book Sections
20044044E	7.4
20044045E	7.1(f)(ii), 7.4, 10.1

General Counsel Memoranda	Book Sections
33912	8.4
35719	8.4
35811	9.1(a)
37257	2.2(c)
38104	6.5(b)(ii)
38168	6.5(b)(i)
38205	6.5(b)(i)
38459	2.2(c)
38878	8.8(a)
38881	7.4
38949	9.3(b)
39061	9.12
39108	1.6
39326	8.4
39598	8.4
39620	5.4(a)
39703	7.3
39715	9.12
39717	9.10
39727	9.6(a)
39744	9.10
39806	9.10
39828	7.3
39865	2.5(b)
39891	2.5(b)

Private Letter Rulings	Book Sections
7741004	3.7
7806039	4.2
7816061	9.12
7823048	1.6
7823062	2.7(e)
7826003	2.7(d)
7833055	5.3(b)
7839042	9.13
7840014	9.4(b)
7840072	2.7(d)
7845029	9.1(b)
7847001	9.4(b)
7851003	9.1(b)
7902006	9.4(a)
7905129	2.5(a)
7908009	2.7(d)
7919053	9.1(b)
7922001	9.1(b), 9.12
7924009	3.13
7926003	3.7
7930043	9.1(b)
7934008	6.4
7936006	3.13
7937002	9.4(b)
7948113	6.5(a), 9.1(b)
8004011	9.2(a)
8006005	3.7
8020010	2.7(d)
8024001	2.7(d)
8025222	9.1(a)
8107006	9.12
8112013	9.12
8116095	4.3
8120006	9.12
8122007	4.3
8127019	9.6(a)
8203134	2.5(b), 9.6(a)
8216009	9.6(a)
8244114	3.1

Private Letter Rulings	Book Sections
8303001	9.13
8303078	9.1(b)
8326008	9.3(b)
8337092	6.1(d)
8349051	9.12
8349072	9.12
8351160	9.12
8417003	9.12
8422168	9.12
8427105	9.2(a)
8429010	9.5
8432004	9.3(a)
8433010	9.13
8442092	9.12
8452074	9.13
8452099	9.2(f)
8503103	9.4(d)
8505044	8.5
8505047	9.12
8511082	9.13
8512084	9.12
8518090	9.12
8523072	9.12
8530043	9.13
8541108	8.11
8606056	8.4
8606074	9.12
8623081	9.12
8624127	9.12
8626080	9.2(e), 9.12
8628049	9.12
8633034	9.12
8640007	9.12
8643049	9.12
8643091	9.12
8708031	3.7
8709051	8.5
8709072	9.12
8725056	9.6(a)

TABLE OF IRS PRIVATE DETERMINATIONS CITED IN TEXT

Private Letter Rulings	Book Sections	Private Letter Rulings	Book Sections	Private Letter Rulings	Book Sections
8730060	9.12	9441001	9.4(b)	199943053	9.2(f)
8736046	9.2(f)	9442013	4.11	199945062	9.12
8747066	9.6(a)	9450028	3.7	199946036	9.2(f)
8749085	9.2(f), 9.12	9505020	2.2(e)	199946037	9.2(f)
8802079	9.12	9535023	2.7(b), 4.1, 9.12	199949045	9.12
8814004	9.13	9535050	9.12	199952086	6.3(a)
8819034	3.15	9539015	9.12	200011063	6.2(b)
8820061	9.12	9544029	4.2	200022056	9.8
8822065	9.2(f)	9603019	5.3(c)	200030027	9.12
8823109	9.6(a)	9615045	3.8(c)	200030033	9.12
8824018	9.12	9619069	2.2(e), 3.10(a)	200033049	2.3
8828011	9.4(b)	9629030	2.2(e)	200037050	9.8
8836038	7.3	9633044	9.12	200044039	7.3
8938001	8.11	9641011	9.8	200044040	8.12(a)
8950072	2.2(e)	9645007	7.3	200051046	6.1(d)
9023081	9.4(a)	9645017	8.7	200101034	9.8
9029047	9.4(b)	9651046	9.12	200101036	9.2(d)
9036025	9.1	9651047	9.8	200102052	8.12(a)
9042038	3.8(d)	9715031	8.4	200108045	9.8
9043001	9.13	9722006	8.4	200118054	8.12(a), 8.15
9108021	3.3	9723046	10.1, 10.2(b)	200119061	2.2(e), 2.3
9128003	9.13	9732032	9.1, 9.2(d)	200124022	8.12(b)(ii)
9137002	9.12	9739043	9.2(c)	200126033	9.12
9145002	9.13	9740032	3.8(a)	200128059	2.5(c), 9.6(b)
9237090	9.12	9746001	9.6(a)	200131034	2.2(d), 9.10
9241055	9.2(e), 9.12	9810038	9.12	200132040	8.4
9242035	9.12	9814051	9.12	200134025	5.4(f), 8.12(b)(i), 8.12(b)(ii)
9245031	8.4, 8.5	9821049	9.12		
9246004	7.3	9821063	9.12	200147058	6.4, 8.17
9246032	3.8(a)	9822039	9.2(f)	200150032	9.12
9247038	3.10(a)	9824048	9.12	200150038	9.12
9249001	9.12	9825030	9.12	200151045	8.11
9252028	6.3(a)	9837031	9.2(a)	200151047	9.12
9252037	9.12	9839039	6.4, 9.8	200151060	10.2(b)
9302023	4.2	9839040	9.2(f)	200151061	2.7
9305026	8.5	9841049	4.1	200201024	8.12(b)(i)
9308047	8.6	9849027	9.8	200202077	8.12(b)(ii)
9316032	2.2(e), 2.2(g)	9851054	9.2(c)	200204051	9.12
9320042	2.7(c)	9853026	9.12	200211051	9.2(a)
9325062	9.12	199905027	9.12	200213027	9.12
9329041	9.2(d)	199905031	9.12	200220028	9.12
9335061	9.2(e), 9.12	199909056	9.12	200222030	9.3(a)
9401031	9.12	199910053	9.12	200222031	9.2(f)
9403022	9.12	199910060	9.8	200223068	6.2(b)
9404029	9.2(a)	199910061	9.12	200225044	9.12
9408002	9.4(a)	199920041	9.12	200227007	8.5
9425030	2.5(a)	199929049	9.12	200230005	4.3
9436002	9.13			200233032	5.4(g)
9438029	8.7				

TABLE OF IRS PRIVATE DETERMINATIONS CITED IN TEXT

Private Letter Rulings	Book Sections	Technical Advice Memoranda	Sections	Technical Advice Memoranda	Sections
200241050	9.12	7851004	9.1(b)	9645004	2.3, 2.7(d), 4.1
200246032	2.2(e)	8040014	4.2		
200249014	8.12(b)(ii), 9.1	8041007	4.2, 4.3	9702004	2.3, 9.1(c)
200301048	9.12	8128004	4.10		
200303062	10.1, 10.3(a), 10.4(b), 10.5, 10.12, 10.13	8211002	4.2	9711002	9.8
		8226019	9.13	9711003	1.6
		8418003	9.4(d)	9712001	2.5(d)
		8433010	4.2	9719002	2.4
		8437014	9.13	9720002	9.3(c)
200304036	8.12(b)(ii), 9.1	8443009	9.12	9742001	4.8
200304041	8.12(a)	8446004	9.13	9751001	4.8
200307094	10.1	8450006	9.12	9811001	9.8
200311034	8.12(a)	8452011	9.2(f)	9821067	9.13
200313024	9.1	8452012	9.2(f)	9822004	9.8
200314030	6.1(d)	8501002	9.12	9822006	9.13
200314031	3.8(c), 9.8	8505002	9.2(d), 9.12	9847002	6.4, 9.2(a), 9.8
200328042	2.2(g)				
200333031	8.12(a), 8.17	8524006	9.4(a)	9848002	9.13
200345041	9.12	8602001	4.7	199922055	9.12
200349008	9.12	8605002	9.3(a), 9.3(b)	200021056	1.6, 1.11, 2.2(b), 2.3, 2.6, 2.7(a), 7.1(b), 7.6, 9.3(a)
200352017	9.12	9147007	2.5(d), 9.1(b)		
200404057	3.8(c)				
200432026	5.3(b)	9345004	4.8		
200439043	9.11	9405004	9.2(a)		
200450037	7.4	9416002	4.8		
200501017	3.4	9440001	9.4(a)		
200501020	7.1(f)(ii)	9502009	4.10		
200504035	10.1	9509002	3.7	200047049	2.2(e), 2.2(g), 2.4, 9.13
200506025	10.1	9540002	9.1(c)		
200510029	2.2(e)	9550001	9.4(a), 9.8, 9.13		
200510030	8.12(b)(ii)			200102051	6.5
200512023	7.1(f)(ii)	9550003	9.3(c)	200151045	8.11
200512025	2.3, 2.7(c), 7.1(f)(ii)	9608003	9.8	200203069	10.1
200512027	7.1(f)(ii)	9612003	2.2(d)	200437040	8.5
200528029	8.15	9635001	4.10	200446033	10.2(b)

Table of Related IRS Private Determinations

The following citations, to private pronouncements from the Internal Revenue Service issued in the context of specific cases, are coordinated to the appropriate footnotes (FN) in the specified chapters. These references are to IRS private letter rulings, technical advice memoranda, and general counsel memoranda, other than those cited in footnotes (see separate table), that are directly pertinent to the material discussed in the text. Five-number items are general counsel memoranda.

Although these pronouncements are not to be cited as precedent (IRC § 6110(j)(3)), they are useful in illuminating the position of the IRS on the subjects involved.

FN	Private Determination	FN	Private Determination	FN	Private Determination
Chapter 1		95	9438040, 9505020, 9509041, 9510039, 200148085	154	8922064, 9407005, 9413020
145	9338043			155	9417003
Chapter 2		104	36827	158	9137002, 9417003, 9509002, 9721001
8	9120029	105	9720035		
13	200027056	131	8651086, 8708052, 8841041	168	8641001
29	8722082, 9735047, 32896, 36827			172	9302023
30	9217001	132	8829003, 8932004, 9309002	177	9539005
34	9325061			178	8819005, 9723046
48	9401031	134	8717002, 8717063, 8733037, 8734005, 8901064, 8934050, 8936013, 9003059, 9017058, 9018049, 9240937, 9337027, 9340061, 9340062, 9349022	184	9535023
53	9242035			189	9750056
54	8822057			190	9641011, 9715041, 9728034
55	8840020, 8841041				
56	8806056, 9318047			191	8732029, 9041045, 9350045
63	9042038			221	9014069
88	9616039, 9619068, 9630031, 9631025, 9631029, 9652028, 9704010, 9745025, 200246032			**Chapter 3**	
				3	9012058
				7	8708031, 9442035
		135	9425031	13	9042038

TABLE OF RELATED IRS PRIVATE DETERMINATIONS

FN	Private Determination	FN	Private Determination	FN	Private Determination
16	8836037	105	9703025,	164	9108034,
24	9826046		9705001,		9108043,
29	199914042,		9709029,		9127045,
	199928042		9714016,		9128030,
41	9030048		9723001,		9132040,
75	9231045		9724006,		9132061,
81	9151001,		9810030,		9144032–
	9306030,		9816027,		9144035,
	9309002, 39827		200046039,		9150047,
93	8839016		200149035,		9204048,
96	9346014		200149037,		9247038,
98	8827017		200149043,		9252028,
102	9316045,		200225046,		9547040,
	9319042,		39615		9551021
	9419033,	108	9139029,	166	9619068
	9503024,		9212030,	170	9108034,
	9552019		9231045,		9108043,
105	8222066,		9234043,		9128030,
	8645050,		9551019,		9132040,
	8717066,		35957, 39568		9132061,
	8717078,	109	9450045,		9144032,
	8721102,		200041031,		9144035,
	8728060,		200147058,		9150047,
	8808002,		200148057,		9252028
	8808003,		200148074		(modified by
	8810097,	111	8950072,		9428037),
	8824054,		9139029,		9308040,
	8828011,		9141051,		9316032,
	8845073,		9146047,		9319044,
	8846005,		9702003		9401029,
	8922084,	112	8445005,		9407005,
	8941011,		8720005,		9411018,
	8941062,		8802009,		9411019,
	8948023,		8925029, 39825		9412039,
	9015038,	119	9450045		9414002,
	9023091,	130	8713072,		9432019,
	9024026,		8822096,		9629032,
	9043039,		8932042		9651014,
	9108021,	138	9245036,		9803024,
	9316052,		9246032,		9826046,
	9404003,		9246033,		9844004,
	9404004,		9301024,		9853034,
	9417036,		9315021,		199952071,
	9417042,		9703025,		200041038,
	9417043,		9850020		200219037,
	9419033,	139	8822057,		200237027
	9436001,		9551019	175	200151046,
	9440001,	140	200032050		200151062
	9441001,	153	9136037	189	8201024
	9450028,			205	199928042,
					199952086

FN	Private Determination	FN	Private Determination	FN	Private Determination
207	8641061, 8831007, 8932004, 8942070, 9033056, 9302023, 9544029, 9605001, 9704012	26	8748064, 8748065, 9024085, 9315021	138	9002030
				139	200224014, 200351032
		30	9651001	144	8721104, 8721107, 9042038
		34	9246032, 9246033		
				147	9619077
		46	8950073, 9047040	148	9637053, 9642051
Chapter 4		48	200125096	150	9717004
6	8736046, 92308113, 9241055	49	9241052	**Chapter 6**	
		60	8044023, 8104098, 8107114, 8110164, 8338138, 8738006, 8807082, 9031052, 9407023, 9703026, 200041038, 200233032	19	8905002, 8943009, 9247039, 9310034, 9344028, 9517035, 9628022, 9721034, 9841003, 199932050, 200003036, 39773
29	39786				
31	8832043, 39752				
53	8915005, 9217001				
59	8728080				
75	39734				
88	9302035, 9303030				
93	9232003	79	9533014	41	8728008, 8728009, 8925091, 9016039,
94	8920084	83	9010025, 9431001, 9533014		
102	9726030				
117	9652004				
119	8721005, 9029047, 9316045, 9321005, 9724006, 39638	96	8822057	41	9310034, 9351042, 9410048, 9413042, 9818001
		104	8945038		
		116	9012001		
125	9847001	118	9042043, 9108021, 9110012, 9527033, 9743054, 200150040, 200233023, 39826	66	9145003, 9328003
153	200029055			75	9141003, 9141004, 9145031, 9145032, 9147059, 9216033, 9242014, 9247039
Chapter 5					
9	8708031, 8717066, 20000348	121	8818008, 8923077, 9031052, 9047069, 9218006, 9218007		
18	8738006, 9144044, 199952089				
22	8522040, 8651091, 8906003, 8935058, 9147058, 9204048, 9726005	123	9450045, 200137061	114	200420029, 200444042, 200448049– 200448051, 200450036
		125	9508031	139	9319044, 9750056
		135	9128020		

FN	Private Determination	FN	Private Determination	FN	Private Determination
144	9847002	58	9438029, 9506046, 9535022, 9547039, 9601047, 9642054, 9705028	70	9110042, 9226055
145	9137002, 9147054, 9205037, 39860			77	9750056
				84	200041030
146	8947002, 9044071, 9234002, 9304001, 9345004, 9724006	84	200325003, 200325004	85	8809092, 8817017
		85	200102053	88	199917084
149	9023003, 199914035	86	200117043	90	8626102, 8640052–8640054, 8640056, 8640057, 8645064, 8833002
150	9302035	87	200304042		
152	8932004	90	200333032, 200333033		
157	8726069, 9302023	151	200333032, 200333033	94	8949093
168	9023001, 9023002, 9204007, 9402005			98	8814001, 9138003
		Chapter 9		100	8641060
		17	9137002, 39860	114	9645027
176	9247001	20	8025222	115	8815002
183	8834006, 8835001, 9023001, 9023002, 9217002, 9402005, 9419003, 9734002	21	8641090	123	9147054, 9527001, 9550001
		26	9231001		
		31	9521004	129	8707003, 8842002, 9037063, 9548001, 39723
		32	8846002		
		37	8650083		
		38	9014069	130	9220054
184	8403013	40	39843	131	9220054, 9306030, 9318005, 9535004 (withdrawn by 9542046), 9612003, 39827
186	9248001	41	39762		
		44	8735004, 8815031, 8817066, 9730941, 9739042		
Chapter 7					
94	9243008, 9316052				
		45	8736046	133	8841003
Chapter 8		51	8736046, 8817017, 9445024	145	8734004, 39735
50	199941048			147	9550001
58	8729005, 8832084, 8833002, 8903083, 8922047, 9010073, 9045003, 9108016, 9308047, 9324026, 9404004,	61	8721103, 8809092, 8921091, 8941082, 9023041	151	9029047
				163	9428035
				164	8852002
		67	9736047	167	9325003
		69	9750056, 9803001	168	9128002
				188	8232011
				202	9623035
				205	8725058

TABLE OF RELATED IRS PRIVATE DETERMINATIONS

FN	Private Determination	FN	Private Determination	FN	Private Determination
206	9736046	267	200108046, 200108047, 200108049	388	9320050, 9323035, 39864
208	9315001, 9321005			389	200147059, 200149044, 200216036, 200222032, 200230004
217	9250001	322	9107030, 9110012, 9137002		
253	9822004				
256	9608003, 9711002, 9718029	326	9428035	395	200150033, 200150035
		332	8432003		
		333	8743081, 8743086, 8743087, 9347036	405	9321072, 9321087, 9323035, 9812031, 9814048, 200234071, 200242041, 200243056
258	9752023, 200108048				
262	200031057, 200033050, 200108048	334	9349024		
		338	9110042, 9329041		
263	9814039, 9819049, 9853026, 199924065, 199943049, 199949038, 200032046, 200036049, 200108048, 200233025, 200238051	339	8643091		
		345	9149002	413	9137049
		348	8643049, 9141053, 9150052, 9152039	419	9128003
				434	9853001
		357	9107030	**Chapter 11**	
		388	9138003, 9145002, 9147005,	18	9147008, 9149006, 39863
264	200108048			20	9324002

Table of Cases Discussed
in *Bruce R. Hopkins' Nonprofit Counsel*

The following cases, referenced in the text, are discussed in greater detail in one or more issues of the author's monthly newsletter, as indicated.

Case	Book Sections	Newsletter Issue
Airlie Found., Inc. v. *United States*	7.1(f)(i)	July 1993, Nov. 2003
Ala. Cent. Credit Union v. *United States*	5.4(e)(i)	June 1987
Alumni Ass'n of Univ. of Or., Inc. v. *Comm'r*	3.7, 9.6(a)	Dec. 1999
Am. Acad. of Family Physicians v. *United States*	2.2(a), 2.2(d), 2.4	June 1995, Oct. 1996
Am. Ass'n of Christian Schs. Voluntary Employees Beneficiary Ass'n Welfare Plan Trust v. *United States*	7.1(f)(ii)	Sept. 1987
Am. Campaign Acad. v. *Comm'r*	8.14	July 1989, June 2001, Feb. 2005
Am. Coll. of Physicians v. *United States*	4.1, 6.5(a)	Oct. 1984, June 1986
Am. Hosp. Ass'n v. *United States*	6.5(b)(i)	May 1987
Am. Med. Ass'n v. *United States*	1.6, 6.5(b)(i)	Oct. 1987, Nov. 1987, Jan. 1990
Am. Postal Workers Union v. *United States*	9.5	Feb. 1990, Apr. 1991
At Cost Servs., Inc. v. *Comm'r*	7.1(f)(i)	Jan. 2001
Atlanta Athletic Club v. *Comm'r*	6.1(b), 6.1(d)	Mar. 1993
The Brook, Inc. v. *Comm'r*	6.1(b)	Oct. 1986
Church by Mail, Inc. v. *Comm'r*	8.14	Oct. 1984
Cleveland Athletic Club, Inc. v. *United States*	6.1(b)	Feb. 1986
Common Cause v. *Comm'r*	3.7	Aug. 1999
CORE Special Purpose Fund v. *Comm'r*	6.5(b)(i), 11.2	May 1985
Disabled Am. Veterans v. *Comm'r*	3.1, 3.7, 4.10	Apr. 1990
Easter House v. *United States*	7.1(e)	Aug. 1987
Ecclesiastical Order of the Ism of Am v. *Comm'r*	7.1(e), 9.6(c)	Dec. 1985
est of Haw. v. *Comm'r*	8.14	June 2001
Executive Network Club, Inc. v. *Comm'r*	4.2	Mar. 1995
Fla. Hosp. Trust Fund v. *Comm'r*	7.3	Sept. 1994, Mar. 1996
Fraternal Order of Police, Ill. State Troopers Lodge No. 41 v. *Comm'r*	3.7, 6.5(a)	Nov. 1986
Harlan E. Moore Charitable Trust v. *United States*	3.8(b), 9.9	Apr. 1993
Henry E. & Nancy Horton Bartels Trust for the Benefit of New Haven v. *United States*	5.4(h)	July 2000
Ill. Ass'n of Prof'l Ins. Agents, Inc. v. *Comm'r*	9.4(b)	Nov. 1986

Case	Book Sections	Newsletter Issue
Julius M. Israel Lodge of B'nai Brith No. 2113 v. Comm'r	4.7	Dec. 1995
Junaluska Assembly Hous., Inc. v. Comm'r	2.2(e), 7.1(e)	Aug. 1986
Knights of Columbus Bldg. Ass'n v. United States	1.2	Sept. 1988
Laborer's Int'l Union v. Comm'r	1.8, 2.2(a), 2.4	Oct. 2001
Living Faith, Inc. v. Comm'r	2.7(b), 7.1(f)(i), 7.6	Nov. 1990, Feb. 1992
Manning Ass'n v. Comm'r	1.6	Jan. 1990
Nat'l Ass'n of Postal Supervisors v. United States	9.5	Oct. 1990, Dec. 1991
Nat'l League of Postmasters v. United States	4.8	Sept. 1996
Nat'l Water Well Ass'n, Inc. v. Comm'r	3.7, 9.4(b)	Mar. 1989
N.C. Citizens for Bus. & Indus. v. United States	6.5(b)(i)	Oct. 1989
NCAA v. Comm'r	2.5(b), 2.5(d)	Apr. 1989, Nov. 1990
Nonprofits' Ins. Alliance of Cal. v. United States	7.1(f)(ii), 7.3	Dec. 1994
Ohio Farm Bureau Fed'n, Inc. v. Comm'r	2.5(b), 9.12	June 1996
Or. State Univ. Alumni Ass'n v. Comm'r	3.7, 9.6(a)	Apr. 1996, Dec. 1999
Paratransit Ins. Corp. v. Comm'r	7.1(f)(ii), 7.3	Aug. 1994
Planned Parenthood Fed'n of Am., Inc. v. Comm'r	3.7	Aug. 1999
Portland Golf Club v. Comm'r	6.1(b)	Jan. 1991
Presbyterian & Reformed Publ'g Co. v. Comm'r	2.2(f), 7.1(e)	Oct. 1984
Prof'l Ins. Agents v. Comm'r	2.2(a), 2.4	Mar. 1987
Redlands Surgical Servs. v. Comm'r	8.11, 8.14	Sept. 1999, June 2001
Rensselaer Polytechnic Inst. v. Comm'r	10.12, 11.2	June 1984
Serv. Bolt & Nut Co. Profit Sharing Trust v. Comm'r	6.4	Apr. 1984
Sherwin-Williams Co. Employee Health Plan Trust v. Comm'r	6.2(b)	Jan. 2001, Aug. 2003
Sierra Club, Inc. v. Comm'r	3.1, 3.4, 3.7, 4.10, 9.6(a)	July 1993, Oct. 1994, Aug. 1996, May 1999
St. David's Health Care Sys., Inc. v. United States	8.11	Aug. 2002, Jan. 2004, July 2004, Aug. 2004
State Police Ass'n of Mass. v. Comm'r	6.5(a)	Nov. 1997
Tex. Farm Bureau v. United States	3.7, 9.4(b)	Aug. 1995
Trust under Will of Emily Oblinger v. Comm'r	3.8(b), 9.9	May 1993
United Cancer Council, Inc. v. Comm'r	7.1(f)(ii), 8.4, 8.14	Jan. 1998, Apr. 1999
Veterans of Foreign Wars, Dep't of Mich. v. Comm'r	9.6(a)	Aug. 1987
Veterans of Foreign Wars, Dep't of Mo., Inc. v. Comm'r	9.6(a)	Dec. 1984
Vigilant Hose Co. of Emmitsburg v. United States	2.2(a), 2.2(d), 8.16	Aug. 2001
W. Va. State Med. Ass'n v. Comm'r	2.4, 6.1(b), 11.2	Nov. 1988
Women of Motion Picture Indus. v. Comm'r	11.2	Mar. 1998

Table of IRS Private Determinations Discussed in
Bruce R. Hopkins' Nonprofit Counsel

The following IRS private letter rulings and technical advice memoranda, referenced in the text, are discussed in greater detail in one or more issues of the author's monthly newsletter, as indicated.

Private Determination	Book Sections	Newsletter Issue
8505044	8.5	May 1985
8512084	9.12	Dec. 1993
8606056	8.4	Apr. 1986
9029047	9.4(b)	Sept. 1990
9042038	3.8(d)	Jan. 1991
9305026	8.5	Apr. 1993, Apr. 1997
9345004	4.8	June 1994
9416002	4.8	June 1994
9438029	8.7	Nov. 1994
9550001	9.4(a), 9.8, 9.13	Feb. 1996
9603019	5.3(c)	Mar. 1996
9608003	9.8	Apr. 1996
9615045	3.8(c)	July 1996
9619069	2.2(e), 3.10(a)	Aug. 1996
9635001	4.10	Nov. 1996
9641011	9.8	Dec. 1996
9645004	2.3, 2.7(d), 4.1	Jan. 1997
9645017	8.7	Feb. 1997, Apr. 1997
9651047	9.8	Jan. 1997
9702004	2.3, 9.1(c)	Mar. 1997
9711002	9.8	May 1997
9711003	1.6	June 1997
9712001	2.5(d)	June 1997
9720002	9.3(c)	Sept. 1997
9722006	8.4	Feb. 1999, Nov. 2002
9732032	9.1, 9.2(d)	Oct. 1997
9739043	9.2(c)	Dec. 1997
9740032	3.8(a)	Dec. 1997
9742001	4.8	Dec. 1997
9751001	4.8	Feb. 1998
9811001	9.8	May 1998

Private Determination	Book Sections	Newsletter Issue
9821049	9.12	Aug. 1998
9821063	9.12	Aug. 1998
9821067	9.13	Aug. 1998
9822004	9.8	Oct. 1998
9822006	9.13	Oct. 1998
9822039	9.2(f)	Oct. 1998
9825030	9.12	Aug. 1998
9839039	6.4, 9.8	Dec. 1998
9847002	6.4, 9.2(a), 9.8	Mar. 1999
9849027	9.8	Mar. 1999
200021056	1.6, 1.11, 2.2(b), 2.3, 2.6, 2.7(a), 7.1(b), 7.6, 9.3(a)	Aug. 2000
200022056	9.8	July 2000, May 2001
200044039	7.3	Jan. 2001
200051046	6.1(d)	Feb. 2001
200108045	9.8	May 2001
200118054	8.12(a), 8.15	July 2001
200119061	2.2(e), 2.3	Aug. 2001
200128059	2.5(c), 9.6(b)	Sept. 2001
200132040	8.14	Nov. 2001
200134025	5.4(f), 8.12(b)(i), 8.12(b)(ii)	Nov. 2001
200147058	6.4, 8.17	Jan. 2002
200151060	10.2(b)	Mar. 2002
200203069	10.1	May 2002
200204051	9.12	Apr. 2002
200222030	9.3(a)	Sept. 2002
200225044	9.12	Sept. 2002
200230005	4.3	Oct. 2002
200303062	10.1, 10.3(a), 10.4(b), 10.5, 10.12, 10.13	Mar. 2003
200304041	8.12(a)	Apr. 2003
200311034	8.12(a)	May 2003
200313024	9.1	June 2003
200314031	3.8(c), 9.8	June 2003, Aug. 2003
200333031	8.12(a), 8.17	Oct. 2003
200345041	9.12	Jan. 2004
200432026	5.3(b)	Oct. 2004
200437040	8.5	Nov. 2004
200439043	9.11	Dec. 2004
200446033	10.2(b)	Jan. 2005
200450037	7.4	Feb. 2005, Mar. 2005
200501017	3.4	Mar. 2005

Private Determination	Book Sections	Newsletter Issue
200504035	10.1	Apr. 2005
200510029	2.2(e)	May 2005
200510030	8.12(b)(ii)	May 2005
200512023	7.1(f)(ii)	June 2005
200512025	2.3, 2.7(c), 7.1(f)(ii)	June 2005
200512027	7.1(f)(ii)	June 2005
200528029	8.15	September 2005
200530029	2.5(e)	October 2005

Index